The Problem of Sociology

The Problem of Sociology

An introduction to the discipline

David Lee and Howard Newby

Hutchinson

London   Melbourne   Sydney   Auckland   Johannesburg

Hutchinson & Co. (Publishers) Ltd

An imprint of the Hutchinson Publishing Group

17-21 Conway Street, London W1P 6JD

Hutchinson Publishing Group (Australia) Pty Ltd
16-22 Church Street, Hawthorn, Melbourne, Victoria 3122

Hutchinson Group (NZ) Ltd
32-34 View Road, PO Box 40-086, Glenfield, Auckland 10

Hutchinson Group (SA) (Pty) Ltd
PO Box 337, Bergvlei 2012, South Africa

First published 1983
Reprinted 1983, 1984, 1985

© David Lee and Howard Newby

Photoset in 10 on 12 Times Roman by
Kelly Typesetting Limited, Bradford-on-Avon, Wiltshire

Printed and bound in Great Britain by
Anchor Brendon Ltd, Tiptree, Essex

British Library Cataloguing in Publication Data
   The problem of sociology.
   1. Sociology
   I. Newby, Howard   II. Lee, David
   301   HM51

ISBN 0 09 151511 4

Long I Have Looked For The Truth

Long I have looked for the truth about the life
   of people together.
That life is crisscrossed, tangled, and difficult
   to understand.
I have worked hard to understand it and when I
   had done so
I told the truth as I found it.

When I had told the truth that was so difficult
   to find
It was a common truth, which many told
   (And not everyone has such difficulty in finding)

Soon after that people arrived in vast masses
   with pistols given to them
And blindly shot around them at all those too
   poor to wear hats
And all those who had told the truth about them
   and their employers
They drove out of the country in the fourteenth
   year of our semi-Republic.

From me they took my little house and my car
   Which I had earned by hard work.
(I was able to save my furniture)

When I crossed the frontier I thought:
   More than my house I need the truth.
But I need my house too. And since then
   Truth for me has been like a house and a car
And they took them.

Bertolt Brecht (1898–1956)

Acknowledgements

The authors and the publishers would like to thank the copyright holders below for their kind permission to reproduce the following material:

'Long have I looked for the truth' from *Bertolt Brecht Poems 1913–56* edited by John Willett and Ralph Manheim, Eyre Methuen 1980

Table 1 from *Structure, Function and Evolution*, readings by H. Spencer, edited with an introduction by S. Andreski, Michael Joseph Ltd 1971

Table 2 from *Essays in Sociological Explanation* by N. J. Smelser, Prentice-Hall Inc., Englewood Cliffs, N. J. 1968

Table 3 from 'The weakest link in the chain? Some comments on the Marxist theory of action' by D. Lockwood, in S. Simpson and I. Simpson (eds.), *Sociological Research in the Sociology of Work*, JAI Press Inc., Greenwich, Conn. 1981

Tables 4 and **5** from 'The sources of variation in working class images of society' by D. Lockwood, in *Sociological Review*, vol. 14, no. 3, pp. 249–63

Table 7 from *Social Theory and Social Structure*, revised and enlarged edition, by Robert K. Merton, The Free Press, a Corporation, N. Y., copyright 1957

Figure 1 from *Royal Commission on the distribution of income and wealth*, Report no. 7, Cmnd 7595, HMSO 1979

Figure 2 from 'Class boundaries in advanced capitalist societies' by E. O. Wright, in *New Left Review*, no. 93

Figure 3 from 'Weber's Last Theory of Capitalism: A Systematization' by Randall Collins, in *American Sociological Review*, vol. 45, no. 6, pp. 925–42

Contents

8 *Contents*

Figures

Tables

Preface

This book is an introductory text in sociology aimed primarily at first-year undergraduate students in British universities.

With that sentence we have probably consigned whatever academic status we possess to oblivion. We are aware of the scorn which has been heaped upon others who have been sufficiently foolhardy to attempt such an enterprise. This is because the conventional wisdom of sociology teaching is that:

a Nobody has ever written a decent sociology textbook.
b Nobody ever will.

By the end of this book the reasons for the widespread scepticism will be apparent. The fact that it is a product of our joint experiences of teaching the first-year course at Essex University between 1975 and 1981 can only be held against us.

So, why offer ourselves for slaughter?

First, because we have become increasingly impatient with those textbooks which offer an 'institutional' approach to sociology – that is, that begin, conventionally, with the family and move on through education, community, work, etc. until most of the subfields of sociology are exhausted. Our criticisms with this approach centre around the fact that it artificially separates 'theory' and 'data' and, more importantly, that it gives students little understanding of how sociology developed historically around the analysis of certain fundamental issues. Most of all, however, such treatments, since they inevitably lack analytical focus, can only confirm the prejudices of the enemies of sociology:

that it is a bibliography in search of a discipline. We utterly repudiate such a judgement of it.

The second purpose in our writing this book follows on from this. We have sought to reassert what we see as the most important issues raised by the history of sociological thought and to demonstrate their contemporary relevance. In other words we have attempted not only to provide an introduction to 'classical' theory but also to show how these theories illuminate present social problems. We intend further to show that the diverse data which have been gathered in the course of social research can be meaningfully organized and ordered by the insights of social theory.

In seeking to pursue these aims we have been selective rather than comprehensive. For example, our selection of social problems is merely illustrative of the relevance of the theories we have chosen. We are aware that a number of topics conventionally included on first-year courses have been omitted or dealt with only cursorily. But we cannot include everything. This book is intended as an introduction, not a comprehensive guide.

Chapters 3 and 4 have appeared in an amended form as an Open University course unit, *Community and Society*, in the course 'Introduction to Sociology' (D201). We gratefully acknowledge permission to use this material here.

Our thanks are also due to a number of people who have made this book possible. Among those who commented on earlier drafts are John Scott, Mary McIntosh, Ken Plummer, Tony

Woodiwiss and Janet Newby. Linda Corcoran, Linda George, Mary Girling, Carole Allington, Betty Salter, Jackie Woodhead and Chris Fox were responsible for typing the manuscript. Students at both Essex University and the University of Wisconsin, Madison, having been exposed to earlier versions, have helped us to clarify our presentation.

David Lee
Howard Newby
Colchester, 1981

Part One: The Problem of Sociology

1 Prologue: to the reader

The purpose of this book is to provide an up-to-date introduction to the study of sociology. It will no doubt help if we begin by describing what the discipline is about and by indicating the scope of the chapters to follow. The simplest way of doing so will be to explain the title of the book: why the *problem* of sociology?

First of all, of course, as with any academic discipline, it ought to be possible to describe the intellectual 'problem' which we are going to tackle. The problem of sociology in this sense is to investigate the many and varied kinds of happenings which are conveyed by the phrase 'human society'. We shall find, however, that this statement is not nearly precise enough. Societies are not tangible 'things' which can be observed and classified like so many butterflies. In order to arrive at a more exact idea of what sociologists study, we must take a closer look at what we really have in mind whenever we talk about 'human society'.

Even in quite ordinary situations people are aware of being, as they put it, under social pressure. Behind this everyday expression is the realization that our relationships with other people can have a curious effect on ourselves. The point has been put particularly well by two British sociologists who undertook a celebrated study of racial conflict in Birmingham over access to housing. They wrote of:

the feeling that individuals were often acting in contradiction of their own ideals and sometimes of their own interests. They adopted discriminatory policies reluctantly, regretfully and sometimes guiltily because they felt compelled to do so by circumstances beyond their control. Sometimes we felt that they

acted as men possessed by some evil demon. (Rex and Moore 1967)

In this description Rex and Moore express what we take to be a common experience of people in many spheres of life: that one is part of a 'system' of forces that one is powerless to interpret or change.

Yet the 'system' itself does change, often with great suddenness, and still we can have that sense of being affected by something which appears to operate outside and independently of ourselves. During times of war, revolution and violent social upheaval the 'thing' seems quite out of control, carrying everyone along in unexpected and unpredictable directions. Here is Nadezdha Mandelstam's vivid account of her feelings as Stalin's purges gathered momentum in the USSR and she and her husband, the poet Osip Mandelstam, were taken into exile:

All of us were seized by the feeling that there was no turning back. . . . all of us were in a state close to hypnotic trance. We had really been persuaded that we had entered a new era and that we really had no choice but to admit to historical inevitability. (Mandelstam 1975, p. 50)

Poor Nadezdha was brought to the point of doubting whether, in the last analysis, individuals are capable of maintaining any distance at all between themselves and society's 'endless pressure' (Pryce 1979). She asks:

Can a man really be held accountable for his own actions? His behaviour, even his character is always in the merciless grip of the age, which squeezes out of

Full references quoted in the text are contained in the bibliography beginning on p. 347.

him the drop of good or evil that it needs from him. (Mandelstam 1975, p. 108)

Of course, people can and do resist 'the merciless grip of the age'. Even under the most extreme conditions of social control we can find examples of the autonomy of the individual asserting itself. S. Cohen and L. Taylor in their study of long-term imprisonment, *Psychological Survival* (1972), explore this aspect of social behaviour. So, too, does Hilde Bluhm (1948) in the analysis of an even more oppressive institution – the Nazi concentration camp. And she concludes:

The ego of the prisoners refused to accept the estrangement it was subjected to. It, therefore, turned the experience connected with the loss of its feelings into an object of its intellectual interests. . . . Those . . . who embarked on a study of the concentration camp proper, turned towards that very reality which had threatened to overpower them; and they rendered that reality into an object of their 'creation'. This turn from a passive suffering to an active undertaking indicated that the ego was regaining control. (Bluhm 1948, pp. 9–10)

Thus even under conditions of extreme coercion the 'system' need not be totally determined, even though the costs of successful resistance may be very high. If it were, if people always acted in ant-like subservience to social discipline, social life would not be the puzzle which in fact it is.

We have said enough, we hope, to suggest that sociology does possess a distinctive 'problem', a subject matter. Nevertheless, it is not easy to describe it in everyday language. This is because ordinary language is rather vague and confusing in these matters and tends to hide not only the precise nature of the issues the sociologist wishes to examine, but also their importance. It encourages us to think of 'society' as if it really were separate from or at variance with the relationships existing between individual people. Providing all that we want is a handy descriptive term to cover the phrase 'relationships between individual people',

terms like 'society' and 'social' will suffice. But exact study requires us to use words carefully. There is, of course, no such object as 'society' with an existence completely removed from individual human beings and certainly not one that could be seen or touched. There is only a set of forces 'exerted by people over one another and over themselves' (Elias 1970, p. 17) and it is with this fact and how it arises that sociology is concerned.

In place of everyday notions like 'society' and 'social pressure', therefore, the discipline has tried to put a more accurate and inevitably more complicated understanding of the experiences and happenings conveyed by such words. We shall be expanding upon the outcome of this attempt, and the questions which flow from it, in the course of the following chapters. We shall consider, for example, the fact that social relationships tend to possess a degree of consistency or stability over periods of time. Sociologists have tried to capture this fact through various metaphors; by talking of social 'structure', 'form', 'system', 'pattern' or 'configuration'. Yet the 'pattern', we know, is quite capable of changing with varying degrees of suddenness; or even of breaking down altogether. What conditions make for cohesion and stability in social relationships and what, on the other hand, bring about disintegration? Then again, it is a familiar experience that at any given moment people vary in their willingness to accept the restraints which the established pattern imposes. Sociologists use the term *deviance* to denote ways of acting which are disapproved of by society at large. What produces deviance and its equally puzzling opposite, *conformity*? One consideration that clearly might be relevant arises out of the observation that in virtually every society individuals and groups come to differ markedly in their access to privilege, opportunity and authority over others. How do we account for this *social differentiation* as it is called? Is a degree of inequality a necessary and inevitable ingredient of 'the life of people together'?

As soon as one does, in fact, examine the

immense variety of human ways, customs and social conditions one cannot help but be struck by the fact that people are very dependent on group life, on their relationship with others. This dependence extends well beyond the level of material needs. In fact, organized economic activity *presupposes*, like other aspects of social life, a more profound dependence, namely, that our relations with others shape that sense of personal uniqueness which we call the individual 'self'. In order to know very basic things about 'ourselves' we are dependent from childhood upon information supplied by other people. It is from others that we learn what sex we are, what words to use, what work to do, which gods to serve, who to love, who to hate – and so on. Sociologists have, therefore, repeatedly rejected the possibility of the totally isolated, non-social individual. If we wish to improve our understanding of human beings, they argue, we will not get very far by confining our attention to the properties of the individual mind as such. We must relate behaviour to its social setting.

Now, we had better make one thing clear. Sociologists recognize that there are some features of people's behaviour that *are* largely dependent on the working of that mysterious entity 'the individual mind'. Processes such as memory, thinking, emotion and so on are capacities of a biological organ, the brain. It is the job of another discipline, psychology, the 'science of the mind', to investigate them. Nothing written in this book should be construed as an attempt to encroach upon its territory. Even so, boundaries between academic disciplines are never rigid and there is undoubtedly a 'grey area' between psychology and sociology. Sooner or later in all investigations of human behaviour we come back to the fact that there is a whole class of effects produced by the interactions occurring *between* minds. Moreover, the interaction takes place not just between those alive now. The minds of the past, great and humble, leave their own legacy of ideas, techniques, customs and obligations.

One way of giving the concept of 'society' a more exact shape, in fact, is to see it as the sum total of these interactions and of their consequence for personal life.

Sociology and the scientific ideal

There is, however, another way to talk of the 'problem of sociology'. Like Bertolt Brecht, in the poem quoted in the epigraph, the sociologist who is faithful to the discipline is someone who '*needs* the truth'. But this demand for 'the truth' is both dangerous and difficult. We are setting out to study something – society – which itself contains and generates its own 'truths' about the world. So sociologists typically find themselves in the position of having to confront, examine and comment upon these generally held 'truths'.

Socially generated ideas can, for now, be put into two rough-and-ready groups. First, there is what we might call 'common sense', which means everyday lore and homespun wisdom about the purpose, nature and vexations of the prevailing way of life. Second, there are more coherent 'ideologies', that is, systems of belief and philosophy which are recurrently introduced to justify some aspect of social life or action.

The trouble is that sociologists themselves are members of society. Sometimes, therefore, their questions and probings threaten powerful interests, disturb the elaborate balance of the status quo or simply upset lay people. Even worse, their own work can become contaminated. Either it suffers an overdose of taken-for-granted 'common sense', or it becomes permeated with the ideologies and assumptions of the apologists of the 'system' – to say nothing of the possibilities of being swayed by those of its enemies. Clearly, we ought to have a clear and accurate set of criteria for distinguishing between rival claims to be telling the 'truth' about social life.

Alas, this is easier to ask for than to provide. The precise basis upon which one might distinguish between 'true' knowledge and false, even in the study of the natural world, has been the subject of controversy among philosophers for centuries. We do not intend to become involved in these unresolved debates here and the reader who is interested in the philosophical problems surrounding the social sciences should consult one of the many introductions available (for example, Ryan 1970; 1973; Lessnoff 1974; Keat and Urry 1975; Benton 1977). We prefer instead to proceed in a more 'down-to-earth' fashion by comparing the way in which we come to hold beliefs simply by participating in social life, with a style of thought that can be described as *disciplined* – and so might serve as a model for our efforts to study society.

As we see it, both 'common sense' and ideological beliefs suffer from certain limitations just because they originate simply from ordinary social activity. First, they tend to be *self-centred*. Their main purpose is to bolster the doings of particular individuals or groups as they endeavour to 'get along' in society (cf. Murphy 1972, p. 6). Second, therefore, the knowledge they offer tends to be *incomplete*. Frequently, it does not even provide a guide to the whole of the individual's society but only that part of it which is of most immediate concern. As for other societies we remain for much of the time with only the most hazy and general notions. Moreover, though social life has always been full of change and novelty, our lay knowledge of society does not cope very well with the unfamiliar. Either our favourite beliefs degenerate into a puzzled but dogged resignation or, and here we come to a third limitation, they tend to promote various forms of *intolerance*. Ideas which have been used to justify costly commitments are abandoned only reluctantly. Ideologies themselves foster a dogmatic style of thought that insists on being right regardless. Even when they have ceased to be serviceable we tend to cling to them for such support as they can still offer.

We are not going to be so foolish as to claim that sociology can completely overcome these limitations. But can one do better *with* its help

than without it? And if so, how? One answer would be to claim, as some indeed have, that sociology is a *science*: the 'science of society'. The notion that there is, in fact, a unity of methods linking recognized natural sciences, like physics and chemistry, to social science is called '*positivism*' and we shall be returning to it repeatedly in the following chapters. Nevertheless, we shall do well to consider now some of the reasons why we ourselves prefer to give positivism a miss.

The word 'science' covers a number of different possibilities. It usually conjures up what is best regarded as a particular technique of investigation, that is, experimental science. Even on practical grounds, it is very doubtful whether sociology could ever aim to be 'scientific' in this sense because it is both physically difficult and, of course, often morally wrong to carry out experiments on groups, particularly large groups, of people. Experiments are not wholly unknown in sociology and up to a point we can and do use variations found within or between actual societies as an approximation to the controlled conditions of an experiment. Let us merely say that formidable practical and logical objections remain.

But not even all of the natural sciences derive their findings from strict and literal adherence to experimental procedure. We may of course talk about 'science' in a wider sense: as the attempt to provide *explanations* based upon a rational appeal to impartial *evidence*. This option is more attractive. Most sociologists would accept that they are in the 'explanation business' in some way. Certainly there is no lack of theories from which such explanations might be culled, nor any lack of research studies which seem to be trying to verify one or more of these theories. But a word or two of caution is necessary before we rush to commend sociological analysis to the reader in these terms.

First as to the theories and 'explanations'. In natural sciences these are usually thought of as being based upon the accumulation of bodies of laws linking given causes to given effects. The laws express general regularities in the natural world. In turn knowledge of them enables the investigator to make predictions about particular instances. Applied to the social context, however, the notion of general causal laws becomes very troublesome. Many of the instances which sociology studies are either unique or at least insufficiently numerous to justify assertions of law-like regularity. Furthermore, in studying physical forces and substances one does not have to worry about the awkward states which in humans we call 'consciousness' and 'experience'. Chemicals in a test-tube are not capable of thought or feeling as far as we know and chemistry has been able to build up the laws of chemical combination without assuming that they are. From time to time it has been suggested that society and human behaviour are, in fact, governed in a similar way, by blind causal forces and deterministic laws. By and large, however, social 'scientists' have accepted that subjective states complicate the chances of showing a simple connection between a given 'effect' and its possible origin in some observable 'cause'. The theories from which our explanations derive, therefore, are performing different 'work' from those in other branches of science, something that comes closer to interpretation than causal explanation alone.

Now for the question of 'evidence'. It is necessary briefly to review here the main sources upon which sociological evidence is based, if only because we shall need to make reference to them in the body of the book. At the same time we shall deliberately emphasize their limitations. Sociological 'evidence', then, falls into four main groups:

1 *Direct observation*. This is the method favoured by those who insist on the need for authenticity in social research and close familiarity with the subject matter. It is the main method used in anthropology, that is, in the study of non-industrial and tribal social systems. In the study of modern life the method often takes the form of 'participant observation' by which the investigator seeks direct involvement in the life or situation of a group (or groups). The problem, of course, is that direct observation cannot be checked or manipulated easily in order to test explanations.

2 *Social survey*. This is a blanket term to describe a variety of methods in which the sociologist attempts one or more 'snapshot' pictures of a significant group of individuals. The best known 'instruments' of the social survey are the questionnaire and the structured interview. In both cases a series of standardized questions is put to all of the subjects of the survey. The survey offers wider and more systematic coverage than direct observation but has been criticized for its formality and relative superficiality.

3 *Official and adminstrative statistics*. For certain purposes the scope of a topic may oblige sociologists to use data collected by the state and similar administrative agencies. Laymen are often very sceptical about such material. But this scepticism is shared by sociologists too. The investigator, for example, has no control over the classification and collection of the data which often reflect quirks of the administrative process. Nevertheless for certain purposes these materials are all that we have available.

4 *Historical and documentary material*. For many types of problem sociologists have to employ the same diversity of materials as historians, relying upon their knowledge of past or present conditions to interpret the sources in question. Needless to say this is a highly precarious exercise since there is again no way of checking the purposes and procedures by which such materials were produced in the first place.

Anyone reading through this list will soon realize that judged by the standards of the orthodox model of scientific procedure our sources are flawed. Quite simply they seem to be riddled with too many ambiguities to enable us always to arbitrate decisively between alternative explanations. Their impartiality is limited too because often they do not yield 'hard facts' but accounts and interpretations given by participants themselves of the situation confronting them. These interpretations then receive a second at the hands of the observer. He or she must form a judgement as to the meaning of what has been said by the participants. Orthodox natural science procedures rely a great deal, of course, upon independent verification of evidence whereas these layers of interpretation are not easily checked.

The 'need for truth' in sociology and how to satisfy it have thus become part of its 'problem'. To admit this is not simply a matter of honesty, of avoiding pretentiousness about what we can achieve. In studying sociology one needs to be constantly aware of the struggle that has taken place between positivism and the various alternatives to it. Some of the latter have in fact rejected the goal of (scientific) 'explanation' altogether. The clash of these perspectives will permeate the pages to follow.

Our diffidence about claiming that sociological findings are based upon 'science', however, does not mean that they are, after all, no better than lay opinions. There are already in existence respectable examples of rational enquiry which are different in character from the methods of the natural sciences and their particular model of causal explanation. Our own appreciation of this fact has come from comparison of sociology with the study of history. Most readers will be accustomed to the discussion of historical affairs in a disciplined and rigorous fashion while also acknowledging the difficulties of obtaining and interpreting historical evidence. We have seen that historical material provides a major source for the sociologist's 'laboratory' and that the accumulation of a working knowledge of relevant history will be found to be fairly essential. The outcome of sociological enquiries has in our view been far more akin to historians' probes into the past than to the controlled experiments of physics. To be sure sociologists study the present at least as much as the past. But why should we not apply to the present the fearless attitudes of the historian? Are we too passionately involved to be capable of adopting some minimal rational attitude or *reasoned procedure* in studying it?

The phrase 'reasoned procedure' indicates the least restrictive sense in which we might describe sociology as a scientific activity or method. It means simply that we adopt the rules of logical thought and the critical attitude to information and opinion which are to be found in any intellectual discipline. Through the application of these rules and attitudes sociology offers a rigorous training in the discussion of social life. We may not be able to 'explain' in the orthodox sense but we can certainly penetrate further than unreflecting dogma or conventional wisdom.

Three aspects of day-to-day sociological method seem especially worth elaborating in order to back up our claims:

1   Unlike egocentric and incomplete everyday knowledge, sociology seeks a systematic and public accumulation of experience and observation of social life.
2   It is also an exercise in comparative investigation.
3   Interpretation of results proceeds by a process of applying 'systematic doubt' to all assertions.

Some explanation of these points is called for.

a   Sociologists do not seek to disparage everyday experience. To experience something is, in a sense, to know it. But the person who relied only on what could be 'known' at first hand would be very impoverished. We take a good deal of what we know on trust from other people because they have told us about their experiences, and sociology is no exception to this. In addition, though, it tries to offer a logical and systematic accumulation of reports on the diversity of social arrangements which have existed in different places and times. Part of the job of any practising sociologist is actively to seek new material of this kind. At the very least, then, sociology offers access to a public literature made up of cumulative observations of social life.

b A mere compilation of 'reports' would hardly justify serious interest of course. In practice, one of the most characteristic procedures of the sociologist is making active comparisons. This can be done in two ways. Sometimes we may wish to contrast arrangements *within* the same set of institutions or within a single society. (We might for instance be interested in the variety of industrial relations as between industries with different technologies.) Other types of study call for comparisons *between* whole societies or between certain types of arrangements – educational, say, or political or familial common to a number of societies. This fundamental work of comparing may not produce anything approaching law-like explanations, but at the very least the effect can be both enlightening and unnerving. It generally makes the observer aware that what one regarded as a natural and inevitable characteristic of human affairs – monogamous marriage, for example – is often restricted to the type of social 'system' in which one grew up. Conversely problems and practices which were thought to be unique and special to one's own place and time may turn out not to be so. Comparative study thus guards against a kind of collective conceit known as *ethnocentrism* – the belief that one's own customs and way of life are somehow more 'natural' and proper than any other simply because one is used to them.

c Obviously it would be naïve to treat all accounts of social life as equally trustworthy. The principle upon which sociological discussion proceeds is one of scepticism or 'systematic doubt' regarding the claim of any statement to be a valid account of its subject matter. As in natural science, the attainment of certainty about 'the truth' is an unrealizable ideal. By means of critical, rational debate, however, one can narrow down the range of *un*certainty. 'Systematic doubt' makes it possible to uncover *some* of the distortions, mistakes, falsehoods

and ambiguities among the competing accounts which claim our attention.

The last point is arguably the most important. It means, of course, that one must be prepared to expose common-sense beliefs and ideologies to 'systematic doubt', even if they happen to be one's own. In this way, for example, one rapidly becomes dissatisfied with the undigested opinions of one individual when based upon purely chance personal experience; nor should one be prepared to accept uncritically the reports of newspapers or impressionistic writings. Above all, one must avoid being restricted to that view of things which people involved in a situation will allow us to have. In short, as with the fictional detective solving a murder mystery, all statements and clues must be treated as equally suspect until they have been systematically cross-checked against each other.

Even so, we cannot pretend that applying 'systematic doubt' to what one has taken for granted is easy, comfortable or foolproof. For that reason we had better insist that we are talking about the relationship of *sociology*, as a method of thinking about society, to everyday belief. This is not necessarily the same thing as the relationship between *sociologists* and other members of society. This point is particularly important in relation to highly controversial matters where vested interest, personal self-respect and/or political, moral or religious beliefs are involved. A rich person, for example, may find it comfortable or convenient to believe that he is overtaxed or that poverty no longer exists. The sociologist who points out that, on the basis of published statistics, the highest income earners actually pay a lower proportion of income in tax than the rest, is likely to be accused, perhaps in the rich person's newspaper, of manufacturing propaganda dressed up as scientific research. And in a sense that is true, for the content of what the sociologist says on such an issue does have political consequences. Sociologists, like journalists, occasionally conduct exposés on issues which some people may prefer to remain secret, or at least un-acknowledged. If sociology is to move beyond common sense and propaganda this will always be the case to a greater or lesser extent because it is *always* bound up with the 'debunking' or *demystification* of a world which would other-wise remain mysterious. But the act of scepti-cism cuts both ways and we cannot always assume in these sorts of debates a clear-cut dis-tinction between the sociologists who are always right and the 'villains' exposed as a result of their work. The data on which such 'proof' rests are often too imprecise or incomplete for that to be possible. And, anyway, good socio-logists need to be their own severest critics.

Sociologists should therefore not pretend to be better or wiser than everybody else: on the contrary, laymen often have insights about society that are clearer, more profound and more in touch with the rules of rational debate than those of the people who are paid to have them. And 'the professionals' are as capable, either unintentionally or deliberately, of dis-torting information as anyone else. In short, *sociology* is not to be equated with the doings of sociologists *per se* but with 'reasoned proce-dure', a style of rigorous critical thought which, hopefully, most sociologists have been trained to apply, to actually use and to urge upon others.

The study of the rules and attitudes of 'reas-oned procedure' within the discipline is now a complex and sophisticated sub-specialism called sociological *methodology*. Readers who wish to pursue the techniques, methods and troubles of social research in greater depth will therefore need to look outside these pages (for example, Bell and Newby 1977; Denzin 1978; Hughes J. 1976). Having done so they may still feel that we have been somewhat disingenuous in our description of the sociologist as someone who 'needs the truth' and that the most difficult inference to draw in sociology is that a particu-lar finding is 'true'. Certainly the methodolo-gist's study of inference very rapidly passes into difficult matters of the philosophy of social

science that lack, and will probably always lack, a settled solution. But the appropriate response to this is *not* despair.

First, it is easy enough on an *intuitive* level to distinguish the ideal of the pursuit of truth from the lies, propaganda, sales talk and other diverse forms of persuasion which we so often encounter in daily social life. Was this not the lesson Brecht drew on behalf of all people from the rise of Nazism?

Second, it is a great mistake to suppose that social research is impossible or without value unless all the methodological and philosophical difficulties have been cleared out of the way first. On the contrary, sociology we believe is a disci-pline which thrives on controversy. The imper-fections and scandals which appear when the discipline is judged by the light of normal models of scientific explanation are often taken by the outsider as a sign of its weakness, 'newness' or 'immaturity'. This we believe to be very mis-taken. In fact, as we shall see, sociology is not particularly 'new'. Its recent past has seen a growth and a greater sophistication in our infor-mation about social conditions and, even if it lacks an overall structure, the presence of this material is a sign of some sort of progress and development in the subject itself. This process we shall now argue is encouraged by controversy between different 'schools' of thought.

Sociology's untidy face

We have come, in fact, to the third and final 'problem of sociology' that we wish to discuss – the untidy face which the discipline presents to the newcomer. For the fact is that there has never been a simple unanimity of view on many of the fundamental questions posed by it and the first experience of this can be perplexing in the extreme. Hence, this book has been arranged as a critical exposition of the principal schools of sociological investigation. It should be stressed that we are not trying to offer the reader a complete or detailed intellectual history of individual social theories. There are far too many of them. Although we do give a brief account of the *origins* of each analytic tradition, the emphasis throughout is on the impact of a certain kind of general theoretical approach upon the conduct of substantive social research. What kinds of research problems does a particular 'school' generate? What methods of study does it favour? Most important of all: what actual results have been produced? By means of this framework we hope to provide a way of ordering the things which sociology offers the student. We also hope to be able to integrate 'theory' with 'methods' and 'findings' in order to show how each is shaped and moulded by the other. In this way, we may additionally demonstrate the relevance of theories, even those developed some time ago, to the analysis of contemporary social problems.

The term 'schools of thought' to describe conflicting positions within sociology has been chosen deliberately. We acknowledge that it is not the one which will appeal to all who currently practise the discipline. Some authors have in fact been anxious to stress the large areas of common ground, the convergences between different perspectives. Unfortunately, recognition of the existence of the supposed common ground usually depends upon favouring the views of one particular 'school', seeing it as the point to which all systems are converging. Or, even worse, sociology is presented as a woolly mishmash of 'perspectives' from which the student of social issues is free to choose at will. To be sure, the danger in stressing 'schools of thought' is that of rigidifying positions which are in reality in flux. Sociologists do not go round wearing badges that state their adherence to a particular 'school'. But the reader who has taken seriously the distinction we have already made between statements by individual sociologists and the processes of sociology will not commit this error. What we shall be discussing is the existence of *logically* separable 'sociologies' which derive from:

1 *mutually incompatible* assumptions about

such matters as the basic ingredients and fundamental character of 'society';
2 *disagreement* about the status of the knowledge to be derived from studying it.

It is true that the lines between the various 'schools' cannot be drawn quite so clearly as in some other disciplines and that, nowadays especially, following an expansion of sociology teaching in higher education, some cross-fertilization and mutual influence is taking place. Nevertheless, the validity of the stress on 'schools of thought' is shown by:

  a the widespread tendency of sociologists to describe research as inspired by a particular approach; for example, 'Weberian action theory', 'functionalist', 'Marxist', etc.;
  b the tendency for schools to view themselves as *either* identical with the whole of sociology (for example, Davis K. 1960) or as a separate venture which has somehow managed to free itself from the limitations of conventional sociology (for example, Atkinson 1977; Shaw 1974);
  c the persistence of certain assumptions and themes and the explicit rejection of others as a basis for the investigation of actual social problems.

Needless to say, since we are not aiming to give a detailed intellectual history of the rival 'schools', it is this last mentioned characteristic which is of principal interest here.

The uses of controversy

We hope, then, that our approach will enable people encountering the subject for the first time to cope with the 'untidy face' of sociological controversy by showing that, appearances to the contrary, it is an *organized* controversy. We can set out some of the functions which this 'organized controversy' performs in the process of the discipline:

1 It provides a very necessary check to the complacently held assumptions about social life

which emanate from society itself. As we have already argued, sociologists can easily be duped by their subject matter and controversy offers the possibility – it is only that – of preventing such 'external' assumptions from penetrating our work and restricting its vision.

2   It offers a continuing element of challenge to the inferences that a single investigation or a single school draws from a piece of research. We have explained that in studying social phenomena the whole process of 'appeal to evidence' which characterizes many other disciplines is made extremely difficult. Competition between radically divergent viewpoints at least offers the possibility of critical scrutiny of research reports and the prospect that narrow or fallacious thinking will be uncovered. In the jargon of the subject we can say that controversy offers the possibility of 'reflexivity' in sociology – some way of building in a critical attitude to the work that is done.

3   It helps to clarify the proper concerns of the discipline. Its 'untidy face' no doubt acquires extra opprobrium in the eyes of the public because the list of topics which have attracted sociological interest looks overwhelmingly ambitious for a single discipline to encompass. Sociologists frequently appear to penetrate the subject matter of history and of the other social sciences on a regular basis. Worst of all they often peruse the same wide range of materials as other groups of investigators – among whom the best example, perhaps, is journalists – who are not practising a discipline, as the term is usually understood, at all. Clearly, this breadth of scope makes it essential – especially if one is attempting to come to grips with the study of the subject – to locate the boundary between sociology and other forms of enquiry.

It is at this point that the controversy within sociology itself plays its part. For it is possible to show – as we are trying to do in this volume – that it is controversy directed and limited by a very finite set of issues, issues of the kind already set out at the start of the chapter and ones to be developed and clarified as we go

along. Hence we would claim that it is the kind of question, albeit asked in different ways of a wide range of information, which unifies the rival schools of sociology, however much they may pretend to ignore each other or argue at cross purposes. And it is the content of the unifying 'problem' within sociology which marks it out from other kinds of activity.

4   Dare we say it in a 'serious' textbook? Sociology is enjoyable. Its 'organized controversy' introduces the student to the life of the mind and the diversity of human achievement in a fashion which some other disciplines, having tamed their 'problems', can no longer offer – certainly not at the elementary level.

For reasons such as these, then, we doubt whether the fragmentation of sociology into rival schools will ever disappear or, if it were to do so, whether the outcome would be particularly welcome or beneficial.

To sum up: this far, we have been at pains to stress the alternative conceptions of 'science' existing within and between academic disciplines. We have defended our own as a reasoned procedure sustained by a controversy between schools of thought whose debates are aimed at a finite set of issues.

What do we wish to get out of such work? It is often said that the control human beings have over natural phenomena has far outgrown their rudimentary understanding of social phenomena, and that it is time that society's capricious and oppressive aspects were alleviated by the development of a 'science of society'. This aspiration has provided much of the momentum behind the positivist perspective in sociology (and elsewhere) of which we have spoken. Surely, though, it would be intolerable if the conduct of social affairs were to be taken out of the hands of the citizen and given over to a group of scientific experts whose opinions were then treated as sacrosanct. Such an arrangement would strike at the heart of any pretensions to democracy that exist in society and create the nightmarish possibility of a manipulative political 'brave new world' based on the use of some sort of pseudoscientific social engineering. On the other hand, if sociology does not lead to 'social engineering', what use is it?

What we are offering in this book is encouragement of a way of thinking which can be brought to bear by anyone upon political and moral debates. Understood in this sense, the sceptical 'scientific' aspiration within sociology is not the enemy of a more democratic or open discussion of social affairs at all but an indispensable preliminary to an as yet imperfectly realized ideal. Neither sociology nor democracy is possible where people are ignorant or misinformed or where they think only in a prescribed, dogmatic or illogical manner.

Thus we may proceed to our 'problem'. Our plan of attack will be simple. The book is divided into seven parts, each part corresponding to a major intellectual tradition of the discipline. Within each part we devote at least one chapter to describing the teaching, theories and ideas contributed by the tradition. This is followed by a selective evaluation of some – by no means all – of the research literature which best illustrates the elaboration and influence of the tradition within contemporary sociology.

As a preliminary to the individual parts of the book, however, we have tried to say something about the historical conditions which encouraged social commentators and scholars to become concerned about those issues which form the common agenda of the schools of sociology. We have already expressed our own inclination to regard sociology as more akin to historical than natural science. Such an approach is sensitive to the fact that science itself is part of the historical process. The way we define its methods and the uses to which we put its findings both reflect wider social developments and contribute to them. This is particularly important in the social sciences where the models of explanation which are put forward reflect the various needs of the age. The schools of sociology are no exception. They brought the discipline into being as a result of a growing preoccupation with an intellectual, political and moral problem that was itself unquestionably historical in character. To this we now turn.

2　Sociology and the growth of industrial society

Although it is possible to trace retrospectively a 'sociological' tradition of thought which goes back to the time of the Ancient Greeks, the word itself – an unhappy amalgam of Latin and Greek roots – is said to have been first coined by the Frenchman, Auguste Comte, as recently as the beginning of the nineteenth century. Like so many words, 'sociology' was introduced in response to a need. It was not a coincidence that sociology began to emerge as a recognized form of enquiry at the beginning of the nineteenth century for there was widespread agreement among observers and commentators at this time that Northern Europe and North America were passing through the most profound transformation of society in the history of mankind. This rupture was regarded as being so profound and so unique that most of the hitherto taken-for-granted assumptions about society and social relationships were thrown into confusion and doubt. We are referring here to the effects of the so-called 'twin revolutions' – the Industrial Revolution of England (and later elsewhere) which occurred roughly between 1780 and 1840 and the Democratic Revolutions of the United States of America in 1776 and France in 1789. Rightly or wrongly, these revolutions were viewed as having precipitated quite unprecedented changes in the organization of society. The tremendous social, economic, political and *ideological* ferment which they provoked forced a whole range of thinkers to come to terms with trying to explain these changes in an apparently novel and distinctive way – a way which we can now call, loosely, sociology.

In many respects we are all, individually and collectively, still trying to come to terms with the kind of society which was forged during this period. The social problems which have been left in its wake remain all around us. And as sociologists we are still trying to grapple with the sociological problems which so concerned the 'founding fathers' of the discipline. This is why this chapter is aimed at conveying something of the flavour of the changes which the early sociologists were trying to explain, principally those which occurred in England between 1750 and 1850 and in France, Germany and the United States somewhat later.

In the previous chapter we referred to the kind of society which emerged in this period as 'industrial society' and, indeed, this period is often referred to as the Industrial Revolution. But this begs some very important questions. Although all the early 'sociologists' were agreed that *something* unique and important had happened during this period, they were by no means in agreement about what, precisely, it was. They characterized the 'great transformation' in different ways and therefore, not surprisingly, sought different explanations of what they observed. From these different explanations we can trace the founding of the main theoretical traditions in sociology.

The important and distinctive features of this period can be interpreted in (at least) four different ways, as representing the growth of:

a　industrialism
b　capitalism
c　urbanism
d　liberal democracy.

A moment's reflection will, of course, show that the first three are closely related interpretations of the *economic* transformations of the 'Industrial' Revolution. The fourth bears upon responses to the political transformations wrought by the 'Democratic' Revolutions. In the remainder of this chapter, then, we will deal with each of these in turn and examine their significance for the rise of sociology.

Industrialism

What, asks Eric Hobsbawm in his book *The Age of Revolution*,

does the phrase '[the] industrial revolution broke out' mean? It means that some time in the 1780s, and for the first time in human history, the shackles were taken off the productive power of human societies which henceforth became capable of the constant, rapid and up to the present limitless multiplication of men, goods and services. (Hobsbawm 1962, p. 45)

Typically when we refer to the Industrial Revolution we are concerned with the transformation of the British economy from one based primarily upon agriculture to one based primarily upon manufacture. With this transformation came the changes to which Hobsbawm refers – changes in the technology of production (for example, new machines) and changes in the social relationships which surround the organization of production (for example, the factory system). It is important to recognize that industrialism is not the same phenomenon as capitalism. Although the two are often merged together, and while we can indeed recognize that in the case of Britain they were closely connected, capitalism clearly predated the Industrial Revolution (see the following section). The same could also be said of urbanism, since there are plenty of examples of cities in the pre-industrial world. However, the growth of cities was obviously accelerated by the Industrial Revolution, just as the Industrial Revolution also aided the spread of the spirit of capitalism.

In some respects the early Industrial Revolution appears a rather modest and insignificant event. It was originally based upon the workshop rather than the factory and was technically rather primitive. New methods of manufacture were founded largely upon the application of simple ideas and devices, often by no means expensive and within the means of the relatively humble artisan or skilled craftsman, but which could, nevertheless, produce striking results. At the centre of the Industrial Revolution was the industry which illustrates this process rather well: the cotton industry. As Hobsbawm again points out, this time in another of his books, *Industry and Empire*:

Whoever says Industrial Revolution says cotton. . . . The British Industrial Revolution was by no means *only* cotton, or Lancashire or even textiles, and cotton lost its primacy within it after a couple of generations. Yet cotton was the pacemaker of industrial change, and the basis of the first regions which could not have existed but for industrialisation, and which expressed a new form of society, industrial capitalism. (Hobsbawm 1969, p. 56)

Cotton manufacture in Britain had grown along with the cycle of international trade during the eighteenth century. The technical problems involved in industrializing cotton production related to the imbalance between spinning and weaving. While weaving had been considerably speeded up by the invention of the 'flying shuttle' in the 1730s, it was not until the 1780s that cotton could be spun in sufficient quantities and at a sufficient speed to supply the weavers. By this time the 'spinning jenny', the 'water frame' and the 'mule' had more than restored the balance, the latter two implying production in new (manu)'factories'. The introduction of power looms for weaving at the beginning of the nineteenth century also placed weaving in factories and virtually completed the technological revolution in cotton manufacture.

For over fifty years 'cotton was king' – even by the 1830s cotton accounted for over half of total British exports. Cotton mills came to epitomize the new 'factory system', a system which was, without any doubt, revolutionary:

A new industrial system based on a new technology thus emerged with remarkable speed and ease among the rainy farms and villages of Lancashire. . . . It represented a new economic relationship between men, a new system of production, a new rhythm of life, a new society, a new historical era, and contemporaries were aware of it almost from the start. (Hobsbawm 1969, pp. 64, 65)

Soon this new factory system spread elsewhere. Technological changes in cotton manufacture both provoked and were provoked by changes in the chemical and engineering industries. The widespread introduction of steam power not only created a new market for machines but in turn stimulated the iron industry and provided an expanded market for coal. In all of these sectors the growth of industrialism brought with it new forms of social organization and new patterns of work, of which two examples follow.

The division of labour

The predominant method of production before the Industrial Revolution was by handicraft. The productive unit was often the family with work being carried out in or adjacent to the family home. Production would also take place *sequentially* – that is, each sequence in the process of production would only be carried out once the previous one had been completed and thus, by and large, a single worker or family unit would see the whole process through from beginning to end. The revolutionary impact of the Industrial Revolution was such, however, that it brought about the change

a   from handicraft to machine production; and
b   from the family to the factory as a unit of production.

This enabled production to be carried out *concurrently* – that is, *all* the processes of production could be carried out *simultaneously*, by machine if necessary.

The Industrial Revolution therefore brought about a tremendous increase in the *division of labour* and this change in the organization of production was in itself sufficient to create a vast increase in productivity – as Adam Smith, the founder of modern economics, set out with great clarity in his book, *The Wealth of Nations*, published in 1776. This increase in the division of labour, and especially mechanized labour, totally transformed the worker's experience of work. The workers, particularly women and children in the early years of textile manufacture, were taken out of the familiar environment of the home and placed in the new impersonal factory, which imposed a regularity, a routine and a monotony that was quite unlike the pre-industrial rhythms of work, which had been largely unaffected by such a rational division of labour. The new factory system

inspired such visions as working men narrowed and dehumanised into 'operatives' or 'hands' before being dispensed with altogether by completely 'self-acting' (automated) machinery. . . . The 'factory' with its logical flow of processes, each a specialised machine tended by a specialised 'hand' all linked together by the inhuman and constant pace of the 'engine' and the discipline of mechanisation . . . *was* a revolutionary form of work. (Hobsbawm 1969, p. 68)

The tyranny of the clock

Organizing the processes of production in such a way that could take place concurrently involved a careful attention to the pacing and timing of machines in order to obtain the maximum possible production in the shortest possible time. Time therefore became money. The Industrial Revolution not only brought about an increase in the division of labour but it also brought about the tyranny of the clock. We see the beginning of a trend which reaches its apotheosis in the twentieth-century specialism of 'time-and-motion' study.

The historian E. P. Thompson has written a

famous paper, entitled 'Time, work-discipline and industrial capitalism' (1967), which traces the changes in the apprehension of time which parallel the new industrial system. Thompson notes that, in the pre-industrial world, work rhythms were determined by the necessities of the job – the changing seasons in agriculture, the changing tides in fishing, and so on. The notion of time which arises in such contexts is called by Thompson 'task-orientation'. He proposes three points concerning this perception of time:

1 There is a sense in which this form of time is more humanly comprehensible than work 'by the clock' because it is based upon what is an observed necessity.
2 Second, a community in which 'task-orientation' prevails exhibits little demarcation between 'work' and 'leisure'. As Thompson puts it:

   Social intercourse and labour are intermingled – the working-day lengthens or contracts according to the task – and there is no great sense of conflict between labour and 'passing the time of day'. (Thompson 1967, p. 60)

3 Third, to those who are accustomed to labour timed by the clock, workers whose attitude to time is based upon 'task-orientation' will appear lazy, wasteful and lacking in urgency.

With the rise of industrialism, as Thompson puts it, 'Time is now currency: it is not passed but spent'. The changes in manufacturing technique demanded a greater synchronization of labour and a greater punctuality and exactitude in the routine of daily work. Much of this was an anathema to the pre-industrial worker, whose perception of time was dominated by 'task-orientation'. Hence we find the characteristic irregularity of labour patterns before the coming of large-scale, machine-powered industry. It is not therefore surprising that one of the major social conflicts which emerged from the Industrial Revolution concerned the

control of time – conflicts over the limitation of the 'working day' (the Ten Hour Movement) and conflicts over the payment of 'over-time'. Similarly workers, brought up under the assumptions of 'task-orientation', were subject to massive indoctrination on the folly of 'wasting' time by their employers, a moral critique of idleness which stemmed from the Puritan work ethic (see Chapter 10) and which sought to inculcate the new time discipline. Thompson is insistent, however, that this conflict over the use and perception of time is not *only* a product of industrialism, but also of *capitalism*:

What we are examining here are not only changes in manufacturing technique which demand greater synchronisation of labour and a greater exactitude in time-routines in *any* society; but also these changes as they were lived through in the society of nascent industrial capitalism. We are concerned simultaneously with time-sense in its technological conditioning, and with time-measurement as a means of labour exploitation. (Thompson 1967, p. 74)

Thompson's reference to 'exploitation' here introduces a wholly separate aspect of the 'transformation', the spread of production for profit on the basis of wage labour. It was a development which, although it accompanied the growth of industrialism, calls for the discussion of a distinct set of views.

Capitalism and the Industrial Revolution

We will be examining the precise nature of capitalism later in this book when we encounter the theories of Karl Marx, and so at this stage we will give only a brief definition of what is meant by this term. Capitalism is first and foremost a system of economic production for a *market* organized around the principle of *profit*. On both counts capitalism differed from the form of society which preceded it, namely feudalism. Under feudalism production was primarily for *subsistence* (with only the surplus over and above subsistence needs being disposed of on the market) and organized around the principle of *use*. Capitalism, however, as the very word suggests, was founded on the investment of capital in the process of production in the expectation that it would eventually yield a return in the form of a profit. The size of this profit was to be regulated, according to Adam Smith, by the conditions of the market for the goods which were produced – that is, by the so-called 'laws' of supply and demand, although we shall see later in this book that many of the founding fathers of sociology (and not only Marx) challenged this view and argued that these 'laws' were in fact dependent upon certain prior *social* arrangements.

It is important to realize that this capitalist system of production did *not* arrive with the Industrial Revolution, although the latter certainly promoted and spread it. In Britain the most thoroughgoing and innovative commercial capitalist system began in agriculture, symbolized by the Agricultural Revolution of the eighteenth century. This revolution ensured the destruction of the peasantry, the most prosperous of whom became *capitalist* (commercial) farmers, producing not for their own subsistence but for the market, while the poorer majority became landless farm labourers, employed on the farms in much the same way that workers were later to be employed in the factories. Capitalist agriculture was ushered in by, for the most part, the 'improving' landowners of the seventeenth and eighteenth centuries, some of whom like Lord 'Turnip' Townsend were to become as famous for their innovations as James Watt or Richard Arkwright were later to become in the sphere of industrial production. It was these landowners who were in the forefront of the movement which epitomizes the transition from feudalism to capitalism in agriculture: enclosure. Enclosure involved the rearranging of open fields and/or common land into self-contained privately owned holdings enclosed by hedges, walls or fences. This enabled capitalist entrepreneurs to proceed with profit maximization on their own holdings

unhindered by the customs and traditions of the village community as a whole. Those on the margins of agricultural production – smallholders, cottagers – often lost their crucial rights over common land to graze their animals and to forage for timber. They were left pauperized and landless. Enclosure itself may only have been part of this process, but the sum total of these changes in agriculture was that social relationships in the countryside became utterly transformed. While previously they were bound by custom and common rights, they now became dominated by what Marx was later to call *cash-nexus* – that is, by payment for commodities. Thus landowners extracted a *rent* from their tenant farmers, who in turn made *profits* from the sale of agricultural produce on the market. Farmers also purchased labour in the labour market whose conditions determined the payment of workers in the form of a *wage*. In each case the payment (at least in theory) was fixed by the so-called 'hidden hand' of the market. These cash-nexus relationships between employer and employee were thus characterized as impersonal and contractual.

The successful establishment of a capitalist agriculture was a crucial prerequisite of the growth of industrialism, principally for two reasons:

1   It enabled the growing proportion of the population who were not engaged in the production of food to be adequately fed and to obtain their food from the market. Of course 'adequately' is here very much a relative term – it means little more than 'allowed them to be kept alive'. It is a matter of vociferous argument among historians as to whether the standard of living of the working population rose or fell during the early years of industrialization (see Hobsbawm 1964, chapter 5) but there is no doubt that the new breed of industrial workers were allowed to subsist and little more. This in itself, however, was sufficient to enable industrialization to proceed.

2   Second, the rise of a capitalist agriculture

enabled thousands of (near-destitute) ex-peasants and rural workers to be released for employment elsewhere in the expanding industries in the towns. It was they who provided a plentiful pool of labour for the Industrial Revolution and who flocked to the towns in search of employment and higher wages.

The Industrial Revolution was therefore capitalist in its nature, even though industrialism and capitalism must be understood as quite separate concepts. The spread of capitalism into industry had exactly the same effects upon social relationships as it had previously engendered in the countryside. The relationship between industrial employers and employees also became primarily based upon cash-nexus – the wage – and the very impersonality of this, together with the manifest short-term conflict of interest between wages and profits, were quite capable of producing the social and political turmoil which also accompanied the Industrial Revolution (see Thompson 1963). This new, impersonal, economically regulated system also produced a very common cultural response over this period – what Raymond Williams (1973a) has called 'retrospective regret'. There was a constant harking back to a largely mythical 'Golden Age' of the pre-industrial era, when the land was alleged, by such influential writers as William Cobbett, to have been peopled by merrie rustics and a happy beef-eating yeomanry. Much of the unrest during the early decades of the nineteenth century was based on a demand for a return to this Golden Age and a restoration of the rights and duties which were believed to have accompanied it. As we shall see in the following two chapters, one important tradition in sociology emerged from this cultural response, founded in a critique of the dehumanizing aspects of industrial capitalism.

These new social relationships also brought forth new social groupings. The word 'class', for example, began to achieve a general currency (see Williams R. 1960; Briggs 1967). Hitherto it had meant little more than 'classification' (like

so many butterflies); now it was to take on entirely new meanings in the wake of the large-scale economic and social changes of the late eighteenth and early nineteenth centuries. As Asa Briggs points out:

There was no dearth of social conflicts in pre-industrial society, but they were not conceived of at the time in straight class terms. The change in nomenclature in the late eighteenth and early nineteenth centuries reflected a basic change not only in men's ways of viewing society but in society itself. (Briggs 1967, p. 43)

In the wake of the Industrial Revolution the language of 'class' became commonplace. To the Victorian 'class' was an obvious social fact and the word was used in common parlance without any of today's reticence or apology. When it came to matters of 'class' each person 'knew their place', for each 'class' was identified by its principal means of monetary return.

a First, there was the upper class, who maintained a virtual monopoly on the ownership of land and who lived off rent. As the nineteenth century proceeded, members of the upper class were to find it increasingly difficult to live in the style to which they were accustomed without recourse to other forms of income than the rents from their estates (unless they were fortunate enough to own the land upon which the new industrial cities were founded). They came also to rely upon the mineral wealth beneath their land and their profitable ventures into various forms of industrial and commercial enterprise.

b Second, there was the middle class, who owned little or no land – but since the new methods of factory production required very little land, this was not an insuperable problem. Their importance lay in the provision of *capital* and since Britain was moving more and more towards a capitalist, industrial economy they were clearly in the ascendancy. Such *parvenus* or *nouveaux riches* (as the landed aristocracy somewhat disdainfully referred to them in a language which few of the new middle class could understand) provided a political threat to the upper class which was not finally settled until the repeal of the Corn Laws in 1846.

   c   Third, there was the working class, who owned neither land nor capital, but who sold the power of their labour in return for a wage. As they became massed together in even larger conglomerations in factories and in cities, so the spectre of class conflict first began to haunt the minority of society who comprised the other two groups. This particularly applied to the great urban centres where, increasingly, manufacture was taking place. As the cities expanded they seemed to threaten the very bonds of society. The cities exemplified *the* key social problem of the age as perceived by the upper and middle classes – the problem of social *order*.

Urbanism

As in the case of capitalism, urbanism did not arrive with the Industrial Revolution. There are plenty of examples of pre-industrial cities, which go back to the ancient civilizations of the East, Ancient Greece and Rome and the urban centres of medieval Europe. However, industrialization promoted urbanization and also transformed the character of cities.

   In pre-industrial Europe the city usually possessed one or more of the following four functions:

1   Cities were garrisons, centres of military protection for the surrounding countryside and often fortified against attack.
2   They were also centres of administration, both secular and ecclesiastical. Thus the city often retained the functions – and the functionaries – of political, religious and economic control.
3   Cities were also centres of trade – and so contained a significant proportion of merchants. Since, during the medieval period, travel across land was usually far slower and more hazardous than travel by sea, the major

trading cities were seaports or cities with easy access to the sea by river.
4   Finally cities were the centres of craft manufacture. This principally involved the production of those articles which were necessities of life in predominantly agrarian societies – tools and implements, clothes, furniture, etc. This ensured that the social and economic connections between the city and the surrounding countryside never diverged very far, since both the city and the countryside depended upon each other for the provision of goods and services.

It was this fourth function of the medieval city which was to expand and dominate the process of urbanization during the late eighteenth and early nineteenth centuries. For this reason those cities which were largely dependent upon the other three functions were bypassed by the Industrial Revolution. In England, for example, medieval urban centres gave way to the new cities which arose from villages and small market towns like Manchester, Leeds, Birmingham and Sheffield. Only London managed to retain the pre-eminence which it had enjoyed before the Industrial Revolution had begun. In 1750 London had been one of only two cities in Britain with a population of over 50,000 (the other was Edinburgh), but by 1801 there were eight such cities and by 1851 there were twenty-nine, including nine with a population of over 100,000. By 1851, in fact, almost one-third of the population lived in towns with more than 50,000 inhabitants.

   The cities attracted such a flow of population partly, as we have seen, because the commercialization of agriculture was expelling the rural poor and leaving a large rural population surplus to the requirements of capitalist agriculture. This rural surplus population was also, however, attracted to the towns by the prospects of a higher standard of living ('streets paved with gold') in the expanding and buoyant manufacturing sector of the economy. The consequent process of urbanization proceeded at such a pace that it was impossible for the amenities of the cities to keep pace with them. Housing was jerry-built close to factories and was frequently damp and insanitary (though perhaps no less so than the equally dilapidated rural hovels that most of their inhabitants had left behind). The crowding together of such large numbers of people also increased the risks to public health (especially in the absence of running water and adequate sewerage) and it was not long before epidemics of typhoid, cholera and other diseases swept through the major cities, especially after 1830.

These epidemics seemed to encapsulate the fear in which the city was held by the vast majority of the upper and middle classes during the first half of the nineteenth century. Despite the fact that the city was not a novel form of social organization, in Britain, at least, there was a widespread assumption on the part of 'responsible' opinion that they were mere temporary necessities which would have no lasting degree of permanence. Evidence for this was culled from the many examples to be found in classical and biblical literature of the rise and eventual fall of city states and of the accompanying decadence of their civilizations. There was, however, no room for complacency. As the nineteenth century advanced, the industrial city showed disturbingly few signs of the decline which the many classical and biblical allusions had predicted. And added to this came a further worry which developed into almost a nineteenth-century upper- and middle-class obsession: that the rise of the city represented a fundamental threat to *social order*.

In many respects this worry was well founded. Urbanization did destroy the established pattern of social relationships in what had hitherto been a small-scale and predominantly agrarian society. The city, by comparison, seemed to consist of a massive conglomeration of working people – a 'great wen', in Cobbett's famous epithet on London – oozing disease, vice and pauperism. The city, it was believed, brought about the breakdown of the *personal* relationships and modes of social control which

had characterized the dealings between the classes in the countryside. As we shall see in the following two chapters, virtually the entire spectrum of the nineteenth-century propertied classes feared that the growth of the city would mean a 'loss of community' and result in society as a whole becoming much less stable. In the city the classes would become segregated and isolated from each other and the 'vertical ties' of community life would be broken. All of this did not augur well for continued social order.

At the beginning of the nineteenth century the typical reaction to the growth of the industrial city was voiced by the poet and essayist, Robert Southey:

A manufacturing poor is more easily instigated to revolt. They have no local attachments . . . a manufacturing populace is always rife for rioting. . . . Governments who found their prosperity upon manufactures sleep upon gunpowder.

Rife for rioting, sleep upon gunpowder: these powerful images expressed the common fear of some volcanic process at work in the city which would unleash chaos and anarchy upon the world. It was a widely held view among the upper and middle classes that a fundamental transformation of society had taken place and one with which they were ill equipped to cope. Overlying this was a revulsion based upon a more humane response. The rise of German and English romanticism taught that in the city man was separated from nature. Therefore the city was 'unnatural' and its inhabitants were dehumanized. The prevailing emotion here was not so much fear as pity. So in addition to the city being 'rife for rioting', there was an additional view, to which many nineteenth-century liberals attested, that the city was also a place where people lacked fulfilling and authentic personal social relationships. In 1844 Frederick Engels, in typically colourful language, expressed this view very well:

The very turmoil of the streets has something repulsive, something against which human nature rebels. . . . And still they crowd by one another as though they had nothing in common, nothing to do with one another, and their only agreement is a tacit one, that each keep to his own side of the pavement, so as not to delay the opposing streams of the crowd, while it occurs to no man to honour another with so much as a glance. The brutal indifference, the unfeeling isolation of each in his private interest becomes the more repellent and offensive, the more these individuals are crowded together, within a limited space. And, however much one may be aware that this isolation of the individual, this narrow self-seeking is the fundamental principle of our society everywhere, it is nowhere so shamelessly barefaced, so self-conscious as just here in the crowding of the great city. The dissolution of mankind into nomads, of which each one has a separate principle, the world of atoms, is here carried to its utmost extreme. (in Coleman 1973, pp. 108–9)

As we shall see in the following two chapters, this kind of imagery was extremely influential on the perspective on the city taken by the early sociologists.

Liberal democracy

Finally, let us turn from the interpretation of economic change to that of political change. The Industrial Revolution brought with it new forms of social organization in the factory and prompted the rapid growth of cities, but it was elsewhere, in the revolutions of the United States of America and France, that a transformation in political *ideas* was also brought about. Both the American Revolution in its Declaration of Independence and the French Revolution with its rallying cry of 'liberty, equality and fraternity' raised in a fundamental way a number of crucial issues which remain relevant to the conduct of politics and society today. Robert Nisbet, in his book *The Sociological Tradition* (1967), lists these issues as follows:

1   *Tradition versus reason.* The American and French Revolutions posed in a stark form the issue of whether society should be organized according to tradition – that is, according to

ideas and values handed down from the past – or whether it was possible to organize society rationally according to some generally accepted principles embodied in a code of law.

2   *Religion versus the state.* One, but only one, dimension of the American and French Revolutions was the attempt to escape from the omnipotence and dogma of the medieval church, including its associated authority over the morality of individual behaviour. An important aspect of the ideal of creating a rational social order was that large areas of society hitherto under the authority of the church should become secularized and that, in particular, the church should be divorced from the ultimate secular authority of the state (embodied, in most cases, in the monarch).

3   *The nature of property.* Property rights became redefined so that those who could lay claim to property were divested of any obligations over how they used it. Thus ideas such as *noblesse oblige* and other such obligations which were imposed upon property holders in medieval times lost much of their significance, especially legal significance. Instead the law became concerned only with establishing a title to property – what the property owner then did with it was left to the freedom of the individual. This was an essential element of the law if the transition to an unfettered market economy was to take place successfully. The interpretation of freedom as freedom of the *individual* was crucial if this was to be carried out successfully.

4   *Relations between social classes.* Labour, as we have seen, became merely a kind of property under capitalism, over which an employer gained title by virtue of a *contract*. This contractual relationship characterized the new era. It applied equally to inanimate property rights and relationships between the social classes where contracts embodied the elements of cash-nexus referred to earlier in this chapter.

5   *Egalitarianism.* In the desire to cast off the yoke of feudal restrictions on individual liberty it was but a short step to conceive of all men as being born equal. 'This truth', as the American

Declaration of Independence put it, was henceforth 'taken to be self-evident'.

The significance of these political notions for the development of sociology cannot be overestimated. They acted like a catalyst upon the currents of speculation and unrest stirred up by the urbanism and industrialization occurring in Britain and elsewhere. Hence the consequences of putting into practice the principles underlying the French and American Revolutions were carefully monitored – both in these countries themselves and abroad. Soon major divisions of opinion had become evident: on one hand various streams of 'progressive' thought greeted the transformations with more or less optimism; on the other writers and commentators offered a largely pessimistic and conservative account of such fundamental political and social changes.

We must now examine certain aspects of these divisions more closely for the debate did not continue to be centred solely around questions of preference. Rival political evaluations of contemporary events encouraged, indeed, relied upon rival *explanations* of them. In this brief account we shall concentrate on three major instances where connection between a recognizable political position and a definite theoretical attitude to industrial society is obvious.

We begin with two 'progressive' accounts.

Classical liberalism

The classical statements of the liberal position in politics drew upon various doctrines stressing the sanctity of the individual person. One of the clearest expressions of this sanctity is contained in the assertions of the American Declaration of Independence that individuals are possessed of certain 'inalienable rights' among which are 'life, liberty and the pursuit of happiness'. Another particularly influential version of this outlook argued that political institutions should be treated as akin to a contract between *equal* partners. Rousseau, for example, expounded the view that political organization of mankind was the result of an actual social contract. In establishing it individuals had emerged from a state of natural savagery to cede some of their personal sovereignty. They had done so in order to create the more effective guarantee that government *ought* to provide of their remaining rights as individuals. The corollary of this emphasis on individual rights was that *each should be free to pursue his (or, less readily, her) own happiness unless it impinged on the happiness of another*.

The merit that liberals saw in the new order lay precisely in the fact that after centuries of tyranny this freedom would at last be possible. The political upheavals attending it were portrayed as an unshackling of the human spirit from centuries of unnatural and often tyrannical restraint. In future the main role of the state would merely be one of providing a useful arrangement whereby conflicting individual interests would be reconciled.

Now, underneath the idealism and optimism to be found in all versions of liberalism was an already established theory of what the human world is, or ought to be, like. It was portrayed as consisting of self-contained individuals, each with certain built-in passions, motives and faculties. Moreover it was assumed that man (*sic*) by nature is a *rational* animal: that his distinguishing and crowning faculty is the ability to think and reason logically from a dispassionate examination of the merits of a case. It was the exercise of reason which had enabled European nations to progress thus far on the road to civilization. The removal of traditional restraints was now urgently necessary and desirable as the next step in the development of reason.

Of course, because of the growing economic dominance of Britain, the liberal credo of the rising British (especially the English) 'middle' class attracted a growing amount of attention from all European social thinkers and critics. Admittedly, the theoretical basis of the 'English System', as it was called, was in some ways merely a variant of the general efforts of European Enlightenment thought to free itself from accounts of natural and social phenomena that still relied on theology, intuition or mere tradition. In their place, as Saint-Simon and Comte in France were to propose, should come a 'positive', that is, a rational-scientific study of human affairs. But for the British, human affairs meant especially *business* affairs, that is, the 'wealth of nations'. Their versions of classical liberalism put especial emphasis on the removal of all obstacles – whether created by tradition or the state – to the growth of trade and profits. Hence the development in Britain of a style of liberal positive or positivist theory which seemed particularly suited to the prosecution of such matters. It is usually referred to as *utilitarian rationalism* or simply *utilitarianism*.

To be sure, the term 'utilitarianism' itself was not coined until quite late in the history of the theory, in association with the moral doctrines of Jeremy Bentham, J. S. Mill and their followers. (As such the utilitarian enjoined law givers and moralists to observe the famous precept of 'the greatest happiness of the greatest number'.) The underlying view of society which it represented had appeared from much earlier on, however, in the writings of Thomas Hobbes, John Locke, James Mill, Adam Smith and many others. Each of these writers was to give the meaning of human rationality a distinctive twist by interpreting all actions as the product of self-interest and the egoistic pursuit of satisfaction and happiness. Out went notions of morality, duty or altruism as causes of human behaviour. All arrangements should be understood as a matter of the calculation and exchange of advantage or 'utility' as it was to become known.

In the hands of the utilitarian theorists the liberal idea of the self-contained sovereign individual was taken to the point where it actually threatened the account of politics which it was intended to support. This possibility was one which Thomas Hobbes had noted in his treatise, *The Leviathan*, at the end of the seventeenth century. If everyone pursued their own ends with scant regard for others, would we not end up with a state of what he called 'a war of all against all'? This chilling vision of chaos and anarchy began to acquire an ominous ring by the beginning of the nineteenth century. It seemed very plausible in the turmoil accompanying industrialization. Hence, what some writers have called 'the Hobbesian problem of order' achieved a peculiar relevance during this period.

This was the first of a number of 'unpleasant surprises' – to use J. B. Burrow's telling phrase – which the rationalist, particularly the utilitarian rationalist, account of human society was to spring on itself. And herein lay a matter of tremendous importance for both the early and the later history of sociological work. But before we can take the point further we must examine some other theories born of rather different political attitudes to the new order.

Utopian socialism

In reaction to utilitarianism a new set of ideas, equally 'progressive' but based upon other premises, began to take hold – the utopian socialism of Claude de Saint-Simon in France and Robert Owen in Britain. The utopian socialists made their case by simply pushing the arguments of classical liberalism beyond the point where most liberals were prepared to go. According to Robert Owen,

The primary and necessary object of all existence is to be happy, but happiness cannot be obtained individually; it is useless to expect isolated happiness; all must partake of it or the few will never enjoy it. (Hobsbawm 1962, p. 286)

The utopian socialists therefore accepted the force of Hobbes's argument. The uninhibited pursuit of self-interest would indeed, they believed, lead to a war of all against all. They therefore rejected the doctrine of the self-contained individual, arguing that human beings were naturally communal and that the greatest happiness of the greatest number could only be achieved collectively. Hence the idea of Owen, for example, was to create co-operative enterprises and 'communist' (in the literal sense) colonies away from the corrupting influences of industrial capitalism. Owen converted his utopia into reality in his settlement of New Lanark in Scotland.

It is important to be clear about the exact sense in which utopian socialism can be described as 'progressive'. Its proponents rejected the nineteenth century because they rejected the dehumanizing nature of *capitalism*. But they quite accepted the growth of *industrialism* as a necessary step in the evolution of mankind. New Lanark, for example, was to serve as an example of the benefits of the new processes of production while at the same time avoiding the reduction of human relationships to those of the cash-nexus.

Liberal democracy: the conservative reaction

Ranged against both of these two 'progressive' reactions to industrialism there stood *classical conservatism*. Notoriously conservatism was not so much a coherent and explicit set of ideas but a gut feeling. Edmund Burke was its most influential exponent in Britain and it is possible to discern in his writing some or all of the following:

1 *An attack upon rationalism*. Instead conservatism placed the emphasis upon instinct, tradition, religious faith and the intractable quality of 'human nature'. Conservatives were thus initially suspicious of liberal democracy or of allowing any semblance of political control to pass to the 'swinish multitude' of the cities and factories.
2 *A belief in the immutability of history*. Radical change was an impossibility because 'the weight of perpetuity' was impossible to cast off. Society was a product of its history and could only proceed in a manner commensurate with that of history.
3 *Society as an organism*. Conservatives regarded the internal relationships of society as 'organic' – that is, based upon mutual dependence. This particularly applied to relations between classes. Like any other organism, society was therefore resistant to rapid change and could only 'evolve' slowly and patiently in a manner which did not create any social disequilibrium and social pathology. Attempts to create revolution were thus not only unwelcome but self-defeating. The growth of cities was also deplored since they provoked both 'disequilibrium' (conflict) and 'pathology' (crime, vice, disease).
4 *Urban industrialism as a 'loss of community'*. Conservatives shared this perception with the utopian socialists, with whom they combined to attack the growth of cities. They did so, however, in a literally 'reactionary' manner by desiring to return to the pre-industrial Golden Age ruled over by a protective and benevolent squirearchy. They yearned for the certainties of a society composed of identifiable 'natural orders' before the confusing and threatening onset of urbanism and industrialism.

Conclusion: industrialism, politics and sociology

Liberalism, socialism and conservatism, then, were overtly 'political' responses to the novel changes which occurred in North America and Northern Europe between 1750 and 1850. Buried within them, however, were recognizable if embryonic theories of how this new form of society worked. And although the writers concerned usually began by speaking about the nature of the new society and the direction of its development, they rapidly found themselves pronouncing on human nature in general and the basis of the bond between individual and society in particular. Gradually the widespread faith in a scientific approach to politics and society brought these assumptions to the surface so that they became a matter of debate in themselves.

In this respect, the influence of liberalism was of great importance, probably outweighing that of either socialism or conservatism. This may seem a somewhat surprising remark, particularly in view of the significance which socialism has come to assume in the modern political context. We concede, too, that it cuts across the lines of a debate on this very issue which is evident among historians of sociology. On one hand a well-known study by Nisbet presents the thesis that much of the nineteenth-century sociology was inspired by a largely conservative and hence hostile attitude to political and industrial revolution as described in this chapter (Nisbet 1967). Zeitlin, on the other hand, has argued that real creative ferment in sociology, the so-called classical period of the late nineteenth and early twentieth centuries, could only take place under the influence of socialism – specifically the scientific socialism of Karl Marx and counter-reactions to it (Zeitlin 1971). It is not, however, our intention to challenge the validity of these interpretations but to supplement them. They do, after all, concentrate attention on the motives which impelled social enquiry forward rather than the issues with which it dealt. The emphasis in this book is rather different. Our main interest we have said is in the emergence of sociology as a discipline, one which despite much internal controversy and diversity may be defended as unified by a distinctive agenda of common problems. Such an approach is bound to recognize the special position of the liberal rationalist outlook:

1   It offered an interpretation of industrialism which was acceptable to aspiring political movements and social groups in several important European states. It was to become the dominant belief system in Britain, the most prosperous and industrialized of these states throughout the nineteenth century. The attention of serious speculative thinkers was bound to be drawn to it even when they themselves were not directly imbued with its assumptions.
2   It represented the dominant form through which people retained at least a nominal belief in the Enlightenment ideal; that in the light of reason the course of human history and the character of political society might be improved. The very idea of a social science was merely an extension of this view and the work of some of sociology's 'founding fathers' may be read as a rearguard effort to defend the Enlightenment ideal against encroaching Unreason (Hughes H. S. 1959).
3   The most fundamental factor, though, lay not in the various aspirations which liberalism expressed but in the successive defects which were uncovered in its *theory* of both human nature and human society. The limitations of the concept of reason – and in particular the limitations of the utilitarian theory of rational self-interest – were brought out in two main ways:
a   Though it claimed to be a theory with universal applications, it clearly could not account for the diversity of customs and moral rules which Europeans encountered as their influence and trade spread over the globe. What then was the origin of moral rules, especially the 'irrational' but entrenched practices of savage and barbarian societies?
b   There was also the problem of the 'lower orders' in the industrial nations themselves. It was not simply that the improvident moral habits of the poor represented a puzzling phenomenon to the apostles of self-interest. It was also that the existence of inequality itself was neither anticipated nor adequately explained by a theory of rational choice (cf. MacPherson 1962).

We shall find these two themes, the origin and effectiveness of moral rules and the causes and consequences of inequality, recurring very frequently in the following pages.

Despite these difficulties, liberalism and utilitarianism represented a remarkable intellectual achievement. Their importance for the history of sociological thought lay in the fact that they stressed the intimate connection between the ways in which individuals make choices and the nature of society. Subsequent theorists in the sociological tradition never denied this. What they did object to was the particular assumption that self-interest is the only ingredient in the making of choices or that only choices involving self-interest may be considered rational. Nor did they consider it to be true that individuals are invariably the most knowledgeable judges of what constitutes their self-interest, nor always act rationally in order to pursue it. For many 'choices' are not based upon complete freedom of will but are constrained by 'society' at large. Choice, therefore, always depends upon antecedent social conditions – and this became the focus of the sociological critique of utilitarianism. Thus, while theories of behaviour based on rational self-interest developed into modern economics, sociology took a different path, investigating the social conditions under which various choices are made and in which particular kinds of rationality thrive. 'Society' rather than 'the individual' became the focus of attention.

Part Two: Industrial Society as Regress – Tönnies and 'Community'

3 Urbanism as a way of life?

Let us now turn to the first of our 'schools' of sociology. We shall begin with a fairly straightforward example, simply in order to show how sociologists take hold of an everyday idea and submit it to careful examination. But our example is not *just* an everyday idea.

In the previous chapter we discussed the various political and ideological reactions which emerged during and after the social turmoil of the 'two revolutions'. We divided these reactions into two: the 'progressives' – themselves divided between liberals and socialists – and the 'conservatives'. We also noted that while they differed over their diagnosis of the changes which they had witnessed, they were in agreement that what was involved was some kind of rupture – that life would never be quite the same again.

So rapid and so widespread were the changes that the temptation to analyse society in 'now-and-then' terms was irresistible. As a consequence the present was constantly being *contrasted* with the past in the belief that what was occurring 'now' was quite unique and completely different from 'then' – that is, before the advent of the Industrial and Democratic Revolutions. Almost all nineteenth-century sociological theorists succumbed to viewing social change in terms of what Nisbet has called 'linked antitheses' – contrasting pairs of concepts, one of which is applied to society before the transformation and the other applied to the subsequent era.

This type of approach to social change is particularly vividly illustrated by the work of the German theorist, Ferdinand Tönnies, and the body of literature influenced by him. Although Tönnies's name is not widely known beyond the bounds of academic sociology, his ideas, even if in a diluted form, remain very influential today. For Tönnies characterized the rise of urban industrialism as involving a *loss of community*.

The pessimistic and somewhat conservative view that modern society is indeed afflicted by such a loss remains a very common everyday belief, often accompanied by a degree of nostalgia for a vanished past of close communal living. But how valid is this outlook? In answering this question we shall be able to illustrate some of the aspects of sociology which we have been considering in the last two chapters and also introduce a number of other basic ideas:

a *'social organization'* – the idea that society as a whole possesses a permanence and regularity which extends beyond the lives of individuals who compose it;

b social *'types'* – the idea that the form of social organization varies between one society and another, especially between traditional and modern societies;

c *typical social relationships* – the idea that the type of social organization will shape the usual or typical character of the relationship existing between one member of society and another.

In Tönnies's work each of these notions is to be found intermingled with the others.

Gemeinschaft and Gesellschaft

Tönnies, then, regarded urban industrial society as representing a contrast with, rather than a continuation of, the past. In order to describe this contrast Tönnies coined the very important twin terms of *Gemeinschaft* and *Gesellschaft* in his book with this title, first published in 1887.

Gemeinschaft is usually translated as 'community' and for Tönnies *gemeinschaft*-like, or 'community-type', relationships were characteristic of the pre-industrial world.

Gesellschaft is more difficult to render exactly in English and is variously translated as 'society', 'organization' or 'association'. Industrialization was associated with the rise of *Gesellschaft* and therefore had, according to Tönnies, been responsible for the decline of 'community' in the modern world.

What did Tönnies mean by these two terms? *Gemeinschaft*-like relationships were intimate, enduring and based upon a clear understanding of each individual's position in society. A person's status was estimated according to *who* that person was rather than *what* that person had done. In addition, members of a society based upon *Gemeinschaft*-like relationships were relatively immobile, both geographically – they did not move around very much from place to place – and socially – there was little mobility up and down the social scale. We can express this sociologically by stating that Tönnies believed that, in the pre-industrial world based on *Gemeinschaft*, the status of an individual was *ascribed* (that is, relatively fixed, given at birth) rather than *achieved* (based on merit or performance). Culturally societies characterized by *Gemeinschaft* were relatively homogeneous since their culture was enforced quite rigidly by well-recognized moral custodians – the church and the family. Both of these institutions were therefore, according to Tönnies, much more important and much stronger in pre-industrial society. The system of beliefs which the church and the family supported were clear to the point of being 'common sense', that is, part of the taken-for-granted, everyday beliefs and values of the entire membership of the society. For example, *Gemeinschaft*-like sentiments placed a high premium on the sanctity of kinship and on territoriality – the solidarity with other members of the family or clan and with those who lived in the same place. Indeed the core of *Gemeinschaft*, according to Tönnies, was the sentimental attachment to the conventions and mores of a 'beloved place' enshrined in a tradition which was handed down over the generations from family to family. Within this territory the enduring, closely knit nature of *Gemeinschaft*-like relationships were also characterized by greater emotional cohesion, greater depth of sentiment and greater continuity, and were ultimately more meaningful.

Opposed to *Gemeinschaft* is *Gesellschaft* – arguably best translated as 'association' – which consists of everything that community is *not*. *Gesellschaft* refers to the large-scale, impersonal, calculative and contractual relationships which, according to Tönnies, were on the increase in the industrial world at the expense of *Gemeinschaft*. Tönnies believed that both industrialism and urbanism had been associated with an increase in the scale, and therefore the impersonality, of society. This impersonality enabled social interaction to become more easily regulated by contract, so that *Gesellschaft*-like relationships were more calculative and more specific – that is, more 'rational' in the sense that they were 'restricted to a definite end and a definite means of obtaining it' (Tönnies 1957, p. 192). Consequently, Tönnies believed, most of the virtues and morality of 'community' were lost under the process of industrialization. In this sense his critique of *Gesellschaft* was a critique of the utilitarian's society of rational individuals and explicitly a reaction against it. For Tönnies, however, the rise of urban, industrial society stemmed from the loss of 'community', rather than vice versa. He regarded the replacement of *Gemeinschaft* by more rational, calculative *Gesellschaft*-like relationships as a prerequisite of the rise of capitalism – and hence of the rise of nineteenth-century industrial society.

Tönnies's greatest legacy, then, was this typological usage of *Gemeinschaft* and *Gesellschaft* –

that is, two contrasting models of pre-industrial and industrial society which enabled some kind of sense to be made of the profound changes which were sweeping across nineteenth-century Europe. Tönnies was generally pessimistic about the consequences of these changes. He feared the breakdown of the traditional social order which the new social forces might engender, regarding *Gemeinschaft* as a source of stability in society. However, it is important to emphasize that Tönnies was not referring to any particular social group when he wrote about *Gemeinschaft* and *Gesellschaft*, but to forms of human association – about how the basis of social relationships had changed from (a) the personal, the emotional and the traditional to (b) the impersonal, the rational and the contractual. For example, Tönnies was careful to argue that both *Gemeinschaft*-like and *Gesellschaft*-like relationships could be found in rural and urban settings, though he did admit to a greater tendency towards *Gemeinschaft* in rural areas – 'it is stronger there and more alive' (Tönnies 1957, p. 35).

Nevertheless Tönnies understood how our sense of place depends on social organization: for him *Gemeinschaft*-like relationships were linked to the 'community of blood' (kinship) and/or a 'community of mind' (friendship) necessary among those who wished to live in reasonable proximity (Tönnies 1957, p. 55). Over the years since Tönnies wrote *Gemeinschaft und Gesellschaft*, particular stress has been laid on his references to the territorial factor, the place, the locality. Yet *Gemeinschaft* as it was originally used by Tönnies, although it included locality, also went beyond it to encompass a type of relationship which could characterize the whole of society: 'communion' as well as 'community'. As Schmalenbach (1961) has pointed out, there is a confusion here in using the same term – *Gemeinschaft* – to describe both the emotive quality of this relationship and its basis in a traditional (by implication rural) community structure. This confusion may have been responsible for the tendency during the twentieth century to identify particular forms of association (e.g. *Gemeinschaft–Gesellschaft*) with particular types of territory (e.g. rural–urban). It has enabled Tönnies's original formulation to become distorted into a rural–urban continuum where *Gemeinschaft*-like and *Gesellschaft*-like relationships become grounded in specific *localities*.

Metropolis and mental life

The first person to relate *Gemeinschaft* and *Gesellschaft* concepts to specific localities was Tönnies's German contemporary, Georg Simmel. In his essay published in 1903, entitled 'The metropolis and mental life' (1950), Simmel applied some of Tönnies's insights to urban society, which, in keeping with the nineteenth-century Romantic tradition, he viewed with thinly veiled hostility. Simmel begins from the premise that, 'The deepest problems of modern life flow from . . . the resistance of the individual to being levelled, swallowed up in the socio-technological mechanism.' (Simmel 1950, p. 409). Simmel attempts to examine the process by investigating the relationship which the city promotes between the individual and the urban world in which he or she lives. Simmel argues that the individual adapts to city life by cultivating a unique kind of personality and that this 'mental life' was shaped by social forces beyond the existence of the single individual. For Simmel, urban life is characterized by the following:

1   Simmel believed that urban life is rational (in the same sense that Tönnies used this term), whereas rural life is based upon feelings and emotional relationships. The rationality of urban society is due to the increased tempo of life which in turn is provoked by the increasing social and economic differentiation. This leads Simmel to introduce a kaleidoscopic view of urbanism: 'the rapid telescoping of our changing images, pronounced differences within what is grasped at a single glance, and the

unexpectedness of violent stimuli' (Simmel 1950, p. 410). Such differentiation creates an increased awareness among urban dwellers that this complex, shifting world is based upon the division of labour, which in turn stimulates thought, rather than a reliance upon habit, as a necessary guide to action in this constantly changing series of encounters.

2   The city is the seat of the money economy. This encourages a purely matter-of-fact treatment of people and things so that social relationships become impersonal and standardized (cf. Tönnies). The crucial intervening factor here is the market: 'Thereby the interests of each party acquire a relentless matter-of-factness, and its rationally calculated economic egoism need not fear any divergence from its set path because of the imponderability of personal relationships.' (Simmel 1950, pp. 411–12)

3   Connected with these first two points, the modern (urban) mind has become much more a *calculating* one. Thus, states Simmel, the world becomes transformed into a mere arithmetical problem, fixing each of its parts in a mathematical formula.

4   These apparently impersonal factors provoke a number of personal consequences. They produce that which, for Simmel, is the prevalent feature of urban life – *the blasé outlook*. The constantly shifting stimuli and the pace of urban living produce so many different and varied experiences that the individual becomes satiated and hence blasé. This blasé attitude leads ultimately, according to Simmel, to an inability to distinguish the individuality of people and things, so that all questions of the quality of experience are reduced to the simple question of 'How much?'

5   Because of the lack of face-to-face contact with known individuals the predominant urban demeanour is a formal 'reserve' – something which, Simmel suggests, is little more than concealed aversion. Thus individuals in the city become isolated from each other.

6   Finally the individual becomes estranged from the other members of urban society and from other social groups.

Thus Simmel provides us with a catalogue of what were later to become familiar urban social evils – impersonality, isolation, alienation. He goes on to argue that this existence produces an exaggerated quest for individuality, a frantic search for self-identity within the amorphous framework of metropolitan life. This leads eventually, Simmel believes, to the emergence of strange personal eccentricities which are employed in a desperate search to be different. These eccentricities of behaviour, which Simmel regards as more prevalent in urban life, are an attempt to overcome the inherent danger of being reduced to a negligible quantity in what appears to be an overwhelmingly vast, immovable and somewhat alien urban culture. As Simmel puts it:

He becomes a single cog as over against the vast overwhelming organisation of things and forces which gradually take out of his hands everything connected with progress, spirituality and value. The operation of these forces results in the transformation of the latter from a subjective form into one of purely objective existence. It need only be pointed out that the metropolis is the proper arena for this type of culture which has outgrown every personal element. (Simmel 1962, p. 422)

Simmel ends his essay with the disingenuous comment that, 'It is our task not to complain or to condone but only to understand.' There is, of course, no doubt where Simmel's own values lie and this is purely a piece of window-dressing. Simmel, like Tönnies, feared the 'loss of community' in modern society, but unlike Tönnies, Simmel related this simply and solely to the growth of the *city* as a unique form of modern social organization.

Urbanism as a way of life

In the first two decades of this century Simmel's ideas were transplanted to the United States, where the first-ever department of sociology was established at the University of Chicago and headed by disciples of Simmel in Albion Small and, later, Robert Park. Park founded the so-called Chicago School of urban sociology, whose detailed studies of urban social processes in the late 1920s and 1930s have, justifiably, become famous as models of diligent empirical research. Simmel's influence on the Chicago School was considerable and therefore his approach reaches its apotheosis in a classic paper by the Chicago sociologist, Louis Wirth, entitled 'Urbanism as a way of life' and published in the *American Journal of Sociology* in 1938. Wirth begins his analysis from a number of assumptions:

1 First, that 'what is distinctively modern in our civilisation is best signalled by the growth of cities' (Wirth 1938, p. 1). In other words, it is urbanism which is characteristic of modern society (rather than, say, industrialism or capitalism or liberal democracy or the growth of a bureaucratic state).

2 The growth of cities has wrought a fundamental break with man's 'natural' situation: 'Nowhere has mankind been further removed from organic nature than under the conditions of life characteristic of great cities.' (Wirth 1938, pp. 1–2)

3 The city is the centre of all that is innovating in the modern world: 'The distinctive feature of the mode of living of man in the modern age is his concentration into gigantic aggregations around which cluster lesser centres and from which radiate the ideas and practices that we call civilisation.' (Wirth 1938, p. 2)

4 Consequently modern culture can be called an *urban* culture because the culture of the city has spread out to envelop all of mankind: 'It is the initiating and controlling centre of economic, political and cultural life that has drawn the most remote parts of the world into its orbit.' (Wirth 1938, p. 2)

5 Urbanization has wrought 'profound changes in virtually every phase of social life'. Thus the city 'wipes out completely the previously dominant modes of human association.' (Wirth 1938, pp. 2, 3)

6 Hence, Wirth argues, 'the city and the country may be regarded as two poles in reference to one or the other of which all human settlements tend to arrange themselves.' (Wirth 1938, p. 3)

Following Tönnies and his twin concepts of *Gemeinschaft* and *Gesellschaft* and building upon Simmel's attempt to root them in a rural–urban dichotomy, Wirth suggests that *where* we live has a profound influence upon *how* we live. As we move from the countryside to the city so we leave behind a 'rural way of life' and take on the values and behaviour of 'urbanism as a way of life'. It is to an analysis of the latter that Wirth devotes his paper.

Wirth's initial task is to furnish a sociological definition of the city. He is reluctant to base this on the size of the population alone since this is too arbitrary and takes no account of the fact that population statistics are frequently based upon administrative boundaries that bear little relationship to the city as a social unit. Moreover,

As long as we identify urbanism with the physical entity of the city, viewing it merely as rigidly delimited in space, and proceed as if urban attributes abruptly ceased to be manifested beyond an arbitrary boundary line, we are not likely to arrive at any adequate conception of urbanism as a mode of life. (Wirth 1938, p. 4)

Urbanism has therefore spread beyond the city as a physical environment; it is a *cultural* rather than physical phenomenon. Any definition must not only take account of this fact, but also embrace the diversity of cities, which will vary significantly according to their industrial, commercial and financial bases. However, Wirth is insistent that urbanism is not *reducible to* an economic base:

It is particularly important to call attention to the danger of confusing urbanism with industrialism and modern capitalism. The rise of cities in the modern world is undoubtedly not independent of the emergence of modern power-driven technology, mass production, and capitalistic enterprise. But different as the cities of earlier epochs may have been by virtue of their development in a pre-industrial and pre-capitalistic order from the great cities of today, they were, nevertheless, cities. (Wirth 1938, pp. 7–8)

Therefore he defines the city simply as 'a relatively large, dense and permanent settlement of socially heterogeneous individuals'.

Wirth then sets out to offer an 'ordered and coherent framework of theory' which accounts for ways of life in the city. He does so by discussing each of the major social characteristics which, he believes, helps to define the city. These three characteristics follow.

Size of population

Here Wirth largely follows the analysis of Simmel in 'The metropolis and mental life'. Wirth, like Simmel, emphasizes that the increased size of population in the city promotes a greater social differentiation. This differentiation is also expressed geographically in the formation of different neighbourhoods according to class, ethnicity, etc. Wirth also agrees with Simmel that in the city 'personal mutual acquaintanceship is lacking' and that human relationships become compartmentalized or 'segmented'. This produces what Wirth calls a 'schizoid' urban mentality. As Wirth points out:

This is not to say that the urban inhabitants have fewer acquaintances than rural inhabitants, for the reverse may actually be true; it means rather that in relation to the number of people whom they see and with whom they rub elbows in the course of daily life, they know a smaller proportion, and of these they have less intensive knowledge. (Wirth 1938, p. 12)

Thus while social contacts in the city may indeed still be face-to-face, they are 'impersonal, superficial, transitory and segmental' – that is, they are what Wirth calls *secondary* relationships which provide only a small fraction of overall human needs. As such, they are to be contrasted with the *primary* relationships characteristic of *Gemeinschaft*-like rural life which fulfil the individual's personal and psychological requirements. In contrast, the city, despite the size of its population, denies the basis for meaningful social intimacy. Indeed, writes Wirth, 'The reserve, the indifference, the *blasé* outlook which urbanites manifest in their relationships may thus be regarded as devices for immunising themselves against the personal claims and expectations of others.' (Wirth 1938)

One consequence of this is that all urban relationships tend to be reduced to utilitarian ones. The superficiality, the anonymity and the transitory character of such relationships make this inevitable. For Wirth, and many other American urban sociologists in the 1930s, the epitome of urbanism was the relationship between the taxi driver and his fare – a 'brief encounter' which exemplified all these factors. Wirth regarded one of the central paradoxes of urbanism to be its tendency to create feelings of individual loneliness in the midst of huge crowds. While the city emancipates the individual from the crushing conformities of *Gemeinschaft*, it also leaves the individual rootless and unintegrated.

Density

Wirth argues that the increasing concentration of people in a limited space also prompts a number of consequences. Some of these are environmental, such as the increase in overcrowding, pollution, grime, etc. Others are more sociological, however. For example, differences among the population, such as those between rich and poor, become much more socially visible. It is not so much that these differences are proportionally any greater in the city than in the countryside, but the greater absolute numbers together with neighbourhood segregation render them more apparent. Wirth also argues that the close proximity to one another of the urban population fosters competition among them. By a process akin to the

Darwinian idea of 'survival of the fittest' aggrandizement and mutual exploitation are encouraged. There are echoes here of the familiar presentation of urbanism as a 'rat race' or a 'jungle'. Indeed Wirth is much taken with analogies drawn from ecology on the consequence of increasing proximity between organisms in a fixed and enclosed habitat. He draws attention to the likely rise in social and interpersonal conflict that will ensue – the friction, irritation and nervous disorder wrought by frequent *physical* contact but decreasingly meaningful *social* contact.

Heterogeneity

The city is characterized by an increasingly heterogeneous population caused by the expanding division of labour. As the urban population becomes more diverse and more specialized, so the class structure becomes more complicated and more opaque. The individual therefore no longer knows his or her 'place', which may contribute to a sense of insecurity and rootlessness. On the other hand, the urban class structure is more 'open' than its rural counterpart – that is, less rigid and less coherent:

No single group has the undivided allegiance of the individual. The groups with which he is affiliated do not lend themselves readily to a simple hierarchical arrangement. By virtue of his different interests arising out of different aspects of social life, the individual acquires membership in widely divergent groups, each of which functions only with reference to a single segment of his personality. Nor do these groups easily permit of a concentric arrangement so that the narrower ones fall within the circumference of the more inclusive ones, as is more likely to be the case in the rural community or in primitive societies. Rather the groups with which the person typically is affiliated are tangential to each other or intersect in highly variable fashion. (Wirth 1938, p. 16)

Urban society is also a more mobile society, both socially and geographically. Both this social mobility and 'physical rootlessness' lead Wirth to describe the urban social structure as a 'fluid mass', a factor which makes urban society unstable and unpredictable. Within this 'fluid mass' the individual is relatively powerless to affect the pattern of urban life and therefore tends to join with other like-minded individuals to form organized groups which attempt to achieve their desired goals. As Wirth concludes this section: 'If the individual would participate at all in the social, political, and economic life of the city, he must subordinate some of his individuality to the demands of the larger community and in that measure immerse himself in mass movements.' (Wirth 1938, p. 18)

Wirth summarizes his paper by stating that urbanism as a way of life may be approached empirically from three interrelated perspectives:

1 as a physical structure comprising a population base, a technology and an ecological order;
2 as a system of social organization involving a characteristic social structure, a set of social institutions and a typical pattern of social relationships;
3 as a set of attitudes and ideas and a constellation of personalities engaging in typical forms of collective behaviour and subject to characteristic mechanisms of social control.

The rural–urban continuum

The aim of Wirth's paper is deliberately *heuristic* – that is, to aid the investigation of various problems, both sociological and practical, which urban society engenders. In this he has been enormously successful, for until very recently Wirth's approach has been extremely influential in urban sociology. There is, however, an implicit contrast running through his paper with 'ruralism as a way of life' which Wirth rarely articulates, but which is assumed to consist of all those attributes which are either absent from or destroyed by urbanism. Indeed the equivalent to Wirth's paper in the field of rural sociology did not appear until 1947 in the form of Robert Redfield's paper, 'The folk society', which was also published in the *American Journal of Sociology* (1947). Redfield was an anthropologist, but he was very familiar with the work of Wirth and other members of the so-called Chicago School of American sociologists. Redfield therefore knew all about the extremely detailed investigations of urban life carried out by Wirth and his contemporaries in Chicago in the 1920s and 1930s. At the same time Redfield was carrying out studies of rural communities, mostly in Mexico. Like Wirth, he wished to offer a general, theoretical appraisal of rural life which would both summarize and make sense of the many *ad hoc* studies hitherto completed.

Redfield's conception of the 'folk society' is very reminiscent of Tönnies's notion of *Gemeinschaft*:

Such a society is small, isolated, non-literate and homogeneous, with a strong sense of group solidarity. The ways of living are conventionalised into the coherent system which we call 'a culture'. Behaviour is traditional, spontaneous, uncritical and personal: there is no legislation or habit of experiment and reflection for intellectual ends. Kinship, its relations and institutions, are the type categories of experience and the familial group is the unit of action. The sacred prevails over the secular; the economy is one of status rather than the market. (Redfield 1947, p. 293)

All of these factors are the very opposite of Wirth's characterization of 'urbanism as a way of life', but what Redfield and Wirth share is a conviction that ways of life are intimately related to geographical locations. This idea was not, of course, a 'discovery' of theirs, for it fitted in with most common-sense ideas of variations in lifestyles between different geographical areas and settlement patterns. Nor was the idea a particularly novel one in sociology. As early as 1929 Sorokin and Zimmerman had attempted to organize a great deal of empirical material about American life around what they called a 'rural–urban continuum' in their book, *Principles of Rural–Urban Sociology*. It is, perhaps, worth quoting their conclusions at some length as a representative illustration of their approach:

Up to recent times, at least for the bulk of the city population, the city environment, as such, has been much less natural and has given much less opportunity for the satisfaction of basic human needs and fundamental impulses than the rural environment. For a clarification of this idea, let us consider the situation of the urban proletariat, its work, its occupational environment, and the essentials of its mode of living. This group works in a closed factory or shop, which has been, especially in the past, often unhygienic, ugly, unaesthetical, and unattractive to eyes, or ears, or to the organs of smell or other perceptions. They are surrounded by the kingdom of dead machinery, steel, iron, coal and oil. Enormous noises, clangs, grinds, knocks, raps, clatters and taps of machinery and tools fill their ears. Dirt, summer heat, and winter cold assail them. Such has been and still is their occupational environment to a considerable degree. The work itself is also tiresome, monotonous, mechanical, half automatic. It furnishes little, if any, creative or interesting outlet for them. It goes on monotonously day in day out, for months and years. . . . Can such a city environment and manner of living satisfy these fundamental impulses and habit developed in quite a different situation and adapted to quite a different environment? The answer is no. Neither the impulses for creative activity, nor for orientation, curiosity, and novelty; nor the lust for variety and adventure; nor the physiological necessity for being in touch with nature; nor to enjoy with eyes the greenishness of the meadow, the beauties of the forest, the clear rivers, the waves of golden wheat in the fields; nor to hear the birds singing, the thunderstorm, or the mysterious calm of an evening amidst nature; these and thousands of similar phenomena have been taken from the urban man. . . . In spite of the enormous improvement of the conditions of the urban labour classes in these respects, the city has a great deal of these elements of 'unnaturality' and through that stimulates dissatisfaction and disorders.

The farmer–peasant environment, on the contrary, has been much more 'natural' and much more identical with that to which man has been trained by thousands of years of preceding history. The basic impulses of man, as they have been shaped by the past, are to be satisfied much easier in the environment and by the occupational activity of the farmer. There is neither the lack of nature, nor the killing monotony of work, nor extreme specialisation, nor one-sidedness. His standard of living may be as low as that of a proletarian; his house or lodging may be as bad; and yet the whole character of his structure of living is quite different and healthier and more natural. (Sorokin and Zimmerman 1929, pp. 466–7)

Although few would be quite so explicit, Sorokin and Zimmerman are merely expressing the assumption which underlay the whole approach to the rural–urban continuum which existed down to and including the work of Redfield. The Romantic cultural perspective is clearly apparent, as is the anti-urbanism. Once these portrayals were accepted then the 'health' of a community could be gauged by locating it on the continuum. However, Wirth and Redfield did depart in one important respect from the analysis of Sorokin and Zimmerman. Whereas the latter were concerned merely to classify communities, both Wirth and Redfield were engaged in a *theoretical*, rather than empirical, exercise. The final sentence of Wirth's paper is a warning against mindless 'fact-gathering'; and Redfield sought to distance himself by referring to the 'folk–urban', rather than rural–urban, continuum. Both were concerned with underlying social processes, particularly the direction of social change, rather than with 'collecting' accounts of rural and urban life. Redfield, for example, was quite emphatic that his 'folk society' was only a model and that it existed nowhere in reality: 'the type is an imagined entity, created only because through it we may hope to understand reality' (Redfield 1947, p. 295). Redfield and Wirth were concerned to see urbanization as a process which changed the structure of social relationships. It was these social relationships which really concerned them and formed the basis for their theorizing (for example, Wirth's reference to size, density and heterogeneity) rather than urbanism/ruralism *per se*. Until at least the mid-1960s (see Frankenberg 1965) this proved to be an enduring idea in sociology, perhaps because it corresponded so well with the prevailing common-sense view that there was indeed something *intrinsically* different about social relationships in the city compared with those in the countryside.

There is, then, a direct continuity between the theories of Tönnies and more recent attempts to gauge the 'health' of community life from the geographical location of the population. Tönnies's original conception has, however, become somewhat distorted in this process. As we have seen, Tönnies was referring to the dehumanizing consequences of contemporary social change in *any* geographical location. For him *Gemeinschaft* and *Gesellschaft* referred to forms of human association which could occur anywhere in society. Tönnies's concern was not urbanization *per se* but the 'loss of community' in a much broader sense – the loss of a sense of identity, meaning and authenticity in the modern world. Attempts to tie this sense of loss to geographical location, by later writers such as Simmel, Wirth and Redfield, risked confusing the issue. As we shall see in the following chapter this proved to be a somewhat mischievous red herring. Nevertheless the tendency to identify settlement types with 'ways of life' and with the presence or absence of 'community' remains a strong one. Consequently we need to look beyond the rural–urban continuum to the more fundamental problems to which Tönnies originally drew attention.

4 A loss of community?

It is a common observation that modern British society is characterized by a 'loss of community'. The phrase is often used in an oblique but poignant way to express the dissatisfaction which many people experience about the quality of life in the contemporary world. There is an implied antithesis between the past, when, so it is believed, the individual was integrated into a stable and harmonious community of kin, friends and neighbours, and the less palatable present, when all too often it is possible to feel like a piece of human flotsam, cast adrift in a sea of apparently bewildering social changes and buffeted by impersonal and alien social forces. The longing for 'community' therefore symbolizes a desire for security and certainty in our lives, but also a desire for identity and authenticity. 'Real communities' are assumed to offer all of these qualities, while their absence is believed to induce a number of disquieting personal and social pathologies. The withering away of a 'spirit of community' as an apparently endemic feature of our social condition is therefore offered as the diagnosis of a wide variety of contemporary social problems, ranging from the incidence of juvenile crime to the loneliness of the elderly. More generally this sense of loss raises doubts about the validity of 'progress' and our fears concerning the direction in which modern society appears to be moving.

Unfortunately, however, it is not always clear precisely what is meant by 'community' and whether, in what ways and how it has been 'lost'. There is, for example, a constant danger of nostalgia in contrasting the past with the present, a tendency to take a highly selective and somewhat rose-tinted view of the 'good old days', which can convey a misleading account of the actual changes which have occurred. However the very persistence of this theme in our literature and social criticism suggests that it cannot be written off as *merely* nostalgia; while an accurate portrayal of the past is frequently absent, what is offered is often an idealization of the past as an implicit criticism of the *present*. In this sense the concern over the decline of 'community' must be taken as a matter of serious sociological investigation, not because it necessarily represents a factual and objective historical process, but because it is an attempt to articulate, albeit somewhat vaguely, the 'private troubles' which many people have experienced in modern society (Mills 1959). Thus many people have recently been engaged in a search for 'community', hoping that it will be the touchstone of authenticity in their lives – the commune movement, for example, might be interpreted in this way. Others are more professionally involved in the creation of 'real communities' – architects, planners, churchmen, social workers, political activists – without being very certain of what they consist or how they are to be engineered. The issue is further complicated by the fact that the word 'community' itself, while it never fails to conjure up a series of warm and favourable connotations, is used in all kinds of ways. We hear about the village community, the scientific community, community care, the Jewish community, the European Economic Community and so on. While we can all agree that 'community' is a good thing, and regret its loss, there is surprisingly little certainty over what it is.

The relevance of community in the modern world

Viewed in this context, it is apparent that the problem which so concerned Tönnies is one which remains very relevant today. However, because the notion of 'community' is not always used in a clear and unambiguous manner, it is first necessary to consider the varying ways in which 'community' has been used in recent social and political debate. In this way it is possible to make explicit some of the values and judgements which underlie the argument that modern society suffers from a 'loss of community', while also placing this pervasive sentiment in some kind of historical and sociological context.

Community as a critique of industrial society

In its most abstract sense the perception of a 'loss of community' in modern society refers to changes in both the structure and content of personal relationships. Here 'community' is used to denote a sense of common identity between individuals, enduring ties of affection and harmony based upon personal knowledge and face-to-face contact. As we have seen in our discussion of Simmel, Wirth and Redfield, it is often contrasted with the impersonal and dehumanizing aspects of modern life, with the rise of a selfish individualism, a calculative approach to human relationships and the sense of social dislocation present under conditions of rapid social and economic change. In Chapter 2 we noted that these judgements were part of the Romantic pessimism of much eighteenth- and nineteenth-century thought, emphasizing the unity of man with Nature, opposing reason with sentiment and offering a thorough critique of the emergent urban, industrial world. The concept of community was used in order to come to terms with this entirely unique and novel form

of society. The scientific and technological advances of the new age were contrasted with man's spiritual and emotional impoverishment, in which the 'loss of community' was taken as emblematic. The term was therefore used in a literally reactionary way – as a reaction to both the material squalor and the spiritual degradation which Romanticism associated with the rise of urban industrialism. 'Community' signified a more humane and intimate existence, more stable, more traditional and less tainted by the rational pursuit of self-interest.

One function of the sociological investigation of various communities is to try to separate the myth from the reality, to 'demystify' our perceptions of social life and to establish a factual basis for arguments about whether modern society does or does not suffer from a 'loss of community'. However, as we have seen, the sociological study of community is confused by the fact that sociology, as an intellectual discipline in its own right, is very much a product of this Romantic critique of urban industrialism. Tönnies, for example, accepted the humanistic concern about the apparently dehumanizing nature of the Industrial Revolution. He, too, used the concept of community as the basis of an attack upon industrial society. Consequently sociologists themselves have not always been immune to the value judgements implicit in this tradition, nor to some of the mythology of 'community' with which it is associated.

Community as localism

A second sense in which a 'loss of community' is said to afflict society concerns the decline of *locality* as a basis of modern social organization. In many pre-industrial societies localism had a particular economic basis in the system of agriculture and craft-manufacturing production. The villages and small towns which grew up around these activities were often small in scale and relatively self-contained. Contact with the outside world was more limited and less common than it is today and control of the most important of life's necessities – food, housing, employment – lay in local hands. Local areas thus retained a fair amount of autonomy and there was a greater diversity of local traditions and customs.

The growth of urban industrialism has, however, brought about the steady dilution of localism as a structural principle in contemporary society. The effect of nationally induced social changes has been to vastly reduce the isolation, the distinctiveness and the self-sufficiency of most local communities. This is not to say that modern society is totally homogeneous nor that a bland uniformity has completely quashed local and regional diversities. However, most localities have become more dependent upon extra-local sources of decision-making, thanks to increasingly nationalized and centralized forms of political and economic control. The locus of important political decisions has, for example, moved progressively from the local Big House to County Hall and thence to Westminster and even to Brussels.

Stein (1964) refers to the way in which locality as a self-sustaining unit has declined as 'the eclipse of community' and he identified its cause in three important social processes: urbanization, industrialization and the growth of bureaucracy. Each of these factors has, in Stein's view, ensured that most of the important decisions affecting the daily lives of individuals are no longer taken in the locality where they live and work. In this context, then, the 'loss of community' refers to the decreasing relevance of locally based social relationships in determining the lives of local inhabitants. Indeed the concept of 'mass society' is often used in contrast to that of 'community' in order to convey the way in which nationally directed changes have successfully reduced the importance of local and regional differences.

As long as localism remained an important organizational principle of society, the notion of 'community' remained unarticulated and taken for granted. As Raymond Williams (1961) has noted, only when the local basis of society was

threatened did a conscious ideology of 'community' emerge and attempts to create 'community' become a publicly debated issue. It is with this paradox that an analysis of localism must begin, for perceptions about the *actual* local basis of social activity have become so intertwined with the *desire* to promote such a basis (often in reaction to the fears of a 'loss of community') that it is important to insist upon a clear separation of the two (Bell C. and Newby 1976a).

Thus there is little doubt that, on the one hand, 'community' had a real social basis in the essentially localized structures of pre-industrial society. This was reflected in the fact that in many pre-industrial societies economic activity was (and is) based upon a struggle for subsistence, so that individuals were tied to their locality by economic dependence (and often legal constraints, too). Under these conditions 'community' became what R. Williams (1973a, p. 104) called 'the mutuality of the oppressed' – the product of a series of often Draconian constraints upon social and geographical mobility born out of a common powerlessness and poverty. On the other hand, as we have already seen in the previous section, 'community' came to be used during the nineteenth century as an ideological interpretation of the quality of the relationships to be found *within* these localized social structures. This ideological usage of 'community' emphasized the *desired* qualities of community life – a common adherence to territory, a solidarity of place, among all the inhabitants of a particular locality, whatever their social or economic differences. 'Community', in this sense, overlooked the actual conditions of existence, such as the presence of any conflicts of interest, but instead offered an interpretation of relationships between all local inhabitants as being characterized by harmony, affection, consensus and stability. The decline of localism therefore presented a threat to social order. The rise of urban industrialism, which could not be contained within the small-scale local communities of the pre-industrial world, thus led to redoubled attempts by those in authority to assert an *ideology* of 'community' as a means of promoting stability and harmony. A diligent search was made for ways of retaining localism and thereby upholding the desired relationships of 'community'.

Such sentiments, as both Ruth Glass (1968) and Norman Dennis (1968) have shown, have remained extraordinarily strong among twentieth-century planners. On the basis of some rudimentary social engineering they have attempted to promote a renewed 'sense of community' in urban life through the creation of 'neighbourhood units', 'garden cities', 'urban villages' and other such local forms of subdivision of the urban environment. They, too, have elevated the *local* basis of 'community' above all others. The long historical pedigree of their value judgements has brought about the taken-for-granted assumption that the desired content of human relationships (affection, integration, identity, etc.) can only be promoted through the creation of *local* forms of territoriality and *local* social structures. Specifically the promotion of localism has sought to do the following (cf. Keller 1968, p. 126; Mann 1965, pp. 17ff.):

1   introduce a principle of physical order into the chaotic, amorphous and fragmented world which is adjudged to constitute modern urban living;
2   reintroduce local, face-to-face, personal forms of interaction and thereby invest the allegedly anonymous and isolated urban world with a renewed sense of 'community';
3   encourage the formation of local loyalties and attachments among an often mobile urban population;
4   stimulate feelings of identity, stability and continuity in an urban setting which appears to threaten such sentiments and promote their downfall;
5   provide a local training ground for the development of larger loyalties to the city and nation.

Whether the reinvigoration of 'community' depends upon a reinstatement of the principle of locality rests, however, upon a number of largely unstated assumptions about urban society which require further scrutiny and which will be examined later in this chapter.

Community, stability and change

To what extent urban planners and architects have been successful in engineering a 'sense of community' in recent years may be judged in part by the third strand in the public debate on this issue. Since the early 1960s a widespread sense of 'loss of community' has arisen in many urban areas, caused either by changes in the social composition of their population or by their physical redevelopment. In many cities old-established, mostly working-class neighbourhoods have been bulldozed aside and their former inhabitants decanted into new housing estates and high-rise flats which have drawn frequent accusations of being 'soul-less' and lacking any of the 'community spirit' which is alleged to have existed among the Victorian back-to-back terraces. The stereotype of the dreary, windswept, monotonous, modern housing development has entered public demonology as the very antithesis of what is commonly understood by 'community'. Ironically many of the old urban neighbourhoods which are now revered as intimate and vital communities were the same areas which were greeted with such suspicion by so many nineteenth-century commentators!

Nevertheless the massive redevelopment of many inner-city areas was held responsible for destroying the closely knit bonds of community life which had become established among families who not only lived together across several generations but who, in many cases, all worked together. The changing occupational structure over the same period was, therefore, also an important factor. Traditional working-class communities based upon coal mining, shipbuilding, the docks, iron- and steel-making and other such industries which have shrunk considerably over the last two decades have consequently been whittled away. With them have declined the strong sense of shared occupational experience, the distinctive local sub-cultures, the overlapping loyalties between workplace and neighbourhood and the closely knit cliques of friends, workmates, neighbours and kin which many of the inhabitants under-stood 'community' to mean.

A sense of 'loss of community' has not, how-ever, been limited to such urban areas, although it has been more visible there because of the actual demolition of Victorian neighbourhoods and their replacement by new housing estates. A similar sense of loss has afflicted the older inhabitants of many rural villages because of the recent transformation in the social composition of the countryside. Rural villages have lost many of their former agricultural inhabitants and received in their place an influx of ex-urban commuters, retired people and second home owners. The impact of these newcomers has been no less disruptive of the established patterns of rural village life than the effects of redevelopment on the urban working-class population. Many farmers and farm workers also feel that their village no longer constitutes the intimate 'community' that it once did. A feeling that 'community' has declined is not therefore limited to those areas which have undergone physical redevelopment. Rapid social change may also bring about a sense of dislocation. The rump of the former population may feel estranged and 'taken over' by such changes. In urban areas, for example, such feel-ings are aroused by the 'gentrification' of former working-class neighbours (that is, their colo-nization by professional and managerial new-comers) or by a rapid influx of overseas immigrants. Nevertheless it is worth pointing out that the newcomers themselves believe that they are creating 'community', albeit among themselves in many cases, rather than attempt-ing to destroy it.

Frequently, therefore, a 'loss of community'

in this third sense refers to the effects of rapid social and economic change. As 'slum clearance' such changes are often welcomed; but as the 'tearing down of inner-city communities' they are criticized. Not surprisingly, therefore, an often fierce public debate has been fought over the desirability of these changes, in which the notion of 'community' has been central. The critics of urban redevelopment, for example, have accused planners and architects of a callous disregard for 'community' while the latter have defended their designs by arguing that a 'spirit of community' cannot be engendered overnight and that in time the new estates will 'settle down' to something like the desired social pattern. Again this is an issue which will be examined in more detail below.

These three examples about how beliefs about a 'loss of community' in modern life have entered public debate are sufficient to give some indication of the wide range of contemporary social problems which the analysis of community raises. In many respects the desire for 'com-munity' symbolizes a desire for personal and social fulfilment, an attempt to close the gap between life as it is actually experienced and life as those who accept that there has been a 'loss of community' would like it to be (or perceive it as having been in the past). In this sense 'com-munity' signifies the Good Life: it is a utopia. However, what this utopian existence actually consists of may vary considerably from person to person according to their aspirations and scale of values. Here 'community' becomes a *normative prescription*: that is, it expresses the values of an individual concerning what life *should* be. As we have already noted, 'community' in this context is inherently ideological.

Although this usage is not without interest to sociologists, most sociological analyses of com-munities are – or, at least, aspire to be – *empiri-cal descriptions* of life in various localities; that is, studies of communities as they actually are, rather than what sociologists feel they should be. This, however, is not as straight-forward as it may seem. To begin with, normative prescription and empirical description are often closely intertwined in sociology – and the history of sociological writings on community clearly bears witness to this. Moreover, sociologists have found it particularly difficult to come to an agreement over how 'community' – their very own object of study – should be defined.

Definitions of community

The concept of community may have been a concern of sociologists for nearly two hundred years, but considerable confusion continues to surround attempts to produce a satisfactory definition. A major problem has been that sociologists, no more than other individuals, have not always been immune to the emotive overtones that the word 'community' consistently carries with it. As we have seen sociologists, too, have tended to regard 'community' as an unmitigated Good Thing, without being too precise in defining what it is, partly because the attraction of 'community' has always centred on its emotional appeal rather than a rational analysis. It is not surprising, then, that the concept of 'community' has proved capable of encompassing any number of contradictory values which different writers have seen fit to include in their normative prescriptions of the Good Life. The problem has been one of too many definitions rather than too few. Indeed, the analysis of the various definitions of 'community' has from time to time provided a thriving sociological sideline. Perhaps the best known example is George A. Hillery's paper, 'Definitions of community: areas of agreement' (Hillery 1955) which considered no fewer than ninety-four such definitions to be found in the literature. Almost inevitably, the quality which was most lacking was agreement: apart from finding that 'all of the definitions deal with people' (Hillery 1955, p. 117) there was no overall consensus.

A perusal of Hillery's paper, together with the many publications dealing with community which have appeared in the intervening years, does enable some conclusions to be drawn, however. Essentially the many and varied definitions of 'community' are reducible to three:

1 'Community' as a 'geographical expression' – that is, as a fixed and bounded *locality*. This is the way in which geographers use the term to denote a human settlement located within a particular local territory. This is not really a sociological usage of 'community' since, apart from the observation that they are all living together in a particular place, there is no consideration of the inhabitants at all, nor of how – or, indeed, whether – they interact with one another.

2 'Community' as a *local social system* – that is, as a set of social relationships which take place wholly, or mostly, within a locality (cf. Stacey 1969). This is a more sociological usage of 'community' since some indication is being given of the social life of the area. Thus a community in this sense may be said to exist when a network of interrelationships is established between those people living in the same locality – for example, where 'everyone knows everyone else'. But note that nothing is being stated about the *content* of these relationships, merely the fact that individuals do relate to one another. It may be, for example, that 'everyone knows everyone else' in the locality, but that they all hate one another! Even if they were in constant conflict, however, they would still constitute a 'community' in this second sense of the word.

3 'Community' as a *type of relationship* – more particularly, 'community' is defined as a *sense of identity* between individuals (even though, in some cases, their mutual identification may never have resulted from any personal contact). This third definition corresponds most closely with the colloquial usage of 'community' – the idea of a 'spirit of community', a sense of commonality among a group of people. In this meaning 'community' may have no geographical (local) referent at all – a 'community spirit' may exist between individuals who are very widely

scattered geographically. This notion of 'community', with its overtones of common identity, is perhaps best called *communion* since this word more clearly conveys what is involved. Most references to a 'loss of community' in the modern world are in fact references to a loss of communion, a loss of meaningful identity with other people and the shared experiences which often accompany this identification.

Unfortunately sociologists have tended in the past to run all three of these definitions together. There has been a largely unexamined assumption that life in particular localities promotes a certain structure of relationships which results in the presence or absence of 'communion'. This, for example, was the assumption upon which the rural–urban continuum rested. Once these aspects of community were considered separately and empirical description began to supersede normative prescription, then the rural–urban continuum came under increasing challenge.

The downfall of the rural–urban continuum

The notion that ways of life could be linked to settlement patterns was first undermined by the American anthropologist, Oscar Lewis, who in 1949 published his account of *Life in a Mexican Village*. The village in question was Tepoztlan, which Redfield had originally studied in the 1930s and which had formed the basis for his conception of the 'folk society'. Whereas Redfield had discovered a homogeneous, smoothly functioning, well-integrated, contented, stable and harmonious community, Lewis, somewhat unnervingly, emphasized

the underlying individualism of Tepoztlan institutions and character, the lack of co-operation, the tensions between villages within the *municipio*, the schisms within the village, the pervading quality of fear, envy and distrust, in interpersonal relations. (Lewis 1953, p. 123)

The discrepancies between the two accounts are very marked and cannot all be accounted for by changes in Tepoztlan itself during the intervening period, nor by Lewis's advantages of working with more personnel and resources and possessing the benefit of hindsight. (A detailed discussion of the Redfield/Lewis debate can be found in Bell C. and Newby 1971, pp. 42–53, 75–8.) Rather the differences are due to the fact that Redfield and Lewis were operating with different theoretical orientations which influenced the selection and coverage of the data and the way in which the data were organized. For Redfield the folk–urban continuum formed the organizing principle of his ethnographic account. Consequently the emphasis throughout his study is on co-operative and unifying factors. He glosses over evidence of violence, cruelty, disease, suffering, poverty, economic and social maladjustment and political schisms. In the tradition of the classical writers on community, Redfield's 'folk society' was riddled with value judgements. As Lewis states,

It contains the old Rousseauian* notion of primitive peoples as noble savages and the corollary that with civilisation comes the fall of man. (Lewis 1949, p. 435)

Later, Redfield attempted to defend himself against some of Lewis's criticisms. He 'confessed' that he had seen

certain good things in Tepoztlan; a sense of conviction in the people as to what life is all about; and a richness of the expressive life of the community. (Redfield 1968, p. 158)

The value judgements then affected the portrayal which he offered to his readers. However, as Redfield points out, Lewis also brought his values into his study of Tepoztlan. Lewis had wanted to improve the material standards of life in Tepoztlan and therefore to substitute scientific for what he called 'superstitious and primitive' understanding.

---

* Derived from the liberal political doctrines of Jean-Jacques Rousseau (1712–78) which proclaimed the essential goodness and reasonableness of human nature.

The Redfield/Lewis debate stands as something of a cautionary tale in sociology, illustrating the ways in which theory, research methods and 'findings' are closely intertwined. Since both Redfield and Lewis are inevitably blinkered to some degree by their values the lessons of this tale are not entirely conclusive. On his own Lewis cannot be said to have completely undermined the rural–urban continuum, but his re-study of Tepoztlan did suggest that the rural–urban or folk–urban hypothesis might at least be inadequate or improperly defined, since it had given Redfield only a very partial, if not incorrect, view of life there. Whatever the reality of Tepoztlan Lewis had persuasively argued that it was something less than *Gemeinschaft*. Indeed Lewis's view of rural society was to be repeated in a number of attacks upon the 'misplaced polarities' of the rural–urban continuum during the 1960s (for example, Gusfield 1967; Avila 1969).

Meanwhile doubts were emerging about the validity of 'urbanism as a way of life'. During the 1950s a number of community studies established the existence of some disturbingly *Gemeinschaft*-like communities in the centre of large cities. In Britain the most famous of these were the studies of Bethnal Green in East London, most notably Michael Young and Peter Willmott's *Family and Kinship in East London*, published in 1957. Here, in the heart of one of the largest cities in the world, there existed not anonymous *Gesellschaft* but something which was later to be termed, significantly, an 'urban village'. In his characterization of urbanism Wirth had chosen to overlook the presence of *Gemeinschaft*-like neighbourhoods within the urban system – even though, thanks to the multitude of studies carried out in Chicago in the 1920s and 1930s, he could hardly have been unaware of them. Rather than a 'fluid mass' Young and Willmott found Bethnal Green to be remarkably stable and homogeneous. For example, on one (notorious) shopping trip which they document, one of their respondents met sixty-three people in all,

thirty-eight of whom were relatives. Kinship, they discovered, was an important aspect of life in Bethnal Green:

Here the family does more than anything else to make local society a familiar society, filled with people who are not strangers. . . . Bethnal Greeners are not lonely people: whenever they go for a walk in a street, for a drink in the pub or for a row on the lake in Victoria Park, they know the faces in the crowd. (Young and Willmott 1957, p. 116)

A similar portrayal of life in Hunslet, a working-class area of Leeds, was also given by Richard Hoggart (1957). In the United States Herbert Gans came up with similar findings in his study of an Italian neighbourhood in Boston, *The Urban Villagers* (1962b). What, then, of the rural–urban continuum, and specifically for Wirth's conception of urban society as an anonymous mass, reliant only upon superficial, transitory relationships? The implication of these and other studies seemed to be that, as Peter Mayer (1962, p. 591) put it, 'While some are born "urban" and others achieve urbanisation, none can be said to have urbanisation thrust upon them'.

If 'urban villagers' were difficult to accommodate within the rural–urban continuum, so were their obverse in the countryside – the fast-growing commuter villages. For example, R. E. Pahl in his study of rural Hertfordshire, *Urbs in Rure* (1965) showed how it was difficult to fit into the rural–urban continuum villages consisting wholly or partly of rural commuters and others who *lived* in the countryside but *worked* in towns and cities. Similarly a series of rural communities studies in the 1960s showed that many rural areas are by no means *Gemeinschaft*-like – that business rationality, geographical mobility, loneliness, anonymity, class conflict, etc. are by no means absent from rural Britain. In 'Ashworthy', an agricultural community in Devon studied by W. M. Williams in 1959, a more fluid and dynamic system appeared to be operating whereby the community was subject to constant change:

Country life, as exemplified by Ashworthy, is subject to piecemeal changes, is constantly in a state of internal adjustment between one part and another. This is a much less neat and tidy concept than the orthodox *Gemeinschaft* view of rural social structure. (Williams W. M. 1963, p. xviii)

In the Cheviot parish of 'Westrigg', James Littlejohn encountered an extremely hierarchical class system in which relationships reflected impersonal, contractual employer–employee ties rather than the kinship characteristic of *Gemeinschaft*. Littlejohn also challenged the assumption that social change in rural areas is a result of the encroachment of urbanism. Although his general conclusion is that social class has increasingly become more important than community as a source of identification among the local population, this is not a result of the impact of urbanism but of national changes upon the *local* social system (Littlejohn 1963). This is an issue to which we shall return below.

Thus by the mid-1960s neither the rural nor the urban 'end' of the continuum was typifying the way of life expected of it. Nevertheless the desire to identify ways of life with particular localities remained strong. Nowhere was this more apparent than in the so-called 'myth of suburbia' which accompanied the continuing suburban development and the increase in working-class affluence during the 1950s and early 1960s. One suspects that the prevailing image of suburbia was inspired as much as anything by the song, *Little Boxes*, popularized by Pete Seeger, which suggested a life of dreary conformity in houses that were 'all made out of ticky-tacky and . . . all /looked/ just the same'.

In sociology Seeger's counterpart was William H. Whyte, whose book *The Organisation Man* (1957) contains a section on 'The organisation man at home' which closely conforms to the stereotype that suburban housing estates represent vast transit camps for upwardly mobile, middle-class executives, concerned only with the conspicuous consumption of consumer durables and keeping up appearances with their like-minded neighbours. Whyte emphasized the homogeneity of suburban life: the serried ranks of identical houses contain lifestyles of similarly relentless conformity. This merely reflects the conformity of modern bureaucratic man – the 'organization man' of his title – commuting back and forth between the arid routines of the office and the bogus neighbourliness of the housing estate. In Britain a similar myth was propagated: that all suburbanites are commuters, that they are devoted to 'keeping up with the Joneses', that suburban life is 'privatized' within the home, with forays outdoors only to mow the lawn and wash the family car. In other words, Wirth's isolated urban man is alive and well and living in a three-bedroomed Wimpey semi.

Again, however, we must ask how much substance there is in this stereotype. The 'myth of suburbia' was subjected to a thoroughgoing critique by Herbert Gans in his second community study, *The Levittowners* (1967). Gans had earlier worked with Whyte and was worried by the growth of an exaggerated and generalized conception of 'suburbanism as a way of life'. Gans was sceptical of the view that people were changed when they moved to suburban communities and was inclined to believe that if there were any changes in lifestyles these were not traceable to the new physical environment, but to broader social factors. *The Levittowners* was a study of a new 'dormitory' suburb in New Jersey, developed by one of America's largest tract building companies, Levit and Sons. Gans bought a house and moved in. What he discovered was in no sense the totally homogeneous community of the suburban myth. Most inhabitants had arrived in Levittown for 'house related reasons' rather than 'job related reasons' and nearly half said that they had come to settle permanently. There were three distinct class cultures identified by Gans, largely on the basis of their lifestyles (that is, broadly speaking, patterns of consumption). Although 56 per cent of the inhabitants were lower white collar workers, there were also substantial numbers of professional (18 per cent) and manual (26 per cent) workers. Gans also discovered that

they wanted more comfortable and modern surroundings but that they did not want to change their old way of life or to make a new one in the community. (Gans 1967, p. 38)

They made friendships on the basis of shared interests rather than residential proximity: 'Propinquity may initiate intimate social contacts but it did not determine friendships.' (Gans 1967) Nor could Gans find much evidence of overt conformity or deliberately changed behaviour to be more like the perceived behaviour of neighbours. Instead Gans emphasizes the diversity and heterogeneity of Levittown which is divided to social class, religious and political affiliation and differences between 'locals' (those interested in and oriented towards the locality) and 'cosmopolitans' (those with extra-local, or national, interests and affiliations). Thus what shaped and moulded life in Levittown

was not the pre-occupancy aspirations of the residents, but rather a complex process of external initiatives and subsequent internal transformation that produced organisations and institutions which reflected the backgrounds and interests of the majority of the population. (Gans 1967, p. 141)

Gans's findings were broadly confirmed by Bennett Berger in his study of suburban Detroit, *Working-Class Suburb* (1969). Berger showed that large numbers of unquestionably working-class people had migrated to the suburbs in the United States and that although suburbia may look from the *outside* to be uniformly middle class, close inspection soon reveals that this is by no means the case. Indeed, more recent work by Samuel Kaplan in his book, *The Dream Deferred* (1977) has revealed the extent to which American suburbia hides quite surprising degrees of poverty, unemployment and multiple deprivation.

In Britain suburban community studies have been relatively few and far between, but again the evidence supports the view that there is no necessary causal connection between a shift in the location of residence to suburbia and the adoption of a particular lifestyle. Willmott and Young, for example, in the 'sequel' to their Bethnal Green study, demonstrated the persistence of family and kinship ties even after the move from Bethnal Green to Woodford. In *Family and Class in a London Suburb* (1960) they showed that close-knit social networks of the kind which they had found in Bethnal Green could be maintained after the move to suburban Woodford with the help of modern technology in the shape of the car and the telephone. Colin Bell, in his study of a middle-class housing estate in Swansea, *Middle Class Families* (1968), also demonstrated how these ties could be maintained over very long distances indeed. In both cases these studies showed how extensive geographical, and even social, mobility did not necessarily involve the dissolution of *Gemeinschaft*-like social relationships, even though it did, of course, often attenuate their *local* basis. 'Community', in other words, is becoming dissociated from locality.

The whole debate concerning the degree of coincidence between locality (*where* one lives) and ways of life (*how* one lives) has been summarized in two important papers: one by Herbert Gans, entitled 'Urbanism and suburbanism as ways of life' (1962a), and the other by R. E. Pahl, called 'The rural–urban continuum' (1966). Gans's paper is a critique of both Wirth and Whyte in the light of more recent studies, including his own. Gans argues that lifestyles are not determined by locality, but by two other variables – *social class* and *stage in the family cycle*. Gans is concerned with social class (which he interprets largely in terms of income level) because it is the best predictor of an individual's ability to *choose* where (and how) to live. Other things being equal, the higher the social class of an individual, the greater the degree of choice over housing – and therefore *where* to live. Stage in the family cycle is important because it is the best indicator of the area of choice which is most likely *within* any given social class. For example, middle-class families may possess the income to gain access to owner-occupied housing, but young couples with small children may lack the capital to purchase anything other than a new house on a modern estate because it is on that type of housing that they can raise the largest proportion of the price. The housing market therefore acts like a series of sieves through which families with appropriate incomes fall to their appropriate place in urban or suburban structure.

Thus observed similarities between residents of the same geographical areas, even where these appear, are not *caused* by living in the same locality. They are caused by the actions of the housing market, which tends to allocate individuals from a similar social class at a similar stage in the family cycle to similar types of housing clustered together in certain districts. It is not 'locality' which causes this; rather, it is the *outcome of a series of constrained choices* on where to live by different individuals. Ideas about urbanism or suburbanism as 'ways of life' are merely spurious correlations (like the belief that policemen cause traffic accidents because every time you see a traffic accident you see a policeman). Gans concludes:

If ways of life do not coincide with settlement types and if these ways are functions of class and life cycle rather than of the ecological attributes of the settlement, a sociological definition of the city cannot be formulated. (Gans 1962a, p. 643)

This implies that no sociological definition of any settlement type can be formulated, and if this is true it would destroy notions of a rural–urban or any other locality-based continuum.

This is the starting point for Pahl's influential paper (Pahl R. E. 1966) for Pahl doubts the *sociological* relevance of the physical differences between 'rural' and 'urban' in highly complex industrial societies. Pahl summarizes much of the empirical work already alluded to in this chapter to demonstrate that, far from there being an exclusive continuum from *Gemeinschaft* to *Gesellschaft*, relationships of both types are to be found in the *same* community. Pahl states that he can find little universal evidence for such a continuum and he doubts its value even as a classificatory device. He points out that there are a number of non-overlapping continua which can be identified as a means of codifying social relationships and that the isolation of *one* process and elevating it above all the others is misleading:

Whether we call the process acting on the local community 'urbanisation', 'differentiation', 'modernisation', 'mass society' or whatever, it is clear that it is not so much *communities* that are acted upon as groups and individuals at particular places in the social structure. Any attempt to tie patterns of social relationships to specific geographical milieux is a singularly fruitless exercise. (Pahl R. E. 1966, p. 328)

Of much greater importance to Pahl is the impact of *national* changes upon *local* areas. The local and the national, he argues, confront each other in towns *and* in villages. Pahl is concerned not with the existence of community, but with the interaction of nationally and locally oriented social groups, with the conflict between the small scale and the large scale:

It is the basic situation of conflict or stress that can be observed from the most highly urbanised metropolitan region to the most remote and isolated peasant village. (Pahl R. E. 1970, p. 286)

In one sense Pahl had merely restored Tönnies's concepts of *Gemeinschaft* and *Gesellschaft* to their original status and divested them of their confusing association with locality. However, his comment that any attempt to tie patterns of social relationships to specific localities was a 'singularly fruitless exercise' can be seen in retrospect to be an overstatement. For in the limiting case, geographical milieux *may* help to determine social relationships through the constraints which they apply to people's access to one another and to scarce material resources – a point which Pahl has since developed himself in his work on urban inequality (Pahl R. E. 1970). For example, in sparsely populated areas a 'tyranny of distance' (Blainey 1966) may operate which heavily constrains social relationships and access to the range of facilities regarded as commonplace in more densely inhabited parts of the country. In other words, if social relationships and institutions are constrained in such a way as to render them locality-based there *may* be a 'local social system' – or mostly self-contained community – where *spatial* factors have some effect upon *social* relationships. Even here, however, this merely stems from the inability of the inhabitants to transcend the spatial constraints imposed upon them, this incapacity usually being linked to a wider, societal system of inequality and/or technological development rather than something specific to the locality *per se*.

The gradual dismantling of the rural–urban continuum has therefore had two main consequences. It created a theoretical vacuum in the sociology of community, which to some extent still persists. But second, and more constructively, it allowed a more rigorous and systematic investigation to begin on the relationship between locality, local social system and communion than had been carried out hitherto. It must be admitted that sociologists still know remarkably little about how, and in what ways, these three factors are connected. Nevertheless recent work on the sociology of community has suggested a number of useful lines of enquiry and it is to these that we can now turn.

Locality, community and network

Another solution to the problem of analysing 'community' has been suggested by Margaret Stacey (1969). She feels that sociologists should avoid the term altogether since it has become too contaminated by value judgements and rendered almost a non-concept by definitional disagreements. Instead she argues, sociologists should concentrate upon institutions and their interrelations in specific localities. If institutions are locality-based *and* interrelated, there may well be, she believes, a *local social system* that is worthy of sociological attention. Stacey's approach is an attempt to introduce some rigour into community studies (she would prefer to call them 'locality studies') so that it is possible to examine systematically:

(i) the establishment and maintenance of a local social system; (ii) local conditions where no such system can be expected; (iii) some circumstances under which an existing system might be modified or destroyed; (iv) certain inter-relations between systems and their parts; (v) the interaction of local and national systems. (Stacey 1969, p. 139)

Stacey is redirecting our attention to an issue that was raised earlier in this chapter – the extent to which locality still remains an important principle of organization in modern society. To what extent are 'local social systems' self-sustaining? Or have they been swallowed up in an amorphous 'mass society'? As we noted earlier, Maurice Stein, in his book *The Eclipse of Community* (1964), argued on the basis of data culled from American community studies that local autonomy was decreasing as the result of the processes of urbanization, industrialization and bureaucratization:

Community ties become increasingly dependent upon centralised authorities and agencies in all areas of life. On the other hand, personal loyalties decrease their range with the successive weakening of national ties, regional ties, family ties, and finally ties to a coherent image of one's self. (Stein 1964, p. 329)

Stein, then, suggests that a series of separate but parallel 'vertical ties' to centralized decision-making bodies are replacing the 'horizontal ties' of local autonomy (cf. Vidich and Bensman 1958; Warren 1963).

The concept which has been used for making sense of these ties is that of 'social network' (Barnes 1954). Relationships are depicted as being like a set of points joined by lines, the lines indicating which individuals, groups or institutions interact with one another. It is a matter for investigation whether or not this network is confined to a particular locality or not – and, indeed, this may vary over time and between different groups of people. 'Urban villages' like Bethnal Green can therefore be conceived of as highly dense social networks based upon particular localities. Avoiding the emotive term 'community', it is possible to investigate the *structure* and *content* of these networks and the extent to which they are changing. In this sense, as Elizabeth Bott has put it:

The immediate social environment of urban families is best considered not as the local area in which they live, but rather as the network of actual social relationships they maintain, regardless of whether these are confined to the local area or run beyond its boundaries. (Bott 1957, p. 99)

The degree to which they are locality-based is often, as we have seen, a function of economic constraint, so that the further up the social scale the more geographically widespread we would expect the individual's social network to be. Similarly, rising living standards would lead more people to break out of the constraints of locality. Thus Bott's conception of contemporary social change is in terms of 'from community to network', but it is an open question as to whether the decreasing significance of locality is the result of rising affluence or the centralizing tendencies which Stein describes.

In either case, social network analysis not only offers a more sophisticated method of analysing these issues (for example, Mitchell 1969; Mitchell and Boissevain 1972) but also warns against undue optimism about the resurgence of 'community' in modern society. As Norman Dennis has written:

Those who live in the pious hope that it is only a matter of time before housing estates settle down and take on the appearance of the Bethnal Green stereotype are therefore probably mistaken. It would be more realistic to predict that in so far as housing estates represent that exaggerated result of processes which are common to our society, it is only a matter of time before our Bethnal Green becomes socially indistinguishable from housing estates. (Dennis 1968, p. 84)

Dennis's remarks are a warning not only against the dissolution of the local basis of social networks, but also against the consequence of this for 'communion'.

However, it is by no means clear how far a 'sense of community' or communion is affected by the changes in what has been called the 'mutuality of the oppressed' – the almost unavoidable communality enforced by a shared existence on the edge of poverty. In Dennis's view the lifting of the constraints deriving from poverty will provoke the decline of communion – a point which, as we have also seen, is echoed in the 'myth of suburbia' and much of the writing on working-class 'privatization'. Old neighbourhood solidarities become dissolved in the move from Victorian terrace to modern semi, aided and abetted by privatized leisure centred around the family car and television set (see Westergaard 1970). It is equally plausible, however, to argue that communion can only be created voluntarily upon the basis of choice of lifestyle or interests. Freed of social and economic constraints, like-minded individuals may come together to share their experiences and develop a meaningful sense of communal identity. It is possible, for example, to regard the commune movement in this light (see Abrams and McCullough 1976) or the many attempts to create communion on the basis of voluntary associations or social movements. Unlike the 'mutuality of the oppressed', however, these are usually quite conscious attempts to recapture a sense of 'belonging' and frequently have resulted from a deep disenchantment with certain aspects of modern society.

Communion is, however, an intangible, precarious and frequently unstable phenomenon, requiring intense mutual involvement which is difficult to sustain on the basis of voluntarism alone. As Schmalenbach has pointed out:

It is indeed the case that communions are borne along by waves of emotion, reaching ecstatic heights of collective enthusiasm. . . . They are bound together by the feeling actually experienced. Indeed, each one is *en rapport*.

Although communions attempt to develop an ethos of loyalty in order to overcome this inherent fragility, they frequently have a mercurial quality. As many community activists and commune members have discovered, it is not easy to sustain a 'spirit of community' without a framework of organizational rules which seems the very antithesis of spontaneous 'community'.

Recently there has been much speculation on whether a sense of communion provides a basis for a new urban politics. In other words, can locality-based social networks be mobilized along the lines of what is often called 'community action' (see Cowley *et al.* 1977). Such a mobilization would be both a cause and a consequence of community. In recent years, writers such as David Harvey (1973) and Manuel Castells (1977) have argued that the formation of homogeneous urban neighbourhoods offers a springboard for the kind of urban social movements characteristic of the modern city – tenants associations, squatters movements, etc.

Many of these groups have indeed arisen in opposition to the role of planners and other 'urban managers' in promoting territorial injustice and they form what David Donnison (1973) has called a new 'micro-politics of the city' mostly outside the ambit of party political organization. At the same time, many of them are mainly *defensive*: they are often concerned to protect *their* locality against changes introduced from outside – whether this involves redevelopment schemes, motorway construction, traffic schemes, or whatever. In this sense they are but a further example of the effects of the national upon the local and the reactions which threats to local autonomy may generate. It is also important to note that many such groups are concerned to protect their already considerable advantages from external threat, rather than wishing to redress the balance of territorial injustice. Although an external threat is often instrumental in promoting a sense of internal cohesion, such a 'sense of community' has normally arisen over very specific

issues, has been limited in duration, and has tended to recede when the threat has been removed. Many of these movements have therefore been little more than briefly spluttering local action groups, short term and populist in character, which have not left behind any permanent residue of communion.

Conclusion

Despite the fact that 'community' has been one of sociology's core ideas, the history of writing on the subject has been marked more by confusion than by conceptual clarity. Community as 'normative prescription' has too often interfered with 'empirical description', with the result that no systematic sociology of community is yet available. It has taken a long time to disentangle ideas about community from prejudices about particular settlement patterns and although the concept of community has been considerably clarified as a result, the work, in many ways, has only just begun. However, there is no tidy classification to replace the rural–urban continuum, only a number of lines of enquiry on the relationship, if any, between locality, social relationships and a sense of identity.

Although this conclusion may appear to be unduly negative, there is little doubt that 'community' continues to have both a substantive and an ideological importance to most of us. No study has yet demonstrated the absence of *any* local relationships from most people's lives. Modern media of communication and transport have *not* rendered local ties completely obsolete and we have a long way to go before we are all absorbed into an amorphous 'global village'. There still remains, therefore, an empirical basis for the local community which is worthy of sociological attention. Moreover it should be apparent that a consideration of 'community' invites us to examine some very important issues in modern society concerning the nature and direction of social change, the effects of macro-social processes upon particular localities and even the gap which often exists between our ideals and aspirations and the reality of the world as we perceive it. While the constraints of locality have been gradually eroded, the ideology of 'community' remains strong, and the desire to reconstitute an idealized notion of 'community' continues unabated.

Perhaps it remains *too* strong and diverts our attention from more pressing and more significant social issues. Does our preoccupation with the intimacy of 'community' deflect our awareness of the wider societal forces which are shaping our lives? In a recent provocative book, the American writer, Richard Sennett, has cast a sardonic eye over our recent concern for 'community'. Perhaps, he argues, our attempts to establish 'real communities' represent what he calls 'destructive *Gemeinschaft*', a 'tyranny of intimacy':

The refusal to deal with, absorb, and exploit reality outside the parochial scale is in one sense a universal human desire, being a simple fear of the unknown. Community feeling formed by the sharing of impulses has the special role of reinforcing the fear of the unknown, converting claustrophobia into an ethical principle.

The term 'gemeinschaft' means, originally, the full disclosure of feeling to others; historically it has come at the same time to mean a community of people. These two taken together make *gemeinschaft* a special social group in which open emotional relations are possible as opposed to groups in which partial, mechanical, or emotionally indifferent ones prevail. . . . This is the peculiar sectarianism of a secular society. It is the result of converting the immediate experience of sharing with others into a social principle. Unfortunately, large-scale forces in society may psychologically be kept at a distance, but do not therefore go away. (Sennett 1977, pp. 310–11)

Sennett is clearly worried by these tendencies. Not only does our concern for 'community' lead us to devalue the macro-social forces which are shaping modern society, but it leads to a form of collective narcissism which is actually counterproductive when it comes to analysing these societal changes:

Localism and local autonomy are becoming widespread political creeds, as though the experience of power relations will have more human meaning the more intimate the scale – even though the actual structures of power grow ever more into an international system. Community becomes a weapon against society, whose great vice is now seen to be its impersonality. But a community of power can only be an illusion in a society like that of the industrial West, one in which stability has been achieved by a progressive extension to the international scale of structures of economic control. In sum, the belief in direct human relations on an intimate scale has seduced us from converting our understanding of the realities of power into guides for our own political behaviour. The result is that the forces of domination or inequality remain unchallenged. (Sennett 1977, p. 339)

At the very least Sennett, in the long tradition of sociological writing, uses the concept of community to say something, however indirectly, about the condition of man in the modern world. He also invites us to consider the nature of the relationship between allegations of 'loss of community' and the broad sweep of contemporary social change. In this he lies very much in the tradition of writing begun by Tönnies.

Part Three: Industrial Society as Progress – Evolutionary Accounts of Society

5 Classic evolutionary doctrines and the diversity of morals

Belief in the inevitability of progress is another assumption about social change which exercises an enormous hold over people's minds. It is a belief which owes a great deal to scholarly efforts in the eighteenth and nineteenth centuries to construct a *scientific theory of progress*. The intention was to show that 'civilization' was the product of certain inevitable processes in history and that contemporary industrial society was the outcome. During the second half of the nineteenth century these efforts gave rise to several different theories of social *evolution*. All of this work received an enormous amount of publicity, especially in Britain and America. Catching the optimistic mood then prevalent, it fired the popular imagination in such a way that it left a permanent mark.

Evolutionary theories are generally considered rather old-fashioned now. For one thing, it has certainly become much more fashionable to be pessimistic about the future. Even so, we still base many of our assumptions about the world on a belief in progressive change, 'development' and other such residues of evolutionary ideas. The growth of sociology was heavily influenced by the notion of evolution – so much so that we can still learn a great deal from the controversy surrounding it about the distinctive ways in which the discipline looks at human behaviour.

Of course, sociology and the social sciences do not have a monopoly over the word 'evolution'. In any case, evolutionary thinking has always taken on a number of *different* forms in the literature of both sociology and anthropology. We shall, therefore, begin with a brief discussion of some core problems around which theories of progress as a whole emerged.

Evolutionism and the problem of culture

Cannibalism is a practice which most people in contemporary industrialized societies would immediately label as uncivilized and barbarous. Yet we know that there have been plenty of cases in which such actions have been not only accepted as part of normal social activity but actually regarded as a duty. For example, an aboriginal tribe in South Australia, the Dieri, apparently believed that fat from the bodies of dead relatives contained beneficial magical power (Leakey and Lewin 1979, p. 206). An important part of their death ceremonial involved ritual removal and eating of all fat from the limbs, belly and face of the corpse. In cases elsewhere the more familiar practice of eating enemies slain in battle rested on a belief that their spirits were thereby prevented from seeking revenge or that their strength would pass into the victor. Such ideas may strike the modern mind as delusions but this does not explain their strength and persistence in tribal society. And, indeed, though *we* have grown accustomed to thinking of our own scientific-technological picture of the universe as the only acceptable one for any rational person to believe, the scientific outlook is, after all, hardly older than industrial society itself. Another problem is that beliefs such as these make the idea that there are universally binding moral standards or an innate sense of right and wrong seem somewhat dubious. Moral diversity need not mean that standards of behaviour are purely arbitrary (Ginsberg 1956). But if they are not, how do we *explain* the fact that actions which surprise, shock or outrage ourselves are performed readily by those with different upbringing and customs?

Obviously, then, comparisons of the dominant customs, beliefs and morals of the society to which one belongs with those elsewhere presents some very tricky problems. This is why we claimed in Chapter 1 that the use of the comparative outlook is one important way in which sociological perspective inevitably differs from everyday thinking about social relationships. What it challenges is our everyday readiness to assume that there is a 'natural' way of doing things.

Broadly speaking, theories of progress were the product of an analogous experience, one which affected a whole group of European intellectuals and commentators at the same time – a growing awareness of the distinction between 'civilized' and 'primitive' morals, beliefs and manners. As we suggested at the end of Chapter 2, the fact that European society became outward looking and expansionist under the influence of industrialism brought it face to face with a variety of beliefs and practices very different from its own. The effect on European thought was dramatic. It became necessary to explain why behaviour and practices which were considered to be normal and natural in the civilized world were not the rule everywhere (Burrow 1966, pp. 1–14). In sociological language, people became aware of the fact of *cultural variation*.

Culture and *cultural variation* are very fundamental ideas in sociology. It is therefore important to point out that the word 'culture' is used in this book in a much wider sense than in everyday speech. Usually, it simply conjures up the idea of refined manners and genteel ideas, fine art, classical music, literature and so on. In sociology these things are seen as no more than a specialized, if important, aspect of 'culture' in general. *All* of the products of a particular way of life are included under this heading. It refers to not just the material objects (tools, clothes, food, etc.) produced in a given society but also its systems of beliefs and ideas, morals and customs, whether mundane or bizarre.

The evolutionists were among the first to realize that although individual cultures exhibit great variety, each one tends to form a whole or *cultural system*. Impressed by the progress which was being made in the study of natural history, they 'borrowed' the idea of classifying cultures in the same way that plants and animals were being classified, that is, into families and species. Contrary to what is commonly believed, however, the idea of arranging these categories into *stages* was *not* borrowed from biology. On the contrary, it was the biologists who did the borrowing in this case, taking the idea of development and stages from a time-hallowed theme of social thought: that *cultures and customs which affront our own should be regarded as the product of a lower or earlier phase of human development* (Harris M. 1968).

Around the end of the eighteenth century this idea had been put forward in one of two ways. Some writers argued that there were different levels and kinds of human nature. Hence the differences between civilization and inferior cultures were fixed and unalterable and the separation of the civilized and the savage mentality was absolute. Others argued that human nature is fundamentally the same everywhere and that differences between cultures can be related to other aspects of social life, particularly the kind of economic, political and military organization adopted by the people. This, however, merely brings us to another problem – the *nature–nurture* controversy.

Evolutionism, nature and nurture

Heightened awareness of foreign ways was a factor in exposing some of the weaker aspects of liberal and utilitarian thought. For example, during the Enlightenment the much vaunted faith in the triumph of Reason in politics left unexplained the fact that, in Rousseau's famous phrase, 'Man is born free but everywhere he is in chains.' How had this servitude come about? Why did 'savages' not behave like Frenchmen? Conversely, how had the societies of Europe attained the state where Reason was preparing to unload its benefits upon all? Modifications to the liberal idea of the universal supremacy of reason and choice inevitably followed.

Many of the explanations, both popular and philosophical, took a form that we should probably regard today as 'racialist'. The capacity for rational thought, it was said, is not present to the same degree in all races and 'savages' especially should be regarded as less human than Europeans. Obviously, such ideas lean heavily in the direction of nature and heredity to account for human variability.

It was more in keeping with prevailing belief in the equality of man, however, to follow ideas which pointed in a wholly different direction. An extreme but highly influential example was to be found in the writings of the English philosopher John Locke. Locke's theory of mind can be seen as an early attempt to depict the malleability of human nature by nurture and cultural factors. Locke wrote:

Let us suppose the mind to be as we say as white paper, void of all characters, without any ideas. How comes it to be furnished? To this I answer in one word, from EXPERIENCE. (Locke 1975)

This famous quotation has earned for Locke's theory notoriety as the so-called Blank Page (*tabula rasa*) theory of human nature. The rather crude view of personal and social life which it offers has reappeared in various forms and under various names in the years which have intervened since Locke's time. Taken literally it adopts an attitude of what would now be referred to as extreme *environmentalism*, in which the uniqueness of each individual is presented as a mere by-product of 'nurture', that is, the circumstances of his or her upbringing.

The argument over 'heredity' versus 'environment', nature versus nurture, has continued ever since, up to and including our own times. In Chapter 6 we shall be considering in depth the reasons why sociologists have been inclined to favour the 'environment' side of the argument and discussing how far they are justified in this. All we need to say here is that, in general terms, it is not very satisfactory to rely exclusively only on 'nature' or only on 'nurture' to explain human behaviour. On the one hand it is virtually impossible to undertake a scientific study of 'pure' biological make-up. How can the fundamental traits and types of human nature be investigated except through the way they work out in practice in the course of responding to culture and environment? On the other hand, the extreme environmentalism of Locke's Blank Page theory is rather unsatisfactory too. It implies that individual people are mere puppets or totally without autonomy – the products of the cultural and other environmental stimuli which have impinged on them. It should not be necessary for the sociologist, in stressing the importance of cultural factors, to deny that the 'natural' capacity for independent judgement and initiative does not belong to human beings at all.

When it first appeared Locke's theory was very influential. From a logical point of view it implied a major change in thought because, as we have just explained, it implied the very opposite of Enlightenment ideas of Reason and rational choice; and it totally undermined the justification for seeing society simply as an aggregate of rational self-centred decisions by individuals. Yet the full implications of this fact were largely ignored – even by Locke himself in other parts of his work (see Chapter 2). Consequently the Blank Page argument was used to provide important backing for many of the theories of progress which began to emerge in the Enlightenment.

These theories began by assuming that although Reason is universal, its exercise is often hampered by the conditions and materials, that is the environment, with which it operates. Before human potential can be fully realized, therefore, a lengthy struggle against the 'state of nature' is necessary. Disparities between civilized nations and the rest have originated from the purely fortuitous willingness of certain European peoples to 'think themselves out of the state of nature', that is, to devise the institutions necessary to progressive economic and political life (Harris M. 1968, pp. 38–40).

In these early accounts of the origins of 'civilization' are buried ideas which later Evolutionary theories were to weld into a full theory. The notion of stages, the struggle for survival and other concepts can be found scattered across the work of Enlightenment thinkers. So, too, can the assumption, known as the Comparative Method, that a careful study of contemporary non-industrial cultures will reveal to advanced nations the origins and the course of their own development. In due course, the theory of progress was to emerge from these isolated fragments into a number of explicitly sociological doctrines.

Auguste Comte and positive society

One of the earliest and most famous examples is the system of sociology associated with the name of Auguste Comte. Comte wrote in the troubled period of French history following the final defeat of Napoleon I in 1815 and with him the last effective remnant of the French Revolutionary ideal.

Comte's work is, in many respects, backward looking. It was motivated by a desire to restore the obligation and orderliness of community feeling which had, he felt, been disastrously undermined by the political revolution and the theories of reason which had inspired it. At the same time, however, he considered that these developments had been necessary ingredients in the long-term historical growth of human knowledge. An inevitable and irreversible transition was now taking place. To understand the nature of this transition involved recognizing that the human mind had passed through three stages in its search for understanding.

In presenting his law of stages Comte put forward an important idea: that the development of knowledge and belief goes hand in hand with a typical form of organization of society and its institutions. Thus, his classification of types of knowledge is simultaneously a theory of the sequence or *order of emergence* of different types of society:

1   *Theological society*. This is dominated by primitive religious thought, particularly animism (the attribution of the spirits and properties of living things to inanimate objects). Theological society is based on intuition, sentiment and feelings. It is ruled by priests and by military personnel and its moral structure is centred around ties of family and blood. (Comte's notion of theological society undoubtedly exercised an influence upon Emile Durkheim – see Chapter 14.)

2   *Metaphysical society*. This involves a limited development of critical thought. It is marked by a transition to belief in a single deity, codification of law and search for some kind of ultimate reality. The political influence of priests has given way to that of churchmen and lawyers. Above all the concept of the state and its defence has emerged as the leading principle of social organization. (Comte was no doubt unduly influenced here by the example of medieval Europe.)

3   *Positive society*. The stage upon whose threshold humankind had recently entered involves the rejection of the religious search for final ends and reasons. It will establish in its place a new 'religion of humanity' based upon the scientific study of the various laws governing the phenomena of the world. This is the characteristic mode of thought associated with the industrial form of society now actually developing. The Revolution had thus been a necessary evil with its sceptical anti-religious currents. But in order to complete the work a *positive* science of society itself, or *sociology*, was required. The appearance of this 'sociology' would complete the study of natural laws which had begun with the physical world.

Comte is frequently, if slightly misleadingly, credited with being one of the first exponents of 'positivism' – a term derived from the notion of 'positive society'. In Chapter 1 we defined positivism as a doctrine in the philosophy of social science which asserts the essential unity of all scientific endeavour and urges sociologists to model their procedures on those of the natural sciences (see p. 18). We also discussed some of the problems associated with such a position.

There are important differences between Comte's views and modern forms of positivism. Nevertheless there is a sense in which all theories of progress and evolution *can* be called positivist – largely because of their naïve assumptions about the prospects for a science of society (and perhaps the possibility of 'discovering' the laws which govern social progress).

The Law of the Three Stages, as it has come to be called, represents a distinct refinement of the theory of progress. But although it contains a worked-out classification of the sequence of social types which accompanied the enlargement of human thought, it fails to explain why either reason or society itself should develop in the direction that they actually have. To do so necessitates turning the notion of 'progress' into something more than a general faith that in the long run the scientific outlook prevails. One must also identify the actual mechanisms by which change occurs and show how these mechanisms operate with a consistent effect over a period of time. As it happened, the concept of evolution, notably via the work of the British evolutionary school, was to fill this gap in the theory of progress.

Yet its arrival was delayed. In early-nineteenth-century Britain, doctrines of social progress had become associated with dangerous political radicalism and treasonable support for the French Revolutionary ideal. For this reason the publication of the principal works of the nineteenth-century evolutionists was preceded by a period of marked prejudice and ignorance about other cultures. The reawakening of interest in cultural diversity did not really become acceptable until the relatively peaceful and prosperous years following the mid-century. Even then it was still permeated with the prejudice that British institutions and culture were superior and more developed than any others.

There was however one crucial difference. This was the growing insistence that the extent and form of variations in human nature was an empirical question to be settled by scientific investigation. A number of scholars and writers more or less simultaneously made the attempt to employ the evolutionary principle as a way of understanding and organizing a growing body of factual information about the ways of different societies.

Herbert Spencer and Social Evolutionism

For present purposes one contribution stands out among these, namely the work of Herbert Spencer. Even judged solely by the painstaking and detailed scholarship with which he tried to collate the knowledge of social customs available at that time and to place it within an overarching evolutionary framework, Spencer would deserve some recognition. But his true originality lies, as we shall now see, in his account of the mechanisms by which social progress occurs. Even today there are very few ideas employed within the mainstream of evolutionary sociology which cannot be traced back to his writings. Likewise, of course, most of the difficulties which have plagued this type of thinking may be found in his work. (The best appreciation of Spencer's importance is Fletcher R. 1971, vol. I; for a modern intellectual biography see Peel 1971.)

Any understanding of Spencer must begin with his conception of evolution itself. Contrary to what was once believed Spencer did not borrow his evolutionary theory from his illustrious contemporary Darwin. On the contrary, Spencer's thinking developed ahead of Darwin's and the impact of so-called 'Darwinism' on social theory is therefore a topic which can only be understood in the light of 'Spencerism' (Peel 1971, Chapter 6). Here we shall concentrate on two aspects of it:

Evolution as the fundamental law of science

Even the most cursory inspection of Spencer reveals the enormous difference in the scope, the range of work, which the evolutionary principle is called upon to do. Darwin's theory of evolution when it appeared involved no more than one kind of process applicable to a limited, if impressive, range of empirical facts – the origin of species. Spencer on the other hand asks us to accept that evolution applies and is of fundamentally the same character at all levels of scientific study. All of the sciences he claims, including sociology, are concerned with *matter* and the ways in which matter tends to move from a state of disorganized flux to one of order and relative stability: or as Spencer puts it, 'from a diffused imperceptible state to a concentrated perceptible state' (Spencer 1971, p. 55). In the course of this movement simple forms and structures give rise to more complex ones by means of two simultaneous processes:

a   differentiation – a breakdown of simple unspecialized structures into many separate specialized parts;
b   integration – development of a specialized function, organ or bond preserving unity among the differentiated parts.

The grandness and generality of Spencer's evolutionary principle, then, is quite different from the relatively limited theory upon which modern biology rests.

Super-organic evolution

According to Spencer, science is a unity. Its apparent divisions rest solely on the different kinds and levels of matter with which each discipline works. Thus, physics, geology and astronomy concern themselves with a level of evolution that Spencer called inorganic. On the next level come the biological sciences whose subject matter is organic evolution. What, then,

is the subject matter of sociology? Since society makes possible an integration of organic with inorganic matter, Spencer argued, there must be a distinctive level of evolution with which sociology deals. This he termed *'super*-organic evolution'.

Super-organic evolution possesses the same properties as are found among other 'bodies of facts'. It, too, conforms to the principles of differentiation and integration. Social development, therefore, brings about:

a   greater institutional complexity based on greater specialization of tasks and processes (that is, the division of labour);
b   the need for some central co-ordinating agency, for example the modern state.

As we shall show in Chapter 7, the notion of social evolution as 'differentiation' and 'integration' has been picked up and reformulated in quite modern work on social change.

We are now in a position to look at the innovations which Spencer was able to contribute to sociology on the basis of this general evolutionary ground plan. His system demonstrates with great clarity the unit ideas of Social Evolutionism: ideas which *must* follow as a logical consequence from the assumption that there are evolutionary processes at work on the 'superorganic' level. The five main ingredients which we shall consider briefly here are: the mechanisms of evolutionary change; the concept of stages; social structure; functional requirements; and industrialism or industrial society.

Mechanisms of evolutionary change

Any evolutionary theory of society must explain the reasons why change and development *necessarily* occur in the way that the theory states. We have already suggested that it was here that an important part of Spencer's originality lay. Thus, it was he and not Darwin who coined the phrase 'survival of the fittest' to describe the competitive struggle which causes more complex and adapted forms to emerge out of simpler ones. He argued that all simple forms of matter are likely in the long run to prove unstable. This includes simple *social* groupings. In social life innovations and complexity occur because of the tendency for environmental conditions to change. By this means he arrived at the idea that even simple social organisms must possess the ability to adapt in order to survive. Adaptation requires greater flexibility and a wider range of activities. It thus continually heightens the degree of differentiation and intensifies the need for regulation and integration. Groups which cannot make the necessary adaptations will be eliminated in favour of those who can. We shall see below, however, that for Spencer the 'survival of the fittest' was more than a scientific hypothesis. It was also part of a moral crusade, a message for his own times.

The concept of stages

As one modern writer, himself sympathetic to the evolutionary position, has observed, the concept of stages is an essential step in introducing evolution into sociological enquiry (Eisenstadt 1964). Watered down into a mere description of a general tendency or trend in human life, the idea of evolution is vague and virtually worthless. Only by trying to distinguish a set of stages or 'jumps' in which a new complex of social arrangements establishes itself, can the investigator demonstrate that the movement towards say greater complexity is a tangible fact. Spencer no doubt appreciated and accepted this challenge. Armed with his general principle of increasing complexity of forms – which he calls 'compounding' – Spencer is able to offer a classification of societies, according to whether they are simple, compound, or doubly compound. A great deal of scholarly effort went into collecting materials from published sources in order to demonstrate the validity of this classification of stages. The problems attached to such a labour were formidable. Like later scholars who tried to follow his example Spencer often could not avoid over-generalizing as a result of the sheer scope of his enquiries and

the unreliability of his sources. He was obliged too, as Table 1 shows, to introduce a cross-cutting principle of political organization into his scheme.

If Spencer's classifications seem unsatisfactory now, however, he had at least established the idea of verifying a general theory of society by means of painstaking empirical work.

Social structure

To take hold of societies which have existed in separate places and historical periods, and to regard them as belonging to the same type or stage within a system of classification, is an audacious procedure. The practice involves placing a line around what may be several centuries of human history to any part of which individual scholars may have devoted a lifetime's research. The procedure can only be justified if it is possible to point to a continuing regularity underlying the tapestry of historical detail and transcending the lives of individuals. This regularity is what certain systems of sociological thought, of which evolutionism was the first, mean when they speak of *social structure*.

Spencer arrived at a concept of social structure because of his wish to demonstrate the importance of evolution at all levels of scientific work. Just as biological organisms have discernible structures which adapt, so, he argued, it must be possible to dispense with the mere chronicle of historical events which historians had provided and demonstrate that society too possesses a 'physiological division of labour'. By this means he hoped to show that an *analogy* with organic growth would aid the understanding of historical change. In practice the biological connotations from which the concept of social structure has developed have proved troublesome for its later users.

Functional requirements

We now come to what was probably the most important of all of Spencer's insights – the notion of 'function'. It was suggested to him by the ideas of competitive struggle and adaptation. How do

Table 1   *Herbert Spencer's classification of societies by degrees of composition* (adapted from Spencer 1971, pp. 150–2)

Simple societies	Headless	*Nomadic*: (hunting) Fuegians, some Australians, Wood-Veddahs, Bushmen, Chépángs and Kusúndas of Nepal *Semi-settled*: most Esquimaux *Settled*: Arafuras, Land Dyaks of Upper Sarawak River
	Occupational headship	*Nomadic*: (hunting) some Australians, Tasmanians *Semi-settled*: some Caribs *Settled*: some Uaupés of the upper Rio Negro
	Vague and unstable headship	*Nomadic*: (hunting) Andamanese, Abipones, Snakes, Chippewayans; (pastoral) some Bedouins *Semi-settled*: some Esquimaux, Chinooks, Chippewas (at present), some Kamschadales, Village Veddahs, Bodo and Dhimáls *Settled*: Guiana tribes, Mandans, Coroados, New Guinea people, Tannese, Vateans, Dyaks, Todas, Nagas, Karens, Santals
	Stable headship	*Nomadic*: *Semi-settled*: some Caribs, Patagonians, New Caledonians, Kaffirs *Settled*: Guaranis, Pueblos
Compound societies	Occasional headship	*Nomadic*: (pastoral) some Bedouins *Semi-settled*: Tannese *Settled*:
	Unstable headship	*Nomadic*: (hunting) Dacotahs; (hunting and pastoral) Comanches; (pastoral) Kalmucks *Semi-settled*: Ostyaks, Beluchis, Kookies, Bhils, Congo-people (passing into doubly compound), Teutons before 5th century *Settled*: Chippewas (in past times), Creeks, Mundrucus, Tupis, Khonds, some New Guinea people, Sumatrans, Malagasy (till recently), Coast Negroes, Inland Negroes, some Abyssinians, Homeric Greeks, Kingdoms of the Heptarchy, Teutons in 5th century, Fiefs of 10th century
	Stable headship	*Nomadic*: (pastoral) Kirghiz *Semi-settled*: Bechuanas, Zulus *Settled*: Uaupés, Fijians (when first visited), New Zealanders, Sandwich Islanders (in Cook's time), Javans, Hottentots, Dahomans, Ashantees, some Abyssinians, Ancient Yucatanese, New Granada people, Honduras people, Chibehas, some town Arabs
Doubly compound societies	Occasional headship	*Semi-settled*: *Settled*: Samoans
	Unstable headship	*Semi-settled*: *Settled*: Tahitians, Tongans, Javans (occasionally), Fijians (since fire-arms), Malagasy (in recent times), Athenian Confederacy, Spartan Confederacy, Teutonic Kingdoms from 6th to 9th centuries, Greater Fiefs in France of the 13th century
	Stable headship	*Semi-settled*: *Settled*: Iroquois, Araucanians, Sandwich Islanders (since Cook's time), Ancient Vera Paz and Bogota peoples, Guatemalans, Ancient Peruvians, Wahhàbees (Arab), Omán (Arab), Ancient Egyptian Kingdom, England after the 10th century

we judge whether an adaptation is successful? One way is to set out a list of essential conditions or 'functions' which must be met if the society is to survive. Admittedly Spencer's ideas on the subject strike us as rather simple and over-general today. He considered that there are three systems or functions which must be present in every society in varying proportions. They are:

a internal regulation – 'managing' and 'co-ordinating' separate activities and ensuring the stability of behaviour;
b a sustaining system – that is, economic arrangements for maintaining the livelihood of members of society;
c a distributing system – for allocating the supply of products and services.

A changing environment will thus lead to the search for new ways of meeting these functional necessities and will even change the relative degree of emphasis given to one or the other. This insight led him to suggest a method of extending his classification of levels of social evolution – as we shall now show.

The industrial type of society

The term evolution can only be used in modern scientific work shorn of any suggestions at all of long-term progress or tendencies to improve-ment. To say that the outcome of evolution does in fact represent progress is to make a moral judgement. Whatever Spencer and his contem-poraries may have thought, there is no scientific way of settling moral issues or of comparing one way of life favourably with another. Yet it was precisely this step that Spencer wanted to make. He hoped to present mid-Victorian industrial society as the necessary outcome of a process whose existence science had established beyond any reasonable doubt. Unfortunately for him the classification of societies according to the level of 'compounding' which was described above fails to fulfil this task. Although civilized

or 'trebly compound' nations appear as the most evolved group the category is very broad and includes the industrialized nations of Western Europe along with the Roman Empire and other ancient civilizations. But his list of essential societal functions offers the possibility of a separate classification on the basis of whichever function receives most emphasis at any given point in the evolutionary scale. For example, he lumped a large number of earlier pre-industrial systems together under the heading 'militant societies' (see Table 2). The fact that, in these cases, coercion and conquest dominate is evidence of a preoccupation with the regulatory function. With the coming of industrial society, however, it has become possible for the regu-lating function to give way to a settled order with an emphasis on the sustaining system. For this type of society to operate effectively the regu-latory principle must be reduced to a minimum. In this way he was able to argue the case for a *laissez-faire* society in which the state plays a minor role and free economic trade – the Wealth of Nations – predominates. The society of rational autonomous individuals thus appears in its proper place at the top of the evolutionary scale. And if the unbridled competition of such a society leaves some individuals worse off than others this is merely the price of allowing the 'struggle for survival' to perform its progressive function.

The problems of Spencerism

At the last then Spencer was a good liberal. There are numerous places where his political and moral outlook points in one direction, his theory in another and in the ensuing confusion his claim to have founded a *scientific* social evolutionism is made highly dubious. His influence over both contemporary and later students of society was such, however, that we are obliged to take the problems raised by his work very seriously. Below we can only describe the most important ones.

Table 2   *The contrast between militant and industrial societies* (constructed from Spencer by Smelser 1968)

Characteristic	Militant society	Industrial society
Dominant function or activity	Corporate defensive and offensive activity for preservation and aggrandizement	Peaceful, mutual rendering of individual services
Principle of social co-ordination	Compulsory co-operation; regimentation by enforcement of orders; both positive and negative regulation of activity	Voluntary co-operation; regulation by contract and principles of justice; only negative regulation of activity
Relations between state and individual	Individuals exist for benefit of state; restraints on liberty, property, and mobility	State exists for benefit of individuals; freedom; few restraints on property and mobility
Relations between state and other organizations	All organizations public; private organizations excluded	Private organizations encouraged
Structure of state	Centralized	Decentralized
Structure of social stratification	Fixity of rank, occupation, and locality; inheritance of positions	Plasticity and openness of rank, occupation, and locality; movement between positions
Type of economic activity	Economic autonomy and self-sufficiency; little external trade; protectionism	Loss of economic autonomy; interdependence via peaceful trade; free trade
Valued social and personal characteristics	Patriotism; courage; reverence; loyalty; obedience; faith in authority; discipline	Independence; respect for others; resistance to coercion; individual initiative; truthfulness; kindness

The comparison of biological and social processes

Parallels and analogies between organisms and societies, between the biological and the sociological, permeate Spencer's thought. Oddly enough, the most well-known criticisms of his work on this score are rather superficial. They concern themselves with the so-called *biological analogy* which he brings in to justify the use of the term 'structure' in the context of both societies and living organisms. Unfortunately there are many important ways in which social 'structures' *differ* from those investigated by biology. For example, a relatively clear set of criteria concerning the healthy functioning and death of organisms can be set out giving the idea of 'survival' some point. Societies, however, do not 'die' in the sense that individuals do and to judge the efficiency of their adaptation and health is to risk slipping in some wholly unsubstantiated judgements about what kind of social existence one personally prefers. Again, even after death, biological organisms retain, for some time at least, a visible structure which can be studied. Even when functioning, social structures prove to be elusive, only amenable to dissection in a metaphorical sense. Finally, it should be pointed out perhaps that the cells comprising biological organs do not 'move around' in the way that individuals move around the institutions within a society. In Chapter 16 we shall see that those who have retained

Spencer's way of conceptualizing social structure have also inherited some of the problems set out here.

However, Spencer himself recognized that comparison between patterns of social behaviour and the bodies of plants and animals is only of limited use to the sociologist – so that the above points do not really get to grips with the chief weakness of his evolutionary scheme.

The central difficulty in his theory of the relation between organic and super-organic evolution arises out of the way in which he employed the concepts of 'struggle' and 'survival'. In Spencer's theories something much less precise is involved than in similar sounding processes described by the Darwinian theory of evolution. For Darwin, the origin of biological species is powered by a process which he initially called 'natural selection'. 'But the expression often used by Mr Herbert Spencer', he wrote, 'of the survival of the fittest is more accurate, and is sometimes equally convenient.' (Cited in Peel 1971, p. 104) Darwin's judgement in this particular matter must be seriously questioned. His readiness to acknowledge Spencer's influence is understandable because of the latter's enormous prestige and the fact that the conversion of biology to evolutionism was a product of the powerful hold of theories of social progress over intellectuals and leaders.

But the scope of the theory which Darwin actually formulated is very specific and far more exact than the speculative works of the 'social scientists' of his time. It made use of a fact that was already known in the animal breeding world – the tendency for spontaneous variations to occur in the characteristics of organic species. From this *observation* he argued that, given a particular environment and a finite food supply, those animals and plants which by chance possess the most favourable characteristics for survival will pass them on to their offspring. What is being described in this model of evolution is indeed a process of natural *selection*. It has none of the implications of a striving of all life towards some sort of ultimate goal or perfectibility which are contained in the phrase 'survival of the fittest'. Darwinian evolution simply proceeds from the assumption that different forms of organism enjoy different relative chances of survival in given environments. Change in an environment implies the possibility that previously successful forms of adaptation may suddenly become obsolete – as when for example climatic or geological changes deprive a group of marine animals of their medium. What was offensive in Darwin's theory to religious interests was precisely the suggestion that human life was not the result of a Divine plan but of a series of haphazard accidents.

Modern biology has substantiated the view that it is only chance mutations in organic structure which are handed on from one generation to the next. Characteristics acquired or learned by an organism during life cannot be inherited by its progeny. Since Darwin offered no explanation of why such variations actually occur, considerable controversy raged over the suggestion that *only* chance variation was needed to account for evolution. Not until much later, when the principles of modern genetics had been incorporated into biology, did the notion of a distinct *genetic* heredity gain force and clarity.

Thus it is that when we come back to examine the theory of super-organic evolution closely we find the themes of nature and nurture, heredity and environment inextricably mixed in a way that is quite foreign to modern ways of thought. Let us start from the problem of heredity. Spencer's references to the 'genetic' cut right across modern-day usage. He spoke of genetic transmission in a loose fashion denoting any study of 'genesis' or origins. He also 'fought a long rearguard action' (Peel 1971, p. 142) against the acceptance of the Darwinian position within biology itself. To have accepted it would have seriously undermined his effort to show the application of evolutionary principles in all branches of science. In fact nothing among either physical or social phenomena corresponds with the biologist's notion of randomly transmitted genetic mutations. Yet to admit this

Spencer would have had to concede at least that evolutionary adaptations occur in dissimilar and perhaps incomparable ways among different groups of phenomena; or even to have abandoned his theses concerning non-biological evolution altogether.

Environment and adaptation in social life

The concept of *environment* has also proved to be rather troublesome when used in the context of social analysis. To be sure in the study of 'simple' (that is, subsistence) societies it might be used in a sense synonymous with the physical or geographical environment, suggesting a struggle for survival that may be analogous to the biological idea. To move beyond such cases is to move almost by definition to situations where the driving force of development has ceased to be pure physical hardship; and where in the very process of adaptation human activity has actually modified, with increasing effect, the nature of the physical environment itself. Moreover, accidents of geography may assume very different degrees of malevolence or benevolence for the same people at separate points in their histories. In short, except at very primitive levels of social organization, it is difficult to define 'environment' in such a way as to avoid including the society itself. Spencer certainly never offered any clear conceptions on this issue (Burrow 1966, pp. 202–3).

Very similar considerations apply to the term *adaptation*. The problem is to set out the *conditions* of successful adaptation. By definition societies which have adapted unsuccessfully will have ceased to exist. But to say that actual societies have survived because they are adapted (that is, they are the way they are) seems rather meaningless.

Human nature and cultural diversity

Spencer's views on the question of a universal human nature and the origin of cultural diversity often appear to be inconsistent. His residual utilitarianism led him on occasions to reject the argument that society is an entity that is somehow more real or more important than the individuals of which it is composed. Hence we find him arguing 'there is no way of coming at a true theory of society but by enquiring into the *nature* of its component individuals' (our italics). Yet as we have seen, it was the variability of behaviour and customs which he wanted to explain. Hence he was also capable of attacking violently the belief in uniform human nature and wrote, 'Man himself obeys the law of indefinite variation. His circumstances are ever altering and he is ever adapting himself to them.' (both cited in Peel 1971, p. 87). From his own point of view there is no conflict between these two statements because it is the study of individual human nature *as it evolves in character* which matters in his sociology. But this position relied on the false assumption that acquired characteristics could form a solid inheritance for future generations of individuals. In the end, therefore, his account of the mechanisms by which one stage of social development succeeds the next breaks down.

Social versus Cultural Evolutionism

Spencer's work represents the most forceful statement of what, at the outset of the chapter, we called *Social* Evolutionism: the thesis that an evolutionary process exists within the social organism as a whole. The distinctiveness of this kind of theory will be made more obvious, perhaps, by contrasting it with an alternative tendency in evolutionary thought which became prominent at roughly the same time. This is usually referred to as *Cultural* Evolutionism, because, as the name suggests, it derived from the belief of certain authors that it would be easier to demonstrate evolution in the *products* of social life (that is, culture) which are relatively more tangible and stable, than in the complexities of social arrangements themselves. It represents a somewhat less ambitious and theoretically innovative perspective than the Spencerian brand. The scholars in question were concerned to a much greater degree simply with identifying and classifying parallel developments across the world in cultural forms than with proving historical laws or with the workings of any one type of society. Cultural Evolutionism is associated in Britain with the writings of E. B. Tylor, a man some ten years younger than Spencer, and with those of L. H. Morgan in the USA. Tylor's influence is perhaps more typical of the genre since Morgan does not use the word culture as such. Morgan however was to have an important influence on Marx and Engels.

Cultural Evolutionism has had more significance for anthropology than for sociology in general. Anthropologists have always been willing to entertain evolutionism as a position with which they should engage for two reasons. First, so many of the cultures which the literature of anthropology describes stem from societies without written history. In this situation the evolutionary perspective offered a kind of substitute for written historical records by suggesting lines along which present-day cultural forms may have originated. Second, in many of these cases the scale of the society was small, with a fairly simple technology. This made the application of the concept of environment and the classification of societies themselves into levels and types a somewhat more meaningful exercise. (An illustration of this possibility is the famous classification of the material cultures of 'simpler peoples' in Hobhouse, Wheeler and Ginsberg 1965.)

Despite these differences, however, Cultural Evolutionism had a great deal in common with 'Spencerism,' not least that like all evolutionary theories of society it was vulnerable to two important criticisms, namely:

a the unilinearity of its theory of stages;
b the adequacy of its methods of comparison.

Unilinearity

By unilinearity is meant the presumption of vulgar evolutionary theories that all societies must pass through a fixed unvarying sequence of stages. It is doubtful whether any of the better-known evolutionists of the nineteenth century ever really believed this. With the possible exception of his earlier work Spencer had clearly argued against it. In fact he compared the evolutionary process to a tree with a single trunk and many branches, some terminating at higher levels than others. He was also of the view that regression and the decay of relatively advanced social forms was a more common process than genuine evolution. The cultural evolutionists, by making some rather extreme sounding statements on the subject, did render themselves liable to charges of belief in unilinear evolution. They have been defended on the grounds that they were really advancing a less ambitious hypothesis: that where a given type of cultural system is found it can always be shown to have originated from the preceding stage.

The Comparative Method

A much more serious problem in evolutionary theories of society in general concerned their *methods* and the *use of anthropological data* from tribal societies to establish hypotheses about the prehistory of humanity. The first major onslaught on this practice came from a now largely discredited school of thought known as the 'diffusionists' or 'ideographic' school. At the centre of the diffusionist case was an objection to the methods employed by the evolutionists to establish their developmental schemes of classifying societies. All of these relied on the assumption that prehistoric society had looked very much like the tribal societies of the present. In this they obtained influential support from the findings of the nineteenth-century archaeologists. But to the diffusionists of the early years of the twentieth century this was a fatal fallacy.

The resemblance of modern savages to a primeval apeman is so important a tenet that we must explicitly expose the error. It lies in failing to understand that even the simplest recent group has a prolonged past during which it has progressed very far indeed from the hypothetical stage. (R. Lowie, cited in Harris M. 1968, p. 154)

In order to tease out this 'prolonged past' the ideographic method entailed putting painstaking fieldwork in the place of a few evolutionary generalizations. No general law-like assumptions were made about the nature or direction of social and historical change. The term diffusionism refers to the simple proposal that change and development of cultures is the result of the spread of influence from certain dominant culture areas to their hinterland.

The disintegration of evolutionary social theory

Despite the enormous initial impact of evolutionary thought on sociology, its decline in popularity was equally dramatic. After the 1920s it was never to regain a major role as a direct stimulus to research. Although several factors contributed to this collapse two were of special importance, namely the spread of Darwinism and the growing reluctance to associate social change and industrialization with progress. We shall conclude the chapter by describing two fairly late developments in evolutionary thought which arose out of the attempt to update or adjust the theory accordingly.

Social Darwinism

We have seen that the Darwinian revolution in biology removed the real basis on which Spencer's sociology had rested. To quite a number of people writing in the harsher light already evident at the turn of the nineteenth century it seemed highly appropriate to replace the self-seeking, self-governing individual of liberal theory by an organism subject to forces of biological heredity and instinctual impulse beyond conscious control. From this source came Social Darwinism, a mode of thought based on the conviction that the conclusions of *The Origin of Species* offered a new evolutionary and scientific basis for the social sciences as well as for biology.

It was an idea highly congenial to interests outside the world of scholarship. Darwin's theory had made notions like 'heredity' and 'genetic' more precise. It was soon used to give 'scientific' legitimacy to an old idea, namely that the capacity for rational judgement, moral behaviour and, above all, business success was not equally distributed among the various races and divisions of humanity. Darwin did not actually dissociate himself from this although he should not be held responsible for the excesses of his followers. Furthermore, quite prominent figures of late-nineteenth-century social science began to state in print their conviction that Africans, Indians, the 'negroes' of North America, paupers, criminals and even women had inherited smaller brains and a reduced capacity for rational thought and moral conduct than everybody else. Such ideas had particular appeal in the United States which was experiencing an influx of immigrants of diverse ethnic background and where people were particularly ready to equate the biological process of natural selection with the competition of an unrestricted market. In *both* Britain and the USA, however, programmes of selective breeding were proposed to encourage progress or to prevent civilization from degenerating (Bendix 1956, Chapter 5, pp. 254ff.; Kamin 1974, Chapter 1; Jones G. 1980). Several decades were to pass before these pseudoscientific doctrines were discredited – to the satisfaction of most social scientists at any rate.

The more unsavoury forms of Social Darwinism should not be allowed to obscure the perfectly serious efforts of several writers to demonstrate that the evolution of the superior mental powers of *Homo sapiens* has not allowed us to escape from our genetic history; and that the mind is therefore *not* a Blank Page. In *The Descent of Man* Darwin himself suggested that there are various social instincts from which the distinctive social life of humans derives. Among the most interesting of those authors who took up the suggestion was Edward Westermarck. Westermarck believed that research would reveal the biological and psychological needs around which moral rules and institutions were built. He tried to show, by dint of much scholarship and even fieldwork, that though customs and morals appear to be diverse there is in fact a set of common elements among them which may be attributed to the biological survival value of the behaviour in question. In the next chapter we shall see that such ideas have enjoyed a revival in recent years although they have not commanded widespread support among sociologists.

For the bulk of sociologists, and many anthropologists too, the insights of modern biology offered a powerful reason for abandoning evolutionary accounts of society altogether. For them, the fact that *Homo sapiens* has developed intelligence and the capacity to create culture meant that little could be learned from studying the contribution of biological heredity to social life. In short, they accepted that human nature is flexible and almost infinitely variable – a function of the matrix of culture and institutions within which the adult and human mind are formed. This matrix could only be made to yield its secrets by employing better conceptual tools than had been forged by evolutionary theories of society.

Technological determinism

This is the somewhat unsatisfactory name given to the form in which the Social Evolutionary type of perspective has enjoyed most support in twentieth-century sociology. At its simplest it denotes the theory that the development and character of a society is contingent upon the level of material culture and technical organization which it has attained. In practice the word 'determinism' is somewhat misleading because few writers in this genre have been willing to assert that there is a one-to-one correspondence between institutions and culture on one hand and 'technology' on the other. The leading representative of this viewpoint is W. F. Ogburn, one of the writers in sociology who continued to put forward a technological evolutionary position during the inter-war years.

Ogburn is famous for the concept of *cultural lag* which refers to the discrepancy between the level of technical development in a society and the conservatism of morals and institutions. Conceptualizing the nature of this cultural lag, however, has proved to be a major difficulty in the theory.

Aside from certain misinterpretations of Marx which we deal with elsewhere, technological determinism derives directly from two features of late-nineteenth-century thought. First came the considerable amount of work on material culture stimulated by the writings of L. H. Morgan, who propounded a whole theory of social stages based on the evolution of tools and technology. Second, certain features of technological 'determinism' can be found in the generation of writers, somewhat younger than Spencer, who were clearly influenced by him. In the works of such writers as L. F. Ward, F. Giddings and W. G. Sumner in the USA, or L. T. Hobhouse and E. Westermarck in Britain, the concept of an adaptive struggle for survival is gradually transformed. It becomes a process in which the growth of mind and intelligent control over the environment makes it possible for the human race to transcend the blueprint of mere biological heredity. Instinctual behaviour based on self-centred impulse gives way to greater altruism, co-operation and morality in social life. In other words morals are the product of successful adaptation to the material environment.

Where this idea leads can be seen most clearly in Hobhouse, whose thought owes much to Comte. Almost unwittingly, Hobhouse propounded a theory of industrial society which completely reverses Spencer's view of civilization as unregulated individual self-interest. For him, it is primitive society, hardly advanced beyond the provision of physical need, which is characterized, or rather marred by, self-centred individualism. Civilized humans, by contrast, are notable for their commitment to systems of co-operation and relative disregard of self-interest.

The broad tone of optimism which such views reflect could not really survive the bloodbath of World War I. Indeed, the fact that the notion of *social* evolution had never been disentangled from pure faith in the inevitability of progress was a major factor in the demise of most sociological theories bearing the stamp of Spencerian thought. Paradoxically, however, the interpretation of social development as simply the story of ever-increasing intellectual and technical mastery over the natural world did not *have* to be bound up with the idea of moral progress. To more recent writers it could simply be regarded as an evident fact whose consequences could be objectively analysed and assessed. This at least was the justification for most of the technological theories of industrial society which have been proposed as the twentieth century has proceeded.

It was an idea which had already been used with devastating effect. According to Thorstein Veblen (1857–1929), the elaborate machine system of industrial society was not a manifestation of moral progress at all. It merely made possible the expression and satisfaction on an unprecedented scale of the most predatory and basic instincts which have been implanted in man (*sic*) by natural selection. The reader who wishes to know more about the place Veblen occupies, or should occupy, in modern social thought is referred to two fascinating recent studies by Seckler (1975) and Diggins (1978), as well as the older biography by Dorfman (1961). For, although it is difficult to know how far to take Veblen seriously, his work is generally considered to contain a version of technological determinism of unsurpassed subtlety (see Banks J. 1959). Many of the ideas contained in it have become commonplace.

Veblen believed that social change is the product of two forces rooted in the human psyche. One, which impels material technology forward, he called 'the instinct of workmanship'. The other, whose influence is mostly conservative, he called the 'instinct of emulation'. It is responsible, at each stage of development, for the growth of a parasitic leisure class whose interests dominate cultural life, determine the division of labour and condemn some members of society, women especially, to a life of drudgery. Eventually, the leisure class is displaced by the effects of 'advance in the industrial arts'. But the consequent increased surplus of material goods and services is merely appropriated by a new leisure class.

This argument is employed with much satire and irony in his most famous work *The Theory of the Leisure Class* to show that little in human society, as represented by the America of his time, has really changed since barbarian times. He was highly sceptical of the belief that the industrializing American business economy was actually efficient. On the contrary, it permitted and encouraged the 'conspicuous waste' and idleness of the modern bourgeois business class. The display of beads and war-paint in savage society finds its counterpart in the ostentation of the symbols of wealth. The use of women as trophies in tribal warfare finds its counterpart in the barbarian status of women amongst the modern rich. Their conspicuous leisure, their coiffure and dress (even their corsets!) serve the purpose of placing in evidence the household's ability to pay. The instinct of emulation on which such practices are founded is as old as human nature itself. (Veblen 1970)

A joke? The first serious theory of the sex war? An alternative materialist theory to Marx's account of the struggles between classes? Veblen's work, undoubtedly eccentric, is probably all of these. Nevertheless his ideas on inequality and the role of business interests in modern society, even shorn of their evolutionary trappings, often seem surprisingly relevant to the modern world. Described as a genius and a failure, the real significance of Veblen surely lies in the fact that he took the theory of progress and turned it against itself – this in a country which had built its way of life around it.

So ended the classic period of evolutionary thought. The orthodox evolutionist had attributed the uniqueness of industrial society to the freedom it allowed to the play of self-interest. Veblen claimed that the competitive struggles of the modern business class offered unprecedented scope for the most primitive instincts. The theory of progress had set out to uncover the prefiguring of civilization in the practices of savagery. It ended by producing a thinker who believed in the essential savagery of the most refined practices.

6 Evolutionary themes in modern social science: nature versus nurture

We must now return to the two basic problems which have lain behind evolutionism from the outset, namely 'cultural variation' and 'human nature' (see pp. 69–72). As we have tried to explain, early evolutionists tended to confuse these two problems. Even Spencer maintained simultaneously that: (a) culture and institutions ultimately determine the characteristics of individuals; and (b) the varieties of social life are somehow a reflection of so many different classes of human nature. We showed that by the late nineteenth century these had become mutually incompatible theses, giving rise to quite separate evolutionary theories of society and social behaviour. On one hand, there were the biologically oriented ideas of the Social Darwinists. On the other, technological determinists continued to maintain that evolution also occurs at the institutional and cultural level.

Our discussion thus falls into two parts. This chapter deals with the legacy of Social Darwinism and examines the reasons sociologists have given for rejecting it. The next considers the claims of so-called 'neo-evolutionism': that is, recent work within sociology itself which looks at industrialization and development in a very similar way to nineteenth-century theories of social evolution. We shall then conclude with an assessment of the general significance of evolutionary thought within sociology.

Blank paper or naked ape? Nature, nurture and industrial society

For much of the period since World War II,

Social Darwinism was considered to be no longer important. In recent years, however, it has undergone a revival and its claims now require careful examination. On the face of it, the 'new' Social Darwinism merely elevates an everyday idea into a scientific theory, namely that there are certain innate and unchanging aspects of human nature which shape social behaviour and affect social organization. It has also, however, challenged conventional social science by advocating the replacement of its usual procedures and established concepts with those of evolutionary biology. Sociologists, to be sure, have been fairly unimpressed with this programme. But perhaps their reaction is mere prejudice and habit? Obviously, much depends upon whether followers of the biological approach have been able to offer evidence of the role of hereditary factors in human behaviour.

We must, therefore, consider some of the relevant research. It will help if we point out here that in ordinary speech the phrase 'human nature' is used in two rather different ways:

1 The first employs nature as some kind of *common* denominator of humanity and human society. The picture of ourselves that emerges from this is frequently uncomplimentary. Human nature left uncontrolled by social discipline is said to be selfish, aggressive, greedy and so on.

2 Sometimes, however, nature is held to explain how individuals come to occupy different positions, opportunities and obligations. For example, differences in nature between the sexes are said to underlie the institutions of

marriage and the family, which are then held to be 'natural', that is, inevitable. The same idea can be used to suggest that inequality of power and privilege is also 'natural', that, say, the condition of various classes and/or racial groups within a society reflects fixed variations in genetic make-up.

We can use this distinction to group the literature on the new forms of Social Darwinism into two categories, the first dealing with the common factors in human nature, the second dealing with the variable factors.

Human nature as a common denominator

Many nineteenth-century scholars thought it would be possible to undertake the study of what J. S. Mill called 'ethology': that is, analysis of the connection between innate traits and forms of social order. The term fell into disuse until the 1930s, when reference to *comparative* ethology began to appear in connection with the pioneering work of certain zoologists whose detailed observations of animals revealed complex patterns of 'social' behaviour entirely imprinted by instinct (Hinde 1982). This posed a new problem for the theory of evolution, shifting attention away from the origin of mere anatomical differences to that of explaining the adaptive significance of the *behavioural* regularities associated with a given species. In due course, the comparative ethologists turned their attention to *Homo sapiens*, who, they rightly argued, is, from the viewpoint of evolutionary biology, simply another animal. Would we not expect to find, as elsewhere in the animal kingdom, that the evolutionary history of our species had had some influence over its present repertoire of social behaviours? One of the most well-known and audacious statements of this theme is contained in Lorenz's popular book *On Aggression* (Lorenz 1963). It has been followed by a number of similar attempts to out-Veblen Veblen by presenting civilized man as 'merely a "naked ape", or a territorial and aggressive baboon in clothes' (Hirst and Woolley 1982, p. 66; cf. Ardrey 1961, 1967, 1970; Morris 1967; Tiger and Fox 1974).

Though popular, these essays in 'human zoology' base their evidence, such as it is, upon two kinds of assumptions neither of which stand up to examination:

1 *That simple parallels can be drawn between human social life and that of animals, particularly the sub-human primates* (for example, baboons, chimpanzees). The worst examples of this practice rely on what is no more than an analogy between human customs and the innate 'social' reflexes of animals. Thus, for example, the term 'ritual' is often used to imply that courtship gestures among greylag geese and, say, fertility rites in African villages have something in common. In fact, the correspondence between zoological and anthropological terminology is far from exact.

True, social behaviour in primates is not just a series of reflexes. Indeed, contrary to what was once believed, hard and fast distinctions between humans (as the creators of culture) and our closest relatives (as creatures of instinct) do not work in evolutionary terms: both early hominids and modern apes have been shown to possess a tool using culture of sorts. On the other hand, the claim of some ethologists, that there is a single 'primate way of life' has been falsified by the advance of ethological fieldwork itself. The social life of each primate species is unique and the differences between human and subhuman society have become immense precisely because the human animal has its own special evolutionary history. (For useful summaries see Hirst and Woolley 1982, pp. 3–91; Reynolds 1980; Washburn 1980; and for a philosophical treatment, Midgeley 1979, 1980.)

2 *That anthropological evidence can be deployed to 'prove' that if an aspect of social behaviour is universal, it is also 'natural', that is, genetically fixed.* There are two problems with so-called 'universals' of human society. The first is whether they exist at all. Much of the

anthropology quoted by ethologists was carried out by investigators who inevitably reported on their materials whilst remaining influenced by Western values, concepts and practices. Their accounts refer to communities facing colonization or some other disturbance from Europe or America. Even so, exceptions can usually be found to so-called universal patterns. Second, the possibility of 'universals' in existing societies does not prove that there is a natural blueprint for human interaction which we break at our peril. On the contrary it begs the question of how much novelty social arrangements can tolerate once industrialization has overcome many of the pre-existing 'natural' limits to human activity.

We are not, of course, suggesting that ethological comparisons between humans and other species are never worth making. Interesting parallels, for example, have been observed between forms of animal display and human phenomena such as play gestures in children or aggressive behaviour among teenage youths. These may well indicate that there are some residual instinctual factors in human modes of communication (Smith P. K. 1974; Marsh 1978). But, in general, it will take much better evidence than this to convince social scientists that whole patterns of organization and disorganization in our collective life are reducible to the hereditary impulses or biological drives which people may feel or express as they participate in them. It would be irresponsible to explain away, say, political tyranny simply in terms of the 'need to dominate', or international war as the product of innate 'aggressive instincts'. In short, the ethological search for genetic common denominators in human social behaviour is set at too abstract a level compared with the shifts and variability of history and culture.

The very latest version of the new Social Darwinism is called 'sociobiology'. It looks upon ethology as pre-scientific, and as far as sociology is concerned it raises somewhat

different issues (see Wilson 1975, 1978; Dawkins, 1976; Sahlins 1977; Caplan 1978; Montagu 1980). Sociobiologists take as their central problem the phenomenon of *altruism*; that is, the willingness of one animal to make sacrifices (of food, say, or life itself) for the sake of another. How could such 'moral' behaviour, though obviously important to the social life of many species, including our own, have resulted from the evolutionary struggle and from natural selection? Sociobiologists usually answer this question with a model of the evolutionary process known as the 'kin selection' theory. According to this, an animal who behaves altruistically is likely to promote the survival and subsequent reproductive success of its own kin who, it is argued, will share at least some of the same genetic 'package'. Though by far the greater part of sociobiologists' efforts have gone into validating this model through observations of nonhuman species, the greatest controversy has surrounded their limited and often naïve remarks about their own kind. Not only have these remarks often been politically tactless (attracting charges of racialism and sexism) but also seemed to assail psychology and social science in a rather arrogant way. For example, anthropologists have reacted strongly against the claim made by E. O. Wilson and others that the various kinship systems of humanity reflect 'universal' genetic pressures towards reproductive success, and that they simply operate to prevent the genetic evils that result from incest. Fieldwork literature on kinship, anthropologists argue, just does not support such a view (Sahlins 1977). This, as we shall see towards the end of the book, is not quite the whole story. But it does seem unlikely that 'evolutionary' methods will *pre-empt* the established procedures of social science; still less that such methods could link given features of social organization to traits of human 'nature' as shaped by natural selection.

Yet sociologists should not jump to the opposite extremes and conclude that the evolution of humanity has no relevance to their work. Fortunately, the controversies described above have led some authors to recognize that there is a need to use the word 'culture' with greater precision. In the past, it has often stood in for various social scientific prejudices, such as that speech and rational thought have enabled humanity to transcend biological controls; that human nature is infinitely malleable through conditioning and training; and, hence, that 'nature' and 'culture' are different orders of facts (Fox R. 1969; Midgeley 1979). The discovery of rudimentary cultural forms among chimpanzees and other primates has shaken these assumptions. The clear implication is that it was the evolutionary value of 'cultural' ways of adapting which produced humanity in the first place. Furthermore, as Hirst and Woolley observe in a sophisticated treatment of the same point:

Biological and psychological capacities clearly do organise and limit social relations. Without the capacity for tool use made possible by the opposable thumb and forefinger and freeing forelimbs from the task of locomotion our social organisations would be very different and very limited. If our average intelligence level were what is measured by an I.Q. of 80, then again, social relations between humans would encounter severe limits. In both cases these biological and psychological capabilities are not independent of and have been shaped by the consequences of humans associating in social organisations. They impose limits nonetheless and cannot be legislated away. (Hirst and Woolley 1982, p. 23)

Hereditary factors in social differences

The question of whether there are 'natural' or innate causes of the differences between members of society will bring us to the same kind of conclusion. The material, however, is much more complex and we shall examine no less than four forms of social division: by sex, by achievement, by race and by conformity.

Sex and gender

The renaissance of feminism in recent years has had important consequences for intellectual life generally. Many people now realize that the ideas and language they take for granted are tainted with the assumption that the male sex is the most important, interesting and/or innovative part of the human race. Sociology itself has woken up to the fact that its theorists and researchers, 'like societal members, tend to define a society and discuss its social organization in terms of what men do and where men are located' (Chodorow 1978, p. 12). In fact, as feminist sociologists insist, the social division of task and privileges between men and women is something to be explained and has a prior claim on our efforts to understand social organization.

This may seem puzzling. Surely, of all forms of social differentiation, the sexual division of activity is most readily accounted for by 'natural' factors? The evidence for this everyday belief, however, is somewhat meagre. For a start, no conclusive psychological data have been put forward which might account for the marked social separation between the spheres of women and men. The variation in cognitive and emotional attributes is greater within each sex than between them and such sex-related traits as have been observed (for example, the finding that rather more girls than boys are bad at maths) could equally well be the consequence rather than the cause of existing cultural assumptions (for example, Maccoby and Jacklin 1975; Flynn 1980, pp. 188–201; Griffiths and Saraga 1979; National Foundation for Educational Research 1982).

For many feminist authors, however, the key issue is the association of 'mothering' and 'maternal instinct' with women. They do not, of course, deny the anatomical basis of sex – though it is not as clear cut as everyday thought likes to pretend – nor do they overlook the role in childbearing and lactation that nature assigns to women. But no research has been able to prove that these obvious differences of biological function and experience have inevitable behavioural implications. Their effect on behaviour is slight compared with that of the *uses to which society puts them*; and compared with the amplification that occurs in the transition from biological organism to fully socialized individual. (For useful reviews of the literature see Oakley 1972; Chodorow 1978, pp. 13–30.)

Feminist writers have been particularly critical of what they see as the speculative and 'androcentric' (that is, male-biased) statements of ethology and sociobiology. These tend to suggest that male dominance and the association of women with childbearing is a characteristic of primates and universal in human groups. Because these ideas are asserted on the basis of very little evidence, they weaken the claims of human social biology to be scientific and hence reduce its ability to contribute useful information to the analysis of the nature/culture interface. To be sure, anthropology and historical records suggest that the association of women with 'mothering' in some form has indeed been a common feature of human groups, one which, in turn, has allowed men to be the universally dominant sex. This evidence, however, does not imply that such a pattern is inevitable, nor in any case have 'the facts' gone unchallenged. There is now a body of counter-evidence indicating that the traits of temperament, aptitude and even physique which we associate with the sexes do not in fact exist in some cultures and are completely reversed in others (Mead M. 1963; Oakley 1972, 1976b; Friedl 1975; Reiter 1975; Lancaster 1976; Hamilton 1978).

Thus the whole question of how biological sex is translated into sex-identities in society is a very important and hitherto neglected one. For this reason sociologists these days try to distinguish sex, in the biological sense, from the social problem of sex-*identity* by employing the term 'gender' for the latter. 'Gender' should not be thought of as a specialized topic that need be discussed only in the context of so-called 'women's issues' such as the family or child-rearing. In this book, we have tried, so far as space and the existing literature of sociology will allow, to show that the concept of gender is relevant to a much wider range of sociological problems than that.

Achievement and intelligence

Some individuals are more successful than others. How far is *this* simply due to 'natural' inequality in the distribution of intelligence between different people?

There is, of course, a hoary scientific controversy surrounding this question, one which goes back to, and was closely associated with, the rise of Social Darwinism. We might, in fact, speak more accurately of Social 'Galtonism', for it was Darwin's cousin Francis Galton (1822–1911) who was primarily responsible for making the role of natural selection and hereditary factors in *human* social differences a publicly debated issue (for details see Jones 1980). In *Hereditary Genius*, Galton ascertained that notable achievements tend to run in families, claiming thereby to have demonstrated that differences in mental capacity are innate (Galton 1962). Galton's evidence, it was soon realized, proves nothing at all. It is to be expected that the advantages of being born into an already successful family atmosphere will be reflected in the achievements of the offspring.

The subsequent development of psychological research on intelligence from the many leads given by Galton, has, however, kept his position alive. The reasons for this will be familiar to many readers already:

1   Mental tests were developed which proved to be quite reliable predictors of what the future intellectual achievements of individuals were likely to be – certainly more reliable predictors than an individual's current *attainment*. Construction of such tests involves a controversial process called 'standardization': the tests are tried out on a large sample of children or adults, ambiguous questions eliminated (in theory) and the average scores (called 'norms') for the sample recorded. Such a procedure, it is claimed, means that the investigator can now compare the score of any new individual or group taking the test, with the test norms. The result is usually expressed as the notorious Intelligence Quotient (IQ). The classic studies in

this genre suggested that scores on intelligence tests do not improve after the age of about 18 and thereafter IQ remains more or less fixed, declining steadily through middle and old age.

2 Investigation of the mathematical structure of the distribution of test scores indicated that beneath the variety of specialized human talents there is a general intelligence factor (*g*) which is the major influence on achievement and this is what IQ tests measure.

3 It was concluded that *g* is overwhelmingly (not entirely) determined by hereditary endowment. A wide body of evidence, all of it pointing in the same direction, has been accumulated to reinforce this finding: kinship studies (analogous to Galton's); adoption studies; and, perhaps most famous of all, some crucial observations of pairs of twins. The latter include a small but famous set of surveys comparing the IQ scores obtained within pairs of *identical* twins, where the individuals concerned had been brought up apart. Identical twins, it was pointed out, come from a single ovum, and so inherit a common set of genes. If intelligence is largely determined by hereditary factors, therefore, we would expect the IQ scores of identical twin partners to be virtually the same regardless of upbringing. If on the other hand it is environment which has the determining influence, we would expect the scores to diverge, especially where separated upbringing has exposed members of the same pair to very different influences. In the event, all of the studies in question reported that identical twin partners do obtain closely similar test scores, more so than fraternal twins or ordinary siblings. These findings provided the main basis for 'heritability estimates' – in simple terms, estimates of the proportion contributed by heredity to IQ. Staunch advocates of IQ testing claim that 70–80 per cent of the variation in IQ scores is due to genetic factors.

4 Testing programmes also showed a concentration of poor intelligence scores and educational subnormality among the 'lower' (that is, less privileged) social classes of Britain and other highly industrialized societies. Several investigations have reported a mild relationship between socio-economic position and IQ and this has led to the further claim that genetic factors cause the division of society into social classes (for example, Eysenck and Kamin 1981, p. 87). It has also been reported that IQ relates less strongly to the socio-economic position from which an individual originates than to the position which he or she achieves. Hence innate intelligence could be a causal factor in social mobility too.

Now, despite this persuasive case, genetic theories of intelligence have always been surrounded by intense controversy and, as one of the more sympathetic of recent surveys of the literature accepts, certainly do not represent the views of the majority of psychologists today (Vernon 1979, p. 181). However, neither would they necessarily endorse the opposite extreme adopted by critics such as Kamin, that IQ is wholly determined by environment (Kamin 1974; Eysenck and Kamin 1981). To complicate matters alternative theories and tests of mental ability have been propounded which do not treat it as a unitary attribute (for example, Guilford 1967; Cattel 1971). This is to say nothing of the growth of an important literature dealing with intellectual development in children (for example, Halford 1974; Donaldson 1980).

To be strictly fair to present-day supporters of intelligence testing, we must also point out that ever since the publication of discussions by Hebb (1949) and Vernon (1955) it has been common to distinguish:

Intelligence A: the basic learning potential of the organism which, almost by definition, is not amenable to measurement.
Intelligence B: the level of ability that a person actually shows in behaviour, the product of the *interplay* of heredity and environment.
Intelligence C: the score or IQ obtained from a particular test.

IQ theory is strictly concerned with C and the

relative contributions to it of heredity and environment.

Obviously, anyone seriously interested in this field must expect to encounter some complex material which we can hardly do full justice to here. We shall thus concentrate upon the strictly sociological aspects of the debate.

Heredity and socio-economic inequality

Sociologists are mainly concerned not with Intelligence C but with Intelligence B, actual differences in achievement. There can be no doubt about the immense overall importance of environment in shaping what individuals accomplish. The best demonstration of this point is to take individuals who have the same measured IQ but who set out from different types of home background. This procedure avoids what is sometimes called the 'sociologists' fallacy' which is the logical opposite of Galton's mistake. Obviously, though people from high-achieving families are advantaged by their home environment, we do not want our findings confused by the possibility that they may also inherit 'high IQ' genes too. Therefore, it is fallacious to relate environmental factors to achievement without controlling for possible genetic factors as well. Some investigations have, in effect, done this. They *have* been able to show that at each level of measured IQ individuals from more privileged ('middle-class') backgrounds achieve on average far more than those from less privileged ('working-class') backgrounds. This relationship holds even at the highest levels of measured intelligence (Banks O. 1976, pp. 69–70).

What, then, should one make of the differences found between social 'classes' in average IQ itself? Several investigators have reported a distinct relationship between socio-economic position and IQ (see Vernon 1979, pp. 115ff.). Sociologists have nevertheless resisted the suggestion that better-off occupational groups differ in their genetic composition from the less fortunate (for example, Halsey 1958; Farber 1965; see also Banks O. 1976, Chapter 4). This

is not mere dislike of the idea. We already know that there are important environmental influences on achievement (Intelligence B), so simple economy of explanation favours the 'environmentalist' side of the argument when we are considering Intelligence C.

It is, in fact, now accepted that individual IQ scores are not as unalterable as was at first claimed (Vernon 1969). The point is of crucial significance when we are considering the possibility of innate differences between whole groups. From the outset, it has been acknowledged that practice in solving typical test items can raise test performance. Even convinced hereditarians are now willing to admit that some cultural environments stimulate the mind in ways that are analogous to practice. Longitudinal studies of age cohorts of children have found that the IQ gap between children from different backgrounds widened over the years (for example, Douglas 1964; Douglas, Ross and Simpson 1968); and there now exists a number of investigations which claim to show that exposure to the right environment can boost – sometimes dramatically – the scores of deprived children (see Vernon 1979; Flynn 1980, Chapter 5; Scarr 1981).

There is some more evidence in favour of the environmentalist explanation of class differences in IQ. It is a well-established fact that the average family size of manual workers is larger than that of better-off sections of the community. Some years ago this phenomenon led supporters of the genetic theory to become concerned about decline in mean intelligence levels as a whole. It was feared that the less 'intelligent' sections of the population were breeding faster. In fact, the results of surveys of long-term trends in intelligence have always indicated that mean scores are rising, the simplest explanation being that improvements in the living standards of industrialized nations during the twentieth century have removed some of the worst environmental causes of intellectual disadvantage (Butcher 1968, p. 165ff.).

Hereditarians have replies to these points, of

course, and the controversy continues (for example, Eysenck and Kamin 1981; Scarr 1981). But many sociologists have objected to IQ testing on more practical grounds. They claim that the tests serve to create a new 'scientific' basis for already existing inequalities of privilege and opportunity. They may even increase the level of *resentment* against inequality, particularly if testing programmes cannot be operated with sufficient efficiency to justify what is claimed for them.

The ideas and writings of the advocates of IQ testing have exercised a heavy influence over government policies towards such matters as education and immigration. In Britain educational policy provides a well-known example. During the first half of this century the notion of measurable IQ lent an aura of 'scientific' authority to programmes that were, according to some writers, merely expressing the traditional hostility of the privileged to the creation of mass secondary and higher education (Banks O. 1955; Simon 1974, pp. 240–50). After the 1944 Education Act IQ tests became part of the notorious 11+ selection procedure for secondary education. Research conducted by sociologists at the London School of Economics (Floud, Halsey and Martin 1956) concluded that the chances of being selected for grammar school varied from region to region according to local authority policy, resources and provision. Their survey results, drawn from two contrasting areas, suggested that IQ testing was to a large extent perpetuating the inequalities in educational opportunity that in previous generations had arisen out of differences in income. These conclusions have since been reinforced by a deluge of work which included a number of influential government reports (Banks O. 1976, pp. 67–97; Halsey, Heath and Ridge 1980). The rigidities of the selective school system, its bias against working-class children and the consequent wastage of talent were all blamed on the tests. Nevertheless, the defenders of intelligence testing remain convinced that use of the tests allowed a greater number of able working-class children to achieve educational success than has been possible since their use was discontinued.

In the United States, the debate has focused on a still more fundamental objection. Several investigations have questioned the presumed connection between the cognitive skills measured by IQ tests and rewarded in schools, on one hand, and the qualities which result in socially recognized achievement on the other (Deutsch 1964; Jastak 1969; Berg 1970; Jencks 1972, 1979; see also Vernon 1979, pp. 115–29). So-called general intelligence, it has been claimed, is not a key factor in economic success, nor can IQ explain why high achievement runs in families (Bowles and Gintis 1973). Hence, IQ testing has encountered widespread suspicion and even, in some states, legal control.

These, then, are some of the reasons why many sociologists and psychologists have in recent decades favoured environmental explanations of group differences in intellectual and socio-economic achievement. Yet the 1970s have seen (along with other Social-Darwinist-type explanations of social behaviour) a revival of genetic theories of intelligence. In order to describe this phenomenon we must now take up the question of ethnic and racial differences.

Heredity and the racial question

It was not until this century that a serious attack was mounted on the idea that variations in the cultural and social achievements of different races were attributable to innate factors. A major landmark was the anti-evolutionist anthropology of F. Boas and his pupils. This sought to reveal, society by society, how so-called 'primitive' social systems were, in their way, equally as intricate as those of industrialized nations. Boas took this as conclusive demonstration of a principle first propounded by Tylor (see p. 81): the 'psychic unity of mankind'. With the rise and fall of Nazism, a consensus developed within social science that the social and genetic meanings of 'race' were not equivalent. Too much intermingling of populations had occurred throughout human history for there to be more than superficial factors (for example, skin colour, facial traits) in so-called racial differences. The explanation of ethnic differences and of course racial prejudice lay, it was assumed, in society itself.

This post-war consensus has been disrupted by the publication of the highly controversial work of Jensen (1969, 1973, 1980). Jensen sets out from the rather sweeping claim that programmes of compensatory education, operating in the USA during the 1960s, had failed to make much impact on the relatively low IQ scores obtained by black as against white children. Thus, there must be a genetic basis to racial differences in intellectual ability. He quotes the findings of the numerous surveys, all of which have shown an IQ 'gap' between the average score of black and white Americans of some 15 to 20 points. Jensen's case has rested on two further arguments, both of them backed up by extensive scholarship:

1   that the overwhelming weight of evidence still supports the view that 70–80 per cent of variation in IQ within the white population is due to heredity;
2   environmentalist scholars have failed to identify any factors in the environment of the black population which would be able adequately to explain the deficit of IQ points between blacks and whites.

Not surprisingly, Jensen has been widely criticized. He has undoubtedly overstated the quality of the evidence and even a relatively sympathetic writer such as Vernon considers that no definitive conclusion from it is possible (1979, p. 325). Yet Flynn, who clearly favours an environmentalist position, acknowledges Jensen's erudition and scientific integrity, arguing that Jensen has been able so far to show that his critics' arguments are mostly fallacious or rhetorical (Flynn 1980; for earlier discussions see Lawler 1975; Loehlin, Lindsey and Spuhler 1975). Nevertheless, Jensen's case, though not yet decisively refuted, has been weakened in two important areas:

a   Heritability of IQ. By now the value of the research on twins on which Jensen's heritability estimates were based has been seriously challenged. The most influential, those carried out by Cyril Burt, have been found to be fraudulent (Hearnshaw 1979). The remainder raise too many questions of method to be acceptable at least without considerable reservations (for the controversy on this point see Kamin 1974, 1981; Vernon 1979, pp. 164–79; Eysenck and Kamin 1981). The latest estimates of heritability, admittedly based on adoption, not twin studies, have settled for lower values – between 40 and 70 per cent (Horn *et al.* 1979; Scarr 1981) and even these have been questioned. Flynn considers this reduction sufficient to render trivial the genetic element in the supposed IQ gap between races (Flynn 1980, p. 158). Geneticists have also questioned the theory of gene transmissions behind hereditarian theories of IQ (see p. 99).

b   Direct evidence on environment. 'Direct evidence' means establishing how black or white genes function when taken out of their usual environment. This condition is approximated in such situations as racial intermarriage, or the adoption of black children by white families. The number of such studies is limited but whereas Vernon considers them inconclusive (1979, p. 298), Flynn claims that to any reasonable person 'an environmental hypothesis about the gap between black and white is more probable than a genetic hypothesis' (Flynn 1980, p. 113). A recent study of a large sample of black children taken into white homes found no reason to support Jensen's position, despite the fact that its author is sympathetic to a genetic hypothesis in other contexts (Scarr and Weinberg 1978; Scarr 1981, pp. 109–315).

Environmental deprivation – a problem for social science?

Today, Jensen's main claim to be taken seriously rests upon his apparent success in arguing that the 'indirect' evidence put forward to establish the environmentalist case against genetic theories of IQ has failed in its objective. But this problem has long been acknowledged in social science itself. Banks, for example, in an influential discussion of the underachievement of working-class children notes that the precise mechanisms which link environmental to mental performance have never been established (Banks O. 1976, p. 67).

To recognize this problem, however, does not mean that the search for environmental influences has been, or will be, pointless. Jensen is in fact guilty of what is sometimes called 'argument by elimination'. What this means is that although we may show a given number of explanations to be false, it does not follow logically that one's own preferred explanation is correct. Furthermore, even hardline hereditarians concede that some variation in IQ *is* environmentally caused. In fact, only when research has identified exactly how environmental factors raise or lower performance will it be appropriate to gauge the size of that influence.

Possible environmental causes for poor intellectual performance have been examined in the context of both socio-economic and racial disadvantage. They may be classified into (i) material, (ii) motivational and (iii) cognitive.

Material Physical hardship presents a number of obstacles to mental development – poverty, hunger, overcrowding are obvious examples. It also usually means greater likelihood of exposure to diverse socio-environmental health hazards, ranging from lead pollution to the effects of smoking. It is highly probable that poor nutrition and similar factors affect development from the prenatal period onward. Though the link with IQ itself is difficult to establish and has yet to be demonstrated conclusively, some scholars are convinced that the apparent 'inheritance' of IQ is explicable by physical prenatal influences on the foetus, including malnutrition during pregnancy. On the other hand, all of the various effects of material deprivation may only be important up to a certain threshold, beyond which they may no longer determine variations in intellectual performance. We certainly cannot explain all such variation in material terms. Thus, the removal of the worst extremes of deprivation during the post-war boom, for example, did not greatly reduce the relative disparities in achievement between, say, middle-class and working-class homes. And it is possible to cite famous individuals who achieved impressive feats despite appalling material handicaps (for example, Eysenck and Kamin 1981, pp. 169–70).

Motivational Attitude studies indicate that many unskilled low-income and black families perceive the educational system in a different way, say, from the white middle class. Why? It is claimed that 'lower-class' values reflect a culture which is adapted to survival in an insecure world. Emphasis is put upon early contribution to family income, an attitude of enjoying whatever opportunities exist in the present and scepticism about the wisdom of a life planned in advance. Middle-class families on the other hand tend to perceive society as a structure of opportunity for any individual who possesses enough diligence and foresight. Gratification is 'deferred' – that is, children are encouraged to forgo immediate satisfaction in order to achieve a better future. These differences in culture and values, it is claimed, account for the low ambition of working-class children and the absence of parental interest in their children's school progress. Ethnic subcultures may have similar effects; research has suggested that black children suffer from problems of poor self-image and their parents are uncertain in their dealings with the education system. In Jewish households, on the other hand, there is an intense concern with intellectual achievement, similar in its effect to the value system of the middle class.

Broadly speaking, however, the picture given by these studies of values and achievement is too simple. The differences in culture, values and aspirations of different sectors of society have not always been found to be as clear cut as the argument of the previous paragraph would suggest. Nor is it wholly free of value judgements – what may appear as 'unambitious' conduct to middle-class school teachers and sociologists may turn out to be intelligible and realistic given the structure of constraints facing any particular low-income family. Furthermore, the school or college itself is an intervening factor which by its behaviour may damp down or confirm the expectations which children derive from home as to the 'real' possibilities available to them (for example, Stone 1981). The *precise* factors in values and culture which encourage mental growth and intellectual achievement, then, are still not properly understood. Sympathizers with the genetic theory of IQ can still object that the relevant research has not overcome 'the sociologists' fallacy'. They also point to the possibility of *covariation*. This means that individuals with a given genetic constitution will seek out or change their environment so that it is compatible with their 'nature'. Thus, the values of different classes *could* be an effect of IQ and not vice versa.

Cognitive   In studying cognitive influences on intellectual growth the aim is to establish the way in which interactions between the individuals in the household facilitate the ability of an individual to learn ideas, make conceptual distinctions and so on. Conversely, disorganized social interaction and low levels of attention to the child, it is believed, can confuse and inhibit the development of thought processes. Various studies indicate that interactions in early infancy between mother or mother-substitute are very important and, in fact, it is frequently reported that the status, race, education or attitude of the mother is a correlate of both intelligence and actual achievement. Of course, hereditarians can still invoke the problem of covariation. An intelligent-seeming baby, may, for example, arouse more favourable maternal response than a less precocious child. However,

research on the interactions between staff and children in orphanages, where clearly no genetic relationship exists, has also found a link between the quality of interaction and talk, and children's IQ (Tizard *et al.* 1972).

One of the most celebrated and interesting of sociological theories of achievement in recent years is that of Bernstein and his colleagues (Bernstein 1971; Lawton 1968). This explores the connection between language style or 'code', family organization and cognitive development. Bernstein's ideas have gone through several different modifications but his basic argument is fairly straightforward. The use of language in the process of communication between members of 'working-class' and less privileged families differs, he claims, from that to be found in the better-off sectors of society. The former employ a linguistic code which he calls 'public' or 'restricted' which is less favourable to the development of abstract thought and to a range of complex concepts and vocabulary than is the 'formal' or elaborated code of the middle class. The difference can be demonstrated on an intuitive level by an early illustration given by Bernstein himself: that of the noisy child who is admonished by a shout of 'shut up' in one family whereas in another he is told 'I'd rather you didn't do that, darling'. These linguistic differences become very important in the school situation where the elaborated code is the dominant style used by teachers and 'academic' children. Children who have encountered only the restricted code at home find themselves literally isolated from what is going on in the classroom.

Bernstein's critics object that the association between background speech patterns and cognition, which he and others claim to have found, is a product of the research procedures used (for example, Labov 1973). They also argue that his treatment of 'class' – a concept we have yet to consider systematically – is defective and has not avoided the imputation that the thought processes and culture of the 'lower orders' are 'naturally' inferior. But it is not Bernstein who is necessarily judging the speech of the deprived so much as official 'society'. Knowledge is closed off to anyone who has not been exposed to the special codes in which it is expressed. That our society does possess a 'public language' in this sense is incontestable (cf. Vernon 1979, p. 127).

Investigation of specific environmental influences will not be very satisfactory unless the concept of 'environment' itself is examined closely. By forcing social scientists onto the defensive, hereditarians have arguably been allowed to get away with a very impoverished conception of how the effect of 'background' on intellectual growth should be studied – as if it were a set of physical variables like temperature, susceptible to a single measurement at a specific point in time (cf. Swift 1972). Many of the factors we have been considering, language, say, or values, are not just individual traits but part of a cultural system in which individuals are enclosed.

We can illustrate the point with reference to an example which is relevant not simply to the race issue but also to some of the other aspects of differentiation and inequality we have been considering. As Flynn points out, in the USA in 1976,

40 per cent of all black children were living in houses in which the father was absent (12 per cent for whites), 25 per cent were being born out of wedlock to teenage mothers (4 per cent for whites) and one-third were receiving welfare benefits under the aid to broken families programme. (Flynn 1980, p. 208)

Such information provides some measure of the disorganization of home and community life which many black children face, aspects of which are demonstrably linked to poor achievement and intellectual performance. The problems of unstable social organization of childcare and sexual relations are, of course, at their worst in the context of deprived inner-city ghetto areas. Both sexes find it difficult to maintain the gender roles expected by the wider society: lack of stable employment leaves men tagged with labels of 'failure' and 'unreliable';

women, on the other hand, bear the brunt of sustaining some kind of household (cf. Liebow 1967). The problems of the ghetto family spill over into the work and discipline of the ghetto school and so on.

'Environment' then must be thought of as a complex and dynamic whole whose effects on the younger generation regularly ensure that the overall pattern tends to be self-maintaining. This is why some writers, having regard to situations such as we have just described, talk of 'cycles of disadvantage' whose effects seem almost indistinguishable from those of heredity in that they persist from one generation to the next (for example, Rutter and Madge 1976). It has even been suggested, somewhat controversially perhaps, that individuals can be more or less permanently damaged by the subcultural milieu in which they have grown up.

Some authors consider, however, that extreme environmentalism can be as dangerous as its opposite, giving rise to over-optimistic expectations of, say, childrearing methods, or educational programmes or political changes. In the present state of knowledge, we accept that it would be mistaken for sociologists to claim that heredity has *no* impact on intelligence and achievement. But this possibility in no way reduces the value of investigating the environmental obstacles to human development which are undoubtedly still numerous. On the contrary:

Too many people believe the myth that if a characteristic is genetic it cannot be changed. This is nonsense. Human behaviour is much more complicated than a particular physical trait such as blue eyes. . . . Genes do not fix behaviour; rather they establish a range of possible reactions to the range of possible experiences that the environment provides. (Scarr and Weinberg 1978, p. 29)

Furthermore, the relative importance of heredity or environment cannot be formulated in any absolute sense but is itself a function of society and the population under discussion. Suppose that all of the material and cultural impediments to mental development were to be eliminated – a possibility that may be close to being realized in the middle class of contemporary industrialized nations – we would then *expect* to ascribe the greater part of any remaining differences in intellectual performance to heredity. With a more deprived population, however, we can make no such assumption. There would, in fact, be good reason to suppose that environmental factors play a more important role in determining the scope for intellectual growth.

The lesson of the Jensen affair ought, perhaps, to be that just as the encounter with ethology and sociobiology is forcing social scientists to recognize the impossibility of the 'purely cultural', so it is time to re-examine the notion of the 'purely environmental'. A corollary, though, would be that hereditarians would have to abandon the possibility of the 'purely hereditary' as well. Before taking this point further we shall briefly examine one further example of Social Darwinism in recent social science.

Is there a criminal 'type'?

During the nineteenth century various efforts were made to uncover defects in the biological make-up of criminals and others who did not conform to accepted ideas of 'proper' behaviour. After a period of relative disfavour, the idea has again been seriously put forward. Items thought to be indices of criminality, for example, have ranged from the crude measures proposed by early investigators (shape of head, size of hands, limbs or musculature) to the more sophisticated biochemical 'measures' and psychosurgical techniques that have been favoured recently (Taylor I. *et al.* 1973; Platt and Tagaki 1980).

Such work remains highly inconclusive and contentious. Isolating the supposed genetic basis of intelligence, which is a relatively identifiable attribute, has proved to be difficult enough. This ought to make us cautious about treating more ambiguous traits such as 'criminality' wholly in hereditarian terms, and we shall not, therefore, go into the matter in detail. What we *shall* try to show later in the book, though, is the fluctuating and problematic nature of official and public ideas of what is 'criminal' and deviant behaviour. Furthermore, we shall see that unlawful and abnormal acts which come to light are not necessarily exhaustive or representative of their 'type' since law enforcement agencies tend to operate selectively. 'Becoming criminal' is not a once for all matching of individual nature with certain kinds of actions. It is a complex and long-term process, analogous to careers in the occupational sphere, requiring us to understand the way individual life histories are patterned by the constraints of social life. Finally, we shall see that here too we cannot ignore the role of home background and social deprivation.

Social Darwinism and forms of reductionism

We have seen that hard evidence of any correspondence between genetic factors and social behaviour is not only difficult to obtain but also inconclusive in content. Social Darwinism is, in fact, built upon a fallacious form of explanation known as 'reductionism'. This consists of trying to explain a complex set of phenomena in a way that fails to account for the full range of observed variation. It is particularly likely when one discipline tries to take over the concerns of another, the risk being that too simple a level of analysis will be used. As Taylor I., Walton and Young (1973) observe in their review of biological theories of crime:

1   Biological reductionism implies a 'steady state' theory of the role of natural selection and hereditary factors in behaviour that fails to do justice to the actual diversity of human history and culture.
2   The 'steady state' theory implies a 'snapshot' view of the individual. Behind every individual, however, lies a history in which each action represents a development of what has preceded it.

3   Reductionism fulfils an ideological need, allowing us to dismiss or disparage the problem or the people we are trying to understand. Those whose actions or customs are different from our own can be written off as 'irrational', 'unnatural' or 'abnormal' with all the authority of 'science' (Taylor I. *et al*. 1973). In this book we shall see that diversity and variability are far more normal than our everyday social world allows us to think.

In any case, many geneticists now consider that biological reductionist 'explanations' of social phenomena have rested upon an incorrect model of gene transference. Though the argument is too technical to summarize here, it seems that the whole idea of a fixed correspondence between given genes and observable behavioural traits may be false. The gene combinations which given individuals inherit are indefinitely variable and thus social attributes are always the product of an indeterminate relation between 'genotype' (that is, genetic potential) and environmental factors (cf. Hambley 1972; King 1980).

These considerations, however, should not trap us into *sociological* reductionism. Sociologists' contributions to the nature–nurture debate have, as we have seen, overwhelmingly stressed the role of the material and social environment in shaping individuality. Pushed too far this also leads to mistakes:

1   It can lead to an over-simple (or 'over-socialized') model of human behaviour which is no better than the Blank Paper theory offered by John Locke and his followers (Midgeley 1979).

2   It can lead to 'reification' of the idea of society, that is, treating society as a wholly self-contained set of forces whose effect takes primacy over or is independent of the individual biological basis of human life (Hirst and Woolley 1982).

The 'cultural' perspective of sociology and anthropology does *not* mean the same as crude environmentalism. The only way to avoid the alternative forms of reductionism is completely to reject the antithesis of nature and nurture, together with theories that give priority to one over the other. The Social Darwinists were, in fact, correct in thinking that culture and society are a product of natural selection. But they were wrong in assuming that as a result the social could be understood in terms of biology alone. The social *is* an autonomous level of reality in which biological factors constitute one, but only one, element. If the reader is still inclined to doubt this, he or she should consider once again the question of intelligence, talent and achievement but this time in a historical perspective. In some periods of history such as the Renaissance there are huge flowerings of human talent in which the natural abilities of individuals are nurtured. Then there are others in which people possessed of an identical nature are condemned to live, as are the 'wretched of the earth' in our own time, through a dark age.

What then brings about the rise and fall of the various cultures and eras? This is a question which other forms of social evolutionary theory have sought to answer.

7 Evolutionary themes in modern social science: cultural variation and technical development

In the recent past, evolutionism has undergone a brief revival within the social sciences themselves. But this 'neo-evolutionism' reverted to the older Spencerian idea that variations in culture can be explained by processes of *super-organic* adaptation – that society as a whole evolves. Largely confined to the USA, the revival first became prominent in anthropology (for example, White 1959; Steward 1955; Sahlins and Service 1960) but in the late 1950s and 1960s it spread to sociology and even to economics (Rostow 1960). Whereas the anthropologists concentrated on cultural evolution, sociologists were primarily interested in economic and social *modernization*. All approaches, however, placed a heavy emphasis upon technology as a determinant of social institutions and culture.

The reason why such a development took place when and where it did invites comparison with the circumstances which gave rise to the first evolutionary doctrines. *Neo*-evolutionism was particularly influential among investigators who, often with financial help from international and governmental organizations, were applying themselves to the problems of the Third World. Their concern with 'under-development' posed the issue of cultural and moral diversity in a new way. It is not wholly unfair to say that the old conundrum of why savages did not behave like Frenchmen was transformed by the neo-evolutionists into one of how people in 'underdeveloped' societies might be induced to behave like Americans.

A precondition for neo-evolutionism was the retrieval of 'social evolution' itself as a scientific concept, by freeing it of moral judgements and invidious comparisons between cultures. A popular solution to this problem was one suggested by Sahlins and Service (1960): the separation of 'specific' from 'general' evolution. As we saw in Chapter 5, the fact that an animal or plant becomes adapted to a given habitat implies nothing about the development (or 'fitness') of species in general. These authors argued that many forms of social change could be treated in the same way: as adaptations to specific and perhaps unique environmental problems. Such a method avoids value-loaded comparisons *between* societies. The only legitimate way to make inter-societal comparisons, in fact, is in terms of the strictly technical features of the adaptation and of the patterns of social organization which correspond to them. Sahlins and Service thus proposed to measure levels of *general* evolution within each culture by the amount of energy transformed by it. They add 'cultures which transform more energy have more parts and subsystems' (Sahlins and Service 1960).

This sentence implies no less than three propositions which are typical of neo-evolutionary comparative research on social development:

1 significant change in societies is the result of technical and economic adaptation;
2 there are only a limited number of ways that this response can be made without threatening the survival of the social fabric itself;
3 successful responses always take the form of an increase in institutional specialization and social complexity.

The writers who put these ideas forward during the 1950s and 1960s were providing, in effect, new variations upon an old theme in social thought known as the Industrial Society theory (cf. Giddens 1972c, 1973 pp. 139–142; 1976). Though it recurs in different guises throughout this book, this idea was one to which the evolutionary school, from Spencer onward, has been repeatedly attracted. Reduced to its most basic, it asserts that industrial technology and the scientific outlook that goes with it will impose a certain uniformity upon social life wherever they appear. The implications of this position are not confined to industrial society itself; it also follows that there is a set of necessary conditions for 'development' which must be realized by any society wishing to industrialize.

We shall now present three distinct variants of the Industrial Society theory, each of them the product of the neo-evolutionary 'revival': (i) the theory of structural differentiation, (ii) modernization theory, and (iii) the 'convergence' or 'logic of industrialism' thesis.

The theory of structural differentiation

The notion which underlies the concept of 'structural differentiation' was first put forward by Herbert Spencer and was encountered in Chapter 5 – namely that evolution involves the change from simple, homogeneous structures to complex, heterogeneous structures defined by increasing specialization. During the revival of evolutionist thought which occurred in sociology during the 1950s this was given more extensive consideration by the American sociologist, Neil Smelser.

Essentially Smelser's theory of structural differentiation closely follows the logic of Spencerian evolutionism, although the language he adopts is that of 1950s American functionalism (see Chapter 15). Simple, traditional societies carry out all their necessary functions (or adaptations) within a single structure – the family, kinship, network or tribe. As societies evolve, however, these functions are performed by specialist structures. For example, work takes place in factories, offices, etc.; education (socialization) is handed over to schools; medical care takes place in hospitals; and so on. Such specialization leads to complexity; in other words the *structure* of societies becomes highly *differentiated* as an *adaptation* to the performance of specialist functions. Rather than all the functions of society being fulfilled by one simple structure (for example, the family), it is performed by many, each one of which is highly specialized. As society becomes structurally differentiated in this way, however, problems of *integration* are created. If the specialist institutions do not fit together, 'structural strain' may ensue which provokes various social pathologies – including, ultimately, revolution. Thus, for Smelser, conflict in society is a product of structural differentiation which has not been accompanied by adequate integration (Smelser 1959, 1963).

Smelser has attempted to apply this general theory to the study of changes in the family during the Industrial Revolution. Directing his attention to the Lancashire cotton industry between 1770 and 1784, he shows that the disturbances wrought by early industrialization upon the closely integrated economic and domestic life of cottage industry resulted in greater specialization of tasks and, simultaneously, a need for greater entrepreneurial co-ordination of the production process. The bulk of the work was removed from the domestic scene into factories and the activity of these was in turn subjected to further fragmentation as successive technical inventions disturbed the organizational balance. Smelser then turns his attention to family structures, showing how:

1   They responded to the pressures of the new system of production and the more impersonal (and urban) way of life in work and community relationships which ensued from it.
2   Specialization developed among the activities of adults, child labour was separated from

adult labour and the workplace was divorced from the home.

3   Specialization also took place within the institutions supportive of family income and consumption patterns, giving rise to such innovations as savings banks, co-operative societies and occupational (trade) unions.

4   These in turn brought forth changes in law so as to ensure the proper regulation and integration of the new institutions.

Seven stages of adaptation, it is claimed, can be discerned in the Lancashire material, which may be generalized onto other cases of social change. In practice critics have reduced these to three:

a   an initial dislocation as the shortcomings of existing arrangements become apparent;

b   a phase in which protest and unrest threaten to induce social disintegration;

c   a final period of *reintegration* in which forces of coercive and regulatory control devise specialized adaptations to contain initial dissatisfaction.

Smelser's study was only the first of a number of attempts to demonstrate that social adaptation and development involve differentiation and reintegration of subdivided parts (for example, Levy 1964; Eisenstadt 1964, 1967; Parsons 1966). Defenders of the approach have insisted that structural differentiation really is a more scientific and objective notion than anything available from traditional evolutionary writings, if only because it is capable of generating research on the way in which societies deal with change in their environment (Eisenstadt 1964). This has not prevented the structural differentiation research from receiving quite rough handling. Apart from the charge that it merely dresses up the ideas of Spencer and others, it has been accused of vagueness and imprecision. The model of adaptation it employs is said to be too general and virtually impossible to prove or disprove (Smith A. 1973; Hoogveldt 1978). After a brief period of

influence it has fallen into relative neglect, for reasons which we will examine in more detail below.

Modernization theory

The term 'modernization' was employed in order to draw attention to the fact that the processes of adaptation could not be *reduced* (see pp. 98–9) to the merely technical and economic. A fully 'developed' economy also depended upon a 'modern' set of political, legal and educational institutions and thus a *value system* conducive to economic advancement. 'Traditional' aspects of the indigenous culture which acted as barriers to the modernization process (for example, autocratic forms of government, inappropriate religious adherence, customs or traditions, poor education, etc.) needed to be discarded before economic development could proceed. To use the key phrases from two influential books on this theme, the 'passing of traditional society' was a prerequisite of 'economic take-off' (Lerner 1958; Rostow 1960). In part this is a modern gloss on nineteenth-century cultural evolutionism ('backward' societies are now termed 'traditional'), while it also rests on an extremely tendentious reading of the writings of the nineteenth-century German theorist, Max Weber, who was also concerned to establish the contribution of cultural factors to the rise of the West in the late Middle Ages (see Chapter 11).

One of the characteristics of modernization theory was the attempt to measure 'modernization' and thereby place the nations of the world on a scale of 'modernity' from the most traditional societies at one extreme to the most modern at the other. In its most naïve form modernization theory tended, so to speak, to 'line up' all societies on a unilinear scale with, say, Australian aborigines at one extreme and the United States at the other, sometimes with the implicit or explicit assumption that, given time and the removal of traditional cultural barriers, aboriginal society would one day be like that of Southern California (see Hoselitz and Moore 1963). Taken even on its own terms, modernization theory ran into some immediate difficulties. The first were methodological: precisely what *were* the best indicators of modernization? In order to utilize the statistical materials collected by international agencies (the primary source of data) these had to be kept fairly simple – for example, per capita income, investment, energy consumption, etc. In practice, however, such indices are not as objective or uncomplicated as they appear. The reliability of the data employed leaves, in itself, a great deal to be desired but this might be tolerable if the conceptual problems attending their use could be solved. Unfortunately, measuring levels of investment and so on tells us nothing about how the resources in question are being used – whether, for example, they are being employed for the extraction of raw materials which will be exported to more developed nations; or for capital-intensive prestige projects that will do little to provide employment for the local population; or for schemes that will really raise living standards among the poor and unskilled. Thus societies classed at the same level might possess very different potential for social 'modernization'.

Studies which have attempted to employ social rather than purely technical or economic indices encountered even trickier problems. Among the range of factors which have been brought into work of this kind are: the degree of urbanization; literacy rates; level of economic and political freedom; type and complexity of occupational structure; amount of social mobility; extent of large-scale bureaucracy and organization; patterns of family relationships; etc. It takes very little examination of such a list to reveal that it is conformity with the Western way of life which is being regarded as the yardstick of development. But simply because industrialization in the West has been accompanied by many of the features listed above, it does not follow that today's Third World societies can repeat the same history or would even

be well advised to do so. One should not assume unreflectingly, as did some of the policy programmes influenced by neo-evolutionary writings, that forcing Western institutions and social patterns on non-industrialized societies will inevitably promote 'development' (Frank 1972; Griffin 1974; Hoogveldt 1976).

This means we should view with some suspicion the main tenet of modernization theory that all 'modern' societies must offer an appropriate core system of values and moral rules (for example, Hoselitz and Moore 1963). This line of argument can be construed as another borrowing from nineteenth-century thought. The source this time is Tönnies (see Chapter 3). But whereas for Tönnies the moral impersonality and individualism of *Gesellschaft* are to be deplored, in the guise of modernization theory they have acquired adaptive functions! Apart from this rather radical change, the 'before–after' contrast is the same. Traditional values, it is argued, are quite opposed to technological innovation and economic growth; by contrast the moral systems of modernizing societies reward material inventiveness and economic enterprise. Thus, the problems of the Third World countries are due to their attachment to time-hallowed communal obligations and customs, to other-worldly beliefs and to emotional attachment to kinship and religious groupings. These provide the so-called 'moral basis of a backward society' (Banfield 1956) which must be displaced by a culture emphasizing the 'need for achievement' (McClelland 1961). The possibility that the problems of the Third World might have something to do with the behaviour of the 'advanced' nations themselves is never seriously considered.

It was for precisely this reason that all forms of neo-evolutionary modernization theory were soon to come under heavy, indeed bitter criticism. For example, in a celebrated paper André Gunder Frank (1972) challenged virtually all of the assumptions of modernization theory – both theoretical *and* political. In many ways Frank's vitriolic attack against modernization theory was analogous to the earlier arguments of the diffusionists against more simplistic versions of evolutionism. It recalls the observation of Lowie (see p. 81) that 'even the simplest recent group has a prolonged past'. The 'prolonged past' which Frank has in mind, however, was one in which today's Third World nations were subject to colonial domination and exploitation by the expanding societies of Europe and, at a later juncture, by the United States. Thus the underdevelopment of the Third World was the direct corollary of the development of the industrialized nations.

According to Frank, underdevelopment (as conventionally defined) is produced by the *dependency* (a key term) of former and existing colonies on their colonial exploiters. Dos Santos, another critic, provides the most succinct definition of this process:

By dependence we mean a situation in which the economy of certain countries is conditioned by the development and expansion of another economy to which the former is subjected. The relation of interdependence between two or more economies, and between these and world trade, assumes the form of dependence when some countries (the dominant ones) can expand and can be self-starting, while other countries (the dependent ones) can do this only as a reflection of that expansion, which can have either a positive or a negative effect on their immediate development. (Dos Santos 1970, p. 231)

In his paper, Frank also argues that the dependence of satellite colonial or neo-colonial economies on the capitalist industrial centres of Western Europe and North America promotes a dual economic system and an associated class structure which accounts for the 'development of underdevelopment' in the Third World (see the important collection of Cockcroft *et al.* 1972; excellent discussions of this literature also include Long 1977; Taylor J. 1979). The urban centres in the Third World, of course, do contain a form of capitalist development (sometimes called clientilist) but it is itself utterly dependent upon the dominant metropolitan economies; meanwhile, these urban centres in turn exploit their rural hinterlands. Thus in Third World countries local elites in urban centres establish dominance over the surrounding rural areas, but are in turn dependent upon the industrial nations for their well-being and political power. This structure, argues Frank, enables us to understand some of the characteristics of Third World societies, such as their typical patterns of industrial organization (little manufacturing industry but an overblown service sector) and the fast rates of urbanization. As a final broadside against modernization theorists Frank accuses them of having aided and abetted the neo-colonial exploitation of Third World countries by providing comforting, ethnocentric rationalizations of underdevelopment.

Within the sociology of development dependency theory is now considered somewhat *passé*, having itself been subjected to a number of thoroughgoing critiques in recent years (see Long 1977, for a more comprehensive discussion). Nevertheless, Frank's demolition of modernization theory has transformed the manner in which problems of the Third World are discussed in sociology, stimulating comparative empirical research into the nature and causes of its distinctive economic and social patterns (for example, Taylor J. 1979). Thus, it is difficult to see how the neo-evolutionary assumptions which underlay the sociology of development can be taken seriously again. The rise and fall of modernization theory not only enables us to see the strengths and weaknesses of neo-evolutionism in sociology, but it also, more soberly, reminds us of how the social scientist rapidly becomes enmeshed in the harsh realities of past and present global politics (Horowitz 1967). Today, the predominant debate among sociologists of modernization is not about *whether* the advanced economies have been, in some degree at least, instrumental in bringing about the problems of the Third World but exactly *how* and *why* they have done so (see, for example, Amin 1974; Wallerstein 1974, 1980). Frank himself has pursued these questions much further in his most recent work (Frank 1981a, b).

This attempts to move beyond his earlier theory of dependency while retaining some of its crucial insights into the general character of development and underdevelopment.

The convergence of industrial societies

Modernization theory flourished in sociology at a time when the political role of its practitioners was frequently concealed behind a façade of bland optimism. This was nowhere more evident than in the thesis of the 'logic of industrialization' or 'convergence' hypothesis as it was also called. It was associated, in particular, with the names of Clark Kerr, J. K. Galbraith, G. Lenski and to a lesser degree R. Aron. It asserts that the idiosyncrasies of different systems of industrialism are gradually diminishing under a set of common internally generated influences. Though this idea has a long history (Weinberg 1969) it exercised a special appeal in the climate of the Cold War, where it represented a liberal interpretation of the political and economic differences between the United States and the Soviet Union.

Why this should have been so will appear from a perusal of the study *Industrialism and Industrial Man* by Clark Kerr *et al.* (1960). Though these authors were clearly influenced by neo-evolutionary ideas, the question of development as such is secondary. Their main purpose is to show that pursuit of the values of technical efficiency and economic growth is bound to modify the distribution of power and privilege in a society, *whatever its formal political complexion*. In effect, Kerr *et al.* were covering a latent difficulty in the neo-evolutionary position: if industrialism requires the kind of adaptations being urged upon Third World nations, how is it that some societies, notably the state socialist societies of the USSR and Eastern Europe, have achieved a high level of industrialism at all? These were acknowledged to be lacking in the open liberal arrangements implied by the model. In Kerr *et al.*'s view, however, revolutionary state socialism should

simply be seen as one among a number of possible legitimations for embarking upon industrialism (a view also to be found in Aron's 1969 polemical 'lectures' on industrial society). Whatever the political impetus which sends societies down various paths to industrialism, however, they may all expect to emerge eventually within a *common* world culture which Kerr and his co-authors label 'pluralistic'. Thus, even the closed regimes of state socialism will become modified by the imperatives of the technological infrastructure which their ruling elite is committed to maintain and develop.

Anyone looking to the main proponents of convergence theory in recent times for extensive and detailed analysis of socialist society will be disappointed, though. Admittedly certain aspects were followed up in the work of Inkeles and Bauer (1959), Brzezinski and Huntingdon (1964), G. Fischer (1968) and others. The main task of substantiating the model of pluralistic industrialism, however, rests on a particular view of the recent social history of Europe and North America. The belief that other areas of the world are likely to repeat Western experience derives from two principal assumptions about it:

a that it bears adequate testimony to the irresistible imperatives which technological development imposes – that is, *technological determinism*;
b that the technological outlook underlying Western institutions is now undergoing a process of *diffusion* throughout the world, especially with the export of military hardware.

The second assumption introduces an important qualification to the straightforward evolutionary position. But, in practice, it is the technological determinist interpretation of the course of Western industrialism which has attracted the most attention and stimulated the most amount of research – largely in rebuttal.

At the heart of the interpretation lies the assertion that, *pace* Marx and Soviet Communism, the inequalities of economic power that marked the early phases of the Industrial Revolution in the West have diminished as time has gone by. First, technological advances become increasingly costly to develop so that the investment process begins to require resources which are beyond the private fortune of a single individual or family. The consequence has been the rise of the public company, a democratization and atomization of share ownership and much greater direct involvement of the state in economic activity (cf. Chapter 10).

Second, the increasingly complex productive and administrative apparatus of companies and the state calls for the services of a body of professional and technical experts. Because of their indispensability the experts present an effective challenge to the authority and control of the owners of private capital or those whose position has rested on birth or fortune only.

Third, the maintenance of expertise in society can only be achieved by ensuring that recruitment to positions of control and authority is based not upon, say, wealth or family connections but upon merit. Society has thus become more mobile as education, 'the handmaid of industrialism', expands and possession of educational credentials forms the basis of selection.

Fourth, extremes of poverty and wealth have tended to disappear because (a) trade unions achieve higher wages for their members (b) mechanization has eliminated heavy manual labour and diverted more and more people into white-collar and service jobs (c) the modern state assumes the role of a welfare state committed to underpinning employment and living standards.

Not surprisingly, therefore, industrial, social and political forms of unrest have diminished with time. Symptomatic of this change is what Bell has termed the 'end of ideology', that is, a diminishing faith in one or other of the older systems of political belief (Bell D. 1960). Trade unions in particular lose their earlier commitment to socialist theory and practice, concentrating instead upon wage-related benefits and improved working conditions. Politics becomes a matter of legally contained conflict between a plurality of institutions and pressure groups none of which has overriding power.

Promulgated in an era of post-war prosperity, this version of convergence theory reflected widespread 'common-sense' beliefs about the course of industrial history in the West which still have not been wholly eroded by the experience of more recessionary times. It could also call on a body of information and research which, at least on a superficial reading, seemed to confirm its analysis of social trends. For example, official statistics or surveys conducted in several highly industrialized nations seemed to confirm that the distribution of income and wealth was indeed becoming more equitable, that the occupational structure was becoming more weighted towards white-collar and skilled employment and that social mobility rates were reasonably comparable (and relatively high) in the major industrial economies.

Alongside convergence theory emerged an evolutionary-style sociology of technology itself, consisting of attempts to classify systems of industrial production in a linear sequence. All of the best-known examples of such work employ approximately the same framework, dividing technical systems into what are basically the same stages (Mann 1973b, pp. 53–6). These are, in simple terms:

a   a 'craft' stage;
b   an assembly line or mass production stage;
c   an automation stage.

Moreover, most of the American and British work in this genre reached conclusions which were highly congenial to supporters of convergence theory. It suggested that work deprivations and conflict brought about by the Industrial Revolution were greatest in the earlier and middle phases of technical development, peaking in the monotony and short job-cycles of the assembly line. The automated forms of modern technology on the other hand were likely to *reduce* workers' sense of 'alienation' from the industrial system by enlarging the scope of jobs and eliminating the hard-and-fast distinction between brain work and manual work (Woodward 1970; Blauner 1964).

These optimistic accounts of the 'logic' of pluralistic industrialization and its technology soon became the object of stringent criticism. One of the earliest and most influential critics was Goldthorpe (Goldthorpe 1967). Goldthorpe develops two principal challenges. The first questions the thesis of a major shift in the relative distribution of power and wealth with advanced industrialism. Using the documentary materials which were available to him at the time he tries to show that the United States and European societies had not become more egalitarian nor more open since the inter-war period, despite a rise in average living standards. More recent material has tended to support Goldthorpe's arguments, as we shall see in Chapter 10. The second challenge concerns state socialist society. Goldthorpe argues that the commitment to industrialism and industrial technology need not constrain the actions of a political elite if it is determined to retain its powers and privileges. On the contrary, as the case of the Soviet Union clearly shows, industrialization and technical expertise can be manipulated so as to bolster up a regime, especially when used to develop military strength. Hence, there is no inherent reason why the political totalitarianism of state socialist societies should succumb to the 'pluralistic industrialism' described by Kerr and his colleagues.

A vital part of Goldthorpe's case rests upon giving a measure of significance and independence to the intentions and autonomous behaviour of the members of a society. Goldthorpe and his students have been at pains to develop this line of attack in subsequent research projects, turning their attention to the prospects of a sociological theory of technology itself. Their work has emphasized the part played by personal goals and culturally generated values in modifying the consequences of new and old forms of industrial production (for example, Goldthorpe 1966; Ingham G. 1970; Gallie 1978).

Despite criticisms of this kind, convergence theory has provided an important stimulus to comparative work on industrial and industrializing societies, even if the encounter with fresh material soon revealed the naïvety of some of its predictions. Japanese society provides an interesting case in point. If the convergence theory was correct, the rapid growth of the Japanese economy should have swept away the unique paternalistic employment systems in Japanese firms and which were, at first, thought to be survivals of feudalism (Ablegglen 1956). But this has not happened. If anything, these practices have spread. In an important comparison of conditions in a British electronics factory with the Hitachi works in Tokyo, Dore suggests that *if* any convergence is taking place it is the Japanese who will provide the example and the West which will 'adapt' (Dore 1973; cf. Cole 1971).

However, the notion that the industrialization of economic production imposes some kind of logic upon society as a whole is a perennial of social thought, and many of the themes raised by the 'convergence thesis' have reappeared in more recent writings on so-called 'post-industrialism'. According to these, the 'advanced' nations are now experiencing a qualitative change (or new stage) in their development in which theoretical knowledge will become a key resource. In the best known of these scenarios, one which is generally optimistic, the 'logic' of the 'knowledge society' is that technical experts will replace industrialists as the dominant decision-makers, service industry will predominate over goods manufacture, white-collar workers will replace blue-collar workers and so on (Bell D. 1973; cf. Kumar 1976, 1978). Not all accounts of post-industrialism are so sanguine. In France, sociologists such as Touraine and Mallet had propounded an 'evolutionary' classification of industrial technology similar to the one outlined above; but they predicted that automation would increase not decrease social conflict, creating a 'new' (educated and sophisticated) working class (Touraine *et al.* 1965; Mallet 1975; for a searching empirical critique,

Gallie 1978). After the disturbances of May 1968 in France, Touraine took this argument further, claiming that the student uprisings were a symptom not only of the growing manipulative potential of an education-based post-industrial order but also of the increasing restlessness of the new class.

Without doubt, though, 'convergence theory' of the kind propounded by Kerr *et al.* has largely been discarded these days, along with the other neo-evolutionary versions of the theory of Industrial Society which we have been considering. Most of them in fact contain a suppressed and somewhat naïve assumption: namely, that the indispensability of one segment of society – the system of economic production, say, or some strategically placed group within it – confers on it the power or influence to shape the remainder. If this were true then the slaves of the ancient empires should have been their leading citizens – a point first made by Max Weber (1968), whose much subtler writings on rational scientific knowledge and industrial society we will consider in Chapter 11.

But in the end, the specific criticisms of neo-evolutionism have been far less important in its recent demise than the spread of a more general refusal to believe that 'industrial' (that is, Western) society contained within itself the solution to its most pressing problems. Newer and more radical voices rejected the notion of 'industrial society' altogether, preferring instead to distinguish between 'capitalist' and other types of economic system. And they sought to move the notions of class and class conflict back into the vocabulary not only of social theory but of practical politics as well.

Thus, we shall shortly turn to examine in some detail Marxism and its theory of Capitalist Development. Much of the critical debate which has surrounded the work of Marx and his followers, however, turns on the question of whether revolutionary socialism can appropriate the technical achievements of capitalism without incurring the same social costs. We shall, therefore, meet the Industrial Society theory again.

But we are running ahead. Let us conclude this chapter with some brief general observations on the long-term significance of sociological evolutionism.

Conclusions

Some of our colleagues might consider that our presentation has been at fault and that to portray social evolutionism as simply one 'school' of sociology among others is misleading. Fletcher, for example, has indicated that even in the nineteenth century there never was a clearly demarcated 'school' of evolutionists and that among many of the pioneers of the discipline there was often frequent interchange of ideas and even personal contact. This was, he argues, the basis from which the main evolutionary assumptions have become the common property of sociology as a whole (Fletcher R. 1971, 1974). Among this legacy, certainly, we might include not only the theory of the Industrial Society but also related notions of 'stage', 'function' and 'social structure', all of which have been assimilated into a variety of later perspectives.

Unfortunately, acquiring the legacy of evolutionary concepts has also introduced certain deficiencies in the exercise of the sociological imagination. In recent years it has come to be recognized, for example, that the notion of structure derived from the evolutionists is still tainted with biological and physical analogies and thus tends to relegate conflict and tension to a secondary role in the shaping of events. Furthermore, the evolutionists' way of thinking about structures encouraged the belief that the principal forms of social change are *endogenous*, that is to say generated from forces contained within the structure itself. This assumption, also found, incidentally, in Marxist and functionalist sociologies, has been subjected to a rigorous critique on both logical and factual grounds in recent years and has been found wanting (for example, Smith A. 1973). That is why in Chapter 3 we used the less contentious term 'social organization' to describe the regularity of social life.

It is surely not coincidental that social evolutionism has declined precisely at a point in time when our faith in 'progress' has dimmed. The self-confidence of the 1950s and early 1960s has been replaced by a growing pessimism and doubt during the recessionary 1970s and 1980s. We are less confident that our own society is more 'civilized' than those of 'backward' or 'primitive' societies: all these terms now make us wince and are used, if at all, with great squeamishness and surrounded by the moral disinfectant of inverted commas. Nevertheless, we should note that commonly used euphemisms like 'underdeveloped' still imply a form of evolutionism. Indeed there is an irony in the fact that while forms of social evolutionism are now disparaged, Social Darwinism, in these tougher economic times, has enjoyed a new lease of life. It thus seems appropriate that we turn to the theorist who was a great admirer of Darwin and whose influence has grown in sociology as that of neo-evolutionism has waned. We are referring, of course, to Karl Marx.

Part Four: Industrial Society as Capitalist Society – Marx and Marxism

8 Marx and the critique of political economy

Among all the major founding fathers of modern sociology there are, by general agreement, three who stand out – Marx, Weber and Durkheim. The following three parts will deal with each of these in turn. We will describe the main ideas of each author and at the same time give some indication of their continuing relevance to the analysis of contemporary social problems.

In this chapter we will introduce the first of the three: Karl Marx. Because of the voluminous nature of Marx's writings, and also because of the intrinsic importance of his work, we shall take two chapters to give even a modest outline of his theories. In a third we shall attempt to apply some of his insights to the analysis of inequality in modern Britain.

We hope we need hardly stress the importance of Marxist thought in the modern world. Karl Marx is probably the single most influential figure in the history of ideas since Jesus Christ. Today hundreds of millions of people live in societies which bear an allegiance, however nominal this may be, to the system of political ideas which bears his name. This indicates that Marx was, of course, much more than a sociologist. Indeed to call him a sociologist would be in many ways to trivialize his thought. Marx developed a body of ideas and theory which encompass the whole of the social sciences and the humanities. Marx's thought is therefore an 'ism' – a systematic doctrine of ideas and, not least, a moral guide to *action*. Marx paid no heed to the irrelevant artificialities of disciplinary boundaries. His work encompasses philosophy, economics, politics, sociology and history. Its intellectual power and its intuitive appeal lie partly in the fact that it offers such a *total* world-view. Its scope is therefore enormous and its complexity is immense. It was developed over four decades in response to changing social and political conditions in Europe and it is not, therefore, an easy or glib philosophy which can be reduced to a few easily grasped nostrums. Moreover, Marxism has developed a language which has to be understood before the full significance of Marx's ideas can be assimilated.

In this part, therefore, we can only introduce Marx's writings in a very sketchy way. We shall be offering not only an introduction to, but also a commentary on, Marx – a few edited highlights and after-the-event summaries, and no more. Those readers who are already politically committed Marxists will have to excuse the superficiality of this. And those who, by contrast, are totally unfamiliar with Marx must *not* take our interpretation – any more than anyone else's – as gospel. The interpretations of Marx's thought are legion and some of them are mischievously misleading. It is *always* better, wherever possible, to read Marx in the original and make one's own judgement, rather than rely on someone else's (including ours). This is important not only in a purely academic sense, but because different interpretations of Marx have very different political implications – as any superficial perusal of those societies which are organized politically according to the application of Marxist principles will make clear.

Historical materialism

We shall begin our discussion of Marx by out-lining the methodological basis of Marxist theory – historical materialism.

Marx refused to recognize the distinction between what we now label as 'philosophy' and 'sociology'. He believed, like most other nine-teenth-century social thinkers, that philosophy and sociology constituted a single field of enquiry. On the one hand philosophy provided a conceptual framework for the investigation of society, while on the other sociological enquiry helped to resolve some philosophical problems which would otherwise be intractable for as long as we relied upon what Marx calls 'speculative reason'. For Marx, the two are inseparable. The investigation of society could never be a uniquely empirical matter of gathering 'facts', for 'facts' only make sense in relation to the presuppositions made within a body of *theory*. In other words, as in any science, the 'science of society' rests upon the sort of concepts that are used, what they mean and how they stand in relation to one another *as much as* the evidence which we collect. Conversely, Marx believed that as long as questions like, 'What is human motive?', and, 'What is society?', were dealt with purely speculatively (that is, without *any* empirical substantiation whatsoever) then there would be no solution to them. Marx is insistent (along with other classical sociologists) that a true 'science of society' cannot be allowed to descend into mere metaphysics. Marx, of all the nineteenth-century sociological theorists, was not going to surrender sociology to mere arm-chair theorizing.

For this reason, among others, Marx refuted the philosophical tradition of *idealism*, which had been most influentially expounded by the German philosopher, Hegel, in the eighteenth century. Idealism was an attempt to explain the nature of society in terms of the development of human consciousness, of 'ideas'. For Hegel society was guided by, and had limits placed on its development by, the human 'spirit' (or

Geist), a kind of quintessence of, and abstraction from, human culture. This 'spirit' was – literally – meta-physical. But where, Marx asked, does this 'spirit' come from? And how could Hegel's claims be substantiated? Neither Hegel nor any other idealist philosopher could, Marx believed, satisfactorily answer these kinds of questions. Their statements were matters of pure meta-physical speculation which could not be investigated scientifically. So Marx, in his early work, in a famous phrase 'turned Hegel on his head'. Ideas, Marx argued, were a *product* of society rather than the other way round. And this simple inversion of Hegel is the starting-point for Marx's historical materialism. For Marx, the doctrine of historical materialism enabled society to be studied empirically and scientific-ally, rather than speculatively and by purely metaphysical deduction.

This 'Hegelian inversion' was not a new 'dis-covery' of Marx. The German philosopher, Feuerbach, had already made this criticism of Hegel. It was Marx's brilliant contribution to develop the implications of Feuerbach's critique in his work, *The German Ideology*, which Marx wrote between 1845 and 1847. As in so many other of his theoretical writings, however, Marx took the ideas of a very heterodox group of writers – Scottish political economists, English political philosophers, French 'physiocrats', German philosophers – reworked and devel-oped them with wonderful facility and produced something that was entirely and uniquely Marxist. In *The German Ideology* Marx com-bined Feuerbach's critique of Hegel with the work of the French utopian socialist, Claude de Saint-Simon, whom we have already encoun-tered in Chapter 2. Marx shared Saint-Simon's basic assumption that *the* most fundamental aspect of human existence is the absolute neces-sity to *produce* the means of subsistence (initially food and shelter). It is the most fundamental aspect of human existence because the produc-tion of the means of subsistence is prior to *all* other human activities. Unless a society is able to organize the production of its subsistence needs there would be no society at all. Hence, according to Marx, the way production is organized determines human existence *in the last analysis*. (The latter qualification is, as we shall see, very important.) Ideas, consciousness, culture, the 'spirit': all are in the last analysis dependent upon the prior capacity of societies to organize the production of the means of their subsistence. Hegel's idealism as a philosophy of human history is therefore inverted by Marx to become his *historical materialism*.

There is a further aspect of historical materialism which needs to be emphasized at this point. Marx not only believed that the way in which production is organized accounts for all the other facets of society. He also argued strongly that this productive activity is impossible without human beings entering into relationships with other human beings. The isolated individual producer, who, as we have seen, was much admired by the utilitarians like Adam Smith, was, Marx believed, a figment of their imagination. Humans were never anything other than *social* beings and in order to overcome the forces of nature they entered into relationships with one another. Work – that is, production – is therefore always a collective social activity. Individuals produce only by co-operating and mutually exchanging their products. Thus the social world is created by interacting productive individuals and the science of society is the study of this process. Therefore an analysis of what Marx calls the 'mode of production' is where an analysis of society must begin. Hence, Marx's philosophy of history is called 'materialism'.

The base/superstructure distinction

The considerations which inform Marx's historical materialism lead him to enunciate his famous distinction between the 'base' and the 'superstructure' of society. The base is the sum total of what we might loosely call the productive activities of society or the 'mode of production'. It is, in the broadest possible sense, the sphere of economic relationships. The superstructure consists of the cultural ideas, or 'ideological' aspects, of society (including politics and the law). The superstructure is, *in the last analysis*, determined by the base.

This base/superstructure distinction lies at the heart of Marx's sociology. It is something which is entirely distinctive about Marx's contribution to sociological theory and is therefore an approach which is uniquely Marxist. Marx himself refers to the base/superstructure distinction as the 'guiding thread for my studies'. Partly as a consequence it is a distinction which is surrounded by intense controversy, as much within Marxism as outside. This is what Marx himself had to say about it in two frequently cited passages:

In the social production of their life, men enter into definite relations that are indispensable and independent of their will, relations of production which correspond to a definite stage of development of their material productive forces. The sum total of these relations of production constitutes the economic structure of society, the real foundation on which rises a legal and political superstructure and to which correspond definite forms of social consciousness. The mode of production of material life conditions the social, political and intellectual life process in general. It is not the consciousness of men that determines their being, but, on the contrary, their social being that determines their consciousness. (Marx 1975, p. 452)

The specific economic form, in which unpaid surplus is pumped out of direct producers, determines the relationship of rulers and ruled, as it grows directly out of production itself and, in turn, reacts upon it as a determining element. Upon this, however, is founded the entire formation of the economic community which grows out of the productive relations themselves, thereby simultaneously its specific political form. It is always the direct relationship of the owners of the conditions of production to the direct producers – a relation always naturally corresponding to a definite stage in the development in the methods of labour and thereby its social productivity – which reveals the innermost secret, the hidden basis of the entire social structure, and with it the political form of

p.112

the relation of sovereignty and dependence, in short, the corresponding specific form of the state. (Marx 1972, p. 791)

For such an important element in Marx's theory, it is a pity that his own writings on the base/superstructure distinction are so tantaliz-ingly obscure – although, it should be added, he himself attached no particular significance to these passages; this has been confirmed by sub-sequent scholars. In the first passage, for example, *precisely* what does Marx mean by his statement that the mode of production 'con-ditions' social, political and intellectual life? Does he mean 'causes', 'determines', 'reflects', 'places limits on', 'specifies', or what? What, for that matter, does the phrase 'guiding thread for my studies' signify? Does it mean that Marx regards the base/superstructure distinction as absolutely crucial or merely a handy metaphor?

Questions like these have been a source of lively (to put it mildly) debate within Marxism since Marx's death. If Marx meant that the base *determines* or *causes* the superstructure this would amount to a theory of *economic deter-minism* – that all social, political and intellectual development is caused by economic changes and even that all human action is economically motivated. Since this is patently not true the charge of economic determinism has long been something of an embarrassment to Marxism. But note that Marx also states that forms of 'social consciousness' merely 'correspond' to the economic structure – that is, there is an affinity but not necessarily a direct relationship of cause and effect. As these ambiguities began to be debated after Marx's death, his collabor-ator, Friedrich Engels, attempted to clarify matters in a letter written in 1894:

Political, juridical, philosophical, religious, literary, artistic, etc. development is based on economic development. But all these react upon one another and also upon the economic basis. It is not that the economic situation is *cause, solely active*, while every-thing else is only passive effect. There is, rather, interaction on the basis of economic necessity, which *ultimately* always asserts itself. . . . So it is not as

people try here and there conveniently to imagine, that the economic situation produces an automatic effect. No. Men make their history themselves, only they do so in a given environment, which conditions them, and so on the basis of actual relations already existing, among which economic relations, however much they may be influenced by the other – the political and ideological relations – are still ultimately the decisive ones, forming the keynote which runs through everything and alone leads to understanding.

Engels's interpretation is one which has subse-quently received widespread acceptance. Engels is trying to draw a careful distinction between historical materialism and economic determin-ism. He is arguing that the base is only *ultimately* determinant – or, as we emphasized above, determinant *in the last analysis*. This does *not* mean that at *any particular point in time* the whole of social life is economically determined or that everyone is guided by economic motives in their actions. Indeed Marx himself regarded the latter as a trivialization of his views, scolding his 'Marxist' followers who had adopted this interpretation by telling them, 'Je ne suis pas un Marxiste' ('I am not a Marxist'). For Marx such 'economic reductionism' was *not* historical materialism and neither was Marxism a de-humanizing theory which reduced all individuals to economic automata and denied them any free will.

What Marx did mean, then, was that, viewed historically, the laws which governed the development of society were *ultimately* deter-mined by material productive forces. Human beings did *not* have complete freedom of action to create a society based solely on their own ideas. This freedom of action was always con-strained within certain limits by the level of development of the mode of production. It was this to which Marx was referring in his famous statement that:

Men make their own history, but not under circum-stances of their own choosing.

There are certain ascertainable laws – material laws – of social development that provide limits upon what individuals can achieve on the basis of ideas. *The base is restrictive, not prescriptive.*

It should already be apparent that historical materialism rides roughshod over some of the most cherished assumptions of liberal individualism. According to Marx individuals do not possess complete freedom of action – indeed, taking the long-term historical view this is quite severely circumscribed by forces beyond their individual control. Even Engels's attempt at a helpful clarification does not entirely remove the taint of economic reductionism, for at times it looks merely like a 'sooner-or-later' kind of argument: superstructural factors may have a transient importance, but sooner or later the base will determine the nature of social development. Numerous critics of Marx have found this a depressing and dehumanizing philosophy of history, and by no means all of them have been unsympathetic to the political ideals of Marxism. The problem is that to call into question the base/superstructure distinction and the determinacy of the base in the last analysis tends to result in a sanitized version of Marxism which is less distinctively Marxist. On the other hand, attempts to assert the centrality of the base/superstructure distinction, while preserving the distinctive contribution of a Marxist sociology, lay the theory open to the charge of economic determinism.

This argument can be illustrated by referring, very schematically and somewhat over-simplistically, to two 'schools' of Marxist thought which have received considerable attention in the twentieth century.

Humanist Marxism

The so-called 'humanist' Marxists tend to deny the importance of the base/superstructure distinction. They believe that Marx used it as a metaphor and little more. Humanist Marxists tend to emphasize the libertarian aspects of Marx's writings – specifically Marx's analysis of the dehumanizing consequences of the rise of a capitalist society. They are concerned with

Marxism as a *method* of analysing and transcending this dehumanization, thereby opening up the possibility of liberating the true productive potential of humanity through political 'praxis' (the unity of theory and action). In particular humanist Marxists pay attention to Marx's writings on *alienation*.

Alienation refers to the process, endemic to capitalism, whereby the products of human labour become expropriated from and appear as opposed – 'alien' – to those who produce them. Workers, indeed, not only become alienated from the products of their labour, but from the labour process itself, from each other and ultimately from themselves. The emphasis placed upon Marxist analysis as a means of enabling workers to overcome their alienation is what designates those who subscribe to this interpretation of Marx as 'humanist' Marxists. Their adoption of Marx's analysis is in order to develop further his critique of the dehumanizing aspects of capitalism. They regard too great an emphasis on the base/superstructure distinction as leading to an equally dehumanizing form of Marxism.

The most polemical of the humanist Marxists was the Hungarian philosopher and critic George Lukacs, especially in his 1934 work *History and Class Consciousness* (1971). Others have included Antonio Gramsci, the founder of the Italian Communist Party, and more recently the historian E. P. Thompson, whose essay *The Poverty of Theory* (1978) is a polemic against recent anti-humanist interpretations of Marx (see below).

Scientific Marxism

This is associated with the French philosopher Louis Althusser and has been extremely influential in the decade after 1968. Scientific Marxists emphasize the capacity of Marx's theory to be truly scientific. They regard humanism as an ideology and therefore 'unscientific'. They acknowledge the existence of Marx's early writings on alienation but attribute this to an immature flirtation with humanistic ideology. They argue that an important 'break' occurred in Marx's work around 1844: thereafter Marx became less concerned with alienation and more concerned with *exploitation* (see Althusser 1969). The exploitation of workers can be measured objectively and, moreover, is not based upon speculative notions concerning the essence of humanity. It consists of the value of the productive activity of workers – or their 'labour power' – which is not retained by them but is taken away and retained by another individual or group. Scientific Marxists argue that as Marx moved away from a concern with alienation to this new 'problematic' of how a proportion of the value of labour power ('surplus value') is removed and retained by non-labourers, so he developed a truly scientific form of historical materialism.

It follows from this that scientific Marxists pay particular attention to the economic 'base' where these exploitative mechanisms are located. It is the 'mode of production' which is given primacy over all elements of the superstructure. While superstructural elements like politics or ideology are granted a degree of 'relative autonomy', it is the 'mode of production' which determines the level of social development. It therefore becomes crucial to define the 'mode of production' in a manner which leaves it untainted by superstructural elements and, *ipso facto*, to draw a clear line between 'base' and 'superstructure'. Thus, for scientific Marxists the base/superstructure distinction is of paramount importance – it renders Marxism a scientifically valid method of analysis.

Scientific Marxists thus shift the emphasis in Marx's work 'from alienation to surplus value'. In doing so they leave themselves open to the charge of economic determinism and although they would hotly deny this, much recent Marxist debate has involved attempts by scientific Marxists to extricate themselves from this accusation. Simultaneously, in placing so much emphasis on the 'mode of production' or 'base'

they have been forced to seek a definition which does not risk superstructural contamination. As we shall now see, this has not been easy.

The mode of production

What actually constitutes the 'mode of production' which forms the base? As the preceding section has already indicated this also tends to be a vexed issue among Marxist scholars, partly because Marx himself was never entirely clear or consistent in what he meant by it. The term itself comes from Adam Smith and, like him, Marx occasionally uses the term very loosely to describe 'how people make things'. This loose meaning can, however, cause confusion. For example, people make things by using tools or machinery – 'the instruments of labour' – which may or may not be defined as their 'property'. Property relationships are clearly part of the mode of production, therefore, for they literally help to define 'how people make things'. Yet 'property' is also a legal matter – and therefore part of the ideological superstructure of society. Can a rigid division between base and superstructure therefore be maintained and with it a clear definition of the mode of production? As we have seen this is clearly important if one takes a view of Marx's work which states that what is uniquely scientific about it is the base/superstructure distinction.

Consequently recent Marxist scholars, especially Althusser, have attempted to offer a much more specific definition of the mode of production. For them the mode of production consists of the following:

1 The *forces* of production – this refers to broader historical factors in the development of human knowledge which can be applied to productive activity. For example, the growth of science and technology would constitute forces of production which have in turn determined the development of new means of production.

2 The forces of production also include the *means* of production – broadly speaking the

tools and machines which people use in order to produce, or the 'instruments of labour'.

3 Social *relations* of production – the way in which the labour process is socially organized.

Scattered through Marx's later work, and especially in *Capital*, there are passages where this schema can be clearly discerned. The general argument is that as the forces of production constantly develop, so the means of production are improved and the social relations of production are constantly changed. Human inventiveness grows and expands as people rise to the challenges inherent in the conquest of nature and the pressure of circumstances which have been handed down through history. New means of production, such as the change in the late eighteenth century from water power to steam power, promote new relations of production, such as the change from handicraft to the factory system, and it is the contradiction between the means of production and the social relations of production which eventually brings about the transformation of the entire *mode* of production.

Marx's theory is therefore a *dynamic* one. He is less concerned to offer a static description of any particular mode of production than to offer a theory of how it changes and is eventually superseded. Marx offers a theory of social development and change rather than a theory of what society is. This, as we have seen in previous chapters, was a common nineteenth-century concern. And in common with many of his contemporaries, Marx accepted the idea that societies develop through an evolutionary process – evolution in Marx's case meaning the progressive human domination over the forces of nature.

But the *logic* of evolutionary development was quite different to the theories we discussed in Chapter 5. The logic of evolution was of a kind which Marx took from Hegel – the *dialectic*. Marx may have 'turned Hegel on his head' by rejecting Hegelian idealism, but he retained Hegel's analytical method. The dialectic is therefore Marx's *method* of analysis. The Hegelian notion of the dialectic holds that all matter (or the *thesis*) always and inevitably creates its own opposite (or *antithesis*). From the contradiction between thesis and antithesis there emerges a transformation which becomes the new thesis, which creates its own antithesis, and so on. *Change therefore results from contradiction* – and, in the case of human social development, human attempts to overcome contradiction.

This dialectical scheme is applied by Marx to his analysis of the mode of production. The mode of production contains inherent contradictions which produce its transformation and ensure the continuity of social evolution. Here is Marx using this dialectical method in another famous passage from his *Preface to the Critique of Political Economy*:

At a certain stage of their development the material productive forces of society come in conflict with the existing relations of production. . . . From forms of development of the productive forces these relations turn into their fetters. Then begins an epoch of social revolution. With the change of the economic foundation the entire immense superstructure is more or less rapidly transformed. (Marx 1975, pp. 425–6)

So the focal point of Marx's thought is the dialectic between the material world and people in society. People progressively subordinate the material world to their purposes but in so doing transform those purposes and generate new needs which require a transformation of their relationships to the material world – and so on. Thus a level of material development which began as liberatory turns into a constraint – 'a fetter' – which must be overcome. In other words, one mode of production which, in the historical evolution of mankind, was once emancipatory must be itself transformed in order to ensure the continuation of the evolutionary process.

Thus, history is divided by Marx into separate epochs (albeit with periods of transition in between), according to the dominant mode of production in each. These are, in chronological order:

a   primitive communism (or tribal society);
b   ancient society (based upon slavery);
c   feudalism;
d   capitalism; and eventually
e   socialism.

(Later Marx also added an 'Asiatic mode of production' which emerged out of tribal societies in the Orient.)

Each epoch is marked by a distinctive mode of production and the transition from one to the next is marked by a social revolution and the transformation of productive relationships. Marx, however, devoted most of his attention to capitalism (as we shall see in the following chapter). His interest in pre-capitalist modes of production was somewhat perfunctory and even his writings on socialism were sketchy and somewhat utopian. Nevertheless Marx regarded capitalism as merely one stage in the evolutionary development of mankind. Just as it had emerged out of the contradictions inherent in feudalism, so capitalism was doomed by its own eventual contradictions. Such teleology is now rather frowned upon among Marxist scholars, for, as we shall see in the Chapter 16, (pp. 276ff.), the philosophical foundations of teleological explanations are, to say the least, shaky. Nevertheless, the view that capitalism contained 'the seeds of its own destruction' was quite central to Marx's analysis. The development of capitalism, like all hitherto existing modes of production, would lead eventually to the revolutionary transformation of the entire society and its material base. How was this to occur? Through the social activity which is absolutely central to Marx's analysis of society: the class struggle.

Marxism and class analysis

It has become commonplace to remark that while Marx never developed a systematic analysis of class, it is nevertheless central to Marx and to Marxism. As Tom Bottomore has pointed out, all of Marx's writings were concerned with class, either implicitly or explicitly (Bottomore 1965, p. 17). Frustratingly, however, the manuscript of *Capital* breaks off at precisely the point at which Marx was beginning to set out in detail his theory of social class. So we are left to infer such a theory from the remainder of Marx's writings. Thus although the concept of class has become an indispensable component of sociological analysis, the precise meaning which Marx gives to it is by no means unambiguous. What is clear is the place of class, and the struggle between classes, in Marx's overall theoretical scheme. For classes perform a decisive function in the evolution of human history: it is through the class struggle that society transforms itself. Every significant social change is therefore related in one way or another to the class struggle. It is in this sense that Marx and Engels assert, in the opening sentence of *The Manifesto of the Communist Party*, that:

The history of all hitherto existing society is the history of class struggles. (Marx and Engels 1969)

What, then, does Marx mean by the term 'class'? In order fully to appreciate his use of the concept, it is necessary first to understand that Marx employed it in two different ways – in a *theoretical*, *sociological* sense; and in a *descriptive*, *historical* sense.

Sociologically, class is defined as 'relation to the means of production' – although Marx himself never used these words (they are Lenin's). Classes, that is, are defined according to the positions which they occupy in the process of production. Under capitalism, for example, one class, the owners of the means of production, is the bourgeoisie; the other, which does *not* own the means of production, is the proletariat. These classes are fundamentally opposed to one another *because* of their different positions within the mode of production. The bourgeoisie, as we have seen, *exploits* the proletariat by retaining part of the 'surplus value' of the production which the proletariat creates (this is discussed in more detail on pp. 125–8). Thus their different relationship to the means of production creates inherently antagonistic class interests. Moreover, class conflict occurs not only over the division between wages and profits, but over the labour process itself and the authority relations associated with it. It is this class struggle, then, which provides the driving force of social and economic development. Hence a sociological analysis of (capitalist) society is *reducible to* a class analysis: society can be explained by the variety of ways in which the class struggle manifests itself.

A number of important points follow from this schema which need to be considered in more detail:

1 First, it is important to note that this is a genuinely *sociological* usage of the concept of class by Marx. 'Class', in this context, refers to a *relationship* based upon the position occupied in the productive process. It is, by definition, an exploitative and an antagonistic relationship. Indeed what makes the relationship a *class* relationship is that it is based upon contradictory interests which stem from differing relations to the means of production.

2 It follows from this that no single 'class' can stand on its own. A class is forged out of its relationship (exploitative, antagonistic) with *another* class, to whose interests it is opposed. There can be no bourgeoisie without a proletariat and vice versa. A society in which there is only one 'class' is a society in which the concept of class is meaningless.

3 The implications of this line of reasoning go even further, however. Class, in this sociological sense, is used as an explanatory concept. Class *explains* the relationship between bourgeoisie and proletariat – and with it the nature of capitalist society. *Thus 'class' is not a group of people.* We could not possibly round up 'the proletarian class' or 'the working class' in some gigantic sports stadium and believe that we had observed 'class'. Class, in this sociological sense, is used as a theoretical *concept* in order to *explain* a certain kind of relationship regarded as central to the historical evolution of society.

4 Because class is here used in this conceptual sense, statements like 'the proletariat is a revolutionary class' are *theoretical*, and not empirical, statements. This does *not* mean that each and every proletarian is a revolutionary. Rather it means that it is the destiny of the proletariat to become the revolutionary class in the overthrow of capitalism, a role which it will assume when the contradictions in the capitalist mode of production cannot be resolved without their fundamental transformation.

It should now be possible to see how Marx is able to reduce a sociological analysis of society to a class analysis. Somewhat over-schematically, Marx's reasoning runs as follows. Class is an antagonistic relationship defined by the relation to the means of production. The ability of one class to exploit the other is to a large degree defined by the capacity of the exploited class to prevent it: hence the class struggle determines the development of the mode of production. Yet the mode of production, as the economic 'base' of society, is what in turn determines (in the last analysis) the superstructure. Thus the totality of society, and the pattern of its historical development, can be understood through an analysis of the class struggle.

We can now turn to the second meaning of 'class' which Marx employed – the purely *descriptive* sense. Here he used the term 'class' simply as a classificatory device – that is, he classified people like so many butterflies according to some relevant criterion, usually an economic characteristic such as income or wealth. Thus in *Revolution and Counter-Revolution in Germany*, Marx distinguishes seven classes – feudal landlords, the bourgeoisie, petty bourgeoisie, rich and middle peasants, poor peasants, the proletariat and the lumpenproletariat – and in *The Class Struggles in France* he refers to six. Here we *are* dealing with actual groups of people. These are simply listed as major social groups, the chief actors on the historical stage. Classes in this sense are bound to be numerous and their number will vary according to the historical situation which is being described. As the above list indicates these classes are to some extent merely sub-groupings, or *fractions*, of the sociological classes referred to earlier in this section (bourgeoisie and proletariat); others may be transitional classes destined to become absorbed into one or other of the sociological classes; still others, such as the peasantry, seem to stand outside the major division between bourgeoisie and proletariat. One problem with Marx's writing on class – and one reason why the fact that *Capital* breaks off at this point is so tantalizing – is that it is not clear how class in this descriptive sense is reconcilable with class in the theoretical sense and we do not know how Marx would have tried to square the circle. It was fundamental to Marx's analysis of capitalism that in the final stages only two classes would remain – the bourgeoisie and the proletariat. Marx believed that all intermediate and transitional classes would disappear and that the class struggle would take this form.

Thus only in the period immediately prior to the revolutionary transformation of society would the two meanings of 'class' elide. Then the two contending classes would become polarized and the class struggle would become a naked conflict between two groups of people defined by their relation to the mode of production. Indeed the observation of a society in this polarized condition would lead one to conclude that a revolution was imminent. It goes without saying that most societies most of the time do not correspond to this form. The class struggle is not, therefore, always directly observable in this sense. For the most part, Marx invites us to look behind the multitude of social groupings and the confusing complexity of the social world in order to comprehend the underlying contradictions which will *eventually* produce a revolutionary transformation. Such a class analysis is therefore a gigantic gamble on the outcome of history. Marx's theory is vindicated not by a description of what society *is*, but by what society *will become*.

It is therefore in no way a test of Marx's theory to discover how many non-owners of the means of production, *here and now*, recognize that they have interests opposed to the bourgeoisie, are exploited by them and are locked into a class struggle which will result in the overthrow of capitalism. It is fair to say, however, that Marx would regard such data as interesting indicators of how the class struggle was proceeding. In fact at one stage Marx even devised his own (unintentionally hilarious) questionnaire as the basis of an enquiry into the state of proletarian politics – or *enquête ouvrière* (see Bottomore and Rubel 1962). This is not to say, then, that contemporary evidence is irrelevant to Marxism – for this would be tantamount to stating that Marxism is irrelevant to an understanding of contemporary society – but that its relevance is somewhat limited. Marxist theory legitimately abjures the narrowly immediate in favour of the broad historical sweep. The ambiguities in the concept of class derive in part from Marx's own attempts to describe existing social reality *and* explain the past and future course of social evolution.

Marx himself was not entirely unaware of this ambiguity. He proposed a twofold distinction:

1   A class-in-itself (*Klasse an sich*) – a class consisting of those people occupying the same relation to the means of production, irrespective of their acknowledgement or awareness of this. They are lacking in any common class identity, political mobilization or other ideological bonds.

2   A class-for-itself (*Klasse für sich*) – a fully fledged conscious class pursuing its own interests against those of the opposing class, aware of their common identity and organized politically.

The observable proliferation of classes, in the descriptive sense, was evidence of a low level of *class consciousness* and an indication of a class (in the sociological sense) existing merely 'in itself'. The key question, of course, was how a class 'in itself' could be transformed into a class 'for itself' and thereby engender the revolutionary transformation from one mode of production to another. Marx never satisfactorily answered this question. In part the contradictions inherent in the mode of production would ensure these changes. Yet Marx was not prepared to regard them as inevitable. They had to be gained through conscious organization and struggle. Marxism has never been merely a desiccated alternative to classical economics – it has also been a rallying cry for political *action*. Capitalism, however, has endured. Does this mean that Marx's gamble on the outcome of history has failed? We can evaluate this question more thoroughly on the basis of Marx's own theory of capitalist development.

9   Marxism and the theory of capitalist development

In this chapter we shall deal with a specific piece of analysis by Marx – his analysis of capitalism. In doing so we hope to clarify many of the issues raised in the previous chapter and to demonstrate how Marx wove them together in a highly intricate pattern in order to form a substantive analysis of capitalist society. Thus many of the concepts which were introduced in the previous chapter – historical materialism, the base/superstructure distinction, the mode of production, the dialectic, the class struggle – will be encountered again. We shall find it necessary to elaborate and extend our discussion of them as well as providing a much deeper understanding of Marx's theoretical scheme within the context of his discussion of capitalist development. Thus by the end of this chapter we should be in a much better position to evaluate Marx's contribution to the history of sociological thought. In particular we shall be able to examine the claims (to which readers of commentaries on Marx's work are frequently exposed) that 'Marxism' is something entirely separate from 'bourgeois sociology' with its own unique and definitive 'problematic'. In doing so we shall also return to the distinction introduced in the previous chapter between 'humanist' and 'scientific' Marxism and seek to demonstrate how Marxism is itself now divided over the same problems of explanation which plague 'bourgeois' (that is, non-Marxist) schools of social theory. In fairness, however, it should be stated that the interpretation offered in this chapter leans more to the 'humanist' rather than the 'scientific' interpretation of Marxism.

Capital is clearly Marx's *magnum opus*. It is a towering monument to his intellectual capacities – the work for which he is best remembered, and deservedly so. It combines sociology and economics by investigating economic life within a social context, all aspects of which are interrelated, and it is upon this foundation that Marx provides an alternative theory of capitalist production to that favoured by 'bourgeois political economy'. Marx, therefore, refused to recognize the distinction between social and economic relations; it is the abstraction of the latter from the former which he regarded as the obfuscating error of conventional economics. Nevertheless Marx, it should be emphasized, agreed with much of the orthodox political economy offered by the Scottish and English utilitarians such as Adam Smith, John Locke, David Ricardo and Thomas Malthus. Where Marx fundamentally diverged from them was in their belief that the economic 'laws' which they had discovered – such as the 'laws' of supply and demand – were indeed natural laws neither made nor alterable by human will. Marx would have no truck with this. Such economic laws, he argued, were dependent upon social relations rather than governed by immutable factors beyond human control. Marx's dominant interest was therefore in ascertaining the laws of social and historical evolution to which capitalist economics was *subordinate*.

The means whereby Marx would undertake such a task should now be apparent from the previous chapter. Since Marx located the driving force of social evolution in the class struggle, it was this struggle which would eventually lead to the overthrow of capitalism. Marx was therefore concerned with social classes rather than individuals as the basic actors on the historical stage and it is implicit in *Capital* that these classes are to be regarded in a conceptual, rather than in a descriptive sense (see pp. 121–2). His theory of capitalism is thus in terms of *capitalist class relations* rather than static class categories or relationships between individuals. Furthermore Marx is determined to discover the 'laws of motion' of capitalist development and the contradictions within the capitalist mode of production which will eventually bring about its transformation into socialism. The three volumes of *Capital* are devoted to this task. They deal with capitalism as a totality rather than adopting a piecemeal approach to the analysis of the problem.

The labour theory of value and the capitalist mode of production

Marx, then, is concerned with a holistic theory of capitalist development in which the role of capitalist class relations is crucial. We have already encountered at the end of the previous chapter some of the problems intrinsic to Marx's conceptualization of class. Nevertheless the broad outline of his theory of capitalist class relations is clear enough. Most obviously, as we have already seen, capitalist class relations (as within any mode of production where class relations exist) are *antagonistic* – meaning they are both conflictual and contradictory. As in all class societies (that is, from ancient society onwards), capitalist society can be understood as consisting of two broad categories:

1   *direct producers* – those who produce the goods and services which enable society to continue in existence;
2   *non-producers* – those who live off the production of others (although by no means all non-producers directly *exploit* producers).

Alongside this distinction between classes is an analytical distinction between two categories of labour:

3   *necessary labour* – labour which is expended by direct producers in order to secure for themselves the means of their subsistence. This, as we have seen in the previous chapter, is a necessary condition for all human existence.
4   *surplus labour* – labour which results in the production of a surplus beyond the requirements of subsistence of the direct producers themselves. It is an important part of Marx's theory of capitalist development that all or part of this surplus is appropriated by the non-producers, creating the fundamental antagonism (conflict, contradiction) in capitalist class relations.

These two sets of distinctions relate to *all* class societies. What distinguishes capitalism from pre-capitalist societies is the *type* of relationship between the direct producers (the proletariat) and the non-producers (the bourgeoisie) – that is, the social mechanisms by which surplus labour is appropriated.

The characteristic class relationship of capitalism involves that between propertyless workers who have effective control over neither the means of production nor the products of their labour and are thus forced to sell their *labour power* – their capacity to produce goods and services – in order to survive. As we saw in Chapter 2 and again encountered in the previous chapter, it is not labour *per se* which is sold – this would constitute slavery, which belongs to ancient societies. Rather under capitalism it is the *power* to produce which is sold (by impersonal, contractual means) while labourers themselves remain formally 'free' – that is, legally capable of transferring the sale of their labour power to the highest bidder. Under capitalism it is the non-producers who own the means of production and the products of the labour process. The capitalist bourgeoisie must, however, purchase labour power on a labour market in order to set those means of production in motion and reap the benefits of production. The bourgeoisie then appropriates the surplus labour from the direct producers (the proletariat) through the creation of *surplus value*. The essential social mechanism which forms the key to capitalist development is therefore the creation and extraction of surplus value. Much of Marx's analysis of capitalism revolves around the concept and his analysis of this issue is in turn known as the *labour theory of value*. Although this is not intended to be a chapter on Marxist economics and neither is this book intended to offer a rigorous analysis of political economy it is nevertheless essential that some of the basic concepts of Marx's labour theory of value be understood.

Capitalism, as Marx emphasizes on the first page of *Capital*, is a system of *commodity* production – that is, production is organized for the purposes of *exchange* rather than direct use or need. This is an entirely unique feature of capitalism, for pre-capitalist modes of production are concerned with exchange only in so far as it is necessary in order to satisfy basic human needs, such as securing the means of subsistence. Under capitalism, however, commodity production – production for the purposes of exchange – becomes an end in itself. Also under capitalism labour power is itself a commodity – that is, human productive capacity is bought and sold (exchanged) like any other commodity. In all cases commodities are bought by capitalists *in order to sell* (and thereby make a profit – see below), having by one means or another increased their *value* in the meantime. Again this is contrary to pre-capitalist modes of production where commodities are only sold in order to buy (the means of subsistence). Pre-capitalist modes of production therefore form a 'closed' circuit of production and exchange. Exchange only occurs in order to secure the means of subsistence; once this is achieved, exchange ceases. The objectives of the system of exchange lie entirely external to it – that is, they consist of the subsistence needs of individuals. Thus exchange is directed only at the satisfaction of these needs and this keeps the act of 'selling-in-order-to-buy' within definite bounds determined by finite consumption needs.

Capitalism, on the other hand, represents the antithesis of pre-capitalist modes of production. Here commodities are bought in order to sell. Exchange becomes an end in itself, for it is through this process that profits are realized. The circuit of production and exchange now becomes a completely 'open' one. The 'needs' which are to be satisfied are no longer external to this system, but part of the system itself: exchange *is* the purpose itself. The system of production (or, more correctly, the circulation of capital) therefore has no limits. The circuit of 'buying-in-order-to-sell' becomes, in Marx's phrase, 'interminable'. The process begins and ends with the same thing: money or, in Marx's term, *exchange-value*.

Questions of value are therefore central to Marx's analysis of the capitalist mode of production. We have already noted that capitalism aims at the expansion of value and that the system of commodity production which characterizes capitalism begins and ends with exchange-value. Marx's analysis of value is extremely complex (and still disputed even by economists sympathetic to Marx) and rests upon assumptions about human purposes or 'philosophical anthropology' which Marx does not examine too closely. However, it lies in direct contradiction to many of the tenets of neo-classical economics which today are often taken for granted. Marx does not see questions of value relating to 'supply and demand' in quite the orthodox way of neo-classical economics. Marx, as indicated earlier, wishes to demonstrate how these so-called 'laws' of supply and demand are grounded in capitalist social relations and it is this factor which leads him to enunciate his 'labour theory of value' which Marx developed from the work of John Locke. It was Locke who had argued that the source of all value was *labour* and Marx used this to attack the notion of Adam Smith that it was the 'hidden hand' of the market (that is, 'supply and demand') which determined value.

Over-simplifying somewhat, the question of value revolves around the questions of whether there is some property of a commodity which determines the rate at which it will exchange with other commodities. It is this rate which is called by Marx the exchange-value of a commodity. According to Marx the exchange-value of commodities is determined by the average number of hours of labour, of average levels of skill, used directly and indirectly in their production. Marx called this the 'socially necessary labour time' required to produce these commodities. Marx also drew an important distinction between exchange-value and use-value. *Use-value* is 'only realized in the process of consumption' – that is, its value is only determined by the needs which it will satisfy. Thus an object has a use-value whether or not it is a commodity. *Surplus-value* is the source of *profit*, though not equivalent to it. Surplus-value refers to the exchange-value of commodities which the capitalist appropriates from labourers during the process of production. The rate of extraction of surplus-value therefore determines the rate of *exploitation* of direct producers – under capitalism, the proletariat. Put another way, under capitalism the workers are involved in the creation of exchange-value through their labour, but part of this – the surplus-value – is retained by the capitalists. From this surplus the capitalist must find his investment in further constant capital (new machines, raw materials, etc.), retaining the remainder as profit. Workers thus do not receive the full exchange-value of the goods they produce.

Now how is it possible for capitalists to make a profit at all? It is because, under capitalism, labour power is itself a commodity. As we have seen, labourers are 'free', in the sense that they are neither slaves nor serfs as in the past and may sell their labour power to whomever they choose. Labour power is thus offered for exchange on the labour market where it becomes a commodity like any other – and where, similarly, its exchange-value becomes determined by the amount of labour time necessary for its production. (We might note in passing here that the conditions necessary for the 'reproduction of labour power' lead to a Marxist theory of the family under capitalism – including the domestication of women. We shall return to this issue in Chapter 10.) In this case what is exchanged is the value of labour power for the means of subsistence necessary to keep the labour alive and functioning. Wages are related to *this* and not to the value of the commodity eventually produced through the application of labour to the means of production. It is the condition of the labour market, and not the exchange-value of the commodities which labourers produce, which determines wages and thus the rate of exploitation.

Let us make this clearer with an example. Let us suppose that the value of labour power is £10 per day and that the worker requires four hours of labour per day to produce the amount of commodities equivalent to his or her wage. Every minute of work beyond this four hours would constitute surplus labour and the surplus-value of this is retained by the capitalist as profit (after paying for raw materials and the cost of machines, which themselves embody the historical value of previous labour required to produce them). Thus, if the worker continues to produce over an eight-hour day and the exchange-value of the commodities which are produced amounts to £20, then £10 will have been retained by the capitalist as surplus-value.

The reason why the capitalist can deprive the worker of this surplus-value is that the capitalist individually – and, equally importantly, capitalists as a class – holds a commanding position in the market for labour. The conditions of the labour market are, in turn, determined by the *class struggle* – hence the importance which Marx attaches to this and which we noted at the end of the previous chapter. In other words workers struggle – usually collectively since they possess little power as individuals – in order to alter the conditions of the labour market and in turn reduce the rate of their exploitation. Capitalists also attempt to pursue their interests and increase the rate of exploitation by changing these conditions to their advantage. This struggle occurs both at the point of production (for example, inside factories) and elsewhere through the broader political struggle to seize control of society. However, as we have seen, it is one of the contradictions of capitalism which Marx identifies that by developing social relations of production which are essentially collective (for example, by herding together large numbers of workers inside factories) it enables the class struggle of the proletariat to be promoted by allowing the mass organization and mobilization of workers to become more easily achieved.

For Marx, then, the purpose of productive activity under capitalism is profit – that is, the appropriation of surplus-value. It is not the satisfaction of human needs *per se* which is the objective of capitalist production but the creation of surplus-value through the production of commodities. In this process the circulation of money as capital becomes an end in itself for the expansion of value takes place only within this constantly repeated circuit of movement. Through this process surplus-value is converted into capital in order to repeat the process of production and the creation of more surplus-value *ad infinitum*. At each stage, therefore, capital is *accumulated* in order to allow the productive process to retain its onward development. Yet at the same time limits are placed upon the accumulation process by the class struggle over the disposal of surplus-value. As Marx believed that he had discovered the 'laws of motion' of capitalist development, so he explored further the consequences of this pattern of determination for the survival of the capitalist system. The central role of the class struggle ensured that capitalism could not be reduced to a set of narrowly economic calculations, but was dependent upon a set of antecedent social relations manifested in the class struggle. Marx's theory of capitalist development therefore entailed both a political economy *and* a theory of social (class) action.

Capitalist development: contradictory and non-contradictory effects

So far we have given only a skeletal indication of how Marx tackled his analysis of capitalist development. The labour theory of value, while being a central part of Marx's scheme, was developed by him only as a preliminary to his substantive theory of capitalist development. Marx used the labour theory of value to explore the likely effect of the 'laws of motion' which he had identified on the future of the capitalist system. This enabled Marx to perceive what he took to be the essential contradictions of capitalist society – the contradictions which would eventually bring about its collapse and make way for the transition to socialism. Following a scheme suggested by Lockwood (1981) the 'system-level effects' discerned by Marx may be summarized as follows.

The falling rate of profit

A crucial conclusion of Marx's analysis of capitalism is that it exhibits a tendency for the rate of profit to fall. For Marx this is a fundamental – if not *the* fundamental – contradiction inherent in capitalist development. It was one of the most important aspects of capitalism, which would eventually bring about its downfall. Why should the rate of profit decline? This is best explained in a number of stages.

Competition between capitalists

We have already discussed Marx's view that capitalism is concerned with the appropriation of surplus-value. Profit is the mainspring of capitalist development and the maximization of surplus-value becomes an end in itself. As Marx expressed it in his typically colourful way:

It is only in so far as the appropriation of ever more and more wealth in the abstract becomes the sole motive of his operations, that he functions as a capitalist, that is, as capital personified and endowed with a consciousness and a will. Use values must therefore never be looked upon as the real aim of the capitalist; neither must the profit on any single transaction. The restless never-ending process of profit-making alone is what he aims at. The boundless greed after riches, this passionate chase after exchange-value, is common to the capitalist and the miser; but while the miser is merely the capitalist gone mad, the capitalist is a rational miser. (Marx 1970, p. 590)

In the pursuit of surplus-value, however, capitalists are brought into *competition* with one another. Each individual capitalist is merely one of what Marx calls the 'wheels' in the overall 'social mechanism' which constitutes the capitalist system. As Marx points out,

competition makes the immanent laws of capitalist production to be felt by each individual capitalist as external, coercive laws. It compels him to keep constantly extending his capital, in order to preserve it, but to extend it he cannot, except by means of progressive accumulation. (Marx 1970, p. 592)

Capitalism is therefore a competitive system, whereby each capitalist strives to maintain a competitive advantage over all others and in doing so hopes to ensure the future security of his or her productive activity. The chief means whereby this competitive advantage is gained is by reducing the costs of production. This may be achieved in a number of ways, but the most common, which Marx noted, is by improving the means of production, mostly through technological innovation. This, indeed, was an aspect of capitalism which Marx much admired. The constant stimulus to technological improvement and the continuing capacity to innovate unfettered by custom and tradition were, Marx recognized, an important step in the human mastery of nature and thus a necessary development in social evolution.

Thus by technological development a capitalist would hope to produce commodities more cheaply than his or her competitors and thereby accrue an increased share of surplus-value. This in turn would provide sufficient accumulated capital to invest in the production of commodities once more and maintain the competitive position of the capitalist within the system as a whole. Thus:

The battle of competition is fought by cheapening of commodities. The cheapness of commodities depends, *ceteris paribus*, on the productiveness of labour and this again on the scale of production. Therefore, the larger capitals beat the smaller. (Marx 1970, p. 645)

The aim of the capitalist is therefore to appropriate an increased share of the available surplus-value and ensure that, in so doing, that it is others who fall by the wayside. However, this process is a constant one: capitalists are placed on a competitive treadmill. For the forces of competition ensure that once any one capitalist achieves a competitive advantage in this way, the remainder will soon follow suit, thus requiring the initial innovator, in order to maintain the initial competitive advantage, to innovate *again*.

Changes in the structure of capital

As the previous quotation indicates, however, each round of the competitive battle does not take place within a capitalist system which remains entirely the same. As the competition between capitalists proceeds, so the structure of capital changes. In the first instance we may note that technological innovation changes the ratio of fixed capital to variable capital – that is, the ratio of fixed investment to labour and new materials. That is to say, in Marx's terminology, the *organic composition of capital* increases. It is this increasing organic composition of capital which produces the tendency in the rate of profit to fall. The forces of competition compel capitalists constantly to extend their capital in order to maintain the long-term competitive position of their productive activity. The increasing organic composition of capital forces an ever-increasing rate of surplus-value in order to keep up the progressive accumulation of capital which is necessary to ensure long-term survival. In other words, the rate of exploitation of labour must be increased in order to provide the necessary capital accumulation required by the increasing organic composition of capital. In the short term, capitalists may be able to achieve this (although this will depend upon their success in the class struggle). In the long term, however, increases in the rate of exploitation of labour cannot completely counteract the rising organic composition of capital: machines cannot be speeded up indefinitely; the length of the working day is not infinitely extendable; and so on. Eventually, inexorably, the rate of profit will begin to fall.

Economic crisis

When the decline in the rate of profit becomes sufficiently serious then an economic crisis ensues. According to Marx, periodic economic crisis was endemic to capitalism. He felt able to assert this not only on theoretical grounds, but on the basis of empirical observation of the trade cycle during the nineteenth century. During the crisis the least profitable capitalists are forced out of business and competition is reduced. Remaining capitalists withhold new investment because there are fewer profitable outlets. Aggregate demand declines as a result of the structural unemployment brought about by the increasing organic composition of capital; yet simultaneously the new means of production are manufacturing goods at a greater rate than before. The coercive laws of competition which produce the rising organic composition of capital and the cheapening of commodities also produce a 'crisis of over-production'. The capitalist is caught between driving down the exchange-value of the commodities produced, and thereby jeopardizing the rate of extraction of surplus-value, or not selling the commodities at all. Capitalists will invariably choose the former course of action and the rate of profit falls still further. A vicious circle of capitalist crisis is engendered which eventually ensures that the least competitive capitalists are rendered bankrupt.

Overcoming the crisis

This crisis is overcome in one or more of the following three ways:

1   The increasing centralization of capital – that is, the merger of capitalist producers and/or the bankruptcy of marginal producers. The structure of capitalist production thus becomes transformed – from many small-scale capitalists to a few, large-scale capitalists. The centralization of capital enables each capitalist to appropriate a larger share of the surplus available and thereby the rate of extraction of surplus-value.

2   Bankruptcy results in the sale of constant capital (machines, etc.) at below existing exchange-value to the remaining producers. This lowers the organic composition of capital and allows the rate of profit to be increased.

3   Unemployment increases, swelling what Marx called the 'reserve army' of unemployed labour. This drives down the exchange-value of labour power and thus increases the rate of exploitation. As noted above, however, there are limitations on this. The success of the capitalist class in achieving this is in part dependent upon their ability to overcome the resistance of workers in the class struggle. More potently, wages cannot be driven below the level necessary to obtain the means of subsistence. There is therefore an absolute limit on the possibility of increasing the rate of exploitation.

Because the second and third of these factors tend to be temporary palliatives it is the first – the increasing centralization of capital – which is the most characteristic way in which the crisis of capitalism is resolved. This is an additional way in which the structure of capitalist production changes. Not only is there a tendency towards a rising organic composition of capital but also a *tendency towards monopoly* as capitalist production becomes more and more centralized.

Termination of capitalism

Marx thus attempted to explain the periodic crises of capitalism identifiable in the trade cycle in these ways. Marx also believed that each successive cycle would become more severe and each crisis more difficult to resolve. At each stage the organic composition of capital would be higher and therefore the rate of exploitation would have to be increased. The outcome of this would be the increasing 'immiseration' or pauperization of the proletariat, which would come to act upon the inherent contradictions in the system (see below). As each crisis became more severe, as the rate of profit continued to decline, as structural transformation was exhausted, so – eventually – would capitalism reach its terminal crisis. No further room for manoeuvre would exist. The falling rate of profit would have brought about an irresolvable systemic crisis. Capitalism could no longer be reformed, it could only be transcended.

Commodity fetishism

The second 'system-level effect' involves the growth of 'commodity fetishism'. This refers not to the capitalist mode of production – or base – but is a theory of *ideology* in advanced capitalist societies.

In the previous chapter we referred to the assertion by Marx that under capitalism each worker is an *alienated* worker. As we noted at that point, the alienation of workers constitutes the alienation not only from the products of their labour but from the labour process, from fellow human beings and eventually from themselves, their own 'species being'. Capitalism increases the alienation of workers by its unremitting tendency to increase the division of labour in the pursuit of surplus value. The increasing organic composition of capital is reflected in the fact that workers become increasingly tied to machines. In the labour process machines run people, rather than people run machines. The consequence of all this is that workers are denied the opportunity to express their creative capacity through their work. Indeed work, rather than being an outlet for human creativity, represents a dehumanizing, meaningless activity. Workers, therefore, come to regard their labour not as a creative and expressive part of their lives, but in an instrumental way – that is, merely a means to pursue an entirely ulterior goal. In particular work becomes merely a means of making money

(exchange-value) in order to purchase commodities.

Thus alienated workers come to regard the purchase of commodities as an end in itself, irrespective of their use or the extent to which they satisfy basic human needs. Alienated workers suffer a displacement of goals – rather than work being regarded as the expression of creative human potential, workers devote themselves to the accumulation of more and more commodities. They make a 'fetish' of purchasing commodities with little consideration for their intrinsic utility. The notion of 'commodity fetishism' thus represents a theory of the ideology of advanced capitalist societies. Commodity fetishism is an unintended consequence of the development of capitalism, but one which brings about a natural identity of interests between capitalists and the proletariat. By turning workers into commodity fetishists capitalism helps to create the conditions for the extension of the market for its products. Moreover, as long as workers maintain their fetish for commodities they will not question the nature of the system which creates their alienation. Basic conflicts of interest over the effective control of production and the disposal of surplus-value are set aside in the desire only to obtain more and more commodities.

It is clear that the growth of commodity fetishism is a factor which affects the transition of a class-in-itself into a class-for-itself. Workers, for example, do not concern themselves with the overthrow of the capitalist mode of production but with the pursuit of goals, such as increases in wages, which lie within the organization of capitalist production. In themselves, of course, wage demands may exacerbate a capitalist crisis and their significance should not be entirely ignored. However, the fetish for commodities clearly hinders the growth of a revolutionary socialist movement in the working class and thus helps to perpetuate the development of capitalism. Unfortunately Marx's own writings on commodity fetishism remain undeveloped. Having outlined its main features and given some indication of how it, develops, Marx does not consider the consequences of commodity fetishism in any systematic way. One may assume that because of the tendency towards the falling rate of profit discussed in the previous section, Marx would look askance at the capacity of capitalism to satisfy indefinitely the fetish for commodities. However, this is an open question. There were, in any case, other, more contradictory, aspects of the ideology of capitalist society to which Marx paid rather greater attention.

Ideological hegemony

The term 'ideological hegemony' derives from Gramsci, but it describes an important aspect of capitalism to which Marx drew attention: the capacity of the dominant class to rule not only by its control over the means of production but by its control of *ideas*.

The bourgeoisie were the revolutionary class of the feudal era. Their triumph in establishing a capitalist society means that they enter the epoch of capitalism as a fully fledged class-for-itself. They represent a truly conscious class, rationally pursuing their interests against those of the dominant class, the proletariat. Class consciousness in this context is much more than just a set of attitudes and values. It is a distinctive ideology, a view of the world and a programme of action – a rational pursuit of goals which may be to uphold, to change or to overthrow society according to the appraisal which is made of class interests. As we have already indicated, a truly conscious class acting in this manner constitutes a class-for-itself, while a class which has not developed a class consciousness exists, according to Marx, only 'in-itself' – that is, it is a class potentially, but not actually. The development of class consciousness within the dominated class is clearly necessary before a revolutionary struggle could take place and overthrow the existing mode of production. Under feudalism the bourgeoisie had achieved this and created a capitalist era through their class struggle with feudal lords.

Under capitalism, then, it is the bourgeoisie who initially constitute both a ruling class and a fully conscious class.

The bourgeoisie rule through their control of the means of production. However, we saw in the previous chapter that an entire ideological superstructure is erected upon the economic base of society which reflects/corresponds to/is determined by (the precise terminology is, as we saw, rather ambiguous) the mode of production. It follows, therefore, that in a capitalist society not only is the 'base' organized around the capitalist mode of production, but the superstructure is, at the very least, commensurate with a bourgeois view of the world. The capitalist class thus rules by its control of the productive process *and* its ability to control ideas. Their class consciousness is reflected in the 'false consciousness' (a term coined by Lenin) of the proletariat, which is frequently unaware of its interests because of the hegemony of bourgeois interpretations of the world. As Marx and Engels put it in *The German Ideology*:

In so far, therefore, as they rule as a class and determine the extent and compass of an epoch, it is self-evident that they do this in its whole range, hence among other things rule also as thinkers, as producers of ideas and regulate the production and distraction of the ideas of their age: thus their ideas are the ruling ideas of the epoch. (Marx and Engels 1970, p. 64)

Given the centrality of the class struggle to Marx's theory of social evolution, the ability of the ruling class to dominate ideologically in this way is clearly important. The class struggle will obviously be affected by the fact that the subordinate class is rendered unaware of its interests by the ideological hegemony of its rulers. As long as the proletariat can be kept in ignorance of its real interests bourgeois control of capitalist society can be reinforced, though it should be emphasized that this need not be a deliberate or conscious process. And the fact that the bourgeoisie enter the capitalist era as a revolutionary class themselves provides the basis of their ideological control.

The rational self-education of the dominated class

The fourth 'system-level effect' of capitalist social relations concerns the rational self-education of the dominated class – that is, the growth of proletarian class consciousness. Given what we have already encountered concerning commodity fetishism and ideological hegemony, how does this come about? Marx offers two reasons:

a As was indicated earlier in this chapter, the development of capitalism would, according to Marx, be accompanied by the growing immiseration of the proletariat. Marx believed that eventually the falling rate of profit and the accompanying and deepening crises of capitalism would so depress the wages of the proletariat as to force them even below the means of subsistence. On the basis of this experience, and by a rational calculation of the fact that the capitalist system could no longer provide the means of subsistence, the proletariat would eventually comprehend that its needs could not be attained under the existing system of capitalist social relations. The proletariat would then overthrow capitalism in order to satisfy its basic needs.

b Equally importantly, however, capitalist social relations of production themselves provide the basis for the perception of common interests among workers. This is because capitalism brings about the *collective* organization of the proletariat at the point of production, in contradistinction to the individual control over the means of production. The proletariat is thereby provided with an objective basis for the overthrow of the capitalist class, while the collective organization of workers also facilitates their political mobilization and the growth of class consciousness. As capitalist production moves towards a progressively more centralized monopoly situation and as the polarization of the classes continues so the class consciousness of the proletariat expands.

These two factors then combine to produce an active, revolutionary consciousness among the proletariat, making it prepared to transform capitalist society through revolution.

The necessity of conscious political intervention: praxis

It is now clear that the class struggle under capitalism is fought out at the level of ideas as well as over the disposal of surplus-value. The ideological hegemony of the ruling class obstructs the growth of working-class consciousness and, where successful, will divert the proletariat from the pursuit of its real interests. The dominant, and highly conscious, position of the ruling class makes this more than a mere abstract possibility. Because of this, direct political intervention in the class struggle is necessary in order to raise the consciousness of the proletariat – that is, in order to appraise its members of its real interests. Marx did not, therefore, regard the growth of a revolutionary working class as *inevitable*. This was something which had to be created by political persuasion and organization.

Marx thus believed in political *praxis* – the unity of theory and action. As Marx commented in his *Theses on Feuerbach*,

The philosophers have only *interpreted* the world in various ways; the point, however, is to *change* it. (Marx 1975, p. 423)

Marx the abstract theorist is therefore also Marx the revolutionary activist. Indeed theory and action lie in a dialectical relationship to each other, so that the ultimate test of the theory lies in praxis. Marxism as a theory is not proved or disproved by this or that empirical fact, but by its direct insertion into the class struggle. The only legitimate test of Marxism is the success of the revolutionary struggle against capital.

Marxism and sociology – some conclusions

It is not easy to reduce three volumes of Marx's *Capital* to an account which will fit within the overall structure of this book. Indeed the above schematic presentation might, with some justice, be attacked as a gross over-simplification of the complex subtleties of Marx's greatest work. We can only repeat the advice we gave at the beginning of the previous chapter: that readers should consult Marx's text for themselves, daunting though this task may seem.

We have presented Marx's analysis of capitalist development in this way, however, in order to highlight certain aspects of Marx's theory which we regard as pertinent to both contemporary theoretical *and* empirical debates within sociology. We have also attempted to present Marxism in such a way that the intellectual power of Marx's work is apparent. It is clear that Marx was extraordinarily prescient in explaining *some* of the subsequent developments in capitalist society – for example, the increasing alienation of workers; the tendency towards monopoly; the persistence of periodic capitalist crises. It is equally apparent that *some* of Marx's expectations concerning the future development of capitalism have *not* occurred – for example, the immiseration of the proletariat; the growth of a revolutionary class consciousness in the proletariat of advanced capitalist societies. Those working within the Marxist tradition are quite aware of these difficulties, which is one reason why Marxism can no longer be considered a monolithic theoretical scheme. Certain aspects of Marx's work have been abandoned by many recent Marxist theorists – most notably Marx's teleological evolutionism – in an attempt to tinker with this or that aspect of Marx's theoretical scheme. It is, of course, possible to argue that where Marx's predictions have not come to pass, they have merely not occurred *yet* – and it is always possible to postpone the culmination of capitalist crisis and the dawn of a socialist era further and further into the future. However, even Marxist scholars, while optimistic, are (rightly) suspicious of this line of argument for it reduces Marxism to an entirely speculative and metaphysical ideology of the kind which Marx

himself so scorned. Marxism cannot forever sustain itself on a prediction which is taking an unconscionable time to occur.

Nevertheless modern Marxism is dominated by an attempt to come to terms with the occurrence of a non-event. In *no* advanced capitalist society has a successful proletarian revolution taken place. Indeed the only case of a proletarian revolution in an advanced capitalist society – the so-called Spartacist Revolution in Germany in 1918 – not only failed to ignite the revolutionary potential of the working class, but also began not in the industrial heartlands but among naval personnel who decided that mutiny was a preferable alternative to inevitable defeat and death in the North Sea at the hands of the British. Moreover, if one wishes to pile up the evidence against Marx, the most advanced capitalist nation in the world, the United States appears ostensibly to be almost a living testament to the falsity of some of Marx's predictions. Not only have the majority of American workers persistently increased their standard of living, there is no significant attachment to socialism among American workers and certainly no widespread revolutionary movement aimed at overthrowing capitalism. In Europe during the 1930s, furthermore, many of the conditions which Marx's writings would lead one to believe would prompt the growth of working-class consciousness were present – the widespread immiseration and unemployment of workers in the midst of a severe economic crisis in advanced capitalist societies. The outcome, however, was not the growth of revolutionary socialism within the working class but, equally often, the growth of Fascism. What all these familiar examples demonstrate is not so much a weakness in Marxist political economy, but in Marx's theory of *action* – the proletariat has persistently failed to act in the ways which Marx both predicted and desired.

So where does this leave Marx's theory? The short answer is . . . relatively unscathed, if the recent resurgence of interest in the thought of Marx (not unconnected with the onset of *another* capitalist crisis) is anything to go by. This is partly because many of the developments which have occurred since the time at which Marx was writing can still be explained by reference to aspects of Marx's own theories. This is a further reason for the way in which we have organized the material in this chapter. Marx's analysis of capitalism enables those factors to be identified which contribute to the collapse of capitalism *and* those which contribute to its persistence. We have listed these again in Table 3 where 'positive' system effects are those which help to perpetuate capitalism and 'negative' effects are those which contribute to its overthrow. Now, one reason why Marxism remains so intellectually powerful is that it explains *both* the destruction (1,4,5) and the persistence (2,3) of capitalism. That is, Marx's 'failure' in predicting the downfall of capitalism can itself be explained by reference to specific and distinctively *Marxist* interpretations of why the proletarian revolution has not occurred (ideological hegemony, the growth of commodity fetishism). It is thus possible to retain the correctness of the theory while conceding problems with this or that empirical application (for further discussion of this, see the provocative critique of Marxist theory by Parkin 1979).

It is the awareness of these kinds of problems, among other things, which has prompted many contemporary Marxists to seek to modify certain aspects of Marx's theory. One approach, favoured by the so-called humanist

Table 3 *System-level effects identified by Marx*

Item	Effect
1 Falling rate of profit	Negative
2 Commodity fetishism	Positive
3 Ideological hegemony	Positive
4 Rational self-education of the dominated class	Negative
5 Necessity of conscious political intervention	Negative

After Lockwood, 1981

Marxists, has been to acknowledge the unfalsifiable elements in Marxist theory as well as its historicism (that is, teleological evolutionism), but to argue that Marxism is fundamentally a *method* rather than a specific theory or set of theories. Scientific Marxists, on the other hand, have been less concerned about the tautological aspects of Marxism, arguing that all sciences consist of an essentially tautological set of conceptualizations constructed to illuminate a particular set of problems (or 'problematic'). It is quite inappropriate, according to this interpretation, to apply a set of evaluative criteria from one 'problematic' – for example, 'bourgeois sociology' – and apply them to another – such as scientific Marxism. Marxist theory thus exists as an ontological and epistemological totality and not as a series of narrowly predictive and empirically falsifiable statements.

In our view the tendency to offer a radical disjunction between 'Marxism' and 'sociology' is not a very helpful one. It leads to an over-simplification of *both* Marxism and sociology while the implication that Marx was not tussling with essentially *sociological* concerns (as we have defined them in this book) seems scarcely supportable. It is true that Marx approached these problems in a distinctive way – but this is a tribute to Marx's genius, not a denial of his sociological relevance. Thus Marx's political economy, while clearly distinctively Marxist, should not be interpreted as a uniquely Marxist preoccupation. Other 'classical' sociological theorists, as we shall see, were concerned with political economy and, like Marx, attempted to demonstrate the reliance of economic organization on antecedent social relations. Indeed the main weakness with Marx's theories concerns the fact that he paid too much attention to classical political economy rather than too little. While Marx's analysis of the capitalist mode of production departs radically in almost every single respect from classical economics, his theory of *social action* remains tied to a fairly conventional *homo economicus* conceptualization which looks remarkably like nineteenth-century utilitarianism. Marx's error appears to lie in his faith that, once he had discovered the crucial, and contradictory, 'laws of motion' of the capitalist mode of production, certain forms of social action would, more or less automatically, ensue. Thus the immiseration of the working class would *ipso facto* promote a 'rational' appreciation of class interest. It is *this* expectation, more than any other, that subsequent historical experience has denied and it is this denial which, in turn, has led to the renewed controversy over the base/superstructure distinction.

Thus, it is ironical to note that while Marx's political economy is a quintessentially sociological account, his theory of social action is scarcely sociological at all. It consists of the familiar utilitarian conception of rational actors (classes) pursuing their economically defined interests deflected only by ignorance or error. The proletarian revolution has not occurred because the proletariat has, stubbornly, been deflected by other 'irrational' (but sociologically explicable) concerns, even under conditions of immiseration. The irony lies in the fact that one important thread in the sociological tradition is the critique of utilitarianism. Subsequent sociological theory *cannot* therefore be reduced merely to a 'debate with Marx' (see Zeitlin 1971). Sociological theory after Marx is a debate both with Marxism *and* with utilitarianism.

10   Marxism and contemporary society

By this time it may have crossed the reader's mind to ask whether it is necessary to learn all this complex doctrine if, as some people claim, its basic approach is outmoded. Can it really be claimed that Marx's theories have any relevance to contemporary society?

Let us be clear first of all that this is a matter which cannot be settled by 'positivist' procedures. Most of Marx's followers would not accept that the propositions of historical materialism and the theory of capitalist development can be treated as if they were like hypotheses in natural science. It is therefore useless to claim to be 'testing', say, Marx's predictions about capitalist development. Not only does Marxism set out with a very broad historical perspective – so that 'cheap refutations' (Dahrendorf 1959) in a particular place and time cut little ice – but it also sets out from very different philosophical foundations from positivism. This is a problem which results in disputes among Marxists themselves about the appropriate role of empirical enquiry. There is nevertheless a general agreement that empirical investigation of contemporary society cannot be considered as simply redundant – no Marxist sociologist would be willing to argue that the implications of historical materialism consist of simply waiting for the inevitable revolution to occur.

We shall argue that the enduring strength of Marxist sociology lies in its *method* of analysis – *class analysis* – rather than in its ability to offer a narrowly empirical range of predictions which can be tested against a given set of data. Instead it seeks to discern the underlying dynamic of class relationships in capitalist societies and to

account for contemporary developments in terms of the contradictions created by such relationships. Consequently, when we come to 'apply' – a term which would make most Marxist theorists wince – Marxism to, say, modern Britain it is to this analysis of class relations that we must turn.

We shall try to show that there is a perfectly reasonable *empirical* case for continuing to analyse Western society in general, and Britain in particular, in class terms. Class is probably the most important single predictor that sociology has 'discovered'. Already we have had occasion to show how educational sociologists, by using economic and cultural aspects of 'home background' as an indicator of achievement potential, were able to offer a major critique of selective schooling policies. This, however, is a *relatively* superficial aspect of class – part of the study of what we shall call class *stratification*, or the unequal 'layering' of individuals and families by economic circumstances which undoubtedly exists throughout all Western societies. It was Marx's insight, however, that class itself is more profoundly rooted than this. For him, class was a source of *power* over others.

Thus, Marxism still draws our attention to certain kinds of data and events in a way which is not significantly emphasized in other approaches. Consequently by no means all of the authors whose work we shall cite in this chapter can be regarded as committed Marxists. It is rather that their material bears upon the kind of empirical issue which, so it seems to us, it is perfectly appropriate to pose in the context of class analysis. But to do this properly, we need to consider the evidence which has been used to criticize Marxist theory as well as that used to support it.

Rivals to the Marxist interpretation of contemporary class structure tend to approach it from a relatively simple* Industrial Society perspective of the kind we have already met. As we saw in Chapter 7, this means that they regard industrialism *per se*, rather than just the capitalist form of it, as the real source of dynamism and change in the modern world. Adherents of the Industrial Society model have spoken of the 'withering away' of class for several reasons, the chief of which we will now examine. They are:

a the disappearance of the capitalist class owing to the separation of the ownership of capital from the control of capital;
b the failure of Marx's 'immiseration' thesis owing to the 'embourgeoisement' of the proletariat;
c the failure of Marx's 'polarization' thesis owing to the growth of social mobility and the rise of the middle class;
d the absence of working-class consciousness and the failure of the working class to become a class for itself;
e the role of the state – the significance of increasing state intervention in civil society.

Our concern here will not simply be with the truth or falsity of these criticisms. We shall be concerned mainly with the efforts made by Marxists and indeed other sociologists to counter them. Their aim has been to show that despite the greatly changed face of contemporary society which the above points reflect, the concept of *class* and the Capitalist Society model are still valid.

---

* The most sophisticated version of this thesis was offered by Max Weber and addresses itself to certain problems within Marxism which we have yet to encounter. Since it does not necessarily deny the importance of class we can safely leave it until Chapter 11.

The capitalist class and the separation of ownership from control

Any assessment of the contemporary relevance of Marxism *must* set out by asking how far the private ownership of *capital* continues to play a dominant role in the structure of contemporary society. This consideration is the source of the biggest challenge to Marxism and is contained in the thesis of the 'separation of ownership from control'. According to this the structure of capital ownership has been transformed since Marx's death from being the foundation of the power of the dominant bourgeois class into a *common asset* of the whole society. Scott has described this thesis as the 'solid backbone' of the Industrial Society model (Scott 1979, p. 19). We shall examine the evidence for it under three headings:

a the rise of the corporation;
b the structure of share ownership;
c the relationship between wealth, shareholding and income.

The rise of the corporation

There can be no question but that Marx foresaw correctly the concentration of capital into ever larger but fewer units. This is most easily seen in the manufacturing sectors of all Western economies all of whom have experienced a growth in the average value and scale of manufacturing investment projects. The proportion of businesses employing large numbers of people with a single unit of organization has grown while the number of small and very small concerns has declined. In Britain these tendencies have been especially marked (Westergaard and Resler 1975, p. 151; Scott 1979, pp. 60 ff.)

It is not only the value and scale of manufacturing activity which has expanded. The concentration of industrial capital has been accompanied, indeed encouraged, by the parallel concentration of money capital, that is, capital placed in firms and banks and moved around in order to maximize the money return on the market-value of the investment. Money capital has also become concentrated: quite different kinds of manufacturing enterprise now belong together in the same financial unit of ownership. Moreover, these concentrations of monetary capital have begun to own foreign subsidiaries and to own overseas businesses. The result has been the rise of multinational corporations and concentrations of capital investment which may exceed the budgets of the smaller nation states.

Curiously enough this apparent vindication of Marx, this concentration of manufacturing and money capital, is to his critics symptomatic of the radical differences between the social structure of Marx's time and our own. In the nineteenth century it was possible to distinguish a class of private family capitalists, each enterprise being owned and managed by a 'Mr Moneybags' as Marx endearingly referred to them. Though such family capitalists have not wholly disappeared they have certainly been relegated to the backwaters of the economy by the requirements of technical change. Modern methods of production call for a team of trained personnel to manage them and require investment resources beyond the fortune of one individual. The result is the rise of the industrial corporation, a large formally run unit of economic organization which boasts a professional management who are themselves its employees.

This leaves open the question of who does actually *own* these vast concentrations of economic power. Here the critics bring into the argument a second factor: change in the legal and institutional structure of company finance, in particular the rise of the *joint stock company*.

The joint stock company was made possible in most countries during the last half of the nineteenth century by legislation which created what is called *limited liability*. This meant that anyone investing their money in a business would only be liable for the debts of the company to the extent of their own investment. No longer need an investor find his own personal property used to pay off company creditors. This change gave a great boost to the institution of *shareholding*. By offering shares in their business the management of a business could simultaneously put to work funds loaned by a variety of different sources.

Shareholding, it is argued, altered the social role of capital by separating control of the business from ownership. On one hand we have the controllers of the business, the professional managers whose obligations are to the efficiency of the business and even its role in the wider society. On the other, we have the owners of capital who are now no longer typically private capitalists but a group of shareholders who will in fact be very numerous. They will include many people with small amounts of savings, plus agencies such as insurance companies and pension funds who will be investing on behalf of their clients. Such a development is believed to have brought about a democratization of share ownership and, combined with the rise of the professional manager, the virtual end of the capitalist class. Obviously then we need evidence on the ownership of company funds to see whether this 'democratization of ownership' has actually occurred.

The distribution of share ownership

The first attempt to gather hard evidence on the ownership/control issue was a celebrated study of publicly quoted American companies carried out in 1929 by Berle and Means. It provided much of the inspiration for theories of the separation of ownership from control (Berle and Means 1932). We shall not attempt to summarize the long critical debate which has followed the publication of this work (see, however, Scott 1979, Chapter 3 as well as earlier studies by Nichols 1969, and Zeitlin 1974) except to make two points:

1   the time when the neo-evolutionary Industrial Society model achieved its greater influence was one when little attempt had been made to

check the methods and findings of the Berle and Means study;

2   the revival of empirical work in this field, some of it stimulated by the Marxist renaissance, has illuminated the many problems of method which bedevil it, to say nothing of the purely practical difficulties of obtaining valid information.

We are fortunate in that most of the relevant literature has now been assembled into a useful critical discussion (Scott 1979) which draws upon material from the United States, Japan, Britain, Canada, Australia and several continental European societies.*

It is hardly surprising to discover that neither the Industrial Society nor the orthodox Marxist view accurately captures the actual development of capital ownership in the twentieth century. This has displayed a complexity and adaptability which is still far from wholly understood. Nevertheless, Marxists could argue that the evidence undoubtedly confirms their insistence upon the continuing importance of *capitalism* in shaping the economic and social structure, albeit in a form which has shown greater resilience than was first envisaged in Marx's theory. This is because:

1   The principles of private property and private investment remain firmly entrenched, despite the enhanced role of the state and public investment in the economy (the significance of which we consider further below).

2   Though new forms of ownership have arisen, the private and family-capitalist pattern of company ownership has far from disappeared.

3   Even in the case of the largest companies, where family ownership does not exist, control

by a *minority* of shareholding interests is still possible because the vast majority of the remaining holdings are in very tiny blocks and their owners do not necessarily attend shareholders' meetings. Forms of minority control, for example, accounted for 93 out of 200 largest American companies according to a recent survey – only 11 were fully controlled by one interest. Admittedly among the 50 very largest firms only 15 were found to be in 'minority' control and it was here that *managerial* control was most important (30 companies).

4   The rate of change to managerial control appears to be very slow and declines in importance as we move to smaller corporations and of course to other medium and small concerns outside the top 200. It also seems to decline in significance as we move from manufacturing to merchandizing and transport companies. And outside of the US the proportion of companies controlled by their owners is higher to start with.

5   In the largest most significant and most concentrated sectors of economy, called the 'corporate sector', there is no question that the personal possession exercised by the family capitalist is of secondary importance. The mistake, however, Scott argues, is to assume that this development has led to a separation of managerial control from ownership interest. On the contrary, 'private ownership control' versus 'managerial control' are not the only possibilities. In fact, the rise of the joint stock shareholder has meant a shift from *personal possession*, in which the wealth of one capitalist was tied up with one unit of capital, to *impersonal possession*. 'Impersonal possession' means that several, maybe many, units of capital are controlled, through the medium of banks, and by impersonal 'constellations of owner interest'.

The significance, Scott shows, of banks and other financial institutions, either as the dominant shareholder group or as holders of important minority blocks of shares, is growing. These financial institutions are beholden neither to one private group of 'finance' capitalists nor subject

* It is worth noting that one of the most striking points which emerges from this work is the degree of economic interdependence between these societies themselves and the less-developed areas of the globe. Much of this has been brought about by the activities of multinational corporations. The result, Scott argues, is an 'anarchic' world economic system, which continually serves to undermine the actions taken by national governments to achieve economic co-ordination (Scott 1979, p. 171). Broadly similar patterns and trends can be found in each case.

to marked democratization of control by those – including insurance policy holders and pension fund members – whose contributions form an important sector of the funds they use for investment. Certainly a few, especially in the USA, seem to be controlled by wealthy families (Zeitlin 1974) but more and more these institutional investors tend to be *owned* and *controlled by each other*. The banks also act as important channels of information which shape and reflect the behaviour of each unit in the company sector. This is done through networks of directorships through which their representatives sit on the boards of many companies. These institutions, then, together with looser financial groupings undoubtedly still *control* the companies that they *own*. All that has changed is that there is now 'an inter-weaving of ownership interests that breaks down the direct link between particular interests and particular companies' (Scott 1979, p. 60).

Very similar conclusions emerge from a slightly earlier study of company directors and the phenomenon of 'asset stripping' in Britain and elsewhere (Pahl R. E. and Winkler 1974). Its authors also point out that the notion of 'managerial' control confuses (a) the autonomy managers might have gained from *particular* ownership interests with (b) the belief that they have gained autonomy from ownership interest as a whole. Furthermore, they show how belief that the second possibility has actually occurred has encouraged excessive optimism about the social role of industry. Managements and corporations, it is claimed, have different interests and sets of priorities, particularly a more 'public spirited' and socially responsible attitude, than private owners. On the contrary, argue Pahl and Winkler, 'the essence of the professional manager is his rigorous and exclusive dedication to financial values'. The transition from family to professional and financial management brings a 'new ethic of hard capitalism'. For the professional in their study 'family owners were . . . clearly objects of derision' (Pahl R. E. and Winkler 1974, p. 119; cf. Francis 1980) because

of their willingness to displace financial priorities.

Shareholding, wealth and income

There can be little doubt then that ownership interest continues to dominate the policies of modern corporations and the broad direction of the capitalist economy. This interest, however, now takes the form of impersonal possession embodied in the shape of 'the shareholder'. The validity of the thesis of the withering away of class as an attack on orthodox Marxism therefore depends to a very large extent on establishing how shareholdings are distributed among the population. Two related issues are involved here: whether share ownership is widely dispensed or retained by a few; and, if the latter is the case, what distinguishing attributes do this select group possess?

Such questions cannot be answered with *absolute* certainty. Indeed, between 1975 and 1979 a Royal Commission on the Distribution of Income and Wealth wrestled with the technical problems of complying with their terms of reference. They confirmed earlier judgements that much of the information concerning ownership of the means of production is shrouded by secrecy and evasion. We have no precise measures of the ownership of capital at all and much of it has to be inferred from data published in the settlement of estates. Nevertheless, we can piece enough information together from British, American and other sources to concur with Scott's conclusion that 'a class of individuals occupying privileged positions . . . by virtue of their participation in units of capital' is a reality (Scott 1979, p. 112). The case rests on seven main considerations:

1 In Britain and America shareholding is not widely dispersed but *concentrated* among a small minority of the population.
2 Private wealth of all forms also remains highly concentrated in a few hands. In America, for example, it is estimated that in recent years 1

per cent of the population held at least 25–30 per cent of the total of all wealth. In Britain the figure is as high if not higher: the richest 1 per cent of the adult population owns between 22 and 29 per cent of private property; the richest 5 per cent owns between 41 and 54 per cent (Atkinson and Harrison 1978).

3   The larger-size holdings of all forms of private wealth include a substantial amount held in company securities, that is, shares of various sorts. Figure 1 gives the latest information for Britain.

4   The top wealth holders are also the top *income* earners and recipients. Shares provide a major proportion of that income. For example, in Britain, the top 1 per cent of all income recipients in 1970 received 7 per cent of all pre-tax income but 17 per cent of investment income (Scott 1979, p. 115; Diamond Report 1979; Noble 1975, p. 180; Noble 1982).

5   The most important category among the wealth-owning minority are company directors and executives. In Britain and the USA they monopolize the ownership of company shares and derive a substantial part of their income from this source (Scott 1979, p. 118). Consequently even when a management do not own a large proportion of shares in their company they nevertheless have a large stake in it, bolstered by an even larger stake in the capitalist system as a whole.

6   Hence, it can be claimed that the wealthy continue to exercise decisive economic *power*. This power is complemented by access to political resources at least in the sense that business interests are well represented, say among MPs in Britain and Congressmen in the United States.

7   Economic power is perpetuated in Britain in various ways, one of which is through the public school system. A disproportionate number of directors and executives have been educated at public schools and this is the form of education that they choose for their children.

Despite problems with access to information, therefore, there seems little doubt that ownership of capital continues to constitute a major basis for the existence of a dominant class in Britain and other Western societies. To this extent the Marxist account of contemporary society is wholly vindicated. What is not explained within the orthodox Capitalist Society model however is the remarkable stability of this system of capitalist relations. In the following sections we shall discuss a number of different aspects of this stability, and consider ways in which Marxists and others have sought to deal with them.

The working class – immiseration or affluence?

Critics of Marx, in an attempt to dismiss the contemporary relevance of his theories, are fond of pointing to the falsity of his predictions concerning working-class immiseration. Rather than the development of capitalism being accompanied by the immiseration of the proletariat, they will declare, it has enabled the proletariat to become ever more prosperous and attain an unprecedented standard of living. This observation has then been used to ridicule Marxism in its entirety, as though it were a set of theories relevant only to the early years of nineteenth-century industrialization and without any merit in its applications to the modern world. While we certainly do not share this view, it must nevertheless be acknowledged that Marx's 'immiseration thesis', in its most simple and superficial form, is a source of some embarrassment.

During the 1950s and early 1960s the economic conditions of most advanced capitalist societies, including Britain, seemed a far cry from the gloomy prognostications of Marx concerning the gradual immiseration of the working class. This was a self-proclaimed 'age of affluence', a period in which – to use a political catch-phrase of the time – 'you've never had it so good!' In the United States, sociologists like Daniel Bell were proclaiming 'the end of ideology' (Bell D. 1960), which they interpreted

Figure 1 *Net wealth, 1976*

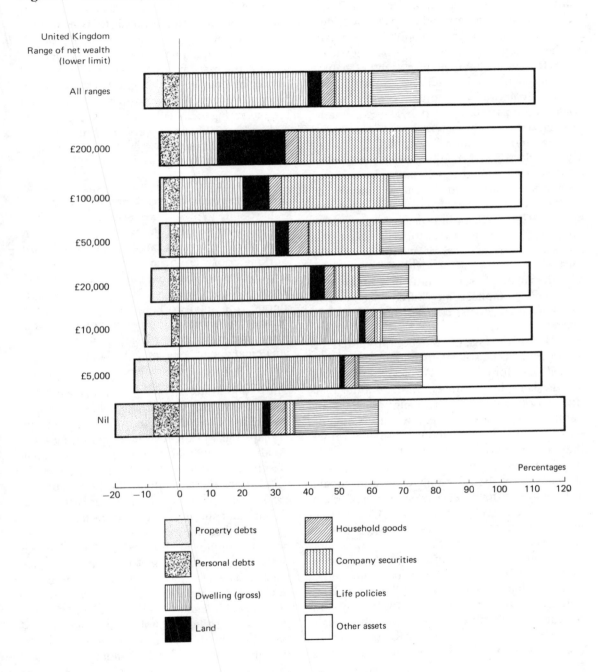

United Kingdom
Range of net wealth
(lower limit)

All ranges

£200,000

£100,000

£50,000

£20,000

£10,000

£5,000

Nil

Percentages

−20 −10 0 10 20 30 40 50 60 70 80 90 100 110 120

Property debts

Personal debts

Dwelling (gross)

Land

Household goods

Company securities

Life policies

Other assets

Source: Diamond Commission (1979), p. 100.

as the end of class conflict and class-based politics. The notion that capitalism was doomed by its own inherent contradictions was derided and in its place a boundless optimism concerning the capacities of capitalism became virtually taken for granted. As we have seen in Chapter 6, an implicitly and sometimes explicitly anti-Marxist evolutionism emerged, centred on the 'logic of industrialization' thesis. According to this the defining characteristic of industrialism (rather than capitalism) was not a sharply divided class-based inequality but a gradation or *stratification* of the population by income, occupation, status and education attainment. With the onset of chronic economic stagnation in the 1970s, such optimism no longer seems justified (Bell himself was to write about 'the cultural contradictions of capitalism (1977) rather than the "end of ideology" ') and the confidence of liberal evolutionists has visibly waned. The emphasis has shifted once more to the analysis of crisis, contradictions and class analysis.

In Britain the 'age of affluence' prompted the emergence of the so-called 'embourgeoisement thesis' (see, for example, Zweig 1961) in direct antithesis to the theories of Marx. Rather than the working class becoming increasingly pauperized, it was argued, it was becoming more 'middle class'. Embourgeoisement rather than immiseration represented the prevailing trend, it was believed. Occasionally one may still hear this belief being expressed today, although with the onset of economic depression from the late 1960s onwards this has become less frequent as well as less plausible. At its simplest and crudest the embourgeoisement thesis consisted of little more than the observation that manual workers were becoming more affluent, that their standard of living was consistently rising and that they were able to purchase consumer durables previously regarded as within the exclusive province of middle-class families – especially those 'status symbols' of the time, the washing machine and the television set. Today such a notion may

seem almost quaint, but in the 1950s it verged upon an obsession: buying washing machines and television sets appeared to constitute a major shift in the class composition of British society, and the phenomenon was widely, if loosely, discussed in just such terms. In Marxist terms, of course, this might constitute commodity fetishism, but it most certainly does not have anything to do with class position *per se*.

A more sophisticated version of the embourgeoisement thesis, however, was that income and wealth differentials were narrowing:

1 The rich, it was argued, were becoming poorer, because of the commitment of the welfare state to progressive taxation.
2 The poor were becoming richer for a variety of reasons – partly because wage rates for the working poor were believed to be increasing in real terms; partly because the 'welfare state' has, in its various manifestations, ended poverty among the non-working poor; and partly because full-employment policies on the part of successive governments together with Keynesian demand management had all but obliterated the problem of unemployment.

Thus optimism about increasing affluence merged with that concerning the reduction of inequality of wealth and income to suggest that perhaps the working class was becoming more middle class and that the possibility of working-class immiseration could be banished forever.

What are the facts about this? Certainly the 1950s was a period of sustained growth in real income and the notion of increasing working-class affluence during this period cannot be dismissed as mythical. By 1965 real income was some 50 per cent higher *per capita* than it had been at the beginning of the 1950s and more than double that of the 1920s. It is also important to note that although the late 1960s and 1970s were marked by rising unemployment and increasingly uneven trends in economic growth, the overall trend in living standards was still upwards – by around 3 per cent *per annum* on average. Such averages can, of course, be misleading, for we also need to know how the benefits of economic growth and rising living standards have been distributed around the population as a whole. This was a point which was often overlooked during discussions of working-class affluence during the 1950s and it was during this period that the *overall* rise in prosperity threatened to disguise the continuing existence of poverty until it was 'rediscovered' in the early 1960s. Thus while it is relevant to note the continuing ability of British capitalism to generate absolute levels of affluence which continue to rise (and this in itself contradicts the 'immiseration thesis'), it is also necessary:

a to look at the *distribution* of income. In other words it is necessary to ascertain whether the absolute increase in income brought about in the post-war period has been accompanied by a redistribution in favour of the middle-income groups;

b to look at relative as well as absolute poverty.

Income distribution

It should be stated immediately that reliable information on the distribution of income is not much easier to obtain than information on private wealth. Summarizing the information available in 1976 Westergaard and Resler found evidence of a distinct shift in income away from the topmost income groups between 1938 and 1949, but there had been little change thereafter. The richest 1 per cent of individuals earned, after tax, 11½ per cent of income in 1938, but only 6½ per cent in 1949. Since that time their share has fallen slowly to just below 5 per cent. These conclusions can be confirmed and updated to 1976–77 from the work of the Diamond Commission. In 1976 the post-tax income of the top 1 per cent stood at 3.5 per cent of all income and for the top 10 per cent it stood at 23 per cent (Diamond Report 1979, p. 15).

How do we explain these undeniable but rather undramatic changes? One thing seems reasonably clear – progressive taxation has had

rather little importance in this regard. The Diamond Commission found that the contribution of the top tenth of income earners to income tax revenue fell from 65 per cent in 1959 to 40 per cent in 1976–7 (Diamond Report 1979, p. 314). The explanation seems to be that suggested in an ageing classic of this area of sociology and social policy by Richard Titmuss (1962). This author pointed to the wide variety of tax evasion devices available to the wealthy. Since his study was written the sophistication of the tax evasion industry has certainly increased.

The same point arises if we consider the intimate connection between the incomes of the wealthy and their ownership of personal wealth (see above). Changes in the distribution of personal wealth since 1911 (when estate duty was introduced and rudimentary statistics became available) indicate a similar pattern of redistribution to that of income. The personal wealth of the richest 1 per cent has declined (from 69 per cent to 42 per cent) but those who have gained are the richest 10 per cent. This can be explained by the redistribution by *individuals* within *families* of their personal assets in order to avoid taxation of personal estates. Overall it is possible to conclude that when families rather than individuals are considered, the distribution of wealth in Britain has remained virtually unchanged since the beginning of this century. As Westergaard and Resler sum up the situation:

There is nothing here to affect property ownership in its crucial form: ownership of the means of production. And the retention of a massive share in all wealth by the top 5 or 10 per cent of the population is very striking. The reason for the shift *within* their ranks – from the richest 1 per cent to those just a little way down the scale from them – is plain. That shift represents, primarily or even exclusively, the measures taken by the very rich to safeguard their wealth against taxation. (Westergaard and Resler 1975, p. 113)

Relative and absolute poverty

The poorest sections of the population have seen their share of income decline, too. Westergaard and Resler (1975) calculated that the poorest third of the population received 14½ per cent of income in 1949, but only 11½ per cent by 1967. The poorest half of the population has seen its share of income remain virtually stable at just over 25 per cent.

More recent statistics are not properly comparable with these earlier estimates. Obtaining accurate information about the less well off is as tricky as investigating the rich, but for rather different reasons. For one thing we have to consider the way in which tax statistics – our principal source of knowledge about incomes – are presented. As Titmuss first observed these tell us about the incomes received by tax *units*, which in very many cases include joint earnings of husband and wife. The post-war trend to more married women working produced a sudden increase in the income share of households. This was real enough but only gained at the price of more hours given by someone to working. (In Chapter 17 we point out that the increased employment of women has not necessarily brought about a sharing of household tasks.)

We have also to consider the impact of social security benefits as well as taxes. Pressure groups on behalf of the poor and low paid have expressed concern that the 'stable' proportion of all income going to the bottom third has changed in make-up as the recession has deepened. The part of 'final' income – income received after taxes and welfare benefits have been included – now shows a greater dependence of the poor upon welfare benefits. The stability of incomes is thus somewhat deceptive.

The issue of 'immiseration' cannot be tackled adequately without considering poverty in relative rather than absolute terms. Today's 'poor' in Britain might be considered affluent in Marx's time, but he himself made it clear poverty always has to be judged relative to the productive capacity of a society and with regard to the disparity in standards between different members of it. Townsend (1979) has recently suggested that substantial relative poverty can still be found in British society in at least three senses:

1   In terms of the state's own standards used in deciding social security benefits. On this basis some 6 per cent of individuals in households sampled by Townsend were found to be living in poverty. This figure rises to 9 per cent if we include people dependent on the income. In addition another 25 per cent are on the 'margins' of poverty. Such individuals are to be found among such groups as the elderly, large families, one-parent families, the disabled and the long-term unemployed. Rising unemployment levels in recent years has undoubtedly added to 'official' poverty of this kind but even at the time of Townsend's survey 'there were between 15 and 17½ million in a population of 55½ million who were in or near poverty' (Townsend 1979, p. 895).

2   In terms of a relative income standard. This means calculating the numbers receiving less than 50 per cent of the national average income for their household type (size and composition). This raises the proportion of 'poor' households to 9 per cent.

3   Townsend's own 'relative deprivation standard'. This complex (and controversial) method looks at exclusion from participation in terms of general standards of provision for needs, rights and citizenship. Such a thoroughgoing 'normative' definition leads to a much higher estimate of persons in poverty – some 25 per cent of households. Not surprisingly these larger estimates have been challenged (for example, Piachaud 1981) and the relative deprivation standard remains a controversial measure.

In *relative* terms, then, the position of the working class has not improved and it is at least arguable that at the present time the position of at least certain sections of it is deteriorating. If at the same time the distribution of personal wealth and income have remained relatively unaffected by attempts to reform them, then this is because the private ownership of the means of production has not been seriously challenged – which is another way of stating that we continue to live in a capitalist society. On the face of it this is not a terribly enlightening conclusion, but at least it warns against undue optimism and unnecessary mystification. It also vindicates a basic Marxist tenet: that the realities of the economic base proscribe the limits of political (superstructural) reform.

This conclusion must be tempered, however, with the acknowledgement that the structure of capitalist relations has proved to be remarkably durable, perhaps more than Marx himself realized. For all the preoccupation with economic stagnation since the mid-1960s, we are still to witness the onset of working-class immiseration in the manner which Marx's theory of capitalist development predicts. Subsequent theorists in the Marxist tradition have felt able to account for this by pointing to a single historical factor – imperialism. One reason, it has been suggested (first by Lenin but by a myriad of subsequent commentators) why the immiseration of the proletariat in advanced capitalist societies has been avoided, or at least postponed, is because it has been exported. As we saw above (p. 104) Marxists argue that advanced capitalist societies *as a whole* have exploited the underdeveloped world in a manner analogous to that which Marx outlined for the purely internal relationship between classes under capitalism. The vehicle for this was colonial domination and, in the latter half of the twentieth century, 'neo-colonialism' (including the activities of multinational corporations) whereby economic control is retained even though political independence has been granted. In this sense the class struggle has become internationalized and we are in the presence of a 'capitalist world system' (Wallerstein 1974) characterized by 'unequal exchange' (Amin 1974) between the exploitative neo-colonial nations and their exploited Third World dependencies. Thus the working class in Britain, as in other advanced capitalist societies, has benefited (albeit indirectly) from the fruits of imperialism – and it is these benefits which have accounted for the absence of absolute proletarian immiseration in Britain.

In this manner Marxist theory attempts to account for the 'disappointment' of its adherents over developments in advanced capitalist societies. For example, the absence of a socialist movement in the United States can be interpreted by referring to American domination of the capitalist world system, both economically and militarily. The United States proletariat can be seen to exist not only in the fifty states of the union but in Taiwan, South Korea, the Philippines, Central America, etc. Thus it becomes less surprising that the major socialist revolutions of the twentieth century have occurred not in the advanced capitalist nations, but in most pre-capitalist societies under the impact of imperialist capitalism – Russia in 1917, China in 1948, Cuba, Vietnam and so on (see Wolf 1969). This line of argument concludes with the analysis of the contradictions of capitalism on an international, as opposed to a solely national, basis. It invites us to consider the Marxist theory of capitalist development in a less parochial and less ethnocentric manner, while presenting a plausible interpretation of both the lack of immiseration in advanced capitalist societies and its existence in the Third World.

Changes in the class structure

In this section we will examine Marx's 'polarization thesis' – that as capitalism develops the class structure becomes polarized between the bourgeoisie and the proletariat, with all intermediate and transitional classes gravitating to one or the other of these groupings.

We shall broaden our discussion out from the 'polarization thesis' itself to consider two separate, but related, issues:

a the growth of the so-called 'new middle class' – that is, non-manual or 'white-collar' employees;
b the degree of social mobility (of individuals) up and down the class structure.

The rise of the new middle class

One of the most difficult issues which has had to be faced by Marxist theorists in the twentieth century concerns the problem of how to interpret the rise of the 'new middle class' – the increasing number of professional, technical, managerial and clerical employees who are often referred to collectively as 'white-collar' workers. Colloquially and subjectively they are often referred to as part of the middle class and although they are all non-manual employees they are not, of course, to be regarded as synonymous with the bourgeoisie, in the classic Marxist sense, for they do *not* own the means of production. On the other hand many of them are in managerial or supervisory positions which, in terms of the social relations of production if not the ownership of the means of production, places them in an antagonistic authority role *vis-à-vis* many manual workers. In other words, many members of this 'new middle class' participate in the *control* of the means of production even if they do not *own* them.

During the twentieth century the proportion of the labour force accounted for by non-manual workers has risen consistently and now stands at over 40 per cent. This makes it difficult to explain them away as a merely transitory phenomenon destined to be absorbed into either the bourgeoisie or the proletariat as classically defined. The new middle class is, moreover, a somewhat amorphous group. Professional and managerial workers alone account for over half of them (21 per cent of the entire working population), routine clerical employees for a further 40 per cent (16 per cent), while only 7.5 per cent comprise the 'entrepreneurial' middle class, who come closest to the Marxist definition of the bourgeoisie (and they account for only 3 per cent of the working population). Their numbers have been increasing for two major reasons:

1   There have been major structural changes in the composition of the economy. Extractive and manufacturing industries have declined as sources of employment, while the service sector has expanded. It is the service sector which employs a high proportion of white-collar workers.

2   As discussed above, there have also been major changes in the structure of the capitalist enterprise – increases in the scale of production, the prevalence of joint stock companies, etc.

Since most of these workers are employees, this places them in the proletariat as far as conventional Marxist categories are concerned, *whatever their subjective feelings on the matter.* Most of these workers, of course, *subjectively* identify themselves as middle class – and are so identified by others. Many of them also maintain very different lifestyles to manual employees, have a highly developed sense of separation from most manual employees, act according to a different set of values and are better paid, more highly educated and possess superior prospects for career advancement. Now in Chapter 7 we indicated that class has to be viewed as a *concept* rather than as a descriptive category. Marxist theory is therefore faced by a tricky *conceptual* problem when dealing with the new middle class – to what extent, if any, does it make sense to regard, say, the managing director of a large industrial company as being in the same class as the employees of that company who work on the factory floor? Because neither may, under modern conditions, actually own the means of production, does this make them equally proletarian?

This kind of problem may be solved in one of two ways:

1   It is possible to argue that, all appearances and subjective feelings notwithstanding, the essential division between the major social classes is precisely where Marx placed it. As indicated in Chapter 7, the concern is with explanatory concepts rather than with groups of people. Class relationships are therefore constructed by the relationship between capital and labour, *whatever its precise organizational form*

(see Poulantzas 1975, 1976). This retrieves the formalism of Marx's theory at the risk of reducing its empirical application and explanatory power.

2 The alternative is to acknowledge that the structure of the capitalist enterprise has so changed since the time in which Marx was writing that, if it is to retain any explanatory utility, the concept of class must be modified. Class, for example, may be defined as the *effective control* of the means of production rather than the solely legal form of ownership. This has the merit of greater analytical value at the cost of modifying Marx's original scheme (see, for example, Carchedi 1977).

It is clear, then, that the new middle class presents Marxist theorists with what Poulantzas (1976) has called a 'boundary problem' – just where, under modern capitalist conditions, is the line to be drawn between the bourgeoisie and the proletariat? Manifestly such a question must be decided upon before the 'polarization thesis' can be settled. Does one opt for the most abstract and purist model, or is one prepared to compromise with the distinctly messier empirical reality?

Perhaps the most ingenious solution to this problem has been suggested by the American sociologist, Erik Olin Wright (1976, 1978). For Wright the heart of Marxist class analysis is to 'decode' the social relations of production within a particular society – the conceptually messy empirical reality which we all observe – in order to uncover the class positions which determine them. Wright argues that capitalist social relations of production can be broken down into three interdependent dimensions:

a social relations of control over money capital – that is, control over the flow of investments into production;

b social relations of control over physical capital – that is, control over the use of the physical means of production;

c social relations of authority – that is, control over supervision and discipline within the labour process.

The fundamental class antagonism between capitalists and workers is represented in each of these three processes, and in the abstract model of capitalist organization they are merged together: capitalists control investment, the physical means of production and authority relations, while all workers are excluded from these forms of control. In empirical reality, however, this is often not the case. For example, self-employed producers – the petty bourgeoisie – are not involved in social relations of authority in the labour process since no workers are employed by them. Similarly the new middle class exercises control over some, *but not all*, of these social relations of production. It therefore occupies what Wright calls a *contradictory class location* – that is, it *simultaneously* shares the position of more than one class. This is illustrated in Figure 2.

More specifically:

1 *Managers and supervisors* occupy a contradictory location between the bourgeoisie and the proletariat. Like the proletariat they sell their labour power and are excluded from control over the flow of investments into production; but unlike members of the proletariat they participate in the control of physical capital and/or the supervision of labour within the process of production.

2 *Semi-autonomous employees* occupy a contradictory location between the working class and the petty bourgeoisie. They include many professional and technical workers. Unlike the petty bourgeoisie they do not own their own means of production and thus must, like members of the proletariat, sell their labour power to capital. But like the petty bourgeoisie they do maintain high levels of control over their immediate labour process.

3 *Small employers* occupy a contradictory location between the bourgeoisie and the petty bourgeoisie. Unlike the petty bourgeoisie they do employ labour, but they do so in sufficiently

Figure 2   *The basic class relations of capitalist society (after Wright 1976)*

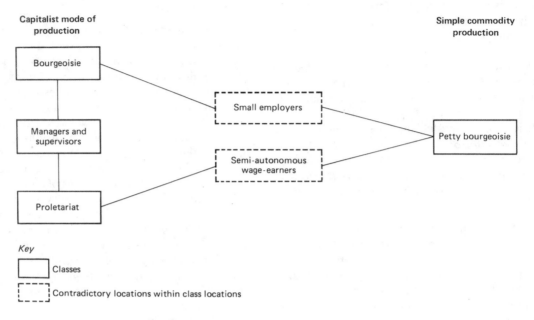

limited quantities that most of their income is still generated by their own labour rather than by the labour of their employees.

Wright argues that the class structure of contemporary capitalist societies is thus much more complex than a simple, polarized two-class model would suggest, but that nevertheless the essential developmental logic of advanced capitalist societies is animated by the polarized class antagonism between capital and labour.

Wright's major concern is to recast classical Marxist theory along lines which take into account what he calls the 'industry-shift effect' on changes in the class structure brought about as a result of shifts in the labour force from industrial sectors with one distribution of class positions to sectors with a different distribution. It is also an attempt to cope with observed changes in the technology of capitalist production, the growth of bureaucracy in public and private sectors and the implications of the rise of joint stock companies as a common form of financial and legal organization. There is,

however, one further factor which needs to be taken into consideration: the extent to which the *content* of occupations conventionally regarded as middle class is becoming 'proletarianized'. In other words, it is necessary to investigate the extent to which occupations which may formerly have involved some control over money capital, physical capital or authority have themselves become reduced to occupations from which these forms of control have been excluded. The most cogent argument for the case that class relations within the labour process have themselves been transformed in this way is that of Braverman (1974). His book, *Labour and Monopoly Capital*, presents a great deal of American material in an attempt to demonstrate that the labour process has become progressively 'deskilled' as a result of increasing efforts on the part of capitalists to retain control at the point of production. According to Braverman, occupations which have been conventionally regarded as middle class have, as a result, lost much of their autonomy, variety, discretion, responsibility and control. Subsequent empirical enquiry in Britain has provided only moderate support for Braverman's claims (see Wood 1981), although the connection (if any) between the proletarianization of certain white-collar occupations and the growth of white-collar unionism is a matter which continues to occupy a central role in sociological enquiries into the new middle class. In this respect the perceived decline in the autonomy of white-collar employees has produced a kind of embourgeoisement-thesis-through-the-looking-glass: that the progressive routinization of much white-collar employment will not only bring about a growth of unionization but a greater propensity to engage in industrial action to press claims for improved pay and conditions. Not surprisingly, therefore, studies of white-collar unionization have taken up a considerable amount of research effort in this area, though differing interpretations of essentially similar findings appear to provoke continuing controversy (see, for example, Blackburn and Prandy 1965; Blackburn 1967; Roberts *et al.* 1972; Bain, Coates and Ellis 1973; Carter 1979; Crompton 1976, 1979, 1980; Banks J. 1978; Heritage 1980).

This concentration on white-collar unionism has tended to obscure other, broader features of the growth of non-manual employment which deserve equal attention. For example, the implications of the fact that the bulk of the expansion of white-collar employment can be accounted for by the increasing participation of females in the labour force has only begun to be explored (McNally 1979; Hunt 1980).

Social mobility and the class structure

Questions concerning social mobility are relevant to considerations of changes in the class structure because increasing *individual* mobility, even within a static or polarizing class structure, could act as a social sedative. People may find inequality and exploitation more acceptable if they can perceive a reasonable chance of upward mobility for themselves or for

their children. As we saw in Chapter 6, this was an assumption of the 'logic of industrialization' thesis. It was assumed that in advanced industrial societies there would be an increase in social mobility owing to the fact that occupations would become increasingly open to individuals on the basis of merit rather than ascribed characteristics. The introduction of universal education would also foster increasing social mobility by allowing the full potential of individuals' aptitudes and talents to be reflected in educational attainment and occupational opportunity. Marxist theory has much less to say about social mobility. This is partly because Marx is concerned with relationships between classes rather than the mobility of individuals. Thus sociologists writing within the Marxist tradition in Britain have paid little attention to the problem of social mobility. The most recent study, the Nuffield Mobility Project (see Goldthorpe 1980) analyses social mobility in terms which are only tangentially related to Marxist categories. Nevertheless the publication of the study's findings has been marked by an iconoclastic stance towards some of the hitherto more plausible accounts of class formation and the stratification system (see especially Goldthorpe and Llewellyn 1977). The findings can be summarized as follows:

1 There is more social mobility in modern British society than sociologists have hitherto suspected. For example, the Nuffield study found that 16 per cent of males in professional and managerial occupations were the sons of manual workers.

2 Most of the mobility, however, is over very small social distances, such as from skilled manual occupations to routine non-manual occupations.

3 Moreover, there is very little mobility into elite positions – that is, top management and the higher echelons of the civil service, the judiciary, the armed forces, etc.

4 Almost all of the mobility is 'induced' mobility. In other words, it is not the result of

any increase in equality of opportunity, but of the expansion of middle-class job opportunities which have had the result of sucking up workers from manual, working-class backgrounds. Thus if upward social mobility has increased across generations this is because changes in the occupational structure (such as those referred to in the previous section in the new middle class) have created more 'room' further up the social scale for individuals to occupy.

5   As a result downward social mobility is very rare and has not become more prevalent.

Goldthorpe and Llewellyn claim that the important phenomenon so far as changes in the class structure is concerned is the rise of the new middle class – a category which they term 'the service class' – rather than social mobility *per se*. The changes in the employment structure consequent upon twentieth-century developments in capitalist organization have had an impact upon individual social mobility, but whether or not this constitutes mobility across social classes is a subject of dispute. In strict Marxist terms the vast majority remain members of the proletariat. However, these very changes have given an appearance of social fluidity which cannot be entirely discounted. Upwardly mobile members of the new middle class – whether induced or not – manifest few signs of identifying themselves with the proletariat. The influence of these changes at the level of consciousness should not, therefore, be entirely discounted.

Class and class consciousness

The centrality of the class struggle in Marx's theory has highlighted the associated problem of class consciousness – under which conditions will the proletariat realize its true interests and mobilize itself politically on the basis of them? As we have already seen, Marx argued that before a class could become engaged in the revolutionary struggle it was necessary for it to become a 'class-for-itself' – truly conscious of its

own material interests and acting in accordance with them. A great deal of recent sociological investigation has been directed towards uncovering the characteristics of working-class ideology in particular and towards an understanding of the sociological conditions for the conversion from a 'class-in-itself' to a 'class-for-itself'.

Marxists themselves, however, are reluctant to use 'snapshot' research methods – for example, surveys – to investigate something which they see as dependent upon a historical process. Eventually, they claim, the necessary awareness of class interests will be provoked by the contradictions in capitalism itself. In general Marxists have preferred to examine the issue of working-class consciousness at a somewhat safer historical distance. The best Marxist studies of class consciousness are therefore historical accounts, including E. P. Thompson's magisterial *The Making of the English Working Class* (1963). These offer important guides to how Marxist sociologists might undertake the task of examining class consciousness, but their direct relevance to contemporary substantive concerns is, perforce, limited. They demonstrate certain continuities in working-class experience and offer an essential contextual understanding of working-class consciousness today, but clearly their findings cannot be extrapolated directly (see also Anderson P. 1965; Thompson 1965; Foster 1973). Even where Marxist sociologists have ventured to explore contemporary settings they are careful to stress the relevant historical background and to look at the setting itself sequentially (for example, Hall and Jefferson 1976; Clarke *et al.* 1979; Willis 1978; Beynon 1973; Nichols and Beynon 1977).

Our first task in this section is to specify what exactly we are looking for in carrying out substantive work on class consciousness. Marx himself offers few clear guidelines about what the main elements are. Michael Mann, in his book *Consciousness and Action in the Western Working Class* (1973a), suggests a fourfold scheme:

1   First, a notion of class *identity*. That is, the first element in the definition of class consciousness must be that the individual does indeed recognize himself or herself as belonging to their appropriate class. Class is not, of course, always the most salient characteristic in an individual's self-identity. Indeed approximately one-third of manual workers in Britain consistently do *not* regard themselves as 'working class', whatever their formal position might be. As we have already noted, the identity of those workers who by a strict Marxist definition are members of the proletariat is even more attenuated.

2   Second, there must be an element of class *opposition*. Thus, in the case of the working class, true proletarian consciousness would involve the perception that capital and its agents constitute an enduring opponent to oneself and the interests of one's fellow workers. Opposition helps to reinforce class identity and vice versa – that is, class consciousness arises out of the class struggle. Colloquially this often manifests itself in a sense of opposition between 'us' (the workers) and 'them' (the bosses).

3   Third, there is an element of class *totality* – the acceptance of the view that class identity and class conflict represent the defining characteristics of contemporary, capitalist society. The class struggle is regarded as a relationship which helps to define and determine every aspect of society, so that no element of social life is entirely immune to the consequences of the class struggle.

4   Finally, there must be present a conception of an *alternative* society – the goal to be achieved as a result of the successful outcome of the class struggle. Such an alternative, for the contemporary working class, would consist of socialism.

Clearly the presence of all four elements of class consciousness is a rare event and would in any case only occur in an immediately pre-revolutionary situation. We shall use the first three of these – identity, opposition and totality – to raise some problems that present themselves whenever we ask why the working class in Britain and other advanced industrial societies has not demonstrated a more highly developed form of class consciousness.

Identity and social imagery

Non-Marxist sociologists have been less reluctant to survey the attitudes and ideology expressed by members of significant groups of workers. Though some Marxists may describe these results as an empiricist irrelevance they are relevant to the question of class identity.

The research has developed in a number of distinct phases. Until the mid-1960s a major concern was the exploration of the many ramifications of the embourgeoisement thesis. Indeed the most striking aspect of sociological research into the working class during the 1960s was the overriding concern with the problems of class awareness and class consciousness. This was a measure of the increasing cross-fertilization between the occasional Marxist-influenced sociology of conventional academic research and the sociologically informed theoretical writing of orthodox Marxist pedigree, particularly among the New Left (for further details see Goldthorpe 1972). Old questions about the relationship between 'objective' class position and class consciousness were reopened and re-examined and within Marxist thought in Britain there was a self-proclaimed crisis and a re-appraisal of many of the fundamental tenets of Marxist theory, signified by the title of Perry Anderson's important paper, 'Origins of the Present Crisis' (1965). There were signs of an increasing impatience with the crude economically deterministic interpretations of Marx's writings and an unwillingness to continue to take for granted the hitherto underexamined connection between class formation and class consciousness. There was some scepticism of the utility of the categories of 'true' and 'false' consciousness, except as ciphers, and a realization that the bases of the variations in class consciousness within the British working class might be related to systematic variations in the structural features of different occupational or other groupings within it (see Wolpe 1970).

The most direct test of the theory of working-class *embourgeoisement* was the 'affluent worker' study carried out in Luton during the mid-1960s (Goldthorpe *et al.* 1968, 1969, 1970). In an important paper published in 1963 Goldthorpe and Lockwood had been able to expose some of the looser assumptions of the *embourgeoisement* thesis even before the empirical research had begun. By breaking down the concept of *embourgeoisement* into its economic, relational and normative aspects, they were able to demonstrate that there was

little basis for the more ambitious thesis of *embourgeoisement* in the sense of the large-scale assimilation of manual workers and their families to middle-class life-styles and middle-class society in general. In particular there is no firm evidence either that manual workers are consciously aspiring to middle-class society, or that it is becoming any more open to them. (Goldthorpe and Lockwood 1963, p. 155)

These conclusions were upheld in the study of affluent workers in Luton, although the results also indicated a degree of what Goldthorpe and Lockwood had called 'normative convergence' between certain sections of the manual and non-manual workers over such issues as the 'instrumental collectivism' of trade union and party political support and an increasing privatization of leisure activities. Moreover, the link between working-class affluence and such admittedly tenuous indicators of class consciousness as trade union membership and voting behaviour were mediated by the social situation in which affluent workers found themselves – it was not a *direct* consequence of increasing prosperity. There was a link here with the same problem that was at the centre of the Marxist debate: what were the social bases of political commitment and class-based identity? As Westergaard pointed out, if the working class was not

becoming more bourgeois, neither was it seething with revolutionary fervour:

If the conjunction of rising expectations and persistent inequalities indicates a potential from which a clear challenge to the established order could emerge, what circumstances account for the apparent repression or dissipation of that potential? (Westergaard 1970, p. 112)

It was in an important paper published in 1966 that Lockwood attempted to answer this question. Lockwood argued that variations in manual workers' 'image of society' – that is, how they perceive and interpret the main structural features of society, which may or may not include the more limited concept of class consciousness – is related to the structure of their 'work situations' (the social relationships they enter into at the workplace) and their local 'status situations' (or 'communities'). Lockwood delineated a threefold typology of working-class images of society:

1   traditional deferential – where the individual both accepts and endorses the hierarchical nature of the class structure;
2   traditional proletarian – where the individual recognizes both a cleavage between social classes and that a conflict of interest exists between them;
3   privatized – where the individual conceives of society as a graded hierarchy based upon differences in financial reward, but with no fundamental cleavage between any one level of the hierarchy and any other.

Lockwood regards certain occupations as being typified by workers with particular images of society – for example, domestic servants and farm workers as traditional deferentials; coal miners, dockers and shipyard workers as traditional proletarians; and car assembly workers as privatized (see Lockwood 1966). This is because workers in certain occupations typically find themselves in certain structural situations which are conducive to certain forms of class consciousness (in its broadest sense). Thus workers' beliefs about society are not, according to Lockwood, developed in a random rashion but are a product of the social *milieux* which typify their work situations and local communities.

This becomes clearer by examining Tables 4 and 5. In Table 4 the concept of work situation is broken down into three dimensions: the extent to which workers are personally involved in their job; the degree of interaction and identification with workmates; the degree of interaction and identification with the employer. These are given positive or negative values according to their high or low ratings. Table 4 indicates Lockwood's argument about how variations in working-class images of society are related to these structural variables – with the typical middle-class work situation included as a comparison. In Table 5 this type of analysis is repeated for the local community. The first dimension concerns the extent to which the local community contains an 'interactional status system' – that is, the extent to which the inhabitants evaluate each other on the basis of *personal* knowledge and acquaintance as opposed to purely impersonal, formal characteristics. The second dimension concerns the extent to which the community is an 'occupational' community – dominated by a single industrial or occupational grouping – and the third involves the extent to which individuals within the community are brought into contact with people from other occupations.

Lockwood's schema provoked a considerable amount of research among particular occupational groups in order to ascertain whether these typologies were empirically verified (much of this is referred to in Bulmer 1975). This led to a new phase of research in the late 1960s and

Table 4 *Working-class images of society by features of the work situation*

Image of society	Work situation		
	Involvement in job	Interaction and identification with workmates	Interaction and identification with employers
Traditional deferential	+	−	+
Traditional proletarian	+	+	−
Privatized	−	−	−
Middle class	+	+	+

After Lockwood 1966.

Table 5 *Working-class images of society by features of the community (status) structure*

Image of society	Community (status) situation		
	Interactional status system	Occupational community	Occupational differentiation
Traditional deferential	+	−	+
Traditional proletarian	+	+	−
Privatized	−	−	−
Middle class	+	+	+

After Lockwood 1966.

1970s, although the basic research problem remained the same: the relationship between the structural features of certain occupational groups and their social imagery. Many of these studies showed, perhaps inevitably, that matters were not quite as straightforward as Lockwood's typologies assume. For example, variations *within* occupational groupings were found to be almost as great as variations *between* them. However, perhaps the most notable conclusion of this research was a set of compatible but rather negative findings – namely that the class consciousness of many workers is neither highly developed nor particularly coherent and that many of them have no fixed ideology at all, but rather a number of opinions, sometimes vague and contradictory, but highly unsystematic.

Earlier research on the 'belief systems of mass public' in the United States had suggested this. Horton and Thompson, for example, concluded from a study of political attitudes that the consciousness of the powerless is 'founded less on accurate political knowledge than on an existential guess' (1962, p. 493). Converse, in the most provocative piece of research to come out of the American literature, argued that as one moves down the social hierarchy 'the contextual grasp of "standard" political belief systems fades out very rapidly' (1964, p. 213). As he continues:

Instead of a few wide-ranging belief systems that organise large amounts of specific information, one would expect to find a proliferation of clusters of ideas among which little constraint is felt, even, quite often, in instances of sheer logical constraint. At the same time . . . the character of the objects that are central in a belief system undergoes systematic changes. These objects shift from the remote, generic and abstract to the increasingly simple, concrete, or 'close to home'. (Converse 1964, p. 213)

In Britain, two pieces of work were relevant to these considerations. In the early 1960s, Runciman had shown that most people had a remarkably restricted conception of inequality in British society. Those at the bottom of the social scale, for example, consistently underestimated the wealth and income of the rich and therefore the extent of inequality (Runciman 1966). This was mainly because their 'reference groups' (those with whom they identified themselves) were very restricted. Then in 1970 Michael Mann published an important article which, drawing upon a large number of studies in both Britain and the United States, argued that working-class consciousness was characterized by a 'pragmatic acceptance' of the concrete and specific issues which affected everyday life rather than a consensus on abstract beliefs and ideologies (Mann 1970). Mann developed the insights of Converse in order to argue that social cohesion in capitalist societies depends upon the *lack* of any sort of consistent commitment to *general* values. The possibility that there was not any one particular articulated set of beliefs, but a set of situationally relevant beliefs, often internally inconsistent though not necessarily perceived as incongruous, was confirmed by further empirical studies (for example, Blackburn and Mann 1978; Davis H. H. 1979; Roberts *et al.* 1977; Cousins and Brown 1975; Newby 1977; Nichols and Armstrong 1979).

Notwithstanding dissenting discussions by Moorhouse (1976) and Hill (1981) there has been a general consensus that successive pieces of research in this vein have yielded essentially compatible findings. Indeed Goldthorpe has gone so far as to suggest that 'the debate on the working class has at the present time reached a serious impasse' (1979, p. 2). It would be more accurate to say that the significance of the debate has changed with time. Increasingly the 'problem' of working-class affluence looked more of a historical curiosity as the contradictions of capitalist development reasserted themselves. For a time the rise in working-class militancy from the late 1960s onwards dissipated the pessimistic interpretations (from a Marxist standpoint) of trends in working-class consciousness in the 1950s. Even then, authors sympathetic to Marxism conceded that the militancy did not extend beyond 'factory consciousness' (Beynon 1973) and that the working class as a political force had been contained by capitalist institutions (Miliband 1977). However, 'the debate on the working class' in Britain has never been entirely reducible to a 'debate with Marx' – (even though, obviously, the work of Marx and scholarship in the Marxist tradition figure prominently). As we shall see in Chapter 15 the problem has resurfaced in the context of inflation and 'disorderly' industrial relations (see also Maitland 1979; Willman 1982).

Opposition and 'trade union consciousness'

Marxists recognize that the oldest, most spontaneous and simultaneously most puzzling manifestation of working-class consciousness is trade unionism. Trade unionism for Engels represented 'the first attempt of the workers to abolish competition'. They therefore threatened the 'vital nerve' of capitalism, namely, the dependence of the power of capital upon maintaining a state of division and hence competition among workers. Neither Engels nor Marx himself, however, expected trade union opposition to the bourgeoisie successfully to break the hold of market forces over the working class. What they did expect, at least in their early work, is that trade unionism would in due course develop into a wider struggle based upon the development of *political* opposition. The importance of trade unions lay (a) in their organizational role as fomenters of discontent and centres of communication; (b) as 'schools of war' – their failure at the economic level was bound to educate workers in the need for political action. It is these developmental links between economic opposition and *political* opposition which have proved troublesome.

If, at least in their early work, Marx and Engels were optimistic about the consciousness-raising potential of trade union opposition, later Marxists have been less sanguine. The most famous example is Lenin whose 1902 pamphlet *What is to be Done?* (1902b) drew a sharp distinction between 'trade union consciousness' and 'social democratic' consciousness. By

themselves, Lenin argued, the proletariat would develop only the former. The realization of full political opposition to the bourgeoisie was a task that must be fomented and implanted in the working class by a self-appointed dedicated group of revolutionaries. This pamphlet is widely quoted, usually out of context. Lenin was referring to the peculiar circumstances facing the Russian Social Democratic Party at the turn of the century. All the same the history of the labour movement of the twentieth century has seemed largely to confirm the wider applicability of Lenin's view of trade union consciousness. For example:

1   In Britain, with the oldest and arguably most powerful trade union movement in the world, political opposition, via the Labour Party, was embraced only slowly and reluctantly. Its main role has been to defend 'trade union rights' which in practice has meant reinforcing the decentralized, amorphous character of the movement and the jealously guarded autonomy of each union. During the 1960s and early 1970s there appeared to be a growing resistance among the rank and file to the staid ways of official established union leaderships. Various efforts at unofficial organization and the politicization of shop floor militancy were begun. These developments were not sustained. Factory consciousness in any case is more politically restricted than trade union consciousness. In the 1974 election a higher proportion than ever (37 per cent) of the working class voted Conservative. Opinion polls suggest that militant unionism is currently unpopular amongst members themselves. (For a valuable summary of sources on class identification and party support see Noble 1981, pp. 261–97).

2   In Germany the apparently united and powerful Marxist Social Democratic Party collapsed and split as a result of the outbreak of World War I. It has been argued that its early commitment to Marxism owed much to the *weakness* of trade unionism in that country. In both Germany and Italy the trade union

movement was later unable to survive the rise of Fascism.

3   In France the high level of political class consciousness among trade union leaders and militants hides a basic weakness *vis-à-vis* employers. The trade union movement is split between Communists and other Marxists, Syndicalists and Catholics. In recent years a non-political unionism based on formulating wage demands has gained in strength.

4   In the United States unionism has had to contend with vigorous and often violent employer opposition. It has tended to be for the benefit of the white Anglo-Saxon, relatively skilled worker minority and has resisted not only direct political involvement but also the extension of federal welfare legislation to cover the whole working class. Currently union membership extends to only one in five of the workforce.

What explains the general failure of political opposition? Various alternatives have been offered:

a   Robert Michels, whose work we consider in greater detail in Chapter 13, attributed the failure of the German Social Democratic Party to what he called 'the iron law of oligarchy' affecting all oppositional organizations (Michels 1962). Sociologists of the 1950s and early 1960s reformulated Michels's arguments to make them apply in the context of trade unions (for example, Lipset 1960).

b   Lenin, in a pamphlet published just before the Russian Revolution, blamed imperialism and the ability of capitalism to export the worst effects of the system abroad while retaining a relatively docile 'bourgeois proletariat' at home (Lenin 1916).

Whatever validity these explanations may possess, the fact is that trade unionism itself remains an important feature of capitalist society. The extent to which it can be understood purely in terms of *class* analysis, however, continues to be hotly debated (Hill 1981, Chapters 8–10).

Totality, race and sex

A further problem for Marxists is that forms of political and economic struggle have arisen in capitalist societies which seem to cut across class allegiances. The issues and grievances conventionally regarded as focal points for the growth of class consciousness often attract less militancy and conflict than these newer developments. Should there, therefore, be a substantial revision of the thesis that capitalist development leads to a growing sense of class *totality* among the proletariat? In order to look more closely at this question we shall briefly consider the two most troublesome examples: *racial* and *sexual* conflict.

Race and class

All of the schools of sociology which trace their origins to nineteenth-century social thought have tended to neglect the problem of race (Lockwood 1970). Marxism is perhaps the least culpable if only because it has been forced by political events to consider problems of ethnicity and nationality. Even so, it cannot be said that there is any settled Marxist account of racial consciousness and conflict. The stumbling block is the problematic relation of race to class. Marxists find themselves virtually compelled to argue that the divisions in society which, on an ideological level, are associated with race do in fact have their origins in the basic *class* tensions of an exploitative order. Failure to make this connection would undermine the base/superstructure relationship which forms such an important part of orthodox Marxist theory. It would imply that important cleavages and conflicts cannot only originate at a purely superstructural level but even override and obscure more 'basic' conflicts of economic interest.

Among the few studies which look at this question both empirically and from a position sympathetic to Marxism are:

a   Leggatt (1968): interviews with a sample of 375 individuals drawn from 'blue-collar', that is, working-class jobs in seven ethnic neighbourhoods in Detroit.

b Phizacklea and Miles (1980): interviews with two ethnically mixed samples of 72 men and 47 men plus 37 women in London.

In general both investigations show that individuals who are the most militant on ethnic issues and most conscious of being discriminated against on racial grounds are also the most class conscious. Thus to a degree empirical work supports a Marxist interpretation of the origins of racial consciousness in a deeper seated class consciousness. There are, however, a number of problems which have not yet been satisfactorily resolved:

1 *The concept of 'totality' is put into question by racial conflict within the working class.* The working class is obviously *not* homogeneous but internally differentiated by the severity with which individuals experience the privations of class society. In comparison with the white working-class racial minorities tend to be much more insecure economically. At the time of Leggatt's survey, for example, unemployment stood at 39 per cent among blacks, compared with much lower levels among whites. These differentiating effects, Leggatt argues, are bound to mean that class colours the opinions of some workers more than others.

2 *The problem of causality.* To show that economic disadvantage coincides with racial disadvantage is not to prove that the former is the cause of the latter. Work by Haddon on housing and employment problems among West Indians in Britain has tended to suggest that in this instance at least there is a pure discrimination factor such that racial disadvantage *per se* intensifies the liability of certain groups to economic insecurity (Haddon 1970).

3 *Conditions of heightening economic crisis,* which should be the most favourable to consciousness of class totality, can (and does at times) greatly encourage instead the growth of ethnic prejudice. Racial minorities, as in pre-war Germany, are cast as scapegoats for the ills suffered by the mainstream working class.

4 *The theory still fails to explain the existence of racial consciousness and racialist ideology in themselves* and why class antagonisms have to emerge in this particular form.

In Chapters 14 and 18 we consider some more recent and more sophisticated Marxist research which has attempted to demonstrate the link between racial and class elements in certain contemporary youth cultures.

Class and gender

Considered solely as problems within social theory, at least, there are many parallels between the racial and sexual forms of discrimination. Again, it can be argued that the classic sociological schools do not really take the issue at all seriously but that the record of Marxism is more creditable on this score than some others. Marxists could at least claim that theirs was the first tradition to recognize that sexual differentiation and inequalities do present very important problems of explanation to social theory. Both Marx and Engels reject wholesale the idea which we considered in Chapter 6, that any social institution or practice can simply be explained away in terms of nature and inborn capacities and talents. In *The Origins of the Family, Private Property and the State*, Engels argues that conflict between the sexes was the first class antagonism (Engels 1972). It was the result of the creation of the institution of the family and this, in turn, was a byproduct of the first growth of private property. The family enabled men to control women and thereby determine quite definite lines of paternity for the transmission of private property. This promising start, however, was not generally followed through by later generations of Marxists. Engels's theories were too reliant on out-of-date evolutionary anthropology and in the critical reception given by later generations to the work, the issue of sex and sexual inequality got lost.

Only recently, with the current revival of

serious feminism, has it finally become accepted by sociology in general and Marxists in particular that the traditional division of roles, power and privilege between the sexes is not simply a result of 'natural' inclinations and capacities but is one of the most fundamental social relationships which the discipline must attempt to *explain* (see Barrett 1980).

Within academic sociology the examination of these issues was hindered by the fact that they arose externally to the discipline rather than from within it. Moreover, arguably the most predominant reaction was initially that succinctly put by Giddens:

Given that women still have to await their liberation from the family, it remains the case in the capitalist societies that female workers are largely peripheral to the class system. (Giddens 1973, p. 288)

A number of critics have not been slow to point out the flaws in this kind of argument. It suggests, for example, that women have their class defined by the family, rather than their relationship to the means of production. This not only runs counter to accepted definitions of class, but it comes perilously close to suggesting that it is quite impossible for women to occupy a different location in the class structure to that of their husbands (see Eichler 1980). It is for this reason that most writers dealing with gender inequality have felt the need to step outside the conventional terms of reference of stratification research and attempt to reconceptualize the entire field of 'structured inequality' on the basis of taking into account the distinctive qualities of gender inequality. As Oakley has commented:

Women are a class, women's class is defined by the family; class, for women as for men, depends on individual occupation – none of these options is satisfactory. Since each of them is suggested by existing stratification analysis with the androcentric, occupationally based logic it is not surprising that they don't solve the problem. (Oakley 1981, p. 291)

Much of the conventional wisdom in sociology about gender inequality has been exploded by Marxist writers. One particularly important aspect of it has been the attempts to show that the modern family, with its powerful ideology of romantic love, and of 'woman's place' as homemaker is not a universal institution but a specific product of twentieth-century capitalism. But if this work has been relatively successful at a descriptive level it poses a number of unresolved analytical issues for Marxists. These have much in common with those we mentioned above in conjunction with the problem of race. For example:

1   *Domestic labour*. The so-called 'domestic labour' debate has been concerned with explaining what it is about the domestic tasks performed by women that contributes to the perpetuation of capitalist relations in society as a whole. Here again it is the question of class *totality* which is at issue. Can it be shown that the subordination of women is not a thing in itself but is simply an aspect of the wider subordination of labour as a whole? This time, however, there is a very precise difficulty. In what sense can domestic labour be shown to be part of or linked to the total exchange value of the labour time which the worker sells to his capitalist employer? Despite the growth of an extensive literature on this subject a solution satisfactory on both Marxist-theoretical and feminist-political grounds has not emerged. Molyneux, for example, has claimed that domestic labour and wage labour are incommensurate (Molyneux 1979). And many feminist sociologists, in fact, wish to argue that the women's struggle cannot in any case be absorbed into the general class struggle by means of theoretical argument.

2   *The problem of causality*. It is clear that the existing inequalities and division of labour between the sexes contain certain 'advantages' for the capitalist class: (1) women perform the task of 'servicing' the domestic needs of the paid worker; (2) they perform childcare duties and thus ensure the literal reproduction of the labour force; (3) they make up a growing sector of the marginal working class by providing a cheap

labour force of casual and disposable workers – women's wages, despite anti-discriminatory legislation, continue to be well below comparable male earnings. To point to these advantages of women's subordination is not, however, the same as explaining the *causes* of that subordination. Hence, it is not clear that the social distinctions between the sexes are explainable by economic distinctions and can, therefore, be fitted into a class theory of society.

3 *Are women a separate class?* One way out of the difficulty is, like Engels, to see sexual inequality as a basic class division in its own right. To conform to the orthodox Marxist position, however, for every class relationship there must be a corresponding mode of production. It is not clear how far sexual inequalities always result from a common mode of production or why this primitive mode survives within more advanced modes, including capitalism itself.

Debates over these issues have largely been conducted in abstract terms. Meanwhile whatever empirical work has been done has confined itself to more concrete aspects of women's present role in society (see Oakley 1981 for summaries). While this has not led to a resolution of the theoretical issues indicated here, there can be no longer any question of perpetuating the androcentric assumption that gender inequality can be 'defined out' of current discussions of class analysis and other approaches to the study of inequality.

The capitalist state and the state in capitalist society

One of the most distinctive features of the period from the mid-1960s onwards has been the growth of government intervention in the running of the British economy. State control has increased over the determination of prices and wages, the control of profits, the promotion of company mergers, the control of labour relations, the restructuring of the British economy,

and so on. Moreover, this has been a trend which is not specific to Britain – a similar tendency can be observed in almost all other advanced capitalist societies. Consequently there has been a growth of interest in analysing the role of the state in capitalist societies, both in order to understand substantive issues in capitalist development, and to address quite basic theoretical issues once more, particularly those surrounding the base/superstructure distinction.

There is, as yet, no consensus on how these issues should be resolved, or even on how to go about tackling them. Indeed the analysis of the state illustrates very well the lively debates which are currently characterizing Marxism (see Anderson P. 1980). Thus quite basic questions, such as how 'the state' is to be defined, remain unresolved. Some writers see it as what might somewhat vaguely be called the 'public sector'; others offer a much narrower definition in terms of the administrative apparatus of the government bureaucracy; still others do not regard the state as a group of people at all, but as a particular fraction of capital with peculiar functions. Here Marx himself is not very helpful, having paid little attention to the growth of the state. In a frequently cited passage from *The Communist Manifesto* (1969, p. 44), Marx and Engels refer to the state as 'but a committee for managing the common affairs of the whole bourgeoisie'. This suggests that the state possesses an enabling role, administering and co-ordinating the various spheres of economic activity in order to ensure that the interests of the bourgeoisie are maintained. It assumes a rather direct relationship between the economic interests of the bourgeoisie and the construction of an administrative apparatus – part of the 'superstructure' – to organize them, and therefore smacks of an economically deterministic theory of the state. Recent Marxist writers have found this simple formulation not so much false as incomplete: it is difficult to maintain the view that 'the state' always and in every way acts in accordance with the immediate interests of the bourgeoisie. Simple inspection will soon reveal that the bourgeoisie, indeed, expends much effort in *combating* the state's encroachment on its interests.

One can infer from some of Marx's later writings that he, too, was not entirely satisfied with the formulation contained in *The Communist Manifesto*. Instead Marx viewed the state as a political institution within which the conflicts between different factions of the ruling class can be represented and fought out. More recently it has been suggested that this can be extended to the class struggle *in toto* – that the institutions and apparatuses of the state reflect the development of the class struggle in 'civil society'. In this way the analysis of the state becomes a microcosm for dealing with general theoretical problems in Marxist sociology. The state as a political institution forms part of the societal superstructure: can, therefore, the state determine the economic activity of the base in an entirely autonomous fashion? Does it make sense to separate 'the state' from 'civil society' in a manner which regards the state as a detached entity suspended above, so to speak, the everyday economic activity of its citizens? How much 'relative autonomy' from the economic base does the state maintain? Is the state merely a politically neutral 'black box' which can be captured by any particular class and used to further its own interests?

Questions like these address not merely the analysis of the state, but the whole relationship between base and superstructure, for it is difficult at times to ascertain how and in precisely what ways the economic base of society determines, even 'in the last instance', the workings of the state. Because the analysis of the state quickly leads to a consideration of fundamental issues in Marxist theory, it is perhaps understandable that the debate has been conducted, for the most part, in highly abstract, theoretical, even speculative, terms. Two parallel sets of issues can be discerned. The first concerns a division between what Wright (1978) calls 'instrumentalist' and 'structuralist' conceptions of the state. The instrumentalist

view of the state is one in which the ruling class uses the political and administrative apparatus of government as an instrument of its own rules and via which the ruling class may maintain its essential political and economic domination (for example, Lenin 1902a; Miliband 1969). The structuralist view of the state is one in which the state expresses and reflects the competing and contradictory interests of various classes and class fractions according to their ability to pursue their interests in the political struggle (see Poulantzas 1975). In the former view the state is an agent in the historical development of capitalism; in the latter it is a functional structure which cannot be reduced to the actions of particular agents (see the celebrated debate over this issue between Miliband and Poulantzas, reprinted in Blackburn 1972). The second issue concerns the historical specificity of the state – that is, whether the state is to be regarded as an institution which transcends particular modes of production, or whether states (in the plural) are peculiar to particular modes of production. In other words, does it make more sense to talk about 'the state in capitalist society' or 'the capitalist state'? (See the various views of, say, Anderson P. 1974; Offe 1975; O'Connor 1976; Therborn 1978; Wright 1978.) Again, the view which is taken on this issue will depend upon how much autonomy particular theorists are prepared to grant to the state from the economic base of society and therefore how far they are prepared to modify the base/superstructure distinction.

Habermas (1975) has approached these issues by arguing that the state has at least three major functions:

1 economic – the regulation of productive activity, including crisis management;
2 political – the maintenance of power, including the monopoly over the use of physical force via the control of the military, law and order, etc.;
3 ideological – the maintenance of the legitimacy of the powerful in society through the

promulgation of ideas which uphold their values; for example, through the control of education, the mass media, etc.

One reason why the state does not act exclusively as an agent of capital, narrowly defined, is that the necessity to maintain its legitimacy and political functions may bring it into conflict with capital – for example, over such important issues as safety regulations, environmental protection, the provision of welfare, etc. For the state to make capitalism 'work' it must ensure stable conditions of production – such as the provision of law and order – and conditions of reproduction of labour power – that is, ensure a continuous flow of appropriately qualified labour and thus maintain educational, welfare and housing provision where private capital is incapable of doing so. The state must also co-ordinate and administer the highly complex structure of capitalist production which is a result of the extensive and interdependent division of labour in all advanced capitalist societies.

Perhaps the most decisive period in modern times for the growth of state intervention in capitalism was during World War II and in the immediate post-war period, owing to the adoption of Keynesian theories of economic management. The advent of Keynesian economics led to state expenditure being employed to regulate demand and thereby promote stable economic growth with minimal unemployment. From the mid-1960s onwards, however, the combination of high rates of inflation, low growth and high unemployment, to which Keynesian economic management has failed to find a solution, has provoked even further state intervention. This has illuminated some of the contradictions in advanced capitalist societies which such intervention creates:

1   There is first created a contradiction between legitimization and the necessity for capitalist accumulation. The state does not serve the function merely of facilitating accumulation through demand maintenance – that is, attempting to avoid the falling rate of profit by creating a mass consumer society; it also serves a vital *legitimating* function – that is, it must ensure the stability of capitalism by maintaining the acquiescence of the proletariat and thus reproducing the class structure. In attempting to manage a capitalist crisis, such as that which has existed in Britain since at least the mid-1960s, the state finds itself in a contradictory situation. For example, *one* way in which the state might be regarded as having attempted to maintain stability over this period has been to co-opt any potential sources of popular discontent (such as the trade union movement) by trying to make them part of the state apparatus, and to convert *political* demands (such as the demand for a socialist restructuring of society) into narrowly economic ones (such as higher wages). Thus a Marxist analysis of the state over this period would note that the attempt to encourage commodity fetishism in this way creates a set of rising expectations with regard to incomes and standards of living which, in a capitalist crisis, cannot be met. The state is then forced to act coercively to curb wage demands (for example, by prices and incomes policies) in which case it threatens to lose its legitimacy, and a *political*, as opposed to a narrowly economic, crisis ensues (see Habermas 1975).

2   Much of the institutional form which state expenditure takes is literally unproductive – for example, military expenditure, welfare payments, etc. These act as a drain upon the surplus created by capitalist production and can promote an accumulation crisis. At the same time the state grants citizenship rights which enable individuals to make claims upon state expenditure – for example, unemployment benefit, old age pensions, medical care, etc. These expenditures are *not* regulated by the market but are granted as a right of citizens. The state may find that in order to control the accumulation crisis it needs to cut back upon unproductive expenditure, yet to do so may impinge upon citizenship rights and therefore jeopardize its legitimating function. Moreover,

since the rights of citizens are essentially un-regulated by 'effective demand' they may well grow at a faster rate than the state can extract a surplus without risking a crisis of capital. The collision between increasing citizenship demands and the inability to extract sufficient surplus to meet them promotes what O'Connor (1976) has called 'the fiscal crisis of the state', which manifests itself at both national (Ginsburg 1979) and local levels (Alcaly *et al.* 1976; Castells 1977; Cockburn 1978).

3   Mechanisms of crisis management by the state therefore result in the politicization of the economy. Despite attempts to separate economic from political demands, state intervention renders 'private' economic activity a concern of the state. Demands which were once a matter of 'private' collective bargaining between employers and trade unions now attract state regulation. The economy thus becomes influenced by 'corporatism' – the setting of key economic parameters (wages, profits, etc.) by negotiation between employers' associations, trade unions and the government (see Winkler 1976; Crouch 1977). Wage claims therefore become essentially claims against the *state* as much as against private employers. Thus wage claims threaten to provoke a *political* crisis in addition to an *economic* crisis. The clearest examples of this occur in those sectors where the state has moved into productive activity (as opposed to mere demand management) in order to retrieve capital from the falling rate of profit – railways, public utilities, coal mining, shipbuilding, etc. The miners' strikes of 1972 and 1974 are opposite examples of this politicization of wage demands producing a crisis of legitimation.

The relevance of much of this analysis to contemporary economic and political conditions in Britain should hardly need emphasizing. It is not, therefore, surprising that the analysis of the state currently occupies such an important role in Marxist sociology and why the former interest in class consciousness has somewhat subsided. In examining the role of the state not only

has Marxist sociology contributed to an understanding of the capitalist crisis of the 1970s; it has also enabled a 'capitalist logic' to be illuminated in the transition from *laissez-faire* to monopoly to state capitalism.

Sooner or later the analysis of the state must return to questions surrounding the class struggle and class consciousness. Thus far the opinion that increasing state involvement will *ipso facto* politicize the consciousness of the proletariat (see Castells 1977) remains wishful thinking rather than realistic expectation. Meanwhile the debate rumbles on, accompanied in many cases by a refreshing readiness to re-examine some of the basic assumptions of Marxist theory which the analysis of the state makes unavoidable. Should, for example, the analysis of the state finally lead the base/super-structure distinction to be discarded (Williams R. 1973b) or does it provide an irreducible 'conceptual threshold and boundary limit for Marxism' (Hall 1977, p. 59)? And what is the alternative?

Summary and conclusions

We began by posing the question of the relevance of Marx's theories to contemporary society. We showed that despite problems of obtaining really conclusive evidence, Marxists could quite convincingly maintain that their class-based model of Capitalist Society remains more applicable than that of their critics. There is plenty of material to indicate the existence of a wealthy class in Western societies deriving privilege and power from the ownership of capital. The Marxist theory of capitalist *development*, however, is in need of substantial revision because of:

a   the tendency for the position of the capitalist class to become stabilized and entrenched by the shift from personal to impersonal possession;
b   the failure of the proletariat to develop revolutionary class consciousness, partly because of the divisive effects of

(i)   trade union consciousness;
(ii) cross-cutting divisions of race and sex;
c   the lack of a fully convincing Marxist theory of the role of the state in late capitalism.

What cannot be denied is the continuing relevance of Marxist concepts and modes of analysis to the phenomena of the modern world. To say this, however, is not to accept the view that Marxism *alone* can offer us a complete account of it. Too many shortcomings have appeared in the orthodox Marxist account of capitalist development. Some of these are not simply weaknesses of substantive interpretation and prediction. They suggest that we can only go so far in our understanding of social life by using the method of historical materialism – whatever its many strengths.

We shall return to this point at the end of the following part, which deals with the work of Max Weber. For Weber, with the benefit of writing after Marx, addressed many of the same problems but came, as we shall see, to rather different conclusions.

Part Five: Industrial Society as Disenchantment – Weber and Rationalization

11 Max Weber and the rationalization of the modern world

Of the three major founding fathers of modern sociology, Max Weber's contribution is arguably the most influential. Like Marx, the work of Weber encompasses more than sociology, extending across philosophy, religion, law, economics, politics and history. But unlike Marx, Weber did not produce a coherent doctrine of theories or develop a systematic philosophy of political action. Thus there is no 'Weberism', but a rather loosely integrated set of ideas, clustered around a few major themes, but not organized into a theoretical system. At times this makes Weber's theories seem frustratingly oblique and incomplete.

Furthermore, though Weber's impact on twentieth-century sociology has been immense, it cannot be said that the appropriation of his ideas has always been accompanied by a clear understanding of them. For the English reader there are especially severe problems: translations of his work have been limited and at times very tendentious. A huge literature of Weber criticism has grown up but part of it at least charges Weber with mistakes he did not make and the genuine difficulties in his position are only now being addressed. For this reason we shall concentrate on exposition, again with the warning that our account is to be treated as far from definitive and that a diversity of assessments of Weber is available (for example, Giddens 1971, 1972a; Sahay 1971; Stammler 1971; Runciman 1972; Mommsen 1974; Lewis J. 1975; Parkin 1982).

Like those of any sociological theorist the products of Weber's thought can be regarded as very much the result of a dialectic between the man himself and his intellectual and social *milieux* (see Aron 1964; Hughes H.S. 1959; Outhwaite 1975; Freund 1968, 1978). This is, perhaps, more apparent in the work of Weber than in that of most others. Many of his writings can only be understood in the context of European, and specifically German, society and social thought around the turn of the century. Moreover, his lifetime (1864–1920) spanned a crucial period in German and European political history – the unification of Germany under Bismarck, with the accompanying emergence of the modern German nation state, founded in part upon the extension of Prussian hegemony. Weber also lived through the phenomenal growth of industrialization in Germany, the attempts to create a German empire, and the culmination of great-power rivalry in the cataclysm of World War 1. Before he died Weber had experienced not only the defeat of Germany, but also the failure of the Sparticist Revolution in Berlin in 1918 and the foundation of the Weimar Republic.

As a keen observer and student of German politics Weber was far from immune to the effects of these events. On the contrary, they were to shape many of his ideas and act as a point of departure for his sociological theories. In this chapter, we shall deal with what are arguably the three most important examples: his methodology; his theory of action; and his sociology of power.

The methodology of the social sciences

Already in this book we have had reason to

encounter something of the flavour of German social thought during the nineteenth century – for example, in our consideration of Tönnies and Simmel in Chapter 3 and in Marx's writings on Hegel in *The German Ideology*. The dominant characteristics of the German intellectual tradition during the nineteenth century were an emphasis on the spiritual, a distrust of the material world and a concern with religiosity (see Hughes 1959, Chapter 8). It was a tradition in which it was conventional to set emotion against reason and community sentiment against technological change, and to protest, either explicitly or implicitly, against capitalism as a force which brought about a dehumanizing, rationalized society. In many respects Weber's work marks an attempt to resolve some of these conflicting concerns. His endeavours often constitute attempts to reconcile apparent polar opposites: idealism and the scientific method; political commitment and objectivity in sociology; material interests and religious adherence; democracy and bureaucracy; individualism and structured social action. It is because these dilemmas remain with us today, rather than because of the success of Weber in resolving them, that Weber's work continues to receive so much attention.

These factors provide a basis for understanding Weber's contribution to sociological methodology. As we shall shortly see, Weber was willing to contemplate the possibility of conflicting explanations and theories. Consequently he places a greater emphasis on methodology than, say, Marx. However, Weber's interest in methodology also stemmed from a long-running debate among German social scientists and historians during the last quarter of the nineteenth century, a debate which involved not only 'the ghost of Marx' but also, equally importantly, profound distrust of the models of human behaviour adopted by classical and neo-classical economists (Eldridge 1971a, p. 18). This broadened out into a much deeper philosophical debate between devotees of idealism and positivism, the *Methodenstreit*

as it was called (see Freund 1968, pp. 37–41; Marshall 1982, pp. 24–5). Weber had joined in the *Methodenstreit* after the termination of a long mental illness in 1903. Not all of his essays have been translated but three of them, largely polemical in nature, have appeared under the title *The Methodology of the Social Sciences*. There is no need at this point to consider Weber's methodological writings in very great detail, but it is necessary to give some indications of his approach in order fully to understand not just his methodology but also his more substantive works.

Ever since the work of the eighteenth-century philosopher Immanuel Kant, the German idealistic tradition had established a radical disjunction between the world of man and the world of nature – and thus between the human (or social) and the natural sciences. One corollary of this German idealistic tradition was a view of people as active, purposive, free agents. Because of this it was argued that the social sciences could not proceed in the same way as the natural sciences because the free will of individuals always introduced an element of unpredictability and a capacity to act in a manner that was utterly unique. The minds of people were not subject to natural laws and therefore the so-called *nomothetic* (that is, analytical and generalizing) methods appropriate for the natural sciences were inapplicable. The social sciences must be *ideographic*, that is, particularizing rather than generalizing. In simple terms, they must limit themselves to an *understanding* of human action and of unique historical events. Since human behaviour is guided by choice based upon free will, rather than determined by natural laws, then the creatures of human behaviour, including society itself, can only be understood in terms of the concrete uniqueness of each specific historical case.

Weber's ideas grew out of this tradition, even though he broke with many, if not most, of its main tenets (see Freund 1968, pp. 3–36 for a clear, if occasionally difficult, account of

Weber's 'vision of the world'). Certain consistent themes can therefore be discerned within his work, even though he himself refrained from conferring any unity on it. In order to understand this it is necessary to emphasize four basic factors which informed Weber's approach to the study of society:

Sociology as science

Weber was passionately concerned to establish sociology as an 'objective' social science. (Precisely what he meant by this term we shall see below.) He was outspoken against the practice of using the university classroom as a platform for political propaganda and was equally insistent that political commitments should not be allowed to intrude into scientific research.

Objectivity/subjectivity

At the same time he was aware that attempts to understand the historical development of a society could only be partial and based upon an incomplete state of knowledge. This is because, for Weber, history consists of a literally infinite chain of cause and effect, in which it is only possible to grasp the sum total of the causes of any unique historical event by replicating the whole of the reality which was antecedent to it. Clearly this is impossible and the social scientist must *choose* those factors which are deemed to be most important. The somewhat paradoxical implications which he drew from this are that:

a All social scientific explanations are partial and preliminary and hence the role of theory in sociology is a rather modest one. Whatever method or theory we use can only impose an *order* on reality, not exhaust it. For this reason Weber profoundly suspected all philosophies, theologies and political doctrines which claimed to be able to deduce reality from a set of a priori theories and concepts. Such philosophies, which he called 'emanationist', were, he believed, highly partial despite their ambitious claims on truth. Instead Weber

consistently favoured an *empirical* approach to sociological research and reserved a limited role for theoretical explanation. Furthermore, all theories undergo a more or less radical correction as enquiry proceeds. Objectivity can be ensured only through the greatest possible precision in research method at this point.

b The choice of factors to be given attention will be based upon the theoretical *problems* of the social scientist. What constitutes a problem, however, will in part be a function of the *values* of the social scientist. Hence the selection of a research agenda is value-laden.

Thus to some degree the apparent lack of synthesis in Weber's work was a consequence of his desire for rigorous, meticulous analysis *and* his recognition that every theoretical system, every 'ism' which claims complete validity, is in part a reflection of the point of view of the social scientist. Other, equally valid, theoretical systems can be constructed to oppose them.

Human agency

This tension also prevented Weber from aligning himself wholly with either the 'nomothetic' view – that the social sciences could simply take over the methods of the natural sciences – or with the idealistic tradition in German philosophy. On the one hand, he accepted that nomothetic propositions might be possible in sociology; on the other, they could never constitute a complete account of human *agency*. That is to say Weber does accept the need for a special approach to human behaviour and this separation of facts from values is mirrored in a second parallel distinction which he drew between human will and human knowledge. What this means is that because each person possesses a free will, they can choose the goals they wish to pursue and social science cannot specify in advance what these goals will be.

In their pursuit of a variety of conflicting goals or *ends* through various *means*, lies all that is distinctive and unique about the subjects of the human sciences. First, causal explanation will be incomplete unless we take this characteristic of goal-directedness or *value relevance* into account. That is why 'nomethetic' explanations (that is, general laws in sociology) will be incomplete. Second, however, the hallmark of the freedom of the human will is not, as the idealists claimed, the element of *unpredictability* and irrationality in our behaviour. On the contrary, our actions have the greatest freedom when they are simultaneously at their most predictable: that is, when they are the result of calculated rational *choice*. But, finally, social science cannot specify the choices that people ought to make or the ends that they ought to want. There is, for Weber, no question of sociologists becoming something akin to secular gurus. He wrote:

In our opinion it can never be the task of an empirical science to provide binding norms and ideals from which directions for immediate practical activity can be derived. (Weber 1949, p. 52)

As far as Weber is concerned, not only are the goals of human action always muddled with contradictions but sociologists cannot even predict what, among the various alternatives, the final choice will be.

Sociology's role

Nevertheless, Weber most emphatically does not mean that value judgements either could or should be removed from the sphere of social-scientific discussion altogether. After the passage just cited he continues:

What is the implication of this proposition? It is certainly not that value-judgements are to be withdrawn from scientific discussion in general simply because in the last analysis they rest on certain ideals and are therefore 'subjective' in origin . . . The problem is rather: what is the meaning and purpose of the scientific criticism of ideals and value-judgements? (Weber 1949, p. 52)

The answer is that the sociologist's role is to be a modest one: not telling people what they *should* want or do, but only *informing* them with a better understanding of how they can go about

achieving their goals and especially the unintended consequences of their *means* for achieving them. It is the task of the social sciences to demonstrate what advantages are to be gained by employing one particular means rather than another for the attainment of a desired end and also the costs that are entailed. These costs may be of two kinds:

a The costs involved in the selection of a given means may bring about a partial rather than a complete attainment of the desired end.

b The employment of a given means may entail certain consequences which negatively affect the other goals which may be held by that individual.

We can clarify these rather abstract formulations by citing the example of revolutionary socialism. Weber argued that those who wished to attain the goals of a socialist society by revolutionary means were subject to a series of dilemmas, some of which could bring about a self-defeating course of action. As we shall see in Chapter 12, as early as 1918 he isolated a number of areas where it seemed that the costs of the 'means' employed to create a planned economy would jeopardize the attainment of other socialist goals. As a result of these insights he may be said to have anticipated the nature of developments in Russian society after the Bolshevik Revolution (see Chapter 13).

The substance, then, of Weber's discussion of the nature of objectivity in the social sciences consists of his attempt to dispel the confusions which, in his view, surround the relevance of value judgements. As has already been indicated, Weber does not advocate the elimination of ideals from scientific discussion. It is, in fact, essential for social scientists to be as clear as possible about their own values and ideals and their relevance to their work. As Weber puts it,

An attitude of moral indifference has no connection with scientific objectivity. (Weber 1949, p. 60)

Scientific activity itself, like any other area of

human conduct, rests upon ideals which cannot, any more than any other set of ideals, be validated scientifically. The crucial problem for methodology is to define limits to the intrusion of ideals into scientific analysis so as to avoid the danger of total subjectivity.

These limits can be understood by reference to the term which Weber borrowed from his contemporary, Rickert: *value-orientation*. Value-orientation means that what one investigator with one set of values regards as a problem, another with another set of values might not. For example, Marxists with one particular value-orientation might regard the absence of a revolutionary class consciousness among the proletariat to be a problem which requires explanation; for capitalists themselves, however, it would be the presence rather than the absence of class consciousness which would constitute a problem and they might appeal to various theories of industrial relations in order to explain it.

The term 'value-orientation', though, should not be equated or confused with simple value judgements. It denotes a many-sided notion whose complexity can be grasped reasonably easily by saying that 'value-orientation' is both a limit on social science and the factor which makes it possible. This can be made apparent by defining the term in three ways:

1   *Value-orientation is the a-rational and subjective basis from which all so-called rational enquiry and scientific analysis proceeds*. In this sense, in fact, the scientist's viewpoint can be no more 'objective' or complete than that of the lay person. Weber writes:

There is no absolutely 'objective' scientific analysis of culture or [social planning] independent of special and one-sided viewpoints according to which . . . they are selected, analysed and organised. (Weber 1949, p. 72)

Thus, belief in the value of science itself is part of this *a*-rational core. But beyond that, what sociologists have to do is to *select*, from the infinite range of viewpoints, from which society

might be studied, some problem that is implicitly or explicitly recognized as worth investigating. However:

2   *Value-orientation is also the factor which renders reality, with its inexhaustible sequences of cause and effect, manageable*. The fact that the *social* scientist starts from a selective perspective is therefore not only inevitable but desirable if the work is to begin at all. Indeed each new value-orientation can shed some new light upon empirical reality. This is particularly true over time, when new value-orientations arise out of contemporary societal – not just sociological – problems, so that fresh questions are asked of society itself. Hence to a considerable degree sociological theory can be regarded as the result of an ongoing dialectic between society and the sociologist. The subject matter of sociology is thus forever in a state of flux and this is reflected in the theoretical eclecticism of sociology. As Weber sums it up:

The stream of immeasurable events flows unendingly to eternity. The cultural problems which move men form themselves ever anew and in different colours, and the boundaries of that area in the infinite stream of concrete events which acquires meaning and significance for us, i.e. which becomes an 'historical individual', are constantly subject to change. The intellectual contexts from which it is viewed and scientifically analysed shift. (Weber 1949, p. 72)

3   *Paradoxically enough, therefore, the relevance of a phenomenon for given values offers a means of constructing value-free concepts and explanations in sociology*. As we have said, no sociologist can be altogether value-neutral because ideals determine the problems to be studied. But for this very reason, these ideals can act as the source of theories and explanations which can then be verified, like any other scientific analysis.

However, ideals are an encumbrance to be discarded once sociological research actually commences. This must proceed according to the usual canons of scientific enquiry and its practitioners should refrain from offering value judgement on their subject matter – otherwise the ethical neutrality and objectivity which Weber was so keen to establish for sociology would be violated.

The ingenuity of Weber's argument at this point can only be appreciated fully when placed in the context of his ideas on the exact nature of sociological explanations. These, he believed, involve the confrontation of one's own value-orientation with that of the subject of study – a process involving 'interpretation' and 'rational understanding'. These much misunderstood but very important ideas will require some further explanation.

The sociology of action

On the opening page of what is arguably his greatest work, *Economy and Society*, Weber defines sociology thus:

Sociology (in the sense in which this highly ambiguous word is used here) is a science concerning itself with the interpretative understanding of social action and thereby with a causal explanation of its course and consequences. (Weber 1968, p. 4)

This statement contains an important term which we have not so far discussed: social action (*Soziales Handeln*). For Weber, human action is social:

in so far as the acting individual attaches a subjective meaning to his behaviour – be it overt or covert, omission or acquiescence. Action is 'social' in so far as its subjective meaning takes account of the behaviour of others and is thereby oriented in its course. (Weber 1968)

Mere behaviour becomes *action*, then, (a) when it derives from dealings with others and (b) when it is meaningful, that is, 'oriented in its course'.

Before going further we should stress that sociology is concerned with the study of social action *alone*. Other forms of behaviour – for example, reflex behaviour – are not the proper object of sociological analysis. Behaviour which is meaningless cannot, by definition, be understood: it is by placing meanings on (interpreting) the behaviour of others that we understand it. However, the meaning of an action is *never* self-evident – it *always* requires an interpretation, even if, in our culture, that interpretation is easily forthcoming. This is a fundamental axiom of Weber's interpretative sociology: actions never speak for themselves – they always require 'the placing of meanings'.

But the problem for the sociologist is: how is this subjective meaning to be discovered? We might add that this is not a problem exclusive to sociologists! Attempting to decipher what people mean by their actions is something that we all encounter in our everyday lives and can be a particularly painful experience when we are placed in strange social contexts. The crucial problem is one which Weber called 'inter-subjectivity': how do I know that what *you* mean by your actions and what *I* mean by them are the same? Similarly, how can the sociologist gain access to the meanings which other individuals and groups place on their behaviour? One method is clearly by sheer intuition, but Weber, wishing to establish sociology as an objective science, is strongly opposed to the use of such a dangerously arbitrary principle other than as a source of 'hunches' about possible meanings. Interpretative sociology must be based upon techniques for the interpretation of meaning which are replicable and thus verifiable. This leads Weber to consider whether there is some objective standard of social action against which actual human behaviour can be measured.

Weber argues that there is an objective standard for action and it lies in the notion of human rationality. The concept of rationality is one which is central to Weberian sociology and it is also one to which we shall have cause to return in this and succeeding chapters. Once again, however, we must pause. This time it is to stress that in using rationality as a standard Weber denied that he was himself making a moral judgement about action. It was, he thought, possible to refer to the rationality of action in a way that did not contain the connotations of 'reason' or reasonableness in the manner of Enlightenment philosophers; nor was he talking of the efficiency, morality or desirability of action as judged by some standard of values or progress – to imagine so has been the source of many mistakes.

The whole of Weber's thought, at this point and throughout his work, turns upon distinguishing what he variously called 'formal' or 'technical' rationality from all of these previous meanings, all of which represent examples of 'substantive' (or 'material' or 'subjective') rationality.

1   By *'formal' rationality* he meant calculability. Formally rational action is action which can be *understood* precisely because it is the result of calculation.

We have a perfectly clear understanding of what it means when somebody employs the proposition $2 \times 2 = 4$ or the Pythagorean theorem in reasoning or argument, or when somebody correctly carries out a logical train of reasoning according to our accepted modes of thinking. In the same way we also understand what a person is doing when he tries to achieve certain ends by choosing appropriate means on the basis of the facts of the situation, as experience has accustomed us to interpret them. The interpretation of such rationally purposeful action possesses, for the understanding of the choice of means, the highest degree of verifiable certainty. (Weber 1968, p. 5)

Calculative rationality is thus the rationality of thought rather than of the conduct itself. It can provide a standard for interpretation because it is also the basis of the scientist's own value-orientation and the meaning of his procedures. It is, in effect, equivalent to the notion of 'logical possibility' which is common to the science of action and to the calculation of action itself.

2   Unfortunately most social action is not calculatively rational. At best it contains a degree of *substantive rationality*. That is, it may still involve the relation of means to ends but the means may be an 'adequate' rather than a logical way of attaining the desired result. This is because the action is governed by ultimate ends, values or principles. Weber writes:

Many ultimate ends or values toward which experience shows human action may be oriented often cannot be understood completely, though sometimes we are able to grasp them intellectually. The more radically they differ from our own ultimate values, however, the more difficult it is for us to understand them empathically. (Weber 1968, p. 6)

3   Finally, there is the problem of acts which are 'irrational', that is, involving no calculation, being purely habitual or emotional reactions.

Weber proposes that the best way to handle cases (ii) and (iii) is to treat them as 'factors of deviation from a conceptually pure type of rational action' (Weber 1968). It is easiest to see what he means where irrational elements have interfered with a calculative course of action. Weber gives the example of a stock exchange panic, arguing that we should first work out what a rational response would have been and then compare with the observed 'irrational components'. It is clear from his other writings, however, that Weber also thought that this method would enable sociologists to verify their interpretations in *all* cases where the meaning of action was not directly accessible. This could be achieved by emphasizing a particular point of view – the sociologist's own, or the significance imputed by the sociologist to the conduct of the actors themselves. We can then ask what are the most (calculatively) rational and logically consistent forms likely to follow from this 'point of view'.

The result will be an example of Weber's famous concept of 'pure' or 'ideal-type'.

Weber describes an ideal-type as follows:

An ideal-type is formed by the one-sided accentuation of one or more points of view and by the synthesis of a great many diffuse, discrete, more or less present and occasionally absent concrete individual phenomena, which are arranged according to those one-sidedly emphasised viewpoints into a unified analytical construct. In its conceptual purity, this mental construct cannot be found empirically anywhere in reality. It is a utopia. (Weber 1949, p. 90)

Thus the calculative or logical application of the 'meaning' or 'point of view' behind a course of action allows a causal sequence of actions to be constructed which can be verified empirically. Such an ideal-type is therefore neither a description of some aspect of reality, nor a hypothesis. It is a model – an aid to interpretation and explanation, or, as it is known technically, a 'heuristic device'.

An ideal-type is, of course, *not* ideal in a normative or moral sense – that is, it is not a one-sided accentuation of those traits which are regarded as most desirable; it is 'ideal' only in the sense that it is a mental construct which may exist nowhere in reality, although it helps to illuminate that reality. We shall look at some examples of Weberian 'ideal-types' in the following chapters, but familiar examples from elsewhere might include the economists' notion of 'perfect competition', Wirth's concept of 'urbanism as a way of life' or Marx's notion of 'class consciousness'.

Weber did not claim that he was creating a new approach for social science methodology by introducing the notion of the ideal-type. On the contrary, he argued that this was essentially what social scientists were doing all the time. However, he did believe that by articulating the methodology of the ideal-type more precisely and explicitly he could contribute to a more rigorous approach to sociological analysis. Ideal-types are thus aids to sociological understanding and, by rendering explicit the nature of causes of action, provide an objective basis for the analysis of empirical problems. They are purely methodological tools which the sociologist forges in order to help empirical investigation. If after subjection to a rigorous attempt at verification they do not work, they must be abandoned, for their value is determined solely by their usefulness and effectiveness in research. If they are not useful the sociologist must construct other, more serviceable ideal-types.

Ideal-types then are neither true nor false, merely useful or useless. They are therefore different in both scope and usage from descriptive concepts. The latter simply summarize common or average empirical features, whereas ideal-types involve the processes of abstraction and recombination of certain elements into a model which is *not* the lowest common denominator. Nevertheless it is possible to construct an ideal-type of virtually any sociological process and then, by comparing it with empirical reality, derive testable hypotheses which account for the various deviations. It is in this process of comparison that Weber attempts to bridge the nomothetic and ideographic traditions in the human sciences. Ideal-type analysis becomes, for Weber, the counterpart of the experimental method in the natural sciences. It helps us to understand the particular by relating it to the general while our analysis of the particular also informs our refinement of generalized theories. From the synthesis of the two emerges, hopefully, sociological theory.

Finally, in order to explicate the degree and the manner with which forms of social action are amenable to sociological analysis, Weber presents a fourfold typology of action. He emphasizes that the typology is not exhaustive. On the contrary each category is itself an ideal-type constructed for the purpose in hand. Thus, the four categories are:

1   *Traditional action*. This lies on the boundary between meaningful and non-meaningful action and hence on the margin of what can be explained by interpretative sociology. This is because traditional action is action carried out under the influence of custom or habit. It is frequently a virtually automatic reaction in unconscious obedience to tradition and therefore contains a number of subjectively unintelligible elements. A great deal of everyday action falls into this category, making it difficult to understand from an objective standpoint.

2   *Affective action*. This is the action which is carried out under the sway of some sort of emotional state. As such it is similar to traditional action in being on the borderline between

meaningful and non-meaningful behaviour because it, too, contains some instinctive, unconscious or unintelligible elements which only psychology or psychoanalysis can explain. Affective action is characterized by the fact that action is not carried out as a means to an end, but as an end in itself and purely for its own sake.

3 *Wertrational* or *rational value-oriented action*. Value-oriented action is distinguished by the fact that the individual is guided solely by an overriding ideal. The value-oriented actor adheres to a religious, political or other cause and takes no account of other relevant considerations. It is none the less *rational* action because it involves the setting of coherent objectives to which the actor orients his or her activities. However, it contains certain irrational elements because it elevates one particular goal over all others and takes no account of the consequences which action taken in the pursuit of a set of objectives may have on the attainment of those goals themselves.

4 *Zweckrational* or *rational goal-oriented action*. This is the most rational type of action for Weber. Here the individual rationally calculates the probable result of a given act on the attainment of a particular goal. Due consideration is given to the appropriate means and full account is taken of the foreseeable consequences which may conflict with the line of action decided upon. Rational goal-oriented conduct is thus the type of action which is most susceptible to sociological understanding. Because it is clearly articulated in terms of a means–ends schema it is the type of action most easily analysed by the methods of interpretative sociology. Thus *zweckrational* action involves individuals constructing their own ideal-type in the form of a calculated, predictive plan. This plan will be the result of having assessed the various means to achieve the required ends and having selected the most suitable means as a course of action. The sociologist is also able to construct an ideal-type of such rational action but has the advantage of being able to employ

hindsight and thus judging the actor's achievements. The construction of this ideal-type enables the sociologist to:

a evaluate the effect of the intervention of irrational elements in the actor's conduct;
b assess the extent to which it was these irrational elements which impaired the actor's accomplishments or whether this was due to a misunderstanding of the situation by the actor;
c measure the deviation between the actual course of conduct and its subjective interpretation by the actor(s) involved.

Weber's typology of social action was not designed to be applied only to individual forms of conduct. For Weber, whole societies could be characterized by the typical forms of action to be contained within them. Thus modern industrial societies, for example, were characterized by a tendency towards rational goal-oriented (*zweckrational*) action – a process which Weber called 'rationalization'. Progressive rationalization had in fact been occurring throughout history and the process, once it had occurred, was irreversible. Once again, however, Weber is at pains to stress that this does not mean any kind of moral judgement or evolutionary 'progress'. Furthermore:

increasing intellectualisation and rationalisation do not . . . indicate an increased and general knowledge of the conditions under which one lives. It means something else, namely, the knowledge or belief that *if one but wished* [our italics] one could learn it at any time. (Weber 1948, p. 139)

In industrial society this process had reached new levels and the result was 'disenchantment', that is, the loss of magical and religious belief in favour of the calculative outlook:

It means there are no mysterious incalculable forces that come into play but rather that one can, in principle, master all things by calculation. (Weber 1948, p. 139)

The following two chapters will look at particular aspects of the rationalization of Western culture. In order, however, fully to appreciate Weber's own value-orientation behind the concern with these topics, we must first turn to another celebrated aspect of his general sociology: the understanding of power.

Weber's sociology of power

Once again the best standpoint from which to view Weber's ideas is that of the milieu within which he wrote. This time, however, we are concerned with a very specific aspect of it: the coming of industrialization to Germany. For Marx, the society which had provided the principal exemplar of capitalist industrialization was Britain. In this case, the new form of society had been the spontaneous achievement of a powerful bourgeois *class* acting through the extension of the market economy. Germany presented Weber with a totally different example, one which Thorstein Veblen was to call a 'borrowing culture' (Veblen 1939). In Germany the bourgeois class remained small and uninfluential; industrialization was the achievement of representatives of a landed nobility acting to maintain its traditional privilege and power through the Prussian unification of the German state (Giddens 1972a, pp. 28–39; Mommsen 1974, pp. 22–46). In the end the German economy developed into a form that was to all intents capitalist; but it was a capitalism achieved through state 'planning' and administration and by the industrialization of the armaments-related industries rather than textiles, as in the British case (cf. Chapter 2).

Thus for Weber there could be no question of seeing history as a succession of class struggles. For him, outcomes which appeared similar because of one's value-orientation could be achieved in divergent ways, many of which were unique. Consequently, a battery of concepts would be needed for their understanding. The only common denominator in history was the struggle for power (*Macht*) which Weber characteristically defines in terms of the will to action and its meaning:

the probability that one actor . . . will be in a position to carry out his own will despite resistance, regardless of the basis on which this probability rests. (Weber 1968, p 53)

The point about such a definition of power is that it deliberately conceives it as 'socially amorphous' (Weber 1968), that is, without content. Before we can apply it to particular cases, therefore, it is necessary to consider ideal-typical forms of (a) the distribution of power and (b) legitimate domination.

The distribution of power

In Marx's writings, all power depends in the last instance on possession of economic resources. Where power is unequally distributed, therefore, all power groupings take the form of *classes* in conflict. Weber greatly complicates the kind of groupings which are possible by distinguishing between *classes, status groups* and *parties*, all of which, he states, are 'phenomena of the distribution of power'.

Class

Class refers to 'the typical probability of enjoying material and social benefits as a result of control over goods and skills and hence benefiting from the fact that these things can be used to produce an income within a given economic order' (Weber 1968, p. 312). Because income presupposes money and fixed values, however, Weber concluded that classes cannot come into existence until the appearance of a market economy and monetary exchange. Subjectively therefore, class is a matter of what *interests* individuals have in common as a result of sharing the same 'market situation'. Weber's use of the term 'market situation' is *not* incompatible with the way Marx uses the term class: the ownership of property (capital) and the ability to command labour power. Both of these capacities can only arise within the context of a market, so that an individual's class is essentially his or her 'market situation'. This in turn confers upon all such individuals within the same class similar 'life-chances' to obtain desired resources.

Nevertheless class is both a narrower and a broader notion for Weber: narrower, because, as we have stated, he wished to emphasize its association with specific historical conditions; broader, because he was sensitive to the different possibilities of establishing power by class means, and because he saw class as a matter of gradations rather than dichotomies stamped by metaphysics upon history (cf. Ossowski 1963, pp. 19–57). Classes can, in principle, be subdivided into

1 *property classes* (*besitzklassen*), deriving their income from possessions;
2 *commercial or 'profit-making' classes* (*erwerbsklassen*), whose income comes from the marketability of goods and services;
3 *social classes*, not in fact defined by source of income at all but as groupings of class situations within which social mobility is 'easy and typical'.

Weber's conception of the social class structure of capitalism resembled the following:

a the dominant entrepreneurial and propertied groups;
b the petty bourgeoisie, who owned property but did not command labour;
c propertyless white-collar workers, technicians and intelligentsia;
d the manual working class (although skill differentials threatened its unity).

These classes are *analytical* categories – it thus follows that many individuals are in the same class, without being aware of it, by sharing the same market situation. Class consciousness arises within the subordinate class, according to Weber, only when the authority of the dominant group is weakened or where the unequal distribution of life-chances comes to be perceived not as an inevitable fact but as something amenable to human will. Class consciousness thus becomes highly developed only when:

1 The class enemy is readily visible and in direct competition for scarce resources. For instance, under capitalism, as Weber points out,

It is not the rentier, the shareholder and the banker who suffer the ill will of the worker, but almost exclusively the manufacturer and the business executives who are the direct opponents in wage conflicts. (Weber 1968, p. 931)

2 Class consciousness also develops where there is a large number of individuals sharing the same class situation.
3 It also arises where communication and assembly are simple to organize – for example, where modern factory production herds large numbers of workers together.
4 Class consciousness also develops where the class in question is provided with leadership – such as from the intelligentsia – which supplies clear and comprehensible goals for action.

Although certain parallels with Marxist and Leninist analysis should be easily apparent, there are no 'contradictory class locations' for Weber.

Status

Status refers to the social (as opposed to the economic) determination of life-chances. It is based upon the distribution of prestige, or what Weber calls 'status honour' – no doubt he had the Prussian nobility in mind. Once again, he rejects the notion that economic phenomena *alone* determine human action, though he recognizes that they are clearly of great importance. Moreover, individuals in a similar class or market situation may be in a quite different 'status situation', which refers to the evaluations which others make of them in terms of prestige or esteem. Status groups, unlike classes, are almost always conscious of their common position – and their differentiation from others. They normally manifest their distinctiveness by adopting a similar 'life style' or pattern of consumption. This also enables them to operate strategies of 'social closure' – that is, they place restrictions on how others may interact with them and erect barriers to entry into the status group. This principle finds its ultimate expression in the case of caste societies, where status based on religious function (and originally the conquest of one race by another) has erected a particularly enduring structure (Weber 1948, pp. 188–90; Srinavas 1962; Dumont 1970). Indeed there is an interesting question, which for lack of space we cannot elaborate here, of whether racial (or ethnic) and gender divisions can be more easily understood as forms of status exclusion than as aspects of class, as other sociologists, both Weberian and Marxist, believe (for example, Rex and Moore 1967; and this book, pp. 158–9).

Weber argued that classes, once they have achieved domination, frequently try to 'usurp' status – that is, redefine the criteria for allocating prestige to their own advantage. In so doing they help to consolidate and legitimate the power they initially gained through economic action. Therefore, empirically, at any particular point in time, class and status hierarchies *tend* to be reasonably consonant, although there are societies and historical periods where this does not apply. Weber also noted that the degree to which status stratification predominates in a society is influenced by the degree of economic stability: during periods of rapid economic transformation or instability class stratification is more prevalent, but in times of economic stability status stratification comes increasingly to the fore.

Parties

Parties differ from both classes and status groups in that they are *rationally organized* for the pursuit of certain goals regarding the distribution of life-chances. But although this means that in principle they might operate in economic terms (as do classes) or in ideal and moral terms (as do status groups) their most likely mode of operation is towards influencing the actions of the state. This is partly because, in the end, questions of power involve the use of physical force and the state is that political structure or grouping which 'successfully upholds a claim to the monopoly of the legitimate use of physical force in the enforcement of its order' (Weber 1968, p. 65). It is also because their rational organization makes them the characteristic form which political activity takes in the modern world. But we must interpret the term loosely because it is clear that what we now call pressure groups are included. Weber believed, in fact, that twentieth-century history would witness the reduction of *all* significant political activity to questions of control of and by the state.

This is why his conceptualizations of the distribution of power reflect a concern with the societal level of analysis and why, too, he was concerned to isolate a separate conception of politics in order to differentiate the state from other dominant institutions such as the medieval church. Political activity, according to Weber, is characterized by the fact that:

a It takes place within a particular territory.

b It involves a form of conduct among those who inhabit this territory which is 'meaningfully oriented' towards some form of authority – whether it is coercive, collective, individual or institutional – which is responsible for maintaining order and which maintains the integrity of the territorial community (or nation state).

c It involves the struggle for domination and legitimacy in a society. The discussion of legitimate domination is, in fact, central to any political sociology.

Domination and legitimacy

There is no guarantee that power will be very great or very permanent if it is based *purely* on physical force, for while it may be effective in the short term it is inherently unstable and therefore has to be constantly reapplied. Thus, it becomes important to achieve *domination* (*Herrschaft* – see Weber 1968, translator's footnote 31, pp. 61–2), that is: 'the probability that a command with a given specific content will be obeyed by a given group of persons' (Weber 1968, p. 53).

How might such obedience come about? Although Weber thinks that it might be a matter of expediency or habit on the part of the subordinates, the most significant case for him was that of legitimacy. The commands issued by the wielders of '*legitimate domination*' or *authority* are not only recognized but accepted as rightful. His threefold typology of the possible basis for such authority has become justly famous.

Traditional authority

This is based upon the belief in the sanctity of age-old rules and powers. In other words, the legitimation of present forms of domination is achieved by reference to the past. In Weber's view there are three kinds of traditional authority:

1   *Gerontology*. This is rule by elders, usually in small tribal or village communities. The elders achieve legitimate power because they are considered to be most steeped in traditional wisdom. They exercise their authority personally and there is no administrative staff.
2   *Patriarchalism*. This occasionally occurs in combination with gerontocracy. Patriarchalism is usually based upon the household unit. The head of the household possesses authority which is transmitted from generation to generation by definite rules of inheritance. Under patriarchalism authority must be exercised in the interests of *all* members of society and thus authority cannot be completely appropriated by the incumbent.
3   *Patrimonialism*. This is similar to patriarchalism and often emerges from it. It is a patriarchal form of domination with the addition of an administrative staff, bound to the patriarch by bonds of personal allegiance. This is the characteristic form of authority among traditional despotic governments. For Weber, the ideal-typical example was the sultanate, although similar forms of authority characterized feudal Europe.

Charismatic authority

In its pure form charismatic authority is, by definition, an extraordinary form of domination. The concept of charisma was given a quite specific meaning by Weber as

a certain quality of an individual personality by virtue of which he is considered extraordinary and treated as endowed with supernatural, superhuman, or at least specifically exceptional powers or qualities. (Weber 1968, pp. 241–2)

Whether the charismatic leader 'really' possesses these extraordinary qualities is, to a certain extent, irrelevant – what is important is that these powers are attributed by the followers. Charismatic authority may arise in any social context and is not limited to specific historical epochs. Consequently charismatic leaders range from religious prophets to modern political leaders and from those who have led movements which have changed the course of history to petty demagogues with a temporary following. In all cases legitimacy is granted on the basis of the followers' belief in their leader's mission.

There is, by definition, no administrative organization involved in the exercise of charismatic authority. Instead there may be a group of intimates who bathe in the reflected glory of the charismatic leader. Indeed – there are no fixed principles around which charismatic authority is built – its whole basis is innovative and unpredictable. It creates or demands new obligations and represents a radical break with the established order. As Weber states:

Within the sphere of its claims charismatic authority rejects the past, and is in this sense specifically revolutionary. (Weber 1968, p. 245)

Charisma, then, is a potentially revolutionary force, capable of driving away the ossified administrations of other forms of domination. For Weber it represents a driving force of social change in human history, but it represents also a strictly *irrational* phenomenon since it in no way deals with the calculation of means and ends. Indeed outbreaks of charismatic domination may occur in reaction to the rationalizing tendencies of the modern world.

Charismatic forms of authority are, however, unstable if not mercurial. They are beset by the insoluble problem of 'routinization'. Because charismatic authority is so revolutionary it is inherently opposed to routine, yet if it is to survive in the long term it must establish a degree of permanence and stability with which elements of routine are inherently associated. One particular problem concerns the 'succession crisis' which accompanies the death of a charismatic leader (and, despite their claims to the contrary, this fate has overtaken all of them). Should the son (or daughter) of the charismatic leader take over, then this becomes a form of traditional authority; if an administrative apparatus is set up in the leader's name, then this is a form of rational-legal authority (see below). Thus charismatic authority eventually reverts to one or the other forms. Although temporary, it can nevertheless be decisively influential.

Rational-legal authority

Weber regarded the growth of rational-legal forms of authority as being a major aspect in the rationalization of the modern world. We spoke above of the progressive disenchantment, the resort to intellectualization and calculation discernible in history. It is a development with important consequences for systems whose legitimacy had hitherto rested on traditional, magical or religious elements. It implies a shift in the beliefs upon which legitimacy rests so that authority itself becomes 'rational': that is, a calculated means of achieving domination or the functional integrity of a society or organization. This, in turn, Weber thought, depends upon:

1   A legal code which claims the obedience of all members of the society or organization.

2   A logically consistent system of abstract rules which are applied to particular cases.

3   The typical person in authority occupies an 'office', which defines his or her responsibilities. This person is also subject to the impersonal regulation of the law.

4   The person obeying authority does so only by virtue of his or her membership of the corporate group (that is, not on any personal basis) and *what* is obeyed is the law (rather than the person in authority).

5   An administrative staff (that is, a bureaucracy) is formally charged with looking after the interests of the corporate body within the limits of the law.

Thus it is law, its precise demands and its administration which encapsulate the element of calculation in rational-legal authority.

Weber considered that the emergence of the Western form of capitalism had given an immense stimulus to rational-legal authority and the calculative attitude. In the next two chapters we shall be developing various aspects of this idea. First, we shall consider Weber's exploration of the historical links between religion and the formally rational spirit of capitalism. And in Chapter 13 we shall consider the consequences of rational-legal authority. For Weber believed that once they were established, the advance of rational-legal authority and bureaucracy would be inexorable.

12 Weber and the origins of capitalism

As we have seen in the previous chapter, Weber's sociological writings were developed in the context of an ongoing intellectual debate in the German social sciences and history concerning the proper conduct of social-scientific enquiry. This debate was tied up with a more substantive set of enquiries into the origins of capitalism, partly influenced by the work of Marx, but affected also by the phase of rapid industrialization in Germany in the latter half of the nineteenth century. Weber entered this debate in 1904 with the publication of his essay, *The Protestant Ethic and the Spirit of Capitalism*, drawing attention to an affinity between certain religous beliefs which had flourished since the Reformation and a rationalistic economic ethic which embodied the 'spirit' of capitalism. Weber was not the first scholar to point to such a possible connection – and he was by no means the last. Indeed 'the Weber thesis', as it is sometimes rather misleadingly called, is at the centre of one of the greatest and certainly longest-running intellectual debates of the twentieth century, still going strong over ninety years after its inception. (The best commentary on this debate is Marshall 1982; but see also Green 1972; Marshall 1980.)

Weber's thesis is often presented as a direct refutation of Marx's analysis of the origins of capitalism, offering an idealistic theory in opposition to Marx's materialistic account (see, for example, Weber 1948). This is a gross oversimplification. Weber was *not* trying to 'refute' Marx. He viewed Marx's theory as an ideal-type rather than as a fully causal analysis, but he wished to add to this ideal-type rather than

refute it. As Weber put it,

It is not our aim to substitute for a one-sided materialistic interpretation an equally one-sided spiritualistic causal interpretation of culture and of history. (Weber 1968, p. 91)

Weber was simply trying to treat 'only one side of the causal chain' in a manner analogous to Marx. Marx had run the causal sequence in one direction – *from* economic *to* ideological factors – whereas Weber wished to run it in the opposite direction in a manner complementary to Marx's analysis. As we pointed out in the previous chapter, Weber believed that all explanations in the social sciences were partial ones. Although historical reality could not be fully understood without replicating it, nevertheless it was possible to approach this reality by combining a number of alternative causal sequences of the kind that both he and Marx were elaborating. Thus, as Weber remarked, both his and Marx's analysis were 'equally possible'.

Weber, however, reserved rather more vitriol for those followers of Marx who, he believed, had vulgarized Marx's historical materialism and turned it into a crude economic determinism. One reason for writing *The Protestant Ethic and the Spirit of Capitalism* seems to have been a riposte against such economically deterministic accounts of the origins of capitalism. Weber was therefore concerned to avoid the accusation of offering an equally reductionist, if completely obverse, argument (see Weber 1978, where he defends himself against such accusations). He did not, therefore, wish to argue that

Protestantism 'caused' the rise of capitalism. Weber was quite clear about this:

We have no intention whatever of maintaining such a foolish and doctrinaire thesis as that the spirit of capitalism . . . could only have arisen as the result of certain effects of the Reformation, or even that capitalism as an economic system is a creation of the Reformation. . . . On the contrary, we only wish to ascertain whether and to what extent religious forces have taken part in the qualitative formation and the quantitative expansion of that spirit over the world, and what concrete aspects of our capitalistic culture can be traced to them. In view of the tremendous confusion of the interdependent influences among the material basis, the forms of social and political organisation, and the ideas current in the time of the Reformation, we can only proceed by investigating whether and at what points certain correlations between the forms of religious belief and practical ethics can be worked out. At the same time we shall as far as possible clarify the manner and the general *direction* in which, by virtue of those relationships, the religious movements have influenced the development of material culture. (Weber 1930, pp. 91–2)

This is Weber's clearest statement of his aims. He was *not* trying to chart a simple causal sequence. He was *not* arguing that capitalism was caused by the rise of Protestantism. He *was* attempting the much more complex task of outlining what he called the 'elective affinity' between Protestantism and certain elements in the culture of capitalism – the large unconscious similarities between early Protestant sects, principally Calvinism, and the required cultural stimuli for early capitalist development.

It is, nevertheless, easy to understand how Weber's thesis has been so consistently misinterpreted. It bears an ambivalent relationship with his other works on major world religions which can look like a controlled historical experiment on the origins of capitalism using the comparative method. Moreover, taken as a whole, his writings on the origins of capitalism show distinct ambiguities. There is a noticeable shift between his essay on the Protestant ethic and his later lectures (collected together as

General Economic History). As Marshall has shown, there are in effect two theses:

The foremost problem is one of specifying the origins of a particular orientation to economic activities. His proposed solution identifies these in the ethical and doctrinal principles of an earlier belief-system. However, behind the overt thesis about the relationship between the Protestant ethic and the spirit of capitalism lies a further thesis which is carried largely by assumption, namely, the proposition that the spirit of modern capitalism was one of a number of factors that were causally effective in the development of modern western capitalism. The new 'spirit' was a necessary, though not sufficient, condition for the new economic system. (Marshall 1982, p. 67)

We shall look at each of these theses in turn – the first, and narrower, one the link between the Protestant ethic and the spirit of capitalism, and the second, broader, thesis concerning the origins of capitalism itself.

The Protestant ethic and the spirit of capitalism

Weber begins the first chapter to *The Protestant Ethic and the Spirit of Capitalism* with a statement of his problem. Why is it, he asks, that in contemporary Europe,

business leaders and owners of capital, as well as the higher grades of skilled labour, and even more the higher technically and commercially trained personnel of modern enterprises, are overwhelmingly Protestant? (Weber 1930, p. 35)

This is something, Weber argues, which is not specific to contemporary Europe, but is also a historical fact. Throughout most of Europe the more freedom that capitalism had had to develop its own mechanisms of allocating individuals to the occupational structure, the more clearly is this effect shown.

There is one explanation for this phenomenon – subsequently disputed if not refuted by historians – which seems plausible, but which Weber dismisses. This is that the abandonment of traditional, pre-capitalist forms of economic organization was accompanied by an abandonment of tradition in other areas of social life – in particular, the overthrow of traditional religious institutions and affiliations. But, Weber, argues, this explanation does not stand up to further examination. The Reformation did not weaken the control of the church over everyday affairs. In fact, if anything, it increased it. Protestantism demanded a much greater degree of regulation of economic behaviour by the individual adherent than Catholicism had hitherto required. Protestantism, for example, adopted a very strict attitude towards consumption, which had to be sober and modest. Relaxation and hedonistic enjoyment were heavily circumscribed. Weber concluded, therefore, that the full understanding of the connection between Protestantism and the spirit of capitalism must lie in the particular *content* of Protestant beliefs rather than in the changing role of religious activity in economic and social life. Weber then isolates an anomaly in these beliefs, an anomaly which represents the theoretical problem which prompts his analysis. The anomaly is this: how was it that a form of economic activity (capitalism) devoted to material gain, and to which religious beliefs appear either irrelevant or even opposed, connected with a religious belief which openly abhorred material gain for its own sake and which, moreover, penetrated more than before into the everyday lives of its adherents? In other words, how can a form of social and economic organization explicitly devoted to the 'material' be connected with a religion which is fundamentally concerned with the 'immaterial' or the 'spiritual'? And – to put it in a way which echoes Weber's theoretical concerns – how can the rationalization of economic life which is characteristic of modern capitalism be connected with apparently irrational value commitments?

Weber was well aware of the fact that capitalism was not a product of early-modern European civilization. Capitalism had existed in an embryonic form in Babylonian, Ancient Chinese, Indian and Roman society, but what was peculiar to Europe were the elements of rationalization which underlay the development of modern capitalism. It was the development of rational goal-oriented (*zweckrational*) behaviour which particularly concerned Weber. For this reason he was interested not so much in capitalist organization, as was, say, Marx, but in what he called the *spirit* of capitalism, of which rationalization was the keynote. The second chapter of *The Protestant Ethic and the Spirit of Capitalism* is thus devoted to describing this dependent variable.

The spirit of capitalism is not simply greed for wealth. Many traditional societies exhibited this:

Absolute and conscious ruthlessness in acquisition has often stood in direct and close connection with the strictest conformity to tradition. (Weber 1930, p. 58)

What is distinctive about modern capitalism is not this pursuit of personal gain, but *the disciplined obligation of work as a duty*. It is this which represents the true spirit of capitalism. Weber describes the principal features as follows:

The acquisition of more and more money, combined with the strict avoidance of all spontaneous enjoyment . . . is thought of so purely as an end in itself, that *vis-à-vis* the happiness of, or utility to, the particular individual, it appears as quite transcendental and wholly irrational. Man is dominated by acquisition as the purpose of his life; acquisition is no longer a means to the end of satisfying his material needs. The reversal of what we might call the 'natural' situation, completely senseless from an unprejudiced standpoint, is evidently as definitely a leading principle of capitalism as it is foreign to all peoples not under capitalistic influence. (Weber 1930, p. 53)

The 'spirit of capitalism' is thus an ultimately irrational value commitment. The point, however, is that it becomes a goal around which capitalist economic activity is rationally organized. For Weber the spirit of capitalism consists of a unique combination of devotion to the accumulation of wealth and the denial of its use for personal enjoyment. The solution to this apparent paradox is to be found in the affinity between the spirit of capitalism and the content of early Protestant beliefs. In particular, Weber pays close attention to the notion of '*the calling*' which became part of Protestant theology at the time of the Reformation.

In order to understand the significance of 'the calling' it is necessary to break off for a moment from Weber's Protestant ethic thesis and refer to his general sociology of religion. Specifically we need to outline two concepts which Weber formulated in his analysis of religious activity – asceticism and mysticism.

1   Asceticism consists of the consciousness that God directs religious activity, so that the believers feel themselves to be the instruments of divine will. It consists of two forms:

a   'This-worldly' asceticism, where individuals not only feel themselves to be the instruments of God's will, but seek to glorify God's name through performing 'good works' in the world. Here success in the world becomes a sign of divine approval.

b   'Other-worldly' asceticism, where the individuals renounce the world so that they may be of service to God alone, as in the case of certain monastic orders.

2   Mysticism consists of a consciousness, not so much of being an instrument of God, but of what Weber calls a 'vessel' of God. Here there is no longer any question of engaging in worldly activities. Instead religious activity is a question of achieving a condition akin to the divine. This is accomplished through pure contemplation, an extraordinary concentration on truths other than those which can be demonstrated in this world.

Religious asceticism and mysticism are clearly opposed to each other. To the ascetic, especially the this-worldly ascetic, mystical contemplation is a form of indolence and self-indulgence, unproductive from a religious standpoint and to be condemned as idolatrous pleasure-seeking. Instead the true objective of religious activity is to fulfil the calling of God by working for the greater glory of His name and by seeking to carry out His will. To the mystic, on the other hand, the ascetic dooms himself or herself to useless conflicts, tensions and compromises by participating in the secular world, the result of which is a separation from God.

It is apparent from this brief outline that Protestantism, and particularly the early sects such as Calvinism, represents an almost archetypal form of religious asceticism. The significance of 'the calling', then, is that it serves to bring into the mundane affairs of everyday life the pursuit of the greater glory of God. The calling of the individual is to fulfil his or her duty to God through the moral conduct of daily life. Life becomes *organized* around the pursuit of this goal. The Reformation therefore played the essential role, according to Weber, of placing the dutiful pursuit of everyday activities at the centre of an individual's life. Weber picks out four early Protestant sects as being of greatest importance in this – Calvinism, Pietism, Baptism and Methodism.

It was Calvinism which Weber believed to be particularly significant although he was concerned not so much with the preachings of Calvin himself as with the elements of Calvin's thought that were incorporated into Calvinist teachings during the late sixteenth and seventeenth centuries. There were four elements of the Calvinist ethic which Weber believed were important in contributing to the spirit of capitalism:

1   The first element is one which we have already considered: the idea that the world is created for the greater glory of God and only has meaning in relation to God's purposes. As Weber puts it:

God does not exist for men, but men for the sake of God. (Weber 1930, pp. 102–3)

2   Because of this, religion has an all-embracing influence on the individual believer's life. It

therefore confers a degree of coherence and systematization to life – aspects which are a precondition of rationalization. (It was the emphasis on this systematization from which Methodism drew its name.)

3   The third important element is the principle that 'God moves in mysterious ways' – that the motives of the Almighty are beyond human comprehension.

4   The fourth element is predestination. Only a small number of believers are chosen to achieve eternal grace. But. because God moves in mysterious ways *no one knows who they are.* Their fate is predestined, but at the same time unascertainable. The consequence of this, according to Weber, is 'an unprecedented inner loneliness'. As he remarks:

In what was for the man of the age of the Reformation the most decisive concern of his life, his eternal salvation, he was forced to follow his path alone to meet a destiny which had been decreed for him from eternity. (Weber 1930, p. 104)

And because God moved in mysterious ways no one, not even a priest, could tell him what his fate would be – hence the elimination of almost all holy ritual:

There was not only no marginal means of attaining the grace of God for those to whom God had decided to deny it, but no means whatsoever. (Weber 1930, p. 105)

The enormous psychological strain to which this exposed the Calvinist believer is obvious. To the unanswerable question, 'Am I one of the chosen?', two responses emerged:

a   The first was that the individual believer should deem it obligatory that he or she was one of the chosen. Any niggling element of doubt was to admit a lack of faith and therefore a lack of grace. This helps to explain the strength of the religious dogmatism of these early Protestant sects.

b   The second response was a belief in 'God helps those who help themselves'. The necessary self-confidence in being one of the chosen could be created through the performance of good works for the greater glory of God. This, of course, was not a way of *attaining* grace, for this could only be achieved by the will of God. Rather, the performance of good works as a duty in one's calling could, if they resulted in material success, hopefully be taken as a sign of grace – although in the last analysis this must remain a hope rather than an expectation.

Thus labour in the material world is given the highest possible evaluation. Wealth itself does not guarantee salvation, but the accumulation of wealth is a symbol of the ascetic pursuit of duty in a calling. Hence it is something to be approved of, but it must under no account be used for idle luxury. Instead it must be used for the performance of further 'good works'.

The relevance of this 'Protestant ethic' to the spirit of capitalism lies in the rationalization of action which it introduces. All aspects of everyday life become a means to an end – the greater glory of God. Indeed, everyday life is organized on just such a basis and hence becomes goal-oriented behaviour. The orientation to wealth and consumption also has an affinity with the necessity to defer gratification by the reinvestment of profits – an important component of the early stages of capitalist accumulation. Weber is careful to disclaim, however, that the Protestant ethic is a necessary component of the functioning of capitalism itself – there is merely an affinity with the 'spirit' of capitalism, the cultural ethos of a capitalist society. Still less is the Protestant ethic necessary for the functioning of twentieth-century capitalism. The divine guidance of Protestant doctrine is increasingly replaced in modern capitalism by the economic and organizational constraints of the division of labour. The specific conclusion of *The Protestant Ethic and the Spirit of Capitalism* is that while the Calvinist, because of religious faith, deliberately chose to work in a calling, the specialized character of the capitalist division of labour *forces* modern men and women to do so. Today most people do not work as a duty but in order to earn money to exchange for commodities produced by other people. As Weber concludes in a famous passage:

Since asceticism undertook to remodel the world and to work itself out in the world, the external goods of this world have gained an increasing and finally an inexorable power over the lives of men as at no previous period of history. Today its spirit – whether finally, who knows? – has escaped from the cage. But, in any case, victorious capitalism, since it rests on mechanical foundations, needs this support no longer. . . . The idea of duty in one's calling prowls about in our life like the ghost of dead religious beliefs. (Weber 1930, pp. 181–2)

The origins of capitalism

Weber's concluding comments give some indication of why he was so outraged by the charge of idealism. Yet some of his more polemical remarks directed against vulgar Marxists certainly give some basis for this accusation, and at one point he describes his aims as 'a contribution to the manner in which ideas become effective forces in history' (Weber 1930, p. 90). Nevertheless Weber was sufficiently affronted by the charge of idealism to return to the subject of the origins of capitalism on a number of subsequent occasions, most notably in his 'Anti-critical afterword' (Weber 1978); his 'Author's introduction' (written in 1920 to the second edition of his essay and confusingly placed at the beginning of the English translation); and in his final lectures delivered in the winter and spring of 1919–20 and published posthumously in 1923 as *General Economic History* (Weber 1961).

In these writings Weber makes it clear that the spirit of capitalism is only one element in the causal chain which brought about the emergence of a capitalist social order in Europe. He devotes much greater attention to the *institutional* development of capitalism, to which the 'spirit' of capitalism provides merely one, albeit important, component: *calculability* (see Collins 1980a, p. 927):

The rational capitalistic establishment is one with capital accounting, that is, an establishment which determines its income-yielding power by calculation according to the methods of modern book-keeping and the striking of a balance. (Weber 1961, p. 207)

Calculability is important because it enables a methodical and predictable form of productive enterprise to be established, one in which the means to achieving the goal of profitability can be calculated with some precision. This enables often complex productive processes to be planned and routinized. According to Weber, the components of a rationalized capitalism are as follows:

a   private ownership of the means of production;
b   technological progress to the degree that production can be calculated in advance – for example, mechanization or automation;
c   formally free labour;
d   a free market for goods and services;
e   the organization of capitalist producers into joint stock companies;
f   calculable law – that is, a universalistic legal system which applies to everyone and is administered equitably.

These elements form the basis of an ideal-type of modern capitalism, as Weber makes clear in a lengthy passage in *General Economic History* which is worth giving in full:

While capitalism of various forms is met with in all periods of history, the provision of the everyday wants by capitalistic methods is characteristic of the Occident alone and even here has been the inevitable method only since the middle of the nineteenth century. . . .

The most general presupposition for the existence of this present-day capitalism is that of rational capital accounting as the norm for all large industrial undertakings which are concerned with provision for everyday wants. Such accounting involves, again, first, the appropriation of all physical means of production – land, apparatus, machinery, tools, etc., as disposable property of autonomous private industrial enterprises. . . . In the second place, it involves freedom of the market, that is, the absence of irrational limitations on trading in the market. . . . Third, capitalistic accounting presupposes rational technology, that is, one reduced to calculation to the largest possible degree, which implies mechanisation. . . .

The fourth characteristic is that of calculable law. The capitalistic form of industrial organisation, if it is to operate rationally, must be able to depend upon calculable adjudication and administration. . . . The fifth measure is free labour. Persons must be present who are not only legally in the position, but are also economically compelled, to sell their labour on the market without restriction. It is in contradiction to the essence of capitalism, and the development of capitalism is impossible, if such a propertyless stratum is absent, a class compelled to sell its labour services to live; and is likewise impossible if only unfree labour is at hand. . . . The sixth and final condition is the commercialisation of economic life. By this we mean the general use of commercial instruments to represent share rights in the enterprise, and also in property ownership. . . .

It is a widespread error that the increase of population is to be included as a really crucial agent in the evolution of western capitalism. . . . Nor can the inflow of precious metals be regarded . . . as the primary cause of the appearance of capitalism. . . . In the last resort the factor which produced capitalism is the rational permanent enterprise, rational accounting, rational technology and rational law, but again not these alone. Necessary complementary factors were the rational spirit, the rationalisation of the conduct of life in general, and a rationalistic economic ethic. (Weber 1961, pp. 275–8, 352–4)

This represents a fairly conventional account of the institutional foundations of capitalism according to the precepts of neo-classical economics. As Collins points out:

He sees the market as providing the maximum amount of calculability for the individual entrepreneur. Goods, labour, and capital flow continuously to the areas of maximal return; at the same time, competition in all markets reduces costs to their minimum. Thus prices serve to summarise all the necessary information about the optimal allocation of resources for maximising profit; on this basis entrepreneurs can most reliably make calculations for long-term production of large amounts of goods. (Collins 1980, p. 928)

Collins also argues that Weber's account of the rise of capitalism in Europe is best considered as a causal chain, as in Figure 3. In the left-hand column are the main components of rationalized capitalism. Two sets of intermediate conditions are responsible for this complex of institutions: a legal system which acts as a buffer between the bureaucratic state and the organization of capitalist economic activity; and the 'spirit' of capitalism that Weber's Protestant ethic thesis was devoted to explicating. Weber traces one causal chain back through the organization of the bureaucratic state to *its* preconditions which he set out in *Economy and Society* (see Chapter 12). The other is traced back to the early theological influences upon the religious transformation of the Reformation. Weber also interposes the notion of citizenship as a set of political rights (originally: membership in a city) which incorporates a formalistic legal code.

It is apparent that this represents a complex set of influences which are to some degree *ad hoc*. They do not add up to any grand theoretical design concerning the origins of capitalism. Indeed many of the 'ultimate conditions' are dealt with as 'just-so' historical facts. Certainly this is a long way from some of the more 'teleological' (Marshall 1981) interpretations of Weber's work, most notably that of Parsons (1969), which purport to discern in Weber's work a common underlying theme. It is apparent, however, that Weber is not offering a systematic *theory* of capitalist development (in terms of 'rationalization' or any other such factor) so much as a theoretically suggestive historical description of a unique event, which depended upon the conjunction of a series of combinations of conditions. In this sense, Weber sees the origins of capitalism as lying in a unique, almost fortuitous, combination of factors which *then* produced the transformations with which we are all familiar. Rationalization is the major vehicle through which these transformations were wrought rather than an *explanation* of these transformations. In the last analysis, therefore, Weber's writings on the origins of

Figure 3 *The Weberian causal chain*

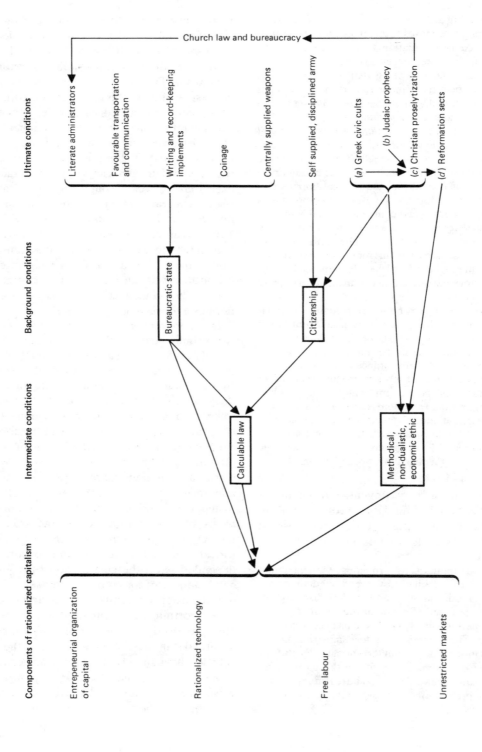

After Collins 1980.

capitalism turn out to be markedly ideographic. Their weakness lies not so much in their idealism, but in their essentially untestable quality. As Weber himself admitted, his analysis is 'equally possible', but it is not clear upon what grounds we can arbitrate between his thesis and that of other writers on the topic.

13   Bureaucracy, democratic politics and socialism

Bureaucracy is frequently regarded as an endemic problem of modern industrial societies. Few observers nowadays accept the growth of bureaucratic forms of administration and government uncritically – indeed the term 'bureaucracy' frequently carries a perjorative connotation. Bureaucracy has been bitterly criticized by political activists on both the Right and the Left of the political spectrum, where on the one hand it is viewed as hindering the freedom of the individual in the market economy and on the other hand as being the key factor which has undermined attempts to create genuinely socialist societies. 'Bureaucracy' has thus become a widely used term of abuse for administration. Nevertheless, the *form* of organization and administration which the term conjures up seems to be a permanent feature of advanced industrial societies. Not surprisingly, therefore, there has been a great deal of discussion in sociology as to whether all such societies, whatever their formal political allegiance, are destined to become dominated by bureaucratic forms of decision-making.

In raising such a question we prepare the way for a more complex and pessimistic version of the theory of Industrial Society which we first encountered in Chapter 6. Max Weber's writings on bureaucracy provide crucial reading in this respect, for they contain a sober appraisal of the prospects for both capitalism *and* socialism in the face of the common threat posed by the advance of technical and administrative *expertise*. In order to appreciate their significance, however, some brief remarks on the history of the concept are required.

The word 'bureaucracy' itself came into European thought about the middle of the eighteenth century and like so many sociological concepts was very much a product of the democratic and industrial revolutions of Western Europe. Yet in the course of the next hundred years or so, as Albrow explains in his excellent introduction to the subject, it came to acquire conflicting meanings, standing for both:

a   a form of government where power is in the hands of officials; and
b   a collective designation for those officials (Albrow 1970, pp. 20–31).

Even today, the word 'bureaucracy' on its own designates a *form* of administration or government; whereas 'the' or 'a' bureaucracy usually refers to a type of administrative unit, a body of officials. On this basic distinction, as Albrow demonstrates, the English tradition of writing has diverged markedly from the Continental – especially the German – tradition. In the former case, especially via the writings of Thomas Carlyle and J. S. Mill, bureaucracy stood for a form of government that should be *contrasted* with the democracy contained in the British constitution. As such, 'bureaucracy' was held to possess two principal flaws: (*a*) concentration of political talent within a class of ruling officials would greatly reduce the possibility of criticism and hence was inherently undemocratic; (*b*) the prevalence of 'red tape' would mean inefficient government. Even though the civil service reforms of the 1870s introduced a measure of continental-style bureaucracy to Britain, the prevailing view remained that good government was the province of the gifted amateur and not of the administrative expert.

In Germany, by contrast, the idea of bureaucracy was intimately connected with the sweeping reforms carried out by Stein and Hardenburg in Prussia following the defeat by Napoleon in 1806. Stein could be said to be the founder of modern bureaucracy by his insistence on the *science* of administration. He castigated France and England for having 'absolutely no science of the State. This is precisely what puts the German genius so high above that of other nations, that we are striving to possess such a science' (cited by Albrow 1970, p. 27). In Germany, then, bureaucracy came to mean administrative *efficiency*, unlike in England where it meant administrative *inefficiency*.

It has been usual among English-speaking sociologists to locate Weber firmly in the German tradition, as admirer of bureaucracy and advocate of its efficiency. This is not quite correct, even though his personal value-orientation to the subject is constructed out of somewhat paradoxical elements. Thus he found it possible simultaneously (*a*) to admire bureaucracy as an intellectual accomplishment, comparing it with the triumph of mechanical over non-mechanical methods of production; (*b*) to regard the advance of bureaucracy in modern capitalist society as inevitable; (*c*) to fear for the encroachment of bureaucracy on individual and national freedom.

That Weber was by no means an unqualified admirer of bureaucracy, however, is indicated by the following passage:

Once it is fully established, bureaucracy is among those social structures which are among the hardest to destroy . . . and where the bureaucratization of administration has been completely carried through, a form of power relation is established that is practically unshatterable. . . . After all, bureaucracy strives merely to level those powers that stand in its way and in those areas that, in the individual case, it seeks to occupy. We must remember this fact – which we have encountered several times and which we shall have to

discuss repeatedly: that 'democracy' as such is opposed to the 'rule' of bureaucracy. (Weber 1968, pp. 987ff.)

The fact is that Weber managed to absorb elements of both the English and the Continental traditions into a wholly new *interpretation* of bureaucracy that, in the end, transcends them both.

Since Weber is often accused of failing to define bureaucracy and of leaving his theory unrelated to his interpretative sociology, it is important to stress that there is, in fact, a direct link both with his methodological writings and his interpretation of power, domination and legitimacy. That link is the concept of *rationality*. Weber describes bureaucracy as 'formally the most rational means of exercising authority over human beings' (Weber 1968, p. 223). Readers who have followed our account of Weber's 'sociology of action' in Chapter 11 should be clear that this has nothing to do with any claim that bureaucracy is necessarily more *efficient*. Unfortunately neither Weber's translators nor his critics have succeeded in keeping the two notions separate (cf. Albrow 1970, pp. 61–6). Yet to conflate 'rationality' and 'efficiency' would be to offend against Weber's view that science cannot arbitrate on questions of value and should not make value judgements about outcomes.

'Rationality' used as a description of bureaucracy refers to the amount of calculation and logical thought used in carrying out administrative duties. Thus it is just like the use of 'rationality' as a value-neutral standard for the interpretation of action which we encountered in Chapter 11. Once again Weber is talking about *formal* and not substantive rationality. In the economic (and administrative) context:

a '*Formal rationality* designates the extent of quantitative calculation or accounting which is technically possible and which is actually applied' (Weber 1968, p. 85) in reaching decisions.

b '*Substantive*' rationality is 'full of

ambiguities' and, in effect, relates to social action guided by 'some criterion (past, present or potential) of ultimate values, regardless of the nature of these ends'. (Weber 1968)

Needless to say it is *formal* rationality which is the distinguishing mark of modern 'bureaucratic' systems of administration. As Albrow notes:

Formal rationality might be realized in either norms or techniques. But even technical formal rationality did not amount to efficiency. Certainly it implied calculability, predictability and stability, but techniques were not in themselves sufficient to achieve the purposes of an organisation. (Albrow 1970, p. 64)

On the contrary, technique 'could even conflict with (substantive) rationality'. (Albrow 1970, p. 65)

The context in which bureaucracy becomes relevant, of course, is that of the rise of rational legal authority and the qualitative transformation of administrative tasks which results from it. We saw that the use of law as the basis of legitimacy greatly expands the calculative element in the administration of authority. This led Weber to formulate eight propositions about the structure of rational-legal authority systems:

1   There is a continuous organization of official functions bound by written rules.
2   These tasks are divided into functionally distinct spheres – which Weber called 'administrative organs' – each furnished with the requisite authority and sanctions.
3   The organization of offices follows the principle of hierarchy – that is, each lower office is under the control and supervision of a higher one. The rights of control and complaint between one office and another are clearly specified.
4   The rules according to which work is conducted are either technical (that is, instrumental or relating to the means adopted by the organization to achieve its ends) or legal. Only a person who has demonstrated an adequate technical training is qualified to be a member of the administrative staff of such a group and only such persons are eligible for appointment.
5   The resources of the organization are quite distinct from those of the members of the organization as private individuals.
6   Administrative actions, decisions and rules are formulated and recorded in writing. The combination of written documents and a continuous organization of official functions constitutes the 'office' which is the central focus of all types of modern corporate action.
7   Such rational-legal authority systems may take many forms, but are seen at their purest in a bureaucratic administrative staff.

The last proposition is particularly important. It shows that Weber was aware that these principles applied to other forms of administration (which Weber also discussed, although more superficially), but that bureaucracy was the most *rational* form of administration because it most closely embodied the *calculated* construction of an organization to achieve the ends laid down in the code from which its members draw their authority. Thus Weber draws up a further list of the characteristics of a rational bureaucracy:

1   The staff members are personally free, observing only the impersonal duties of their offices.
2   They are organized in a clearly defined hierachy of offices.
3   The functions of the offices are clearly specified.
4   The office is filled by an individual on the basis of a free contractual relationship. Thus, in principle, there is free selection of office holders.
5   Candidates for office are selected on the basis of technical qualifications. In the most rational case this is tested by examination or guaranteed by diplomas certifying technical training or both. They are appointed, not elected.
6   Office holders are remunerated by fixed salaries in money, with a right to pensions. The

salary scale is primarily graded according to rank in the hierarchy. The official is always free to resign and under certain circumstances his or her position may also be terminated.

7   The official's post is his or her sole, or major, occupation.

8   The official's occupation constitutes a career. There is a system of promotion according to seniority or achievement or both. Promotion is dependent upon the judgement of superiors.

9   The official may appropriate neither the post nor the resources that accompany it. Thus the official is entirely separated from the ownership of the means of administration.

10   The official is subject to strict and systematic discipline and control in the conduct of the office. The discharge of duties is to be 'sine ira et studio' that is, proceeding impartially in terms of 'cases' *without regard for persons*.

These ten features constitute Weber's ideal-type bureaucracy. It is bureaucratic organization in this form which represented the most rational form of administration because it was methodical and predictable, producing a routinized form of administration based upon practical means–ends calculations and expertise in technical matters.

Since, as we shall shortly see, Weber had some critical things to say about socialism, it is important to emphasize that his view of capitalism is equally harsh and bleak. It is the capitalist market, not bureaucracy, which encourages the impersonal calculative attitude in the first place. 'Without regard for persons' is 'the watchword of the market and in general of all pursuits of naked economic interests.' (Weber 1968, p. 975) But the very large modern capitalistic enterprises are themselves strict models of bureaucratic organization because business management throughout rests upon increasing precision, steadiness and above all, speed of operations. Thus, capitalism by itself is quite capable of enmeshing humanity in a network of formal rationality that lacks overall direction.

Nevertheless, it was the *political* expressions of formal rationality that in his view presented the gravest threat to freedom. The reason lay in the growth of the bureaucratic adminstration of rational-legal domination within the state itself and one aspect of it in particular: the inherent tendency of bureaucracy to accumulate power by its ability to exercise a *monopoly over knowledge* (Mommsen 1974). As a democrat, Weber feared the consequences of bureaucratization, leading to a despondent pessimism over the future of liberal democracy which Gouldner (1965) calls 'metaphysical pathos'. For while the very rationality of bureaucracy demanded that the administrative apparatus should function like a smoothly running and precisely maintained machine, this in itself could contribute not only to the attenuation of popular democratic control but also to the dehumanization of modern society. The process of rationalization, as embodied in bureaucratic forms of control, would form an invisible 'iron cage' constraining the free will of the individual. Weber uses a familiar German metaphor to describe his gloomy prognostication – society as a machine, in which the human spirit (*Geist*) has been rationalized out of existence. The ultimate expression of this possibility was the 'Administrative Secret' – the tendency of bureaucratic administration to exclude or manipulate the public, especially those most affected by the outcome of its machinations. Novels such as Kafka's *The Castle* and Heller's *Catch* 22 represent literary testimonies to the validity of Weber's point.

His fears were exacerbated by his knowledge that the rationality of bureaucracy left little alternative – indeed, the idea of eliminating the bureaucratic organs of capitalism becomes ever more utopian. If its functions are interrupted by force the result is chaos (Weber 1968, pp. 987–8). The only ways in which the scope of bureaucratic authority could be limited and democratic control maintained would involve introducing an element of *substantive* rationality (that is, considerations of particular values) which might reduce the effectiveness of decision-making in the short run and only serve to increase the domination of bureaucratic *formal* rationality in the long run. To some extent this possibility is built in to the very idea of democracy itself with its stress upon *equality before the law*. The paradoxical corollary of this substantive principle must be the formulation of impartial rules and administration 'without regard to persons' – in a word, *bureaucracy*. (For an empirical illustration of this outcome in the context of Australian society see the important study by Encel 1970, pp. 49–78).

Nevertheless, Weber did attempt to sketch some mechanisms whereby some kind of popular control over bureaucratic authority could be retained. These were:

1   *Collegiality*. Here, while bureaucrats would retain their responsibility for decision-making, any questions which demand some form of executive action would first be placed before a collegial body. This would, however, reduce the speed of decision-making.

2   *Separation of powers*. With an eye to the constitution of the United States, Weber suggested that bureaucratic hierarchies might be functionally divided rather than contained within a single organization. For any decision to emerge, a compromise or accommodation would then have to be reached based upon collective rather than sectional interests.

3   *Amateur administration*. Frequent turnover to bureaucratic personnel would prevent bureaucrats from becoming an administrative caste beyond democratic control.

4   *Direct democracy*. Officials should be guided by, or answerable to, a popular assembly. Various other devices could be introduced such as short-term tenure of office, selection by lot and the permanent possibility of recall.

5   *Representation*. Officials could be directly appointed by the people, usually through the aegis of political parties (which are themselves, however, bureaucracies).

In each of these cases there would be a reduction in the rational organization of bureaucracies – expertise would be reduced, routines would be disrupted, decision-making would be slowed down, and so on. Weber was trying to show, however, that a balance had to be struck between the threat to democracy which the growth of bureaucracy entailed and the functional necessity of rational forms of administration in large-scale complex and advanced industrial societies.

Weber left open the question of what the outcome of the confrontation between these conflicting value-orientations might be, though it is clear that his 'metaphysical pathos' left little room for optimism. And he warns:

Where administration has been completely bureaucratised the resulting system of domination is *completely indestructible* (Weber 1968, p. 987)

and will work for anyone who can get control of it.

The question we now have to ask, therefore, is how far events since Weber's death have born out this pessimism and the theory underlying it. As with our discussion of Marxism, we shall begin with developments in contemporary Western societies. But in order to deal properly with the problem it will also be necessary to broaden our comparative focus to include the socialist industrial states that have arisen during this period.

The dysfunctions of Western bureaucracies

Not surprisingly, Weber's writings on bureaucracy have subsequently been the subject of considerable criticism and elaboration. Predictably, much of the criticism of Weber has come from the direction of those writers who subscribe to the contemporary equivalent of what, earlier in this chapter, we called the 'English tradition' on bureaucracy: the American Functionalist School (see also Chapter 15). There has been, as we noted, a tendency to portray Weber as advocating bureaucracy as the most efficient form of administration and to proceed from this to an easy demolition of such a notion on the basis of documenting the many manifest inefficiencies (or dysfunctions) of bureaucracy (for example, Selznick 1943; Parsons in his introduction to Weber 1947). As we have also seen, this criticism is misplaced. True, Weber *does* talk about the efficiency of bureaucracy in places but this is always in terms of a very strict historical comparison with the personal and patrimonial systems of administration to be found in the more complex forms of traditional authority. Compared with these, modern bureaucratic efficiency is a *by-product* of its rationality and arises with specific reference to the effective maintenance of domination (see also Weber's parenthesis, 1968, pp. 974–5).

Nevertheless, the work of those who, since Weber, have drawn attention to the 'dysfunctions' or inefficiencies of Weber's ideal-type has contained some important empirical material in its own right, making an important contribution to industrial sociology and to the specialized area of social science known today as Organization Theory (Etzioni 1961, 1965; Mouzelis 1967; Perrow 1972; Salaman 1979). If we set aside the issue of 'efficiency', these studies have shown Weber to be vulnerable on two grounds:

a the inseparable empirical connection he asserted between modern administration and hierarchical organization;
b his lack of attention to the actual activities of bureaucrats.

How far do these potential weaknesses in the theory undermine his dread of the inexorable advance of rational-legal bureaucracy in the form in which he described it?

Empirical features of the ideal-type

The problem here is whether Weber's ideal-type would in practice find its *formal* rationality (its calculativeness) impaired by inflexibility, so that modern administration does not *necessarily* attempt to achieve its goals in the manner

described. For example, the French sociologist Michel Crozier, in his book *The Bureaucratic Phenomenon* (1964), argues that it is essential for modern forms of administration to be flexible and adaptable in relation to technological changes and continuing social development (cf. Burns 1969). Both Crozier and Peter Blau (in his book *The Dynamics of Bureaucracy*, 1963) seek to construct alternative ideal-types to that of Weber by asking what, in a given situation, would constitute rational administration and then, on the basis of empirical case studies, go on to compare their answers to this question with Weber's. Blau, for example, takes two examples of bureaucracy – the American federal law enforcement agency (the FBI) and a state employment agency. In each case he concentrates on the ways in which formal regulations are implemented. In the case of the employment agency Blau discovered that groups of officials who circumvented the formal regulations and co-operated with each other on an informal basis, though no less *calculative* or *logical*, achieved a higher rate of success than those who adhered to the rules. Blau's investigation of the FBI (principally the section dealing with business embezzlement and fraud) showed that those officers who persistently infringed the rules achieved higher success rates in the enforcement of the law. Blau concludes that bureaucracy is often too inflexible to be a rational form of administration.

An equally famous example is *Patterns of Industrial Bureaucracy* by A. Gouldner (1954). This is a detailed case study of the consequences of the tightening up of supervision and discipline with a gypsum mine subjected to a take-over by a larger corporation. The result of the managerial *putsch* was to create a system of *punishment-centred* rules. Not only did this result in 'inefficient' administration of the plant but it introduced an element of irrationality into relations between workers and management increasing the perceived need for disciplinary rules themselves and leading in the end to industrial conflict (Gouldner 1955). Both Blau and

Gouldner conclude that the most rational (that is, stable and calculable) administrative rules will contain some element of discretion and representation (see also Burns and Stalker 1961).

All that can be said in Weber's defence on this point is that in general both the extent and the formal rationality of modern administration *has* increased not decreased over the years and that too wide a departure from the accountability and responsibility of subordinates to superior authority, especially in the political sphere, is unlikely to be tolerated. Indeed, in the latter case giving discretion to officials might have the effect of making them even less accountable to the public than where they *must* subscribe to formal rules!

Bureaucracy in practice

The foregoing examples nevertheless show that there is a hiatus in Weber's theory. That is, he may have been aware of the inefficiencies of bureaucracy but he never felt it necessary to ask how a formal organization would be interpreted, both by its officials and its clients. When one considers the nature of Weber's interpretative sociology it seems odd, to say the least, that the actual activities of bureaucrats were merely implied by reference to the defining characteristics of the organizational structure of bureaucracies. One result was an important ambiguity in his conception of the expert knowledge within bureaucracy. That is, expertise may consist of general knowledge possessed by professional experts which the organization makes use of to carry out its tasks – for example, scientists, accountants, lawyers or it may consist of the specialist knowledge of the particular administrative processes that comes from long service in one organization. Subsequent empirical work has shown this to be an important source of conflict *within* organizations. Again, however, in Weber's defence, it must be said that it is the 'line' officials or management who usually seem to manage to prevail over the

'professionals' because the latter's loyalties principally lie outside the bureaucracy.

Furthermore, in what is arguably the most famous essay in sociology on the meaning of officialdom to the official, Merton brings out the element of so-called 'goal displacement' which results from the pressure upon individuals for precision and accountability in their actions. He argues that the tendency in such a context is for strategies of personal survival to displace the official purposes of the decision-making process (Merton 1968c). An analogous 'goal displacement' process was observed by Selznick in a study which showed how the ostensibly democratic managerial philosophy of the Tennessee Valley Authority was 'taken over' by particular departments of its bureaucracy. Doing so enabled them to ward off encroachment from both higher authority as well as from sectors of the community (particularly the black members of it) and to advance their own interests (Selznick 1966). As Albrow notes (1970, pp. 64, 133, fn. 51) these studies, offered in criticism of Weber, in fact bear out the one 'dysfunction' which he certainly did not neglect – 'that the most perfect formal system might operate to defeat the purposes and values which animated it. This was of course implicit in his recognition that bureaucrats might arrogate the highest positions in the state for themselves.' (Albrow 1970)

We shall now consider this possibility directly. That the capitalist society of Western Europe and North America might be falling into the hands of a bureaucratic class has formed the subject of speculative work from Weber's time onward. An early example was G. Mosca in *The Ruling Class*, published before Weber's work on bureaucracy. Mosca argued that all societies are inevitably divided into a ruling minority and the majority who are powerless (Mosca 1960; cf. Meisel 1962; Bottomore 1964). In the (modern) bureaucratic state power falls into the hands of a body of salaried officials and hence society as a whole could be characterized as bureaucratic in nature. Mosca's analysis concentrated on governmental bureaucracies but subsequent commentators have drawn attention to the growing interpenetration of private bureaucracies – especially large-scale industrial bureaucracies – and government administration. The theme of such work is that bureaucratic interpenetration permits a 'managerial revolution' (Burnham 1945); or the rise of a 'technostructure' (Galbraith 1967) to occur.

The alleged tendency of modern capitalism to move in the direction of interpenetration or 'corporatism' as it is now called has also stimulated empirical work in recent years on the extent to which the state now plans and directs the allocation of resources and rewards within the broad framework of capitalism, leaving conventional mechanisms of the market as a façade or a 'peripheral' part of the economy (for example, Winkler 1976; Crouch 1977). The authors of these empirical studies are, for the most part, content to detail and record an empirical trend without implying that 'corporatism' is inevitable. Others detect a slide into some form of more or less benign totalitarianism (Marcuse 1964; Moore B. 1969; Habermas 1975); but even so, the appropriateness of Weber's 'metaphysical pathos' remains one of those issues which are probably too grandiose to settle definitively – except by observing whether people are still allowed to write books on the subject!

The notion that society *should* be run as one large bureaucracy is, in fact, totalitarian in origin – its most eloquent exponent having been Benito Mussolini. The attempt to construct a 'corporate state', rationally planned around an assumed organic identity of interests, hierarchically organized and obedient to rules laid down by a leader who was the embodiment of society's destiny, was a common feature of Fascist regimes in the inter-war period. And, according to some twentieth-century Marxist writers, Fascism is the inevitable outcome of the contradictions in those capitalist societies which have managed to postpone the inevitable

revolution into the indefinite future (see, for example, Sweezy 1956, pp. 329–47).

There is a curious irony here. For the trajectory taken by the avowedly Marxist regimes in Russia, Eastern Europe and elsewhere has raised exactly the same issues: the role of bureaucracy in an industrial economy; and whether, as some claim, the unique circumstances in which these regimes came into being has affected their subsequent evolution; or whether, as Weber thought, domination by a bureaucratic class is the inevitable consequence of a planned economy.

Marx himself had very little to say on the concept of bureaucracy, using the term only to describe the administrative apparatus of the state. Since the state itself was conceived as being nothing more than the form of organization which the ruling class necessarily adopts in order to pursue its interests, then the bureaucracy could only be the agency of class domination. Bureaucrats in themselves had no autonomous basis for their power, merely exercising the power of the ruling class on its behalf. Albrow (1970) suggests that Marx's lack of concern for bureaucracy stems from his reluctance to admit that any basis for bureaucratic domination was possible unless it could be assimilated into his overall conception of the state as being founded on class relations and personal possession of the means of production. As we shall see (pp. 200–7) this problem has become crucial in the debate with and among Marxist scholars about the nature of contemporary Marxist states.

The problems of the Bolshevik model of revolution – capture of state power by an organized party of professional revolutionaries – had certainly been anticipated. For example, in his book *Political Parties* (1962), Weber's contemporary Robert Michels offered what has become the classic analysis of 'goal displacement' among organizations of the Left, as a result of the professionalization and acquisition of expertise by the leadership. Michels's famous 'iron law of oligarchy' ('who says organization, says oligarchy') is really a statement that organization, instead of being merely a means to an end, such as socialism, becomes an end in itself. Thus, for officials in the German trade unions and the Social Democratic Party the possibility of loss of office implied return to the kinds of occupations pursued by the rank and file, and hence loss of power, status and, usually, income. Furthermore, the actual activity of leadership, maintaining organizational viability, forced different perspectives and values upon the leadership, as against the rank and file. Thus organization had created and reinforced conservatism and opportunism in the running of organizations formally committed to radical social change.

Although Weber did not accept all of Michels's assumptions, he was undoubtedly impressed by his arguments. Writing in 1918, he predicted that the Bolshevik Revolution of the previous year would be likely to evolve towards a form of totalitarian bureaucratic domination by the victorious party. He based his argument in the following grounds:

1   Revolutionary socialism involves the establishment of a socialist society by the use of force. But the application of force must necessarily involve political repression after the revolution in order to secure the desired social changes. This, however, will negate some of the freedoms which are embodied in the very ideal of socialism itself.

2   The construction of a socialist economy in a predominantly capitalist world is likely to entail a series of economic difficulties which are neither accounted for nor desired by socialists. Attempts to cope with these economic difficulties will bring about a diminution of socialist organization.

3   Third, according to Weber whatever the means whereby a socialist society comes into being, the result will almost certainly contravene socialist ideals by creating a *bureaucratic* state out of the necessity to create a rationally planned socialism. Indeed, the abolition of the property-owning entrepreneurial class will remove the one group which has managed so far to resist the total domination of society by bureaucratic knowledge.

Weber's admirers regard the third point as the most prescient of his comments on socialism. But is bureaucratization inherent in socialism? And is it accurate to characterize state socialist society as 'totalitarian bureaucratic domination'? Both issues have been extensively discussed since and no more than in the recent past. In the process, a welter of alternative descriptions have been coined including 'degenerate workers' state', 'state capitalism', 'totalitarian state capitalism', 'rational redistribution', 'bureaucratic collectivism' . . . to name but a few. Below we can only give a brief indication of the important analytical and empirical issues which lie beneath this war of concepts.

Class and legitimacy under state socialism

From the very early days of Bolshevism in the Soviet Union, the phenomenon of bureaucracy provided an apparently intractable problem. Lenin – whose theory of the state and the bureaucratic apparatus actually concurs in several respects with that of Weber (see Wright E. O. 1978, pp. 204–7) – believed that rational organization was necessary in order to seize power. Lenin termed bureaucracy 'the organizational principle of revolutionary social democracy', through whose agency the new socialist order could be constructed. His admiration for the bureaucratic state soon attracted vehement criticism, however. Rosa Luxemburg quarrelled directly with Lenin, accusing him, in what was to become a common criticism, of enslaving the workers to an intellectual élite.

Lenin attempted to answer many of his critics in *The State and the Revolution*, published in 1917. His recipe was for workers' deputies to supervise the administration of the state apparatus. These deputies were to be elected and subject to recall and their pay was not to exceed that of a worker. By this means, Lenin hoped, everyone might become a bureaucrat and therefore the bureaucracy would not become a privileged caste. These proposals were, however, undermined. Lenin himself was partly responsible by introducing formally rational ('scientific') management techniques in order to boost productivity in Soviet factories. With the advent of Stalin a wholesale and rapid centralization of power occurred and in the process the remnants of the Leninist system of controls, along with other possible sources of localized power, were swept away.

The emergence of bureaucratic domination in the wake of a socialist revolution led Marxists outside the Soviet Union to ponder on what had gone wrong. How could a purportedly socialist revolution have produced a society in which some of the most basic tenets of socialism appeared to have been overthrown? The answer to this question was made more difficult by adopting a literal interpretation of Marx's own categories of analysis. If societies were to be understood by means of a class analysis and if the class structure was determined by the ownership of the means of production, how then was the Soviet Union, which had abolished the private ownership of the means of production and thus eliminated social classes, to be explained without significantly departing from a Marxist analysis?

One of the first to tackle the problem was Trotsky in *The Revolution Betrayed* (1937), and in his *History of the Russian Revolution* (1934) Trotsky's argument was that, for a mixture of historical and political reasons, the Bolshevik Revolution had not succeeded in establishing socialism in the Soviet Union. The first step, the appropriation of the privately owned means of production, had been achieved, but a socialist political order had not been created. Instead an embryonic workers' state had *degenerated* into a form of state-run capitalism. Within this structure the bureaucracy had emerged as a privileged and commanding stratum taking on the values of the bourgeoisie without possessing the

latter's ownership of the means of production. This outcome is transitory, the result of trying to build socialism in one country, against an imperialist world economy and from a feudal base (that is, bypassing the capitalist mode of production). But the degeneration into state capitalism should not be seen as an inherent result of the socialist experiment itself.

In this fashion, a whole brand of (mostly Western) Marxist analyses have managed to remain faithful to the historical materialist tradition by introducing 'special factors' to account for the rise of 'state capitalism' in Bolshevik Russia (arguably the most distinguished example is Cliff 1964).

During the 1950s, especially in the wake of the Hungarian uprising in 1956, the interpretation of Soviet society (and by extension the other Communist regimes in Eastern Europe) became once more the subject of intense debate not least among East European intellectuals. The most influential account was that of the Yugoslav writer, Milovan Djilas, whose book *The New Class* (1957) offered a candid appraisal of the relationship between bureaucracy and the dominant political order in Eastern Europe. The 'new class' of Djilas's title is the Party bureaucracy which, though it does not own state property, uses, controls and disposes of it. Apart from its critical overtones, this theme offended orthodoxy in two directions:

a the power of the 'new class' was ascribed to its total ideological control and its monopoly of political force rather than to material factors in the conventional sense;

b bureaucratic state domination is *not* just a transitory staging post between capitalism and socialism but permanent and *inherent* in all of the communist systems of Eastern Europe.

The respective writings of Trotsky and Djilas represent ideal-type alternatives for understanding so-called 'existing' socialist societies (Bahro 1978). Either one appeals to special 'distorting' factors in Russian, European or world history, or one concludes that centralization of power is inherent in the very idea of a planned economy and even in Marxism itself. In recent years, however, both types of explanation have been called upon within the same analysis, even though to at least one author the result is 'paradoxical' (Vajda 1981, p. 108). This tendency is most apparent in the work of a number of East European dissidents, many of them now expelled to the West, including R. Bahro (East Germany), M. Hirszowicz (Poland) and a Hungarian 'school' influenced by the work of the twentieth-century Marxist, G. Lukacs (cf. Boella 1979). Lukacs was at one time a student of Max Weber and in the works to which we refer there is a remarkable tendency, explicitly or implicitly, to introduce Weberian-style hypotheses and evidence into the analysis.

First, then, there are the various special distorting factors which must be considered due to the fact that the first Marxist state was founded in Russia. It was not possible to reproduce here the details of the arguments which have been deployed with or without reference to Trotsky but they include the following suggestions:

1 The Bolsheviks in government were constrained by the absorption by the Bolshevik party of organizational tendencies already evident in the West European workers' movement. Thus, the elitist ideas of Lenin were quite compatible with the oligarchic tendencies noted by Michels and others (Bahro 1978; cf. Vajda 1981, pp. 107ff.).

2 The relative backwardness of Russian society in the period leading up to the Revolution promoted homogeneity and a will to power among the revolutionary intelligentsia. Their counterparts in West Europe by contrast were increasingly distracted and divided by the conflicting market pressures of capitalism. The absence of such pressures in Russia meant that intellectuals were a relatively homogeneous group ready to occupy a leading political role (Konrad and Szelenyi 1979).

3 The traditions and social forms inherited from pre-revolutionary Russia carried over into the post-revolutionary situation and so made the emergence of a centralized autocratic regime highly probable. Although these traditions and forms include religious and political differences from Western Europe, the main legacy was the so-called 'Asiatic mode of production'. This was the economic and command system of traditional despotisms originating in Asia whose influence spread westward as far as Eastern Europe. For present purposes its main feature was the dominance of a military nobility which functioned as an all-powerful tax-collecting bureaucracy. Thus the revolution merely introduced a change from a system of 'traditional redistribution' to one of 'rational redistribution' under the Bolsheviks. (Marx had struggled with difficulty to incorporate 'Asiatic mode of production' into his theory of class struggles – a thought that is not congenial to 'official' Marxism–Leninism.) (Konrad and Szelenyi 1979)

4 Observers from Lenin onward have noted that the Prussian model of state-induced industrialization (see p. 178) tended to recur throughout Eastern Europe in marked contrast to the spontaneous growth of capitalism in Britain, the United States and elsewhere. (Konrad and Szelenyi 1979; Hirszowicz 1980)

Factors such as these indicate a marked difference between the pre-industrial social history of today's communist states and that of Britain and America. Furthermore, they introduce considerations which are reminiscent of many themes to be found in the work of Max Weber, ones which had underlain his rejection of dogmatic historical materialism and which stimulated his original concern with bureaucracy.

The most 'Weberian' aspect of the recent work we are considering, however, lies in its recognition of the pervasive role of power relations in social life. As Vajda notes this must lead to a 'profound revision of Marxism' (1981, p. 66). In fact, the revision amounts to a recognition that Marx grossly simplified the forms which power relations can take and the ease with which power inequalities can be ended simply by abolishing private property. This revision has 'cleared the ground' of too literal an adherence to the assumptions of official Marxism. It has enabled the authors in question to bring their 'insider' knowledge of existing socialism to bear on the key question of whether and in what way centralizing and bureaucratic tendencies of state socialism are inherent in the system itself?

Much of this 'revision' of course recalls Weber's own gloss on Marxism and we shall find it convenient to employ his approach in summarizing recent work on the power structure of Soviet and East European society.

Class and the distribution of power under state socialism

Despite the difficulties of working from the official statistics of existing socialist societies, it is generally accepted by Western scholars that a considerable degree of inequality is to be found in them. True, the abolition of private property has meant that the stark differences in ownership of capital found in Western society do not exist. Nevertheless, there remain substantial inequalities in the distribution of income between town and country; and between workers and peasants on the one hand and the intelligentsia (as they are officially described) and other non-manual employees on the other. Some writers point out that the gradient is not as steep as in Western societies, particularly the USA. Lane has even claimed that this difference between socialist and non-socialist societies is an indication that 'rewards on the American level are not "necessary" to the maintenance of modern economy' (Lane 1971, p. 74). From more recent studies, however, it has emerged that the question of income does not exhaust all aspects of inequality. Examination of the official income distribution has to be supplemented by a consideration of the administrative privileges enjoyed by party bureaucrats. At the very least it is also necessary to

include favoured access to apartments and housing not easily available to the ordinary citizen, together with perks and payments in kind available through the contacts of party members, particularly cars and other consumer durables. Finally, there are said to be opportunities for (a) profits from direct or indirect market transactions (b) embezzlements, 'corruption' and illegal deals including opportunities for benefiting from a substantial black market (Matthews 1972; Yanowitch 1977; Zukin 1978; Zaslavsky 1979; Hirszowicz 1980, pp. 87–126).

In addition to material inequalities, a number of other non-monetary benefits have to be considered of which arguably the most important is access to the education system – because qualification is a key element in occupational recruitment (if not *absolute* as Konrad and Szelenyi claim; 1979, pp. 24–38). Research suggests that there is a preponderance in higher education of children from the homes of party officials and elite professional groups. A crucial factor seems to be the amount of money spent by better-off cadres on expensive *private* tuition for examinations. This has clear implications for social mobility so that despite the absence of direct inheritance, the better-off cadres are self-recruiting to a considerable degree. However, the evidence here is conflicting; some authors claim that the situation in this respect is worsening, others that Soviet society at least is becoming more open (cf. Yanowitch 1977, Chapter 3; Zaslavsky 1979; Hirszowicz 1980).

How is the persistence of inequality in societies which have abolished private property to be explained? Is it valid to follow Djilas and refer to the intellectuals and party functionaries as a *class*; and if so, how? The official explanation of such inequalities as these regimes will admit to is that the inequality reflects the presence of 'non-antagonistic' classes in socialist society, preparatory to the realization of full communism. The writings of their sociologists have reflected this explanation by falling back on a utilitarian or functionalist account of the need for different skills to be rewarded (for example, Wesolowski

1969). Recent, more critical, writings are divided on the question. For present purposes the most interesting (and influential) accounts are those which lean in a Weberian direction. Konrad and Szelenyi argue, for example, that a class does exist in state socialism in Weber's sense of 'a position which derives from the relative control over goods and skills and from their income producing uses within a given economic order' (1979, p. 302). All we need to do is relax Weber's insistence that such a situation could only arise with a system of free markets, because obviously the planned monetary economy of existing socialism is quite capable of producing unequal opportunities for the control of goods and services. For the authors the class which results is one which is able to enjoy a form of 'collective' ownership. This they do by virtue of the bureaucratic knowledge and expertise which they possess in their capacity as 'rational' redistributors of the surplus product of the worker's state. Konrad and Szelenyi argue that if we maintain Weber's identification of classes with market conditions 'then we must abandon the use of the concept of class in dealing with socialist societies' (1979, p. 45).

This is the alternative favoured by Hirszowicz. Her solution has the merit of both simplicity and accord with everyday ideas about Soviet and Eastern European regimes. For her, existing socialist society is not a class society but a *party* state. Weber, it will be remembered, included 'parties' among his list of 'phenomena of the distribution of power' and predicted that they would rise in importance in modern times owing to their rational organization aimed at influencing or capturing the activity of the state. Hirszowicz shows how the dominant position of the bureaucratic intelligentsia is paralleled by domination within the party organization. The resulting system of stratification is the product of

an organizational society whose complexity of horizontal and vertical division is perhaps comparable to a large-scale company with its many branches, divisions, chains of command, and departments . . . etc. . . . all of which intersect formal boundaries. Inequality is characteristic of such a system but whether these are conflicts whose origins are to be sought elsewhere, is another question (Ossowski 1963, pp. 100–3). (Hirszowicz 1980, p. 94).

This analysis assumes, of course, that it is possible to explain how 'the mass party is . . . both an instrument of power and its social basis' (Hirszowicz 1980, pp. 100–1). We thus turn to the question of domination and legitimacy.

Party domination and bureaucratic legitimacy

In order to understand the precise mechanisms by which party domination is maintained it becomes necessary to explain how potential opposition is neutralized. Western political scientists have long since become dissatisfied with Cold War descriptions of communist party rule as 'totalitarian'. Such a label leads to an oversimple view of the actual structure of politics in state socialist societies and obscures the process by which policy is formulated, political socialization is achieved and change is effected – as it undoubtedly is. On the other hand, the transposition of concepts such as 'pluralism' or 'corporatism' from the Western political context is not very helpful either. Soviet society is not monolithic – it is 'plural' in the sense that it is made up of diverse nationalities and interest groups. On the other hand, it is not 'pluralistic' in the sense that compromise or mutual accommodation of conflicting interests underlies the political decision-making process. The power of making and enforcing commands (that is, domination) remains with the Party.

There seems to be a fair measure of consensus in recent literature that this domination is due to the operation of a 'sovereign bureaucracy' – or more accurately perhaps 'bureaucratic sovereignty' – in which rational bureaucratic administration is appropriated by the bureaucracy itself as Weber feared.

Even so, we should not think of this as deriving from a single bureaucracy permeating society but in terms of the special role of the *Party* bureaucracy as the point of reference for other bureaucracies administering particular functions of state such as the military, government, economic planning and so on. The origins of this form of domination lie with the so-called 'bureaucratic reconstruction' of the Stalin period in which potential opposition within particular arms of government and societal officialdom were coercively crushed. This has since been maintained by a thoroughgoing interpenetration of Party and officialdom at all levels including the local level (Hough 1969). If need be the Party can act as arbiter of the conflicting claims of different sectors or even reconstruct whole servant bureaucracies afresh.

The most pressing questions surrounding such a system arise in connection with the problem of *legitimacy*. Here there has been further room for debate. Konrad and Szelenyi consider that in what they call modern rational redistributive (that is, socialist) systems those who are able to formulate the goals and objectives of the society are also able to control the disposal of the surplus product which the state exacts from its citizens in various ways. 'In order to become one of them an individual must possess specialised knowledge, or in other words must be an intellectual.' (1979, p. 42). Though this is faithful to the spirit of Weber and his writings on bureaucratic formal rationality, Vajda (1981, p. 112) has questioned the accuracy of this account of the basis of *legitimacy*. Legitimacy of the Party in fact rests on its claim to represent the *interests of the workers*.

It is this very issue that Vajda and a number of others see as the weakest link in the chain of party domination. Indeed, Konrad and Szelenyi themselves point out the nature of the economic problem which domination by a sovereign party bureaucracy creates; namely, the tendency for the bureaucracy to place as large a proportion as possible of the national product under its own control, thus expanding the investment goods market over that of consumption. The result is that consumer goods – even basic items like meat – are in constant short supply and the experience of endemic shortage undercuts the claim of the regime to be operating in the interests of the workers (1979, pp. 149ff.: cf. Marczewski 1979). Hirszowicz goes further, claiming that the process of economic growth actually accentuates the shortages because it is 'self-consuming': that is, the positive effects of industrial growth are in varying degrees 'consumed' by the growing needs of the productive and administrative apparatus itself at the expense of the living standards of the population (1980, pp. 159ff.). The problem is exacerbated by the reappearance on a societal level of all of the classic 'dysfunctions' of bureaucracy observed in the West, not least the tendency towards defence mechanisms by bureaucrats. This encourages corruption and inhibits possibilities of real reform.

These problems can be ameliorated in various ways: the claim to be implementing socialism can be maintained by putting 'the end of the road' into the indefinite future; or it can be maintained through the achievement of technically spectacular 'collective' goods – space research and armaments provide the obvious example (cf. Bailes 1978, pp. 409–10). Nevertheless the crisis points, particularly in East European regimes, seem to occur around economic shortages and have to be met either with coercion or decentralization. The recent Polish crisis has provided a working example of this.

Of course, the above remarks are schematic and introductory only. They are no substitute for detailed studies of the particular circumstances of individual Communist states. A particularly important application of this point is Yugoslavia which deliberately decentralized its political structure and established workers' councils in a series of reforms subsequent to its expulsion from the Warsaw pact in 1948 (for example, Blumberg 1968, pp. 168–87). This system has probably received more attention from Western sociologists than any other 'existing' socialist regime, and some optimistic claims have been made about the extent to which it has overcome the defects of a centrally planned economy. More melancholy assessments, however, have concluded that the decentralization of administration has only served to enhance the dominant role of the party, creating a series of 'satrapies' or local bossdoms in place of the single sovereign bureaucracy of centrally planned economies (Benson 1974). It is also maintained that the system of workers' councils interferes with the formal rationality of economic processes in a manner analogous to the 'self-consuming growth' elsewhere (Estrin 1982).

To sum up: in this section we have been considering a body of contemporary work which regards bureaucracy and bureaucratic domination as *inherent* in planned economies. By seeking to identify the means by which the sovereign party bureaucracy maintains its power in socialist society, the authors in question have in effect built upon and rendered more precise Weber's inevitably rather general statements on the subject. Such views, of course, contrast markedly with orthodox Marxist attempts to account for what has happened in the Soviet Union and elsewhere as the consequence of historically specific circumstances. To argue that inegalitarian tendencies are inherent in socialism is to modify greatly the assumptions of Marxist theory. But the themes in Weberian sociology have always represented a commentary of some kind upon the claims of historical materialism.

Epilogue: Marx and Weber compared

It has been an abiding sociological pastime to debate the extent to which Weber's work is an attempt to present an alternative to Marx or whether it merely 'rounds off' what Marx had to say. The numerous references to Marx in Weber's work (particularly *General Economic History*) attest to the seriousness with which Weber approached Marx's work. As we have already indicated in Chapter 11 Weber was as much concerned to correct many of the vulgarizations of Marx's theory as he was to attack the

work of Marx himself. Weber also attempted to clarify some of the customary problems of Marxist analysis, but this is not to deny that there are also many points on which they are opposed:

1   The point which arises most directly out of the material considered in this and preceding chapters is Weber's emphasis on the struggle for power and in particular the growing importance of the state in the modern world. Weber, of course, had the benefit of writing after Marx and indeed many of their differences can be related to the continuing problem of establishing socialism in Germany, which if anything seemed more remote by the time that Weber began to consider such matters than in the recurrent revolutionary crises which beset Europe during Marx's heyday. Not surprisingly this led Weber to re-examine in a critical fashion many of Marx's assumptions concerning future political developments and, as we have seen, to view the concentration of formally rational structures of industrial and bureaucratic domination with pessimism.

2   This in turn brings us to the problem of historical materialism. The relation of Weber to Marx on this point is more complex than has often been assumed. As we pointed out in Chapter 12, materialist accounts of the origins of capitalism in particular are by no means straightforward. Weber certainly rejected 'crude economic determinist arguments' – but then so did Marx. It would even be possible to present the differences between Marx and Weber as rather trivial – Marx arguing that the economic was determinant in the last analysis, Weber denying this while recognizing the importance of such factors – but this would be to overstate the case. The base/superstructure distinction, which is fundamental to Marxism, is regarded by Weber as merely an ideal-type, with other 'equally possible' causal explanations available. Weber's political economy (in so far as it was explicit) was founded upon an essentially neo-classical conception of *competition* for resources in a market, rather than, as in the case

of Marx, contradiction between forces and relations of *production*. Weber did not see any fundamental contradiction in the competitive process: on the contrary he believed capitalism was quite capable of enduring indefinitely as an economic system, notwithstanding the fact that it could be toppled by an organized seizure of political power.

3   Weber was less than convinced that even in periods of capitalist crisis there would be a tendency towards revolutionary socialism. He was sceptical of the idea, implicit in Marx, that social action was a function of economic change in this straightforward manner and he gave some attention to Marx's tendency to elide 'economic', 'economically conditioned' and 'economically relevant' behaviour. Weber also attempted to clarify some of the ambiguity in Marx over 'economic' and 'technological' factors in social change. Weber gives more attention to the elements of calculability consequent upon technological change, enabling production to be further rationalized. Marx, on the other hand, emphasizes the sheer increase in productive power that becomes available.

4   Weber maintained the neo-Kantian disjunction between fact and value – between questions of what is and questions of what ought to be. This leads Weber to adopt a voluntaristic theory of action which insists upon the irreducibility of competing values. Marx's work, on the other hand, involves the commitment to the scientific ethic of 'ultimate ends', the unity of theory and practice and a totalizing conception of history which invests it with a coherent meaning.

5   Obviously, then, there is a fundamental and inescapable conflict in their conception of the social sciences as intellectual disciplines and of what their capabilities are. As we discussed in Chapter 11, Weber was firmly set against any overall systematization of sociology. He placed due weight upon the particularizing as well as the generalizing aspects of the social sciences; and paid much more attention to subjective interpretations of social situations than to the 'objective' characteristics of social structures. He was thus able to be more sensitive to the contingent and elusive nature of consciousness, whether it arose from class interest or some other, than was Marx.

In making these points, we are aware of the numerous objections which have, in turn, been raised against Weber's sociological *weltanschauung* and his methodology in particular. Without making the discussion unduly long we have not been able to refer to most of these. It seems to us that merely presenting and understanding Weber's diffuse and complex writings must suffice for an introductory book. We will, however, conclude by monitoring one critical observation which will, in turn, serve as prologue to the next chapter.

If the strength of Weber's sociology lies in its emphasis on the irreducibly subjective element in social action, it presents us with a problem. This is its tendency to – indeed open acceptance of – what is called *methodological individualism*. In simple terms this means that Weber was willing to treat all social forces and pressures as if they could be explained (or reduced) to the actions and purposes of seemingly isolated individuals. This position has always been vehemently rejected by a large body of social scientists, not all of them by any means committed Marxists (see Lukes 1977). In turning to the work of Emile Durkheim, however, we encounter a scholar whose reputation rests on his sense of the irreducibly *collective* element in meaning, subjectivity and consciousness itself.

Part Six: Industrial Society as Organic Solidarity – Durkheim, the Division of Labour and Moral Science

14   Moral obligation and individual life

In the work of Emile Durkheim we find neither the optimism of Marx, the revolutionary, nor the pessimism of Weber, the despairing liberal. Although he was clearly troubled by the strains and conflicts evident in modern society, Durkheim nevertheless remained convinced for most of his life that grounds for cautious optimism about the future existed. Only the terrible events of World War I, which he did not live to see concluded and in which his son was killed, may have shaken his confidence in scientific reason (Lukes 1975, pp. 402–3). In general, however, Durkheim's name is associated with the view that by the adoption of a rigorous scientific sociology the problems of modern society could be understood and overcome. On this, and indeed many other points, his writings have always been the centre of intense controversy.

Certain details of Durkheim's life are invaluable in the understanding of his sociology. Durkheim lived between 1858 and 1917, almost an exact contemporary of Max Weber. During his youth came the conclusion of a long period of debilitating instability in French political life which commenced with the great French Revolution of 1789, saw the rise of Napoleon and the Napoleonic wars, the restoration of the Bourbon Monarchy, further revolutions in 1830 and 1848 and the *coup d'état* of Napoleon's nephew. Two events of 1870 ended this period; a crushing military defeat by Prussia, and the last brief flowering of the Parisian insurrectionary tradition known as the Paris Commune (which Marx regarded as a true proletarian uprising). The Third Republic, inaugurated in

1871, was to last until the German invasion of 1914. Durkheim, though never really actively engaged in politics, was one of its stalwarts.

The manner in which Durkheim's personal biography meshed with these events does much to explain the political and social perspectives which underlay his intellectual position. The most important are:

Nationalism

Durkheim was born a Jew in the Rhineland province of Alsace which had changed hands between Germany and France during the nineteenth century and was ceded to Prussia in 1870. Durkheim's family had had to choose French nationality as a consequence. He was thus in many ways a 'marginal' member of French society and, like many marginal people, compensated by identifying strongly with his *'reference' group*, that is, the society and culture to which he sought to belong. His work betrays a concern with the reconstruction and stabilization of French life. It also shows a preference for French modes of social thought, particularly via the writings of Comte and Saint-Simon.

Reformism and individualism

Durkheim rejected altogether the case for further revolutionary politics. Reconstruction was to be achieved by means of (and not in the face of) the institutions of the Third Republic. Marxism did not really impinge on his thought in an important way until relatively late in his career. A self-styled socialist, he was most strongly influenced by the thought of Jaurès. Followers of Jaurès espoused a so-called 'administrative socialism', not entirely dissimilar from the ideas of the Fabians in England. The most fundamental clue to Durkheim's political attitudes, however, lies in his moral individualism, which means belief in the sanctity of the individual person and the inviolability of individual rights. This had been the leading ideal of the first French Revolution. Durkheim sought for this ideal to be fully and finally realized in the new republic.

Anti-clericalism

Durkheim has been described as the 'theologian' of the new 'religion of humanity' which was first propounded by Comte. Certainly, like a true follower of the revolutionary tradition his hostility to the clergy and to Catholicism ran deep. This was to motivate his only involvement in political activity during the celebrated Dreyfus case in 1894. It was not, however, the only factor. The central figure in the case, Dreyfus himself, was, like Durkheim, an Alsatian Jew. This fact had played a major role in Dreyfus's arbitrary arrest and conviction for spying. The case thus brought together for Durkheim a number of key issues besides anti-clericalism. There was in particular the question of anti-semitism, indigenous in Alsace but becoming more strident in France generally (see Cobban 1975, pp. 48ff.). And there was the fundamental question of individual rights.

These highly specific contemporary influences affected his scholastic output profoundly. Why though should his writings be taken seriously today? There is no easy answer for, truth to tell, assessments of his ultimate significance diverge widely. Some critics, though acknowledging his immense influence on this history of the discipline, assert that his work is now largely surpassed. His ideas, they argue, essentially belong to outdated nineteenth-century modes of thought; his hypotheses, where they lend themselves to stringent examination, fail to stand the test; and his data and evidence were inadequate, used naïvely or were based on sources now rendered obsolete. Others see him as an 'inexhaustibly interesting scholar' (Stanmer 1975, p. 217). For many of them his writings are a watershed, setting out definitely much that is intrinsic to modern sociological perspectives.

In this situation, therefore, our own account will inevitably be selective and influenced by personal judgement. We shall argue that despite the numerous imperfections which have been revealed by critical examination of his output, Durkheim's sociology remains of crucial significance. This significance lies in the powerful arguments he put forward for the view that the manner of ordering and grouping in society is, as Fletcher puts it, 'psychologically creative' (Fletcher R. 1971, vol. II, p. 271). Admittedly, the boldness of his arguments often result in a hopeless overstatement of his case and seem to suggest that sociology makes the existence of a separate discipline of psychology unnecessary. This must obviously be rejected. But mental life cannot be understood in terms of individual psychology alone. As we have seen in Weberian sociology, *social* action derives its subjective meaning from the fact that it occurs within a context of relations with others. Durkheim, however, ventures into territory that Weber regarded as almost impenetrable, advancing explanations of the origin not only of moral values but also of the 'irrational' forms of conduct which Weber had associated with tradition and affect. Consequently, his work emphasizes the *collective* aspects of subjectivity, including collective thought and collective experience (for an important discussion of this point cf. Fletcher R. 1971, pp. 269–82).

Durkheim's general approach

Sociology as a discipline

The most obvious common denominator running through Durkheim's writings can be simply stated. It is the attempt conclusively to demonstrate that social forces exist as a distinctive level of reality. Sociology, which takes these forces as its subject matter, is therefore a legitimate and meaningful scientific discipline. For the most part Durkheim was to make this demonstration through the study of substantive aspects of social organization. But relatively early in his career he did write in a more formal, albeit polemical, way about sociological procedure.

The views set out in *The Rules of Sociological Method* (Durkheim 1964a) do not contain a set of subtly worked out doctrines. They contain none of the philosophical manoeuvrings of a Weber in debate with his German contemporaries. And in the actual course of his own research Durkheim was not always faithful to his own methodological teachings. The reason, however, is simple. At this stage, at least, Durkheim regarded sociology as 'entirely independent of philosophy' (Durkheim 1964a, p. 141) and was thus prepared to cut through long-standing philosophical arguments about the nature of the social sciences. It is thus easy to pick philosophical holes in his prescriptions but somewhat beside the point.

This fact probably explains for example the difficulties which have been encountered in pigeon-holing his views. Many people have been tempted to label him a 'positivist' because he clearly believes that the principle of causality can be applied to social phenomena. Never mind the fact that what exactly we mean and imply by the term 'cause' has been hotly debated by the philosophers. It is enough that 'the law of causality has been verified in other realms of nature' for the sociologist to feel justified in claiming its applicability to the social world. Durkheim himself, however, denies that this is a piece of positivism. And his most recent biographer has argued that it should rather be seen as a statement of 'scientific rationalism' (Lukes 1975, p. 72). This phrase should be understood as referring to an attitude that is more general and less stringent than out-and-out positivism. It means simply that we do not need to resort to mysticism in understanding social life any more than in the study of the physical world.

Social facts as things

Arguably the best known of Durkheim's *Rules* is his insistence that the sociologist should treat *social facts* as if they were *things* (*comme les choses*) (Durkheim 1964a, p. 14). Shortly after this was written Durkheim's views underwent a process of subtle modification (see p. 228), one important difference being apparently that he became more aware of the interpenetration of sociology and philosophy. It is, therefore, instructive to note what he had to say in the preface to the *second* edition of the *Rules* published in 1901 after this change had had its effect. Durkheim did not retract his earlier advice but asked:

What precisely is a thing? . . . Things include all objects of knowledge that cannot be conceived by purely mental activity, those that require for their conception data from outside the mind, from observations and experiments, those which are built up from the more external and immediately accessible characteristics to the less visible and more profound. To treat the facts of a certain order as things is not, then, to place them in a certain category of reality, but to assume a certain *mental attitude toward them* (our italics) on the principle that when approaching their study we are absolutely ignorant of their nature and that their characteristic properties, like the unknown causes on which they depend, cannot be discovered by even the most careful introspection. (Durkheim 1964a, p. xliii)

Durkheim, then, is commending an attitude, not a dogma, to the investigator, in order to impress upon us that our very familiarity with society is the source of our ignorance of its workings.

The term *social fact* should also be seen in this light. In the *Rules* he stipulated that social facts are to be recognized by virtue of two properties:

a   they are 'external' to individuals;
b   they exercise 'constraint' over individual behaviour.

Now this will not do. Both terms, 'externality' and 'constraint', are ambiguous. For example, externality could mean 'external' to any one individual, or 'external to *all* individuals' – as if 'society' possessed its own independent organic and mental life, a clearly absurd idea (Lukes 1975, p. 11). Again, 'constraint' seems to imply that social conformity is 'caused' in the same way that physical events have causes. If this were true, society would seem to operate in a wholly coercive way in which people would be literally forced to conform. We rejected this view in Chapter 5. In a much later work Durkheim made it clear that this was not what he had in mind (Durkheim 1976, p. 208, n. 4). He was at pains to point out that the 'constraining' effect of society on individuals is no more than the *outward sign* that we are in the presence of a social fact. In reality this is no more than 'the material and apparent expression of an interior (that is, subjective) and profound fact, namely that society possesses a degree of *moral* authority over the individual'. But this moral authority cannot be understood in terms of individual personality and circumstances alone. In the jargon of modern philosophy moral authority is the product of an 'emergent' level of facts. This refers to a very common aspect of scientific work. For example, combinations of molecules in a certain way have produced a new 'emergent' level of biological organisms that for certain purposes need not, indeed cannot, be studied in terms of molecules at all. Similarly the intercommunication of minds which forms a society is never a wholly individual matter. On the contrary it extends its regularities beyond individuals in time and space. The investigator should therefore treat them 'as if they were things'.

There is an obvious danger in this position. It is perfectly reasonable, indeed necessary, to see sociological problems as the product of an emergent level of reality (see pp. 98–9). But Durkheim's account of 'social facts' and how to study them has, with some justice, been held responsible for the tendency towards *reductionism* in sociology and anthropology. As we saw in Chapter 6, this means the fallacious claim that the sociological level of analysis can adequately explain *all* aspects of human behaviour without any reference at all to bio-logical and social factors.

Moral science

In the preface to the first edition of his first major work, Durkheim proposes to 'treat the facts of moral life according to the method of the posi-tive sciences' (Durkheim 1964b, p. 32). He insists that the chief aim of moral science is *not* to establish universal standards of right and wrong. On the contrary its rationale would be the recognition that moral standards vary according to causes originating within the collectivity as a whole.

But what exactly does Durkheim mean by the 'moral'? Though Durkheim's argument is rather self-contradictory, it seems reasonably clear that the 'moral' does refer to two aspects of the very idea of 'society':

a solidarity – that is, the achievement of cohesiveness or integration in society;

b regulation – that is, restraint upon the wholesale pursuit of self-interest and including *self*-restraint or altruism.

In effect, these two criteria are merely differ-ent aspects of the same thing for Durkheim. What he is denying is once again the utilitarian view that society can develop from the unbridled pursuit of purely individual interest. He viewed such thoroughgoing 'egoism' as wholly incom-patible with group cohesion. Any strengthening of the latter implies the imposition of *restraint* on purely individual goals. The work of the moral scientist, therefore, sets out from the fact that morality acts as a powerful determinant of the character of individual mental ('psychic') life.

It would be quite false, however, to imagine that we have here a reformation of the old philosophical problem of how to reconcile the opposition of individual and society. On the contrary, as Giddens puts it:

The key to Durkheim's whole life's work is to be found in his attempt to resolve the apparent paradox that the liberty of the individual is only achieved *through* his dependence on society. (our italics) (Giddens 1972b, p. 45)

The solution lay in making a radical separation between *egoism* or unrestrained individual self-interest on one hand and the moral idea of *individualism* on the other. Under the former 'the strongest conquer the weakest but the conquered do not consent to it and consequently this cannot constitute a stable equilibrium'. Under the latter 'liberty is the product of regulation' (Durkheim 1964b, pp. 2–3). Let us explain this further.

The acceptance of industrial society

Durkheim was a 'progressive' in his attitude to industrial society. His work, as we have said, reflects a political commitment to the ideals underlying the French Revolution – ideals which had stressed the intrinsic solidarity and fullest development of all that is potential in the individual. Thus it was that he rejected the diagnoses of contemporary ills which had been offered by all *three* strands of political philosophy which we reviewed in Chapter 2.

1 *Traditional conservatism* he rejected because it advocated a return to the conformist (*gemeinschaft*-like) morality appropriate to a small-scale, agrarian and largely outmoded way of life. Such a morality is the very antithesis of individual self-fulfilment and had indeed been a prime target of the anti-clericalism of the Revolution itself.
2 But equally, he could not, as we have seen, accept the *liberal-utilitarian view* that simply by removing traditional restraints and giving free play to unrestrained egoism a satisfactory and cohesive society would result.
3 Finally, although Durkheim applied the label *socialist* to himself, he was convinced that

prominent (that is, mostly Marxist) versions of socialism had not really transcended the limitations of utilitarian thought. By seeing the problems of industrial society solely in terms of the clash of material, that is, *economic* class interests, the socialists obscured the source of the ills of modern civilization.

These ills for Durkheim are essentially moral. They stem from the way in which the development of exchange, the division of labour between specialized activities, had transformed the relationship of individuals to collective obligations. The dangers inherent in this change are most evident in relation to the economic world of market transactions. He wrote:

If in the work that occupies almost all of our time we follow no other rule than that of our well understood interest, how can we learn to depend upon disinterestedness or self-sacrifice or discipline? In this way the absence of all economic discipline cannot fail to extend its effects beyond the economic world and consequently weaken public morality. (Durkheim 1964b, p. 4)

Under what conditions then can individuals *achieve* that 'genuine liberty which it is society's duty to have respected' (Durkheim 1964b, p. 3)? The search for an answer to this question, one that would be compatible with the industrial way of life, underlay all of his sociological writings (Giddens 1977, pp. 273–91). We still seek the solution today.

These then are the preoccupations of Durkheim's thought. We shall now trace them in the context of three of his best known works, drawing attention in each case to the critical response that each has stimulated.

The division of labour in society

The argument

In this book, arguably Durkheim's most famous work, he set out for the first time in full his views on the moral consequences of the specialization of activities and functions which industrialism –

or as Durkheim calls it, 'civilization' – brings about. His argument starts out from the observation that the specialization of activities has extended well beyond the purely economic context in which the phrase 'division of labour' had so far been used. It was extending rapidly into all departments of social life. Work had become separate from the home: politics, education, all had become specialized spheres of activity. Even science splits into a series of specialisms. It is this wider fragmentation, this *social* division of labour, which has changed the relation of the individual to the moral order. Hence, the initial subtitle of the work: 'A study of the organization of the advanced societies'.

Almost inevitably, posing the problem in this way invited some kind of 'before–after' contrast, industrial versus traditional, along lines which we have met before and whose limitations will, by now, be evident. Durkheim's 'linked antithesis' contrasted what he called *'mechanical'* with *'organic'* types of social solidarity.

1   *Mechanical solidarity* denotes the form of cohesion underlying primitive and traditional social systems and is characterized by the fact that it emphasizes the homogeneity of the group, likenesses and similarities between individuals and common moral sentiments binding one member to another. Social solidarity realized in this way places rather severe restrictions on any given individual's ability to develop a sense of personal identity or uniqueness. On the contrary co-operation within the group is restricted to what can be achieved through the close conformity of each member to a single stereotype.

2   *Organic solidarity*: the situation is quite different in the complex modern order. Here whatever cohesion exists depends on a type of solidarity which is 'organic'. It is the opposite of the mechanical type because it depends upon accentuating and regulating complementary *differences* in individual characteristics and for that matter subgroups within the social whole.

A diversity of interests and perspectives develops and herein, of course, lies the significance of the division of labour. It is not simply, as in the works of the political economists, the cause of 'the wealth of nations'. *It is the source from which they derive whatever cohesion they possess.*

Durkheim then launches upon his first attempt to grapple with a problem that was to dominate his career. What he struggled to clarify was the manner in which different types and conditions of social organization will vary in their psychic consequences for members of the collectivity. Unfortunately in this relatively early work, what Durkheim is saying is not at all clear. His argument is obscured by his introduction of a concept which has proved extremely troublesome, especially to English readers: the *'conscience collective'*. The problem arises in part because the French word *conscience* translates into English both as 'conscience' and 'consciousness'. Even his compatriots, however, have accused him of believing in the entity which seems to be conjured up by such a phrase, that is, some kind of group mind independent from and 'above' individual minds. This he denied and in fact used the term very little in later writings (Lukes 1975, p. 51).

The idea behind the term *'conscience collective'* might, we suggest, be rendered in English by using some long-winded phrase such as 'collective moral awareness' or 'sense of mutual obligation'. This however would probably be too flattering to the coherence of his thought at the time. One problem in understanding Durkheim in general is his tendency to use the language and assumptions of evolutionism even though he rejected many aspects of evolutionist thought. In the *Division of Labour in Society* he was not averse to using biological analogies as metaphors to characterize social processes – even though he certainly did not believe in a real similarity between biological organisms and social structure. But this fact may help us to understand why he refers to the *conscience collective* as a 'determinate system *that has its own life*' (Durkheim 1964b, p. 79) (our italics) – and why the concept aroused accusations from critics that he had proposed the existence of a group mind. This was not helped by a further definition he gives of it as 'the psychic type of society, with its own distinctive properties, conditions of existence and mode of development' (Durkheim 1964b, p. 80).

Durkheim was not talking about a group mind and, for all the imprecision, his use of 'conscience' is interesting and important. In simple terms we can say that he is trying to describe the varying nature of moral obligations. The 'conscience', he maintains, has four dimensions:

1   *volume* – or the extent to which individual conscience is wholly permeated by collective feelings and standards;
2   *intensity* – or the energy and sincerity with which individuals observe collective sentiments;
3   *rigidity* – or the relative sharpness or vagueness in collective moral ideas;
4   *content* – the actual nature of the moral ideas themselves.

In Table 6 we have tried to summarize how each of these will be affected by the type of solidarity.

Under 'mechanical solidarity', the volume, intensity and rigidity of the collective conscience will all be high. This is because the dependence of the individual upon group life is almost total and the scope for 'individuality' almost nil. Members of society will hold very precise ideas of right and wrong with intense fervour. But the most important aspect of morality lies in the content of the collective conscience: the fusion of social duty and religious duty. Originally, says Durkheim, religion 'pervades everything; everything social is religious' (1964b).

Under 'organic solidarity' the first three dimensions of collective moral awareness become weakened:

Table 6   *The effects of solidarity type on the 'collective conscience'*

	Mechanical solidarity	Organic solidarity
Basis	Likeness	Complementary differences
Division of labour	Low	High
Conscience collective:		
Volume	High	Low
Intensity	High	Low
Rigidity	High	Low
Contents	Collectivity as sacred	Individual as sacred (imperfectly realized in contemporary society)
Individual conscience	Low	High
Index:		
type of law	Repressive	Restitutive

—————————Increase in moral density—————————→

1   More and more scope is given to individual conscience, aptitude and freedom of action.
2   Sentiments relating to the collectivity lose their intensity.
3   They become the focus of vague feelings and ideals as opposed to rigid notions of duty.

Now before we move on to the fourth aspect, content, let us remind ourselves of the arguments which had been put forward by nineteenth-century political conservatives and which also underlay the sociology of Tönnies and his school. For these writers it was precisely the decreasing *volume, intensity* and *rigidity* of communal sentiment which so troubled them. To many of them, too, the answer lay in re-establishing religious sentiments and values. Not so with Durkheim. For him the division of labour is a progressive phenomenon. Its appearance signals not the inevitable collapse of morality but the emergence of a new *content* for the *conscience collective*, a content appropriate to the modern age. This centres around the obligation of society to the individual person (rather than the individual's obligation to society as under mechanical solidarity). It enshrines the fact that *the individual is the repository of the sentiments of sanctity once attributed to the collectivity as a whole*.

To give the maximum possible encouragement to individual rights does not however mean that altruism (that is, self-sacrifice for others) is destined to become 'a sort of agreeable ornament to social life'. On the contrary, moral individualism is *not* self-interest. It imposes its own set of reciprocal obligations on the individuals in a society. 'Human beings cannot live together', wrote Durkheim, 'without acknowledging and, consequently, making mutual sacrifices. . . . Every society is a moral society. In certain respects, this character is even more pronounced in organised societies.' (Durkheim 1964b, p. 228)

These words bring us to the essential novelty of Durkheim's treatment of the division of labour. The economists, he states, have seen in the specialization of economic exchange simply an effect of the growth of wealth and the free play of economic self-interest. On the contrary: the true significance of division of labour lies in its *moral* role. It is a source of restraint upon self-interest and thereby renders society cohesive.

Belief that unbridled egoism could ever become the basis of a civilized order is, for him, quite absurd. In a famous chapter he takes Spencer and the utilitarian economists to task for assuming that a stable society could possibly be built up of nothing more than a series of private exchanges between individuals. He goes on: 'There is nothing less constant than interest. Today it unites me to you; tomorrow it will make me your enemy. Such a cause can only give rise to transient relations and passing associations.' (Durkheim 1964b, p. 204) Even the 'purely economic' business contract, he points out, is not wholly built upon self-interest but in fact contains a moral basis. As the scope and number of such contracts has expanded, so has the sphere of social regulations – a fact which can be shown in a number of ways. First, the activities of the state have actually increased not decreased and so has the quantity of administrative law. Second, even the most mundane of business exchanges presumes that there are certain well-understood standards of good business behaviour – not least the purely moral agreement to refrain from defaulting on the terms of the contract itself which have been fixed in advance. Finally, society sees fit to regulate the content of contracts so that 'the agreement of parties cannot render a clause just which by itself is unjust' (Durkheim 1964b, p. 216). Thus, not everything in the contract is, in fact, contractual. If the moral basis is missing, organic solidarity is itself impaired.

This then in broad outline is the principal argument of *The Division of Labour*. In addition there are a number of important secondary themes which we have not so far considered. However it will be better to consider these in the light of some of the chief criticisms which have subsequently been made of the whole book.

Critical discussion

Any evaluation of Durkheim's writings has to start out from an acceptance that the anthropological and historical materials from which he tried to prove his case have dated badly. The consequences are often extremely serious. For example, his assertion that small-scale tribal societies lack a division of labour is, to say the least, over-simple. Anthropological studies from Malinowski onward have presented many counter-examples of the quite elaborate specialization of tasks and functions to be found in these types of collectivity. It is therefore not surprising that some writers have argued that to treat Durkheim's work as a contribution to modern thinking on occupational specialization and social solidarity would 'yield rather meagre results' (Barnes 1966, p. 172).

Another difficulty is one with which Durkheim himself wrestled. His analysis depends on the basic assumption that 'in the societies in which we live it is from the division of labour that the solidarity they possess principally derives'. The need to 'prove' this hypothesis created trouble in several ways:

1   It took up a large proportion of the early part of the book, thus obscuring the argument as a whole.
2   It involved examining an entity – 'organic solidarity' – which, on his own admission, did not lend itself to exact observation, or measurement.
3   He was forced, as a result, to introduce a second unproven hypothesis, namely that law is an accurate reflection of the internal condition of society. Armed with this assumption the development of different *types* of law is used to measure the growth of organic solidarity.

According to Durkheim there are two main classes of law:

1   *Repressive law* applies to crimes and similar actions which offend against the *'conscience collective'*. This 'repressive' law is so called because the sanctions it contains take the form of punishment. The offender is held to have infringed beliefs and practices which are imposed upon all members of society and whose hold on society the act of punishment actually strengthens. A dominance of repressive law in a society, Durkheim thought, is a clear indication that its solidarity is of the mechanical type. He then tries to show that as the division of labour has developed, repressive laws have been supplemented by a second type called:
2   *Restitutive law* In this case, the sanctions imposed on the offender do not concern society as a whole. They are not punishments but merely seek to restore to the plaintiff what he has lost as the result of the failure of the defendant to keep to an agreement or contract. The obvious application of this principle is in the field of civil law. For Durkheim the growth of restitutive civil law represents the visible symbol of the rise of organic solidarity and he presents evidence to 'prove' that it is a singularly modern phenomenon.

Unfortunately, subsequent research and criticism has suggested that Durkheim was wrong. The consensus of recent opinion is that repressive law *diminishes* in importance as we move away from the case of modern nation states and in the simplest societies it is almost wholly absent. As Barnes puts it, 'it is governmental action that is typically repressive' (1966, p. 169). In a more recent version of the same argument Sheleff (1975) claims that Durkheim's use of law as an index of social organization is in fact justified, but only if we reverse the relationship between types of law and types of solidarity (cf. Jones T. A. 1981). In primitive (mechanical) societies law is wholly restitutive. Growth in the repressive forms of law is a concomitant of modernization. Durkheim was too sanguine about the extent to which organic solidarity would bring about the liberation of the individual. And he seems to have overlooked the possibility that sentiments of sanctity might not be transferred from the collectivity to the individual. Instead they have, in varying degrees, been attached to the nation state which in our own times has often been the source of repressive acts *against* the individual (Sheleff 1975; Jones T. A. 1981)

Durkheim has also been accused of failing to explain how the transition from mechanical to organic solidarity occurs. This is not quite true. At one point he tries to show that modifications in the structure and organization of a society will occur as a result of an increase in its size and in the number of other groups with which it has to compete. Such an effect has, in fact, been brought about by the increase and concentration of human population. As a result the 'moral density' of social life – the number of contacts and the intensity of the struggle for survival – has increased. Now, earlier writers such as Thomas Malthus had greeted the growth in the population of European societies with pessimism. They regarded a competitive struggle for scarce resources as inevitable because prosperity would only increase the population to the point where countervailing tendencies would set in. Durkheim's argument challenges this view. The 'natural checks' to prosperity will be overcome because society has responded to population growth and greater moral density by developing new, more effective forms of organization, that is, the division of labour and organic solidarity. Alas, this theory will not do as it stands: it is put forward in too cryptic and imprecise a fashion; far more evidence would be required to substantiate it; and it implies a rather deterministic view of the relation between the growth in moral density and the organizational form of society. Hence, the criticism that he gave the problem of change insufficient attention can, to some extent, be sustained.

Lastly, Durkheim's definition of 'morality' is suspect. He was anxious, of course, to treat the term scientifically and to free it from judgements of the satisfactoriness or rightness of purely individual states of behaviour, motivation and thought. He also wanted to attack the utilitarians for their lack of a sociological perspective. In the process, however, morality becomes confused with mere conformity. This is wholly to ignore the type of behaviour covered by the Weberian concept of *Wertrationalität* (see Chapter 11). Or as Pope puts it, 'the possibility that man (*sic*) might find meaning in serving some transcendent end other than society' (Pope 1976, p. 18). Durkheim is also rather naïve about the degree of benevolence in systems of morality. As both Weber and Marx were all too aware, such systems usually function to legitimate inequalities of power and privilege. This is a possibility which is not really considered within the main argument of *The Division of Labour* as we have so far described it.

It would be misleading, however, to suggest that Durkheim ignores the problem altogether. In the final section of the work he turns to a consideration of what he calls the 'abnormal' forms of the division of labour. These are cases where for some reason or other the creation of organic solidarity by means of the specialization of activities has failed. As we shall see, he considers that widespread or systematic inequalities and injustices must be seen as major cause of this state of affairs.

Before examining the details of this thesis we must note that most subsequent commentators have found the distinction between 'normal' and 'abnormal' conditions of social organization quite untenable. Precisely because society is *not* like an organic body it is impossible for sociologists to diagnose states of 'disease' in society or to devise a pathology of social systems. Such an activity would presuppose that there was some scientific way of overriding or transcending the inevitable and continual conflict of political and moral perspectives which exists within groups. There is in fact *no* scientific way in which questions of good and evil, justice or injustice can be resolved. To pretend otherwise conflicts with Durkheim's own concern to protect individual dignity. It is also to abuse the scientific approach to society which he did so much to promote.

A further problem with his use of the normal–abnormal typology is that it has the effect of relegating his thoughts on the consequences of inequality to the status of a subtheme, indeed almost an afterthought. At this time of his life Durkheim clearly shared some of the optimism of his surroundings and hence he gives the impression that in due process of social evolution, impediments to organic solidarity would disappear. Today, with our somewhat more jaundiced attitude to the idea of progress, we are likely to recognize that the so-called 'abnormal' forms of the division of labour have become its *typical* forms. As a result the last section of *The Division of Labour* has received attention out of all proportion to its position in the book as a whole.

The abnormal forms

Undoubtedly Durkheim regarded the cohesion of nineteenth-century *laissez-faire* society, with its wholly unregulated markets, its arbitrary inequalities, its restrictions on social mobility and its 'class' wars, as in a dangerous condition. This is clear from the two major 'abnormal' forms which he describes, namely the *anomic* and the *forced* division of labour. Let us briefly consider each of these.

The anomic division of labour

Durkheim's famous concept of *anomie* has become the subject of a vast literature. Along with Marx's notion of alienation, with which it is often compared, it has come to symbolize the characteristic problems of the industrial world and the modern mind. It is important, therefore, that Durkheim referred to anomie in different ways in the course of his writings. In the context of the abnormal forms of the division of labour it denotes two ideas:

a the absence of regulation or rules so that the parts of the social order are insufficiently co-ordinated. Anomie in this sense is a property of society, not a psychological condition;

b the consequence of this state of affairs for individual life in producing a sense of the isolation and meaninglessness of life and work. Even here, psychological factors reflect a condition of the collectivity as a whole.

We shall see that the second of these ideas acquired increasing significance for Durkheim in the course of his studies of suicide (see below).

Durkheim argues that the economic structure of *laissez-faire* society, with its powerful inducements to self-interested behaviour, must be regarded as a major source of anomie. For example, the occurrence of periodic commercial crises provides tangible evidence that there is no stable control or regulation of the number of businesses or the level of output in a trade. Hence 'social functions are not adjusted to one another'. Recurrent industrial conflict especially in large-scale industry is another symptom of lack of regulation. Unjust contracts have resulted from the system of wage labour between masters and servants who, at one time, worked in harmony alongside one another. Admittedly, economic life is not the only cause of anomie. Durkheim talks of the way in which unregulated specialism in the scientific community leaves each scholar enclosed and may in the end lead to 'the ruin of all science'. We are left in no doubt however that the unregulated character of the industrial economy should be regarded as the major cause of anomie.

The forced division of labour

The problem here is not the lack of rules but rather the excess of them in that 'the rules themselves are the cause of evil'. The rules have in fact arisen in order to enforce the division of labour *coercively*. Individual 'specialism' and occupations are not freely chosen, but thrust upon each person by custom, law and even sheer chance. Once again unpleasant consequences ensue for personal life. Individuals find themselves estranged, resentful and aspiring to social positions which have been arbitrarily closed off to them. This is clearly the case, Durkheim observes, where a person can enjoy a special advantage owing to possession of inherited wealth or where 'thanks to the persistence of certain prejudices, a certain distinction is attached to some individuals independent of their merits'. The forced division of labour, then, brings about a situation which one modern author has called the 'anomie of injustice' (Merton 1964; cf. Young J. 1974). It is this which has produced class conflict and not, as Marx would have it, the inherently exploitative nature of capitalism. Nor did Durkheim consider that all inequality could be abolished. But whereas some inequalities are 'natural' and occur spontaneously, others are external and 'all external inequality compromises organic solidarity'. What in effect he is urging is the creation of what today is called 'equality of opportunity' or a meritocracy. For this to be possible all forms of hereditary privilege should be abolished. 'There cannot be rich and poor at birth', he wrote, 'without there being unjust contracts.' (Durkheim 1964b, p. 384)

The anomie of isolation

In a brief chapter almost at the end of the book appears a discussion of 'another' (nameless) abnormal form. What is described here is the isolation of the worker whose task is too highly specialized for its relation to the whole to be intelligible. The discussion anticipates much modern writing on the meaningless, routine character of industrial work and the moral breakdown which threatens to occur because of the hierarchical nature of factory life.

To cure this and other forms of anomie Durkheim proposed the establishment of representative corporations for each specialist occupation or industry. These would interpose a level of regulation between contracts and agreements made by individuals on one hand, and the overall legislative regulation given by the state. In this way the anomie produced by modern economic life would be contained. It has been argued however that such measures would merely produce at best a false sense of contentment, leaving the basic problem of capitalism untouched (for example, Friedmann 1961, Chapter 5).

On the whole, however, the theme of inequality occupies a subordinate place in Durkheim's work. If the above proposals *in toto* constitute a justification for regarding him as a socialist – a label he applied to himself – it was not this aspect of his discussion of the abnormal forms which he carried forward into his later substantive writings. Instead it was the other aspects of his critique of *laissez-faire* capitalism which he chose to emphasize: the association between lack of social regulation, egoism and the condition of collective mental life. This is foreshadowed in a passage towards the end of the book. Taking the utilitarians to task for automatically associating the growth of division

of labour with an increase in human happiness he shows that the propensity to self-destruction as shown by rates of suicide becomes far greater with the advance of 'civilization'. And it was through the study of suicide that he was to develop still further his thesis that personal life is affected profoundly by the nature and extent of social solidarity.

Suicide

The argument

The story goes that Durkheim undertook this work as a challenge to his sociological perspectives, especially his insistence that the discipline studied an emergent level of forces existing and explainable in their own terms (cf., however, Lukes 1975, pp. 191ff.; Pope 1976). Suicide is the ultimate individual act. The perpetrator by definition perishes in the attempt and in doing so mocks the utilitarian idea of the pursuit of self-interest, the search for pleasure and the avoidance of pain. To show that such seemingly asocial behaviour is, in fact, imbued with the impress of social forces would have been a great achievement. Whether or not this story is true, the sociological theory of suicide which resulted has become justly famous. The question of its ultimate success as an explanation of the phenomenon however remains open.

The raw material of the book is an analysis of variation in *rates* of suicide in

a   different nations;
b   different subgroupings within French society.

The stress upon rates is rather vital. Durkheim did not intend – despite some lapses in his logic in places – to investigate the many *purely* individual factors which would have to be taken into account in order to explain why a given person takes his or her life. His point is rather that we cannot understand why suicide is a recurrent feature of modern life by means of a study of individual cases. Only a sociological analysis of rates can illuminate the social element in suicide. But as we shall see later his insistence on studying rates raises a methodological problem of how secure our knowledge of them is. It also raises the problem of how we define the term suicide itself. For the moment, however, let us step over these issues and outline Durkheim's main argument.

The first part of the book is devoted to establishing – not altogether successfully in the opinion of recent critics – two major points in connection with the rates:

1   That they remain constant for a given society or group for a substantial period. What explains this phenomenon? Only, argues Durkheim, some reality which is external and superior to the suicidal individuals themselves each of whom, after all, perishes in the act of self-destruction.

2   That various extra-social and individual causes which might explain why a particular individual commits suicide cannot account for the stability of the rates as a whole. The list of factors examined in this connection are 'psychopathic' states including alcoholism; heredity; imitation; and lastly 'cosmic factors', that is, climate, temperature and *times and seasons*.

Discussion of the 'cosmic factors' acts as a prologue to the main drama Durkheim has prepared. The majority of suicides, he shows, occur in the daytime. But to explain this curiosity one could not refer to the action of the sun and the temperature. He concludes that 'day favours suicide because this is the time of most active existence when human relations cross and recross, when social life is most intense'. Similar considerations explain the increase of suicide with the onset of summer (Durkheim 1952, pp. 116–27).

Having 'eliminated' possible non-social explanations to his own satisfaction Durkheim sets out his own, by now, very famous sociological theory of suicide rates. What he tries to establish is that the social elements of self-destruction consist of three major types and one minor one. These can be understood as the product of 'suicidogenetic' social currents. These will impel certain individuals to take their own lives whenever the condition of society departs from a state of balance. This state of balance is defined in terms of two dimensions which we give in Figure 4.

The two dimensions are: (1) *integration* – the extent to which individuals experience a sense of belonging to the collectivity; (2) *regulation* – the extent to which the actions and desires of individuals are kept in check by moral values.

A society which possesses too much or too little of these will favour different varieties of types of suicide. Durkheim tries through the statistics of suicide rates to show that these different types have a real existence in society.

Integration

Let us begin with the 'integration' dimension since it occupies the larger share of Durkheim's attention. This gives us two corresponding types of suicide:

1   *Egoistic suicide* is the product of insufficient integration. It is a distinctively modern phenomenon. It can be illustrated by showing how suicide rates vary according to (*a*) religious affiliation (*b*) marital status (*c*) political events. The common denominator among these empirical variations is the level of integration in the relevant social groups. Consequently integration is a key factor in the prevention of suicide. Thus Protestantism which tolerates individualism and free enquiry into the basis of religious belief induces a higher suicide rate among its followers than does Catholicism. Rates are high among bachelors and the widowed but lower among the married, that is, those integrated into a family group. Then again at times of heightened collective political fervour, such as in wartime, suicide rates in general fall.

2   *Altruistic suicide* We should avoid the conclusion, however, that individuals can only benefit the more they are subject to integration

Figure 4   *Suicide types and the balance of society*

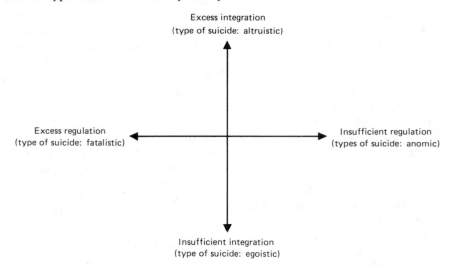

into social groups. That it is possible to have *too much* integration is shown by the second type of suicide, called *altruistic* suicide. It typically occurs in traditional and primitive social orders but is also found in the modern military context. In these cases, individuals kill themselves out of a sense of overwhelming moral obligation, classically illustrated by the heroic suicide – the Roman collapsing on his sword – or by the case of the wife who is supposed to perish gladly on the funeral pyre of her husband.

Regulation

Now let us take the other dimension, regulation. This also gives us two forms:

1   *Anomic suicide* is the production of insufficient regulation and in modern society its effects are added to those of the lack of integration. The main example which Durkheim gives of this variety of suicide recalls the discussion of the anomic forms of the division of labour and the effect of economic and commercial crisis. These, so he claims on the basis of his data, much influence the suicide rate. In times of economic depression more individuals are impelled to self-destruction than at others. But anomic suicide may be found as well in the

domestic context. For it can be shown that throughout Europe the number of suicides is much higher among the divorced and separated than among the married.

2   *Fatalistic suicide* This type is only mentioned by Durkheim in a brief footnote and he clearly had problems finding examples. It is included here for logical completeness. Fatalistic suicide is the product of excessive regulation and is the counterpart of the altruistic case.

Suicide in modern society

Considerable debate surrounds the relationship Durkheim saw between the rise of egoistic and anomic forms of suicide and the nature of modern society. This much is clear: in general terms suicide has become a problem due to the 'sweeping away of older forms of organisation' (Durkheim 1952, p. 388). Moreover he seems to have agreed with a prevalent view of his time that the greater emphasis on individualism, 'the cult of man', had been partly responsible for this dissolution. Nevertheless the solution did not lie in reassertion of tradition controls because as the case of altruistic suicide indicated, insufficient individuation was equally undesirable. A humane solution must be found, one which did not 'concentrate each separate person upon himself' but in accordance with the new religion of humanity would 'subordinate him to the general interests' (Durkheim 1952, p. 337; cf. Lukes 1975, pp. 198–9). This was to be found in the creation of occupational associations.

Durkheim's preoccupation with drawing these general conclusions and with championing his discipline undermined, in various ways, the satisfactoriness of the details of his theory. There is clearly some sort of connection with the discussion of the .abnormal forms in *The Division of Labour*, but the fit is not exact. In effect the notion of anomie in the earlier work has become split:

a Anomic suicide, as before, is due to 'lack of regulation' but its effect on the individual is to produce an excess of desires and greed. Some interpretations, particularly older ones, have taken this statement as evidence of Durkheim's rather pessimistic and conservative view of human nature – as if individuals were seething with insatiable passions that are only kept in check by social rules. Such a reading conflicts with his view of society in general; and even in this passage we are discussing it seems reasonably clear that it is modern society itself which is the source of insatiable human desires. He actually singles out for blame 'the development of industry and the indefinite extensions of the market' (Durkheim 1952, pp. 285–7).

b The sense of meaninglessness which, in his earlier work, Durkheim has associated with anomie is, in this book, attributed to egoism. Egoism is used to denote lack of integration into group life, but the causes of this lack of integration are left rather unclear and seem only to have intellectual and psychological effects in common.

This brings us to another problem. Durkheim believed that his research would reveal the autonomous nature of social causes. In practice he was unable to describe these causes without referring to their effects on the psychological

condition of *individuals*. We can illustrate this in two ways:

1 The 'modern' types of suicide both depend upon an intervening mental condition as the precipitating factor in self-destruction. Thus:

| Lack of regulation (social cause) | → | uncontrolled desires (mental state) | → | *anomic suicide* |
| Lack of integration (social cause) | → | sense of meaninglessness (mental state) | → | *egoistic suicide* |

This is a perfectly reasonable theory: that mental states often have social causes. But his argument often reads as if the sociologist could study social causes without any reference to their mental effects.

2 *The definition of suicide* We have deliberately not considered Durkheim's definition of suicide until now although it appears at the beginning of the book. Durkheim wanted to offer an 'objective' definition which did not depend on the consciousness or intentions of the suicidal individual. But his definition contradicts this: 'all cases of death resulting directly or indirectly from a positive or negative act of the victim himself, *which he knows* (our italics) will produce this result' (1952, p. 44). Here Durkheim has run immediately into the problem of the 'mental' nature of social phenomena. And there is a further problem: how do we establish after the event what it is the suicide 'knows'?

Critical discussion

What significance, if any, is there for the modern sociologist in all this? More than in relation to any other of Durkheim's works, this question is not easily answered because of the intense critical raking over which *Suicide* has received. It is fairly clear what significance Durkheim himself saw in it. In the section following upon the exposition of the types of suicide he claims to have proven by the use of 'moral statistics' the theme of the *Rules*, namely the 'fundamental principle of the sociological method' that 'social facts are objective'. Such a purpose can only be said to have been achieved in a lasting sense, however, if the reasonings of the investigator are sound and his data adequate for the purposes imposed on them. On neither score can *Suicide* now suffice to present the discipline of sociology to the unconvinced enquirer.

The types of criticism which have emerged from the voluminous literature on *Suicide* may be divided into four categories:

1   There are first of all those of a general logical nature. Durkheim's failings as a dialectician are all too evident in the work. He frequently begs the question, defines his terms in such a way as to suit his own arguments and presents contradictory assertions (for example, see Lukes 1975, pp. 30–4).

2   Closely connected criticism concerns his *use of the data* and the *relationship between theory and evidence*. The most recent and exhaustive treatment of this issue is to be found in a study by Pope (1976). This author sets out by questioning established judgements of the worth of *Suicide*. The work has been taken, particularly by those who believe that sociology should be modelled on the example of the natural sciences, to be a research classic. Against this view Pope presents detailed evidence that in large measure Durkheim's theory is not borne out by a close examination of the data which he assembles. For example, if a correlation coefficient is calculated on the figures relating to the association between bankruptcy and suicide a small *negative* relationship is found. Again, in discussing economic anomie Durkheim confined himself to showing that the overall suicide rate increases in crisis period. He failed to consider whether the impact upon suicide rates is at all related to the severity of the crisis and in the only attempt which he presents, the results are negative (Pope 1979, pp. 116–17).

3   There is, however, a still more fundamental difficulty which is that the theory of the different types of suicide is itself made untestable by its *ambiguity and by the diversity of different and unrelated causal statements* made in the course of the analysis. Pope argues that in fact the two types of suicide called egoism and anomie are not really different. Thus the conditions of 'meaninglessness' and 'uncontrolled passion' said to ensue from the different types of modern suicide are frequently confused in Durkheim's text. He alleges that the 'regulation' dimension and, with it, the category of anomic suicide was invented to cover certain inconsistencies between Durkheim's theory of egoism and the actual data. Lukes has also argued that:

Durkheim's characterisation of the adverse social conditions (producing meaninglessness etc.) is problematic. He saw them entirely in terms of the relative absence or excessive influence of social goals and rules; he never saw the importance in this context of discriminating between different types of goals and of rules. He never clearly conceived of the possibility that there might be socially given goals that are non-integrative, and social rules or norms that do not lead in general to social harmony and individual contentment. (Lukes 1975, p. 217)

Small wonder then that much time has been spent in trying to decide what, if any, difference exists between 'lack of integration' (egoism) and lack of 'regulation' (anomie).

4   The most startling criticism of recent years, however, has been that of Douglas (1967). He too begins by questioning whether, in the context of the great interest in the suicide problem in the France of his time, Durkheim's contribution is as original as has been claimed. He argues that Durkheim's handling of the statistical data adds very little to what had already been 'discovered' by his contemporaries. But it is Durkheim's 'realism' – that is, his belief that society may be treated as a reality in its own right – which Douglas wishes to attack. He claims that Durkheim ignores the necessary element of shared meaning which is part and parcel of all social acts. The notion of social facts forced him to argue that only 'external' social elements in the fixing of suicide rates should be considered. On the other hand, as we have seen, in defining

these very 'external' elements he finds it necessary to talk about internal states or the meaning which the act has for the individual. Similarly, the categories of egoism, altruism or anomie can only be identified in the statistical materials used by making assumptions about what group membership *means* to individuals; for example, that membership of a Protestant sect means 'free enquiry' and 'isolation' to the person concerned. Douglas's most telling criticism, however, is that the statistics of suicide rates themselves, which Durkheim uses to prove the reality of social facts, are not free of the problem of shared meanings. The fact that they depend on administrative categorizations, not 'scientific' classifications and concepts, introduces an element of uncontrolled bias. Thus for example among Catholics suicide is a disgrace and will lead them to conceal the fact of suicide if they can when registering a death. The social fact of a lower suicide rate among Catholics will thus be an artefact.

Now these criticisms raise issues for sociology in general. They go well beyond the limited question of the merits of one work into the problem of how in fact the discipline is to handle the problem of the subjectivity of much that occurs in social life. Douglas's own writing is vulnerable from this point of view. How, one might ask, can we ever know what the meanings which people attach to their actions 'really' are (Hindess 1973)? The concept of meaning with which he operates threatens to undermine the entire notion of collective life altogether. In Douglas's society each individual is locked inside his or her own private world of social meanings and he does not explain how it is that the mental life of a person, the 'meanings' attached to social behaviour, are formed as they certainly are as a result of participation in group life. It was this aspect which Durkheim sought to understand and which, as he rightly insisted, has in some way to be analysed as a totality, that is, as minds in interaction. Much of the criticism to which he has been exposed stems from the

fact that he does not make a clear enough separation between:

a the 'subjective' or psychological which, as we argued above, is a necessary 'intervening' element in the chain of causes linking the condition of society to any individual acts, including suicide;

b the 'individual', which is a purely philosophical abstraction that certain liberal moral philosophers have tried to oppose to society (Lukes 1975, pp. 19ff.). The non-social individual does not exist and the concept of individual reason, as Durkheim realized correctly, can never be sufficient to account for social processes.

What Douglas's study does usefully show up is the built-in epistemological uncertainties surrounding data on suicides. By definition we cannot determine the nature and motives of the dead. The judgements and classification by others of 'what has happened', however, are only arrived at through a further set of social processes. They therefore cannot be used as a source of neutral, objective facts. If, as Durkheim claimed, suicide cannot be understood simply in terms of individual mental states it is not clear that there is any 'scientific' way of uncovering the nature of the social causes of the phenomenon.

On balance, then, why continue to read *Suicide* eighty or more years after it first appeared? Barnes suggests that there are two chief reasons for continuing to read Durkheim's work and they apply as much to *Suicide* as to the rest.

First, of course, for clarification of the validity of the many diverse criticisms levelled against him as a sociologist.

Second, and more importantly, as an indication that 'Durkheim's efforts to make sociology scientific have not been wholly successful and that we can still read him for help in interpreting the results of current enquiries'. (Barnes 1966, p.159).

A third reason for continuing to read *Suicide* is

contained in his own statement that 'a people's mental system is a system of definite forces not to be disarranged or rearranged by simple injunctions. It depends really on the grouping and organisation of social elements'. (Durkheim 1952, p. 387). *Suicide* represents an advance in Durkheim's thought over the *Division of Labour* because of the greater precision with which it captures the social element in mental life, connecting it with the actions of individuals. To prove this connection with empirical materials and conceptual argument was bound to be beyond the resources at his disposal.

The elementary forms of the religious life

The argument

The final work we shall consider in this review of Durkheim's thought is *The Elementary Forms of the Religious Life*. A relatively long interval separates it from *Suicide* but in that time Durkheim had not been idle. In addition to carrying a heavy teaching programme he had acted as Editor to *L'Année Sociologique*, contributing articles and an immense number of reviews to it. He also oversaw the publication of second editions of several of his major works to date, of lectures on education, on philosophy and socialism. The importance of his output during this period has only recently been fully recognized and its content absorbed into the understanding of Durkheim within the English-speaking world. The consequence has been a greater appreciation of the political element in his ideas, his concern for the ideal of moral individualism and above all the essential consistency and coherence of his intellectual output which earlier evaluation had understated (Giddens 1977, Chapter 7).

All of these activities, however, were merely incidental to his most basic preoccupation after about 1895. Around that time he seems to have experienced his own kind of 'epistemological break' (cf. p. 118). He wrote:

The course of 1895 marks a line of demarcation in the development of my thought so much so that all previous researches had to be taken up again with renewed efforts in order to be placed in harmony with these new views. (cited in Lukes 1973, p. 237)

The heart of this change, already in fact anticipated in the theory of the *conscience collective* was the conviction that religion is the most primitive of all phenomena. In the beginning all thought is religious and stems from society's need for a moral classification of men and things. The first full statement of where this insight had led him is contained in a famous article in *L'Année* published with his distinguished nephew M. Mauss in 1903. Its subject is the forms of primitive classification (Durkheim and Mauss 1963). But the final product of his insight, *The Elementary Forms*, did not appear for another nine years.

This work has become a classic for two reasons. First, alongside Max Weber's analysis of the sources of economic rationalization in religious activity it represents a major breakthrough in the establishment of the sociology of religion. Its arguments have been debated and utilized in research up to the present day. Second, it achieves at the same time the double feat of helping to establish a sociological, as opposed to a philosophical, theory of knowledge. That is to say it proposes a wholly different kind of answer to a question which philosophers had debated for centuries; what is the source of the certainty which enables us to accept the truth of a statement or a piece of reasoning? Durkheim was one of the first authors to argue in detail that certainty derives from society and socially approved ways of thought rather than from disembodied universal standards of truth as such. The entitlement of the sociologist to make such a claim of course remains a hotly disputed matter.

Sociology of religion

Let us set out first Durkheim's contribution to the sociology of religion. The actual topic which provides the fodder for his arguments might seem far removed from his preceding interests – it is totemism among the aborigine tribes of Australia. Durkheim soon makes clear, however, that his purpose is to use these aborigine societies, so remote in distance and organization from our own, as a way of highlighting the exact difference between modern and traditional social systems. This will allow the sociologist to locate those things which industrial societies still need if they are to overcome their lack of moral cohesion. Aborigine tribal societies represent the simplest type of organization known to ethnography. Hence they, and their religion, will reveal all that is essential to social organization in general and religion in particular. This essential element is merely compounded in the process of civilization. The pernicious influence of evolutionism upon Durkheim will be evident here. He has been justly criticized for confusing two meanings of 'simple' or 'elementary'; namely, in the sense of 'first' or 'original' and in the sense of 'lacking complexity'. But it was this which provided his reason for focusing his attention on totemism.

For Durkheim the distinguishing features of totemism were as follows:

1   It is to be found in societies organized on a clan basis, that is, groupings united by recognition of a kinship.
2   This kinship is not derived from any blood relationship but from acceptance of a common name.
3   The name 'is also the name of a determined species of material things with which it [the clan] believes that it has very particular relations . . . especially relations of kinship' (Durkheim 1976, p. 102). This species of things is the *totem* itself.
4   Both the clan and its totem form part of a wider system of bonds known as the phratry. Totem religion is in fact a religion of the whole phratry since it involves recognition of the identification which other clans feel with their totems and not just recognition of the sacredness of one's own totem.

Durkheim aligns himself strongly with those previous scholars who had seen in totemism the ancestor of all religions and spends many pages attacking those who had refused to recognize its religious character or who saw it as an amalgam of other beliefs. All this, however, is a mere prologue to his attack on existing definitions of religion itself. These had located the essence of religious thought either in its attention to the 'supernatural' and the 'mysterious' or to association with diversity and spiritual beings. Durkheim does not have much trouble in showing to his own satisfaction that there are important cases which do not fit such definitions. Furthermore they all suffer from a common fault, namely, 'it would be necessary to admit that a whole world of delusive representations has superimposed itself upon the other, denatured it to the point of making it unrecognisable, and substituted a pure hallucination for reality' (Durkheim 1976, p. 87). On the contrary, he insists with remarkable originality and persuasiveness, religion is *not* based upon delusion. We must accept the statement of the multitude of believers that they have experienced something real and it is the sociologist's task to apprehend that reality.

Seen in this way the significance of totemism as the germ of all religious systems becomes apparent. For what is most basic to religion in general and totemism in particular is a profound sense of 'a bipartite division of the whole universe known and knowable into two classes which embrace all that exists but which radically exclude each other' (Durkheim 1976, p. 40). These two classes are Durkheim's famous categories of *sacred* and *profane*. Religious systems consist of:

a compulsory beliefs, 'which express the nature of sacred things and the relations which they sustain, either with each other or with profane things' (Durkheim 1967, p. 37);
b compulsory rules, which are 'rules of conduct which prescribe how a man [i.e. a person] should comport himself in the presence

of these sacred objects' (Durkheim 1976, p. 41).

Both of these elements, untrammelled by the overlay and mixing of different systems, exist in purest form in the aborigine totem.

What then is the basis of the sacred force which the totem possesses? If we can answer this question we shall have understood the source of the idea of the sacred in all religions. Predictably, perhaps, Durkheim insists that the 'sacred' is the reflection of society itself:

Religious force is only the sentiment inspired by the group in its members, but projected outside of the consciousness that experiences them and objectified [that is, made into objects]. To be objectified they are fixed upon some object which thus becomes sacred; but any object might fulfil this function. (Durkheim 1976, p. 229)

He offers two kinds of justification for this opinion:

1   In terms of the moral power which social pressure exerts upon any individual and the need which that individual feels to understand what is controlling him. The workings of society are too complex and abstract for the ordinary person to see the true source of this moral power. 'As long as scientific analysis does not come to teach it to them, men know well that they are acted upon but they do not know by whom.' (Durkheim 1976, p. 209)

2   In terms of the coincidence of religious organization with social organization. Religions, unlike magical superstitions, are always associated with the existence of a moral community or 'church' with which the believer identifies. In totem religion this moral unit is the clan itself. The totem is the flag or emblem denoting the unit to which individual interest is subordinated.

But the social concomitants of religion extend deeper than this. To understand them we must turn to the contribution of *The Elemenatary Forms* to the sociology of knowledge.

Sociology of knowledge

The basic principle of Durkheim's sociology of knowledge is that the catgories of thought with which the mind works are first and foremost social categories. That is, they reflect and uphold the organization of the society itself. This was an idea which Durkheim and Mauss had first propounded in 1903: 'The first logical categories were social categories; the first classes of things were classes of men . . . etc.' At around the same time he had begun to use the term *collective representation* to refer to these socially derived categories of thought. The term represents a refinement of the earlier very general *conscience collective*. In simple terms *collective representations* are specific items or states of the conscience as manifested in the thought processes of individuals. Throughout his career Durkheim had sought ever better ways to express the idea that the study of mental life is not exhausted by what can be known about individuals in themselves. An additional level of analysis is required which today is known as 'inter' or 'macro-subjectivity' (Lukes 1973, pp. 6–8; Ritzer and Bell 1981). In *The Elementary Forms* we find a clear statement of the *necessity* for such *representations*:

If men (i.e. people) did not agree upon these essential ideas at every moment, if they did not have the same conception of time, space, cause, number etc. all contact between their minds would be impossible and with that, all life together. Thus society could not abandon the categories to the free choice of the individual without abandoning itself. If it is to live there is not merely need of a satisfactory moral conformity but also there is a minimum of logical conformity beyond which it cannot safely go. For this reason it uses all its authority upon its members to forestall such dissidences. (Durkheim 1976, p. 17)

We must now recall Durkheim's argument that social authority is represented to the individual, especially in the most humble society, in the form of religious ideas. Consequently, 'when primitive religious beliefs are systematically analysed the principal categories are naturally found' (Durkheim 1976, p. 9). We can now see the essential connection Durkheim makes between the growth of human thought and the existence of religion. The former owes its very formation to the latter. Religion provided fundamental ideas on such matters as cosmology (the constitution of the universe) and time and space. All of these elements are found within totemism. In addition we find something even more fundamental to thought; in the organization of society into clans and phratries is represented the first notions of classification and arrangement; in the imitative rites of the clan we find the notion of causal force or relation 'implied in the power . . . attributed to the like to produce the like' (Durkheim 1976, p. 363). Thus philosophy and the sciences had their origins in religious thought as did the notions of necessary and causal connection upon which these forms of knowledge depend.

Critical discussion

Of course, neither the sociology of religion nor the sociology of knowledge have gone unchallenged. The bold arguments of *The Elementary Forms* are open to objections on at least five major counts.

Anthropological evidence

The first and perhaps least damaging concerns the anthropological evidence. Modern anthropology, able to draw upon a wider range of source materials has, as with Durkheim's earlier work, been able to challenge the picture he gives of aborigine society as built upon homogeneous tightly organized clans. In fact the clan structure was loose and the proposed coincidence of clan and totem extremely dubious. The same goes for the evidence of correspondence between classificatory system and social organization. It is not even clear that aborigine systems of thought were unified within single units of social organization as his arguments suggest. And, of course, many objections have been raised to Durkheim's assumption that Australian totemism may be regarded as representing the most primitive or elementary stage of either social organization or religious thought.

Sacred/profane distinction

A second group of criticisms surrounds the distinction between sacred and profane. Critics have objected that the distinction is faulty at an empirical level, that is, as an account of what aborigine religious thought was actually like. They also complain that it fails at a conceptual level as well. For example it is not clear why there can only be *two* classes of objects. Is there not also at least one other class which consists of things which are neither sacred nor profane, but simply 'mundane'? (Stanmer 1975). Again, is the relationship between the two classes of objects one of total hostility or one of a division between two *complementary* systems of thought?

Religious beliefs and rituals

A third group of criticisms concerns Durkheim's explanations of religious beliefs and rituals. Despite the length and detail of *The Elementary Forms* the explanation is cast in very general form. The origins of the actual content of religious systems are not accounted for at all but treated as if, say, the choice of sacred objects or the actual ritual prescription themselves were arbitrary or unimportant. This is especially regrettable in the case of rituals since it has been argued that rituals do, in fact, always contain an important material basis in the agricultural technology of the tribe or group which employs them (Worsley 1956).

Religion and society

Durkheim is irritatingly ambiguous on the subject of the exact relation between religion and society or between society and the conceptual order. At various points he seems to be claiming that social organization exerts a causal influence over religious thought. At others, as when he asserts that 'nearly all the great social institutions have been born in religion' (Durkheim 1976, pp. 418–19), it is religious thought which is the determining element. At still other points he appears to be arguing that religion and society are the same thing. This does not exhaust the list. Lukes has identified no less than six distinct hypotheses, none of them reducible to the others, about the relation between society and ideas which can be found within Durkheim's sociology of knowledge as a whole (1973, p. 75).

Knowledge and reason

Finally, there are the philosophical problems raised by Durkheim's attempt to place the source of our notions of validity and truth within the social order. This is of course a general problem facing any sociologist who wishes to say something more than the commonplace that knowledge always develops within a social context. To assert that the actual logical rules and criteria which we use to distinguish genuine knowledge from mere thought in general are also social artefacts is to enter a philosophical minefield. The trouble centres around what is called *relativism*. Relativism is a philosophical doctrine which asserts that there is no way in which humans can escape the limiting, selective and relative effects of the conditions in which knowledge is produced. Though it sounds a very plausible belief it has the apparent effect of undermining

1   the basis of scientific knowledge in general which is the appeal to independent and objective evidence;
2   the idea of sociology as the rigorous and scientific study of social facts – a particularly serious problem for Durkheim;
3   the very proposition itself, which is stated in the form of a universal law; that is, that the criteria of knowledge are always relative to the conditions of their production.

Durkheim certainly did not wish to embrace such a heterodox doctrine and at the end of his life was seeking ways to defend the notion of rational enquiry while simultaneously giving full credit to the social foundations of reason.

Durkheim's influence and the rival interpretations of his thought

Having completed our review of Durkheim's major pieces of substantive work our final task will be to form some assessment of his significance for sociology. The problem with this, however, is that later generations have used his work in diverse ways in order to legitimate their *own* views about what is significant in the discipline. A study of various competing interpretations of Durkheim's thought is thus equally as important as study of the works themselves. Here we shall briefly consider three alternative strands of social theory, all of which have at various times been said to have been derived from or enriched by Durkheim.

Conservative sociology

According to some accounts Durkheim's work gave a major boost to conservatism in sociology in general. It has been portrayed as part of an attempt by 'bourgeois' intellectuals at the turn of the century to challenge and neutralize Marxism (Zeitlin 1971, pp. 231–7). This interpretation of Durkheim's thought introduces some criticisms of it which we have already considered and rejected because they do not tally with the most recent accounts of his views. Whilst no revolutionary, he did not favour the conservative politics of his time and in fact propounded major changes in economic institutions and the distribution of wealth. He drew upon a tradition of conservative thought in order to criticize its fundamental thesis, namely, that the ills of industrial society should be cured by a return to traditional religion and morality. Durkheim has also been accused of holding, like other conservatives, a pessimistic view of human nature which insists upon the necessity of moral control as a way of restraining the instincts and passions of the pre-social individual. Giddens has argued convincingly and in detail that none of these charges reflects accurately the actual content of Durkheim's endeavours (Giddens 1971, 1977, pp. 208–91). As we shall see in the next chapter, Durkheim's authority has been cited by certain management theorists in order to justify conservatism in the workplace. But Durkheim himself was by no means a thoroughgoing conservative.

The founder of functionalism

This phrase encapsulates what has been, until recently, the most widespread assessment of Durkheim's true significance. After Spencer he has been regarded as doing more than anyone to bring into sociology the functionalist method of explanation (examined in the next part of the book). According to this method social phenomena and institutions are explained in terms of their functions for the continuance of society as a whole. There is, in fact, fairly solid evidence of Durkheim's functionalist mode of thought to be found in his actual work. Thus he writes of the need 'to determine whether there is a correspondence between the facts under consideration and the general needs of the social organism'. Examples of the use of this procedure exist in both the early and the late works. His theories about the *Division of Labour* in society as well as the analysis in *The Elementary Forms* are clearly designed to show the functions of the object of study for social solidarity as a whole. And at the end of the latter work appears a passage which anticipates a key functionalist notion, that of a central value system (Durkheim 1976, p. 422). With all of these examples, however, it must be carefully borne in mind that Durkheim was always insistent upon the difference between causal and functional explanation. Furthermore, he stressed the desirability of achieving a satisfactory understanding of the *causal origins* of social phenomena before establishing their functions. This advice was not always observed by those who claimed to be his heirs. We shall return to this problem in Chapters 16 and 17.

The originator of structuralism

It is misleading to see Durkheim as *no more than* the precursor of modern functionalism. In recent years increasing prominence has been given to those aspects of his work which may be described as anticipating a so-called *structuralist* perspective. Structuralism represents a number of analogous tendencies in modern social thought which we have hesitated to treat as a separate school of thought. This is partly because of its fragmentary character, partly because of the difficulties which substantive structuralist work would present in an introductory text, and partly because, *pace* functionalism, the structuralists should, if anything, be classed among the true inheritors of the Durkheimian position. And, as we shall see, structuralism has exercised a greater hold in Durkheim's country, France, than elsewhere.

The word structure may be employed in sociology in two different ways which we shall term the 'architectural' and the 'implicit'. The 'architectural' sense refers to the obvious and observable sense in which an object or an organism may be said to possess structure. The 'implicit' sense is best understood by analogy with language. Language possesses structure in so far as it conforms to a series of rules of grammar. The latter are not directly observable but only discoverable by analysis of what is actually present, that is, actual speech and writing.

Both uses have been imported into sociology. The architectural metaphor has been taken up by both anthropological and normative functionalism and also underlies the cruder versions of the Marxist distinction between base and *superstructure*. Modern structuralists, however, wish to distance themselves from this usage or even reject it altogether. According to one account their aim is to elucidate the underlying principles by which a social system works and this involves recognizing that communication forms the basis of all social transactions (Leach 1961, p. 6). Thus even economic exchange is not *just* exchange. As Durkheim himself noted, it also communicates something about the cohesion of society as a whole.

This stress on the analysis of communication entails:

1   Attention to the system of ideas rather than (or as well as) the structure of a society: 'a system of social ideas bears the same sort of relationship to what actually happens as does a musical score to the performance. The score is, in a sense, the cause of what happens but we . . . cannot reliably infer the score from direct observation of any single performer's behaviour.' (Leach 1961, p. 5)

2   An analogy between speaking a language – which is after all itself a form of social behaviour – and the conduct of social intercourse. Structuralist sociologists have been impressed by advances in linguistics, notably the work on the 'deep structure' of language and transformational grammar associated with Naom Chomsky (for example, Lyons 1970).

3   An interest in how far patterns in the structure of cultural ideas reflect a common unchanging set of rules by which the human mind, in its traffic with others, always operates.

Much in Durkheim may be read as an anticipation of this way of thought even though it is combined with his functionalist perspective (Bottomore and Nisbet 1978; Glucksman 1974, pp. 25–6).

The subsequent growth of structuralism owed a great deal to Durkheim's actual teaching. This manifested itself in the immediately following generation of scholars, notably Mauss and Halbwachs. Apart from his collaboration with Durkheim, Mauss is famous for his essay on ceremonial gift exchanges which, again in truly Durkheimian fashion, emphasizes the underlying significance of such acts for the maintenance of social cohesion, communication and reciprocity between giver and taker.

In acknowledging the work of Durkheim and his followers, Levi-Strauss writes of their 'attempt to break up the categories of the layman and to group the data into a deeper,

sounder classification' (quoted in Glucksman 1974, p. 26). This is worthy of a similar passage at the end of the *Rules of Sociological Method*. In this Durkheim claims that sociology asks its followers 'to discard the concepts they are accustomed to apply to our order of facts, in order to re-examine the latter in a new way'. This insistence that sociology is more than the naïve understandings possessed by the layman represents the very essence of the Durkheimian attitude to society itself.

Conclusion

In this chapter, then, we have tried to present the sociology of Emile Durkheim as an attempt to reconcile two potentially conflicting demands. On the one hand there was his attempt to provide sociology with a rigorous and objective method. On the other was the desire to portray society as an interaction of minds that would have consequences for the subjective life of each individual. His major works develop this second notion in ever more audacious and precise terms.

In *The Division of Labour* the collective consciousness merely determines the extent to which people develop a sense of themselves as individuals.

In *Suicide* the mental system of a people actually is capable of affecting their conduct.

In *The Elementary Forms* collective life penetrates to the very categories and rules according to which people think.

Inevitably this programme involved making statements about elements in subjective mental life itself, elements which involved conceptions of a 'self'. But the 'self' of any given individual is logically and empirically distinct from the forces which weld separate selves into a collectivity. Failure to make this distinction caused Durkheim increasingly to violate the more unrelenting aspects of his *Rules of Sociological Method*. By the end of his career he had abandoned the rather simple view of social facts as characterized by exteriority and constraint. He wrote:

The problem of sociology – if we can speak of a sociological problem – consists in seeking, among the different forms of external constraint, the different sorts of moral authority corresponding to them and discovering the causes which have determined these latter. (Durkheim 1976, p. 2084)

'Moral authority' on this view restrains individual self-interest but its force does not possess the inevitability of physical causes. In Chapters 18 and 19 we shall consider a number of theories which set out from the point where this notion of 'moral authority' leaves off.

But first we must consider some of the many ways in which Durkheimian sociology has influenced research and thinking in the mainstream of the discipline he did so much to establish.

15   Anomie, disorder and conflict

The legacy which Durkheim left to later generations of sociological investigators defies easy summary. As we tried to show at the end of the last chapter, quite separate traditions of enquiry have claimed him as their mentor. Furthermore, 'the spirit if not the detail' of his theories (Swanson 1960, p. 17) still continues to stimulate work on the topics which he himself had written about – suicide, religion, law and crime. Above all, few sociologists, whatever their opinions, have been wholly untouched by his general example and his stalwart advocacy of his discipline.

In selecting material for this chapter, therefore, we have been able to draw upon only a very small part of post-Durkheimian writings and research. Our judgement of what is most significant in this literature is inevitably a highly personal one, shaped by the objectives which we have been pursuing in this book as a whole:

a   We have sought to show that sociology derives its *rigour* from a debate about a determinate and related set of issues.
b   In reviewing the contribution of each particular school of thought we have sought to defend the *relevance* of sociology as a guide to public events and personal experience in the modern world.

In terms of these criteria, certain topics almost select themselves – as we shall now explain.

The *core problems within the discipline* which we have so far encountered may be roughly divided into two groups. On the one hand, finding its clearest expression in Marxism and in the Weberian critique of Marxism, there is the theme of inequality, constraint, power and *social conflict*. On the other, there is the theme of morality, integration and *social order*. The last is especially central to the 'community' school, of course, but it also provides much of the impetus behind classical evolutionary writing, to say nothing of modern functionalism which we shall be discussing in the next chapter.

On the face of it, Durkheimian sociology also appears to be focused on the latter set of issues. After all, Durkheim himself claimed to be founding a science of 'morality' and 'moral authority'. But if we follow this view exclusively we shall miss some of the subtler aspects of his work. We shall also fail to catch the special significance of one particular topic to which it has given rise, namely the sociology of *anomie* and the consequences of anomie for individual behaviour and social cohesion.

In Durkheim's various discussions of anomie, the themes of morality and inequality, order and conflict are always either fused together or, at the very least, considered in relation to each other. Of particular significance are those passages where he points to the consequences of inequality for the degree of integration or cohesion in society. An unjust or forced division of labour, he points out, implies a society held together not by organic solidarity but by coercion. Inequality, in short, presents acute problems of justice and morality. Since Durkheim's death these ideas have attracted continued discussion and development.

The 'sociology of anomie' also offers a means of furthering the second of our objectives:

relevance to contemporary society. During the past decade or so it has become a cliché of popular political discussion that Britain is becoming 'ungovernable'. Among the diversity of stirrings which have been taken to indicate the waning of public order, two have become particularly acute recently, namely:

a disaffection among the young;
b disorderly industrial relations.

One influential way of interpreting these troubles, not surprisingly perhaps, is to see them in Marxist terms. For Marxists, both forms of unrest are indicators of the inherent contradictions of British capitalism, its precarious solidarity and the potential growth of class consciousness among disaffected sections of the population. We shall have more to say about this kind of analysis later in the chapter. But this is not the only account that is available. Among non-Marxist alternatives the most important, without doubt, can be described as 'neo-Durkheimian'. This is because some sociologists have attempted to analyse *both* the youth problem *and* industrial relations troubles as manifestations of anomie. Thus by comparing modern anomie theories with the Marxist alternative we shall be discussing matters of considerable topical interest.

Although it is not usual to say so, the modern theory of anomie represents, in fact, the neo-Durkheimian counterpart of the great 'debate with the ghost of Marx' posed by Weberian sociology. It originated not in Britain but in the United States of America. Even the vaguest acquaintance with twentieth-century American social history should serve as a reminder that problems of unrest in industry and among youth are not confined to Britain alone. The USA, however, has been a society in which few intellectuals, or for that matter, few members of the labour movement, have really taken to Marxism. It has also been a society which has fitted only with difficulty into the Marxist theory of capitalist development, particularly in relation to the thorny question of the growth of

proletarian class consciousness. And lastly, of course, post-war American sociology has been dominated by the view that Marxist perspectives on the development of capitalism and class are simply out of date (see Chapters 7, 10 and 16). For all of these reasons, therefore, Durkheim's ideas on the anomic division of labour have, at various times, offered an attractive alternative to Marxism as a way of accounting for the existence of conflicts and strains in American society.

The first uses of Durkheimian thought in this context were of a somewhat conservative cast, the most renowned example being the 'managerial' sociology of Elton Mayo. Mayo was an Australian who emigrated to the USA and who became associated with the so-called Hawthorn 'experiments' on the behaviour and productivity of industrial workgroups. These were conducted from the Western Electric Company by a Harvard University team during the 1930s; but Mayo's reflections on social tensions in industry, like most of the other literature inspired by the experiments, were not published until after World War II (Mayo 1949, 1959; Bendix and Fisher 1965; Rose 1975). There are many superficial similarities between Mayo and Durkheim. Mayo believed for example that trade union militancy and industrial conflict were a symptom, not of a conflict of interest between employer and employee, but of the moral 'rootlessness' of industrial civilization. The solution, he thought, lay in:

a an enhancement of the role of the company as the basis for the re-emergence of community;
b managerial leadership as the basis for better 'human relations'.

Durkheim is actually cited in support of this thesis. Careful inspection shows, however, that Mayo and his disciples in the Human Relations movement were, in fact, advocating almost the reverse of what Durkheim had favoured. Their prescription is for a return to the kind of group ties which constitute a denial of the moral individualist idea. Mayoism really fits in better with the 'loss of community' school of thought than with the ideas propounded in *The Division of Labour*.

A number of well-known fieldwork investigations grew out of this early industrial sociology, however. As Eldridge points out in a useful résumé, these contained a more critical and truly Durkheimian outlook than Mayo's own. In the works of Cottrell (1951) and Lloyd Warner (Warner and Low 1957) we are presented with evidence of the weakening of both communal ties and *moral authority* by the capricious economic forces of the market. These authors did not fail to point out that the resultant anomie was built into the American way of life (Eldridge 1971b, pp. 100–11).

Another well-known study in the same genre is Ely Chinoy's *Automobile Workers and the American Dream* (1955). Chinoy interviewed in depth sixty-two male assembly line workers, a group who, in their own eyes as well as of others, were deemed to have failed to realize the success ethic of the wider society. His book reports the various ways in which his respondents had tried to come to terms with the monotony, low status and limited prospects associated with their jobs. Some rejected the success ethic itself; others redefined it in some way, usually by stressing the relatively good wages they received in comparison with other types of semi-skilled work; still others had sought, in fantasy or in fact, to 'escape', notably via self-employment; a few sought compensation by means of a union career. Chinoy's theme of adaptation to the failure of ambition and the absence of opportunity reflects not so much the influence of Elton Mayo, however, but of Robert Merton. And it is with Merton's work that any serious study of modern writings on anomie must begin.

Deviance, delinquency and opportunity

Merton's much discussed and frequently misunderstood reworking of the theory of anomie looks beyond the relatively narrow problems of the factory worker and the world of employment to the wider issues of deviance and the breakdown of conformity in general (Merton 1968b).

First, a word of explanation. The term 'deviance' is not easy to explain or define. In practice the so-called sociology of deviance has concerned itself not simply with crime and delinquency but also with such phenomena as drug-taking, suicide, marital breakdown, sexual abnormality, stuttering, wife-battering and so on. At one extreme it has sought to understand counter- and subcultures of various sorts; at the other it examines society's *response* to deviance, that is, not just attempts to control social 'problems' but also why people come to define them as such and why they worry about them. A number of different perspectives in this field have a common origin in Durkheim's writings (Jones 1981), anomie theory being just one of them. Other schools of sociology have also made their mark upon it, of course, notably Chicago sociology, and, as we shall soon see, Marxism, psycho-analysis and symbolic interactionism. Yet despite the volume of research produced by these various influences the precise common denominator behind these different manifestations of deviance remains unclear. Merton's theory of anomie represented an early and very influential attempt to impose an overall framework. It has been said of it that its widespread use and acceptance 'testified to the need' for such a scheme. But the near-monopoly which it enjoyed for some years 'testified to the paucity of original thinking' which existed in the field as a whole (Cohen A. K. 1959, p. 464).

All societies make two general kinds of moral demand upon their members, Merton argues. First, they establish certain culturally approved goals such as economic success, which individuals are encouraged to strive towards. Second, they set out certain approved ways or 'institutionalized means' (for example, 'hard work') of achieving these goals (and by implication throw disapproval on other illegitimate forms of access; for example, cheating). In a perfectly functioning society there should be no strain or inconsistency between goals and institutionalized means. But in actual societies there is no logical reason why this should automatically happen. In some cases, for example, the original purposes (or goals) are forgotten and close adherence to institutionally prescribed conduct (the means) becomes a matter of ritual. In others 'exaltation of the end generates a literal *demoralisation* of the means' (Merton 1968, p. 190). It is from the second of these 'disorders' that modern America suffers: there is great emphasis upon certain success goals but a lack of attention to the availability or propriety of ways of getting them. The anomie or 'normlessness' of such a system is hidden from the participants by an ideological smokescreen which acts upon them in two main ways. First, it will not allow anyone to give up: 'Americans are bombarded on every side by precepts which affirm the right or often the duty of retaining the goal even in the face of repeated frustration.' (Merton 1968, p. 191) Second, failure is held to be a personal flaw not a product of the system. (Chinoy's fieldwork materials were in fact later to provide powerful demonstration of the effectiveness of this ideological 'smokescreen'.) But Merton himself suggests that the main consequence is *that the system is protected from criticism*.

The 'ideological smokescreen' can, however, be penetrated by scientific analysis, showing how the strains of anomie lead to deviant patterns of adjustment. It used to be argued that in offering his own view of what this scientific analysis should look like, Merton *betrayed* Durkheim, twisting and watering down the concept of anomie (Horton 1964). More recently, however, the assessment has been more favourable. The critical cutting edge of Merton's arguments has been acknowledged and recognition given to the fact that he manages to *improve* upon Durkheim in ways that are consistent with Durkheim's own stated aims (Eldridge 1971b, pp. 119–35; Taylor I. *et al.* 1973; Young 1974). As Young observes, for Merton anomie results from two failings of modern social organization:

1 *Distributional arbitrariness*. In Durkheimian terms the society is 'unjust'. Merton writes: 'in this same society that proclaims the right and even the duty of lofty aspirations for all, men (*sic*) do not have equal access to the opportunity structure.' Unequal social origins due to class, race and, of course, sex ensure that merit and opportunity do not coincide.

2 *Regulative weakness*. The moral system is 'utilitarian' in that it concentrates on the ends, leaving the individual only loose guidance as to the means of achieving them.

In this situation restraints upon the range of tactics that may legitimately be used to achieve success are in constant danger of being eroded. It is as if the players in a game ceased to abide by the official rules and began to adopt a variety of underhand devices in order to guarantee victory. Since 'the pressure of such a social order is upon out-doing one's competitors' (Merton 1968, p. 211) cultural taboos recede before the adoption of *any* tactic that is technically efficient in achieving the desired end. Merton drives home the point:

With this attenuation of institutional controls, there occurs an approximation to the situation erroneously held by the utilitarian philosophers to be typical of society, a situation in which calculations of personal advantage and fear of punishment are the only regulating agencies. (Merton 1968)

A social structure with these characteristics produces a strain towards anomie and, hence, deviant behaviour. Merton describes five types of adaptation which individuals will make in the course of performing roles in society (Table 7). Which one of these adaptations is in fact adopted depends on:

a the type of relation between means and ends generated by the position of the individual in the social structure;

b the kind of role being performed – in this case Merton claims to be interested primarily in economic activity.

The types of adaptation are as follows:

Table 7   *Merton's typology of modes of individual adaptation*

Modes of adaptation		Cultural goals	Institutionalized means
I	Conformity	+	+
II	Innovation	+	–
III	Ritualism	–	+
IV	Retreatism	–	–
V	Rebellion	±	±

+ = Acceptance;   – = rejection;   ± = rejection of prevailing values and substitution of new values.

Conformity

The simplest case to understand, and also the most frequent, involves straightforward acceptance of both the cultural goal and the approved means. Its relative frequency in a society is a measure of the stability of that society. In the American case, however, there are two problems with acting in a conformist manner. First, as we have already noted, use of approved means requires access to the requisite opportunities and resources. Second, Merton recognizes that the accumulation of money symbolizes and indeed facilitates many other forms of success; in turn it can and does become an end in itself. 'But the accumulation of money is an indefinite limitless and unsubstantial measure. . . . The anomie of the successful results from the futile pursuit of a nebulous and ever retreating end.' (Young 1974, pp. 174–5; Merton 1968, p. 190) There is little doubt, however, that this 'anomie of the successful' receives less attention from Merton than the 'anomie of injustice' to be found in the remaining types of adaptation. Each of these is anomic or deviant responses brought about by strain in the relation between means and ends.

Innovation

Brendan Behan once observed that 'A crook is only a businessman without an office.' Merton draws attention to the thin line between legitimate and illegitimate ways of earning money with a more ponderous epigram: 'The history of the great American fortunes is threaded (*sic*) with strains toward institutionally dubious innovations.' (1968b, p. 195). 'Innovation', then, means *acceptance* of the success goal so stressed by the culture but *rejection* of legitimate means in favour of deviant ones. If a fortunate few become millionaires in this way, however, it remains generally true that 'the greatest pressures towards deviation are exerted upon the lower strata' (1968b, p. 198) for the simple reason that at this point in the social structure opportunities to achieve legitimate success are relatively few and far between. And this he claims is borne out by the crime statistics which, allowing for their many faults, show a clear increase in crime and delinquency as we descend the social scale. This is not due to the deviant 'natures' of the lower orders but to the social strain placed upon the individuals concerned.

Ritualism

This case is the contrary of 'innovation'. Individuals scale down or abandon their attempt to realize the goal of success but continue to 'go through the motions', as it were, persisting in a formal compliance with the 'institutionalized means'. Merton thinks that such adaptations generally will be congenial to members of the lower middle class especially those who have been brought up to conform and be respectable and who, at the same time, are not as well endowed with opportunity as the upper classes. Middle-class economic and work environments reinforce this tendency: 'ritualism' is the hallmark of the 'bureaucratic personality', and, as Merton notes in another essay, threatens the rationality of bureaucracy itself (Merton 1968c). Hence relative failure of career and lifestyle engender fatalism, resignation, lowered hope and a spirit of 'playing safe'.

Retreatism

A further alternative response to strain is to drop out of society altogether, rejecting both means and ends. In this category Merton includes 'psychotics, artists, pariahs, outcasts, vagrants, vagabonds, tramps, chronic drunkards and drug addicts'. What these forms have in common, he argues, is that their response is individual and 'asocial'. In fact, this is highly contentious. Quite often, as subsequent fieldwork has shown, these forms develop in conjunction with group subcultures which, on investigation, prove to be intricate and even colourful. To assert that retreatism is always 'asocial', therefore, is misleading.

Rebellion

'Rebellion presupposes alienation from reigning goals and standards' and the possibility of the pursuit of new ones: first, by means of countervailing myths; second, once new myths exist by organized political action.

This, then, is Merton's schema. Though highly influential, as we have said, it contains many flaws. We shall list the most important:

1 *It is too abstract and tidy* Several authors have noted that Merton does not even exploit the full range of adaptations logically possible within the classification itself. Others have attempted various refinements and amendments (Clinard 1964b, pp. 23ff.; Eldridge 1971b, p. 222).
2 *It appears to make deviance an individual act* – alternatively it fails to spell out the role of groups in the creation of individual deviant acts.
3 *It fails to criticize or question the factors which give rise to the goals of material success in the first place.* Merton, in fact, casts the sociologist in a rather manipulative role, advising governments on how to 'reform' the opportunity structure so that there will be less strain in the system. He also seems to assume that there is a universal consensus in society as to the desirability of material success and the 'deviance' of rejecting it. This leads to an 'all or nothing' view of the way individuals are taught societal values.
4 *Its treatment of rebellion is superficial* This is especially relevant given the 'debate with Marx' that we are emphasizing in this chapter. Merton's model implies that rebellion is just another way of responding to anomie. In effect, his classification defines away the possibility thrown up later by fieldworkers, that the forms of behaviour classified as 'innovation' might also contain a greater or lesser degree of countermythology and rebellion. Moreover, it begs the question which, as later Marxist critiques were to point out, is the basic bone of contention between their approach and 'neo-Durkheimian' explanations of social tension. For, as we have said already, to the Marxist class consciousness is a real and ever-present possibility. 'Anomie', in so far as Marxists acknowledge it at all, is merely a symptom of class conflict. Durkheim's view, and by implication Merton's as well, is the exact opposite; class conflict ('rebellion') is a symptom of anomie. Merton, in fact, avoided the issue. The implication of his position is that anomie, if it reached serious proportions, could lead people to reject the American way of life altogether – an end result little different in practice from Marxist revolutionary theory. In later writings he seems to have sought to divorce anomie from possibilities of open revolution. In these he distinguishes between:

a *non-conformity*, 'in which the non-conformist announces his dissent publicly'; and
b *aberrant deviance* (that is, innovation etc.) in which the non-conformity is hidden (Merton 1964, 1966).

Merton's equivocation over this point would (and for a time *did*) impose severe limitations on the sociology of deviance, leaving underexplored the relation of 'hidden' individual and subcultural non-conformity to publicly declared dissent. Yet there are not only some interesting parallels between these two but also some awkward borderline cases. The most germane perhaps is the case of organized industrial militancy by workers, particularly in the form of 'unofficial' action. Marxists see industrial conflict as clear evidence of revolutionary potential among ordinary workers. Although non-conformity to industrial relations practice is publicly proclaimed, sometimes with the rhetoric of class conflict, however, it could equally well be *explained* as a case of innovatory response to strain between ends (higher wages, group status) and restricted means (including low wages and unsatisfactory formal grievance procedures). But we anticipate.

Despite its shortcomings, Merton's reworking of anomie theory formed the basic reference point for a large number of empirical studies of types of deviant behaviour (Clinard 1964b, p. 216). Undoubtedly though, the most celebrated instances were to be found in research into *delinquency among urban youth*. For present purposes, therefore, we can concentrate upon significant developments on that particular problem.

First, some background. Teenage delinquency and gang violence had already been well studied long before Merton's paper appeared. Most of the important contributions, however, had been cast within the 'Chicago School' perspective which we discussed in Chapter 3. The emphasis, as the reader might expect in this work, is upon the *ecological* factors in delinquency. The city is depicted as a product of struggle for territory and resources between several distinct zones formed on the basis of either natural or (later in the theory) cultural characteristics. Rapid immigration and turnover of population, however, undermine the community structure of a zone. Crime and delinquency will be the result. Thus, Shaw and Mackay explain the concentration of these phenomena in inner city-areas in terms of the 'social disorganization' which had occurred there (Shaw and Mackay 1942). The consequences, as Sutherland pointed out, will be that the inhabitants, particularly the youth of such areas, will be exposed to 'an excess of definitions favourable to violation of law over definitions unfavourable to violation of law'. This aspect of the inner-city environment, in which

the young criminal grows up and learns deviant perceptions of the social world, he termed '*differential association*' (Sutherland and Cressey 1966). Delinquency as such, therefore, is the product of a 'delinquent subculture' offering 'delinquent solutions' (as they later came to be called; see Downes 1966) to the problems of living in a particular area.

Thus an impressive body of work was already in existence, one which had already managed to conceptualize behaviour as the product of collective factors. Yet in the 1950s these early subcultural theories were rejected by many of the younger sociologists because: (*a*) they made the individual appear as a passive recipient of subculture; and (*b*) they neglected the flow of influence between deviant and mainstream culture.

It was in this context that Merton's version of anomie theory made its appearance. Its applicability to the problem of delinquency, therefore, soon became the focus of extensive discussion and has continued to do so until the present day. Three major phases in this debate can be discerned. The first, building on Merton's example, consists of attempts to rework the concept of delinquent subculture in broadly Durkheimian terms, stressing its 'psychically creative' role in the face of the inequalities confronting different classes of youth. The second consists of various 'reactions' to these efforts within orthodox academic sociology. The third, and most recent has arisen out of the Marxist revival of the 1960s and 1970s. Its point of departure is the failure of all previous delinquency theories, including anomie theory, to carry their account of the origins of delinquency in inequality through to its 'logical' conclusion. Let us consider each of these phases.

Anomie and delinquent opportunity

Applying Merton's model of deviant behaviour to a specific example, delinquency, soon revealed its more important flaws. One difficulty – not the only one, as we shall see – was the problem of fitting the diversity of delinquent behaviour observed by fieldworkers into the single (and rather general) category of 'innovation'. An important attempt to deal with this problem is to be found in the work of Cloward and Ohlin (1960). These authors accepted the general proposition that deviance results from the anomie caused by discrepancy between institutionalized goals and available means. Legitimate forms of opportunity are not the only ones which are unequally distributed, however. Illegitimate forms are also concentrated in certain districts where, as Sutherland and others had argued, 'delinquent association' makes illegitimate opportunities available in a fashion which is not open to disaffected youth elsewhere. There will thus be at least three kinds of delinquent subculture:

1 *Conflict* subculture where, as in the classic Mertonian case, legitimate opportunity is closed off without presentation of an alternative. Hence we find that delinquency takes the form of irrational violent behaviour.
2 *Criminal* subculture, where legitimate opportunity is closed off but illegitimate opportunity is available and taken up. Here gang delinquency functions as an adjunct to organized adult crime.
3 *Retreatist* subculture, which represents a closing off of both legitimate and illegitimate opportunity. It is expressed in the world of drug-taking, vagrancy and so on.

As the reader will appreciate this represents an ingenious fusion of the earlier Chicago tradition *with* anomie theory and at the time was heralded as something of a breakthrough.

Status frustration and lower-class values

The 'anomie' theory nevertheless met with formidable objections. One of the more influential critics was A. K. Cohen who complained that Merton had represented the resort to deviance as a product of an isolated individual decision whereas most youth delinquency is committed in and through groups. Merton had also distorted reality by making deviance appear calculative and rational. Actual delinquency is marked by destructiveness, versatility, zest and 'negativism' – a hostile, dismissive attitude to orthodox society. For these reasons, Cohen himself repudiated the notion of anomie altogether, replacing it with his key concept of 'status frustration' (see below).

This was a somewhat hasty decision. For one thing, Merton had little difficulty in showing that he had anticipated many of Cohen's arguments, even if, as he himself later admitted, his original formulation of his theory had been unclear. Nevertheless, he insisted there is nothing integral to the theory 'which requires it to be atomistic and individualistic'. On the contrary, 'anomie is a condition of the social environment, not of the isolated self' (Merton 1964, p. 234). But, we may ask, how exactly does this 'condition of the social environment' come about?

Paradoxically, by pointing to the need for the concept of a delinquent subculture, Cohen contributed towards overcoming this deficiency in anomie theory. Therefore, his account of how the subculture arises and produces its effects is sufficiently analogous to Merton's model to invite comparisons. Thus, whereas Merton concentrates on the discrepancy between *monetary* success goals and the differential availability of means, Cohen focuses on the discrepancy between:

a the 'universalistic' standards which in theory determine *status* in modern society;
b the limited opportunity available in practice to lower-class youth that leads them to experience 'status frustration'.

The school is the focal point of the tension. Here the lower-class boy experiences acute problems of status as he encounters universal standards and middle-class culture to which he cannot respond adequately. The key difference from Merton is the observation that there will be at any one time a number of individuals in close proximity who experience *the same problem*.

Together, they elaborate a subculture based on 'reaction formation'; that is, a deliberate inversion of middle-class norms and values. And the bearer of this culture, the delinquent gang, provides a structure in which alternative forms of status can be realized through daring and violent behaviour.

Cohen in fact is describing a rather extreme delinquent subculture which, so his critics in turn argued, accounts for a mere 10 per cent or so of known delinquency. W. Miller, for example, questioned whether the delinquent subculture is simply a negative reversal of middle-class values. On the basis of extensive field studies using anthropological techniques, and using a conceptual framework that implicitly revives the notion of 'delinquent association', he argued that delinquency is better viewed as an extension of a separate and self-contained value system borne along by adult working-class culture. This culture embodies a tradition of *sustained* resistance to the middle-class world. Delinquent behaviour merely represents an extension of this culture and an affirmation of its continuance in the rising generation. Consider, for example, the violent style which, so Miller claimed, characterizes the adult culture. This, as his fieldwork showed, typically expresses itself not in the rather exceptional violent gang of Cohen's account but in the commoner looser-knit 'street corner' gang in which aggression is directed inward towards the members of the peer group rather than against conventional middle-class society (Miller 1958).

Of course, these different interpretations of 'subculture' are not necessarily incompatible. It is rather to be expected that a diversity of subcultural responses creates in turn a diversity of types of delinquency. Downes (1966) suggests that much of the difference between Miller and Cohen can be resolved by distinguishing between:

1 *subcultural elements* formed outside or independently of a dominant culture, for example in the case of immigrant groups, or building upon pre-existing communal ties and traditions of resistance;

2 emergent *'cultural solutions'* that appear in response to conflict situations as in Cohen's example of the school.

These, then, were the theories; but what of the evidence? The broad impression to be gained from the voluminous research inspired by anomie and subcultural interpretations of deviancy is that the modifications and developments from Merton's initiative still fail to capture the complexity of real life situations. The work of Short is among the best known of the American studies (Short 1964; Short and Strodtbeck 1965). He contacted sixteen gangs (covering five hundred and ninety-eight boys) via the YMCA of Metropolitan Chicago. In addition to detailed observations made by the authors, the subjects of the study were encouraged to complete personality tests and questionnaires and from the results Short and Strodtbeck examined no less than ten propositions relevant to the Cohen/Miller/Cloward debate. The findings confirm none of the theories fully. Their key conclusion was that the gang boys *do* use the gang to create alternative status systems but that delinquency arises almost as a chance by-product. Evidence that it is produced by 'reaction formation' against the middle-class world was lacking, nor did an individual's association with the gang necessarily coincide with a rejection of conventional values. Likewise, those groups subject to the most strain between ambition and opportunity did not necessarily show the highest rate of offences (as measured by the police record). Similar findings as to the complexity of the factors in delinquency are reported by Spergel (Spergel 1964).

Further complications present themselves when the theories are applied outside of the American context. In a review of the theories and their compatibility with the then available British material, Downes found almost no evidence of the existence at the time of writing of organized criminal gang subcultures as suggested by Cloward and Ohlin; nor of the relevance of the contra-culture of Cohen's model. The somewhat thin material indicated a straightforward conformity to the expectations of lower-class 'slum' culture, which if anything fits closest to the arguments of Miller. A number of intervening factors, however, complicate the picture, not least the rate of unemployment among juveniles which at that time was very *low*. This was still a period of relative prosperity, and exploitation of the teenage market constituted not only an important focus of commercial interest but also a source of pressure on the young people themselves. If anomie and strain between goals and ends was felt by lower-class youth at all it was in the area of *leisure*. On one hand they were exposed to the usual advertising which preached the desirability of leisure commodities. On the other, contrary to popular belief, they often lacked sufficient means to obtain these goods – particularly in the kind of depressed area observed in Downes's own fieldwork.

Downes's report, in fact, marks something of a watershed. In America, interest in anomie theory waned around that time (Rock 1979b, p. 60). It was displaced by a new critical approach which we consider in Chapter 18, known as *labelling* theory. Meanwhile, more *British* investigations began to appear. Like Downes they emphasized the importance of specific historical factors, in particular the level of economic activity. And times were changing. As a later author put it, the new work appeared in the context of a welfare state society which had gone 'sour'. It attacked the entire corpus of existing deviancy theory 'which had patently not delivered the goods' (Cohen S. 1980, p. iv). Rooted firmly in the Marxist tradition it rejected the separation of scientific and political activity so dear to Durkheim and his successors.

Of course, we cannot hope, in a chapter devoted to 'neo-Durkheimian' sociology, to do justice to the important insights provided by this 'neo-Marxist' work on deviance and subculture.

Nevertheless, it is necessary to form some kind of judgement as to whether the new studies succeeded in displacing the preoccupations of the older 'anomie' literature.

Neo-Marxism, disaffected youth and spectacular subculture

The 'new' wave of neo-Marxist writings was a reaction to *all* of the established sociological interpretations of youth which had been produced in the 1950s and 1960s – not just to anomie theories (for example, Hall and Jefferson 1976; Clarke and Jefferson 1976). The common failing of these interpretations, it was argued, is their inadequate treatment or even downright neglect of the problem of *class*. Especial scorn was reserved for the view, a by-product of the optimistic 'Industrial Society' perspective of much post-war sociology, that the problems of youth cut across questions of class. In these older theories adolescence was seen as a time of ambiguous status; not fully fledged adults, teenagers nevertheless wielded enormous spending power. 'Youth culture' (so-called) was seen as a product of conflict between generations not conflict between classes. Anomie and subcultural explanations of delinquency came out of the Marxist critique rather well, precisely because they progressively focused attention back to the real inequalities of the 'affluent' society – and thus to the continuing significance of class (Mungham and Pearson 1976, pp. 1–9). Merton was even credited with having 'used Marx to prise open Durkheim' (Taylor I. *et al.* 1973, p. 100), that is, for bringing out the cutting edge of Durkheim's attack upon individualism and economic competition.

Nevertheless, the post-Merton literature was held to contain four related faults. First, it displayed a tendency to assume a fundamental consensus in society on the question of success values. With the possible exception of Miller, all interpreters had assumed that resort to illegitimacy extends only to means, not ends. Second, its 'unhistorical' character: by this was meant that the delinquent responses of youth are explained in terms of a model that refers to no particular time or place other than 'American society' in general. Third, in consequence, the model fails to ask why status or monetary success goals should be so important in the first place. Individualism is, in fact, a feature of *capitalist* market society and exists in conjunction with inequalities of wealth and power to which the subcultural model does not directly point. Finally, therefore, the remedies offered are inadequate. Like Durkheim, Merton and many of his followers see the creation of a more equal opportunity structure, such that social position is determined more effectively by merit, as a sufficient remedy. To Merton, the planned intervention of the social scientist using objective knowledge to enable the 'system' to work more effectively is a form of 'rebellion'. But real rebellion against an unjust class-based order is a mere residual category to be illustrated, say, by remote examples from the French Revolution (Merton 1968b, pp. 244–5).

When we turn to examples of the substantive work produced by the Marxists themselves, we find, of course, that the question of rebellion looms large. The general style of it contrasts markedly with the material reviewed above. For one thing, the authors in question refuse to entertain the distinction between disinterested social science and political commitment which orthodox sociology derived from Weber and, of course, Durkheim. An early and highly influential account by P. Cohen of skinhead culture, for example, was written 'in the light of the writer's own work as a radical community worker' (Cohen P. 1972). There is also an emphasis on authenticity and relevance to the struggles of contemporary working-class youth (for example, Corrigan 1979). For this reason, fieldwork has tended to rely heavily on ethnographic and observational techniques directed at small groups placed at what are held to be strategic points of crisis – kids (*sic*) leaving school, black inner-city youth and so on. These features will not recommend themselves to

everyone (Rock 1979b). So it is important to point out that much of the work undertaken from this perspective does, by any standards, possess some obvious merits in comparison with the earlier literature:

1 it has succeeded in injecting an important and, it is to be hoped, permanent concern with the historical and environmental context in which deviant acts occur;
2 it has demonstrated the need to be concerned with the fine details of 'style' – symbols and coded meanings – adopted by youth (and other) subcultures;
3 it has emphasized the male gender bias of previous research and stimulated useful ethnographic accounts of female adolescent subculture and delinquency (for an overview see Brake 1980, Chapter 5).

Some influential examples will serve to illustrate the above points. First let us look at an area which is crucial both for orthodox anomie and neo-Marxist theories; the interface between school and class society. For A. K. Cohen, it will be recalled, it is in school that the aspiration of lower-class youth for status becomes thwarted by the middle-class goals and ideas. By contrast, neo-Marxist work emphasizes the way in which individuals encountered during the fieldwork had rejected the aims and authority of the school *from the start*. This argument of course recalls the Chicago tradition and W. Miller on lower-class subculture, except that the latter had treated individuals as if (like 'blank paper'!) they were stamped with the values appropriate to their circumstances. It is the 'reproduction' – that is to say, the acceptance and renewal of working-class subculture in each generation – which the Marxists wish to explain.

According to Corrigan, for example, school remains an *imposition* upon most working-class youngsters. The educational process is about controlling, moulding and changing character in conformity with a view of how society works which the youngsters in question do not share. This is because they and their families experience the 'opportunity' structure of the labour market as restrictive and uncompromising and they consequently reject the middle-class values that go with careerism. Consequently they resist the school's discipline by 'mucking about' and playing truant. Attempts to assert the authority of the teacher merely bottle up the resistance which will then find ingenious alternative means of expression (Corrigan 1979). A subtler version of the same thesis is offered by Willis (1977). In a much praised ethnography of the 'counter-school' culture he tries to show that, as he puts it at one point, 'counter-school culture has many profound similarities with the culture its members are mostly destined for – shop floor culture'. The act of resistance inherent in the refusal of school lessons and discipline arises from the fact that the culture of the 'difficult' working-class lads 'denies that knowledge is in any sense a meaningful "equivalent" for the generality of the working-class kids. . . . It knows better than the new vocational guidance what is the real state of the job market.' Yet, in this very act of resistance exists a curious kind of 'self-damnation' by which techniques of insubordination provide an unofficial preparation for labour within capitalist industry. One of the most basic things that 'the lads' learn from their culture is the sameness and uniformity of the work alternatives supposedly open to them. This is something that official school culture cannot admit. Instead: 'The culture allows this realisation to surface in one form or another because it provides an alternative to finding, and needing to find, satisfaction and particular meaning in work.' (Willis 1977, pp. 101–2) In this way not only are the values of adult male-oriented working-class culture sustained and 'reproduced' but so too are the central economic relationships between labour and capital.

A second and overlapping area of attention has been the 'spectacular' cultural styles – teds, mods, rockers, punks and so on – adopted by working-class youth of both sexes. But whereas the work of Corrigan and Willis could be applied fairly widely (and not just in Britain even), these movements call for attention to the particular times and context where they appear. In the work of P. Cohen, already alluded to, we find the basic idea that 'has literally transformed the study of spectacular youth culture', namely 'the idea of style as a coded response to changes affecting the entire community' (Hebdige 1979, p. 80). In this case the changes in question are developments in post-war society which led to the break-up of the cohesive East London community as depicted, say, in the famous surveys of the Institute of Community Studies (see Chapter 4). The *destruction* of the local economy, re-planning and rehousing led to the destruction of the very units through which the traditional working-class culture had always been expressed, that is, the local street, matrilocal residence, and recruitment into an established job structure. The predicament, Cohen argues, registered most deeply in the young. He tries to show that 'mods, Parkers, skinheads, crombies, all represent, in their different ways, an attempt to retrieve some of the socially cohesive elements destroyed in the parent culture'.

The idea that youth counter-cultures are an attempt to reassert control in the face of implacable social change has also been applied to the phenomenon of football hooliganism. Against the commercialization and professionalism of football the 'hooliganism', it is said, represents:

a an attempt to influence the actual outcome of the match; and, in consequence,

b to achieve a symbolic reassertion of social control over a game which was once a local working-class sport (Ingham R. *et al.* 1978).

Now these examples do offer extremely constructive insights into significant features of contemporary life (Brake 1980). Nevertheless from the point of view of a rigorous approach to social problems they have attracted a number of criticisms, of which two seem especially important.

Validity

The explanations *sound* plausible, but are they true? For example, how should we choose between explanations, which though offered within the same Marxist perspective, cut across each other or even conflict? Thus, Hebdige (1979) has proposed substantial modification to P. Cohen's account of spectacular subcultures among white working-class youth. For him, skinheads, mods, punks and so on should be seen as a response to the parallel growth of a black (especially West Indian) working-class youth counter-culture in British society. After the major phase of black immigration to this country, a second black generation, born and bred in Britain, grew up in the inner areas of large cities. As it did so, 'a new West Indian style began to emerge. . . . behind it lay the suggestion . . . that Britain had failed to supply the promised goods and that the disaffected immigrants had psychologically moved out' (Hebdige 1979, p. 42). Disaffection showed itself in the cultural style adopted: reggae music, emphasis on African influences and so on. But even more important, elements of this expression of disaffection, notably music styles, conveyed themselves to local white working-class youngsters and were taken up into their own counter-culture. The facilitating link is the fact that in popular mythology 'youth' and 'Negro' *both* symbolize 'values (the search for adventure and excitement) which co-exist with and undercut the sober positives of mainstream society' (Hebdige 1979, p. 44). Identification may or may not be conscious. 'It can be recognised and extended into actual links (the mods, skinheads and punks) or repressed and inverted into an antagonism (teds, greasers)' (Hebdige 1979). Nevertheless, at the 'deep structural level' the various subcultures are connected.

Again, no one can question the plausibility of this analysis nor its relevance to recent events in Britain's inner cities. But how are we to view it in relation to P. Cohen's explanation or choose between the two? Furthermore, how are we to validate the coincidence of the two cultures at the 'deep structural level'? Because Marxists tend to reject the distinction between the activity of the analyst and the practice of politics it becomes impossible to tell whether the account given could be confirmed by an uncommitted observer, or whether the whole thing is a piece of political wishful thinking. But this brings us to a second crucial point.

Class consciousness or anomie?

For similar reasons we might ask whether the new Marxist studies have actually produced a better *explanation* or whether, as Stanley Cohen argues, they merely offer a 'political re-translation of the conventional assumptions of the old theories' (Cohen S. 1980, p. vi). To be sure the delinquent, formerly portrayed as a 'frustrated social climber' has become a 'cultural innovator and critic'. But there are problems with this. It presupposes what was, as we have seen, a matter of contention previously; namely, that deviance is some kind of act of defiance or rejection of conventional society – an interpretation which in fact remained unsubstantiated in that literature (Downes 1966, p. 11). So on what grounds are neo-Marxists convinced of its aptness?

The problem is, as we saw in Chapter 9, a crucial one for Marxism: the failure of the proletariat to develop a truly political revolutionary consciousness. The danger in the 'new' subcultural theories is their implication that in fact 'mass proletarian resistance did not die out – it survives as deviance' (Cohen S. 1980, p. x). Hence, they tend to 'explain away' evidence that disaffection and disorder among youth may also contain conservative, racialist, divisive, irrational and downright vicious elements. This is to gloss over features of delinquency which the older subcultural perspectives did face up to, albeit inadequately.

Thus, defenders of the Durkheimian tradition might argue that no really fundamental objections have been raised against the view that delinquent subculture is a symptom of anomie, provided, like Durkheim himself, we recognize that the *moral breakdown is inherent in the individualist structure of capitalist society as a whole*. This is not in any way to obscure the class nature of that society but rather to offer an alternative (and perhaps more sober and realistic?) appraisal of how class is experienced by the young.

Inequality and the British sickness

Neo-Durkheimians might also argue that the Marxist tendency to 'romanticize' delinquency finds its parallel in some Marxist interpretations of industrial relations. In representative Marxist works on this topic, work group norms and control over the level of effort are also seen as containing an irreducible element of proletarian opposition and consciousness (for example, Beynon 1973; Hyman 1975; Hill 1982). Such an interpretation of shop floor culture is in fact integral to Willis's study too (1977, pp. 52ff.). But as we have seen earlier in the chapter, there is an alternative neo-Durkheimian analysis (not necessarily confined to the conservative perspectives of Elton Mayo), which interprets the experience and behaviour of the industrial worker as the embodiment of anomie. This viewpoint has made an important resurgence in the discussion of Britain's recent industrial relations problems. It forms the subject of this next section.

The starting-point of the work we wish to discuss is one in fact *shared* with Marxism and which we ourselves endorsed earlier – the survival of substantial concentrations of wealth and of marked inequality in the social structure of late-twentieth-century Britain. The key point of divergence, however, is once again over the question of the level of political consciousness in the working class. It has been expressed by Goldthorpe as follows:

The most far reaching implications of inequality for the integration of British society occur not in the political sphere but rather in that of economic life;. . . they are manifested not in a situation of fundamental class struggle but rather in a situation of anomie. (Goldthorpe 1974, p. 222)

In order to show in detail how this idea has been brought by various writers to bear upon recent events we shall, once again, need to go over some basic, albeit familiar background.

Growing concern over industrial relations problems has been a feature of political life in Britain for some time but it intensified from the early 1960s onwards. At its centre was a widely shared diagnosis that the unreformed character of bargaining between unions and management was having severe consequences for the performance and efficiency of the national economy. The effects were said to be both direct and indirect. The indirect effects stemmed from the growing success of strikes as a means of pursuing wage claims. It was argued that the post-war boom had allowed certain key groups of workers to become exceedingly powerful. These groups pursued and obtained abnormally high wage demands which, in due course, forced others to follow suit. The result was a general upward drift in money wages thus increasing manufacturing costs. This, in turn, brought about inflation at home and loss of competitiveness abroad. It is important, in passing, to observe that economists' explanations of this state of affairs were not all of one piece. Some argued, to put matters crudely, that wage demands were a consequence rather than a cause of rising cost and price levels. But all tended to agree that the only way out of the vicious circle of wage and price rises lay through the exercise of some limitation on the power of workers to pursue demands for more money and better hours and conditions. This in turn implied a political as well as an economic restriction of the right to strike, and of the associated legal privileges for which trade unionists had fought for over more than a century.

The distinctive character of the British industrial relations 'system' is in fact its so-called 'voluntarism'. That is to say, 'collective' bargaining between representatives of employers and employees is not restricted by elaborate legislation or various forms of state intervention and regulation, as in many other countries. The parties to negotiation have been free to make whatever kind of compromise is acceptable to both sides and without reference to any formal considerations of wider public or national interest. Debate over the advantages or disadvantages of this system is complex. It does not really concern us here except to note that in the opinion of many well-informed students of labour history the balance of advantage until the post-war period lay with employers and the state, which explains its persistence. In other words the voluntary system tended to be productive of order rather than disorder largely because union weakness and economic depression meant that employers could usually impose their own terms upon workers. Hence, industrial conflict only occasionally presented the state with serious problems of social coercion.

In the post-war period, however, the balance of power undoubtedly began to shift, partly because labour shortages, brought about by the economic boom, coincided with the growth of union membership to an all-time high. According to one prominent diagnosis, however, this was not the whole story. The interpretation in question will be found in the pages of the Donovan Report, so-called after the Chairman of the Royal Commission set up in 1965 to examine possible reforms in industrial relations (Donovan Report 1968). The report argued that various changes in the organization of management and industry itself had precipitated the need for reform. In the past, employers had sought to contain union power by working through a system of nationally based agreements on procedures, wages and conditions. Changes in the structure of ownership, pay systems, new technology and altered management philosophies had undermined this national system. It had in many cases shifted the effective unit of collective bargaining from national level to the individual plant or firm. This was the catalyst which had enabled key groups of workers, often through unofficial action, to exploit the current labour shortage and the interdependence of modern industrial life. As a result a second or 'informal' system of industrial relations had developed whose anarchic character constantly disrupted the formally recognized national agreements.

The most controversial aspect of the Report concerned its proposals for reform. Popular opinion, it seems, has tended to favour what would be in effect an abandonment of the voluntary system, replacing it instead with greater use of law and compulsion. The Donovan Commission, however, decided in the light of its analysis not to recommend legal penalties at all. Instead it proposed a series of measures to strengthen the status of voluntary *plant* agreements. The use of law simply imposed upon the current system might well be counter-productive. Penalties against a determined mass of strikers might bring the law itself into ridicule. But this view did not find favour in many quarters. In the years since the Commission reported, as most readers will know, a variety of innovations has been tried with varying success in an attempt to limit strikes, control the level of wage increases and combat inflation. These include both voluntary and statutory incomes policies, the Industrial Relations Act, repealed in 1974, and the recent Employment Act, 1980. Each of these developments has created or at least attempted substantial modification to the status quo which existed under the voluntary system. Yet the controversy which they have excited threatens to be as divisive as the conditions they were designed to treat.

It is in this context that 'neo-Durkheimian' arguments have resurfaced. First we must consider some common features of the approach. In particular we shall focus on their acceptance of Durkheim's view that economic life rests on a moral foundation which modern industrial forms tend to disrupt. Consequently neither the working of the labour contract in general nor the particular problems of the British economy can be understood solely in terms of conventional economic theories. Flanders, for one, argued that collective bargaining by employees with the employer wholly alters the nature of wage fixing.

It ceases to be a transaction dominated by the regulative processes of the market and becomes instead a political process of rule-making. The economic transactions of the market are replaced by 'a power relationship between organisations' (Flanders 1975, pp. 218–19; Fox A. 1975, has criticized certain aspects of this argument).

Other writers have objected to a more fundamental aspect of economic theories; namely, their dependence on the view that the *economy contains inherent self-regulating tendencies* (for example, Lipsey 1979, p. 62). They argue that on the contrary the self-motivated pursuit of economic advantage implied in the notion of the competitive market economy contains inherent tendencies towards breakdown and social disorder. This, as we have said above, is a position derived from Durkheim. A major theme of *The Division of Labour* is about the moral disruption caused by modern economic life because of the lack of regulation and the individual egoism which it entails. It can be argued that the situation is more serious than in Durkheim's time. As Crouch points out, we can roughly divide the sources from which most societies derive their cohesion into three groups: economic, social (that is, moral) and political. But modern society is somewhat unusual in this respect:

It was the extraordinary achievement of advocates of *laissez-faire* political economy to outline a system that placed overwhelming stress on the economic. The achievement within capitalist societies of an unprecedented degree of political and moral freedom resulted from the liberation of these areas of action (i.e. political and social forms of control) from detailed involvement (with the economy). . . . The achievement was always in part illusory. Capitalism depended on the survival of political institutions from an earlier (generally absolutist) period which made it possible to create the coercive legal framework it needed . . . while the pursuit of amoral individualised ends through the market system assumed reinforcement by a framework of moral restraint similarly inherited from the past. (Crouch 1978, p. 220)

In company with a number of other writers

Crouch is saying that the cohesion of market societies rests on a legacy of past political and moral traditions which it simultaneously tends to destroy. This process is now reaching a critical point. Nor can the problems of contemporary economic life itself be any longer understood and *analysed* in terms of purely *economic* doctrines, whether classical, monetarist or Keynesian. We are *not* confronted with a self-regulating economy which has been disrupted by outside imperfections such as trade union power or too much state interference. We are confronted with an economy that has undermined the sources of social cohesion upon which it depends and which has nothing to put in their place.

Neo-Durkheimian analyses offer a variety of models of the process of breakdown. In each case moral regulation collapses under the influence of egoism born of market pressures. This, in turn, gives rise to moral anomie and problems of political order. Specific features of contemporary economic life – industrial conflict, inflation – can then be explained in terms of the general model. Let us describe the leading examples.

Industrial conflict

The first and earliest example is contained in an article by Fox and Flanders, two writers with detailed knowledge of British trade unionism who were themselves heavily involved in the work of the Donovan Commission (Flanders and Fox 1969). They argued that what the Commission had uncovered was not simply a breakdown in industrial relations but *anomie*, a profound attenuation of the processes of social regulation determining rewards in society. In industrial relations there are two major types of 'norm' or moral rule (see Chapter 15) which they call substantive and procedural:

1 *Substantive norms* regulate the actual content of collective bargaining such as standard wage rates, working hours, overtime and holiday arrangements.

2   *Procedural norms* include both precise constitutional provisions, that is, machinery for negotiation and dispute settlement and also rather vaguer methods and criteria for determining just levels of rewards, rights, duties and discipline.

Taken together, disorder in industrial relations can occur because of substantive conflict (asking for a wage rise) or procedural conflict (demanding trade union recognition or an extension of bargaining rights).

In Britain, however, disorder results from the peculiar nature of the relationship of substantive to procedural. As the Donovan Commission had tried to show, the largely unofficial form assumed by substantive conflict had had the consequence of breaking the larger unit of procedural regulation – the national agreement – into a number of smaller integrated units. The result had been the progressive fragmentation and breakdown of the whole regulative order. Fox and Flanders attribute a special 'gravity and intractability' to this form of disorder for a number of reasons:

1   There is the cumulative and endemic nature of the causes which have brought the situation about and which will require 'wholesale reconstruction' of the procedures by which wage fixing and negotiation are conducted.
2   There is the fact that the fragmentation process is contested by *none* of the participants. It is the *system* of regulation which has drifted out of control.
3   Finally, there are the enormous resentments built up in such a situation and which ensure its prolongation. For the initial conflicts upon which it has fed have been resolved according to accidents of power. Extreme frustration, therefore, builds up among groups who have the same aspirations but who lack the same strategic opportunities. This is, in fact, a unique distributional conflict occurring, not between classes, but *within* them.

We shall now turn to certain evaluations of Fox and Flanders's analysis. In doing so we come back to the theme with which the chapter began: the relationship between inequality in a society and its moral cohesiveness (or lack of it). To Goldthorpe, for instance, the Fox/Flanders account is valuable in so far as it shows that conflicts over the distribution of incomes, which are the stuff of industrial relations, raise problems of morality and justice as well as economic management (Goldthorpe 1974). Valuable, too, is the stress upon the size of the task of reconstruction. But he argues that by the same token the central weakness of their analysis emerges. Reconstruction will be doubly difficult if it remains preoccupied only with the problem of conflicts *within* classes. This is to ignore 'the context of the *overall* degree of economic inequality (that is, between classes), which statistics on the distribution of wealth reveal' (Goldthorpe 1974, p. 224). At the same time it is to fail to exploit Durkheim's basic insight that 'all external inequality compromises organic solidarity'. Britain's problems are symptomatic of the fundamental problem of order in modern society expressed in *The Division of Labour*.

Of course, Goldthorpe is not suggesting that the typical worker reads statistical publications regularly or even knows what they contain. But the unrecognized inequalities of birth and fortune which exist in a market society do lead to more visible inequalities of opportunity in the educational and occupational spheres. They also encourage a process of comparison across limited ranges of the social order which, once begun, cannot be restrained by principles of distributive justice for there are none to appeal to. On the contrary, the mass of wage and salary earners have thrown off the moral restraints upon acquisitiveness which existed in the past. They have learnt from capitalism the practice of exploiting one's market position to the full (Goldthorpe 1978, pp. 200–1).

Thus, only when we understand that inequality *between* classes lacks an accepted moral basis, can we also understand why a competitive struggle also develops *within* classes. Or, as Goldthorpe puts it, 'the absence of an accepted moral basis for economic life as a whole . . . must always render precarious the norms which at any time prevail in any specific area – a plant, company or industry etc.' (1974, p. 225).

The empirical validity of this thesis and the interpretation of working-class consciousness on which it rests has recently been strongly challenged (Maitland 1979; Willman 1982). But another writer, M. Gilbert, suggests that Goldthorpe's argument does less than total justice to the radicalism of Durkheim's thought (Gilbert 1978). For this we need to remember that Durkheim's account of the abnormal division of labour and moral anomie operates on a number of different levels. Gilbert reworks these into:

1 the social isolation of individual workers brought about, for example, by excessive specialization of tasks;
2 the breakdown of regulation and order in society as a whole – for example, the absence of rules under capitalism which fix the number of economic enterprises or the relation of production to consumption;
3 the problem of excessive individualism.

At first sight, the last form of anomie does not appear to result either from factors working upon individuals themselves or from factors operating at the level of society as a whole. In Gilbert's view though it does have a definite origin: it results from the strain or contradiction from conflicting moral rules. How does the conflict arise? It arises out of the fact that society stresses different virtues on different levels of the economy:

a Individual people are encouraged to participate in economic life on the basis of the virtues of *competitiveness and self-help*. It is commonly recognized that economic activity fundamentally rests upon a calculation of personal economic advantage to be gained from a given contract – in particular the employment contract.

b The complex and technical character of the industrial system as a whole, however, requires a certain willingness to co-operate and restrain self-interest. This is particularly apparent in large corporations with their ethos of dedication to the company; and at times of economic crisis when workers are urged to indulge in restraint from 'greedy' wage claims – say in the interests of national/international competitiveness or profitability.

Conflict between these two opposed moral ideals emerges whenever particular economic, technological or organizational factors give some groups an element of strategic importance – and hence potential power – over society at large. 'It is this contradiction', Gilbert argues, 'which gives rise to the various manifestations of industrial and economic disorder which are frequently termed "the British sickness" – industrial disputes, low productivity, inflation, etc.' (Gilbert 1978, p. 734).

Incomes policy

Analogous and related problems arise in connection with the administration of incomes policies. The fact that a number of different attempts to operate such a policy have run into difficulties is, in itself, evidence that some rather fundamental problems exist. Within a neo-Durkheimian framework this problem is again seen to be a moral one. In operating incomes policy, the government or its agents, confronted by growing and irreconcilable demands of different groups of workers, actually seeks to impose standards regulating the general growth of wages and salaries; and also to judge the merit of particular claims in the light of them. The fact that the standards themselves are set out in economic and quantitative terms obscures, for a time at least, the true situation – which is that the state has allowed itself to become dragged into an unresolvable moral debate about the social justice of the levels of remuneration of sectors of society. Incomes policies seem, in fact, to make matters worse, for they publicize the principle of comparison and encourage people to widen the range of occupations with which they compare themselves. Yet they leave untouched the deepest problems of the society, such as the question of whether income control is to be applied to the better-off sectors of the population whose income is derived from personal wealth and distributed profits.

That the standards of social justice which people apply to existing income differentials conflict has long been known both in the practical operation of industrial relations and in social science. A pioneering study by Wootton brought out the incommensurable nature of these conflicting judgements – how should we rate, say, the performance of unpleasant and dangerous work, as against say, long training, responsibility, comparability with 'similar' work elsewhere, inconvenient hours, seniority and so on. Wootton also was one of the first to show how different moral arguments are used as weapons in the course of collective bargaining, a factor which makes the work of arbitration exceedingly difficult (Wootton 1955; cf. Lockwood 1955).

Incomes policies inherit the full disruptive potential of this moral anomie. This can be illustrated from the detailed examination by Crouch of the work of both the National Incomes Commission and the much more ambitious National Board of Prices and Incomes set up by the Labour Government of 1965 (Crouch 1975, 1977). Both bodies found themselves attempting to override the factors which had hitherto been responsible for determining incomes, namely, the operation of the market and time-honoured standards of consensus and compromise in collective bargaining. The NBPI in particular attempted to imply a rational set of standards for determining pay which largely reflected its own desire to reward managerial responsibility and skill. In order to create a new consensus on which to base the policy, however, it also adopted the criterion of 'productivity' as a fresh moral element in determining pay

awards. Furthermore it was committed to the criterion of 'fairness' by the general political ethics of the time; and to assisting low-paid groups by the policy of the Labour Government itself. The actual experience of the Board brought out the contradictions between these aims and brought it into conflict with the powerful legacy of custom and practice surviving from earlier settlements.

The central difficulty in mounting incomes policies, however, is that the attempt to apply rational criteria of income determination starts out with an existing wage structure that lacks any kind of clear moral foundation. This, it is argued, is why such efforts fail in their attempt to win voluntary consent and precipitate instead a move towards state compulsion and legal penalties as a way of regulating wage and salary increases. This is precisely what happened to labour incomes policy in the 1960s.

Inflation

Moral anomie is also seen by neo-Durkheimians as explaining the persistent inflation which has troubled Britain and other Western societies since the war. At the time of writing considerable ambiguity exists as to whether these sociological models of what has been central territory for economics are intended to replace or merely complement ones which use only economic variables. Goldthorpe claims that although his theory begins with certain 'residual categories', or unexplained gaps in economists' accounts of inflation, it is bound ultimately to come into conflict with them (1978). The reason is that, as explained above, economists see the capitalist economy as containing its own self-stabilizing forces. Their proviso is that 'irrational' factors – moral aspirations, trade union power, 'unreasonable' political objectives – are not allowed to disrupt the economic order. Sociological models of all schools, however, tend to see industrial society, and capitalist versions of it in particular, as containing *built-in* self-destructive tendencies. Goldthorpe's own account of the factors which have produced endemic and cumulative inflationary tendencies include:

1   decay of the traditional status order;
2   the achievement of citizenship rights which create demand for 'expensive' state services;
3   the emergence of a working class which is 'mature' in two senses:

a   it has had several generations' experience of industrial society;
b   rather than develop revolutionary political and economic consciousness it has developed institutions which reflect its full absorption of capitalist economic values – individualism, egoism and economic calculation.

For Goldthorpe then economics and neo-Durkheimian explanations of inflation are not reconcilable.

Gilbert is less abrasive, partly because of his recognition that sociological accounts of inflation would be unlikely to be in a position to dispense with the contribution of other disciplines entirely (Gilbert 1981) and partly because of the residual imprecision of the sociological theories themselves. His latest work, in fact, is directed towards remedying one major ambiguity – whether the explanations are meant to hold for *all* capitalist societies or whether there are a number of specific factors which make Britain peculiarly liable to moral anomie of the kind considered above. In order to examine this question he draws upon a distinction first put forward by Fox. According to this we should distinguish:

1   on the one hand, employment and collective bargaining contexts in which the degree of trust which the parties have in each other steadily deteriorates;
2   on the other, situations where mutual trust is maintained and even improves.

Britain, he argues, has been particularly liable to bouts of excessive inflation because as a society it has become trapped in a process of long-term decline in trust between and within classes and work groups (see also Fox A. 1974). By contrast societies such as Japan and Germany have developed institutional arrangements within the fabric of their industrial life which ensure maintenance of a level of trust in the face of the otherwise inevitable moral anarchy of the market economy *per se* (Gilbert 1981, cf. Maitland 1979 for empirical evidence). Of course, no one can say how well such arrangements will fare in the long run. Their mere existence provides an important corrective to the idea that moral and political collapse is inevitable and *inherent* in capitalist society. Thus, although there can be no simple way of validating Gilbert's general approach, we can at least say that it introduces a new and valuable *comparative* element based upon attention to historical and institutional detail into the study of inflation and other economic problems.

One consequence of the comparative perspective will almost certainly be to throw considerable doubt upon the suggestion that problems of moral anomie are found *only* in capitalist economies of the West. In a review of the social and political factors underlying the last decade in Poland (1970–80), Kolankiewicz illustrates some of the ways in which a discrepancy between institutionalized goals and available means can arise under existing socialist regimes. We saw in Chapter 13 that the legitimacy, both moral and political, of such regimes rests upon an ideology of total dedication to working-class interests. In practice, it is perfectly possible for the regime to fall far short of such an ideal, with the consequence that the working class finds itself not only materially and politically disadvantaged in relation to the white-collar workers and the Party elite but also subject to a process of *demoralization* which above all affects the working of the economy. In the Polish case the factors giving rise to such 'anomic' socialism included:

1   strong evidence of corruption within the political and administrative structure of society combined with insensitive flaunting of personal

privileges and benefits gained through corruption;

2 'socialist consumerism' growth in the possession of consumer goods in Polish society served to heighten awareness of income differentials between different sectors of the population and the arbitrary factors on which these are based.

3 the disparity between:

a an ideology equivalent to the 'citizenship rights' of Western welfare states and

b the actual standard of provision of public and social services;

4 'demoralization' of the wages structure. Kolankiewicz writes of how:

blue collar workers came to believe that the quality and the results of their work were unrelated to the rewards or sanctions received. The latter, they felt, was largely in the gift of management, who could dispose of the rewards as they saw fit . . . the effort–reward equation was lost in a morass of thirteenth and fourteenth month bonuses, various premiums and reward funds which left workers unclear as to what they were being paid for and obscured the already dim perception of what constituted legitimate expectations as to the relationship between work and pay . . . two-thirds of workers in a national study . . . declared that the majority of their colleagues could work better or much better. (Kolankiewicz 1981, p. 141)

Kolankiewicz calls this later piece of evidence 'a subjective reflection of the objective decline in productivity'.

Obviously, it is tempting to emphasize the analogies between this situation and the so-called 'British sickness'. But whereas British trade unionists possessed a means of expressing their grievances, Polish workers did not. On the contrary, disenchantment with the role of the 'official' trade unions in Poland was a major factor in the rise of Solidarity and the crisis of Polish politics since 1980. The 'solution' adopted by the authorities to the problem of order created by anomic socialism was to use force.

In Britain, such an extreme situation does not exist, of course. Yet the question of reliance upon coercion and state power as a solution to the inherent tensions of *capitalist* society is topical enough. 'Law and order', for example, is an important issue in a number of Western societies. Many people besides our own in this country consider that today's social and industrial problems should be tackled coercively – through 'discipline' and various forms of legal restraint. The use of law and legal penalties to deal with industrial troubles is also growing.

Durkheim's basic thesis, however, was that social order depends first and foremost upon *moral* restraint, not force. Recent neo-Durkheimian treatments of Britain's industrial relations problems have not only taken up this theme but also argued that greater use of coercion will only increase the tendency to what Durkheim would have called a *forced* division of labour. A forced division of labour possesses only a troubled solidarity because the cohesion achieved is gained at the price of resentment. The 'solution' offered by coercive methods is counter-productive because it is not based upon consent. We shall return to this point in a moment.

Conclusion

In this chapter, then, we have found that the application of the concept of anomie to some contemporary problems has involved us in a dialogue with Marxist sociology. Let us try to sum this up.

We have found that there is little disagreement between neo-Durkheimian and neo-Marxist positions about the existence of substantial inequality in our society and others like it. The Marxists could successfully sustain their charge that anomie theories do not really contribute much to understanding the deep causes of that inequality. Neo-Durkheimians, on the other hand, could argue that the anomie of injustice is not necessarily ended with the abolition of class society. And they would probably defend their approach in two ways.

First, they could argue that their work does not so much conflict with the Marxist account of the class nature of capitalism as complement it in an area where it is weak, that is, in providing a detailed account of the moral and ideological consequences of a free market economy. For this reason, it is necessary to emphasize that the neo-Durkheimian view does *not* rest on a simple thesis that people have been somehow 'indoctrinated' into acceptance of materialism and consumer values. It is, first and foremost, offering a relatively sophisticated account of the paradoxes of moral order which are produced as unintended consequences of the market economy itself. The model states that where social inequality lacks a moral basis, such as that existing between and within social classes, the result will be to encourage preoccupation with the personal grievance – the narrowly sectional and the private. The main result is a weakening of solidarity and moral authority. Delinquency, for example, arises because the competitive goals and standards, which everyone is encouraged to emulate, conflict with the deprivations and inequalities which youngsters face in practice. But the cohesion of the system as a whole is threatened, too. As we saw in the discussion of incomes policy, the encouragement of a 'self-help' ideology undermines the winning of the kind of co-operation required to regulate the economy.

Second, they could claim that their account fits in better with the historical record of the Western working class than does classical Marxism. The growth structure and policy of the labour movement suggests that the demoralization of established society which we have been describing is, at the same time (and for similar reasons), inimical to the growth of organized political consciousness. The 'maturity' of the working class is signified instead by the extent to which people have wholly absorbed the individualism and the material values of capitalism. This argument, we might add, is wholly compatible:

1   with the sceptical approach of the Weberian tradition as to the possibility of an automatic connection between class position and political expression;
2   with the particular findings of studies of class imagery in the contemporary British working class (see Chapter 9; also Goldthorpe *et al.* 1968; Roberts *et al.* 1977). These have stressed the 'privatized' and 'fragmentary' consciousness to be found in large sectors of the working class in Britain during the post-war period;
3   and even with empirical work critical of the neo-Durkheimian position. Maitland for example reports that 'British workers generally saw the existing structure of income and power as legitimate' (1973, p. 353).

To be sure, the current industrial relations scene in Britain cannot be understood without recognizing the existence of a measure of solidarity among groups of workers and what Beynon calls 'factory consciousness'. We saw that Willis perceptively describes how this consciousness is anticipated and reaffirmed in the counter-culture of the school. The problem for neo-Marxism though, as Beynon himself recognizes, is why this 'factory consciousness' does not extend itself to full political expression of the interest of the class as a whole (Beynon 1973, pp. 317ff.). The neo-Durkheimian account of industrial relations accepts the existence of such localized and segmental solidarity while seeing the political significance of such solidarity in its capacity, not to unify the working class, but keep it permanently fragmented. More recent Marxists have, as we saw in Chapters 8 and 9, displayed a greater pessimism about the development of political consciousness of the working class. In varying measure they acknowledge the effective incorporation of the contemporary working class into the materialism and individualism of capitalism itself. As such they have come more and more to resemble the neo-Durkheimian view.

Thus, the differences between Marxist and neo-Durkheimian analyses of contemporary society should not be stressed at the cost of concealing the similarities between the two perspectives. Marx himself, it will be remembered, argued that capitalism tends to reduce all contact between human beings to the level of a cash transaction (see p. 126). Therefore, as Westergaard has argued, in a frequently quoted review, empirical studies such as Goldthorpe and Lockwood's survey of 'affluent' car workers amounted to no more than a 'rediscovery' of the 'cash-nexus' (Westergaard 1970). What they reported was the domination of workers' outlook by the size of the pay packet. In Britain of the post-war boom the solidarity of the traditional working-class community of lifestyle had all but gone. In its place stood 'instrumentalism' and 'privatization'.

But what if the cash-nexus suffers rupture, notably under the impact of economic recession and unemployment? At such times there is no force of moral cohesion for society to fall back upon. There is, at best, the coercive power of the state. The Marxist thesis of how the cash-nexus pares away pre-existing moral bonds is then, in this respect, remarkably *close* to the position adopted by the neo-Durkheimian school.

Thus we come back to the question of whether a society which attempts to ensure the authority of its institutions through an enhanced use of force can offer any long-run guarantee of stability? There is, almost from the beginning of sociology, an inclination to answer to this question in the negative. Marx expected the political stability of capitalism to decrease, not increase. Weber, despite his fears of bureaucracy and the growth of the modern rational legal state, argued that force alone was not a sufficient basis for stable domination. As for Durkheim, the only lasting solution to the problems of contemporary society lay in the removal of the deep-rooted inequalities and injustices which continued to compromise organic solidarity. This is a prescription which, we think, would be endorsed by most contemporary sociologists, whatever their theoretical allegiances. It is also the solution which we, the authors, would ourselves prefer.

Nevertheless, the assumption that coercive regimes are unstable seems to us premature – at least in the context of later twentieth-century states with their vastly improved powers of surveillance; information control, retrieval and storage; persuasion, enforcement and mortification of 'trouble-makers'. The preference for the just, rather than the coercive, solution is precisely that – a preference, not a historical necessity. To imagine otherwise is to remain, like Durkheim, in thrall to the remnants of the theory of progress.

The themes of order and control, particularly in the contexts of injustice and inequality, will recur frequently in the remainder of the book. In the next part we shall examine a relatively modern school of thought known as Functionalism. Functionalists have sought to build a scientific explanation of behaviour from the premise that any society is a 'functioning' whole, resting upon a consensus of morals and values. But our studies will oblige us to consider the institution of the family and some questions about the origin and justice of moral rules which prescribe divisions of society by *gender*.

In the final part of the book we shall be dealing with various theories of the social self and of the social factors which can elevate or destroy it. Here too we shall confront problems of state control, consciousness and order in a modern society.

Part Seven: Industrial Society as Structural Differentiation – Functionalism and its Discontents

16 Societies as systems: functionalist models of social order

During the 1950s and 1960s the school of thought known as functionalism provided the nearest thing to an orthodoxy that has ever existed in sociology, certainly within the English-speaking world. It held sway at a time when sociology was undergoing enormous expansion in university teaching programmes and when the number of people professionally engaged in sociological research projects was likewise growing rapidly.

Yet as we examine the functionalist approach, it is important to be aware that, even in its heyday, it was never without strong critical opponents. It never, in fact, held a total monopoly over courses and institutions even in the United States, the country which felt its influence to the greatest extent.

In the late 1960s, the criticism of functionalism acquired a new extent and intensity. Accusations were made that the leading functionalists had led the discipline into serious difficulties, enough to discredit many of the achievements of the post-war years. To begin with, most of the discontent was expressed by leading functionalists themselves as they attempted to adapt their perspective to fresh problems. They were soon joined by a number of other sociologists, mostly, but not entirely, Europeans. These 'conflict theorists' as they were called sought to revive one or more of the earlier classical traditions of analysis from which many of the ideas contained in functionalism had been borrowed. They also sought to argue, albeit in a relatively gentle way, that more serious consideration should be given to the perspectives of Marxism – a school of thought for which, as we explained in Chapter 10, the majority of functionalist and neo-evolutionary writers had had little sympathy. In the late 1960s the 'conflict theorists' were themselves overtaken by a far more strident resurgence of Marxist thought. The immediate catalysts of this ferment were world events such as the crisis in American society over civil rights, the Vietnam War, Watergate and the upheavals on campuses throughout the Western hemisphere. 'Post-68' sociology has meant a return of the discipline to the inherently controversial, divergent and amorphous character which it had in fact possessed in earlier times. The only honest way to teach the subject was to explain systematically its divisions. The days of the orthodoxy were over.

Nevertheless it is still essential to understand functionalist theory and research, provided we reject its pretensions to be equivalent to sociology as a whole (Davis K. 1960):

1 In order to understand the debates which have been going on in recent sociology a familiarity with its concepts and methods is essential.

2 Preoccupation with the 'findings' which this school claimed to have established has formed the backdrop to much of the substantive research done in the past decade or so – admittedly this period is now coming to an end.

3 Arguably, functionalism has addressed itself to some important problems in social theory even if it has not succeeded in resolving them (cf. Giddens 1977, pp. 96–128).

Functionalism in outline – the problem of 'functional imperatives'

The common denominator of all versions of functionalist theory is the expectation that whatever adjustments and changes occur in social behaviour and organization, there are a set of basic underlying pressures which work towards the maintenance of stability, the co-ordination of activities and even the conformity of individuals with the life of the group. It is a basic tenet of this school that whatever happens in one department or area of society will entail compensatory adjustments throughout the rest of the network and vice versa. People themselves and the groups to which they belong may not be aware that maintenance of social stability will be the consequence of their actions. Nevertheless, functionalist sociology aims to reveal the functions which each part of the social structure plays in relation to the whole, in the belief that *integration*, rather than disintegration, is the fundamental direction in which all society tends.

The earliest attempts to treat society as a self-maintaining structure or system depended upon the old analogy between societies and biological organisms, as found for example in the writings of Herbert Spencer (see Chapter 5). Indeed, it was Spencer, it will be recalled, who argued that just as plants and animals have certain essential needs which they seek to satisfy, so do social 'organisms'. These essential needs of social functioning he called 'functional requirements'. Twentieth-century functionalists, however, have sought to discard evolutionalism and the organic model of society that went with it. All the same they have continued to speak of society as if it possessed a 'structure' made up of 'parts' which contribute certain essential functions to the whole. They have in fact *insisted* that there are certain necessities or prerequisites of normal social organization and that any society which fails to meet these conditions is faced with the risk of disruption and ultimately collapse. But before the process of disintegration can get too far, powerful pressures will be set in motion to restore some kind of stability and 'normality' again. The first job of the sociologist, then, ought to be to identify what this set of minimum conditions or *'functional prerequisites'* consists of.

Unfortunately, most attempts to identify these 'functional prerequisites' have been rather unsatisfactory. For example, one of the doyens of functionalist anthropology, Bronislaw Malinowski, argued that the list of prerequisites essential for social functioning would simply reflect the conditions most favourable to the biological and mental welfare of each member (1944). But what is individual welfare? Moral philosophers have never managed to agree about what basic human needs exist. In any case, it would not be too hard to cite examples where society had maintained itself in equilibrium only at the price of overruling individual welfare. This is to say nothing of the possibility that society itself is often a major influence upon the way individuals *define* their own well-being – so there is a serious risk of the reasoning behind Malinowski's theory becoming circular. Obviously we cannot base substantive research on such shifting sand.

Another more recent approach, one which fits in better with the belief of many sociologists that their discipline should not depend on too many psychological assumptions about the way in which people are motivated, starts out from the idea of *scarcity* (Johnson 1961). In the end human desires are unlimited and welfare is indefinable. They are certainly always unlimited in relation to society's capacity to satisfy them. Every individual thus develops a new *kind* of need, namely, for society to regulate the competitive struggle that would otherwise develop for the desirables which are in short supply. The functional prerequisites, then, *are* needs of individuals, but they represent an emergent or new level of needs brought about because we need society itself. As a consequence the needs of a given 'part', be it individual, group or institution, are subordinated to the regulation of the whole. This, too, is an old argument going back at least as far as Hobbes. It expresses an essentially pessimistic picture of society arbitrarily restraining individuals and, indeed, the absolute necessity for it to do so if recognizably human existence is to continue.

In practice the lists of functional prerequisites which have been proposed from time to time have been very 'armchair' exercises, lacking any research basis. Typical items include:

1   *adaptation* – the need to maintain 'adequate' food and material provisions;
2   *socialization* – the need to instil society's values and rules into the membership;
3   *social control* – the need to 'police' non-conformity and reward conformity and devotion to the group;
4   *reproduction* – the need to provide a stable structure within which sexual activity is allowed and the young are reared;
5   *a belief system* – the need to provide members with a shared set of meanings and understandings and to pass on society's knowledge;
6   *a polity/leadership* – the need to co-ordinate and motivate energies of the entire collectivity.

The list is potentially endless. Unfortunately such prerequisites do not tell us much about actual societies and they beg the question of whether social life is really ordered like this. For example, there are plenty of societies which continue to 'function' in the sense that they continue to exist and yet their provision for material adaptation of the majority of the population could not be described as adequate by anyone's standards. In short, the functionalist theory that society contains fundamental self-maintaining tendencies rests upon rather insecure foundations.

We now come to a further difficulty which is that there are actually *two* versions of functionalism. The distinction between them turns on whether the hypothesis of 'self-maintenance' is simply a 'heuristic' device – that is, a methodological assumption that enables us to ask

interesting questions about society; or whether the hypothesis is meant to be taken literally.

Version number 1

The older of the two, which we will call general or 'soft' functionalism (Lockwood 1964; Morgan 1975, p. 18), really says little more than that societies can be regarded as 'structure' composed of interrelated parts. Tracing the mutual relations and dependency between one part and another forms a useful mode of enquiry, though not the only one. It was first developed in British anthropology, after 1930, in the study of tribal societies (Malinowski 1944; Radcliffe-Brown 1952; Rex 1961; Harris M. 1968, Chapter 10). It was encouraged by the fact that such societies were usually small and self-contained. Those who developed it objected to the way in which the classic evolutionary writers had treated their anthropological materials and in particular to the attempt to fit such societies into grand classificatory arrangements by 'stage' of development. Features of social behaviour and institutions, they maintained, must be explained by their 'function' in relation to the present form of social organization, not by their relation to supposed adaptations in the past. In any case – and this was a vitally important consideration – such societies lack the necessary historical records to enable us to verify evolutionary ideas. A functional approach becomes inescapable. In modern sociology, the writer whose work comes closest to our description of 'soft' functionalism is Robert Merton (see below).

Version number 2

We will call this version normative or 'hard' functionalism. It asserts first of all that society and the actions of its members *must* be viewed as a total system or even a set of systems. The primary task of sociology is to understand the conditions which give rise to stability and order within any such system. This is sometimes referred to as 'the Hobbesian problem of order'. Change can then be understood as the result of the absence of the conditions of order.

The principal condition of stability is the existence of a persistent consensus among the members of society over moral ideals and abstract values. The central core of shared values provides the means whereby the social conduct of actual individuals is regulated and integrated. Hence the description: 'normative' functionalism.

Given the limitations of space which are inevitable in a book of this nature, it is the *second* of these two versions we shall mostly be talking about here. This is because it was 'normative' functionalism which became so influential in post-war sociology, finding expression in a wide range of treatises and textbooks. Furthermore, normative functionalists developed a characteristic 'language' of terms and concepts which have now slipped into general use in the discipline. (We shall describe these as we go along.) Finally, normative functionalism offered its *own* solution to the problem of explaining why it is that societies are self-maintaining systems. This was placed alongside the notion of functional imperatives, as we shall now see.

'Hard' functionalism: conformity, norms and institutionalization

The logical starting-point of the 'hard' functionalist position is with a commonplace of modern sociology, so fundamental that it is barely discussed these days, namely: rejection of the possibility of a non-social individual. The corollary, however, is that a minimum degree of conformity with group demands is a necessity for satisfactory personal life. How is this achieved? The functionalist answer, in sociological shorthand, is that it is realized by means of *conformity to institutionalized norms*. Let us look at the meaning of this phrase.

Conformity

The most familiar word here will be 'conformity'. Functionalists are anxious to stress, with some justification, that conformity is a fundamental part of our being. Basically, they argue, what we learn to do as children is to conform in countless ways and whatever happens to us in later life some part at least of this conformity is retained. Even individuals who become criminals, rebels or revolutionaries may be said to conform in certain key respects. Obvious examples can be found in the way they continue, say, to wear clothes, adhere to the customary diet, speak the same language, observe sexual customs and so forth. A subtler form of 'conformity' may be said to arise out of the fact that their crime, rebellion (a decision *not* to wear clothes in order to shock?) or revolution is always made in response to typical problems of a status quo, a common area of discourse, which is shared with others. Quite frequently, for example, rebels express the ideals of the society in a purer form than their more conventional contemporaries. The cloak of social conditioning is never wholly discarded.

Norms

The term norm refers to the basic pattern which this conformity, however it is directed, takes. Loosely speaking, it may be understood as any type of rule that is actually recognized and followed by a substantial portion of the membership of a group. However, the functionalist is not just making the banal assertion that conformity consists of obeying rules. A more exact definition regards a norm as 'an abstract pattern, held in the mind that sets certain limits for behaviour. . . . "Conforming" to the norm means guiding one's conduct in relation to it.' (Johnson 1961, p.8) There are, in fact, for the functionalist two kinds of order in society: the ideal or 'normative' order (deriving from a core of shared values in society) and the day-to-day or factual order (that is, what people actually get up to). The two do not coincide. But neither can they diverge too widely. Their relationship is a functional one. The normative order can only continue in so far as it finds expression in the actual doings of individuals. But we have seen that individuals actually need the integration which comes from observing and upholding the normative ideal. To depart from it is in the end to raise questions about one's *self*.

Institutionalization

Before a rule or ideal can be considered as part of the normative order it must become institutionalized. That is to say, it must possess two characteristics:

1 First, it must be *widely sanctioned*. In other words conformity will be rewarded and non-conformity will be punished. It hardly needs to be said that sanctions give rise to the full play of human ingenuity. But it is useful to group them into a few simple categories according to whether they emphasize:

a physical constraints including, of course, force;
b material inducements – gifts, payments or penalties;
c moral (verbal) approval or disapproval. The range of items that might be included in the last-named group of course defies all but the most general classification because they employ the whole range of beliefs, values and symbols which arise in the course of social life. Underlying them all, however, is the use of integration into group life itself, conveyed via approval or disapproval, as a sanction over the individual.

2 Second, norms must be *widely internalized*. By themselves, external sanctions can never guarantee conformity. Prevention of violations of the normative order would call for an immense amount of supervision and control were it not for the fact that, for much of the time, individuals can be relied upon to supervise themselves. The second formal characteristic of institutionalized norms, therefore, is that they should have become to some degree internal in the sense that the members of the group have made these ideal rules of society part of their own personalities. In this way, much conformity will become automatic and unreflecting,

producing a sense of disorientation and shock if challenged.

The business of learning the normative standards of society is referred to as *socialization*. It has three forms, primary, secondary and adult:

1 The most significant learning (or *'primary' socialization*) occurs during early infancy. It is at this time that we internalize the more fundamental facts about ourselves and the repertoire of behaviour which society expects of us. We also learn to discriminate between the various objects which go to make up the social as well as the physical world we inhabit. It is certain that without this fundamental learning of the constitution and organization of the groups to which we belong, no individual would develop a stable sense of personal identity.

2 *Secondary socialization* refers to the learning of norms which takes place among equals or 'peers' rather than in the unequal relationships between parent and child. Our first peer-group contact will consist of age peers, playmates and brothers and sisters, school companions. Informal peer groups, however, continue to play an important part in later life and for this reason secondary socialization merges in practice with:

3 *Adult socialization*. Learning after childhood is usually taken to be less important than the critical experiences of childhood. Usually, at least for functionalist theory, which tends to rely on the ideas of Freud (Chapter 18), adult socialization merely reinforces what has been learned earlier. (It has been claimed that the aged go through a fourth process of *'desocialization'* or *'disengagement'*, but this idea has been much criticized in recent years.)

We can now set out some important conclusions which the functionalists drew from the points we have been describing. Conformity to institutionalized norms, they argued, satisfies the basic need of each person to possess a sense of their own identity and to communicate and co-operate with others in order to obtain the means of life. *Groups will therefore contain an inbuilt tendency to defend established rules and customs*. This tendency is called '*social control*'. It should not be confused with the control one person might exercise over another. 'Social control' refers to the spontaneous control over non-conformity which the group exhibits. It is analogous to the way in which Durkheim spoke of mechanical solidarity (see Chapter 14).

The normative order possesses another property which serves the process of social control, namely, that it makes it possible to live a routine of daily social existence. Without the guidance of shared norms we would find it difficult even to make a short shopping expedition. It would for a start be uncertain whether we could guarantee personal security other than through sheer force. Rules of courtesy, which regulate the behaviour of passers-by on, say, a crowded pavement, would be in abeyance. Once at the shop we would discover that we would have to negotiate the whole structure of business transactions from scratch – and so on. The fact that such points are 'obvious' is precisely what functionalists want us to notice. Organized society depends on a whole set of integrative behaviours of which we are not aware unless, with some tedium, they are pointed out to us. Once again we seem to reach the conclusion that merely by participating in group life we give our support to the continuance of its integrative aspects.

Now let us consider one final and highly significant aspect of the functionalist account of normative order. Norms rarely make much sense in isolation. By far the more usual situation is that each has some bearing on a whole context of social behaviours which has been created by observing a set of *related* rules. For example, it only makes sense to say 'parents should look after their children' in a context where the rules have already established the existence of people called parents (and children) on a fairly stable basis. Because of this, functionalists talk of the tendency of norms to occur in 'bundles' which they refer to as *status-roles*, or 'roles' for short. This somewhat

clumsy label serves to indicate that there are two very basic types of norms in any group of permanence. The first type, norms of 'status', prescribe what positions exist to be filled. In our society, for example, the statuses of mother, student, postman, friend, politician have continued to exist for much longer than the lifespan of the individuals who at various times have happened to occupy them. The same is true of what are called norms of 'role'. In this case, however, the norms prescribe how the occupants of social statuses are to perform their duties. The dramatic metaphor is intended here. It is as if, in conformity with Shakespeare's observation that 'all the world's a stage', society assigns us all to preordained parts and with each part a script which we are only free to vary up to a point.

In practice status-roles differ greatly in the amount of variation which society will tolerate: surgeons performing abdominal surgery have less opportunity to depart from the script than parents socializing their children.

Furthermore, it is too much to hope that all norms will be perfectly unambiguous: still less that they will be harmoniously compatible at all times. Thus functionalists talk about role *strain* arising out of the fact that all of us occupy many different roles at any given point in our lives and that the relevant norms often make conflicting demands. A common source of such strain nowadays, for example, arises out of the way in which the traditional structure of family roles assigns clear obligations to both sexes; whereas the structure of roles assigned to women and men outside of the family – in the economy, say, and the educational system – appears more and more to be calling this traditional pattern into question. (In the next chapter we shall consider this issue in more detail.)

The normative functionalist model of society has sometimes been compared to a set of Chinese boxes, in which each box is enclosed within another slightly larger box. Just as norms are said to occur in related clusters called status-roles, so the status-roles themselves occur in co-ordinated units which are denoted by the everyday term *institution*. The familiarity of this word should not be allowed to obscure the fact that the sociological usage is wider and more abstract than in ordinary conversation. We are not simply talking about a particular organization or building. We would also want to include such examples as, say, the institution of marriage, or spectator sport, or foxhunting – all of which may equally well be treated as focal points for the co-ordination of status and role clusters. (Modern society, of course, is remarkable for the fact that it has developed very complex institutions – for example, armies, bureaucracies and industrial firms – in which the way the component roles are to be brought together is quite intricately specified.)

Some of the more prominent functionalist writers go one stage further. They argue that there is yet one more 'box' (or even 'boxes') in the 'Chinese puzzle' because institutions themselves form part of still wider complexes of co-ordinated social activity which they refer to as *functional subsystems* of the society as a whole. But we will go into the details of this idea in the section on Talcott Parsons.

The sum total of all of the 'Chinese boxes' is referred to as the *social structure*. It is simply the combination of all the individual units 'in motion' as it were – that is, the status-roles, institutions and functional subsystems which go to make up the normative order. This way of talking about society possessing a 'structure' is somewhat old-fashioned. We have seen that so-called 'structuralists' use the term in a more subtle sense of 'implicit' structure – just as we might describe the grammatical rules of language as its 'implicit' structure (see pp. 233–4). The functionalists' usage of structure, on the other hand, is 'architectural': it relies on an analogy between:

a   the arrangements which give stability to visible objects;
b   the regularities which, though they undoubtedly exist in social life, cannot be regarded as forming a visible object in quite the same sense.

Functionalists would defend themselves by insisting that they are concerned with actual behaviour, unlike the structuralists who emphasize culture or communication. Beneath the surface events which occur in society, people's actions do exhibit a regularity. This is achieved by following norms (rules) which make it possible for people who may never have met each other to co-operate and predict each other's behaviour in an organized fashion.

This, then, is a general description of the basic model of social structure common to the 'normative' functionalist orthodoxy in post-war sociology. We must now say something about the social theory of Talcott Parsons who by any standards must be regarded as the 'guru' of this kind of approach. Parsons either developed or incorporated all of the terms, concepts and ideas which we have been considering in these two sections (for example, Parsons 1969, 1951; Parsons and Shils 1951; Parsons, Bales and Shils 1968; Parsons and Smelser 1956).

Talcott Parsons: systems of action

Parsons's writings are difficult, often unnecessarily so. (It may, therefore, be necessary to 'work at' this section rather more than usual.) As a result not only he, but also sociology, have acquired a reputation for pretentiousness and triviality. But, in fact, the problems which Parsons addresses are not trivial, and to understand his work properly an extensive knowledge of both nineteenth- and twentieth-century social theory is required.

The structure of social action and the problem of order

Parsons's first and arguably his greatest work, first published in 1937, was called *The Structure of Social Action*. It sets out from a problem which he refers to as the 'utilitarian dilemma'.

This will, we hope, strike the reader by now as a very common kind of starting point for a sociological theory. Parsons's discussion, though somewhat tortuously written, is one of the most perceptive accounts of why sociology *must* reject the utilitarian theory of society (cf. pp. 35–9; Parsons 1969, Chapter 2). The belief that society is founded on the self-interested actions of rational individuals cannot, he argues, explain the nature and origins of the theory's most fundamental notion, that is, self-interest. In order to do so it would be necessary to account for *ends*, that is, the values and purposes which make the term 'self-interest' meaningful. Parsons then shows that every attempt to modify the theory in order to explain the origin of ends has finished by denying the idea of human choice altogether:

a either ends and purposes are said to be determined by instinct and other hereditary factors, that is, Social Darwinism;
b or ends and purposes are said to be determined by environment and social conditioning, that is, the 'Blank Page' theory.

Parsons rejects both alternatives because they represent quite unacceptable forms of positivism and because, like all positivist positions, they deny what he calls the 'voluntaristic' character of social behaviour. This means that social theory must be able to handle the role of subjective intentions and choices – people are the puppets of neither heredity nor environment.

The alternative to the utilitarian dilemma, Parsons maintains, is to understand society as the expression of systems of values and norms which have been mutually evolved and institutionalized by the membership. He argues that in the works of the classical social theorists can be found a convergence of thought towards this solution. Here we shall single out the treatment given to Durkheim.

Parsons is especially concerned with Durkheim's contribution to the 'convergence' of theory in three respects:

1   Durkheim grappled with the problem, first raised in the work of Hobbes, of setting out the conditions of social order. He realized that such an order must presuppose an element of moral consensus about the purposes and conditions of social life.
2   He was able to show that under conditions of mechanical solidarity social order is derived from the moral sentiments embodied in the collective conscience.
3   But he failed to find a satisfactory account of social order in the case of societies with a developed division of labour. For, according to Parsons, Durkheim thought that this order *presupposes the disappearance of the 'collective conscience'*.

The accuracy of this interpretation has been challenged. Giddens, for example, has little difficulty in showing that Durkheim was actually somewhat contemptuous of Hobbes and not at all interested in understanding social order in the abstract. His concern was very specifically related to the conditions for the development of a morality of individualism. And on this score, Parsons has misread his sources. The 'collective conscience' does not disappear altogether with the development of the division of labour but, as we have seen, possesses a changed content. The result is a new organic type of order (or solidarity) (Giddens 1977, pp. 235–91).

Parsons's position is not as hopeless, however, as it may seem. Durkheim's actual discussion of the relation between moral individualism and the collective conscience is, to say the least, unclear and passages which seem to support Parsons's account of it undoubtedly exist (cf. Durkheim 1964b, pp. 171–3). Furthermore, the issues raised by Parsons in his account of the 'utilitarian dilemma' are not to be lightly dismissed, whatever the textual accuracy of his reading of Durkheim (Adriaansens 1980). It is hard to evisage a sociology that was not somehow concerned with, on the one hand, moral ideas and their restraining effect on individual conduct; and on the other, with the realization of orderliness in the life of social groups. Adriaansens has gone so far as to argue that Parsons's own theories represent an attempt to set out an 'ideal-type', as it were, of total moral consensus or normative order. What they show is that even under such extreme and unlikely conditions, social life would still contain fundamental strains and tensions (Adriaansens 1980, pp. 169ff.).

The disciplinary status of the social sciences

Another aspect of Parsons's work is the possibility that it represents an attempt to put the viability of the social sciences beyond all reasonable doubt (Rocher 1974). Like Spencer, Parsons has sought to uncover the grand principle unifying all scientific enquiry. Admittedly the writings themselves do not make this particularly obvious. In the first paragraph of *The Structure of Social Action* Parsons declares 'Spencer is dead'. Yet viewing Parsons's output with hindsight we can see that certain Spencerian themes have been taken up again. Admittedly, the grand unifying principle is not evolution – although late in Parsons's career he did return to the evolutionary perspective and proposed a classification of levels of social development (see Parsons 1967). But evolution will no longer do as a linking principle between social and natural science. Human action is 'voluntaristic' – in other words it contains a subjective element in which purposes and meaning come into play. Parsons himself, of course, shows that evolutionary *explanations* of 'voluntaristic' actions are inadequate.

It is the notion of *system*, not evolution, which he uses to link social and natural science. By system we mean whole complexes or sequences of mutually linked events. This principle is already well established in the study of the natural world. It also applies to the social world, however. Although human actions are 'voluntaristic' they are at the same time interdependent and this makes the use of systems analysis a peculiarly appropriate method of

studying them. Therefore the system perspective of functionalism is simply the counterpart in the social sciences of the scientific approach already used in the natural sciences. The finishing touch to this argument is contained in a work written with Smelser called *Economy and Society* (Parsons and Smelser 1956). This aims to show that economics (rational choice theory) is simply a special case of the more general theory of social systems.

A theory of the social system

What then would a theory of systems of social action look like? For Parsons, what we loosely call 'society' is actually the end product not of one system of action but *four*, which are:

1 the organism – that is, the human body;
2 the personality;
3 the culture;
4 the social system.

Each of these systems is directed towards the securing of four requirements, which Parsons regards as essential to the continuation of human life as a whole. (Actually, they are a digest of earlier lists of functional prerequisites of the sort already given above, p. 263.) These requirements and their corresponding system are:

1 *Adaptation.* The fulfilment of the function of adaptive survival. It resides ultimately in the *organism*. It should be noted, however, that many aspects of the organism (for example, breathing, heartbeat) do not concern Parsons directly because they do not affect action and choice as such.

2 *Goal attainment.* This means the sense of purposes or ends which in human beings is not reducible to mere biological impulse. The fulfilment of this function ultimately resides in the *personality* which programmes the mind and body towards the realization of various objectives.

3 *Pattern maintenance.* The 'pattern' here is that of action in the future – contemplated but

not yet carried out. Neither the organism nor the personality can exist on their own as utilitarianism has implied. This is where the *cultural system* comes in. For Parsons, culture is not just an accumulation of objects and ideas. It is a living system made up of all the different kinds of symbols – material, linguistic, moral, etc. – which are created out of and modified by social action, and which are transmitted from one generation to the next. The cultural system is also the repository of the core value system of society as well as of the normative order based upon it. As we have seen above, both of these have the function of socially integrating individuals with collective life.

4 *Integration.* In actually using the term 'integration', Parsons is not talking about individuals but society as a whole and the way in which the three other systems of action are brought together. This function is fulfilled by what he calls the *social* system. The social system consists of the functioning patterns of behaviour to be found in actual social life. Strictly speaking, only the social system constitutes the proper subject matter for sociology.

At this point we meet up again with the 'Chinese box' motif. We have just said that there are four systems of action, each dominated by one of four prerequisites of human action as a whole. Each system will seek equilibrium in relation to the prerequisite which dominates it. Yet we can take any one of these systems, Parsons claims, and show that although one function does indeed dominate, the other prerequisites will also be present.

Let us illustrate this in the case of the social system. What Parsons is arguing is that inside the Chinese box called the social system we can find the pattern of prerequisites repeated. The social system has its own 'needs' for adaptation, goal attainment, pattern maintenance and integration. Likewise there will be a specialized subsystem to deal with each prerequisite. Furthermore, we can show that the activities of each one of these specialized subsystems

corresponds to our everyday understanding of the object or 'function' of familiar complexes of institutions. Thus:

a the primary function of the *economy* is adaptation;

b that of the *political* system is goal attainment;

c *cultural and religious institutions* and the family express and cement our commitment to the normative order, that is, to pattern maintenance;

d the institutions of law, order and social control monitor events in the factual order and thus ensure *integration* in the whole collectivity.

Activities and functions

The next step is to classify the type of activities ('action') which take place in the social system. Parsons offers two dimensions:

1 *instrumental-expressive*, that is, whether activities are concerned with *means* or with *ends or purposes*.

2 *external-internal*, that is, whether they relate to the environment of the system or group, or whether they relate to its internal structure.

These different types of activity can then be fitted in to the functional prerequisites as shown in Table 8.

To complete our account of the Chinese boxes, we need only add that Parsons thinks it possible to take each of the subsystems of action and find within it further sub-subsystems again

Table 8 *Functional prerequisites for social activity*

	Instrumental activity	Expressive activity
External relevance	Adaptation (economy)	Goal attainment (polity)
Internal relevance	Pattern maintenance (culture)	Integration (social system)

specialized according to the four functional imperatives, and so on. In fact, at any given level of individual or social action at which we care to look, we shall find the conflicting demands of the four functional imperatives behind the surface pattern of events. The point is important because Parsons and the 'hard' functionalists have often been accused of ignoring conflict, tension and change within social life. On the contrary, whatever else might be unsatisfactory in the theory, it *is* built upon the idea that society presupposes competing, even irreconcilable, elements and that constant changes and adjustments have to be made as a result.

Traditional versus modern

Finally we can put these abstractions to work by asking how they help us to explain the difference between industrial and non-industrial social systems. Alas, in order to understand Parsons's answer there are two more concepts we need to consider. They are:

1   pattern variables;
2   structural differentiation.

The pattern variables

These are devices for describing and comparing the norms and values of all known cultures. They are designed to replace 'linked antitheses' (notably Tönnies's concepts of *Gemeinschaft* and *Gesellschaft*) with sets of dimensions or variables which express the whole range of possibilities from which actual societies develop complexes of rules and roles.

Once again, it is tension and the insolubility of the demands which social life places upon individuals and institutions which dominate Parsons's thought. The moral choices which lead to human action are, we have said, guided by norms. In practice, however, each norm will represent an imperfect solution to what is ultimately a moral dilemma or series of dilemmas. The pattern variables are, in fact, what Parsons

thinks is an exhaustive list of these dilemmas put in their most general form. The idea is that armed with this list we can compare the pattern of norms which have arisen in any number of actual societies in order to see how, in each case, the dilemma has been resolved and what has made that particular 'solution' acceptable. Let us, first of all, see what the dilemmas behind the pattern variables actually are (see also Table 9).

Dilemma number 1 relates to the problem of how people are to be motivated to perform any particular item of social behaviour. Parsons accepts that in the end all human conduct is motivated by the level of gratification of wants or impulses which can be expected. There is, however, a difference in principle between gratification obtained directly from the object of action and indirect gratification, where the individual actually defers enjoyment in order to perform some action which will lead to even greater gratification in the long run. The first type Parsons calls '*affectivity*'. Examples include eating a meal, seeking comfort from a parent or friend, participation in religious ritual. The second type Parsons calls '*affectively neutral*'. Examples include cooking the meal or performing dull work for the sake of a wage.

Dilemma number 2 asks what kind of standard is used to judge the behaviour and performance of individuals as they carry out various roles. For example, performance in engineering

Table 9   *The pattern variables – 'dilemmas of action'*

'Traditional' orientation		'Modern' orientation
1 Affectivity	versus	Affective neutrality
2 Particularism		Universalism
3 Ascription		Achievement
4 Diffuse		Specific
————Structural differentiation————→		

examinations and assignments must be assessed strictly according to the knowledge of engineering which each candidate shows. We can therefore speak of the *universalism* of the examiner's role. Some societies which have tried to adopt Western technology and skills have encountered problems with this universalism, Parsons argues. This is because it conflicts with a widespread and deeply held belief found in traditional societies that one ought to give especial favours to relatives, friends or members of particular religious groups. He calls this type of behaviour standard *particularism*. Even in modern society, of course, the family still remains an important source of particularistic values which clash with the dominant universalism of the wider society (see next chapter).

Dilemma number 3 is about what we make of the persons actually carrying out the action. In some cases we judge them by their performance or *achievement*. Examinations again give us the obvious illustration here, but the same can be said of the way we relate, say, to shop assistants, or the doctor, or the applicant for a job. On other occasions what matters is that the characteristics of a person cannot be changed by anything they themselves do. Age- and sex-related roles are the obvious case in point because they represent roles in society which are shared out by fixed 'natural' characteristics. It is very important to emphasize that Parsons is *not* adopting a Social Darwinist standpoint. He is not claiming that certain roles *have* to be handed out on the basis of biological ascriptions but pointing out that cultures vary in their use of ascriptions and in their choice of the 'natural' attributes which are given emphasis. Ascriptive roles usually carry very strong and enduring attachments. A son is a son regardless. Kingship provides a common example of a political role being filled on the ascriptive principle.

Dilemma number 4 refers to the scope which a role possesses in relation to the system of which it is part. Again family roles may be used to illustrate one 'pole' of the range of possible alternatives. There is hardly any limit to the range of services which the members of a family may perform for each other. In other words family roles are *functionally diffuse*. The duties of an employee, however, incline towards the other pole – the *functionally specific*. He or she is paid to carry out a task and there, to all intents, the relationship ends.

Now, we have already suggested that each of these fundamental dilemmas will enable the investigator to classify either whole societies, or subsystems, and/or even individual roles according to the pattern of solutions which they represent. What we also need to do, however, is to explain what *causes* the pattern adopted by different societies to vary. There are actually *two* problems to be considered – the causes of variation within societies and the causes of variation between them:

1 *Variation within societies* can be explained in terms we already know. The nature of the norms which predominate within a subsystem of society will depend on the functional prerequisite which it serves. For example, in the economy, which is a subsystem ordered around the function of adaptation, the norms express affective neutrality, self-orientation, universalism, achievement and functionally specific action. In the family, on the other hand, which has the function of integration, the norms emphasize affectivity, collectivity orientation, particularism, ascription and functionally diffuse action. And so on for the other subsystems.

2 *Variation between societies* cannot be explained in this way. Instead we need the concept of structural differentiation.

Structural differentiation

We have encountered this concept already in Chapter 6 where we pointed to the Spencerian origins of the idea behind it. It refers to the most general way of all in which societies can vary from each other, namely: the degree of specialization found in the activities, institutions and subsystems of societies.

1 *Societies with a low degree of structural differentiation* will, almost by definition, not be in a position to emphasize the pattern variable solution given in the right-hand column of Table 9. For example, one cannot, in an undifferentiated society, distance oneself from particularistic obligations (dilemma number 2) nor greatly restrict the scope of roles (dilemma number 4).

2 *Societies with a high degree of structural differentiation* will have a much greater range of variation in their normative patterns since each subsystem will tend to gravitate towards the type of solution most favourable to its basic function. However, Parsons also asserts that all societies possess a fundamental or 'core' value system which prevents conflicting subsystem demands from threatening the cohesion of the whole. This core value system works by giving primacy to one functional imperative over the rest. The shift to the modern structurally differentiated pattern, for example, implies placing a high value upon adaptation (that is, material and economic well-being) and hence in many areas of life an abandonment of the dilemma resolutions on the left-hand side of the diagram in favour of those on the right.

Parsons is open to the charge that he has merely reformulated the problem which had to be explained: he may be able to account for why particular sets of norms differ but we still need to know why cultures adopt one core value system rather than another. Perhaps it was this criticism which led him to identify with the (hardly new) thought that in all societies, the function of adaptation is, in the last instance, the primary one; and under this influence to reintroduce, late in his career, the concept of evolution (Parsons 1966). The irony of this Spencerian 'regression' has not gone unnoticed.

An interesting failure?

Parsons's elaborate schema has been the object of a vast critical literature which we cannot hope to summarize here. His work is currently unfashionable and in some quarters is regarded as no more than a cover for deep-rooted political conservatism. Among those still prepared to take Parsons seriously the job of evaluation boils down to a few basic questions. How successfully does his theory deal with the problem of the non-determined, subjective or 'voluntaristic' element in human social behaviour? Can it deal more effectively than utilitarianism with the nature of ends, goals and purposes? In particular can it do so without betraying the commitment to a non-positivist 'voluntaristic' view of the social actor?

In these terms the theory seems to be an interesting failure. It implies for example that the way in which people come to accept certain values and purposes is wholly understandable by reference to the normative system. The internalization of norms is the fundamental process by which individuals are socially integrated into groups and into society. But these norms also form the building blocks of institutional and social systems. Their content, therefore, will not be fixed by the actions and choices of individual people at all but by the functional prerequisites of system integration.

This way of looking at social behaviour is not wholly wrong. We have argued all along that social choices and meanings are always fixed in relation to the context of group life as a whole. But normative functionalists, Parsons among them, lean too far in the opposite direction. As a result they have been charged with offering what Dennis Wrong calls an 'oversocialized concept' of social behaviour (Wrong 1967). People have become puppets of the roles and institutions they belong to. Not only does such a view smuggle into sociology the simplifications of the 'Blank Page' theory of social forces which we discussed in Chapter 5. It also begs the question of the origins of order which the theory is committed to deal with.

Robert Merton – intentions and dysfunctions

It has always been the case that functionalists

have themselves never been wholly satisfied with their way of explaining social phenomena. Much of the literature of the school, therefore, consists of constructive criticism. A classic example of this tendency is a famous paper called 'Manifest and Latent Functions' by Robert Merton, which, in fact, appeared well before the bulk of Parsons's writings had been published(Merton 1968a). Merton's aim in presenting the paper was to remove some of the obscurities which older functionalist interpretations inherited from anthropology and to present a revitalized 'paradigm' or model of the proper procedure for pursuing functionalist analysis. With the passage of time, his arguments have more and more been taken to represent, on the most favourable view, a rather different 'softer' kind of functionalism from that of Parsons. To Merton's critics, however, they represent an early statement of the inherent weaknesses which are contained in *any* functionalist approach to conformity and social integration.

Even the mildest 'soft' commitment to functionalism as a mode of analysis implies some acceptance of the idea of society as a self-maintaining system. (Moore W. E. 1978, pp. 323–4). Merton's essay still remains the best starting-point for understanding the difficulties which such an idea runs into. Quite early in the piece we are presented with three fallacious hypotheses to which functionalism is prone – and to which, we might add, Merton himself failed to find any generally acceptable remedy. In describing them we shall, at the same time, give some of the solutions which other functionalists besides Merton have offered.

Fallacy number 1

Merton calls this the *postulate of indispensability*. To what extent can any particular institution be said to reflect 'functional' or 'essential' prerequisites for social order? There are two possibilities:

1   When we offer a functionalist explanation we could be claiming that a basic function gives rise to (is the cause of) the particular item of social structure that we observe *in its existing form.*

2   Alternatively we might argue that an observable part of the structure of a society just happens to have acquired a particular significance in relation to the whole and thus may be said to possess a 'function'.

Whereas Parsons opts for the former solution, Merton himself clearly prefers to begin with the actual features of a structure or part. This enables us, as we have seen, to ask whether there exist any *functional alternatives* to it, say, in similar kinds of societies? But it weakens considerably the theory that the nature of the part is to be understood principally in terms of its relation to the social structure as a whole. It is this idea which is supposed to provide much of the explanatory muscle in functionalist analysis. If, however, there are alternatives the part only belongs to the structure in a descriptive sense. Indeed Giddens points out that the term 'structure' 'is often used as more or less equivalent to system in the functionalist literature' which makes the idea of a structure composed of systematically related 'parts' rather pointless (Giddens 1977, p. 113).

Fallacy number 2

Merton calls this the postulate of *functional unity*. This means simply that it is quite naïve for sociologists to assume that society is a completely integrated, smoothly functioning whole – even for the sake of argument. Societies are just not like that. But in that case is there any sense in regarding them as 'systems' at all?

The fact that societies cannot be regarded as comparable with organisms shows that they do not correspond to one type of system which is known in the jargon of modern cybernetics as a *closed* system. Post-war functionalists, however, under the influence of cybernetics, have suggested instead that a more appropriate analogy can be found in other parts of the natural world where what we observe is the operation of various open or partially open systems. In such cases, the actual structure of the system readily undergoes modification as a result of external influences. We might, for example, point to the behaviour of systems of weather or the systems of turbulence that develop in liquids. As a number of authors have observed, though, the distinctive assumption of the functionalist account of social systems is that they are functionally unified by virtue of the fact that they are to a degree self-maintaining. The concept of open system, by contrast, merely denotes a set of causal influences linked in a complex fashion to produce an enduring result but *not* one which is necessarily functionally unified or self-maintaining.

Merton himself tried to resolve the problem by treating the hypothesis of functional unity simply as a *method* of investigating the unintended consequences of particular forms of behaviour. He pointed out that in conforming to a particular practice individuals are likely to have a diversity of purposes in mind. It is by no means clear that their conscious intentions always include an accurate assessment of the likely consequences of their actions for the integration of society. For example, in observing a particular religious ceremony the participants may be intending to produce rain or obtain a sense of spiritual salvation. These then, are possible *manifest functions* of the practice. The sociologist, however, may wish to point out that the rituals have the *latent function* of cementing a sense of cohesiveness among the members of the sect and this, rather than the manifest function of the ceremony, may better explain the reasons for its persistence. By means of the distinction between manifest and latent functions then, Merton calls for the efforts of sociologists to be directed principally at the *unintended consequences* of social action. This argument leaves two unsolved problems:

1 *Methodological*: how are the pure speculations which sociologists might have about the possible latent functions of a piece of behaviour to be turned into valid analysis? Merton might reply that this is not just a problem for functionalists. The problem of dealing with unintended consequences arises in sociology generally – for example, when Marxists refer to false consciousness, in connection with Weber's ideal types or in Freud's theory of unconsciousness motivations (see Chapter 18).

2 *Substantive*: the relation between intentions, integration and unintended consequences is usually far less straightforward than in the example above. Merton himself makes a great deal out of the kind of self-fulfilling prophecy underlying cases such as a stock-market panic where actions intended to avoid a threatened disaster actually bring about the result which was feared. And it would be equally possible to point to other examples where people's behaviour has brought about the direct opposite to their intentions, where conformity, say, to inappropriate norms has had the effect of *dis*integrating society.

Fallacy number 3

This arises from the '*postulate of universal functionalism*' which early versions of the theory tended to make. To put the matter simply again: why should it be taken for granted that *every* social practice can be understood as making a contribution to the maintenance of society? It is not hard to think of examples which, on the face of it, are either neutral (stamp collecting?) or positively harmful (gang warfare, unemployment?) from the point of view of system integration. Merton proposes to meet this difficulty in two ways:

1 *By distinguishing between functions (or eufunctions; Levy 1964) and dysfunctions*. Given that for Merton the notion of functional integration is not necessarily a hypothesis about how society actually works, but a method of analysis, of probing the relationship between one part of social life and another, it is perfectly feasible to accept that some social relationships are *dysfunctional*, that is, systematically *dis*integrative.

To be sure, this does not wholly dispose of all criticisms. In particular it is not clear how Merton intends to distinguish between functions and dysfunctions except by applying purely arbitrary moral judgements about the state or 'health' of integration in society. But his approach does allow us to recognize that social problems, non-conformity and deviance may not be the result of individual intentions but systematically generated by their location in the wider social structure or by strain between conflicting norms.

2 *By confining his method to substantive cases*. We have already encountered examples where Merton can claim to have made contributions to particular fields by applying his method. One example is in the study of organizations and the dysfunctions of the bureaucratic personality (p. 198). The most impressive example, however, is to be found in the revised theory of anomie and deviance which we discussed in Chapter 15.

A comparable solution which appears to be morally more neutral than Merton's is contained in an article published by Alvin Gouldner shortly before the radical attack on functionalism had begun in earnest. Gouldner suggested that the fallacy of universal functionalism might be avoided by undertaking an analysis of the causes of what he called 'functional autonomy' (Gouldner 1959). Conformity to integrative patterns, he goes on, depends on the differing extent to which individuals and groups have an investment in the system. Those with a low investment possess the basis for a degree of autonomy from it. Alternatively, as Moore was to point out later, some organizations and groups benefit more from whatever system exists than do others and thus possess the autonomy to manipulate it. What is good for General Motors is *not* necessarily good for the community. All this, however, does not leave much of the notion of a self-maintaining system which, as Moore notes ruefully: 'is put further in doubt if circumstances permit "subsystems"

with sufficient degrees of independence or autonomy so that what is eufunctional or dysfunctional for the part does not have the same consequences for the broader society' (Moore W. E. 1978, p. 332).

In grappling, not wholly successfully, with these three problems or 'fallacies', then, Merton can be seen as providing a seminal critique of functionalism. In fact, each 'fallacy' he describes arises because basically it has never been clear in sociology whether one can be said to have explained a phenomenon by identifying its 'function' or 'functions'. In short, how *valid* is a functional explanation? To find an answer to this question is as important to functionalism's critics as it is to functionalists themselves, as we shall see. In the remainder of this chapter, therefore, we shall consider, on a fairly simple level, (a) the logical and (b) the substantive, validity of functionalist explanations.

Functionalist explanations

Logical problems

The logic of functionalist explanation is unorthodox, breaking an important principle which holds in the natural sciences. This stipulates that there is a definite sequence in the relationship between cause and effect so that the cause must always occur before the event which is held to be its consequence. For the functionalist sociologist, however, social structure is already in existence: we cannot, for instance, treat social structure as an effect of the actions of individuals since individuals can only develop within a social structure that is already 'given'. Furthermore, whatever features or changes occur within it have to be interpreted in terms of *their* consequence for the whole collectivity. This has attracted the criticism that functionalist explanations are *teleological*: which is a piece of philosophers' jargon meaning 'explaining in terms of consequences', that is, in terms of what comes after and not what comes before.

One way to avoid this charge might be to accept that causal explanations in sociology are simply not like the causal explanations to be found in natural sciences – an argument which incidentally puts at risk a thesis popular with functionalists: the essential unity of all science. Max Weber's methodology, as we have seen, states that causally adequate accounts of social action depend upon understanding the *intentions* of actors. The distinction between manifest and latent function, however, rules out this type of solution: functions and intentions are not simple equivalents. But it was Durkheim no less who pointed out that there is also no equivalence between accounting for a phenomenon by its functions and explaining the *causes* from which it originated. The latter, he argued, must take logical priority over the former. Functional and causal explanations then are not necessarily the same even in sociology (Durkheim 1964a; cf. Cohen P. 1968, pp. 34–7).

Stinchcombe (1968) insists that a certain class of causal explanation in all sciences *does* rely on the use of consequences. Known as 'equifinal' explanations, we encounter them in observing the behaviour of a cat looking for its plate of food; or in watching the 'feedback' which results from the operation of a thermostat. Both explanations require the ability of the investigator to identify some kind of drive or momentum which creates a 'feedback loop' between effect and cause. In the first example it is the animal's *need* for food. In the second case it is the fact that the instrument is part of an engineered *system*. We have seen however that neither the concept of individual need nor that of system offers much help to the sociologist.

Thus it might be argued that the functional form of explanation is of a fallacious kind which sociology ought to avoid.

Substantive problems

The logical problems which we have just been considering become particularly serious in the case of certain substantive issues all of which, in various ways, concern what Merton had called the 'dysfunctional' aspects of social life. Consider, for example, the question of why conflict and power struggles develop. A lack of interest in such matters is rather evident in all functionalist writing until the appearance of works by Parsons and by Coser in the 1950s (Parsons 1951, 1967, pp. 240–65; Coser 1956). Even then what dominates is rather unrecognizable in comparison with 'common-sense' understandings of these phenomena. For Parsons, power is to be understood as a 'facility' for operating the political (that is, goal attainment) subsystem. Without this facility certain objectives which all parties consider desirable (for example, law and order, public health) would never be realized. But Parsons does not ask whether these benefits of power are equally distributed in society. Coser uses a similar argument to explain conflict. It is to be understood as an advanced warning of strain in the social structure which has the latent function of restoring integration.

In both of these examples the 'dysfunctions' are explained by asserting that what appears manifestly dysfunctional does in fact have latent functions. We shall now look in more detail at two further instances of the same theory.

Deviance

Merton was not the only functionalist theorist to tackle the problem of deviance. In fact *the* functionalist theory of deviance proper claims its authority from Durkheim. In a famous passage in the *Rules of Sociological Method* Durkheim challenged the conventional idea that crime is a symptom of social malfunctioning and incipient disorder. On the contrary, though (as he admits) it may seem 'quite paradoxical', crime 'is a factor in public health, an integral part of all healthy societies'. Its effect is to strengthen collective sentiments in the law-abiding majority. The acts of the wrongdoer serve to solidify and strengthen the collective conscience. He points out that different societies vary in the classes of actions which are considered criminal. If one kind of law-breaking were to be wholly eliminated it would be necessary to find others. Thus:

Imagine a society of saints, a perfect cloister of exemplary individuals. Crimes, properly so called, will there be unknown: but the faults which appear venial to the layman will create there the same scandal that the ordinary offence does in ordinary consciousness. (Durkheim 1964a, pp. 65–75)

It is arguable that what Durkheim anticipates in this passage is *not*, in fact, the functionalist theory at all but another, known as the 'labelling' theory of deviance which we shall be discussing in Chapter 19 (cf. Jones T. A. 1981). The functionalist theory is, nevertheless, similar to Durkheim's. It states that deviance, apparently symptomatic of the failure of social integration, in fact promotes it by fulfilling the following functions:

a it defines the boundaries of acceptable conduct;
b it highlights 'weak spots' in the social order which can then become the concern of law enforcement agencies;
c it cements a sense of identification with the culture among members of conventional society.

One of the most successful and well-known applications of the theory is to be found in Kai Erikson's book *Wayward Puritans* (1966). This work is of interest because it takes a 'new' community and, in Durkheimian style, asks how the boundary between acceptable and unacceptable conduct became established. The Puritans in question, seventeenth-century settlers on the East Coast of the USA, in fact had much in common with Durkheim's community of saints. The primary 'evils' which emerged were in the first instance failures of religious probity. Quite minor departures from the Puritan code would become inflamed into crimes of heresy and witchcraft. Such strong reactions to infringements might seem trivial to the modern mind. But they functioned to maintain a very rigorous

sense of right conduct and cohesion in a settler community, faced as it was with constant possibilities of external novelty, invasion by new cultures and internal disruption.

The idea that deviance has 'functions', however, is full of ambiguities. Do we mean that the function is the 'cause' of the deviance; or that 'society' has an 'intention' of creating deviance; or that deviance is a prerequisite of social 'functioning'? How, empirically, can we validate such a theory? Can we wholly ignore the possibility that deviance does not cement the social order at all but, as Merton had already argued, arises from the systemic strains and tensions of the order itself? In fact not all deviance does promote social integration. Some deviant acts are the product of laws which have become obsolete or anachronistic. Others reach such a level of severity that they genuinely threaten the breakdown of social order. The latter seems particularly likely where the society possesses a plural structure (for example, South Africa) or is highly stratified. In such cases the laws and rules do not reflect common sentiment but the interest of a minority.

Inequality and stratification

In a much debated paper written as long ago as 1945, Davis and Moore assert that inequality is a phenomenon to be found in all societies and hence stratification must serve a necessary and definite function (Davis and Moore 1967).

From this highly contentious beginning Davis and Moore attempt to account for the inevitability of the mechanisms that result in stratification. Some roles, they argue, are more functionally necessary than others; the skills and attributes to fill those roles are relatively scarce and unequally available; hence those who do possess them must be motivated by above-average material and emotional rewards so that 'the most important positions are conscientiously filled by the most qualified persons'.

Davis and Moore's arguments were adapted, revised but not substantially altered by Parsons

(1951, pp. 69–86, 386–439; 1954). They also became the centre of debate that has raged until quite recently (Bendix and Lipset 1967, pp. 47ff.; Coser and Rosenberg 1964, pp. 413ff.). Numerous criticisms of this theory have been offered. The two basic objections however are:

1 *Factual*: Is stratification universal? In a recent review of the whole controversy Moore (1978) states that in none of it 'has the universality of inequality been challenged'. This disingenuous remark seems to have been made without reference to the rather neglected discussion by the anthropologist M. G. Smith (1966). Smith points out that although it would be surprising to find a society where individuals were all completely equal to each other, the anthropological evidence does not support the view that all societies possess systems of *stratification* in the sense defined above.

2 *Methodological and logical*: How should the investigator decide which positions are 'functionally necessary' or 'important'? *Either* we must make a wholly arbitrary decision about the value of each contribution which members make to society, *or* we measure importance by the actual distribution of rewards which society gives to individuals and groups. The first carries a serious risk of smuggling in moral assumptions; the second makes the theory circular – it was the distribution of rewards which it was designed to explain.

It is perhaps hardly surprising, in view of the way in which particular functionalists have gone about explaining inequality, conflict and power, that the school as a whole has attracted the criticism of being incurably *conservative*. To concentrate on the 'functions' of the more divisive aspects of social life and to say nothing of the suffering and injustice to which they give rise is to invite accusations of using social theory to legitimate the status quo. It is also said that the functionalist model as a whole is excessively *static*. By emphasizing institutionalized norms and value consensus in its account of social order it minimizes the significance of change

and fails to explain it. Finally, for similar reasons, a great deal of functionalism appears to be *unhistorical*: the society it describes is abstracted from the actual human drama.

Conflict theory and the problem of order

In fact we do not need to assume that the sharing of norms and values is an essential condition for social order. It is possible to start out from the conviction that society always contains fundamental conflicts of interest and that order is achieved by a balance of power in which the interests of the stronger successfully contain and channel the demands of the weaker. But this model also enables us to see that social order is essentially precarious and that the likely consequence of struggles to alter the balance of power is social change.

This was the position put forward in opposition to functionalism in the late 1950s and early 1960s by a group of European writers who became known as 'conflict theorists':

Ralf Dahrendorf (1959) argued that it is the stabilization of a system of authority which is the most important aspect of social order. Conflict of interest is always present in social life but authority means that some way of resolving these conflicts within the existing framework of institutions has been found (for example, the settlement of labour disputes through collective bargaining). In other words conflict has become *institutionalized*. Dahrendorf also argues that Marx was incorrect to see property as the basis of class; classes and stratification derive from the division of institutionalized authority between leaders and subordinates.

John Rex (1961) claims that Dahrendorf does not go far enough. Behind the stabilization of authority lies a more fundamental balance of power. Rex proposes to treat social systems as involving conflict situations at central points – ranging from, say, market competition to open violence. From this derives a social order composed of two or more classes each with its own self-contained normative system. Since there will be an unequal distribution of power, however, one of these emerges as a relatively secure ruling class.

David Lockwood had already observed, in a major review of Parsons's work (1956), that the latter's attention to conflict and tension in society is confined to *normative* strain. This restricted view ignores the probability that genuine conflicts of material interest and power distribution exist which the normative order will actually 'function' to conceal. Lockwood's most telling critique of functionalism, however, certainly for present purposes, appeared in 1964: the distinction between 'social' and 'system' integration.

Social and system integration

Why should functionalists attach so much importance to self-maintenance or 'integration' in social systems? Lockwood shows that in fact normative functionalists had actually been compounding two forms of integration which cannot be regarded as equivalent. In order to make clear what the distinction between social and system integration is getting at let us consider the problem of throwing a party.

A party may be a disappointment for a number of reasons. Some of these have to do with each guest's response to the occasion. Suppose one of the guests is called Harry. Maybe the party was fine for most people but Harry did not know anyone and was too shy to join in. Or perhaps there was some external influence (the bank statement came that morning); or maybe they expected him to behave at the party in a way that conflicted with his puritanical upbringing. All of these examples lead to the failure of a given individual to 'click' with others and thus refer to the problem of social integration, which, if it arises for too many guests, can ruin the party. But this is not the only hazard. Trouble may also arise because of the way the party was organized. Maybe the host forgot to send out the invitations on time; or failed to order enough food or

drink; or insisted on organizing games even though the guests clearly wanted to dance. These failures of the basic arrangements are like the kind of problem in society which reflects lack of so-called system integration.

In general terms we can say that:

1   *System integration* is about the co-ordination of groups' activities and functions. It is to this type of integration that the notion of functional prerequisites is addressed.

2   *Social integration* is about the problem of persuading individuals that they belong to a group and indeed derive responsibilities and even benefits from belonging. It is to this type of integration that we refer in speaking of a consensus of values and the conformity of individuals to institutionalized norms.

The originality of Lockwood's discussion therefore lies in showing that (a) the hypothesis that societies function in accordance with certain prerequisites and (b) the hypothesis that individuals conform to norms, need not both be true at once.* Indeed if they were, we would be confronted with a society in which individuals were 'oversocialized' in perfect accordance with social needs. But in the following chapters we shall repeatedly come back to the point that the calibre of personal social experience and the functioning of society represent two totally different levels of analysis, even requiring 'two sociologies'. This is especially true in an unequal society which may 'function' perfectly as a system and yet create immense problems of integration for the individuals and groups within it.

Conclusion

Functionalism today is a very unfashionable

---

* Many functionalists were aware to a degree that these two need not coincide. For example, there is much discussion in the literature on role theory of the tension between roles considered as set demands which social structure imposes on individuals; and roles considered as actual performances where individuals negotiate their precise rights and benefits.

school of thought. In recent years, as Martins has observed, 'the demolition of functionalism is almost an initiation rite of passage into sociological adulthood or at least adolescence' (1974, p. 247). Yet the attack on Parsons, Merton and others has merely produced a 'succession crisis' in which the various rivals have often tended to repeat functionalist arguments in a number of conceptual languages which, however radical, often possessed the same teleological, static and unhistorical character. Conflict theory suffers from this problem. Percy Cohen (1968, p. 62) for example observes: 'The so-called anti-functionalist theory is . . . in a sense functionalist for it explains how structures of power persist by showing how they are part of a wider *system* [our italics] of interdependent processes'.

Conflict theory, which drew somewhat eclectically from the work of Marx and Weber was, as we noted earlier, soon displaced by a thoroughgoing Marxism. But the resilience of 'late capitalism' to political upheaval has meant that much of the new Marxist writing has been concerned with the 'reproduction' of the capitalist system and with the role of ideological (normative and consensual?) forces as a major element in this. The result has been a functionalism in all but name.

The troubles of functionalist explanation, then, are *still* part of the problem of sociology as a whole. If it constitutes a fallacy or fatal error of sociological analysis it is one which seems remarkably difficult to avoid.

17 Functionalists, family and gender

Although we have described a number of basic weaknesses in functionalism as a theory, it could be argued that they are not very important. The allegiance of many sociologists to functionalism has in fact been based on its 'heuristic' value – that is, its usefulness as a way of asking questions – and they have been rather suspicious of the inclination shown by some of their colleagues to go in for huge systems of speculation unrelated to evidence. Merton himself appealed for the creation and scientific testing of 'theories of the middle range' – in other words, explanations, directed at strictly delimited topics.

This, at times somewhat naïve, belief that sociology, like other branches of science, should submit its explanations to empirical test, stimulated an extensive research literature which in many ways is the main achievement of functionalism. Even today, when so many of the earlier 'middle-range' theories have been called into question, there is hardly any substantive area of sociological enquiry where the student is not obliged to engage with some set of functionalist monographs simply in order to appreciate the point of later work. Indeed, sociology is still somewhat over-reliant on the evidence these monographs yielded, because functionalism's critics have been less than enthusiastic about what can be achieved through empirical enquiry.

We cannot hope, in a single chapter, to summarize the entirety of this research tradition. We have, in any case, been drawing upon it in various ways elsewhere in the book. In what follows, therefore, we shall concentrate on one key 'middle-range' problem, the analysis of the family.

The family – problems of definition

What do we mean by the family? Such is the diversity of culture that this question is almost impossible to answer. One of the most famous attempts at a definition is to be found in the work of G. P. Murdock, according to whom: 'the family is a social group characterised by common residence, economic co-operation and reproduction. It includes adults of both sexes at least two of whom maintain a socially approved sexual relationship and one or more children, own or adopted, of the sexually cohabiting adults.' (Murdock 1949, p. 2) This is a good example of the problems caused when social scientists wrench an everyday word out of the specific everyday context in which it was coined and try to give it some analytical meaning. Murdock has attempted to include all of the great variety of activities around which, as his own research testified, real cultures have woven patterns of 'family' organization. In order to accommodate them all the definition has become complex and somewhat general. There are several problems with it. For example:

1 We cannot be sure whether it is the particular activities as such which constitute the common denominator of family life – a doubtful argument – or whether it is the recurrence of a certain form, that is, cohabiting parents plus children, that is so important.

2 If the latter then the definition is probably

still not inclusive enough. For instance, one-parent families, which are largely disapproved of, even now, in our culture, have been the rule in some others.

Greater precision and usefulness is gained by making some simple distinctions. Thus Murdock himself was careful to follow the practice of separating the *nuclear* or *elementary* family on one hand and the *composite* family on the other. The nuclear family, 'the type of family recognised to the exclusion of all others in our own society', is made up of 'a married man and woman with their offspring, although in individual cases one or more additional persons may reside with them'. In the majority of non-industrial cultures, however, the typical family form is *composite*: that is to say, 'nuclear families are combined, like atoms in a molecule into larger aggregates' (Murdock 1949). The principles upon which the combination is made fall into two broad subtypes, both of them reflecting activities/relationships which intuitively we recognize as part of, though not confined to, family life as we know it. The first principle is that of *sexual* relationship between a man (or men) and a woman (or women). The second is the *age* relationship between generations. As principles for the compounding of nuclear into composite families, however, they tend to be mutually exclusive. If, in a given society, we find two or more nuclear families joined by the sexual bond by having one parent common to each, then we have an example of the composite form known as the *polygamous family*. The example best known to Westerners is probably polygyny – where a man takes several wives. But examples of polyandry, where the wife is the common partner, are far from unknown. By contrast with these cases, composite family forms built around the parent–child relationship are known as the *extended family*. In such cases sexual relationships, though obviously important, are subordinated to the overriding question of who is related to whom. In a later section we shall see

that a prominent area of controversy is whether anything of the extended family form survives in our own culture.

This brings us to the confusing term *kinship* which is often used in conjunction with this particular controversy as if kin and extended family were interchangeable terms. This is rather misleading since, to scholars of Murdock's generation, the extended family denoted an actual social group whereas kinship did not. It was thought of as a set of highly salient labels denoting relationship rather than organization (just as in our culture we distinguish people to whom we are or are not 'related' whether or not we meet them socially). As such the discussion of kinship falls outside the scope of this chapter (see Murdock 1949, pp. 91–2; Fox 1967; Harris C. 1969, Chapter 1).

Functionalist sociology of the family

Now that we have sorted out some terminology we must ask why 'the family' attracted so much attention from functionalists. The answer is that it presented a challenge to very basic functionalist ideas about the conditions of social order. In order to be more precise about this, however, we will find it useful to remember Lockwood's distinction between 'system' and 'social' integration which we explained at the end of the previous chapter. The point of this distinction, it will be recalled, was to show that functionalists had unwittingly been talking about two kinds of order and, hence, two kinds of explanations of it. From this it follows that the family is a key problem for functionalists from more than one viewpoint:

System integration

Does it help to understand the family from the viewpoint of the theory of functional prerequisites of self-maintaining social systems? In a sense, the family is a form of group which is certainly to be found in many different societies. At the same time actual examples are endlessly differentiated from each other on the basis of a few simple principles concerning relations of men to women, children to parents and so on. What prerequisite explains both the prevalence and the variety of the family? Not surprisingly, certain functionalist treatments tend to fall back upon biology in order to deal with this question. Nevertheless, the elaboration of the hard or normative functionalist position in the post-war period indicated that functional accounts of the family need not employ the idea of pure biological necessity at all. Instead it was argued that the family may be seen as an example of society *making use* of easily understood biological relationships in order to provide the conditions 'necessary' for stable, organized and co-operative group life. As Coser puts it: 'the family ensures the *victory* of the social over the biological' (quoted in Morgan 1975, p. 23) (our italics).

Social integration

We saw in the last chapter that normative functionalists went beyond the notion of functional prerequisites, arguing that social order also requires conformity to institutionalized norms and norm 'bundles' called status-roles. This suggests a definite hypothesis, namely that people are taught and share certain fundamental values which lead them to maintain broadly similar expectations about the behaviour appropriate to roles.

This *hypothesis of role consensus* as we shall call it can, in principle at least, be investigated empirically. One method of doing so which has been tried (and which tends to support the hypothesis) is to use a laboratory situation. Experiments can be done which monitor carefully the development of role expectations among groups of hitherto unacquainted people who have been brought together for the purpose. The objection to such work, however, is that by definition it cannot tell us how far the laboratory situation corresponds to real life, nor can it throw much light upon the question of

how roles performed by individuals in one group are integrated with the structure and functioning of society at large.

Another famous study of role consensus employed the device of choosing a real-life role (Gross, Mason and McEachern, 1958). Ideally this should be one occurring on a widespread basis. The investigation should aim to survey the expressed attitudes to that role of people whose lives come into frequent contact with it. The status role which Gross and his collaborators chose was that of school superintendent – a position within the US educational system which involves interaction with different schools, their boards of management, class teachers, parents etc. Although the findings of this particular investigation failed to find much support for the hypothesis of role consensus, with hindsight one can argue that the failure may have lain in the investigation itself. Not only were the survey techniques employed and the way they were analysed too arid and impersonal by present-day standards, but also it could be argued that the school superintendent role is one which is *likely* to be surrounded by conflict. We should choose a more deeply rooted set of behaviours and employ a wider range of investigative strategies.

It should now be possible to see why the family acquired such significance for functionalism. If family life cannot be shown to be founded on a deep-seated consensus it is unlikely that consensus will be found within other less intimate and enduring structures. Indeed, is it not likely that processes within the family perform vital functions for individuals to acquire capacities and skills for role learning in general?

System and social integration in industrial society

Many proponents of 'middle-range' theories of the family were interested in certain moralistic critiques of modern society which suggested and deplored the fact that the family is in decline. According to these the 'pressures of modern living' have placed traditional family values and loyalties under increasing strain. No doubt this kind of argument will be familiar. We are all accustomed to hearing and reading complaints that there has been a devaluation in the quality of home life and consequently a loss of parental control over the young. To sociologists, what is interesting about these diagnoses of contemporary ills is the underlying *functionalism* they contain. It is assumed that a 'healthy family life' performs an irreplaceable 'function' in the integration and cohesion of society. But such questions apart, we know that important changes *are* taking place in the relations between men and women and in the wider society. It is important, therefore, to subject our everyday ideas about family life to as rigorous a test as we can. Functionalists have certainly been anxious to examine their validity in view of their obvious relevance to the problem of how industrial society is 'integrated'.

As we pointed out earlier in this chapter, the older traditions of sociology tended either to ignore the family and the differences in activities between the sexes altogether or else tended to explain them away in purely biological terms (Goode 1965, p. 178). Undoubtedly, then, the functionalists under the pressure of the considerations we have just listed made a major contribution to the discipline: they took what we call the family seriously, as requiring a place within a general theory of society. But we shall find that the middle-range theories that have come to be associated with the zenith of functionalism did not carry this attitude far enough. In advancing explanations of the functional necessity of the family they made, implicitly or explicitly, unwarranted assumptions about the functional necessity for the association of particular tasks with each sex and the degree of consensus surrounding *gender* roles. They also tended to imply that these 'natural' gender divisions are required in the context of relations between generations, particularly those through which the young learn to conform to norms and values. In short, they failed fully to

realize that the term 'family' itself obscures rather than illuminates the real scientific problems which arise in this area. In recent years, therefore, 'middle-range' functionalist theories have been subjected to a rigorous critique from the viewpoint of a thoroughgoing sociology of *gender*.

Despite these remarks, the importance of functionalist family sociology cannot be denied. The contribution of one major functionalist in particular, namely Talcott Parsons, has been said to have 'not only provided a framework to argue within or against but . . . (also) defined the rules within which people argue' (Morgan 1975, pp. 25–6). We shall now turn to a detailed consideration of all of this work, together with developments in the post-functionalist period. We may usefully begin with the three problems above: family functions, family roles and the family under industrialism.

System integration: the family and functional prerequisites

What necessary condition or functional prerequisite, then, underlies the family as an institution? This is really two questions. First we must enquire whether it is in fact true that the family is a universal institution? Second, is this universality to be explained by the functions which the family fulfils for the social system in general? Obviously the functionalist answer to both questions is 'yes'. But it is possible to distinguish, within the corpus of functionalist literature, two distinct styles of approach.

Listing of functions

The first, and somewhat earlier and simpler 'style', began with a fairly untheorized or descriptive list of functions, based on known activities within the family. Undoubtedly, the most celebrated attempt to do so is to be found in G. P. Murdock's book *Social Structure* (1949). A tendency to conflate activities and functions is already apparent in Murdock's definition of the family which we discussed above. Murdock has in fact taken a battering from later critics, many of whom take his list of family functions out of context and ignore the remainder of the book. It is therefore desirable to redress the balance somewhat.

Murdock's contribution was both methodological and conceptual. His methodological contribution was to develop, to a new level of sophistication, a procedure known as the 'statistical cross-cultural survey', a device which appealed to the functionalist desire to develop scientifically tested explanations of social variation. Over several decades he established what became known as the Human Relations Area Files, really a vast catalogue of all available information about individual societies, arranged under appropriate headings and which in 1968 stretched to 240 cases (Harris M. 1968, pp. 612–15). These files were then used as a basis for studying some aspect of society – for example, the family – by sampling cases from the files, rather in the manner in which an opinion poll samples the voters' register in order to cover the range of voting intentions.

It was, in fact, in connection with Murdock's work on the family that the files received one of their best known uses. Here we must recall the distinction between nuclear and composite family forms. Using the files together with additional materials painstakingly extracted from various other sources, Murdock claimed to have established that *the nuclear family is indeed a universal form*. Societies which display composite family arrangements do not violate this finding, Murdock argued, because they use the nuclear unit as their basic building block. Now there are undoubtedly many objections to this argument, the most obvious being that the research results must be a foregone conclusion: in large measure the discovery of a universal nuclear family is a trick of definition. Lengthy debates have taken place too as to whether certain cases, notably the Nayar caste of the Malabar coast, India, represent an important exception to the rule (see Harris C. 1970, pp.

49–52). Most fundamental are the objections to the cross-cultural survey method itself. The files, it might be said, do not constitute a true basis for statistical sampling and the quality of the information they contain is very variable. Comparisons of case with case involve wrenching aspects of social organization out of their particular historical context and hence the conclusions drawn may be extremely misleading. To some sociologists the major significance of this method of comparing societies is simply as an awful warning of the amount of resources and energy, as well as the problems of rigour, involved in making comparisons on too grandiose a scale. These criticisms, though important, should not be allowed to obscure the fact that Murdock's findings are not without all interest. Systematic arrangement of existing knowledge always represents some kind of gain and his work is still widely quoted.

Murdock's second contribution is conceptual. The best-known aspect of this is his list, stated briefly at the beginning of his book, of functions of the family. They are: the sexual, the reproductive, the economic and the educational. Two things must be made clear. Murdock was not a thoroughgoing functionalist and 'did not hold a functional theory of society' (Morgan 1975, p. 21; see also Harris M. 1968). Further he was perfectly aware that all of these activities are performed outside of the family as well. For him, however, a problem which any community finds it necessary to solve is simply that of residence – who may live with whom. Thus, it is in combination with the convenience of the family as a unit of residence that the list of functions makes sense. In particular his much criticized statement that:

By virtue of their primary sex differences a man and a woman make an exceptionally efficient co-operating unit. (Murdock 1949, p. 7)

should be seen in this light. Standard criticisms of Murdock tend to ignore his emphasis on residence and they lose some of their force as soon as it is reintroduced into the discussion.

Two basic problems, however, remain:

1 Murdock tends to neglect the individual, assuming that what is necessary for the benefit of society will also be of benefit for a particular person. For the majority of women this may not have been true of their involvement with the family.

2 Murdock begs the question of what we mean by society. His families seem to be functioning within orderly, peaceful, stabilized and self-contained social units. But much human history has not been like that (Murphy 1972). What happens to the family in periods of upheaval is not discussed.

Other writers besides Murdock have attempted to provide multiple lists of family functions and they are far more guilty than he of the charge that the functions are not true explanations at all, but uncritically presented descriptions. It will be found that the lists do not even always agree with each other, a fact which reflects on the implication of 'self-evidence' which some writers adopt to their lists. Nevertheless, as Table 10 shows, it is possible to compare other lists with Murdock's and find a measure of agreement that the family (1) provides a sense of *organized* biological reproduction (2) organizes the provision and consumption of basics such as food and shelter (3) facilitates the learning of cultural patterns and approved behaviours (4) initiates individuals into positions within the social structure. The

Table 10 *Functions of the family*

Murdock	Goode	Davis
Reproductive	Reproductive	Reproductive
Economic	Physical maintenance	Maintenance
Educational	Socialization	Socialization
Sexual	Social control	Appropriate reproduction situations
—	Placement	Placement

contemporary attitude in sociology to such lists tends to be that they are vague and unhelpful. Many would now argue that, as far as gender divisions are concerned, this early functionalism is especially conservative. The most serious criticisms, however, from the point of view of sociology as a discipline must be that of a failure to explain the connection between such general and vaguely specified prerequisites and the wide variety of possible structures that actually exist. If one form of the family is simply to be considered as one functional alternative among others, why has the society adopted it and why does it persist?

Selection of root functions

Many of these criticisms may also be applied to the second style or variety of functionalist treatments which we wish to consider. These have grown up around Talcott Parsons's attempt to incorporate the family into the 'Chinese Box' schema discussed in the last chapter. What distinguishes Parsons's work is his awareness of the need to distinguish certain 'root functions', 'which must be performed wherever there is a family or kinship system at all', from other functions which may be 'present or not according to the *kind* of family or kinship system under consideration' (Parsons and Bales 1956, p. 9) (our italics). Thus he sets out a basis for understanding the precise relation between general functional imperatives and actual structures. Unfortunately, his failure to keep problems of system and social integration separate means that this promising opening is not followed up. His discussion of the link between system function and family remains at the most general level. From this he slips, as we shall see, to the quite separate problem of how individuals are integrated socially by means of family life into the structure of one type of society: the industrial.

Parsons's selection of the 'root function' of the family, then, is guided by very abstract considerations. It will be recalled there are four functional prerequisites of 'systems of action': adaptation, goal attainment, integration and pattern maintenance. Each system of action 'specializes' in one of the four prerequisites yet in turn has a requirement for each of the four to be met at its own particular level of operations. Thus the social system specializes in integration but also contains its *own* mechanisms of adaptation, goal attainment and pattern maintenance. The family's concern is with the latter. Its root function is to sustain the pattern of norms, roles and institutions which express and perpetuate the cultural heritage of the whole society. This is realized in part, as is clearly the case in modern society, because the adult members of the family also perform roles outside the family and wish to minimize the degree of strain between the two sets of demands.

Parsons is mostly concerned, however, to show how the family encourages and enables individuals to make the correct kind of decisions when relating to others. This is a problem of social integration not system integration. Indeed, Parsons specifically states that in modern society it falls to the family to perform functions in relation to the *personalities* of the members of society. In the next section we shall concentrate only on the implications of certain aspects of this theory: as an explanation of age and gender roles within the family itself.

The family and social integration

In order to procure and use the commitment of individuals to society and its customs some very powerful forces must come into play. There is, among both psychologists and sociologists, a wide measure of agreement that the forces in question have to do with the formation of individual personality. Only participation in society itself can give us a sense of personal identity. Apart from society it might be argued the 'person' as such does not exist. Thus, in treating the personality as one of his four systems of action Parsons was merely acknowledging the established wisdom and research in social

science. Parsons then goes on to argue, however, that:

1   There are certain universal social prerequisites of 'normal' personality development, particularly those related to the existence of sexuality in infants and the sexual attributes of parents.
2   Since these are universal and inescapable, the group in which personality formation takes place, which is usually the family, will *have* to be organized on primarily *ascriptive* lines – that is, in terms of 'natural' attributes that an individual cannot hope to control.

These ideas are derived from three very different traditions of research and theory in social science. The first is the *psychoanalytic*, that is, that based on the writings and clinical evidence provided by Freud and his followers. Parsons deserves quite a lot of credit for appreciating that psychoanalysis does have considerable relevance for sociology, particularly with reference to socialization, role conformity and gender. It is only recently in fact that students of gender divisions have caught up with him. But at the same time it has become clear that Parsons does not look critically enough at one assumption made by orthodox psychoanalysis, namely, that there is a universal process of personality formation underlying the diversity of cultures. This assumption had been seriously questioned by Malinowski, Mead and several other anthropologists and became the subject of lengthy controversy. By the mid- to late 1950s when Parsons was writing on the family, however, the anthropological movement was 'moving closer to the universalism of psychoanalytic theory and away from an exclusive preoccupation with differences' (Singer 1961, p. 19).

Since that time, under the impact of feminist sociology, the controversy has opened again. The argument in this latest phase concerns the 'universality' of one particular aspect of personality formation, namely feelings towards the female parent. Freud had claimed that strong feelings of attraction and attachment in infancy to the mother figure supply the dynamism of the whole process. As we shall see in the next chapter these feelings have a crucial 'sexual' (libidinal) momentum, with the implication that because an individual's sex is biologically fixed, certain aspects of mothering and of the social integration of male and female personality will be universal and inevitable ('natural'). To many contemporary writers this 'inevitability' is highly contentious and Freud's ideas describe, at best, certain consequences of the mystique surrounding the institution of motherhood in Western industrial societies. By association with Freud, Parsons risks being found guilty of the same charge and in fact says nothing to dispel the criticism.

The second source upon which Parsons drew was quite different – it was the *experimental work* of Bales which we have referred to above. In a series of studies of leadership roles, Bales claimed to have shown that groups develop not one but two kinds of leadership figure (Parsons and Bales 1956, Chapter 1). On the one hand, the dominant leader is concerned with the accomplishment of group tasks, notably those involved with adaptations to external physical and social conditions. This he termed 'instrumental'. But, on the other, groups also evolve a second generally less dominant leader figure who is concerned with 'expressive' problems. These problems are internal in nature and revolve around the maintenance of the esprit or warmth of group relations themselves, or the gratification that comes simply from belonging.

Parsons's use of these findings depended upon the assumption that what occurs in experimental groups is directly transferable to the dynamics of real groups, including, of course, the family itself. The link with Freudian theory is that the ties of infantile attraction surrounding the mother's role clearly belong within the domain of expressive relations. The implication is that it is the female adult in the nuclear family who will in normal circumstances become the expressive leader and females in general who will become accommodated to expressive role behaviours. By contrast, it is the male adult who takes the dominant role of expressive leader and male children who, in imitation of the father, take up instrumental tasks and identifications outside the family itself.

In confirmation of this, Parsons and his collaborator Zelditch deployed a third body of evidence, consisting of *cross-cultural survey data* in the Murdock style and drawing, in fact, upon some of the Area File material (Parsons and Bales 1956, Chapter 6). Asking the somewhat ethnocentric question 'Why after all are two parents necessary?', Zelditch claims that in forty-six out of a final sample of fifty-six societies differentiation of expressive and instrumental family roles occurs between the sexes in the expected direction.

These, then, are the sources from which Parsons tries to explain how the demands of personality development and the requirements of the social system are reconciled with each other in the course of the performance of family roles. The group will divide into leaders and non-leaders on the basis of the parent–child division; and into instrumental and expressive leadership specializations on the basis of the mother–father division. The resultant fourfold classification of family roles ('the Parsonian family') is shown in Table 11. It is important to emphasize that originally Parsons's theory was *not* propounded in relation to the family in general. It was devised to explain the basic dynamics of the *modern* family, in particular that of white middle-class America. It is clear, however, that what he is doing here is making a

Table 11 *The Parsonian family: differentiation of roles*

Power	Group goals	
	Instrumental priority	*Expressive priority*
Superior	Father	Mother
Inferior	Male child	Female child

simplifying assumption for the sake of argument. The family of middle-class America, or a somewhat idealized version of it, is explicitly treated as if it contained all that is essential to family life throughout the world and nothing peripheral or superfluous. The reason for this will be examined in a later section. A second point is that in the interaction of adults and children it is not simply the personalities of the latter which are socialized. Parsons assumes that living with children, that is, socializing them, is a key means of sustaining adult identity. Yet the fact is that a majority of adults do not live in this fashion at any time, with the result that the schema seems to relegate the remainder to some kind of subsocial existence. Third, what of the division of tasks between husband and wife? In sociology this is termed the *conjugal relationship*. In this case it is not clear whether Parsons intends the instrumental/ expressive division of conjugal roles to be one of equality or not. On one hand he asserts that egalitarianism is a dominant norm of industrial society and this implies that conjugal roles are 'separate but equal' as foci of decision-making. On the other, he recognizes that the family places severe limitations on career possibilities for women, making them economically dependent on the husband's career.

All three research sources for the model are, in fact, highly controversial and have serious weaknesses from the viewpoint of today's more exacting methodological standards (Edgell 1980, p. 21). We are thus confronted with the problem of how far Parsons's ideas have been substantiated by more recent or more rigorous evidence? Unfortunately, testing the Parsonian theory has long since ceased to be the direct object of research projects but what evidence there is has, as we shall now see, been largely negative. It will come as no surprise to learn that investigators have found many families that do operate in the above fashion. What has also emerged, however, is that there is far more room for flexibility and deviation from the stereotyped pattern than

can be accommodated within Parsons's framework.

In the remainder of this section we shall provide a brief summary of material relevant to social integration, and age and gender relations within the family. The sources we can draw upon for this purpose include two out of the three kinds of evidence used by Parsons himself, namely clinical and cross-cultural.

Clinical evidence

The overwhelming impression to be gained from clinical studies of the family even as Parsons's work appeared is of the relatively naïve nature of his approach and of the strains and tensions, rather than the functional harmony, which can arise from too close a conformity with the ideal family role structure depicted above. The work of Vogel and Bell, for example, showed that under certain conditions maintenance of conjugal role relations between spouses in a conflict-free condition is only achieved at the price of emotional disturbance in the children of the marriage (Vogel and Bell 1968). This is especially likely to arise where the partners hold distinct but unacknowledged disagreements on moral-evaluative issues. The child is used as a scapegoat: aggression which is really intended for the spouse is directed at the child who is encouraged by one partner to behave in ways which will irritate the other. Furthermore, as Slater showed in a damning if ageing review of the clinical evidence, role discrepancy and childhood disturbance are far more likely to occur when the allocation of family tasks among the adults in the family are strictly segmented into instrumental and expressive after the Parsonian mould (Slater 1974). Another indictment of the Parsonian version of the old adage that 'women's place is in the home' is provided by recent discussion of the high incidence of mental depression among women who are, in fact, confined to hearth, children and home (Brown and Harris 1978).

There is also reason to question the automatic

association of women with motherhood as the focus of the expressive aspects of family life in general and personality development in particular. Here we should turn to recent clinical evidence surrounding a much-discussed issue: the so-called *maternal deprivation hypothesis*. The phrase 'maternal deprivation' derives from the work of Bowlby (1965). It is often vulgarized as the thesis that 'only twenty four hours of care, day in, day out by the same person' who happens to be the biological mother of the child, can guarantee the healthy maturation of the child and, by implication, social order and stability. This is inaccurate and unfair. Bowlby's thesis, supported by long and carefully documented clinical experience, is that what is essential for mental health is that 'an infant and young child should experience a warm, intimate and continuous relationship' with his mother (*or permanent mother-substitute* – one person who steadily "mothers" him)' (Bowlby 1965, p. 13; our italics). Sociologically this should be understood as describing a social activity which in many societies happens to be a female-gender role, that is, 'mothering'. Subsequent work in this area supports the idea that it is lack of one or more close bonds, rather than maternal deprivation as such, which is a critical factor in disturbance. Perfectly healthy individuals may form their main attachment to their fathers or non-family individuals. And of course as we have already hinted, healthy development is also perfectly possible in contexts such as the kibbutz where social arrangements do not sanction the mother-centred family ideal as the norm. One authoritative review of the maternal deprivation literature concludes:

In most families the mother has most to do with the young child and as a consequence, she is usually the person with whom the closest bond is formed. But it should be appreciated that the chief bond need not be with a biological parent, it need not be with the chief caretaker and it need not be with a female. (Rutter 1972, p. 125)

Obviously, to identify the components of

satisfactory 'bonds of attachment' with respect to such a complex organism as the human infant is an extremely difficult matter.*

It would seem from more recent clinical evidence, then, that human beings are able to adapt to a much wider range of family situations than people often think (Rutter 1972; Schaffer 1977; Chodorow 1978). The implications for Parsons's arguments are, of course, fairly serious.

Cross-cultural and comparative evidence

The fundamental problem, questions of reliability apart, with the kind of mass cross-cultural evidence offered by Zelditch, or for that matter Murdock, is that it can, at best, only inform us as to the facts of the division of family type tasks by gender. It can never really throw any light on the question of *why* uniform patterns do or do not emerge. Thus it is possible for other investigators to look at the same sort of information, or to produce additional material, and in doing so 'prove', to their own satisfaction at least, some new explanation of the evidence. It is, therefore, not very surprising that feminist scholars, dissatisfied with the implications of the Parsonian theory of instrumental and expressive gender roles, have been able to challenge it with their own preferred account of the matter, namely: that the differences in role allocation are the result of the worldwide subordination of women to men, and the exploitation of the former by the latter (Mitchell 1971; Oakley 1972). We are not suggesting that such a view is false; rather that faced with a wide range of source materials, both the terms exploitation and subordination, just like the distinction between 'instrumental' and

* At least six elements of adequate 'mothering' have been identified. These include not only the undefinable and ultimately mystical notion of love, but also: the amount of reciprocity on the part of the individual concerned; the degree of continuity in the relationship; the degree of stimulation concerned; whether bonding is 'monotropic', that is, to one person, and the existence of a definite site for the relationship – the home. The contribution which each of these aspects can make to mental health has been the subject of investigation.

'expressive', are simply too general to help us to explain what actually happens in any *given* society.

For this reason studies which offer in-depth comparisons of one or two societies only can often be more illuminating. An excellent example of this type of work is that of Safilios-Rothschild whose very thorough survey of marital patterns in the United States and in Greece cast considerable doubt upon the necessity of the division of tasks by gender implied in Parsons's theory. Covering several hundred couples in both countries, this author found that *both* sexes tended to define their roles in instrumental and expressive terms. Just *how* the division of activities was derived depended upon the social, familial and cultural circumstances of the spouses, not from any common general functional imperatives (Safilios-Rothschild 1969; Safilios-Rothschild and Georgioupoulos 1970).

Another style of comparative analysis involves using 'utopian' experiments and unusual situations as a kind of laboratory substitute for the testing of propositions about the universal roots of institutional life. It is not a very safe procedure since the real world is not in fact a laboratory and the investigator can be no more certain than the visionaries who make the experiment that contaminating influences have not invalidated the exercise. This point is very important because such experiments tend universally to show one thing: that it is very difficult to break away from accepted and time-hallowed practices especially where gender divisions are concerned (Skolnick and Skolnick 1974; Abrams and McCullough 1976). The Israeli kibbutz provides a cogent illustration in the area of family studies. Kibbutzim communities were established under the impetus of a radical egalitarian and anti-family ideology which sought to impose the ideal of community attachment as a substitute for the narrow private and mother-centred family life of traditional Jewish society. It was held that the latter resulted in the oppression of women and in future women were no longer to be tied to the performance of traditional domestic tasks. Women worked at heavy labouring tasks alongside the men. Children were reared communally in mixed-sex dormitories within the 'children's house'. During the early history of the 'experiment', enthusiastic reports were received, emphasizing the extent of the sexual tolerance and emancipation already achieved by these changes. Children reared under this system, it was claimed, were devoid of the oppressive sense of attachment found in the typical middle-class child in the United States and elsewhere, with its concomitant mistrust of unfamiliar faces; or the sense of personal and irreparable loss which accompanies the break-up of such a household. And it remains the case that delinquency, crime and disturbance are virtually non-existent in the kibbutzim (Bettelheim 1971; Spiro 1979).

What has subsequently occurred in these communities as they have grown to be established is the gradual reassertion of traditional gender divisions and many of the forms associated with family and marriage as practised in the society generally. The parental room of the old pioneer days has become an apartment filled with personally owned consumer goods and children have begun more and more to sleep there, with their parents rather than in the children's house.

No simple explanation of why this has happened is likely to suffice. To a degree it might be seen as a vindication of Murdock's view that the nuclear family is likely to be a more effective residence arrangement than any alternative that can be devised. Some commentators have been fairly outspoken in their opinion that here is clear confirmation of the instinctual basis of the family and the conventional division of tasks between men and women (Tiger and Shepher 1976; Spiro 1979). To this extent, therefore, it might also be claimed as a vindication of the Parsonian theory that it is functionally necessary for societies to allocate family roles in the manner described in his model.

It is also possible to argue, however, that the

kibbutz attempt to create a new order within the framework of a more conventional one was bound to fail and that it has become corrupted from without by the consumer values of industrialism. All that has been achieved by the kibbutz experiment is that 'the individual dependency of each woman on her husband in such a society has simply been transferred (within the kibbutz context) to a collective dependency of all women upon all men' (Talmon 1977, p. 627). This solution is also undoubtedly too simple. A crucial factor in the early stages of kibbutz life which made for rapid return to differentiation of work tasks by gender was the dominance of heavy agricultural work as the major economic activity (Talmon 1972, p. 10). But the example does illustrate again the importance of studying specific conditions of *social* integration rather than generalizing about the universal functions of gender roles for the social system as a whole.

Precisely the same point emerges from comparisons made within societies. One of the most celebrated examples is *Family and Social Network* by Elizabeth Bott. Admittedly the fieldwork basis for Bott's arguments leaves a lot to be desired but there can be no questioning their influence. Rejecting the instrumental/expressive distinction Bott argues that Parsons 'underestimates the amount of variation in conjugal segregation' particularly in the kind of family situation which he had considered most typical of modern life, that is, where it is forced to become a self-contained unit with relatively loose-knit outside bonds. In fact, Bott found none of the existing methods of classifying husband–wife relations useful. Instead she settled for a simple division of conjugal styles into:

1 *Segregated role relationships*. These are ones in which, as in the Parsonian model, 'complementary and independent types of organization predominate. Husband and wife have a clear differentiation of tasks and a considerable number of separate interests and activities'.

2 *Joint role relationships*. These occur where 'husband and wife expect to carry out many activities together with a minimum of task differentiation and separation of interests' (Bott 1957).

Bott claims that her evidence (only twenty families) suggests that whichever of these forms of relationship is adopted will depend on the wider social network, particularly the kinship network, with which the couple are connected.

There are two important concepts here:

1 *Network* is a term which we have met already in this book (Chapter 4). Bott points out that a social network is not the same thing as an organized group. In the latter:

the component individuals make up a larger social whole with common aims, interdependent roles and a distinctive sub-culture. In network formation. . . only some, not all of the component individuals have social relationships with one another. (Bott 1957, p. 58)

2 Thus networks vary in the extent of their social integration, or as Bott calls it, their *connectedness*, by which she means 'the extent to which the people known by a family know and meet one another independently of the family' (Bott 1957, p. 59). (Bott's usage of the term 'connectedness' poses problems; see Price 1981.)

This brings her to her central proposition: '*The degree of segregation in the role relationship of husband and wife varies directly with the connectedness of the family's social networks.*' (Bott 1957, p. 60; author's italics) 'Close knit' networks produce informal pressure on members to observe values and feelings of solidarity. Hence they favour the segregation of conjugal role relations within the marriages of the members. 'Loose knit' networks permit greater variation in norms to occur and at the same time offer a lower likelihood of mutual assistance and companionship. Thrown back on their own resources the couple gravitate towards joint conjugal role relations. Note that if this ingenious theory were found to be true it would imply the opposite of Parsons's model – his instrumental–expressive segregated couple are to be found *par excellence* in a context, the American middle class, which as he himself admits, is likely to favour loose rather than close knit networks.

Real life, unfortunately, is more complex than either author recognizes. Attempts to confirm or falsify Bott's hypothesis have produced conflicting results. Several studies have appeared which seem to contradict. These, however, have been attacked for not providing an adequate test of the thesis. On the other hand what is said to be 'the only satisfactory attempt to verify Bott's hypothesis' (Harris C. 1969, p. 175) is not claimed by its author to be a rigorous test at all (Turner 1970, p. 258) but a retrospective examination using data produced for other purposes (pp. 245–60). Turner concludes that network connectedness *as such* is not the key predictor of conjugal role segregation. What matters is connectedness among same-sex members of the network. Of considerable interest too is the recent survey by Hannan and Katiaouni (1977), contacting 408 families in the least prosperous areas of Ireland. The findings completely reverse Bott's own. The most segregated conjugal role relationships occurred among couples who had lowest involvement with kinship and neighbour networks. The conclusion to be drawn from this is not that Bott's thesis is false but that she fell victim to her own complaint against Parsons: that of underestimating 'the amount of variation in conjugal segregation' and of course the extent to which this is affected by idiosyncrasies of culture and by circumstance. But at least, as Harris observes, 'the really lasting significance of Bott's study is that she has made impossible the proliferation of studies of the internal structure of the family which take no account of its social environment' (1969, p. 176).

Summary

To sum up the arguments of this section. We have several times pointed out above that functionalists like Parsons have been criticized for failing to distinguish between social and system integration. In this section we have been considering research evidence which shows very clearly the folly of assuming that the two will coincide. On the contrary we saw that the internal structure of the family is intelligible more from a study of the network of relationships surrounding it than in terms of general functions and universal processes of personality formation. Such processes may exist but human beings will tolerate considerable diversity in the role structure of the family. To judge by the clinical evidence, one of the least satisfactory arrangements is that of a highly segregated instrumental–expressive division of conjugal tasks. That being so we might ask why such an arrangement is so prevalent and is the object of so much approval in our own type of society?

The family and types of integration in modern society

In this section we shall begin by considering another celebrated 'middle-range' theory of post-war functionalism. This asserts that there will be a determinate pattern of family organization, corresponding to each type of society. Hence, there is a definite form which fits the particular conditions of industrial society.

Once again our discussion will begin with Talcott Parsons. We have already stated that Parsons views the American middle-class family as somehow representative of all that is essential, in a theoretical sense, in family life. We must now investigate what exactly this means. On the face of it, it seems rather strange: we have, throughout this chapter, been alluding to moralistic opinions and fears that family life in industrial societies, such as the United States, is in a threatened condition if not actually in a state of crisis. Parsons makes clear that he is actually very critical of such views. The main targets for his arguments are certain discussions in the older functionalist style. These had located the cause of the decline of the family in the fact that many of its functions – as represented, for example, in the lists given in Table 17.1 – had been taken over by special purposes outside agencies. For example, economic activity typically takes place outside the family; socialization falls more and more to the education system; and so on.

Parsons rejects the whole thesis of the declining functions of the family. What he asserts is that the family is no exception to the basic principle of structural differentiation which industrialization brings to its fullest development. The deep-seated changes now occurring within family life are due not to impending total collapse but to an adaptation to new conditions. As a result of these 'the family is now a more *specialised* agency than before' (Parsons and Bales 1956, p. 11; our italics).

This important argument is supported by an examination of then-available family and demographic statistics for the USA. He shows, for example, that the rise in divorce rates which had appeared alarming in the previous and inevitably disturbed period surrounding World War II had levelled off and was in any case concentrated among childless couples and during the first few years of marriage. Marriage itself remained popular:

1   The proportion of the population married had never been higher and the average age at first marriage never lower.
2   A high percentage of divorcees remarry, itself indicating that it was the collapse of a relationship and not the institution itself which had produced the divorce.
3   Birth rates, a rough reflection of what we might call 'family building', have recovered from the all-time low to which they had sunk under the influence of war and pre-war economic depression.
4   Ownership of family homes had increased.

Much of Parsons's case remains in this respect intact despite the ageing of his sources. The reader will find a more up-to-date discussion of statistical material on the family in a widely available article by M. Anderson (1980b). The merit of this source lies in the fact that it brings together data from a number of different Western industrial nations. From this it is clear that whatever trends manifest themselves do so on a relatively uniform basis across national boundaries. By and large it is also true to say that many, though not all, of the tendencies discussed by Parsons have continued to operate. The chief points of *contrast* with his findings do not really undermine the drift of his overall argument. It is true for example that in recent years both the overall rate of marrying and the average age at which people marry have begun to rise once more. This, however, is not necessarily an indicator of the imminent moral collapse of marriage but of the influence of economic factors, notably recession, in preventing individuals from realizing their plans. Economic conditions tend to influence most trends in demographic and 'family' statistics in a parallel fashion. Hence, the birth rate and the average size of completed families have also begun to fall under the impact of harsher times.

Of course, economic factors are not the *only* causes of the trends to be found in published demographic statistics. The fall in the birth rate, for example, has obviously been intensified by the availability of the contraceptive pill and other improvements in contraceptive techniques. It could be argued that such developments actually *help* to strengthen family life. The most marked drop in 'unwanted' conceptions due to the pill, for example, seems to have been among low-income groups where additional children place an undue strain on the financial and emotional resources of the household. Another example is the rise in abortions owing to easier availability of this operation in some countries. Much controversy surrounds this issue and the only point we wish to make here about it is that the rise in abortions which appears in published statistics, a development which Parsons does not anticipate, cannot be taken as an index of the worsening of contemporary family morality either. This is because in the past abortions *did* take place but in dubious surroundings and in secret because of their illegal nature. We can have no accurate idea of the scale of this activity except that comparisons with the present are likely to understate the extent of the practice in the period before abortion was legalized.

In using official sources we should in any case be aware of an important ambiguity in the very notion of the 'decline' of the family. There are signs that willingness to observe the administrative and legal formalities surrounding marriage and childbearing *may* be on the wane, at least among the younger members of certain segments of certain societies. On the other hand, it does not follow from this that the actual nuclear pattern of familial residential organization as such has declined. The best illustration of this point is to be found in the evidence of an increase in what are termed 'consensual unions', that is, 'unmarried' couples living together in what is a stable and enduring relationship. The growth of this practice has undoubtedly contributed to a rise in the relative number of births officially classified as illegitimate. But it would require considerable moral assertiveness on our part to argue that such consensual unions provide a worse psychological or moral environment for the family to function than, say, a 'proper' but unhappy marital relation between a husband and a wife. As Anderson observes such considerations serve rather to indicate the limitations of what can be learned from the study of administrative data, namely that social conduct does not necessarily take its cues, nor give up its secrets, in conformity with a set of official classifications.

We must now, however, examine a more audacious and characteristic aspect of the argument which bears on the themes of integration, consensus and gender roles.

What Parsons wishes to establish is that there is a specific functional 'fit' between the form of the family organization under industrialism and the overall nature of the social system. He argues that the *structural differentiation* which proliferates in modern institutions has two major consequences from this point of view, namely:

1   The isolation of the nuclear family from organized extended kinship bonds such that it becomes self-contained, that is, no longer dependent upon material or emotional services from the spouses, parents or other kin.
2   It becomes organized around a willing consensus based upon the provision of expressive support for the husband's and children's instrumental participation in the outside world.

Let us take each of these in turn.

Family and kinship in the Western world

Parsons claims that the isolation of the American nuclear family is a product of the dominant values of industrial culture. These place a high premium on material efficiency, prosperity, occupational careers and personal achievement. The result is a universalistically oriented society which requires, even of the moderately successful, that they put aside all particular considerations of birth and kin when performing occupational tasks. Such a society frequently expects in addition that families will undergo geographical and social mobility in order to further the husband's occupational career. The result is that the family is forced to become self-reliant and self-contained. Any kinship ties which remain will be very loose and 'multilineal', that is, not favouring either the husband's or the wife's family. These effects are seen to the fullest extent in the middle class where stress on successful careerism is particularly common. Parsons was not the only functionalist scholar to talk of the isolation of the modern nuclear family unit.

A less audacious and much better researched version of the thesis of family modernization is to be found in the work of W. J. Goode (1970). Goode, unlike Parsons, is reluctant to suggest an exact connection between family form and social type; merely that there is a discernible trend towards the modernization of family life. This conclusion Goode derives from a detailed and valuable comparison of traditional with modernizing and industrial nations. It is on this empirical contribution to the sociology of the family, in fact, that Goode's reputation has largely rested. But another important difference, compared with Parsons, is his emphasis on the connection between property and family structure. Modernization of the family, he maintains, is more likely to appear first within the lower classes of modernizing societies. This is because the elders of upper-class families will still have control over inheritable property and thus be in a position to control the behaviour of younger members.

There is no reason, in fact, why Goode's stress on property transmission as a source of cohesion for the extended family should not also apply within industrial society itself. We discussed earlier the concentration of wealth which exists within, say, America, Britain and Europe. Holdings of wealth provide an important reason why upper-class families might *retain* their extended kinship structure. Not all facets of 'modern' society imply increasing isolation of the nuclear unit.

But in any case the thesis of the isolation of the nuclear family from kinship ties in industrial society is not widely accepted among sociologists today. There are two classes of objections to it:

1 *Historical*. There has by now been a great deal of work by social historians casting doubt upon the rather nostalgic view of past times which, despite various *caveats*, permeates the functionalist theory of a 'fit' between family and industrialism (Anderson M. 1980a, pp. 33–63). This picture of the past had, it is true, been based upon evidence, albeit of a limited kind. The evidence included a much cited

anthropological study of a rural Irish community by Arensberg and Kimball. Like a number of similar investigations of peasant life in Europe and elsewhere these authors had found that extended family relations were the basis for a range of community activities and that ties outside the nuclear family between relatives and neighbours of the same sex were, in many ways, as important as conjugal relations within the nuclear family itself. Conjugal relationships were organized along segregated lines in accordance with Bott's model (Arensberg and Kimball 1948).

That this is a typical representation of the pattern of family life in Europe in the past has been thrown into doubt by historians, notably by Laslett and his colleagues at Cambridge (Laslett 1971, 1977). This work is a splendid illustration of the need for sociologists to be careful and informed when making statements about the past and of the benefits which accrue when a sociological perspective is allied to painstaking use of the historical method. Laslett establishes that in Europe at least the 'isolated' nuclear family predates the Industrial Revolution by many years. Moreover, family life was often highly unstable, being affected by liability to high death rates and rapid fluctuations in economic conditions. The clear division between adult and child of today's family often did not exist (Aries 1962). Life was hard, communications poor and the opportunities for *Gemeinschaft-like* family solidarity frequently lacking.

2 *Contemporary*. Another class of objections is to be found in the results of numerous survey investigations of extended family relations in the *present*. Generally speaking, such work shows that organized kinship bonds have not been destroyed by industrialism but are, rather, in the process of constantly adapting themselves to it. One standard review by Sussman of much of the older American literature on the subject concludes that there can be no question but that extended kinship networks occur widely in modern urban society. Sussman argues that we

must consequently reject the thesis of family units being isolated or entirely dependent for their maintenance upon the activities of formal institutions and systems. The surveys which he reviews show that aid and assistance, particularly financial aid, still flows from parents to adult children and more usually on the daughter's than on the son's side (Sussman 1965). Later research both in America and Europe has confirmed this general picture. Recent British examples include the well-known studies of Young and Willmott in East London and the successive investigations of family life in Swansea by Rosser and Harris and by Colin Bell (Young and Willmott 1957; Young and Willmott 1973; Rosser and Harris 1965; Bell C. 1968).

Several functionalists have attempted to produce a modified theory to account for the above objections without wholly abandoning the proposition that there is a type of family structure which 'fits' the nature of industrial society as a whole. One of the better known examples is Litwak (1965). Rather than seeing the family as totally isolated, Litwak sees it as sharing the functions which formerly it would have monopolized, with other institutions (for example, schools, work organizations, hospitals etc.). Furthermore, kinship ties have changed rather than totally disappeared. Field research – including his own – indicated the existence of the 'modified extended family' in which generations and siblings still exchange services despite occupational and geographical mobility.

According to Harris, however, Litwak has confused the *activities* which members of the family get up to with the *functions* the family has for society (Harris C. 1969, p. 109). This point really relates back to the problem we have had with functionalism as a whole: the activities people undertake together and the bonds they develop are an aspect of social integration. On the other hand, when Parsons talks about the isolation of the nuclear family he has slipped back into a discussion of the functions of the family for the system as a whole. What is significant for him about the nuclear family in modern society is the fact that it alone is the source of intimate 'particularistic' and expressive role relationships. Outside of the oasis of close family contact, roles are organized by norms which are predominantly 'universalistic', achievement-oriented and instrumental.

What we have been saying here is that, at least in the context of the family, empirical research has found patterns of activity within the broad framework of industrial society to be very diverse. It has not found anything suggesting the emergence of a single or typical pattern that 'fits' the functioning of the society as a whole.

Parsons's arguments on this score also, of course, depend on a further assumption: the hypothesis of role consensus. Is it true that members of the family, particularly the adults, accept the central values (priority of occupational achievement and so on) on which the whole system rests? Moreover, does this acceptance take the form of a consensus within the family itself – particularly between husband and wife? The drift of the most recent investigations has been to suggest that this assumption wholly neglects the problem of power relationships, not only within the nuclear family but within the wider society.

Family solidarity – consensus or power relations?

Instead of universal functions and prerequisites let us this time take social relationships within the nuclear family as our starting-point. What is it that holds it together? Even Parsons recognizes that some element of power inequality rather than automatic consensus is involved in the relation of parents to children (Table 11). He implies, however, that the instrumental/expressive differentiation of gender roles has been taken up voluntarily and in such a fashion as not to conflict with egalitarian values. More recent work has tended to pour scorn on this view. It starts out from the perspective that the division of labour between the sexes in the family is also determined by underlying inequalities of power.

This work has, of course, been associated with the rise of the women's movement in most advanced industrial societies since the 1960s. Indeed the growth of feminist writing during this period has presented the academic discipline of sociology (most of whose practitioners are, of course, male) with a range of difficult personal, political and theoretical problems. This is because the issue of sexual inequality was not something which emerged from within sociology as a substantive problem. Rather it emerged in society at large via the women's movement and then forced sociologists to confront the issues which it raised. These issues were both empirical – little was known about the 'social facts' of sexual divisions in society – and theoretical – how were sexual divisions to be conceptualized? In Chapter 9 we discussed the significance of these questions for Marxism. In so far as conventional (that is, mostly functionalist) sociology could find a niche for the consideration of them it was via an extension of the sociology of the family. However, this 'ghettoization' of sexual divisions in society, so that 'women' are considered a separate subcategory along with education, stratification, industrial sociology, etc. is inadequate and is now increasingly under attack. Sexual inequality is something which pervades *all* aspects of modern society and cannot be consigned to a separate substantive category very meaningfully. As a historical fact, however, sociological investigation of sexual divisions has tended to be associated with the sociology of the family – and thus we must now examine the ways in which recent work has sought critically to examine the link between sexual divisions in the family and sexual divisions in the wider society (see Barrett 1980; Delamont 1980 for further discussion).

Let us, by way of background, begin with some fairly elderly material. The suggestion that 'the most important aspect of the family structure is the power position of the members' had in fact appeared in a work published by two functionalists, colourfully named Blood and Wolfe. Their account of the determinants of marital relations is set out within a framework of standard assumptions, starting from the position that changing relations between husband and wife must be seen from the point of view of a fairly conventional list of functions of the family. Nevertheless they argue that the family can also be seen in terms of the resources which each participant can bring to the group. If, in the case of children this is relatively unproblematic, it has become much more uncertain in the case of husband and wife. Blood and Wolfe's so-called resource theory of family power states that: dominance or equality in marriage will follow the distribution of resources and not the existence of particular ideologies of the justice of rights and duties of each partner. In general 'that particular partner is most powerful who is the instrumental leader', who 'gets those things done which most urgently need doing if the family is to survive'. In traditional society that role has *largely* fallen to men. In modern marriage, however, the position is changing. Blood and Wolfe took a range of important marital decisions and asked couples how these decisions were taken in their household. Armed with the results of a sample survey of over one thousand married couples they argue that the power balance is much more finely poised these days. This is because wives have, to a much greater extent than before, acquired a range of power resources themselves; for example, through education and by going out to work (Blood and Wolfe 1960).

Since the appearance of this particular study many commentaries and research monographs have taken up the theme of the distribution of power within conjugal relationships. Of course, the resurgence of a more militant kind of feminism has greatly encouraged this development, sufficient that at least one author has been moved to publish a feminist critique of feminist sociology (Eichler 1980). Even if we allow for the dangers which an excess of zeal may present to standards of rigour, however, there can be no question that the new emphasis on 'women's sociology' and the sociology of women in modern society has revealed serious intellectual weaknesses and lacunae in conventional sociology in general and functionalist family sociology in particular.

In the process the limitations of Blood and Wolfe's functional study of marital power have emerged:

1 *Methodological.* Blood and Wolfe were rather naïve about their choice of key domestic decisions and their probing of how they were settled. By selecting an appropriate range of decisions or domestic tasks it is possible to produce measures of the relative power of husband and wife which favour the investigator's own beliefs as to where the true power lies. But obviously some decisions (such as major items of expenditure still largely monopolized by husbands) do not involve so much power play as others (for example, meal planning, largely the prerogative of wives) (Edgell 1980). There is also a marked difference between people's *beliefs*, as expressed in answers to survey questions about what goes on in their homes, and behavioural data, that is, what they actually do. A classic study in this context is that by Kerckhoff who found that a majority of respondents claimed to have joint conjugal role relations. Probed to talk about the performance of specific tasks and decisions it emerged that the roles were in practice segregated (Kerckhoff 1965).

2 *Substantive.* Many recent researchers have pointed to the distinction between what Gowler and Legge call the 'open' and the 'hidden' contracts in marriage. By this they mean the distinction between the legal aspects of the marriage and the actual aspects of gender division and conjugal role division which go well beyond any legal commitments (Gowler and Legge 1978). They argue that the hidden contract involves women in an almost inescapable element of subordination to and dependency upon the husband. Let us take two different but typical marital situations and illustrate how the case has been presented by such critics.

Conventional marriage

Our first situation is that of conventional marriage, that is, where the wife does housework but is not employed. Even quite recently commentators were asserting that power relations within marriage and family had become more symmetrical both in the making of decisions and the sharing of household tasks (Young and Wilmott 1973). A broad corpus of sociological survey literature pointed in the same direction (Dennis 1962). This picture is now challenged in three ways, all relating to the hidden contract in conventional marriage:

1 *Domestic labour.* Of key importance here is the question of housework – its lowly status and yet its vital importance in enabling other members of the family to participate in the wider society (Chapter 10). This 'unpaid domestic labour' has been the subject of an important series of pioneering studies by Oakley (Oakley 1976a and b) and has stimulated other work which largely confirms her findings (see Edgell 1980). Oakley found that even in supposedly 'symmetrical' families the sharing of household jobs between men and women is in general confined to the pleasanter duties. She argues that when the full range of housework tasks is fully taken into account the existence of two marriages, 'his' and 'hers', remained, for most of the sample, impressively strong and was accompanied by powerful feelings of guilt and obligation on the woman's part.

2 *Economic dependence.* If the wife does not herself work, the extent and nature of cash transactions and the flow of resources from husband to wife become crucial. Reporting on a preliminary study of the problem, based on a small sample of battered wives, Pahl distinguishes three different styles of domestic cash transaction which she calls: the whole wage system,

the allowance system and the pooling system. The first, in which the husband hands over his whole wage packet to the wife, is believed to have declined rapidly during this century in favour of the second – the allowance. In this case the wife is given an amount fixed by the husband's judgement of what she needs. In effect, Pahl argues, the wife is 'kept'. This arrangement seems to have become more common and one factor fuelling it is the stress on mobility and careerism. Parsons, of course, singles this out as central to the position of the 'typical' industrial family (Pahl J. 1980). It comes as no surprise, therefore, that several studies have concluded that the power of husband over wife peaks in the case of middle-class couples and may even be increasing (Blood and Wolfe 1960; Edgell 1980). Pahl's third category, the pooling system, is chiefly found, she maintains, among couples where both partners are earning (see below).

3 *The ideology of the expressive female*. A third group of issues concerns socialization and the way in which little girls are brought up to think of themselves as charged with the duty of being attractive to men and expressive in nature. Bell and Newby have employed the term 'deference' to classify the power transaction that underlies this flow of ideas. Deference is a type of power relation that can exist in a number of contexts (Newby 1977) and is particularly appropriate to the kind of time-honoured inequality that has undoubtedly existed between men and women. It is based upon a paradox (or 'dialectic') between *differentiation* of roles and mutual *identification* (or sense of 'togetherness'). Because it is easiest to maintain in close intimate groupings it is particularly appropriate to describe the effects of the myth of the 'ideal woman', the 'perfect mother'. Both are defined by their basic subservience to male interests. Thus 'the ideology of the home . . . (is) a social control mechanism in the sense that escape from the home threatens access to alternative definitions of the female role' (Bell C. and Newby 1976b, p. 160).

Working couples

Our second situation concerns 'working couples' and the thesis of Blood and Wolfe that as soon as the wife acquires her own earnings the balance of power in the 'hidden contract' is altered. This interpretation is too simple. J. Pahl, in the source cited above, argues that a wife's income cannot simply be assumed to confer the same economic independence upon her as upon her husband. In many cases, the evidence is that her earnings will be used for whole household expenditure or joint luxuries. In others, the husband simply reduces correspondingly the amount of the allowance from his own income. Moreover, most wives still remain responsible for the majority of housework tasks despite being employed as well.

The significance of the wife's employment and its consequence for power relations between the husband and wife lies, in fact, not so much in the wife's possession of an income; it arises only in the relatively unusual case where the wife claims the right to a sustained career. This 'strikes at the heart' of the traditional instrumental–expressive division of tasks, of course, yet it does not really figure in functionalist accounts of the forces modernizing family structure.

The implications of 'dual career' families, as they are called, have received a fair share of attention from sociologists in recent years, notably in the distinguished writings of R. and R. N. Rapoport. These authors cite an estimate that in the USA as many as 20 per cent of couples now run what must be called dual households. In Britain the proportion is unlikely to be so high. The most recent survey of graduate women, a group more likely to seek careers for themselves than any other, found that only 34 per cent were working. Many of the respondents, however, reported experiencing conflicts between the demands of work and motherhood (Kelsall *et al.* 1972). Most of the studies of dual career families have so far tended to suggest that in the case of conflict between the two careers it is that of the wife which is sacrificed (Pahl J. and Pahl R. 1971). This is particularly likely where the husband works for what is termed a 'greedy' occupation, that is, where his job makes excessive demands on his time and energy (Handy 1978). In their latest work, however, the Rapoports write:

Whereas the couples that we studied in the 1960s tended, with some exceptions, to encourage equal career developments for the wife, so long as it did not entail too much change for the husband's life style, young couples in the 1970s seemed to engage more in a dialogue that involves joint planning and equitable exchanges on balances of advantages. (Rapoport R. and R. N. 1978, p. 298)

In Norway some partners have initiated the practice of sharing a job either jointly or with an outsider in order to avoid the pressure of both partners working full time. And there is evidence from United States that as the wife continues to work the attitudes of husbands become more sympathetic. Thus we can agree with the Rapoports' judgement that dual career families 'have an intrinsic interest as a variant pattern (of marital organisation) that was previously regarded with some suspicion but is now widely accepted' (Rapoport R. and R. N. 1978, p. 298).

If, however, these new developments in family life appear to take us some way from the simple notions of 'fit' put forward by Parsons and the post-war functionalists, it is important not to overstate the extent of change in society. Most dual career families where the wife works have to struggle against the absence of an infrastructure – nurseries, day care centres etc. – which such a lifestyle really requires. The risk of overload on one or more partner is high and initial plans to maintain career equality may for various reasons come unstuck (cf. West 1982).

From this brief discussion of the hidden contract in two typical marital situations we can draw out some fundamental differences between the treatment of conjugal power in Blood and Wolfe's study and that of more recent discussions:

1   Blood and Wolfe's attention is focused (in a fairly simple way at that) upon *personal* power resources, that is, the 'bargaining' strengths that each partner brings to the 'internal' division of labour within the marriage. This is to neglect the fact that relations between men and women in modern urban-industrial society still contain many elements of a caste-like system where members of the subordinate group are believed to possess an inferior or different 'nature' from the superior caste (Gillespie 1971). Thus the power of the partners within marriage is mirrored and reinforced by relations of domination between the sexes in society as a whole. We have described some, but not all, of the factors which sustain this situation – the socialization of girls and women, inequality in the legal and in the hidden marriage contract, educational differences and, above all, important differences in the economic position of women, brought about by discrimination in the labour market.

2   Blood and Wolfe subscribe, albeit in a limited fashion, to the remnants of the functionalist *hypothesis of role consensus*. The feminist critique of women's traditional position in society, on the other hand, has brought this hypothesis into considerable doubt, certainly as far as sex-related roles within the family are concerned. We suggested earlier that if this hypothesis could not be sustained in the context of an institution which is considered to be so basic and which affects individuals for long periods of their lives, the consequences for the functionalist model of society – or at least the 'harder' versions of it – are serious.

With these points in mind let us consider one final problem in functionalist treatments of the family.

The family, inequality and the class structure

Functionalists, such as Parsons, who have written extensively about the family, cannot be accused of wholly ignoring inequality and its effect on family life. Their treatment of it, however, is relatively narrow and grudging, a fact which reflects:

1 the belief of many functionalists that *class* inequality would diminish in importance with the transition of societies to 'mature' industrialism;

2 their not unrelated preoccupation with the problems of family life in middle-class America.

The fact is, however, that the existence of inequality in one form or another is extremely relevant to an examination of family life and the questions of power and role allocation which we have been considering. We shall briefly illustrate this thesis with two examples.

Class and the extended family

We have seen that since the publication of Bott's work it has been necessary to recognize that the dominant kind of conjugal relationship which exists between parties to a marriage is undoubtedly affected by nature of the wider circle of contacts in which they are enmeshed. Now these kinship and other networks themselves do not vary randomly. Though the many surveys which have looked at this matter do *not* suggest that the relationship is a simple one, they do indicate quite conclusively that among groups who do not have the advantages of a middle-class lifestyle, extended family relations continue to be very significant as a means of support and defence against the threat of poverty and against the capricious behaviour of the economy.

In work on black families in the USA, for example, it has been repeatedly argued that the extended family functions to enable individuals to cope with times of financial or personal crisis and thus retain an element of continuity in their lives (for example, Willie 1976; Shimkin, Shimkin and Trate 1978; Scanzoni 1977). In inner-city ghetto areas, to be sure, it may not be possible to sustain even this network of support. In such a context, as a famous study by Liebow found, the multiplication of problems brought about by the deprivation of the whole neighbourhood has made the stabilization of either extended or 'isolated' nuclear family patterns

virtually impossible. Thus relations between the sexes were not 'regularized', were sometimes violent and were marked by sharp power inequalities between men and women (Liebow 1967). Some authors in the past have been tempted to explain these findings away as the residue of 'slave' patterns of culture but historical research has not borne this idea out (Anderson M. 1980a, pp. 36–7). The ghetto pattern of family and sex relations is attributable to the effects of inequality *per se*.

The effect of inequality can also be seen from the fact that patterns of family relations show a consistent relationship to position in the *class structure*. Much of the supporting information on this point is by now well known. Surveys in Britain, America and Europe have revealed that the extended family is a major ingredient of 'respectable' working-class life in all industrial societies (for example, Klein 1965, vol. 1, section I; Komarovsky 1967). What is true in the particular case of black families, then, tends also to be true on a more general scale in industrial society. The lower the income and occupational status of the household, the more likely is it to adhere to an extended rather than an 'isolated' pattern. Below a certain threshold neither operates. Why should it be thought that the middle-class nuclear family ideal is the arrangement which typically 'fits' industrial society? This is to ignore the lifestyles of large sectors of the population who are hardly marginal members of industrial society but are persistently present, as workers and subordinates, within it.

It is also to neglect the role of the extended family in the transmission of property, opportunity and positions of power in the higher echelons of society. Although we still know relatively little about the role of the extended family at the very top of the class structure, what we do know suggests that there are extensive family connections between top decision-makers in different spheres of life (Lupton and Wilson 1973; Scott 1982).

Functional for whom?

By confounding system and social integration
Parsons and other functionalists were able to
minimize the fact that in an unequal society
what is functional for the social system may not
be advantageous from the viewpoint of the individual. In this chapter we have been in effect
dealing with aspects of this point in relation to
the perpetuation of gender divisions. But
gender is after all but one facet of inequality and
the family also functions in the reproduction of
class, status and power. For example, the transmission of inequality of achievement (and
hence of social position) cannot, as we have
seen in Chapter 6, simply be explained away by
differences in the inheritance of *genetic*
capacity. The *family environment* also affects
achievement in various ways:

a   It acts to transmit *capital* and other material
resources which affect opportunity.
b   It acts to transmit what Bourdieu calls
'cultural capital' – in simple terms this means all
of the paraphernalia which go towards educational and intellectual success and development
(Bourdieu and Passeron 1977) such as books,
cultural activities, 'know-how' with regard to
the system and so on.
c   It is the focus of class-related differences in
linguistic skill (see pp. 96–7).
d   It is the source of class-related differences in
values instilled in the course of 'normal' family
life. Whereas the middle-class child may be
brought up to see society as an 'open' structure
of opportunity within which he may pursue a
career, the lower-class child will be more likely
to be taught a more fatalistic view of life, reflecting the experience his parents had had of the
world as essentially unpredictable and certainly
not 'open'.

Thus, even in its own terms, the 'normative'
account of the functions of the family in industrial society was not only incomplete, but insufficiently sensitive to the fact that it was
dealing with the problem of order in a context of
inequality.

Conclusions

We began this chapter with the point that the
majority of functionalists regarded theory in
sociology as a device for asking questions and
something to be discarded if, in the light of
evidence, it proved unequal to the complexities
of the actual working of society. We have
examined a number of middle-range theories of
the family as propounded by Parsons and other
functionalists in the 1950s and early 1960s and
have indeed found them wanting. Their value
now is primarily as a vehicle for summarizing the
voluminous body of research which has
appeared on the subject since they were first put
forward. But we have shown that their explanatory power is low and that they omit certain
complicating features of the real social world.

Perhaps our discussion has not been altogether fair to the functionalist position,
however. Though it may be the case that *these*
particular early functionalist theories have been
found wanting it does not at all follow that we
can reject the functionalist position as a whole. It
is widely accepted in British sociology now that
the principal weakness of functionalism was its
inability to account for systematic inequalities
and conflicts over the distribution of power,
particularly economic power, in society. We
have tried to show how attention to such factors
greatly alters the way in which sociology would
look at the family. The functionalist might well
argue, however, that in placing more emphasis
on power and inequality the basic assumptions
of functionalism have not been refuted but taken
up in new ways. Though the focus is on conflicts
of interest society is still of necessity viewed as a
total system that in some measure at least possesses properties of self-maintenance. For
example, Edgell's recent study of middle-class
families draws attention to the interdependence
between (a) family life and the division of
conjugal task, and (b) the structure of ideas and
economic relations in the wider society which
maintain family and gender relations in their
present form (Edgell 1980).

Those who have sought to forge a (mainly Marxist) theory of gender relationships within present-day society concede that they have not wholly avoided reintroducing functional notions and ideas into their work (Molyneaux 1979; Barrett 1980). Some writers in fact actively welcome this development (McIntosh 1978) drawing upon the implicit functionalism of certain modern 'structuralist' versions of Marxism. Of course, there is no reason why individual sociologists should not find both Marxism and functionalism interesting. Furthermore perhaps we should even accept that functional interdependence is a feature of the actual course of social development. As Anderson remarks, changes of family structure during industrialization:

are a direct reflection of changes in the family's relation with the wider society . . . we cannot go back to a strict conformity to the family morality that we have inherited from the past without also – which is clearly impossible – reverting to the economic and social relations of the past. (Anderson M. 1980a, p. 58)

In merging hitherto distinct modes of explanation, however, there are bound to be logical and conceptual problems. Are we, for example, to assume that Marxist students of gender divisions accept the validity of the teleological form of explanation to which functionalism tends? And how do they propose to handle the distinction between system and social integration which normative functionalists tended to conflate – with unfortunate results?

The last-mentioned problem is particularly relevant at this point in our discussion. Many Marxists – and even Marx himself – have been inclined to work with a model of society in which individual 'subjects' (that is, people) appear as no more than the bearers (*träger*) of the dominant mode of production and its associated ideological and political structure. The analogy with the 'oversocialized' conformist of functionalism is obvious.

But we are now going to consider briefly some writings which in a sense 'conflate' system and social integration in the opposite direction. That is to say, they ignore or even deny the notion that society is 'structured' or functions as 'system'. Yet arguably they do have considerable relevance for sociology – not least because they concern themselves with the family and other areas of close interaction in which the question of control and orderliness is critical.

Part Eight: Industrial Order and the Fragmentation of Self

18   The fragmentation of consciousness

In this chapter we will be concerned with theories whose starting-point is the *social self* and not, as with functionalism, the idea of society as a 'whole' or system. By the social self we mean those aspects of the personal life of each individual which have been created through social participation, which shape the way in which we come to experience the world and which contribute to a consciousness of being a member of society.

The case for considering the problem of the social self stems from a complaint, not just against functionalism but against *all* the 'mainstream' schools of sociology. As Dawe puts it: 'In the end, in Marx, in Weber, in Durkheim, in Parsons it is always systems which act, disembodied systems torn from their roots in the human agency which created them.' Yet the challenge presented by industrial society – and to which sociology itself was a response – points in quite the opposite direction. How can we establish human control *over* a system which in fact threatens to control its creators? (Dawe 1978, p. 408).

No doubt the overemphasis on 'system' in mainstream sociology stems from an obsession with defining and defending the discipline. This once-justified concern has undoubtedly placed too great a distance between sociology and psychology. Such a separation would have been unthinkable to many of the great figures of late-nineteenth-centry social science (Fletcher R. 1971; Bocock 1976, pp.128–9). Both disciplines deal with a single entity, the human being. Therefore, any sociology of 'system' must, at the very least, be complemented by an account of how the social is constructed within the personal, to say nothing of the possible problems and ambiguities that arise in the course of this.

In considering the two best-known attempts to offer a theory of the social self we shall be taken back to themes and influences with which the book began. The theories we shall discuss are:

a   Psychoanalysis. This confronts us once again with relation of the biological to the social in human nature.
b   Interactionism. With this we return to the Chicago School, the decay of community and ensuing crisis of personal identity.

We do not of course intend to give a *detailed* account of these two traditions. Our aim in what follows is merely to show briefly their relevance for some of the key 'problems of sociology' which we have already considered.

Freud and the renunciation of instinct

To sociologists the distinctive feature of Freudian theory must be that it tackles directly the question of how our essentially open-ended biological 'nature' becomes structured. The entity that we term the 'personality', that is, the total organization of individual mentality, is treated as the outcome of a struggle. On the one hand there is the 'polymorphous perversity' of our biological drives; on the other, the standards of acceptable conduct imposed by the particular group. Psychoanalysis claims to explore the nature and manner of the individual's subjection to the group by looking at the 'psychic repercussions' of this struggle. Thus it 'tells us something about the inner workings of society itself in the very act of turning its back on society and immersing itself in the individual unconscious' (Lasch 1978, p. 76). Study of the relationship of the conscious to the unconscious mind reveals the intrinsic instability at the heart of society – its uneasy relationship within the individual's psyche with the eternal forces of instinct. We thus have in principle a basis for understanding the troubles, changes and transformations of the social order.

The notion of the 'unconscious' has slipped into everyday language, yet its precise meaning is often not fully grasped. The unconscious is *the* primary 'discovery' in the psychoanalytic account of mental processes. It means that our physical feelings and social actions can be affected to a major degree by psychic activity that is not noticeable by our waking, reality-based and 'reasonable' selves – and it certainly cannot be understood by utilitarian-style theories. It is created by the repression, very early in the life of each individual, of all impulse and thought that is too painful, frustrating and threatening to be admitted into the stream of consciousness. Yet its presence can be detected in symbols, in dreams, fantasies and impulses. In short the unconscious mind represents the primary source of *irrational* influences on behaviour and, hence, within society and culture.

Two of these irrational impulses are of especial importance, namely:

1   instincts of bodily pleasure – the so-called 'sexual' instincts (or, in the terms of Freud's later theory, Eros);
2   the instincts of destruction and death (or Thanatos).

We shall here avoid becoming ensnared in the long-standing debate about what exactly Freud meant by these terms or why he attached such significance to them (see for example Bocock 1976, p. 104). Instead let us concentrate on what is sociologically most relevant, namely, the paradox these instincts represent in society. On

one hand, the energy they mobilize is necessary to social cohesion. Thus sexual energy or *libido* is the basis of social attachment; and destructive violence is a necessary aspect of the defence of both the external integrity and the internal order of the group. On the other hand they have to be repressed and contained in forms acceptable to the social order (indeed, unrepressed they represent a *threat* to the social order).

Because 'becoming social' involves the repression of instinctual wishes which are inherited and thus not removable, the prospects of creating a social order which can guarantee human happiness must be regarded as limited. It is certainly not the case that for Freud greater happiness results from the enhanced material security and technical superiority of industrial society. On the contrary in *Civilisation and its Discontents* he maintained that the amount of instinctual repression demanded by a society actually increases in relation to the complexity of its achievements. Industrial life requires new degrees of mutual co-operativeness and long periods of renunciation for the purposes of education and training. It follows that the more educated, successful and 'civilized' the individual the greater the level of repression and the greater the likelihood of affliction by guilt and neurosis (repressed anxiety). Freud also considered that with this insight he could explain the unrest which he detected among the more articulate and intelligent sectors of the population. The problem of repression, however, is one which besets the whole civilized order (Freud 1930).

It is now possible to set out a broad (and necessarily simplified) outline of Freud's account of the structure of human personality. Freud maintained that the personality is made up of three conflicting centres of activity:

1   The *id* is wholly unconscious and is made up of the instinctual energy of Eros and Thanatos. It operates with complete disregard to moral standards or any kind of realistic appraisal of the external situation of the individual. It is, in

fact, dominated by the 'pleasure principle', the insistent demand for bodily sensation, excitation and gratification. To Freud's contemporaries – and maybe even to ourselves – the suggestion that everyone, not just evil people, contains within themselves such powerful asocial forces ('a cauldron of seething excitations') was unacceptably shocking. Freud himself is convinced of the self-deception behind such responses. Each of us, he points out, begins life as an organism ('His Majesty the baby') which is essentially *narcissistic* – that is, unable and unwilling to experience the rest of the world except as an extension of itself. It is with this primary narcissism that culture struggles with only limited success.

2   The work of repression is the task of the *ego* and to a large extent its monitoring and controlling of irrational instinctual demands also occurs at an unconscious level. The importance of the unconscious censor can be seen in dreams where repressed thoughts *are* allowed to surface into consciousness, albeit in disjointed and symbolic form. The ego also includes, however, the *conscious* mental processes of perception, learning, reasoning and of course the very *sense* of self. For the function of the ego is to protect and maintain the life of the individual, and adapt to the environment. Consequently it must operate according to the 'reality principle': if, as the Enlightenment philosophers proposed, human beings possess a faculty of rational and controlled thought, it is here. It has in fact been suggested that Freud's whole work can be seen as an attempt to retrieve something of the Enlightenment ideal. That is, the aim of psychoanalysis was to help strengthen the ego in its battles against id and to harness its energy in the face of the external world (Hughes H. S. 1959, pp. 27–9). (Indeed, our own culture is arguably itself narcissistic in that, for reasons that Durkheim would have appreciated, it fails in its task, producing adult men and women who remain unable to accept the 'otherness' of the world; Lasch 1978).

3   Yet the ego has a complex task for it must also confront the pressures contained in the third and final aspect of personality structure. Freud termed this third aspect the *super-ego*. It corresponds to what in everyday life we think of as 'conscience'. The psychoanalytic view is that 'conscience' is the outward manifestation of an ego-ideal or ideal self which is also mainly unconscious, but which sets 'perfect unrealizable standards' for the ego to attain, and which punishes failure with a sense of guilt (Freud 1923).

Even quite recently many sociologists took very little effective notice of this model of personality and the theory of the social self which underlies it. A too-literal reading of Freud's work was but one of the factors which prevented them from seeing how psychoanalytic ideas might complement and contribute to their discussions. Another was the sociological *reductionism* which we described in Chapter 6, the belief that human behaviour can be uniquely understood at the social level without reference to the biological and pyschological materials with which society and culture are obliged to work. This, we have argued, is no longer tenable. Today it is possible to illustrate the relevance of Freud and psychoanalysis in at least three ways.

Freud and gender

The most immediately significant example is the way in which interest in psychoanalytic theory has grown within the sociology of gender (Mitchell 1974; Strouse 1974; Chodorow 1978; Barrett 1980). Freud himself, of course, did not make a clear distinction between biological sex and social gender. Furthermore his ideas on the family appear to imply that the father–mother–child grouping is some kind of biologically given universal of human culture. This and the fact that, as we shall see, Freud's account of the development of female personality is far from flattering, has caused many feminists to be hostile to his work.

The reappraisal of psychoanalysis within the sociology of gender is due to two factors. First, the idea that the family is the most desirable or beneficent means of socializing the human personality has come under critical attack within psychiatry. Psychoanalytic notions have been appealed to in support of the claim that family socialization is the source of many deformations of personal mental life, not least among women (for an overview see Morgan 1975). Second, certain writers have been prepared to argue that Freud, whatever his limitations as judged by present-day feminism, was in fact grappling with a wholly novel problem. How does the developing infant, which initially is an asexual being, acquire its psychic sense of what we now call 'gender'? In other words, what Freud wants to explain is how individuals come to feel, behave and identify with objects that correspond to and accord with their biological sex.

The beginnings of an answer to such questions, it is argued, can be found in his account of family life. This contrasts markedly with the 'moralist' treatment of family love as the pattern for all harmonious human relationships. On the contrary, states Freud, the family is the principal medium for the social repression of instinct, for the internalization of socially approved objects of attachment and hence of much subsequent trouble and pain. Fundamental to this is the infant's 'primary narcissism' which rests upon powerful erotic drives, the first and chief object of which is the mother. The dynamics of 'normal' family life, then, are centred around conflict and the repression of desires which are *incestuous* in all but name.

Freud's emphasis on the normality of incestual cravings and the structuring of adult personality around the survival of these cravings in unconscious life is liable to evoke outrage, shock, ridicule or all three. But the idea is not as far-fetched as it seems. First, there is the observation, well known to anthropology, that powerful taboos on incest are one of the very few moral rules that occur in some form in all cultures. A diversity of explanations of this has been offered. Some are wholly cultural and thus deny in a reductionist manner the relevance of biology and instinct to the problem. Others, equally reductionist, imply that groups are somehow programmed to be aware of the genetic damage to the species that would result from incest. (A standard review of these theories is Fox R. 1967, pp. 54–76; see also Hirst and Woolley 1982, pp. 154ff.). But, Freud asks, why should there be such strong taboos against this act unless secretly we all *wish to commit incest*? That this is not a wholly outlandish suggestion is shown by the recent evidence that incest is more common in our own society than we have been prepared to admit (for example, Renvoize 1982).

The use to which Freud puts the idea is contained in the celebrated theory of the Oedipus complex which purports to describe the 'normal' routes by which individuals are psychically differentiated into male and female.

In the male, the infantile desire to possess the mother as a source of bodily pleasure (libidinal gratification) encounters the rivalry of the father and consequently engenders feelings of hostility and aggression towards him. Yet the end result will be identification with the father, with the 'maleness' and the world of men. The means by which this occurs is the formation of the ego ideal (super-ego) and it is the direct product of the infant's conflict with his erotic feelings towards his mother. In the normal case the hopelessness of the Oedipal wish in the face of the father's rivalry takes the form of fear of castration. The conflict between reality and pleasure principles is resolved by giving up the mother, and recreating the father within his own mind. *The super-ego, in other words, is the strong parent, taken within the self, through whose agency irrational impulse is buried in the unconscious*. Yet Freud asserted that although these primitive dispositions towards both parents become repressed and overlain with more 'acceptable' ones, they never disappear. They can persist to cause trouble later in conscious life. For example, they may impair an adult male's ability to achieve intercourse with a 'respectable' woman. And guilt feelings over the death of a father are a recurrent theme in mythology, literature and individual case histories. It was indeed Freud's view that in archaic times an actual parricide had occurred and its consequences survived as an inherited (and again repressed) folk memory (Freud 1912).

In the female the resolution of the Oedipus complex is less straightforward and defies easy summary. Freud himself offered several different versions and his followers have added their own ideas. Basically psychoanalysis presupposes that young infants are aware of the anatomical differences in the genitals of both sexes and assumes that girls suffer from 'penis envy' and a deep sense of inferiority because of having been already castrated for their erotic feelings. It also assumes that the mother is 'held responsible' for the missing penis. But there is a diversity of psychic paths out of this early training which the female experiences. One of these psychic paths may be revulsion and a denial of sex. Or there may be a submissive identification with the father analogous to the formation of the super-ego in boys: first in hope of restoration of the lost penis; and later as potential provider of a baby which can function as a 'penis substitute'.

The reader who wishes to understand the theory properly is advised to consult one of the many excellent summaries now available – or read Freud himself. A useful collection is Strouse (1974).

In the end then the result is broadly the same: the ego ideal of the adult individual originates from an infantile internalization or identification with a gendered parent in resolution of the Oedipus complex.

This last point, rather than the literal details of the Oedipal resolution, seems to us the most significant aspect of the theory from the point of view of recent sociological consensus. The way in which individuals act, think and experience

themselves as men and women, so it implies, is derived from the precise manner in which the disorganized instinctual desires of the infant are repressed. In the course of this painful forgotten process we identify with and, therefore, perpetuate one or other of the gender 'styles' present in the culture and represented by the actual father and mother.

Culture, of course, includes symbols of one kind or another. Psychoanalysis claims that these symbols correspond to patterns of mental life which, in an uneasy way, organize the social self and produce a kind of troubled order in society itself. It also insists that the phallus, which, in various guises, occurs widely in the symbolic structures of human culture, represents the pre-eminent symbol of the psychic organization of what sociologists call 'gender'. And to some students, therefore, what Freud described was the symbolic system of a patriarchal (that is, male dominated) sexual politics.

The corollary of this is the fundamental importance of the perpetuation of the institution of motherhood and the intense feelings which it arouses in both men and women. Whether the mother is renounced (as with boys) or incorporated into the self (as with girls) adults of both sexes grow up with deeply rooted feelings of what a 'proper mother' should be. But in turn the feminist writers argue that the ideal of the loving mother is bound in with gender-related inequalities within and without the family, and the adulation she inspires provides a crucial component of the subordination of women in the social structure as a whole (for example, Chodorow 1978, pp. 77–91).

At the present time this is no more than an interesting hypothesis, of course, which does not command complete assent even among feminist students of gender. There are, in any case, difficult methodological problems in attempting to validate an explanation derived originally from clinical observation. It has been a standard criticism of Freud that the patients who presented themselves in his consulting room were a specially selected group drawn from a narrow segment of late-nineteenth-century society. From this narrow base he presents a sweeping theory that seems to claim validity for all cultures and historical periods. This aspect of his work is quite unacceptable even to those who consider that psychoanalysis does have something to offer to the sociology of gender. They are far more inclined to argue that 'families', and the set of parent–child roles and relations described by Freud, are very much the product of our own unique times. As Barrett puts it, 'families' are

an achievement of industriousness, respectability and regulation, rather than a pre-given or natural entity and it was only later that these aggregations of co-residing kin came to be seen as the only natural form of household organisation. (Barrett 1980, p. 203)

Using historical sources Barrett and others have claimed that the emotional domestication of women as mothers is a result of the separation of workplace and home brought about by the factory system:* and in any case the relations between men and women were affected in different ways in different classes. The Freudian family, like the Parsonian one, is pre-eminently a middle-class institution. Its account of the reproduction of gender is accordingly limited. But this is not a new problem.

Culture and personality

There was, in fact, already a literature which had developed a dialogue with psychoanalysis about the relation between culture and personality (and which we met briefly on p. 288). There are actually two problems.

Variation between cultures

Is there a 'basic' or 'typical' personality type? If, indeed, there are certain psychic universals in socialization – as suggested by the theory of the Oedipus complex – what happens when these

---

* This argument resembles the functionalist structural differentiation thesis (see p. 101).

encounter the great variety of childrearing practices which can be found throughout the world? For example, cultures with relatively 'easy-going' attitudes to what we call toilet training will presumably inflict less instinctual repression than Western culture with its traditionally harsh attitudes to such things. Unfortunately the methodological problems involved in tracing the relation between personality and the cultural construction of childhood are extremely difficult. The inconclusiveness of this line of enquiry has meant that it has been relatively neglected in recent years (cf. Singer 1961; Erikson 1963; Hirst and Woolley 1982, pp. 154ff.).

Variation within cultures

Childrearing practices vary *within* each society of course, not least our own (Newson J. and E. 1963, 1968, 1976; Klein 1965) and this may mean that there is a systematic personality factor in the differentiation of societies into classes and strata. Again, however, the methodological problems of demonstrating this conclusively are large.

One classic investigation which *did* bring enormous empirical resources to bear on questions of this sort explores the psychic sources upon which those who seek coercive domination over others may be able to draw. The study in question is *The Authoritarian Personality* conducted by T. W. Adorno and his collaborators at the University of California just after the end of World War II (Adorno *et al.* 1950). Adorno was a member of the so-called Frankfurt School of Social Research whose concern has been with adapting and revising the Marxist perspective in the light of twentieth-century developments. Freudian ideas figure significantly in this work, functioning to overcome the neglect of psychological factors by orthodox Marxism. The rise of the Nazis to power forced the members of the School to leave Germany and *The Authoritarian Personality* was therefore a work carried out in exile and shows the influence of American empirical traditions of social research.

A major preoccupation of the study is to explain anti-semitism and racial prejudice. What it tries to show is that such prejudice is not a purely isolated aspect of a person's attitudes but part of an authoritarian personality type produced by harsh and threatening home discipline. Authoritarian individuals, it was argued, fail to develop a normal 'internalized' super-ego. They respond readily to external authority, which 'takes over' as it were the work of self-imposed restraint. But they are also easily induced to displays of uncontrolled release of instinctual tendencies, notably those involved in aggression and destructiveness. Furthermore, whatever identification has occurred is with the 'power' parent, usually the authoritarian father. The result is that displays of aggression are particularly directed at the inferior and weak (Adorno *et al.* 1950, pp. 385–7).

The relevance of this analysis to specific periods in contemporary twentieth-century history hardly needs to be stressed. This should not, of course, blind us to the fact that this is an old study and its claims to validity raise the usual crop of methodological problems (Christie and Jahoda 1954). Nevertheless, it is a substantial and, these days, unduly neglected piece of work which impressively demonstrates the power of psychoanalytical ideas in the study of public issues, as well as private troubles.

Psychoanalysis and mainstream sociology

We began the chapter by observing that sociology has tended to be a sociology of system whereas the most pressing problem of our time is the search for a means to bring that system under control. Psychoanalysis appears, on the face of it, to thwart this, offering instead a pessimistic theory of the social self that complements or even goes beyond the Marxian image of the alienated individual or the prisoner of Weber's 'iron cage'. Furthermore, the way in which the ideas of Durkheim and Freud complement each other has often been commented

upon. For example, the theory of the super-ego explains how it is that social facts come to possess their apparent externality and constraint in the eyes of the individual and why conscience possesses collective content and moral authority. It might also be said that Durkheim agrees that social life calls for 'pure' self-interest (that is, Freud's instinctual 'pleasure principle') to be dominated by moral rules (that is, by the 'reality principle'). The chief difference is that for Freud the guilt feeling which social repression produces is responsible for much of the misery of our times.

This is too stark. More than any other modern thinker Freud's greatness lay in probing the cause and the cure of that misery – the enormous layers of self-deceit from which that misery springs. And like the classic sociological theorists he places his hopes on the belief that the development of a scientific analysis can offer humanity the ability to recognize, if not to transcend, the source of its discontents.

Great concern, therefore, must surround the nature of his claim to be offering a *scientific* account of the mind. We are entitled to ask how the psychoanalyst can be certain that mental events originate in the manner indicated in the theory. Much of the latter cannot be easily proven or disproven by recourse to the usual appeals to empirical evidence. But problems of validity, never conclusively settled in sociology, become particularly acute when we enquire about our individual experience of a common life.

Interactionism, phenomenology and the problem of shared meaning

In moving from the ideas of Freud and psychoanalysis to those of interactionism we encounter not so much a radically different kind of theory as a shift in emphasis. For Freud the true locus of the self is in the unconscious mind with its drives and repressions. The conscious forces of the ego, the sense of self, can at best maintain some kind of holding operation against the determination of these unconscious forces. For the interactionist, however, the self is treated in the consciousness and is more truly social. This tradition does not deny the existence of biological nature and instincts but regards them as malleable through the effects of culture and the conscious efforts of the individual. Indeed it is the unique property of the human mind not to be wholly programmed by blind biological force but to be able to come to know oneself, to gain an identity, through the social world of shared symbols and meanings.

Thus, symbolic interactionism offers a solution to the age-old philosophical problem of free will versus determinism. Put at its simplest, this portrays the human self as if it were like a conversation with a single topic: the identity of the individual. Interactionists call this conversation 'the dialectic of the self' and they employ a number of metaphors to convey what they mean. They talk of the 'looking-glass self', of the mirrors which society holds up to us and of the 'masks' we don to convey or hide, that is to *manage*, the image which others have of us. Each human being does possess a degree of free will and spontaneity, an element of the self which is termed the 'I'. But the 'I' is only one end of the conversation. It can only formulate its message in terms that are not of its own choosing – which is where the mirrors and masks come in. They are the symbols of identity common to the group and as such are also available to the other 'partner' in the conversation. This second element of the self is termed 'Me': it is ourself as we try to see it *through the eyes of others*. The fact that the self comprises a conversation of 'I' and 'Me' means that we do not possess complete freedom but neither are we wholly subservient to the external world.

More than any of the other theories we have encountered, therefore, interactionists approach society with due allowance for human agency. The problem is where to go next. They tend to disparage the thesis that society has a 'structure' and have constituted a kind of official opposition to functionalism in American sociology, with its images of conformity and system. In its turn, the interactionist emphasis on human volition has attracted the criticism that it is unhistorical. It underplays the significance of the distribution of power and privilege in society as a whole and it seems careless of the causes of inequality, concentrating instead on the strategies people employ to cope with it.

Interactionists by and large reject the 'scientific' pretensions of mainstream sociology. They prefer complete authenticity, achieved by means of participation in the interaction under study, 'telling it like it is' on the basis of personal experience of fragments of the social world. This raises acute problems of the validity and reliability of 'evidence' produced in this way: how do they know? The reply is disconcerting. How does anyone know?

The informality of these methods recalls much of the urban sociology of the Chicago School (Chapter 4) and formed part of the intellectual climate of the University of Chicago as a whole. One of the members of faculty was the psychologist and philosopher, George Herbert Mead.

G. H. Mead and 'social behaviourism'

The significance of G. H. Mead to the interactionist is comparable with that of Freud for psychoanalysis. His model of the self fuses together a number of different psychological and philosophical ideas from the intellectual milieu of the USA of the early twentieth century (see pp. 319–20 and also Mead G. 1934). At the same time it provided the starting point for several different interpretations (Meltzer *et al.* 1975, Part 11). All the more curious then that much of what we know of his ideas is filtered through the collated notes of his students. Mead himself never published a book.

To appreciate the significance of the actual processes which he took to constitute the self we must set out the general principles upon which his approach to behaviour and experience is based.

1   The label which he applied to himself: 'social behaviourist'. Just what he meant by this term is a matter of some dispute but one thing is clear. His theory is about the scientific analysis of actual human *behaviour*, and only indirectly about social institutions and structures. It begins with a problem already raised by Darwinism and biology, namely the distinctive evolutionary properties of humanity as a species. According to Mead it is the *capacity for reflection* which enables us to reason and learn on the basis of past experience – to stand outside that experience as it were and look at the present situation in the light of it.

2   The mind then is a device which works on the present *selectively*. The meaning and significance of current events and objects is selected out of an infinite range of possibilities by the filter of reflective intelligence. To illustrate: to the modern mind lightning signifies a discharge of static electricity; to the ancient Greek it was the wrath of Zeus.

3   Like other writers we have encountered Mead rejects the idea of society as a group of autonomous individuals. On the contrary the individual and his or her identity develops out of interaction with others in the present and, through culture, others of the past. But:

4   The individual self is no more wholly programmed by social interaction than by biological impulse. Individuals of course possess various intentions. Mead argues, however, that these intentions have to be communicated back into society through the medium of 'gestures', that is, symbolic acts whose meaning has to be interpreted by other individuals. In the simplest case gestures may consist of an actual bodily movement – a wave, or a clenched fist. But the most significant group of gestures is represented by language and the complex possibilities of symbol formation opened up by it.

5   We now come to a key idea which Mead and interactionists call '*taking the role of the Other*'. What this means is simply that gestures, symbols, language all have a double aspect. On one hand they are the common property of a group. On the other, they actually go to make up an important part of each individual personality. They have as it were been 'internalized' and guide and inform an individual's conduct as they relate to his or her own intentions. Mead called this aspect of individual consciousness the Generalized Other. To fix exactly the idea let us quote a later commentator:

Each socialized person . . . is a society in miniature. Once he has incorporated the culture of his group, it becomes his perspective and he can bring this frame of reference to bear upon all new structures. . . . The fact that most people are able to control themselves in this manner is what makes society possible. (Shibutani 1962, p. 132)

6   Like Freud, Mead places great importance upon childhood and play as the time for acquiring the control of the Generalized Other and simultaneously taking up personal identity. Thus the Generalized Other is transmitted through the agency of Significant Others, for example, parents, members of the peer group. From these we learn about different roles which are absorbed into the self through the childhood game. This is best illustrated by the classic favourite of 'Mothers' and 'Fathers' which can be seen as putting oneself into the place of (taking the role of) another and thereby perpetuating the idea of those roles within one's own private 'map' of the social world.

For Mead, then, the self is a process. He was the first to describe the self as an interplay between two poles which he called the 'I' and the 'Me'. The latter is the simplest to explain and understand. It is merely the sum total of definitions of oneself given by society and above all *oneself* seen through the eyes of significant others. Thus an individual will recognize such descriptions as John Robinson, man, son, postman, strong, 'a bit of a lad' as attributes of 'Me'. The 'I' on the other hand is the moving centre of all of these descriptions which are derived from others. It is the source of impulse, energy and *reflection*. It therefore contains the uniqueness of the individual. The individual is never wholly fixed by the labels, projects and obligations which society gives. Corresponding to society's 'conversation of gestures' there is an internal conversation which uses the given language of the 'Me' but may create wholly new meanings out of it. As a recent commentator puts it, 'The self is a peculiar construction of consciousness which translates a person into his own object' (Rock 1979a, p. 106).

H. Blumer and 'symbolic interactionism'

Mead's most conspicuous interpreter has been H. Blumer and it was he who coined the phrase 'symbolic interactionism'. Blumer's perspective is usually summarized in terms of three main propositions put forward by the author himself (Blumer 1969, p. 2: Plummer 1975, Chapter 2).

1 *'Human beings act towards things on the basis of the meanings that things have for them.'* At its face value this proposition does no more than adopt Mead's view of the reflective character of the human mind and its tendency to interpret present reality on the basis of past experience and learning. In the hands of Blumer and his followers, however, this is developed into a fairly radical critique of normative functionalism, especially its dependence upon what D. Wrong had called the 'over-socialized' concept of social behaviour (see Wrong 1967, and p. 273). For Blumer and his followers 'meanings do not reside within objects, nor within the psychological elements of the person, but rather emerge out of the (social) process of interpretation by which definitions of objects are created and used' (Plummer 1975). They therefore *start* from a view of society which is very close to the concept of 'collective representations' developed by Durkheim in the course of his later career. But whereas Durkheim's concept is a static 'moral classification of men and things', Blumer's is dynamic. Using Mead's I–Me model of the self the classification of meanings becomes *negotiable* and the fixity of the norm-following

individual is replaced by the conversational dialectic of the social self. Hence:

2 *'The meaning . . . of things is derived from, or arises out of, the social interaction that one has with one's fellows.'* Blumer and his followers were responsible for developing the thesis that the functionalist view of social life as 'structured' is too rigid. In its place they advocate a perspective which they describe as 'processual'. Social order understood as an ongoing *process* immediately becomes more precarious, more pliable, more unpredictable, and, it is claimed, more vital than in hard functional interpretations. It is hardly surprising therefore that the major focus of interactionist studies is on the *negotiation of social reality*, usually at the level of groups and face-to-face dealings. We are led through the sequences by which individuals initiate action, come together and monitor the responses of others against a background of meanings and expectations called the 'definition of the situation'. That is to say, if individuals have a *sense* that social life possesses a structure it is because their identity – or 'career' – has become 'lodged' in a recurrent sequence of encounters. This should not be allowed to obscure the fact that personal identity can only be confirmed in the course of the concrete processes of social life.

3 *'Group action takes the form of a fitting together of individual lines of action.'* It is in fact only after we have acknowledged that social interaction consists of individuals interpreting each other's behaviour through shared symbols and meanings that we can entertain the notion of group life being orderly at all. Even here we are directed inward, as it were, to the social self, rather than outward to social structure, in order to explain how relative stability is arrived at. The explanation of order lies in the presence of the 'generalized other' in the self through which the individual forms and aligns his own action on the basis of 'taking the role' of others. Blumer writes: 'Practically all sociological conceptions of human society fail to recognise that the individuals who compose it have selves in the sense

spoken of.' They thus omit the vital element in explaining how the interconnections of group life are possible in the first place, that is, through the sense of 'otherness' embedded within the self. This implies that social organization is the *framework* within which social action takes place rather than its cause or determinant.

These three propositions have led Blumer and his school to reject the idea that society can be studied through the methods of the natural sciences, that is, by operating through a crude notion of 'social facts' and using these to test general laws. The aim of symbolic interactionism is far less ambitious: merely to understand the process of interpretation being used in a given context, one which may have no consequence in any other. The aim should be to see things from the actor's point of view, no more. For this purpose the student must do his own role-taking, standing in the place of the 'acting unit' under investigation. The affinity between this style of work and the urban sociology of Park and Burgess is that both typically rely upon personal documents, autobiographies, case studies, life histories and participant observation. Formal surveys and statistical analyses are out.

Formal sociology and the origins of interactionism

In Blumer's hands, then, interactionism becomes more than just a social psychology of the individual self. It builds upon Mead's ideas, selecting for especial emphasis the role of *shared meanings* and how they provide us with a sense that our relations with others do possess a degree of orderliness, if not actual structure. Symbolic interactionism thus constitutes a variety of interpretative sociology.

And, in fact, the German neo-Kantian type of social thought that so influenced Weber provided one of the sources from which interactionism also developed. The history of symbolic

interactionism has, to be sure, become a matter of some controversy because its adherents have apparently had their own oral tradition in communicating their ideas and methods. Much of the information about 'who influenced whom' is no longer available, especially to anyone who is not 'on the Circuit' (Rock 1979a). Blumer, for example, has been accused of overstating the importance of G. H. Mead and of twisting Mead's ideas to suit himself – a charge which Blumer vehemently denies. Undoubtedly, the key figure in bringing the ideas of German sociology to Chicago was Robert Park, who was a member of the 'Chicago School' of urban sociology described in Chapter 3 (Fisher and Strauss 1978). Yet it was not Weber but Georg Simmel, Weber's enigmatic contemporary with whom Park had studied and who remained the major influence on Park when he returned to the USA.

In Simmel's writing we certainly find ideas which anticipate the interactionist position. For example, in an early essay entitled 'The problem of sociology' we find what is arguably the clearest statement of what this problem is (Simmel 1971). For Simmel, the unity of society is not something detachable from the individual's sense of belonging to society. Indeed the two are, in a logical sense, merely the same thing viewed from different perspectives: the human condition is one of 'sociation' (*Vergesellschaftung*), a consciousness of forming a unity with others. In every individual there is an irreducible element which comprises his or her individuality yet paradoxically what we know about any individual, including ourselves of course, is only possible by comparison with others. In other words the individual self is a unity of purely individual and purely social elements. Simmel calls the latter the general value of individuality.

He then goes on to argue that if there is to be a science whose subject matter is society and nothing else it must be exclusively concerned with the kinds and *forms* of 'sociation'. The study of these forms is to be detached from a particular content: just as geometry studies the properties of abstract spatial forms so formal sociology will fix upon the general properties of social forms. After all, in everyday life we still speak of 'good form'.

Unlike geometry, however, the study of social form will have to rely a great deal upon the use of intuitive procedures and methods. On the face of it, this conception of the problem of sociology is wholly different from that adopted by Durkheim in his best-known works. Indeed, Durkheim was very critical of Simmel's ideas. Paradoxically, however, it has been argued that in his work on religion, collective representations and moral authority, he had moved to a position which, like Simmel's, anticipates symbolic interactionism (Stone and Farberman 1967).

Today, formal sociology's most active representative is Erving Goffman, who is arguably the most popular, and certainly the best known, of the modern symbolic interactionists. In the substantive work of Goffman (which we shall examine more closely in the next chapter) interpretative sociology becomes a wry, insightful, sometimes bitter, sometimes cool, observation on our everyday lives. It provides us with some valuable insights on the human condition, but ones which we are asked to accept almost *intuitively*. Because of the emphasis on the *interpretation* of behaviour (that is, its meaning) we are forced to trust the empathetic skills of the sociologist.

Consequently as sociological theory moves further along the interpretative path a number of tricky methodological and philosophical problems have loomed. How can sociologists claim a more valid understanding of social behaviour than the agents possess themselves?

Phenomenology and relativism

In the natural sciences day-to-day work is almost wholly free from entanglement with philosophical problems. Only rarely is it necessary to raise the question of how the procedures of science themselves are to be validated (Kuhn 1962). In the social sciences, as this book will have already made clear, this has never been really true. Indeed, in this chapter we seem to have reached some kind of limiting case which flies in the face of all 'proper' scientific procedure. But this is not all. It seems that the closer we come to understanding any society the more important it becomes to take seriously the fact that its members are themselves in possession of their own stock of knowledge concerning what their life together is about. As observers we may regard this knowledge as limited or false but the basis on which sociologists claim to have better insight is far from clear. On the contrary the sociologist's own perspective is coloured by the social conditions under which it is produced and is itself a social product. The result is that the distinction between sociology, the study of human action, and philosophy, the study of human thought, tends, in the course of our work, to break down.

In fact this tendency had become apparent by the end of the classical period of sociological thought. For example, in Chapter 14 we saw that Durkheim's later writings gave rise to what we called the problems of *relativism*. Thus Durkheim's own substantive work brought out the inherent difficulty of his intention to develop sociology as the study of social facts founded on agreed procedures as in other areas of science. Interactionism takes us much further down this road. It draws upon and in fact uses two 'isms' in philosophy which cast still more doubt upon the possibility of unambiguous social facts and the special status of sociological knowledge.

1   The first is called *pragmatism*, a largely American system of philosophy which greatly influenced Mead and his students. Although there are several different variants of pragmatism, as a doctrine it implies that truth is always relative to human purpose and the validity of knowledge determined by its 'satisfactoriness' in accomplishing human ends. The pragmatists attracted the attention of Durkheim who recognized that they had addressed certain problems raised by his own work – the origins of

our notions of *reality*, truth and logic through social activity. However, he deplored what he saw as the attack upon Reason implicit in pragmatism and sought to counter it (Lukes 1975, Chapter 24).

2 The second is *phenomenology* and can loosely be traced back to the philosophy of Kant. The most influential proponent of sociological phenomenology was Alfred Schutz who took up a number of problems relating to *verstehen* and ideal types where Weber had left them. Schutz maintains that Weber did not go far enough with his theory of meaningful social action. Thus while accepting Weber's critique of positivism that behaviour can only be understood by discovering its *meaning*, Schutz went further. Schutz argued that our sense of reality – our perception of this world around us – is *only* a social construct. In itself the world is meaningless. Thus in order to make sense of it, *we* impose a meaning upon it. Moreover we construct this meaning socially out of our interaction with others. In this way we share a set of 'taken-for-granted' assumptions about the world which makes 'society' possible. The very notion of society therefore resides in a set of shared meanings and consequently the analysis of society must begin with the investigation of these meanings. Sociology begins from the investigation of the 'taken-for-granted' (Schutz 1964).

Now there are some clear parallels here with Weber's own methodology, which can be expressed as follows:

a Reality is not self-evident; the problem is to interpret it.

b In their everyday lives, individuals interpret the world by imposing meanings on it – that is, they create *ideal-types* of how the world operates. Schutz called these 'first-order typifications'. We might call them 'common sense', or, in Schutz's terms, the 'world of We'.

c Sociologists then analyse these first-order typifications by the methods of interpretative sociology. This, too, involves the use of ideal-

types. *These* ideal-types Schutz calls 'second-order typifications'.

A number of consequences, both positive and negative, flow from this:

(i) Sociologists cannot (and should not) attempt to judge what is 'really' real. It is not the task of sociology to ascertain the 'reality' of a phenomenon; rather, phenomena *are* 'real' if they are defined as such by individuals who then act on that basis.

(ii) Hence the positivist goal of *objectivity* is abandoned (since we can never penetrate the reality which lies behind our interpretations of the world) and replaced by the ascertaining of meaning. This is essentially the nature of the debate between Douglas and Durkheim which we encountered in Chapter 13.

(iii) There is an obvious charge of what philosophers call 'infinite regress'. If sociologists are involved in constructing second-order typifications, what is to stop others constructing 'third-order' typifications from the ideal-types of sociologists – and so on *ad infinitum*? In other words there is a danger of complete *relativism*, whereby we cannot arbitrate between *any* claims about the world around us.

At this point we are in danger of coming to a dead end. We must either retreat from the interpretative approach or push on still further in the hope that this last problem will resolve itself. The latter course has been adopted by the devotees of a brand of sociology called *ethnomethodology*. This was coined by Harold Garfinkel (1967) and achieved some notoriety during the 1970s (for a sympathetic treatment see Turner 1974; Silverman 1975; Atkinson 1978; for hostile criticism see Goldthorpe 1973; de Mille 1980). Ethnomethodologists argue that *all* expressions of reality are 'indexical' – that is, based upon a set of assumptions which are specific only to the social context in which they are used. Even our most cherished 'taken-for-granted' views of the world do not reflect reality but our own fragile assumptions (or *categorizations*). Thus no single version of reality contains any more truth than any other and Garfinkel invented some diabolical schemes (called 'ethnomethodological experiments') for demonstrating this. For example, Garfinkel developed 'breaching' techniques whereby the 'taken-for-granted' assumptions of others were deliberately overthrown in order to reveal how social interaction demands shared understandings. Examples of this included students being sent home and told to act like boarders; or deliberately to mistake other people's social roles. Not surprisingly Garfinkel was able to demonstrate that indeed the social world is thrown into chaos if common assumptions are disrupted.

But he then applied this to sociology, arguing that sociologists *also* depended upon shared and unarticulated assumptions which rendered *their* explanations indexical. Garfinkel's solution was then to sweep aside the whole of conventional sociology as representing little more than a 'fairy tale' of sociologists and begin a complete reconstruction. This must begin from recognition that society represents an 'intersubjective achievement' based upon common categorizations of reality. We see the uses of this in the following chapter when we examine official categorizations of deviant behaviour.

Ethnomethodology thus makes very ambitious claims to be involved in a qualitatively different *kind* of sociology (Mennel 1974). This distinguishes it from interactionism and phenomenology, which imply fairly modest claims about the kind of knowledge that sociology can provide. In the view of the latter, the accounts we can offer of the social world cannot be shown to be 'better' or more rational than the understandings which members of society hold as they go about social life – simply different. On the contrary the best hope is that we can, to a limited degree, reconstruct these understandings through our own empathy and acquaintance with the 'other' point of view.

Needless to say this outlook is not palatable to everyone, not least those sociologists who wish to continue looking at problems and topics more traditionally associated with sociology. They deplore what they see as a shift and a narrowing of focus to a smaller-scale perspective, the focus upon social encounters, the neglect of structural issues. Nor are they happy to be led towards relativism. For example both functionalists and Marxists, albeit for very different reasons, would both wish to claim that their work can penetrate *beyond* the 'manifest' meanings and the 'false' consciousness of the taken-for-granted world and, in doing so, offer a superior kind of knowledge.

We cannot offer any ready-made general solution to such difficulties. We shall however make some brief observations.

First, even approaches like phenomenology and ethnomethodology presuppose, by their very existence, that there is some point to recording and thus *comparing* the 'taken-for-granted assumptions', the everyday knowledge which comprise society itself. We suggested in Chapter 1 that this exercise of comparison can itself be a *reasoned* procedure. By this we mean a process of the kind which Weber would have described as *formally* rational (see p. 175). This rational comparison of points of view provides a means by which we can hold relativism in check. By the same token it enables sociology to offer to those who study it a method of self-understanding that is more *reasonable* than any which is available from common sense or ideological dogma.

Second, many of the doubts we have about the status of our knowledge in the social sciences can be traced to various forms of *reductionism*. We saw in Chapter 5 for example how both biological and sociological types of reductionism lead to a situation in which one set of 'findings' is played off against another, with no real overriding method for arbitrating rival claims. But much the same sort of thing can be found *within* sociology itself. The complexity of the phenomena with which we have to deal makes it necessary for us to distinguish separate but equally necessary, equally valid, levels of analysis.

Reductionism occurs whenever this separateness remains unacknowledged or where the 'levels' are confused.

We began this chapter by accepting that there is a common tendency, among the mainstream schools of sociology, to assimilate questions of human agency into a sociology of system. There is always a danger that this will, in turn, lead to what we will call *holistic reductionism*: that is, society and the social categories to which people belong are made to appear too much as if they were 'things' and hence, like physical objects, explainable by mechanical laws of cause and effect.

But there is another danger which is the exact opposite and which we will call *individualistic reductionism*. The mistake here is to regard human action or 'agency' as an absolute and in so doing to absorb collective processes into a chaos of private meanings and subjective knowledge. But just as the self is a 'conversation' of the 'I' and the 'Me', so society is the product of the meeting between 'agency' and 'structure'. We would, therefore, accept the thesis that there are 'two sociologies', one of social systems or social wholes and one of human agency (Dawe 1978). We would also accept that they often seem to be saying different and incommensurate things. But we would resist the inference of despair that is commonly drawn, namely that sociological knowledge will, as a result, be hopelessly contested and subjective. What the presence of the two (or three (Benton 1977) or more) sociologies really shows is that we cannot study everything at once. If we do, the result will be a wholly unnecessary philosophical perplexity.

Third, philosophical uncertainty need not prevent us from examining substantive problems and we shall now try to show that at this level interactionism has, appearances to the contrary, something to offer the student of the mainstream problems of sociology. Yet only occasionally has it been suggested that the dialectical approach of Mead and his followers to the problem of self and society might actually help to round out more strictly sociological traditions of thought and illuminate the conundrums they have encountered (Berger P. and Luckman 1967, pp. 217–18).

19 Consciousness and control

The major substantive contributions of the approaches which we discussed in the previous chapter have been in the field of social deviance, relating social consciousness to the perpetuation or breakdown of order. The aim of such work has been to minimize the 'otherness' of what Howard Becker (1963) calls *Outsiders*, that is, deviants and rebels against conventional society. It has attempted to render their world of meanings understandable to the uninitiated and to reveal the role of conventional society in perpetuating this same world. We shall argue that in following this programme interactionists and phenomenologists have, albeit unwittingly, offered important 'leads' through which to understand the characteristic mechanisms upon which control and order in contemporary society depend.

First, however, it is necessary to discuss the conceptual impact of these two approaches upon deviancy research itself.

Interactionism and labelling theory

In so-called labelling theory the centre of interest shifts away from the qualities of the deviants in themselves and towards society's *response* to deviance. At the core of the approach is a distinction between mere rule-breaking, understood simply as a class of common individual actions which may have no further significance, and *deviance*. According to one of the more sophisticated definitions, deviance:

is created through processes of social definition and rule making, through processes of interaction with individuals and organisations, including agents and agencies of social control that affect the development of deviant self-concepts among rule breakers. (Schur 1971, p. 3)

Early versions of the approach have been much criticized because they appeared to be trying to explain all non-conforming behaviour in terms of social reactions. Thus in the formulation of Becker's *Outsiders*, 'deviance is *not* a quality of the act the person commits but rather a consequence of the application by others of rules and sanctions to an offender' (Becker 1963, p. 9). Thus the approach seemed to be claiming that the question of how individuals become attached to non-conforming behaviour as well as the intrinsic quality of their actions – that is, their violence or other anti-social features – could be ignored. More recent advocates of the position have insisted that 'labelling theory' is not intended to brush aside these problems and indeed is not a theory in the strict sense at all. It should rather be seen as an attempt to single out and define certain processes in society itself which patently must occur before separate individual acts become classified by society as particular kinds of happening (Plummer 1979). For example, the many different occurrences which are classified as 'thieving' involve a labelling reaction on the part of society which once attached to given individuals has long-term power to affect the way these individuals will be treated; and, more importantly, the way in which they will regard themselves. As a way of emphasizing this point Lemert (1972) distinguishes between 'primary' and 'secondary' deviation. Primary deviation denotes the original significance which the rule-breaking act has for the individual. Secondary deviation, on the other hand, 'refers to a special class of socially defined responses which people make to problems created by the societal reaction to their deviance . . . essentially moral problems which revolve around stigmatisation, punishments, segregation and social control'. Thus a person's life and identity become organized around the facts of deviance (Lemert 1972, p. 63) and includes a process of 'self-labelling'.

During the 1970s labelling theory came under heavy attack from the new wave of Marxist criminology and deviancy theory, examples of which have already been encountered in Chapter 14. Writers like Becker and Lemert were accused of ignoring the political significance of the deviant act, of being excessively preoccupied with the exotic details of deviant subcultures. The stated intention of examining society and its labelling process did not, it was said, go very deep. Whilst there may be some justice in these criticisms, it is important to stress that the study of labelling does not have to be confined to the perspectives of the particular interactionists who pioneered it. As Plummer observes, it 'may be dealt with by Marxists, ethnomethodologists, functionalists or positivists. There is no endemic link to interactionism and it is interactionist imperialism to suggest otherwise' (Plummer 1979, p. 88).

Phenomenology and becoming deviant

On the face of it, phenomenological approaches have turned 'inward' towards the deviant rather than outward towards society. But in fact the effect of their work is comparable to that of the labelling perspective.

One of the best-known phenomenological writers on deviance is David Matza. Matza has insisted on the need for naturalism, that is, to present a picture of the deviant which is authentic and which deviants themselves would recognize. Matza criticized the failings of subcultural and anomie theories from this point of view and, instead of imposing an abstract category of anomie upon the deviant imagination, set out to reconstruct it through his investigations (Matza 1964, 1969). In this way, Matza concluded that the values of the deviant were no different from those of conventional society but, rather, represent a heightening of certain 'subterranean' elements already present in the culture. For example, the element of irresponsibility and pleasure-seeking characterizing much delinquency finds its counterpart in the leisure values of respectable society. The difference is that restraints upon certain ways of expressing such values have become subject to techniques of neutralization.

Paradoxically, the focus upon deviant *meanings* has involved recognition that becoming 'labelled' ought in principle at least to affect the way deviants see themselves. Hence, much interest has focused on 'the imposition of unwelcome status' through (a) the generation of rules by the state and (b) the administration of these rules. Attention has therefore widened to include the creation of deviant meanings by 'legislating, defining and policing agencies which collectively make up the formal structure of a society and system of social control' (Rock 1973, p. 122).

Phenomenological approaches are the centre of considerable controversy and, again, Marxists have been prominent among the critics. They argue that phenomenological perspectives distract attention away from the political and economic factors conditioning the state's social control. Advocates of phenomenology might reply that it is dealing with a problem ignored by orthodox Marxism and which we have already suggested is important, that is, how political and economic domination is reflected and reproduced at the level of individual consciousness. Matza's later writings, for example, seem to be offering an account of the process of becoming deviant that has much in common with the 'self-damnation' observed by Willis in his work on 'why working class kids get working class jobs'

(Willis 1978). The state function, he argues, 'is the authorised ordering of activities and persons as deviant, thus making them suitable objects of surveillance and control'. But this depends upon the complicity of deviants in their own fate. 'Without building and conceiving the meaning of his own deviant identity the subject would be unprepared for the constructive use to which he is to be put . . . conceiving himself as an essential deviant prepares him for meaningfully representing the deviant enterprise. . . . The thief will stand for theft.' (Matza 1969, p. 169).

A second reply might be that the Marxist criticism only holds if the assumptions of the Capitalist Society model can be carried into deviance studies (see p. 137–8). The implication would be that there is something unique to the way in which *capitalism* defines and polices offenders which is not found in other societies. Phenomenologists could argue that their focus challenges this. Their concern is with the 'meaningfully adequate' conditions of 'becoming deviant' which are necessary to the exercise of control *per se* regardless of the kind of economic or political order for which it is being obtained. In practice, their work has much in common with Weber's variant of the Industrial Society perspective. Industrialism involves the use of rational bureaucratic procedures that can be employed to identify and control 'troublemakers' and 'irresponsible elements' regardless of who controls the bureaucracy. By implication, such procedures will be just as relevant to the study of contemporary Marxist states as to anywhere else.

In general then the labelling and the phenomenological approaches tend to complement each other. Schur has summarized the elements that they hold in common (1971, p. 132) as follows:

a   deviance is seen as a socially contructed act;
b   the primary focus is upon societal reaction to deviance;

c   there is a simultaneous and complementary effort to approach deviance from the point of view of the 'other';
d   there is heavy reliance on the concept of the 'definition of the situation' and this definition is negotiated;
e   there is great use of intensive observation as a research technique.

Undoubtedly all of these ingredients raise numerous and as yet unsolved problems. What we have been trying to show, however, is that the discussion of deviance and control from the perspective of the *self* reveals a dimension which is relatively neglected in the general mainstream debate in sociology about order and disorder, morality and inequality. In order to illustrate and amplify this theme we will now turn, briefly, to examples of research inspired by these approaches.

Outsiders: whose side are we on?

In his book *Outsiders*, Howard Becker calls upon case material gathered in the course of investigating two deviant subcultures, dance musicians and marijuana users. The report on the latter study has probably been the most influential. Based upon unstructured interviews obtained through informal contacts with fifty marijuana users, it aims to illustrate Becker's thesis that 'instead of . . . deviant motives leading to deviant behaviour, it is the other way round; the deviant behaviour in time produces the deviant motivation' (Becker 1963, p. 42). He argues that marijuana use does not involve the addiction and side effects associated with narcotics. This is borne out, he maintains, not only by medical evidence but also by the history of the activity. The use of the drug was not illegal until the advent of the Marijuana Tax Act which brought about a classic labelling situation. He then tries to show that becoming a marijuana user may be regarded as a 'career' in an analogous fashion to the pursuit of an occupational career. This career must be thought of not as an inevitable sequence of psychological states but as a sociological sequence of stages, any one of which may be 'failed' by a given individual (who would then cease to use the drug). These stages are (a) learning the technique of 'pot' smoking (b) learning to perceive the effects (which are not always immediately obvious to the individual) (c) learning to enjoy the effects. In each case the reassurances and advice of the user subculture are vital in order to present to the newcomer a series of identities. Thus the drug user is not in possession of psychologically abnormal motives but is someone who has learned, through group participation, to perceive the marijuana as something that can give him pleasure.

The group is equally vital in rendering the sanctions of orthodox society ineffective. Thus it offers means of (a) overcoming restrictions on the supply of the drug (b) avoiding behaviour which might betray one's deviance to significant members of conventional society (c) replacing conventional notions of morality with an 'inside' view acquired through experience with the drug in the company of users. In short what Becker seems to be arguing is that an act which becomes externally labelled by conventional society as 'deviant' also involves deviants themselves in a process of self-labelling, in which the creation of a subculture specific to that activity is crucial.

Becker's work brilliantly exemplifies many of the strengths of symbolic interactionism. It vividly conjures up the 'world of the other' and enables the reader to empathize with this world. It does, however, raise both sociological *and* ethical problems which critics have not been slow to take up. For example, labelling theory, in its extreme form, *appears* to absolve the actor from moral responsibility for his or her actions — *tout comprendre* becomes *tout pardonner*. As Gouldner has forcefully stated in his essay 'The sociologist as partisan' (1968), the outcome is, ironically, a conception of human action which comes very close to that of orthodox functionalism:

The deviant is made by society in two senses: first, that society makes the rules which he has broken and secondly, that society enforces them and makes a public declaration announcing that the rules have been broken. The making of the deviant, then, entails a process of social interaction. That being the case, the deviant making process cannot be understood unless rule [author's note: or *norm*] making and rule-enforcing procedures or persons are studied. (Gouldner 1968, p. 31)

Official categorizations and the labelling of deviants

In *The Social Organisation of Juvenile Justice*, A. Cicourel looks at the labelling process from the point of view of conventional society, or rather that part of it which is actually called upon to enforce society's rules. Here we are back with the problem of delinquency which we discussed in Chapter 14. How in practice do the representatives of law enforcement actually decide whether or not a particular event is an example of delinquency and how do they go about assigning it to a particular class of offence? Cicourel claims that his ethnomethodological perspective 'directs the researcher's attention to the theories of delinquency *employed by laymen* (our italics) and particularly to theories employed by police, probation and court officials when deciding the existence of delinquency' (Cicourel 1968, p. 24). His own fieldwork reports on an in-depth observational study over a number of years of this decision-making process in two Californian cities. It is significant from at least three points of view.

First, it brought out the importance of what Cicourel calls 'background expectancies'. Thus what to the individual appears as harassment is a product of expectations which, say, the police officer regards as part of his or her normal skills. Cicourel's investigation, albeit in an American context, was able to throw light upon the self-confirming nature of these skills. Because police and other officials (for example, social workers) operate with 'lay' theories as to the typical delinquent, they *concentrate* their activity on certain individuals and areas. For youths from middle-class homes who happened to be drawn into the net the scope for the negotiation of justice was far wider than for 'typical delinquents' and their liability for actual conviction lower. Curiously enough while this chapter of *The Problem of Sociology* was being written a topical and vivid illustration of Cicourel's point was supplied gratuitously by the deputy head of West Yorkshire CID. The police, he maintained, must be *prejudiced* if they are to do their job properly: 'Prejudice is a state of mind brought about by experience.' (*The Guardian*, 14 September 1981) For example, searching West Indian youths wearing jeans and T-shirts 'often turned up handbag snatchers and muggers'.

Second, Cicourel exposed the naïve way in which existing studies of delinquency had regarded official statistics of delinquency as non-problematic reflections of 'the facts'. The existence of 'background expectancies' raised the difficult problem of whether the presumed association between class and delinquency is an artefact of the law enforcement process. Cicourel was not the first to challenge conventional widom on this issue but the novelty of his theoretical perspective and the thoroughness of his research certainly brought a fresh urgency to the debate about the relation between class, deviance and crime, which has continued to the present day (for example, Braithwaite 1981; Box 1981). For example, it revived interest in the work of the Chicago sociologist Sutherland on white-collar crime (Sutherland 1961). Marxists have joined in the debate, drawing attention to the crimes of the powerful which do not meet with immediate opprobrium or appear in statistics (for example, Chamblis and Seidman 1971; Pearce 1976). It seems fairly clear then that society's labelling process is directed downward. But this argument cannot be carried too far. If there were no 'real' relationship between class and deviance or delinquency it would be difficult for Marxists to claim that such acts are symptomatic of latent rebellion in, say,

working-class adult culture or among lower-class youth.

The need to examine the production of statistics (and hence the production of 'delinquency' itself) was further brought out by comparing the two cities of Cicourel's study. Both had similar size populations and appeared to have similar socio-economic characteristics. Their delinquency rates, however, were very different.

This brings us to the third aspect of this work, namely, as a *study of organization decision-making and the application of bureaucratic rules*. Cicourel's argument is that people-processing bureaucracies, such as police and legal organizations, are presented with a problem of reducing a bewildering variety of everyday 'happenings' to a series of categories prescribed by procedural rules. 'Members of these organisations develop and employ their own theories, recipes and shortcuts for meeting general requirements acceptable to themselves and (to) . . . "supervisors" or some form of external control.' (Cicourel 1968, p. 1) In developing these 'recipes and short cuts' careful attention has to be paid to the organizational context. Thus the difference in recorded delinquency rates between the two cities is explained by Cicourel in terms of (a) the different relationships existing between the respective police department and local political bosses (b) the effect of this relationship on day-to-day routines.

Finally, Cicourel's work illustrates what is undoubtedly the most controversial aspect of ethnomethodology itself. This is its attitude to the relationship between common-sense or everyday understanding on one hand and sociology on the other. Put simply, ethnomethodologists question the idea that sociology aims to make descriptions of social reality which are different from the explanations which members of society themselves possess. Cicourel would hold, for example, that when orthodox sociological treatments of delinquency took delinquency statistics at their face value they did *not*, as they thought, uncover some latent aspect of social structure which was obscured from those dealing with the problem. They in fact 'discovered' the 'causes' that police and law enforcers *themselves* believe give rise to delinquency. These lay theories are not by-products of social process, however; they *are* social process. They are taken-for-granted procedures for 'making sense of a potentially senseless world', of rendering into order the passage of events which is itself disordered. Sociologists themselves unwittingly rely upon such common-sense procedures which are shared with the 'lay' world.

Is sociology, then, no more than common sense? The solution to this problem, ethnomethodologists argue, lies in taking these procedures, these ways of 'making sense', as the object of study in their own right. This approach seems to be particularly fruitful when applied to legal classifications and decision-making, because there is an obvious problem in the legal context of deciding 'what happened'. In Britain, one of the best examples is Atkinson's work on the way in which coroners reach verdicts as to the occurrence or non-occurrence of suicide. Using fieldwork material Atkinson maintains that such decisions are *not* reached by applying a known formal definition or definitions of suicide. Coroners work by assimilating 'cues' from the case history under examination which lead them to conclude whether or not the case conforms to their notions of what constitutes suicide:

Coroners, to an admittedly unknown extent, share the prevalent definitions of suicide in a society at any one time (and) . . . they are also in a position to reaffirm these definitions publicly and even perhaps introduce new ones. By defining deaths as suicides they are in effect saying to others in society: 'These kinds of deaths are suicides, these are the kind of situations in which people commit suicide and these are the type of people who commit suicide'. (Atkinson 1978, pp. 144–5)

The Durkheimian tradition of explaining suicide by examining variations in *rates* fails to examine the process by which the suicide rates are produced. It merely succeeds, as in the delinquency example above, in making explicit the explanations used implicitly by the legal agent – in this case the coroner. Once, however, we have uncovered these lay explanations, what else is there to understand about the suicide rate?

Used in contexts where there is a recognized problem of reducing disorderly events to some acceptable framework this is a powerful approach. The effect of ethnomethodology, for example, has been to encourage further study of various aspects of legal deliberations (Carlen 1976; Taylor L. 1972; Emerson 1969; Baldwin and McConville 1981). In a more recent publication Atkinson and Drew examine language use in court proceedings (Atkinson and Drew 1979) and this particular study shows the general drift of all ethnomethodological work towards ever greater preoccupation with language or 'naturally occurring talk'. In this respect it is approximating some of the concerns of anthropological structuralism with the basis of cultural order (see Chapter 14).

Ethnomethodologists, indeed, claim for their work that it is centrally concerned with the orthodox 'problem of order', whilst rejecting orthodox ways of solving it. Their critics, however, could maintain that not all aspects of social life can be simply reduced to members' interpretations. If, instead of moral classification, we concern ourselves, say, with inequality, class and poverty, we might wish to reserve the option of disputing everyday interpretations of 'what is happening'. And even with moral and legal classifications we might wish to ask what is the *source* of the rules by which members of society make sense of the world and in whose interest they operate. Power, privilege and social hierarchy are 'facts' of social 'structure' in some sense which sociology may still acknowledge in *preference* to *common* sense.

The neo-Marxist challenge

We are now in a position to focus upon one particular problem: the split which is evident in treatments of deviance and control between, on the one hand, interactionism and related approaches and, on the other, its neo-Marxist critics. We described the nature of the neo-Marxist challenge to existing deviance research and the proposed alternative in Chapter 15. Here, we are principally concerned with consequences. Interactionists have continued to explore the micro-world of the powerless deviant and his encounters with authority. They argue that this is a valid area of work in its own right. Impatient with this preoccupation with what they see as the least pressing problem, Marxists have turned to the study of *crime*. They have particularly focused upon the question of how notions of what is legal or illegal reflect the overriding structure of class interests. And they have looked for potential rebellion in the acts of criminals and other 'organized' deviants. This split, it seems to us, is symptomatic of an unnecessary and regrettable competition between micro and macro sociology, when in fact they both offer important insights albeit at separate levels of explanation.

Yet certain of the recent work in the area of deviance and conflict research offers the possibility of a *rapprochement*. The common denominator in each case is the application and development of interactionist concepts to the problems of social control at the 'macro' level. It entails the use of these concepts *in conjunction with* a sense of social structure and in the context of particular moments in contemporary social history. We shall be careful not to claim too much for such work which at present is neither extensive nor wholly convincing in its methods of reaching conclusions. Nevertheless it has progressed far enough to demonstrate the potential of insights gleaned from the study of the social self in illuminating the relation between agency or consciousness and social structure. Or in the terms of another debate, between social and system integration. Let us consider some examples.

We shall begin with the treatment of labelling as a phenomenon of system rather than social integration. *Pace* Marxists, the work of Howard Becker has included consideration of this point, particularly his work on the Marijuana Tax Act. Becker's fundamental purpose is to draw attention 'to the people who make and enforce the rules to which outsiders (deviants) fail to conform' (Becker 1963, p. 121). Enforcement and rule-making are not, as functionalists might claim, activities which 'society' produces in the abstract. It requires 'moral entrepreneurs', that is, someone or some group willing to bring the behaviour to the attention of others, to define it as a 'problem' and to make that definition stick by means of a moral crusade. This requires both motivation and resources the origins of all of which can be investigated. In the case of the Marijuana Tax Act: 'The Treasury Department's Bureau of Narcotics furnished most of the enterprise that produced the Marijuana Tax Act. While it is, of course, difficult to know what the motives of Bureau officials were we need assume no more than that they perceived an area of wrongdoing *that properly belonged to their jurisdiction* and moved to put it there (our italics).' (Becker 1963, p. 138) This example is important because it reveals two characteristically modern phenomena: (1) the use by the 'moral entrepreneur' (the Bureau) of the press and communications media in order to draw attention to and provide 'information' about the 'problem'; (2) the pursuit of the role of moral entrepreneur by a state bureaucracy in the course of its 'normal' activities. We will now illustrate both.

Moral enterprise and the media

The theme of the media as a factor in moral entrepreneurship, rule creation and enforcement, and in the creation of labels and stereotypes on a society-wide basis has received considerable attention from British sociologists recently. S. Cohen and J. Young, in an edited collection of some prominent examples (1973), stress the inadequacies of existing approaches to the mass media. The media, they maintain, are neither 'mass manipulators' nor, on the other hand, are they simply 'giving the public what it wants'. Their effect, rather, is to *narrow* the range of choices and perspectives which are acceptable and respectable. This is achieved by means of

1   Their ability to affect the quantity and quality of the stock of information available in society;

2   Their ability to affect the 'consensual' image of society': that is to say that those who are abnormal, who deviate or who present problems to the dominant value system 'are presented as inhabiting a territory beyond the boundaries of society. They are allowed no history, no real alternative conception of reality and no status other than objects of social control' (Cohen S. and Young 1973, p. 341).

3   Their effect on social control itself, for example by providing the members of control agencies with stereotypes and 'background expectancies' which we discussed above.

These authors have also, through their own respective researches, drawn attention to examples of further aspects of labelling processes, which they call *deviancy amplification* and *moral panic*. We shall illustrate the use of these concepts in the context of issues which have figured prominently in the course of this book, namely, (a) troublesome youth and (b) industrial relations.

The first of these forms the subject of *Folk Devils and Moral Panics* in which Stanley Cohen examines the disturbance at Bank Holiday resorts caused by rivalry between mods and rockers (Cohen S. 1980). A moral panic may be said to exist when 'a condition, episode, person or group of persons emerges to become defined as a threat to societal values and interests'. Cohen offers a detailed account of how this particular moral panic developed and was focused by the media as agents of moral indignation. Their effect was to cast mods and rockers in the role of 'folk devils', that is 'visible reminders of what we (youth especially) should not be' (Cohen S. 1980, p. 10); and thereby they

polarized the deviants further against the community. To be sure they provided magistrates and police with a legitimation for their severity but the severity was arguably not very effective and the moral panic was, on the face of it, counter-productive in that it provoked more trouble and 'amplified' the otherness which lay behind the deviance. In his conclusion, however, Cohen points out that in the end social control probably did have its intended consequences. 'After being put off the train by police before even arriving at your destination and then being continually pushed around and harassed by the police on the streets and beaches, searched in clubs, refused service in cafés, you might just give up in disgust. The game was simply not worth it' (Cohen S. 1980, p. 202). The moral panic then is in the hands of the media who actively foment it, an important social control device. Its immediate effect is to amplify the behaviour but its likely long-run effect is to de-amplify it.

As Cohen himself acknowledges, however, the most novel twist to the theory of labelling and the notion of moral panic is to be found in a study by Hall *et al.* of media reaction to the mugging phenomenon (Hall 1978). In fact 'it is extremely difficult to discover exactly what was new in mugging – except perhaps the label itself' (Hall 1978, p. 6). What is undoubtedly new however is that here we have concepts originating wholly within the interactionist tradition taken into an explicitly *Marxist* account of the matter in question. In a complex and subtle study Hall argues that the moral panic in this case involved a mobilization of the whole control culture as a way of fending off the crisis which British society faced in the 1970s – and of course still faces. The moral panic over mugging was in effect taken over from the American press where mugging had come (without any justification) to symbolize *black* crime. In fact, both in the USA and in Britain many of the social and economic problems had borne especially heavily on the black population in the inner cities even at the time of this particular investigation. This had resulted in greater ethnic consciousness, politicization (cf. p. 248) and hostility to the police. The latter for their part responded to the moral panic over mugging with the kind of intensive policing of inner-city areas which already in 1974 had led to community rioting in places like Brixton. We now know that these were mere dress rehearsals for later events.

Hall's analysis is not above criticism nor wholly backed up by sufficient evidence. It does, however, recall earlier arguments by the interactionist Lofland on the subject of the difference between deviance, social movements (for example, trade unions) and political conflict. Lofland argued that the boundary should be fixed not by the inherent qualities of events themselves but *by the extent to which the well-organized majority of conventional society feels fearful or threatened* (Lofland 1969). The studies reviewed in this section, then, have provided a certain amount of evidence that in contemporary society these feelings of threat are focused and mobilized via the mass media and that further study of how this is managed, by whom and under what conditions will yield important information.

The political and social significance of containing trouble through the media can be seen vividly if we turn to their role in reporting industrial relations news. In three highly controversial studies the Glasgow University Group (1977, 1980, 1982; cf. Schlesinger 1978) have maintained that press and television have 'amplified' the industrial relations problems of the country, creating a moral panic over strikes and turning trade unionists and shop stewards into 'folk devils'. The result, it could be argued, has been to intensify union unpopularity and if this view is correct the political ramifications are highly disturbing, highlighting the ability of the media to determine the state of public consciousness in regard to industrial relations issues and to influence the outcome of political debate. For in a climate of moral panic on the subject, any politician who promises to 'do something about the unions' possesses an electoral advantage of some weight.

Bureaucratic hierarchy and personal identity: the world of Erving Goffman

Further sources of moral enterprise and social control emanate from the welter of administrative institutions of modern life, in particular those forming part of the bureaucratically organized states which, as Max Weber observed, characterize highly industrialized societies. Most interactionist writing on the subject is speculative and impressionistic but offers fruitful possibilities for future work. Nowhere is this better exemplified than in the work of Erving Goffman.

Goffman is a highly controversial figure whose work is accorded the highest respect by some sociologists and wholly discounted by others. Differing sharply in spirit and style from functionalists and mainstream sociology it relies upon anecdote, biography, literary allusions, and excerpts from journals and newspapers for evidence. It appears to be almost exclusively preoccupied with the minutiae of social life; the conversation, the chance encounter in the street, 'embarrassment, uneasiness, self-consciousness, awkward situations, *faux pas*, scandals and mental illness'.

At the heart of Goffman's writings is a metaphor of society as theatre – hence the grotesque term 'dramaturgy'. We should make clear what this does *not* mean. It does not depend upon a literal comparison of social roles with acting a script or of social life with a play. Goffman's point is a subtler if cynical one, namely that in order to engage in social life the individual requires skills analogous to those of the actor in putting on a performance:

Thus interactants [that is, people!], singly or in 'teams' give performances during which they enact 'parts' or 'routines' which make use of a 'setting' or 'props' as well as both the 'front region' of the 'scene' and the 'back stage' (hidden from the 'audience'). *The outcome of each performance is an imputation by the audience of a particular kind of self to the performed character.* (Meltzer, Petras and Reynolds 1975, p. 68; our italics)

The 'dramaturgical analogy' provides a succinct

example of the fusion of several of the systems of ideas discussed in the last chapter. This is most clear in Goffman's first major work, *The Presentation of Self in Everyday Life* (1958) which was based in part upon anthropological fieldwork in the Shetland Islands. Goffman noted how interaction takes the form of the communication of symbols – or 'gestures' as Mead called them – which are both linguistic (speech) and non-linguistic (demeanour, body language, gesture, etc). Individuals present a 'self' by *over*-communicating those gestures which reinforce their desired interpretation and under-communicating those which would detract from the 'presentation of self' they wish to convey. Goffman calls this process 'impression management'. It can be observed and analysed by comparing 'on-stage' with 'off-stage' behaviour – here lies Goffman's affinity with the formal sociology of Simmel. But Goffman, like Durkheim, also recognizes the importance of ritual and ceremony as factors in cementing collective social life (see Ditton 1980; a full bibliography of Goffman's publications will be found in this work).

In so far as the 'presentation of self' is a conscious performance, then Goffman presents a somewhat manipulative portrayal of human interaction. 'Impressions' are deliberately 'managed' in order to have the desired effect. In Goffman's early work this manipulation takes a somewhat benign form – we recognize ourselves on the pages of Goffman's books with an affectionate amusement. However, where power relations are involved such manipulation clearly carries the potential of being much more sinister. And while Goffman, like all symbolic interactionists, has frequently been accused of ignoring the issue of power and social hierarchy in his work, he has nevertheless devoted a great deal of attention to the dark underside of interpersonal relations between the powerful and the powerless. Rogers, for example, has argued on the basis of careful examination of Goffman's entire output that no less than four themes recur in it which are very relevant to the vexed question of how power, hierarchy and class status inequalities are reproduced (Rogers 1980, pp. 101–2):

1   Hierarchy and inequality in the wider society pose problems of self-respect and opportunity for certain individuals (a thesis shared with the 'anomie' perspective on deviance).
2   Formal organizations of modern society, including especially work organizations, may so limit the autonomy of lowest-level subordinates that proper demeanour becomes a problematical undertaking.
3   One consequence will be that some individuals will attempt to maintain 'face' by means of acts of deviance.
4   Hierarchy also however implies an unequal social distribution of information. The result is false consciousness of which deviance is but one manifestation. Rogers talks of the possibly misguided but understandable efforts of individuals to achieve through 'false consciousness' a (psychic) security which is systematically denied to them by the social structure they thereby serve to perpetuate.

This, as Collins observes in a companion essay, is why classes persist – because they give rise to unequal possibilities of self-presentation to individuals in the course of the ordinary encounters of life. He goes on:

The overall structure of stratification is the result of the ongoing activities by which some people idealise themselves (that is, 'perform') better than others in the everyday . . . world of work. . . . The solid economic and political organisations of society must . . . be *enacted*.

Ordinary macro-level social theory tends to take such organizations for granted, as if they were things with a permanence that exists apart from the people who perform in them. 'Organizations' and 'positions' are thinglike in their solidity only because they are repeatedly *enacted* in a series of micro situations (Collins 1980b, p. 190, our italics; see also Collins 1981). The clue to these day-to-day situations is, as Goffman suggests, their role as 'stages' for the realization of 'rituals' of class and power:

Ritual creates solid seeming realities, social symbols which are not to be questioned and which leave a strong and compelling sense of exteriority . . . well performed rituals create and recreate the stratified order and hence underlie the distribution of material power and status privileges. (Goffman 1958)

Goffman's best-known contribution to the analysis of these issues is his book *Asylums* (1968). Here he sets out the general characteristics of what he calls '*total institutions*'. An ideal-typical total institution is a hierarchical organization whose control of its 'inmates' has become absolute in that:

1   They are concerned in some way with 'processing' or 'treating' individuals.
2   There is a defined class of inmates – individuals in the charge of the institution who (i) are cut off more or less permanently from the wider society (ii) lead an 'enclosed, formally administered life together' (Goffman 1968, p. 11).
3   There is a clear distinction between inmates and *staff*, reinforced by mutually antagonistic stereotypes of each other.

Goffman writes: 'Prisons serve as a clear example (of a total institution) providing we appreciate that what is prisonlike about prisons is found in institutions whose members have broken no laws.' (Goffman 1968, p. 11) His major example is, in fact, the mental hospital. In the course of his discussion however we come across many others: military institutions, concentration camps, boarding schools and monasteries are just some of the examples used.

Total institutions tend to have a clearly defined sense of purpose or treatment. It is common for the inmates' response to their incarceration (that is, to the institution itself) to be taken as a sign of their need to be where they are, subject to the organization's ministrations. The ethos of treatment also, Goffman claims, provides a valuable rationalization or excuse for the closely administered life which keeping people in an institution encourages.

Goffman's stated aim in making this study is 'to develop a sociological version of the structure of the self' (Goffman 1968, p. 11). Total institutions are 'the forcing houses for changing persons; each is a natural experiment on what can be done to the self' (Goffman 1968, p. 22). On one level, therefore, they represent a somewhat extreme, if not alas particularly uncommon, social situation. On another level, however, we cannot be sure that Goffman does not have a deeper purpose in mind. There are always moments in 'normal' social life which approximate to the conditions of a total institution. *Asylums* may be intended as a metaphor for society as a whole.

How, then, do total institutions act on the 'self' of the inmate? Their effect, we are told, is one of 'disculturation'. By this term Goffman intends to convey a process of progressive removal from the individual of the elements and signs of what the individual was in his or her pre-admission life. The object is leave a self which can be administered and is submissive to the requirements of the institution. As a consequence, we can describe what is done to the inmate in terms of a 'moral career' – just as Becker speaks of the 'moral career' of the marijuana user. Among the phases of this 'moral career' are the following four.

Admission

The emphasis in this phase is to establish the absolute control of the staff over the inmate. This is accomplished by a process of very obvious 'disidentifying' with past associations, including removal of personal property, and clothing; quite often literal stripping; issue of standard equipment and apparel; etc. Obedience is enforced by extreme severity including (a) violation of personal space (for example, through medical examination, 'bathing', shaving of hair, etc. (b) examination of the inmate's past history and 'record' (c) degradation rituals – enforcement of some particularly menial task or routine designed to emphasize the inmate's lowly status.

Mortification

The institution exhibits certain well-known routines which have the effect of continuing the mortification of the inmate's self which began in the admission phase. In general these have the effect of regimentation and tyrannization of their object but they can be further subdivided into different categories including (a) the multiplication of actively enforced rulings to the point where the inmate is uncertain where next to expect discipline and must concentrate the whole attention upon staying out of trouble (b) 'looping' – that is, strategies for incorporating the inmate's response to discipline into the disciplinary net itself (c) use of meaningless tasks and activities (d) keeping the inmates ignorant of what decisions have been made about them (e) use of a system of privileges to encourage compliance with the long-term objectives of 'treatment'.

Adaptations

The range of adaptations available to inmates is restricted by the close supervision to which they are subject. They may include what Goffman calls 'situational withdrawal', removal as far as possible of all emotional investment in the present. There is also a likelihood of 'colonization' or 'conversion' of the self either to the maximum satisfaction procurable within the institution or to the role of 'perfect inmate'. The characteristic adjustment, however, is 'playing it cool' – 'a somewhat opportunistic combination' of several forms of adjustment and loyalty to the inmate group 'so that the inmate will have a maximum chance of eventually getting out physically and psychologically undamaged'.

Release

Not every inmate of a total institution is presented with the opportunity of release from its clutches. If he or she is to be released, then the event may be anticipated with considerable anxiety brought on by two sources (a) the disculturation process itself which has induced a sense of the need to 'relearn' about everyday life (b) the *stigmatization* of having been associated with the institution and of accepting in some measure its definition of one's self. The result is the phenomenon of 'institutional dependency', that is, uncertainty about one's ability to 'cope' in the 'real' world.

We said earlier that total institutions may at times serve as a metaphor for society as a whole. Their fundamental mode of operation is the violation of personal space. To be sure, in much of Goffman's work the theme is quite different. In ordinary life, he seems to be saying, individuals are constantly engaged in resisting the imposition of too much social order. Impression management and self-presentation are aimed at preserving personal space. Their object is the maintenance of 'distance' between self and role. Alan Dawe, among others, has noted, though, that this emphasis on an analogy with gamesmanship has gradually been displaced. As society itself has displayed less and less order the image has changed to that of predator and prey. In an increasingly violent world:

the very possibility of personal space has disappeared, because the established surrounds and rituals which used to protect it now protect its invaders. When your home can be bugged you can no longer trust it as your 'informational preserve'. When it can be invaded by the rapist posing as the gasman, or bank robbers intent on using you as a hostage, it is they and not you it shelters. When others, whose very presence you do not even notice, can contrive your normal social surroundings to set you up, your ability to scan and so to control the situation is gone. And when the house opposite, your neighbour's preserve, can conceal the sniper, then there is no longer any place for anyone to hide. The world is turned upside down, its rituals, its tacit understandings, even its physical barriers against invasion, all are turned against it. (Dawe 1973, p. 249)

Inside or outside the total institution the

question of personal space is problematic. For Dawe, Goffman's work is about the condition of America. But is this all? Some of the worst problems of personal space in modern times have occurred where society and the total institution have coincided. In the *totalitarian* society the invasion of the self attains new levels and metaphor is metaphor no longer.

The fragmentation of self

It may come as no surprise to the reader to discover that the theories of the self which we have been revealing in this chapter see the problem of selfhood and identity in modern society as inherently problematic. Modern men and women suffer what psychoanalysts call the 'narcissistic' or self-obsessed personality; to interactionists and phenomenologists we live in an abstracted society in which the mind suffers feelings of fragmentation and 'homelessness'. In *The Homeless Mind*, Berger and Berger (1973) suggest that there are certain key 'carriers' of this singularly modern form of consciousness and their framework offers a useful way of summarizing the drift of this and previous chapters.

Berger and Berger distinguish what they call primary and secondary carriers. *Primary* carriers are the institutions of social structure, the economic and political 'base' of society. Each contributes to the fragmentation process affecting selfhood. Market forces, as neo-Durkheimian theories of anomie also point out, weaken the hold of traditional constraints and encourage egoism and 'privatization' of key sectors of life, work and consumption. Technology, with its ever-growing scale, creates a structure of 'anonymous social relations' defined in functional and not personal terms. And both market and technological forces create the need for what Berger and Berger call 'self-engineering'. By this they mean the variety of devices which become necessary to protect the real from the less real aspects of self, particularly the correlation of work identity with other aspects of selfhood. The result, they argue, echoing Freud, is emotional management and repression.

All of these experiences are intensified by the main primary carrier which is the pervasive *bureaucratization* of modern life. Bureaucracies create a diversity of abstract formal identities in which the individual will either be a subordinate or 'client'. The overall meaning of bureaucracy is that it locates the individual in society more precisely than work roles in themselves. The individual is threatened not simply with meaninglessness and anonymity in the world of work but in wide sectors of his or her relations with other people.

The general effect of the primary carriers then is to make more and more social relations opaque to the individual and to encourage a sharp separation between an anonymous highly structured public world and a 'private' world into which the individual retreats but which is underinstitutionalized and creates a troublesome separation of personal identity from institutional roles. These tendencies are intensified by the secondary carriers of consciousness which transmit information, particularly urbanism and the mass media. These heighten the separation of the public from the personal and create a diversity of life worlds which further fragment what Mead would have termed the 'Me' phase of selfhood. The 'I' becomes, in consequence, peculiarly reflective and individuated.

Paradoxically, the individualistic values of modern society, the development of the 'religion of humanity', which Durkheim considered would solve the moral problems of organic solidarity, do not alleviate these problems but intensify them. For example, as Weber noted, the ethos of political democracy and a certain degree of equality before the law encourages the growth of rules and the rise of bureaucracies, including rule enforcement bureaucracies. Thus, if these arguments are correct, the fragmentation and privatization of self is a fundamental aspect of the conditions which give modern society its troubled stability. By examining the characteristic carriers of self-consciousness we can begin to understand the precise way in which the incorporation of vast masses of people into an acceptance of hierarchical society is effected. Because it is a society which always seems to *threaten* a 'loss of community' we cling ever more tenaciously to those areas of private communion which are still left to us; and we leave the wider public spaces to the care of others whom we pay but never meet.

Of course sociologists do not actually 'know' these things with the certainty of natural facts. We can only take hold of the possibilities and ask if they are true of the time and place and circumstances where for us history and biography intersect. Nevertheless there are many echoes here of a common twentieth-century preoccupation in art and literature, namely the problem of how personal identity and authority can be retained in an increasingly dehumanized, impersonal and alienating modern world. Much of the work we have considered in these two chapters takes this as an implicit theme. From Weber's concerns over the 'iron cage' of rationalization to the 'homeless mind' of Berger and Berger, interpretative sociology has struggled with the existentialist doubt which is prompted by the contemporary social world (Craib 1976). In this sense 'the personal' is closely linked to 'the political'. Major issues concerning the nature of social change have been examined via a consideration of interpersonal relationships. Thus in examining issues which might appear to be more in the province of social psychology, these writers have sought to say something much more general about the nature of society.

20 Epilogue

At the beginning of this book we warned that sociology is a discipline which thrives on controversy. By now this, at least, should be apparent. Hopefully it is also clear why, when sociologists are asked to solve some manifest social problem, they seem to be congenitally incapable of giving a straight answer to an apparently simple question. Instead they tend to challenge the assumptions which lie behind the question. This is not due merely to perverseness or evasiveness (though doubtless each may play its part on particular occasions) but to the requirement of sociology to penetrate behind the taken-for-granted, common-sense assumptions which are built into our perceptions of contemporary society.

This leads to the classic dilemma which faces all students of society. The sociologist, as Robert Merton once pointed out, is widely regarded as someone who spends £50,000 on discovering something which everyone knew already. But if the sociologist discovers something which is not 'known' then there is a refusal to believe in the findings, since 'common sense' decrees that it cannot be true! More recently the image of the sociologist as someone who expends Herculean labour on discovering the monumentally trivial has been replaced by something altogether more sinister – most tendentiously portrayed in Malcolm Bradbury's novel, *The History Man* (1975). Here sociology is regarded as little more than a thin veneer on radical politics. Not only is sociology regarded as lacking in any academic integrity, its practitioners appear bereft of personal integrity. Like Howard Kirk, Bradbury's egregious, sociologist anti-hero, they are sociologists only for ulterior personal or political motives, without commitment to the disinterested advancement of knowledge which befits the true social scientist.

Surprising though it may seem to some, sociologists have been more than aware of the limitations of their discipline. Indeed there has recently been a spate of books on 'the sociology of sociology' which have attempted to reflect upon the limits and uses of the discipline (discussed in Bell C. and Newby H. 1977, Introduction). Such introspection has been prompted by the collapse of functionalism as a generally accepted scheme, leaving behind a variety of competing, and sometimes incompatible, approaches to sociology no one of which has gained universal recognition. The general trend in sociology since the 1960s has therefore been towards increasing fragmentation – and thus introspection. In itself, however, this is not a reason for pessimism. As we have tried to indicate in this book, the history of sociology is marked by a plurality of theoretical approaches. Functionalism, for a short time, appeared to be within striking distance of theoretical hegemony only at the cost of suppressing the consideration of many of the issues which formed an essential part of the sociological tradition. In the post-functionalist era there has, therefore, merely been a return to the theoretical and philosophical pluralism which has traditionally characterized sociology.

These changes have not, however, been solely the result of the conceptual inadequacies of functionalism. As we pointed out at the beginning of Chapter 15 it is difficult to understand the demise of functionalism without referring to the external political events of the 1960s with which it was ill-equipped to deal. In a very direct sense, then, the current fragmentation of sociological thought cannot be dissociated from the aftermath of this period. It is impossible to consider sociology on a purely 'internalist' basis – that is, as a self-contained body of ideas whose development takes place without reference to the outside world. As Merton has put it:

The concrete development of sociology is of course not the product only of social processes imminent to the field. It is the result of social and intellectual forces internal to the discipline with both of these being influenced by the environing social structure. (Merton 1959, p. 29)

The 'environing social structure' of the 1960s meant that sociology would never, and *could* never, be interpreted and implemented in the same way again.

With the benefit of hindsight these comments seem obvious; indeed they have become almost clichés. But they account for the preoccupation of sociology during the 1970s with its own self-doubts. In part this is due to sociology's rigorous pursuit of its own weaknesses – both positivism and functionalism have been subject to ruthless *self*-criticism. But more importantly it is due to the fact that during the 1960s many of the 'domain assumptions' (that is, taken-for-granted premises) of post-war functionalism were found irretrievably wanting (see Gouldner 1971). These assumptions were largely those of the liberal polity (see Chapter 2), whereby the emancipation of the individual was guaranteed, ascriptive social differences (class, sex, race, etc.) were declining and the state was merely the representation of the people. Within the liberal polity the role of the sociologist was clear: to argue, on the basis of rational enquiry, for piecemeal social engineering in order to redress the imbalances of a perfectable society.

In the wake of events in locations as widespread as Watts, Chicago, Paris and (for devotees of 'convergence') Prague, the classic liberal assumptions about the nature of politics and society were difficult, if not impossible, to sustain. They were seen to be inadequate *empirically* as well as theoretically. Sociologists came increasingly to question their technocratic role (see Becker 1967) – what was the point of conducting 'objective', 'scientific' sociology if, in the last analysis, the findings would only be acted upon if they served the ulterior political motives of those in power? It was only a short step from this uncomfortable, if relevant, question to the advocacy of the 'sociologist as partisan' (Becker 1967). It was Alvin Gouldner (1968, 1971) who best perceived the significance of this, writing as early as 1971 of *The Coming Crisis in Western Sociology*. In a memorable phrase – 'theorising in the sound of gunfire' – he captured the essence of the liberal dilemma. To Gouldner's proclamation of 'crisis' at least three reactions have occurred, all of them involving, however, as we see it, a risk of Unreason:

1 There has been a political radicalization of sociology which has involved the complete overthrow, not only of functionalism, but of many of the liberal assumptions which underlay it – in particular the separation of scholarship from political advocacy. There has been a resurgence of interest in Marxism, which has, despite its own internal problems (New Left Review 1977; Anderson P. 1980), at least appeared *relevant* during a period of worldwide economic recession.

2 The second reaction has been to renounce the search for any 'grounded theory' with, instead, an increasing interest in various forms of ideographic interpretative sociology (see Chapters 17 and 18). By its nature this will increase the fragmentary appearance of sociology.

3 Third, there has occurred a retreat from holistic theories of *any* kind in the hope that a viable theoretical sociology might be reconstructed piecemeal on the basis of *methodological* rigour. The result, particularly in the United States, has been a sociological practice which

emphasizes *technical* competence in research methods at the expense of imaginative sociological thought.

With the increasing fragmentation and/or specialization in recent sociology, it is not surprising that quite basic issues relating to how sociological research should be conducted have once more received so much attention. Much of this discussion is as old as sociology itself. It concerns, fundamentally, the age-old question, is a *science* of society *possible*? Sociologists continually worry about whether there are any obvious criteria for certifying sociological knowledge, for judging the appropriateness of methodological procedures and even for judging the suitability of topics for investigation. To use a distinction in C. Wright Mills's magisterial book, *The Sociological Imagination* (1959), these are the 'private troubles' of sociology which always lie just beneath the surface of the analysis of 'public issues' (see also Fletcher C. 1974).

But we can play the conventional sociological trick and turn this question back on itself. What is 'science'? Is a 'science of society' desirable? In other words, what attitude should be adopted to the differences which, a century and a half after the appearance of Comte's appeal for a positive social science, obviously still exist between sociology and the natural sciences? It is easy enough to make a few generalizations about the embarrassed way contemporary British sociologists themselves handle the problem in front of each other, in front of their students and among the informed public. Their stance may be described as simultaneously over-apologetic and over-abrasive. On one hand they display complete agnosticism – even despair – about the integrity of the discipline and its lack of agreed procedures. On the other they adopt what Becker would call an 'Outsider' stance towards lay explanations and interpretations of social phenomena – especially if these emanate from authority. The uncertainty of the first mocks the arrogance of the latter. Members of the public

and those students who do not get drawn into the 'Outsider' subculture do not take long to sniff out the ambivalence. Their feelings, whether unspoken or openly expressed, that sociology is a bogus discipline, a soft option, are understandable.

Understandable, but nevertheless wrong. Anyone who has seriously tackled the literature outlined in this book will have no doubt that they have learned something – even if it is only to think in a different kind of way about the web of social relations in which we are all involved. The problem is not that sociology is vacuous or lacking in rigour. *The problem is the failure of sociologists to appreciate that what appear to be its weaknesses are actually its strengths.*

This failure arises because, in spite of the enormous amount of effort devoted to the question, sociologists and their public are still blinded by the example of the natural sciences and the successes of physics and chemistry. Even elsewhere among the social sciences (*sic*) there stands the distraction offered by economics whose practitioners are resolutely devoted to the ideal of the unity of scientific method and who seem on the face of it to have built up an impressive body of quantified theory. It is time to accept once and for all that the natural science comparison will lead to a number of false criticisms of sociology, forcing its devotees to be diffident about their own knowledge and insecure about their achievements. Let us amplify the point by considering two complaints about sociology each of which stems from the belief that the natural science method offers the only paradigm for procedural rigour.

Unity versus diversity of procedure

The procedure of natural science depends upon the fact that the principles which underlie the natural world are assumed by the investigator to be beyond human control. This is not to state the obvious nonsense that people cannot change the physical environment, but that they can do so only by discovering the general laws which determine particular happenings of nature and manipulating them in accordance with human ends and purposes. These laws are 'given' – it is Canute-like to pretend otherwise. This being so natural science sets up a single yardstick to prevent as far as possible human feelings and desires from contaminating its observations and so impeding its search for the actual rather than desired state of affairs. We know that in practice individual scientists do not stick to the rules of this procedure and that its coherence is not absolute (for example, Kuhn 1962). But this can always be countered:

1   by arguing that too radical a departure from the 'rules' will be uncovered eventually by the scientific community as it attempts to replicate the findings of others;
2   by pointing to the obvious fact that natural science 'works'. It is intimately linked with a technology that has succeeded in bending nature to human will to a dramatic extent. The world is round and does go round the sun even if we would prefer that the universe were less indifferent to human egos.

Sociology and the other social sciences have sought a comparable yardstick in vain. We would suggest that the futility of the search can be explained by the fact that their object of study is fundamentally different from the natural world and therefore cannot be understood by imposing a single procedure as a yardstick for all investigations to follow. The principles of the social world are not fixed or incapable of being altered by human agency. For example, sociologists have sought to understand or discover the conditions or elements which enable an individual or group to exercise power over others – almost as if we could then proceed to devise a 'recipe' or 'prescription' for gaining and retaining power. But probably the only thing we can say in general about power is that its most fundamental condition is the capacity for novelty and surprise; or the ability to transform old sources of control into new as the situation changes.

If then we set out using the unified procedures of natural sciences to discover the 'laws' which govern the social world, we shall find that in doing so we have always arrived too late. 'Laws' of social behaviour are always yesterday's laws and while we were uncovering them the rules of the current game have been changed. For, inevitably those who are the real participants in the action will always be ahead of the 'imaginary friends' (to use a phrase from another fictional account of sociology) who come to expose their doings (Lurie 1967). We therefore need a method in sociology that reflects the nature of the reality being studied and its vulnerability to human intervention. This is not the place to attempt a formal solution to the problem, but we do think it is necessary to indicate how perceived 'weaknesses' of sociology are in fact part of its strength.

1   Sociology is the only 'social science' discipline in which the 'natural science' model is routinely questioned and debated. Other social sciences are able to appear more 'objective' and 'scientific' precisely because they suppress the discussion of philosophical and methodological issues. This is not an advantage but a disadvantage. Awareness of the limitations of what can be known from, say, official statistics or a survey questionnaire is not a loss but a gain.

To be sure, this can be carried too far. For sociologists to dwell on the 'private troubles' of the discipline (questions of method, rules of evidence, criteria of validity, etc.) *at the expense* of the analysis of public issues is, ultimately, self-defeating, for it provokes a kind of narcissistic self-pity. Equally, however, to build up a set of established findings on blithely unconsidered, and invalid, procedures is a denial of rational enquiry.

2   Sociology is the only 'social science' discipline which would not be seriously impeded and undermined by the 'natural science' model being jettisoned. For there are other ways of studying society than by seeking elusive 'laws' of the social world. For example, many of the method-

ological problems which beset sociology have long been familiar to historians. Indeed historians have been forced to confront problems of evidence and method in a much starker form than sociologists because historians are incapable of creating their own data. As E. P. Thompson once remarked, 'You cannot interview tombstones'.

Consequently historians have developed an enhanced awareness of

a The extent to which enquiry is *disciplined* by the presence or absence of appropriate evidence;
b The extent to which the evidence stands in need of interpretation -- that is, 'theory' and 'data' are by no means separate entities. As Alan MacFarlane has observed:

'Data' is not just 'out there' to be harvested, it is not a finite quantity, but rather an organic and infinite growth. Its quantity and quality will depend very considerably on the simple techniques whereby it is collected. (1978, p. 22)

Thus historians have recognized that methodological issues cannot be arbitrated on an a priori basis but only via immersion in a process of rational enquiry – that is, corroboration or contradiction by other sources, internal logical coherence, inherent probability, etc. These matters are in turn the subject of the cut and thrust of rational debate. While in the end sociology may, like history, thus be little more than 'constructive speculation', nevertheless, to echo E. P. Thompson, 'We must reconstruct what we can'. (Thompson 1963, p. 542) Sociology warts-and-all is better than no sociology at all if we are to develop a proper understanding of the human condition.

Unified theory versus schools of thought

Sociology is not the *same as* history, however. Again there is room for much debate about the precise nature of the difference between the two disciplines. Suffice it to say that it has something to do with the fact that sociologists do try to erect a more theoretical set of explanations than historians; ones which will facilitate comparison between different times and places; ones that will systematize the particular explanations historians give for individual events. While the *primary* purpose of history is to narrate and to evoke, that of sociology is to *explain*. Is this search for theory not as vain as the search for a unified method? As we have clearly seen in the above chapters there are many rival explanations, many rival theories. Is this not tangible proof of the impossibility of the whole exercise?

Our own view would be that some of the diversity of explanations is indeed superfluous. The only remedy is to step up the empirical research effort in face of the doubters of recent times. An excessive tendency to speculation can be cured by more and better information – which, as Dr Johnson said, is the enemy of good conversation.

It is useless, however, to think that the genuine logical and conceptual divisions between the schools of sociology will some day be finally resolved. This is again to be seduced by the natural science view of things which expects the passage of scientific progress to bring about greater cohesion and unity in the edifice of validated theory.

Things are quite different in sociology. The reason for this lies once again in the lack of unity in the subject matter under investigation. Whereas the natural world is all of a piece, and a law that holds in one part will hold in another, society by contrast *is* a tissue of incompatible meanings and points of view and this is the only general account which can be given of it. Our argument implies a number of very definite characteristics of sociological explanation:

1 As the symbolic interactionists recognized more clearly and simply than anyone else, sociological explanations depend upon the ability to 'take the role of the other'. This is also the fundamental discipline of sociological method, the

ability to strip off preconceptions, personal interests and prejudices in order to discover as completely as possible the structure and meaning which social action possesses from a perspective that is different from one's own. Considerable effort and rigour are required for the task. But such a procedure does enable us to discover the intelligibility if not the rationality of behaviour that otherwise appears irrational, less than normal, less than human to the lay mind untrained in this skill of 'switching' perspectives.

2   It is necessary to add an important rider to this. The methodological doctrines of symbolic interactionism are unnecessarily restricted by having too simple a view of the 'other' which we have to try to capture in order to understand society. With some notable exceptions the interactionists concentrate on the level of social integration. The 'others' which they consider are those of particular individuals and groups whose failure to integrate attracts the sociologist's interest. For the most part they deny any significance to the problem of structures and systems. We see this as a needlessly modest programme. There are 'others' whose viewpoint can be rendered intelligible even though they are not individuals or self-conscious groups. These 'others' represent aggregates of whom it may be said that their common or shared position *in the structure* offers the key to rendering intelligible their characteristic modes of behaviour. Two obvious examples present themselves. The first, which it was the contribution of Marxism to recognize, is that of a *class*, an element in the social structure whose members may be quite unaware of what it is they hold in common but who exhibit similar characteristics and behaviour precisely because they do have a common relation to economic production and distribution. The second, most closely approached in the work of Durkheim and the functionalists, is that of the whole collectivity – the Generalized Other where the problems of integration assume an overriding importance. After the revolution every Marxist will become a functionalist!

3   We can now see the role of theory. Its task is not to contribute to a steadily accumulating pile of laws but something very different. Each new school of theory represents a new 'discovery' in the sense that each contributes a new and different perspective to the sociologist's attempt to understand all of the separate meanings which go to make up the social world as it is. This is the resolution of the apparent paradox that sociology can actually progress by adding to the number of different theories.

4   We do not of course mean to suggest that sociologists can simply 'make up' or invent new perspectives at will. Max Weber offered a powerful argument that our interpretations of the meaning which social action has for others can be conducted with due deference to all the normal rules of evidence and proof. And this is what we ourselves would wish to argue. The established schools of sociology have achieved eminence precisely because they have shown that they can point to significant classes of information. They are significant because they show that the perspective in question is one which genuinely holds for some or other category or group of individuals in society itself.

5   Sociology is always more than the sum of its various 'isms'. The sociological imagination is distinguished by the fact that it is not tied down to one point of view. It is not content with the ordered conventional lay view of the world, nor is it content with the dogmatism that insists that one account of the structure of social action will serve for all. Sociology is never reducible solely to Marxism, functionalism, interpretative sociology though it can encompass them all. Indeed it insists that the trained sociologist be able to look equally through the eyes of any one of these without confusing or confounding them.

To say that is not to deny the possibility of personal commitment to a point of view. On the contrary it is an essential element in the choosing and exploration of a research problem. What it does mean is that the willingness to shift perspectives or to discover new ones is the closest we can come in the social sciences to the open-minded enquiry of pure science. Refusal to acknowledge this fact is the hallmark of the *closed* mind.

The 'natural science' paradigm for sociological enquiry, then, is misleading and should be laid to rest. One final reason for burying it should be that it is an affront to human dignity. If it is true that the social world is ruled by 'laws', we place a corresponding limit upon human responsibility and moral choice. Certainly there are many features of social life which are unalterable at least in the short run and many constraints that force us to follow one course of action rather than another. In the last analysis, however, these imponderable forces are monitored within the private world of the self and our response to them is our own product and our own responsibility.

Durkheim was thus correct to describe sociology as a 'moral science'. Not only however can it tell us, as Durkheim claimed, why morality and self-control are necessary to human life. It can also inform us as to the likely consequence of serving particular ends or of adopting given means. It offers us, in fact, the most basic choice of all. Either we make moral and political choices on the basis of a rational attempt to make sense of the social world. Or we can make them on the basis of self-deceit, ignorance, dogma and blind prejudice. To deny the possibility of a rational sociology is to close off one of these options and to deny that there ever was or can be reason and responsibility in human life.

Sociology is a difficult, stringent discipline. It is not that the concepts and information it comprises are particularly hard to grasp. Many of its discoveries, such as the cramping effect of inequality upon human potential, are almost 'obvious'. The problem for the would-be sociologist lies elsewhere. It is that our taken-for-granted beliefs, however they arise, provide a comfortable, convenient and necessarily simplified picture of the social world. The effort required to place them under critical review and to keep them there, is almost superhuman.

Bibliography

Abegglen, J. (1956), *The Japanese Factory*, Glencoe, Ill.: The Free Press

Abrams, P., and McCullough, A. (1976), *Communes, Sociology and Society*, Cambridge: Cambridge University Press

Adorno, T., Frenkel-Brunswick, E., Levinson, D. J., and Sandford, R. N. (1950), *The Authoritarian Personality*, London: Harper & Row

Adriaansens, H. P. M. (1980), *Talcott Parsons and the Conceptual Dilemma*, London: Routledge & Kegan Paul

Albrow, M. (1970), *Bureaucracy*, London: Pall Mall Press & Macmillan

Alcaly, R. E., and Mermelstein, D. (1976) (eds), *The Fiscal Crisis of American Cities*, New York: Vintage Books

Althusser, L. (1969), *For Marx*, Harmondsworth: Penguin Books

Amin, S. (1974), *Accumulation on a World Scale*, 2 vols, New York: Monthly Review Press

Anderson, M. (1980a) (ed.), 'The relevance of family history', in M. Anderson (ed.), *Sociology of the Family*, Harmondsworth: Penguin

Anderson, M. (1980b), 'Quantitative indicators of family change', pp. 11–30 in M. Anderson (ed.), *Sociology of the Family*, Harmondsworth: Penguin

Anderson, P. (1965), 'Origins of the present crisis', in P. Anderson and R. Blackburn (eds), *Towards Socialism*, London: Fontana

Anderson, P. (1974), *Lineages of the Absolutist State*, London: New Left Books

Anderson, P. (1980), *Arguments within English Marxism*, London: New Left Books

Ardrey, R. (1961), *African Genesis* – a personal investigation into the animal origins and the nature of man, London: Collins

Ardrey, R. (1967), *The Territorial Imperative* – a personal enquiry into the animal origins of property and nations, London: Collins

Ardrey, R. (1970), *The Social Contract* – a personal inquiry into the evolutionary sources of order and disorder, London: Collins

Arensberg, C., and Kimball, S. (1948), *Family and Community in Ireland*, Mass.: Harvard University Press

Aries, P. (1962), *Centuries of Childhood*, London: Jonathan Cape

Aron, R. (1964), *German Sociology*, London: Heinemann

Aron, R. (1969), *Eighteen Lectures on Industrial Society*, London: Weidenfeld & Nicolson

Atkinson, A., and Harrison, A. J. (1978), *The Distribution of Wealth in Britain*, Cambridge: Cambridge University Press

Atkinson, M. (1977), 'Coroners and the categorisation of deaths as suicides', in C. Bell and H. Newby (eds), *Doing Sociological Research*, London: Allen & Unwin

Atkinson, M. (1978), *Discovering Suicide*, London: Macmillan

Atkinson, M., and Drew, J. M. (1979), *Order in Court – the Organisation of Verbal Interaction in Judicial Settings*, London: Macmillan

Avila, M. (1969), *Tradition and Growth*, Chicago: University of Chicago Press

Bahro, R. (1978), *The Alternative in Eastern Europe*, London: New Left Books

Bailes, J. (1978), *Technology and Society under*

Lenin and Stalin, Princeton: Princeton University Press

Bain, G. S., Coates, D., and Ellis, V. (1973), *Social Stratification and Trade Unionism*, Oxford: Basil Blackwell

Baldwin, J., and McConville, M. (1981), *Courts, Prosecution and Convictions*, Oxford: Oxford University Press

Banfield, E. (1956), *The Moral Basis of a Backward Society*, Glencoe, Illinois: Free Press

Banks, J. (1959), 'Veblen and industrial sociology', *British Journal of Sociology*, vol. 10, pp. 231–43

Banks, J. A. (1978), 'A comment on Rosemary Crompton's "Approaches to the study of white-collar unionism" ', *Sociology*, vol. 12, no. 1

Banks, O. (1955), *Parity and Prestige in English Secondary Education*, London: Routledge & Kegan Paul

Banks, O. (1976), *The Sociology of Education*, London: Batsford

Barnes, J. (1954), 'Class and committees in a Norwegian island parish', *Human Relations*, vol. 7, pp. 39–58

Barnes, J. A. (1966), Durkheim's 'Division of Labour in Society', *Man*, (NS) (1), pp. 158–75

Barrett, M. (1980), *Women's Oppression Today*, London: Verso Editions

Becker, H. (1963), *Outsiders – Studies in the Sociology of Deviance*, NY: Free Press

Becker, H. (1967),'Whose side are we on?', *Social Problems*, vol. 14, no. 3

Bell, C. (1968), *Middle Class Families*, London: Routledge & Kegan Paul

Bell, C., and Newby, H. (1971), *Community Studies*, London: Allen & Unwin

Bell, C., and Newby, H. (1976a), 'Community, communion, class and community action: the social sources of the new urban politics', in D. T. Herbert and R. J. Johnston (eds), *Social Areas in Cities*, vol. 2, pp. 189–207, London: Wiley

Bell, C., and Newby, H. (1976b), 'Husbands and wives – the dynamics of the deferential dialectic', in D. Barker and S. Allen (eds), *Dependence and Exploitation in Work and Marriage*, London: Longman

Bell, C., and Newby, H. (1977) (eds), *Doing Sociological Research*, London: Allen & Unwin

Bell, D. (1960), *The End of Ideology*, Glencoe, Illinois.: Free Press

Bell, D. (1973), *The Coming of Post Industrial Society*, New York: Basic Books

Bell, D. (1977), *The Cultural Contradictions of Capitalism*, London: Heinemann

Bendix, R. (1956), *Work and Authority in Industry*, Berkeley and London: University of California Press

Bendix, R., and Fisher, L. H. (1965), 'The perspectives of Elton Mayo', in A. Etzioni (ed.), *Complex Organisations – a Sociological Reader*, New York: Holt, Rinehart & Winston

Bendix, R., and Lipset, S. (1967), *Class Status and Power: Social Stratification in Comparative Perspective*, London: Routledge & Kegan Paul

Benson, L. (1974), 'Market socialism and class structure – manual workers and managerial power in the Yugoslav enterprise', in F. Parkin (ed.), *The Social Analysis of Class Structures*, London: Tavistock

Benton, E. (1977), *The Philosophical Foundations of the Three Sociologies*, London: Routledge & Kegan Paul

Berg, I. (1970), *Education and Jobs – the Great Training Robbery*, Harmondsworth: Penguin Education

Berger, B. (1969), *Working-Class Suburb*, Cambridge: Cambridge University Press

Berger, P., and Berger, S. (1973), *The Homeless Mind – Modernisation and Consciousness*, New York: Random House

Berger, P., and Luckman, T. (1967), *The Social Construction of Reality*, London: Allen Lane, Penguin

Berle, A., and Means, G. (1932), *The Modern Corporation and Private Property*, NY: Harcourt Brace

Bernstein, B. (1971–7), *Class, Codes and Control*, 3 vols, London: Routledge & Kegan Paul

Bettelheim, B. (1971), *Children of the Dream*, St Albans: Paladin Paper Back

Beynon, H. (1973), *Working for Ford*, Harmondsworth: Penguin

Blackburn, R. (1972), (ed.), *Ideology and Social Science*, London: Fontana

Blackburn, R. M. (1967), *Union Character and Social Class*, London: Batsford

Blackburn, R. M., and Mann, M. (1978), *The Working Class in the Labour Market*, London: Macmillan

Blackburn, R. M., and Prandy, K. (1965), 'White-collar unionization: a conceptual framework', *British Journal of Sociology*, vol. 16, no. 2, pp. 111–22

Blainey, G. (1966), *The Tyranny of Distance*, Melbourne: Cheshire

Blau, P. (1963), *The Dynamics of Bureaucracy – a study of interpersonal relations in two governmental beaurocracies*, Chicago: Chicago University Press

Blauner, R. (1964), *Alienation and Freedom – The Factory Worker and His Industry*, Chicago University Press

Blood, R, and Wolfe, D. (1960), *Husbands and Wives*, London: Collier–Macmillan

Bluhm, H. (1948), 'How did they survive. . . ?' *American Journal of Psychotherapy* (January) vol. 2, no. 5, pp. 3–32

Blumberg, P. (1968), *Industrial Democracy – The Sociology of Participation*, London: Constable

Blumer, H. (1969), *Symbolic Interactionism – Perspective on Method*, Englewood Cliffs, NJ: Prentice–Hall

Bocock, R. (1976), *Freud and Modern Society*, London: Nelson

Boella, L. (1979), 'Eastern European societies', *Telos*, no. 41, Fall, pp. 59–75

Bott, E. (1957), *Family and Social Network*, London: Tavistock

Bottomore, T. (1964), *Elites and Society*, Harmondsworth: Penguin

Bottomore, T. (1965), *Classes in Modern Society*, London: Allen & Unwin

Bottomore, T., and Nisbet, R. (1978a), 'Structuralism', in T. Bottomore and R. Nisbet (eds), pp. 557–98, *A History of Sociological Analysis*, London: Heinemann

Bottomore, T. B., and Rubel, M. (1962), *Karl Marx: Selected Writings in Sociology and Social Philosophy*, Harmondsworth: Penguin

Bourdieu, P., and Passeron, J. C. (1977), *Reproduction in Education Society and Culture*, trans. R. Nice, London: Sage

Bowlby, J. (1968–80), *Attachment and Loss*, 3 vols, London: Hogarth

Bowles, S., and Gintis, H. (1973), 'I. Q. in the class structure', *Social Policy*, vol. 3, Jan./Feb., nos 4 and 5

Box, S. (1981), *Deviance, Reality and Society*, 2nd edn, London: Holt, Rinehart & Winston

Bradbury, M. (1975), *The History Man*, London: Secker & Warburg

Braithwaite, J. (1981), 'The myth of social class and criminality reconsidered', *American Sociological Review*, Feb., vol. 46, no. 1

Brake, M. (1980), *The Sociology of Youth Culture*, London: Routledge & Kegan Paul

Braverman, H. (1974), *Labour and Monopoly Capital*, New York: Monthly Review Press

Briggs, A. (1967), 'The language of "class" in early-nineteenth-century England', in A. Briggs and J. Saville (eds), *Essays in Labour History*, pp. 43–73, London: Macmillan

Brown, G. N., and Harris, T. (1978), *The Social Origins of Depression: A Study of Psychiatric Disorder in Women*, London: Tavistock

Brzezinski, Z., and Huntington, S. P. (1964), *Political Power, USA/USSR*, London: Chatto & Windus

Bulmer, M. (1975) (ed.), *Working-Class Images of Society*, London: Routledge & Kegan Paul

Burnham, J. (1945), *The Managerial Revolution*, Harmondsworth: Penguin

Burns, T. (1969) (ed.), *Industrial Man*, Harmondsworth: Penguin

Burns, T., and Stalker, G. (1961), *The Management of Innovation*, London: Tavistock

Burrow, J. W. B. (1966), *Evolution and Society*, Cambridge: Cambridge University Press

Butcher, H. (1968), *Human Intelligence, its Nature and Assessment*, London: Methuen

Caplan, A. L. (1978), *The Sociobiology Debate – Readings on Ethical and Scientific Issues*, New York: Harper & Row

Carchedi, G. (1977), *On the Economic Identification of Social Classes*, London: Routledge & Kegan Paul

Carlen, P. (1976), *Magistrates' Justice*, Oxford: Martin Robertson

Carter, R. (1979), 'Class, militancy and union character: a study of ASTMS', *Sociological Review*, vol. 27, no. 2, pp. 297–316

Castells, M. (1977), *The Urban Question*, London: Edward Arnold

Cattell, R. B. (1971), *Abilities – Their Structure, Growth and Action*, Boston: Houghton Mifflin

Chamblis, W. J., and Seidman, R. B. (1971), *Law, Order and Power*, Massachusetts: Addison–Wesley

Chinoy, E. (1955), *Automobile Workers and the American Dream*, New York: Doubleday

Chodorow, N. (1978), *The Reproduction of Mothering*, Los Angeles: University of California Press

Christie, R., and Jahoda, M. (1954), *Studies in the Scope and Method of the Authoritarian Personality*, Glencoe, Illinois: Free Press

Cicourel, A. V. (1968), *The Social Organisation of Juvenile Justice*, New York: Wiley

Clarke, J., and Jefferson, T. (1979), 'Working class youth cultures', in G. Mungham and G. Pearson (eds), *Working class youth culture*, London: Routledge & Kegan Paul

Clarke, J., Critcher, C. and Johnson, R. (1979) (eds), *Working Class Culture*, London: Hutchinson

Cliff, T. (1964), *Russia – A Marxist Analysis*, London: Socialist Review Publications

Clinard, M. B. (1964a) (ed.), *Anomie and Deviant Behaviour*, Glencoe, Illinois: Free Press

Clinard, M. B. (1964b), 'The theoretical implications of anomie and deviant behaviour', pp. 1–56 in M. B. Clinard (ed.), *Anomie and Deviant Behaviour*, Glencoe, Illinois: Free Press

Cloward, R., and Ohlin, L. (1960), *Delinquency and Opportunity – a Theory of Delinquent Gangs*, Chicago: Free Press

Cobban, A. (1975), *A History of Modern France* (1965), 3 vols, Harmondsworth: Penguin

Cockburn, C. (1978), *The Local State*, London: Pluto Press

Cockcroft, J. D., Frank, A. G., and Johnson, D. L. (1972) (eds), *Dependence and Underdevelopment: Latin America's Political Economy*, Garden City, NJ: Doubleday Anchor

Cohen, A. K. (1958), 'The sociology of the deviant act – Anomie theory and beyond', *American Sociological Review*, vol. 30, no. 1, pp. 5–14

Cohen, A. K. (1959), 'The study of social disorganization and deviant behaviour', in R. K. Merton, L. Broom and L. Cottrell (eds), *Sociology Today*, New York: Basic Books

Cohen, P. (1968), *Modern Social Theory*, London: Heinemann

Cohen, P. (1972), 'Sub-cultural conflict and working class community', Working Papers in Cultural Studies 2, University of Birmingham

Cohen, S. (1980), *Folk Devils and Moral Panics – the Creation of the Mods and Rockers*, 2nd edn., Oxford: Martin Robertson

Cohen, S., and Taylor, L. (1972), *Psychological Survival*, Harmondsworth: Penguin

Cohen, S., and Young, J. (1973), *The Manufacture of News*, London: Constable

Cole, R. (1971), *Japanese Blue Collar – the Changing Tradition*, Berkeley and London: California University Press

Coleman, B. I. (1973), *The Idea of the City in Nineteenth-Century Britain*, London: Routledge & Kegan Paul

Collins, R. (1980a), 'Weber's lost theory of capitalism – a systematization', *American Sociological Review*, vol. 45, no. 6, pp. 925–42.

Collins, R. (1980b), 'Erving Goffman and the development of modern social theory', in J. Ditton (ed.), *The View from Goffman*, London: Macmillan, pp. 170–209

Collins, R. (1981), 'On the micro-foundations of macro-sociology', *American Journal of Sociology*, vol. 86, no. 5, March

Comte, A. (1976), *The Foundations of Sociology*, readings edited and with an introduction by K. Thompson, London: Nelson

Converse, P. E. (1964), 'The nature of belief systems in mass publics', in D. E. Apter (ed.), *Ideology and Discontent*, Glencoe, Illinois: Free Press

Corrigan, P. (1979), *Schooling the Smash Kids*, London: Macmillan

Coser, L. A. (1956), *The Functions of Social Conflict*, Glencoe, Illinois: Free Press

Coser, L. A., and Rosenberg, B. (1964), *Sociological theory – a book of readings*, London: Macmillan

Cottrell, L. (1951), "Death by dieselisation – a case study in the reaction to technological change', in N. J. Smelser, *Readings on Economic Sociology*, Englewood Cliffs, N.J: Prentice–Hall

Cousins, J., and Brown, R. (1975), 'Patterns of paradox: shipbuilding workers' images of society', in M. Bulmer (ed.), *Working-Class Images of Society*, London: Routledge & Kegan Paul

Cowley, J., Kaye, A., Mayo, M., and Thompson, M. (1977) (eds) *Community or Class Struggle*, London: Stage One Books

Craib, I. (1976), *Existentialism and Sociology*, Cambridge: Cambridge University Press

Crompton, R. (1976), 'Approaches to the study of white-collar unionism', *Sociology*, vol. 10, no. 3

Crompton, R. (1979), 'Trade unionism and the insurance clerk', *Sociology*, vol. 13, no. 3

Crompton, R. (1980), 'The double proletarianization thesis', *Sociology*, vol. 14, no. 3

Crouch, C. (1975), 'The drive for equality – experience of incomes policy in Britain', in L. N. Lindberg, R. Alford, C. Crouch and C. Offe (eds), *Stress and Contradiction in Modern Capitalism*, Lexington: D. C. Heath

Crouch, C. (1977), *Class Conflict and the Industrial Relations Crisis*, London: Heinemann

Crouch, C. (1978), 'Inflation and the political organisation', in F. Hirsch and J. H. Goldthorpe (eds), *The Political Economy of Inflation*, Oxford: Martin Robertson, 1978

Crozier, M. (1964), *The Bureaucratic Phenomenon*, London: Tavistock

Dahrendorf, R. (1959), *Class and Class Conflict in Industrial Society*, London: Routledge & Kegan Paul

Davies, J. G. (1972), The Evangelistic Bureaucrat, London: Tavistock

Davis, H. H. (1979), *Beyond Class Images*, London: Croom Helm

Davis, K. (1960), 'The myth of functional analysis as a special method in sociology', reprinted in H. J. Demerath and R. Peterson (1967) (eds), *System Change and Conflict*, New York: Free Press/Macmillan

Davis, K., and Moore, W. E. (1967), 'Some principles of stratification', in R. Bendix and S. Lipset, *Class, Status and Power*, London: Routledge & Kegan Paul

Dawe, A. (1973), 'The underworld view of Erving Goffman', *British Journal of Sociology*, vol. 24, pp. 246–53

Dawe, A. (1978), 'Theories of social action', in T. Bottomore and R. Nisbet (eds.), *A History of Sociological Analysis*, London: Heinemann

Dawkins, R. (1976), *The Selfish Gene*, London: Oxford University Press

Delamont, R. (1980), *The Sociology of Women*, London: Allen & Unwin

De Mille, R. (1980), *The Don Juan Papers*, Santa-Barbara, Calif.: Ross-Erikson

Dennis, N. (1962), 'Secondary group relationships and the pre-eminence of the family', *International Journal of Comparative Sociology*, vol. 3, pp. 80–90

Dennis, N. (1968), 'The popularity of the neighbourhood community idea', pp. 74–92 in

R. E. Pahl (ed.), *Readings in Urban Sociology*, Oxford: Pergamon Press

Denzin, N. (1978), *The Research Act – a theoretical introduction to sociological methods*, New York: McGraw–Hill

Deutsch, M. *et al.* (1964), *The Disadvantaged Child*, New York: Van Nostrand

Diamond Report (1979), Royal Commission on the Distribution of Income and Wealth, *Report No. 7*, Cmnd 7595, London: HMSO

Diggins, J. P. (1978), *The Bard of Savagery – Veblen and Modern Social Theory*, New York: Harvester

Ditton, J. (1980), *The View from Goffman*, London: Macmillan

Djilas, M. (1957), *The New Class – An Analysis of the Communist System*, NY: Praeger

Donaldson, M. (1980), *Children's Minds*, Harmondsworth: Penguin

Donnison, David (1973), 'Micro-politics of the city', in D. Donnison and D. Eversley (eds), *London: Urban Patterns, Problems and Policies*, London: Heinemann

Donovan Report (1968), Royal Commission on Trade Unions and Employer Associations, 1965–8, Chairman Rt Hon. Lord Donovan, Cmnd 3623, London: HMSO

Dore, R. (1973), *British Factory/Japanese Factory*, London: Allen & Unwin

Dorfmann, J. (1961), *Thorstein Veblen and His America*, New York: F. Cass & Co.

Dos Santos, T. (1970), 'The structure of dependence', *American Economic Review*, vol. 60, no. 2, pp. 231–6

Douglas, J. (1967), *The Social Meanings of Suicide*, Princeton: Princeton University Press

Douglas, J. W. B.(1964), *The Home and the School*, London: McGibbon & Kee

Douglas, J. W. B., J. M. Ross and H. R. Simpson, (1968), *All Our Future*, London: P. Davies

Downes, D. (1966), *The Delinquent Solution*, London: Routledge & Kegan Paul

Dumont, L. (1970), *Homo Hierarchicus: the Caste System and Its Implications*, trans. M. Sainsbury, Chicago: Chicago University Press

Durkheim, E. (1952), *Suicide* (1897), London: Routledge & Kegan Paul

Durkheim, E. (1964a), *The Rules of Sociological Method* (1895), NY: The Free Press; London: Collier–Macmillan

Durkheim, E. (1964b), *The Division of Labour in Society* (1893), New York and London: Free Press/Macmillan

Durkheim, E. (1976), *The Elementary Forms of the Religious Life* (1915), London: Allen & Unwin

Durkheim, E., and Mauss, M. (1963), *Primitive Classification* (1901–2), English translation with an introduction by R. Needham; London: Cohen & West

Edgell, S. (1980), *Middle Class Couples*, London: Allen & Unwin

Eichler, M. (1980), *The Double Standard: A Feminist Critique of Feminist Social Science*, London: Croom Helm

Eisenstadt, S. (1964), 'Social change, differentiation and evolution', *American Sociological Review*, vol. 29, no. 3, pp. 375–86

Eisenstadt, S. (1967), Modernization, Protest and Change, New York: Prentice-Hall

Eldridge, J. E. T. (1971a) (ed.), *Max Weber: The Interpretation of Social Reality*, London: Nelson

Eldridge, J. E. T. (1971b), *Sociology and Industrial Life*, London: Nelson

Elias, N. (1970), *What is Sociology?*, London: Hutchinson

Emerson, R. (1969), *Judging Delinquents: Context and Process in the Juvenile Court*, Chicago: Aldine Press

Encel, S. (1970), *Equality and Authority*, Melbourne: Cheshire

Engels, F. (1972), *The Origins of the Family, Private Property and the State*, London: Lawrence & Wishart

Erikson, E. (1963), *Childhood and Society*, New York: Norton

Erikson, K. (1966), *Wayward Puritans*, New York: Wiley

Estrin, S. (1982), 'The effects of self-management on Yugoslavian industrial growth', *Soviet Studies*, vol. 34, no. 1, Jan., pp. 69–85

Etzioni, A. (1961), *A Comparative Analysis of Complex Organisations*, Glencoe, Illinois: Free Press

Etzioni, A. (1965), *Complex Organisations – A Sociological Reader*, New York: Holt, Rinehart & Winston

Eysenck, H. J., and Kamin, L. (1981), *Intelligence – the Battle for the Mind*, London and Sydney: Pan Books

Farber, B. (1965), 'Social class and intelligence', *Social Forces*, vol. 44, pp. 215–25.

Fischer, G. (1968), *The Soviet System and Modern Society*, London: Atherton

Fisher, B., and Strauss, A. L. (1978) 'Interactionism' in T. Bottomore and R. Nisbet (eds), *A History of Sociological Analysis*, London: Heinemann

Flanders A. (1975), 'Collective bargaining – a theoretical analysis', in A. Flanders, *Management and Unions*, London: Faber & Faber; first published in *British Journal of Industrial Relations*, March 1968

Flanders, A., and Fox, A. (1969), 'Collective bargaining – from Donovan to Durkheim', in A. Flanders, *Management and Unions*, London: Faber & Faber; first published in *British Journal of Industrial Relations*, July 1969

Fletcher, C. (1974), *Beneath the Surface*, London: Routledge & Kegan Paul

Fletcher, R. (1971), *The Making of Sociology – a Study of Sociological Theory*. Vol I: *Beginnings and Foundations*, London: Maxwell Joseph. Vol II: *Developments* London: Nelson

Fletcher, R. (1974), 'Evolutionary and developmental sociology', in J. Rex (ed.), *Approaches to Sociology*, London: Routledge & Kegan Paul

Floud, J. E., Halsey, A. H., and Martin, F. M. (1956), *Social Class and Educational Opportunity*, London: Heinemann

Flynn, J. R. (1980), *Race, I.Q. and Jensen*, London: Boston & Henley, Routledge & Kegan Paul

Foster, J. (1973), *Class Struggle and the Industrial Revolution*, London: Methuen

Fox, A. (1974) *Beyond Contract, Work Power and Trust Relations*, London: Faber & Faber

Fox, A. (1975), 'Collective bargaining, Flanders and the Webbs', *British Journal of Industrial Relations*, vol. 13, no. 2

Fox, R. (1967), *Kinship and Marriage*, Harmondsworth: Penguin

Fox, R. (1969), 'The cultural animal', in J. Eisenberg and W. S. Dillon (eds), *Man and Beast*, Washington: Smithsonian Institute Press

Francis, A. (1980), 'Families, firms and finance capital', *Sociology*, vol. 14, no. 1

Frank, A. G. (1966), 'The development of underdevelopment', in J. D. Cockroft, A. G. Frank and D. Johnson (eds.), (1972), *Dependence and Underdevelopment – Latin America's Political Economy*, Garden City, N.J.: Doubleday Anchor

Frank, A. G. (1969), *Capitalism and Underdevelopment in Latin America*, New York: Monthly Review Press

Frankenberg, R. (1965), *Communities in Britain*, Harmondsworth: Penguin

Freud, S. (1912), *Totem and Taboo*, vol. 13 of *The Complete Works of Sigmund Freud*, London: Hogarth

Freud, S. (1923), *The Ego and the Id*, vol. 19 of *The Complete Works of Sigmund Freud*, London: Hogarth

Freud, S. (1930), *Civilisation and its Discontents* vol. 21 *The Complete Works of Sigmund Freud*, London: Hogarth

Freund, J. (1968), *The Sociology of Max Weber*, London: Allen Lane & Penguin

Freund, J. (1978), 'German sociology in the time of Max Weber', in T. Bottomore and R. Nisbet (eds), *A History of Sociological Analysis*, London: Heinemann

Friedl, E. (1975), *Women and Men – and Anthropologist's View*, New York: Holt

Friedmann, G. (1961), *The Anatomy of Work*, London: Heinemann

Galbraith, J. K. (1967), *The New Industrial State*, Boston: Houghton Mifflin

Gallie, D. (1978), *In Search of the New Working Class*, Cambridge: Cambridge University Press

Galton, F. (1962), *Hereditary Genius* (1869), Cleveland and New York: Meridian Books, World Publishing

Gans, H. (1962a), 'Urbanism and suburbanism as ways of life', pp. 625–48 in A. M. Rose (ed), *Human Behaviour and Social Processes*, Boston: Houghton Mifflin

Gans, H. (1962b), *The Urban Villagers*, Glencoe, Illinois: Free Press

Gans, H. (1967), *The Levittowners*, London: Allen Lane

Garfinkel, H. (1967), *Studies in Ethnomethodology*, London: Prentice–Hall

Giddens, A. (1971), *Capitalism and Modern Social Theory*, Cambridge: Cambridge University Press

Giddens, A. (1972a), *Politics and Sociology in the Thought of Max Weber*, London: Macmillan

Giddens, A. (1972b) (ed.), *Emile Durkheim: Selected Writings*, Cambridge: Cambridge University Press

Giddens, A. (1972c), 'Four myths in the history of social theory', *Economy and Society*, vol. 1, no. 2

Giddens, A. (1973), *The Class Structure of the Advanced Societies*, London: Hutchinson

Giddens, A. (1976), Classical Theory and Modern Sociology, *American Journal of Sociology*, vol. 81, no. 4, Jan.

Giddens, A. (1977), 'Durkheim's political sociology', pp. 235–72; 'The 'individual' in the writings of Emile Durkheim', pp. 273–90; 'Durkheim on social facts', pp. 291–6; 'The suicide problem in French sociology', pp. 322–32; 'Functionalism: après la lutte', pp. 96–128; in *Studies in Social and Political Theory*, London: Hutchinson

Gilbert, M. (1981a), 'A sociological model of inflation', *Sociology*, vol. 15, no. 2, May

Gilbert, M. (1978), 'Neo-Durkheimian analyses of economic life and strife – from Durkheim to the Social Contract', *Sociological Review*, vol. 26, no. 4, Nov.

Gillespie, D. (1971), 'Who has the power? The marital struggle', *Journal of Marriage and the Family*, vol. 133, no. 3, pp. 445–58

Ginsberg, M. (1956), 'On the diversity of morals' (1953). Reprinted in M. Ginsberg (ed.), *Essays in Sociology and Social Philosophy*, vol. 1, London: Heinemann

Ginsburg, N. (1979), *Class, Capital and Social Policy*, London: Macmillan

Glasgow University Media Group (1977), *Bad News*, London: Routledge & Kegan Paul

Glasgow University Media Group (1980), *More Bad News*, London: Routledge & Kegan Paul

Glasgow University Media Group (1982), *Really Bad News*, London: Routledge & Kegan Paul

Glass, R. (1968), 'Conflict in the Cities', in CIBA Foundation Symposium, *Conflict in Society*, London: Churchill Press

Glucksman, M. (1974), *Structuralist Analysis in Contemporary Social Thought – a Comparison of the Theories of C. Levi Strauss and L. Althusser*, London: Routledge & Kegan Paul

Goffman, E. (1958), *The Presentation of Self in Everyday Life*, Harmondsworth: Penguin

Goffman, E. (1968), *Asylums* (1961), Harmondsworth: Penguin

Goldthorpe, J. H. (1966), 'Attitudes and behaviour of car assembly workers – a deviant case and a theoretical critique', *British Journal of Sociology*, vol. 27, no. 3, pp. 227–44

Goldthorpe, J. H. (1967), 'Social stratification in industrial society' in R. Bendix and S. Lipset (eds), *Class, Status and Power*, London: Routledge & Kegan Paul

Goldthorpe, J. H. (1972), 'Class, status and party in modern Britain: some recent interpretations, Marxist and Marxisant', *European Journal of Sociology*, vol. 13, pp. 342–72

Goldthorpe, J. H. (1973), 'A revolution in sociology?', *Sociology*, vol. 7, no. 3, pp. 448–62

Goldthorpe, J. H. (1974), 'Social inequality and social integration in modern Britain', in

D. Wedderburn (ed.), *Poverty, Inequality and Class Structure*, Cambridge: Cambridge University Press

Goldthorpe, J. H. (1978), 'The current inflation – towards a sociological account', in F. Hirsch and J. H. Goldthorpe (eds), *The Political Economy of Inflation*, Oxford: Martin Robertson

Goldthorpe, J. H. (1979), 'Intellectuals and the working class in modern Britain', Fuller Lecture, Department of Sociology, University of Essex

Goldthorpe, J. H. (1980), *Social Mobility and Class Structure in Modern Britain*, Oxford: Clarendon Press

Goldthorpe, J. H., and Llewelyn, C. (1977), 'Class mobility in modern Britain: three theses examined', *Sociology*, vol. 11, no. 2

Goldthorpe, J. H., and Lockwood, D. (1963), 'Affluence and the British class structure', *Sociological Review*, vol. 11, no. 2

Goldthorpe, J. H., Lockwood, D., Bechhoffer, F., and Platt, J. (1968), *The Affluent Worker: Industrial Attitudes and Behaviour*, Cambridge: Cambridge University Press

Goldthorpe, J. H., Lockwood, D., Bechhoffer, F., and Platt, J. (1969), *The Affluent Worker: Political Attitudes and Behaviour*, Cambridge: Cambridge University Press

Goldthorpe, J. H., Lockwood, D., Bechhoffer, F., and Platt, J. (1970), *The Affluent Worker in the Class Structure*, Cambridge: Cambridge University Press

Goode, W. J. (1965), 'The sociology of the family', in R. Merton, R. Broom and L. Cottrell (eds), *Sociology Today*, vol. 1, New York: Harper

Goode, W. J. (1970), *World Revolution and Family Patterns*, New York: Free Press

Gouldner, A. (1954), *Patterns of Industrial Bureaucracy*, Glencoe, Illinois: Free Press

Gouldner, A. (1955), *Wildcat Strike*, London: Routledge & Kegan Paul

Gouldner, A. (1959), 'Reciprocity and autonomy in functional theory', in L. Gross (ed.), *Symposium on Sociological Theory*, New York: Harper & Row

Gouldner, A (1965), 'Metaphysical pathos and the theory of bureaucracy', in A. Etzioni (ed.), *Complex Organizations – a Sociological Reader*, New York: Holt, Rinehart & Winston

Gouldner, A. (1968), 'The sociologist as partisan – sociology and the welfare state', *American Sociologist*, pp. 103–16. Reprinted in A. Gouldner (1973), *For Sociology*, London: Heinemann

Gouldner, A. (1971), *The Coming Crisis of Western Sociology*, London: Heinemann

Gowler, D., and Legge, K. (1978), 'Hidden and open contracts in marriage', in R. Rapoport, R. N. Rapoport and J. Bumstead (eds), *Working Couples*, London: Routledge and Kegan Paul

Green, R. W. (1973), *Protestantism, Capitalism and Social Science*, Lexington Mass.: D. C. Heath

Griffin, K. (1974), *The Political Economy of Agrarian Change*, London: Macmillan

Griffiths, D., and Saraga, E. (1979), 'Sex differences and cognitive abilities – a sterile field of inquiry?' in O. Hartnett, G. Booth and M. Fuller (eds), *Sex – Role Stereotyping – Connected Papers*, London: Tavistock

Gross, L., Mason, W. S. and McEachern, A. W. (1958), *Explorations in Role Analysis*, New York: Wiley

Guilford, J. P. (1967), *The Nature of Human Intelligence*, New York: McGraw–Hill

Gusfield, J. (1967), 'Tradition and modernity: misplaced polarities in the study of social change', *American Journal of Sociology*, vol. 72, pp. 118–34

Habermas, J. (1975), *Legitimation Crisis*, London: Heinemann

Haddon, R. F. (1970), 'A minority in a welfare state society: location of West Indians in the London housing market', *The New Atlantis*, vol. 1, no. 2, pp. 80–133

Halford, G. S. (1974), 'The impact of Piaget on psychology in the seventies', in B. Foss (ed.),

New Perspectives on Child Development, Harmondsworth: Penguin

Hall, S. (1977), 'The "political" and the "economic" in Marx's theory of classes', in A. Hunt (ed.), *Class and Class Structure*, London: Lawrence & Wishart

Hall, S. (1978), *Policing the Crisis – Mugging, The State and Law and Order*, London: Macmillan

Hall, S., and Jefferson, T. (1976) (eds), *Resistance Through Rituals*, London: Hutchinson

Halsey, A. H. (1958), 'Genetics, social structure and intelligence', *British Journal of Sociology*, vol. 9, pp. 15–28

Halsey, A. H., Heath, A. F., and Ridge, J. M. (1980), *Origins and Destinations*, Oxford: Clarendon Press

Hambley, J. (1972), 'Diversity – a developmental perspective', in A. Gartner, C. Greer and F. Riessman (eds), *The New Assault on Equality*, New York: Harper & Row

Hamilton, R. (1978), *The Liberation of Women*, London: Allen & Unwin

Handy, C. (1978), 'Going against the grain – working couples and greedy occupations', in R. Rapoport, R. N. Rapoport and J. Bumstead (eds), *Working Couples*, London: Routledge & Kegan Paul

Hannan, D., and Katiaouni, L. (1977), *Traditional Families? From Culturally Prescribed to Negotiated Roles in Farm Families*, Dublin: The Economic and Social Research Institute

Harris, C. (1969), *The Family*, London: Allen & Unwin

Harris, C. (1970) (ed.), *Readings on Kinship in Urban Society*, Oxford: Pergamon Press

Harris, M. (1968), *The Rise of Anthropological Theory*, London: Routledge & Kegan Paul

Harvey, D. (1973), *Social Justice and the City*, London: Edward Arnold

Hearnshaw, L. (1979), *Cyril Burt, Psychologist*, Ithaca: Cornell University Press

Hebb, D. O. (1949), *The Organisation of Behaviour*, New York: Wiley

Hebdige, D. (1979), *Subculture – the Meaning of Style*, London: Methuen

Heritage, J. (1980), 'Class situation, white collar unionization and the "double proletarianization" thesis: a comment', *Sociology*, vol. 14, no. 2

Hill, S. (1981), *Competition and Control at Work*, London: Heinemann

Hillery, G. A. (1955), 'Definitions of community: Areas of agreement', *Rural Sociology*, vol. 20, no. 2, pp. 111–23

Hinde, R. (1982), *Ethology*, Oxford: Fontana Master Guides

Hindess, B. (1973), *The Uses of Official Statistics*, London: Macmillan

Hirst, P., and Woolley, P. (1982), *Social Relations and Human Attributes*, London: Tavistock

Hirszowicz, M. (1980), *The Bureaucratic Leviathan – a study in the Sociology of Communism*, Oxford: Martin Robertson

Hobhouse, L., Wheeler, G., and Ginsberg, M. (1965), *The Material Culture and Social Institutions of the Simpler Peoples* (1915), London: Routledge & Kegan Paul

Hobsbawm, E. J. (1962), *The Age of Revolution*, 1789–1848, New York: Mentor

Hobsbawm, E. J. (1964), *Labouring Men*, London: Weidenfeld

Hobsbawm, E. J. (1969), *Industry and Empire*, Harmondsworth: Penguin

Hoggart, R. (1957), *The Uses of Literacy*, London: Chatto & Windus

Hoogveldt, A. (1978), *The Sociology of Developing Societies*, 2nd edn., London: Macmillan

Horn, J. M., Loehlin, J. C., and Willerman, L. (1979), 'Intellectual resemblance among adoptive and biological relatives: the Texas Adoption Project', *Behaviour Genetics*, vol. 9, pp. 177–207

Horowitz, D. (1967), *The Rise of Project Camelot*, Cambridge, Mass.: MIT Press

Horton, J. (1964), 'The dehumanisation of alienation and anomie – a problem in the ideology of sociology', *British Journal of Sociology*, vol. 15, no. 4, pp. 293–300

Horton J. E., and Thompson, W. E. (1962), 'Powerlessness and political negativism: a study of defeated local referendums', *American Journal of Sociology*, vol. 67, no. 5

Hoselitz, B., and Moore, W. (1963), *Industrialisation and Society*, The Hague: Mouton

Hough, G. (1969), *The Soviet Prefects*, Cambridge, Mass.: Harvard University Press

Hughes, H. S. (1959), *Consciousness and Society*, London: MacGibbon & Kee

Hughes, J. (1976), *Sociological Analysis: Methods of Discovery*, London: Nelson

Hunt, P. (1980), *Gender and Class Consciousness*, London: Macmillan

Hyman, R. (1975), foreword to 1975 edition of C. L. Goodrich, *The Frontier of Control*, Pluto Press

Ingham, G. (1970), *Size of Industrial Organisation and Worker Behaviour*, Cambridge: Cambridge University Press

Ingham, R. (ed.) (1978), *Football Hooliganism*, London: Inter-Action Imprints

Inkeles, A., and Bauer, R. (1959), *The Soviet Citizen – Daily Life in a Totalitarian Society*, Cambridge, Mass.: Harvard University Press

Jastak, J. F. (1969), 'Intelligence is more than measurement', *Harvard Educational Review*, vol. 39, pp. 608–11

Jencks, C. (1972), *Inequality – a reassessment of the effect of family and schooling in America*, New York: Basic Books

Jencks, C. (1979), *Who Gets Ahead?*, New York: Basic Books

Jensen, A. R. (1969), 'How much can we boost I.Q. and scholastic achievement?', *Harvard Educational Review*, vol. 39, pp. 1–123

Jensen, A. R. (1973), *Educability and Group Differences*, New York: Harper & Row

Jensen, A. R. (1980), *Bias in Mental Testing*, London: Methuen

Johnson, H. M. (1961), *Sociology: A Systematic Analysis*, London: Routledge & Kegan Paul

Jones, G. (1980), *Social Darwinism and English Thought – the Interaction between Biological and Social Theory*, Brighton: Harvester Press; New Jersey: Humanities Press

Jones, T. A. (1981), 'Durkheim, deviance and development – opportunities lost and regained', *Social Forces*, vol. 59, no. 4, June 1981

Kamin, L. (1974), *The Science and Politics of I.Q.*, Poltimac, Ma: Erlbaum Associates

Kamin, L. (1981), 'Commentary', pp. 477–81 in S. Scarr, *Race, Social Class and Individual Differences in I.Q.*, NJ: Erlbaum

Kaplan, S. (1977), *The Dream Deferred*, New York: Vintage Books

Keat, R. and Urry, J. (1975), *Social Theory as Science*, London: Routledge & Kegan Paul

Keller, S. (1968), *The Urban Neighbourhood: A Sociological Perspective*, New York: Random House

Kelsall, R. K., Poole, A., and Kuhn, A. (1972), *Graduates: the Sociology of an Elite*, London: Tavistock

Kerckhoff, A. C. (1965), 'Nuclear and extended family relationships', in E. Shanas and G. Streib (eds), *Social Structure and the Family*, Englewood Cliffs, NJ: Prentice–Hall

Kerr, C., Dunlop, J. T., Harbin, F. H., and Myers, C. (1960), *Industrialism and Industrial Man*, London: Heinemann

King, J. C. (1980), 'The genetics of sociobiology', in A. Montagu (ed.), *Sociobiology Re-examined*, Oxford: Oxford University Press

Klein, J. (1965), *Samples from English Cultures*, 2 vols, London: Routledge & Kegan Paul

Kolankiewicz, G. (1981), 'Poland 1980 – the working class under anomic socialism', in J. F. Triska and C. Gati (eds), *Blue Collar Workers in Eastern Europe*, London: Allen & Unwin

Komarowski, M. (1967), *Blue Collar Marriage*, New York: Random House

Konrad, G., and Szelenyi, I. (1979), *The Intellectuals on the Road to Class Power*, Brighton: Harvester Press

Kuhn, T. (1962), *The Structure of Scientific Revolutions*, Chicago: Chicago University Press

Kumar, K. (1976), 'Industrialism and post industrialism reflections on a putative transition', *Sociological Review*, vol. 24, no. 3, pp. 439–78

Kumar, K. (1978), *Prophecy and Progress*, London: Allen Lane

Labov, W. (1973), 'The logic of non standard English', in N. Keddie (ed.), *Tinker, Tailor . . . the Myth of Cultural Deprivation*, Harmondsworth: Penguin

Lancaster, J. B. (1976), *Sex Roles in Primate Societies*, pp. 22–61 in M. S. Tedelbaum (ed.), *Sex Differences*, New York: Anchor Books

Lane, D. (1971), *The End of Inequality*, Harmondsworth: Penguin

Lasch, (1978), *The Culture of Narcissism*, New York: Abacus Books

Laslett, P. (1971), *The World We Have Lost*, 2nd edn., London: Methuen

Laslett, P. (1977), *Family Life and Illicit Love in Earlier Generations*, Cambridge: Cambridge University Press

Lawler, I. R. (1975), *I.Q. Heritability and Racism – A Marxist Critique of Jensenism*, London: Lawrence & Wishart

Lawton, D. (1968), *Social Class, Language and Education*, London: Routledge & Kegan Paul

Leach, E. (1961), *Rethinking Anthropology* London: Athlone Press

Leakey, R., and Lewin, R. (1979), *The People of the Lake*, London: Collins

Leggatt, (1968), *Class, Race, and Labour*, New York: Oxford University Press

Lemert, E. (1964), 'Social structure, social control and deviation', pp. 57–97 in M. B. Clinard (ed.), *Anomie and Deviant Behaviour*, Gencoe, Illinois: Free Press

Lemert, E. (1972) (ed.), *Human Deviance, Social Problems and Social Control*, Englewood Cliffs, NJ: Prentice–Hall

Lenin, V. I. (1902a), *The State and Revolution*, Moscow: Progress Publishers

Lenin, V. I. (1902b), *What is to be done?*, Moscow: Progress Publishers

Lenski, G. (1966), *Power and Privilege*, New York: McGraw–Hill

Lerner, D. (1958), *The Passing of Traditional Society*, New York: Free Press

Lessnoff, M. (1974), The Structure of Social Science – a philosophical introduction, London: Allen & Unwin

Levy, M. (1964), *The Structure of Society* (1952), Princetown University Press

Lewis, J. (1975), *Max Weber and Value Free Sociology*, London: Lawrence & Wishart

Lewis, O. (1949), *Life in a Mexican Village*, Urbana: University of Illinois Press

Lewis, O. (1953), 'Controls and experiments in fieldwork', in A. R. Kroeber *et al.* (eds), *Anthropology Today*, Chicago: University of Chicago Press

Liebow, E. (1967), *Tally's Corner*, Boston: Little Brown

Lipset, S. M. (1960), 'The political process in trade unions', in W. Galenson and S. M. Lipset (eds), *Labour and Trade Unionism*, New York: Wiley

Lipsey, R. (1979), *An Introduction to Positive Economics*, 5th edn., London: Weidenfield & Nicolson

Littlejohn, J. (1963), *Westrigg*, London: Routledge & Kegan Paul

Litwak, E. V. (1965), 'Extended kin relations in an industrial democratic society', in E. Shanas and G. Streib, *Social Structure and the Family*, Englwood Cliffs, NJ: Prentice–Hall

Locke, J. (1975), *An Essay Concerning Human Understanding* (1689), Oxford: Clarendon Press

Lockwood, D. (1955), 'Arbitration and industrial conflict', *British Journal of Sociology*, vol. 4, no. 4

Lockwood, D. (1956), 'Some remarks on "The social system" ', *British Journal of Sociology*, vol. 7, no. 2

Lockwood, D. (1964), 'Social integration and system integration', pp. 244–56 in G. Zollschan and W. Hirsch (eds), *Explorations in Social Change*, London: Routledge & Kegan Paul

Lockwood, D. (1966), 'The sources of variation in working class images of society', *Sociological Review*, vol. 14, no. 3. pp. 249–63

Lockwood, D. (1970), 'Race, conflict and plural society', in S. Zubaida (ed.), *Race and Racialism*, London: Tavistock

Lockwood, D. (1981), 'The weakest link in the chain? Some comments on the Marxist theory of action', pp. 435–81 in S. Simpson and I. Simpson (eds), *Research in the Sociology of Work*, vol. 1, Greenford, Conn.: JA1 Press

Loechlin, J., Lindsey, G., and Spuhler, J. N. (1975), *Race Differences in Intelligence*, San Francisco: Freeman

Lofland, J. (1969), *Deviance and Identity*, Englewood Cliffs, NJ: Prentice–Hall

Long, N. (1977), *An Introduction to the Sociology of Rural Development*, London: Tavistock

Lorenz, K. (1963), *On Aggression*, London: Methuen

Lukacs, G. (1971), *History and Class Consciousness*, (1934), London: Merlin

Lukes, S. (1975), *Emile Durkheim*, Harmondsworth: Penguin

Lukes, S. (1977), 'Methodological individualism reconsidered', in S. Lukes, *Essays in Social Theory*, London: Macmillan

Lupton, T., and Wilson, C. (1973), 'The social background and connections of top decision-makers' (1959), in J. Urry and J. Wakeford, *Power in Britain*, London: Heinemann

Lurie, A. (1967) *Imaginary Friends*, Harmondsworth: Penguin Books

Lyons, J. (1970), *Chomsky*, London: Fontana

McClelland, D. C. (1961), *The Achieving Society*, Princeton: Van Nostrand

Maccoby, E. E., Jacklin, C. N. (1975), *The Psychology of Sex Differences*, London: Tavistock

MacFarlane, A. (1978), *Reconstructing Historical Communities*, Cambridge: Cambridge University Press

McIntosh, M. (1978), 'The state and the oppression of women', in A. Kuhn and A. M. Wolpe (eds), *Feminism and Materialism*, London: Routledge & Kegan Paul

McNally, F. (1979), *Women for Hire*, London: Macmillan

MacPherson, C. B. (1962), *The Political Theory of Possessive Individualism*, Oxford: Oxford University Press

Maitland, I. (1979) 'Disorder in the British work-place – the limits of consensus, *British Journal of Industrial Relations*, vol. xviii, no. 3, pp. 353–64

Malinowski, (1944), *A Scientific Theory of Culture*, Chapel Hill: University of Carolina Press

Mallet, S. (1975), *The New Working Class* (1969), Nottingham: Spokesman

Mandelstam, N. (1975), *Hope Against Hope*, Harmondsworth: Penguin

Mann, M. (1970), 'The social cohesion of liberal democracy', *American Sociological Review*, vol. 35, no. 3

Mann, M. (1973a), *Consciousness and Action in the Western Working Class*, London: Macmillan

Mann, M. (1973b), *Workers on the Move*, Cambridge: Cambridge University Press

Mann, P. M. (1965), *An Approach to Urban Sociology*, London: Routledge & Kegan Paul

Marcuse, H. (1964), *One-dimensional Man*, London: Sphere

Marczewski, J. (1979), 'The problem of consumption in Soviet-type economies', *Soviet Studies*, vol. 31, no. 1, Jan., pp. 112–17

Marsh, P. (1978), *Agro – the illusion of violence*, London: Dent

Marshall, G. (1980), *Presbyteries and profits: Calvinism and the Development of Capitalism in Scotland, 1560–1707*, Oxford: Oxford University Press

Marshall, G. (1982), In *Search of the Spirit of Capitalism*, London: Hutchinson

Martins, H. (1974), 'Time and theory in sociology', in J. Rex (ed.), *Key Problems of Social Theory*, London: Routledge & Kegan Paul

Marx, K. (1970), *Capital, vol. 1*, London: Lawrence & Wishart

Marx, K. (1972), *Capital, vol. 3*, London: Lawrence & Wishart

Marx, K. (1975), 'Preface' to A Contribution to the Critique of Political Economy, in *Karl Marx: Early Writings*, Harmondsworth: Penguin

Marx, K., and Engels, F. (1969), *The Manifesto of the Communist Party*, Harmondsworth: Penguin

Marx, K. and Engels, F. (1970), *The German Ideology*, London: Lawrence & Wishart

Matthews, M. (1972), *Class and Society in Soviet Russia*, London: Allen Lane, Penguin

Matza, D. (1964), *Delinquency and Drift*, New York: Wiley

Matza, D. (1969), *Becoming Deviant*, Englewood Cliffs, NJ: Prentice–Hall

Mayer, P. (1962), 'Migrancy and the study of African towns', *American Anthropologist*, vol. 64, no. 4, pp. 572–92

Mayo, E. (1949), *The Social Problems of an Industrial Civilisation*, London: Routledge & Kegan Paul

Mayo, E. (1959), *The Human Problems of an Industrial Civilisation*, Cambridge, Mass: Harvard University Press

Mead, G. (1934), *Mind, Self and Society*, Chicago: University of Chicago Press

Mead, M. (1963), *Sex and Temperament in Three Primitive Societies*, New York: Morrow

Meisel, J. (1962), *The Myth of the Ruling Class*, Ann Arbour: Greenwood Press

Meltzer, B. N., Petras, J. W., and Reynolds, L. T. (1975), *Symbolic Interactionism – Genesis, Varieties and Criticism*, London: Routledge & Kegan Paul

Mennel, S. (1974), *Sociological Theory: Uses and Unities*, London: Nelson

Menzies, K. (1977), *Talcott Parsons and the Social Image of Man*, London: Routledge & Kegan Paul

Merton, R. K. (1959), 'Social Conflict over styles of sociological work', *Transactions of the Fourth World Congress of Sociology*, vol. 3, pp. 21–44

Merton, R. K. (1964), 'Anomie, Anomia and Social Interaction – contexts of deviant behaviour', in M. Clinard (ed.) *Anomie and Deviant Behaviour*, Glencoe, Illinois: Free Press

Merton, R. K. (1966), 'Social Problems and Sociological Theory', in R. K. Merton and R. Nisbet (eds) *Contemporary Social Problems*, New York: Harcourt Brace & World

Merton, R. K. (1968a) 'Manifest and Latent Functions' (pp. 73–138), (1968b), 'Social Structure and Anomie' (pp. 185–214), (1968c), 'Bureaucratic Structure and Personality' (pp. 249–60), in R. K. Merton (ed.), *Social Theory and Social Structure* (1957) Enlarged edition, Glencoe, Illinois: Free Press

Michels, R. (1962), *Political Parties* (1911), New York: Collier

Midgeley, M. (1979), *Beast and Man – the roots of human nature*, London: Harvester

Midgeley, M. (1980), 'Gene-juggling and rival fatalisms', in A. Montague (ed.), *Sociology Re-examined*, Oxford: Oxford University Press

Miliband, R. (1969), *The State in Captialist Society*, London: Weidenfeld & Nicolson

Miliband, R. (1977), *Marxism and Politics*, Oxford: Oxford University Press

Miller, W. (1958), 'Lower class culture as a generating mileu of gang delinquency', *Journal of Social Issues*, vol. 14, pp. 5–19

Mills, C. W. (1959), *The Sociological Imagination*, Oxford: Oxford University Press

Mitchell, J. (1971), *Woman's Estate*, Harmondsworth: Penguin

Mitchell, J. (1974), *Psychoanalysis and Feminism*, Harmondsworth: Penguin

Mitchell, J. C. (1969) (ed.), *Social Networks in Urban Situations*, Manchester: Manchester University Press

Mitchell, J. C., and Boissevain, J. (1972) (eds), *Network Analysis: Studies in Human Interaction*, Paris: Mouton

Molyneux, M. (1979), 'Beyond the domestic labour debate', *New Left Review*, no. 116

Mommsen, W. J. (1974), *The Age of Bureaucracy*, Oxford: Basil Blackwell

Montagu, A. (1980) (ed.), *Sociobiology Re-examined*, Oxford: Oxford University Press

Moore, B. (1969), *The Social Origins of Dictatorship and Democracy*, Harmondsworth: Penguin Books

Moore, W. E. (1978), 'Functionalism', pp. 321–61 in T. Bottomore and R. Nisbet (eds), *A History of Sociological Analysis*, London: Heinemann

Moorhouse, H. R. (1976), 'Attitudes to class and class relationship in Britain', *Sociology*, vol. 10, no. 3

Morgan, D. (1975), *Social Theory and the Family*, London: Routledge & Kegan Paul

Morris, D. (1967), *The Naked Ape – a Zoologist's Study of the Human Animal*, London: Jonathan Cape

Mosca, G. (1960), *The Ruling Class* (1939), New York: McGraw–Hill

Mouzelis, N. (1967), *Organisation and Bureaucracy*, London: Routledge & Kegan Paul

Mungham, G., and Pearson, G. (1976), *Working Class Youth Culture*, London: Routledge & Kegan Paul

Murdock, G. P. (1949), *Social Structure*, New York: Free Press; London: Collier Macmillan

Murphy, R. (1972), *The Dialectics of Social Life*, London: Allen & Unwin

National Foundation for Educational Research (1982): Assessment of Performance Unit, Primary Survey: *Report no. 2: Mathematical Development*: Secondary Survey Report no. 2, London: Department of Education and Science

New Left Review (1977) (ed.), *Western Marxism – a Critical Reader*, London: New Left Books

Newby, H. (1977), *The Deferential Worker*, London: Allen Lane

Newson, J., and Newson, E. (1963), *Patterns of Infant Care in an Urban Community*, Harmondsworth: Penguin

Newson, J., and Newson, E. (1968), *Four years old in an Urban Community*, London: Allen & Unwin

Newson, J., and Newson, E. (1976), *Seven years Old in the Home Environment*, London: Allen & Unwin

Nichols T. (1969), *Ownership, Control and Ideology*, London: Allen & Unwin

Nichols, T., and Armstrong, P. (1979) *Workers Divided*, London: Fontana

Nichols, T., and Beynon, H, (1977), *Living with Capitalism*, London: Routledge & Kegan Paul

Nisbet, R. (1967), *The Sociological Tradition*, London: Heinemann

Noble, T. (1975), *Modern Britain*, London: Batsford

Noble, T. (1982), *Structure and Change in Modern Britain*, London: Batsford

Oakley, A. (1972), *Sex, Gender, and Society*, London: Maurice Temple Smith

Oakley, A. (1976a), *The Sociology of Housework*, London: Martin Robertson

Oakley, A. (1976b), *Housewife*, Harmondsworth: Penguin

Oakley, A. (1981), *Subject Women*, London: Martin Robertson

O'Connor, J. (1976), *The Fiscal Crisis of the State*, New York: St Martin's Press

Offe, C. (1975), 'The theory of the capitalist state and the problem of policy formation', in Leon Lindberg *et al.* (eds) *Stress and Contradiction in Modern Capitalism*, Lexington, Mass: D. C. Heath

Ogburn, W. F. (1964), *On Culture and Social Change: Selected Papers*, Chicago and London: Chicago University Press

Ossowski, (1963), *Class Structure in the Social Consiousness*, London: Routledge & Kegan Paul

Outhwaite, W. (1975), *Understanding Social Life*, London: Allen & Unwin

Pahl, J, (1980), 'Patterns of money management within marriage', *Journal of Social Policy*, vol. 9, no. 3, pp. 315–35

Pahl, J., and Pahl, R. E. (1971), *Managers and*

their Wives – a Study of Career and Family Relations in the Middle Class, London: Allen Lane

Pahl, R. E. (1965), *Urbs in Rure*, London: Weidenfeld & Nicolson

Pahl, R. E. (1966), 'The rural–urban continuum', *Sociologica Ruralis*, vol. 6, no. 3/4, pp. 299–329

Pahl, R. E. (1970), *Whose City?*, London: Longman

Pahl, R. E., and Winkler, J. T. (1974), 'The economic elite: theory and practice', in P. Stanworth and A. Giddens (eds), *Elites and Power in British Society*, Cambridge: Cambridge University Press

Parkin, F. (1978), *Marxism and Class Theory: A bourgeois critique*, London: Tavistock

Parkin, F. (1982), *Max Weber*, London: Tavistock

Parsons, T. (1951), *The Social System*, London: Routledge & Kegan Paul

Parsons, T. (1954), 'A revised analytical approach to the theory of social stratification', in T. Parsons, *Essays in Sociological Theory*, Glencoe, Illinois: Free Press

Parsons, T. (1957), 'The distribution of power in American society', *World Politics*, vol. 10, no. 2, pp. 123–43

Parsons, T. (1967), *Social Theory and Modern Society*, New York: Free Press

Parsons, T. (1966), *Societies: Evolutionary and Comparative Perspectives*, New York: Prentice–Hall

Parsons, T. (1969), *The Structure of Social Action*, (1937), McGraw–Hill; New York: Free Press

Parsons, T. and Bales, R. F. (1956) (eds), *Family, Socialisation and Interaction Process*, London: Routledge & Kegan Paul

Parsons, T., Bales, R. F., and Shils, E. A. (1968), *Working Papers in the Theory of Action* (1953), New York: Free Press

Parsons, T., and Shils, E. (1951), *Towards a General Theory of Action*, Cambridge, Mass.: Harvard University Press

Parsons, T., and Smelser, N. (1956), *Economy and Society – a Study in the Integration of Economic and Social Theory*, London: Routledge & Kegan Paul

Pearce, F. (1976), *The Crimes of the Powerful*, London: Pluto Press

Peel, J. (1971), *H. Spencer – the Evolution of a Sociologist*, London: Heinemann

Perrow, C. (1972), *Complex Organisations – a Critical Essay*, Glenview, Mass.: Scott Foresman

Phizacklea, A., and Miles, R. (1980), *Labour and Racism*, London: Routledge & Kegan Paul

Piachaud, D. (1981), 'Peter Townsend and the Holy Grail', *New Society* (10 September), pp. 419–21

Platt, T., and Tagaki, P. (1980), 'Biosocial criminology – a critique', *Crime and Social Justice*, Spring/Summer, pp. 5–13

Plummer, K. (1975), *Sexual Stigma*, London: Routledge & Kegan Paul

Plummer, K. (1979), 'Misunderstanding labelling perspectives', in D. Downes and P. Rock (eds), *Deviant Interpretations*, London: Martin Robertson

Pope, W. (1976), *Durkheim's Suicide – a Classic Analysed*, Chicago: Chicago University Press

Poulantzas, N. (1975), *Political Power and Social Classes*, London: New Left Books

Poulantzas, N. (1976), *Classes in Contemporary Capitalism*, London: New Left Books

Price, F. V. (1981), 'Only connect? Issues in Charting social networks', *Sociological Review*, May, vol. 129, no. 2, pp. 283–312

Pryce, K. (1979), *Endless Pressure*, Harmondsworth: Penguin

Radcliffe-Brown, A. (1952), *Structure and Function in Primitive Society*, London: Oxford University Press

Rapoport, R., Rapoport, R. N., and Bumstead, J. M. (eds) (1978), *Working Couples*, London: Routledge & Kegan Paul

Redfield, R. (1947), 'The folk society', *American Journal of Sociology*, vol. 52, no. 3, pp. 293–308

Redfield, R. (1968), *The Primitive World and its Transformations*, Harmondsworth: Penguin

Reiter, R. (1975), *Towards an Anthropology of Women*, New York: Monthly Review Press

Renvoize, J. (1982), *Incest – a Family Pattern*, London: Routledge & Kegan Paul

Rex, J. (1961), *Key Problems of Social Theory*, London: Routledge & Kegan Paul

Rex, J. (1974) (ed.), *Approaches to Sociology*, London: Routledge & Kegan Paul

Rex, J., and Moore, R. (1967), *Race, Community and Conflict*, Oxford: Institute of Race Relations and Oxford University Press

Reynolds, V. (1980), *The Biology of Human Action*, Oxford: W. H. Freeman

Rickert, H. (1962), *Science and History*, trans. G. Reisman, Princeton: Van Nostrand

Ritzer, G., and Bell, R. (1981), 'Emile Durkheim – examplar for an integrated sociological paradigm?', *Social Forces*, vol. 59, no. 4, June, pp. 966–95

Roazen, P. (1969), *Freud, Social and Political Thought*, London: Hogarth

Roberts, B. C. *et al.* (1972), *Reluctant Militants*, London: Heinemann

Roberts, K., Cook, F. G., Clark, S. C., Semenoff, E. (1977), *The Fragmentary Class Structure*, London: Heinemann

Rocher, G. (1974), *Talcott Parsons and American Sociology*, London: Nelson

Rock, P. (1973), *Deviant Behaviour*, London: Hutchinson

Rock, P. (1979a), *The Making of Symbolic Interactionism*, London: Macmillan

Rock, P. (1979b), 'The sociology of symbolic interactionism and some problematic qualities of radical criminology', in D. Downes and P. Rock (eds), *Deviant Interpretations*, London: Martin Robertson

Rogers, M. F. (1980), 'Goffman on power hierarchy and status', pp. 100–33 in J. Ditton (ed.), *The View from Goffman*, London: Macmillan

Rose, M. (1975), *Industrial Behaviour*, London: Allen Lane, Penguin

Rosser, C., and Harris, C. (1965), *The Family and Social Change*, London: Routledge & Kegan Paul

Rostow, W. (1960), *The Stages of Economic Growth*, Cambridge: Cambridge University Press

Runciman, W. G. (1966), *Relative Deprivation and Social Justice*, London: Routledge & Kegan Paul

Runciman, W. G. (1972), *A Critique of Max Weber's Philosophy of Social Science*, Cambridge: Cambridge University Press

Rutter, M. (1972), *Maternal Deprivation Reassessed*, Harmondsworth: Penguin

Rutter, M., and Madge, N. (1976), *Cycles of Disadvantage*, London: Heinemann

Ryan, A. (1972), *The Philosophy of the Social Sciences*, London: Macmillan

Ryan, A. (1970), (ed.), *The Philosophy of Social Explanation*, Oxford: Oxford University Press

Safilios-Rothschild, C. (1969), 'Family sociology or wives' family sociology?', *Journal of Marriage and the Family*, vol. 31, vol. 2, pp. 290–301

Safilios-Rothschild, C., and Georgioupoulos, (1970), 'A comparative study of parental and filial role definitions', *Journal of Marriage and the Family*, vol. 32, no. 3, pp. 381–9

Sahay, A. (1971), 'The importance of Weber's methodology in sociological explanation', in A. Sahay, *Max Weber and Modern Sociology*, London: Routledge & Kegan Paul

Sahlins, M. (1977), *The Use and Abuse of Biology*, London: Tavistock

Sahlins, M. D., and Service, E. R. (1960), *Evolution and Culture*, Michigan: University of Michigan Press

Salaman, G. (1979), *Work Organisations – Resistance and Control*, London: Longman

Scanzoni, J. H. (1977), *The Black Family in Modern Society*, Chicago: University of Chicago Press

Scarr, S. (1981), *Race, Social Class and Individual Differences in I.Q*, New Jersey: Lawrence Erlbaum

Scarr, S., and Weinberg, R. (1978), 'Attitudes, interest and I.Q.', *Human Nature*, vol. 1, no. 4, pp. 29–36

Schaffer, R. (1977), *Mothering*, London: Fontana

Schlesinger, P. (1978), *Putting Reality Together*, London: Constable

Schmalenbach, H. (1961), 'The sociological category of communism', pp. 331–47 in T. Parsons and E. Shils (eds), *Theories of Society*, vol. 1, Glencoe, Illinois: Free Press

Schur, E. (1971), *Labelling Deviant Behaviour*, New York: Harper & Row

Schutz, A. (1964), *Collected Papers*, 2 vols, The Hague: Nijhoff

Scott, J. (1979), *Corporations, Classes and Capitalism*, London: Hutchinson

Scott, J. (1982), *Property and Privilege: the Development of the Privileged Classes in Britain*, London: Macmillan

Seckler, D. (1975), *Thorstein Veblen and the Institutionalists – a Study in the Social Philosophy of Economics*, London: Macmillan

Selznick, P. (1943), 'An approach to the theory of bureaucracy', *American Sociological Review*, vol. 8, pp. 47–54

Selznick, P. (1966), *T.V.A. and the Grassroots: a Study in the Sociology of Formal Organisation*, New York: Harper & Row

Sennett, R. (1977), *The Fall of Public Man*, Cambridge: Cambridge University Press

Shaw, C., and Mackay, H. (1942), *Juvenile Delinquency and Urban Areas*, Chicago: Chicago University Press

Shaw, M. (1974), *Marxism versus Sociology – a Guide to Reading*, London: Pluto Press

Sheleff, L. S. (1975), 'From restitutive law to repressive law – Durkheim's *The Division of Labour in Society* revisited', *Archives Européennes de Sociol.*, vol. 16, no. 1, pp. 16–45

Shibutani, T. (1962), 'Reference Groups and Social Control', in A. M. Rose (ed.), *Human Behaviour and Social Processes*, London: Routledge & Kegan Paul

Shimkin, D. B., Shimkin, E. M., Trate, D. A. (1978) (eds), *The Extended Family in Black Societies*, The Hague: Mouton

Short, J. F. (1964), 'Gang delinquency and Anomie', pp. 98–127 in M. B. Clinard (ed.), *Anomie and Deviant Behaviour*, Glencoe, Illinois: Free Press

Short, J. F., and Strodtbeck, F. L. (1965), *Group Process and Gang Delinquency*, Chicago: Chicago University Press

Silverman, D. (1975), *Reading Castaneda*, London: Routledge & Kegan Paul

Simmel, G. (1950), 'The metropolis and mental life', pp. 409–24 in K. Wolf (ed.), *The Sociology of George Simmel*, Glencoe, Illinois: Free Press

Simmel, G. (1971), 'The problem of sociology', in G. Simmel, *On Individuality and Social Forms*, edited with an introduction by D. Levine, Chicago: University of Chicago Press

Simon, B. (1974), *The Politics of Educational Reform*, London: Lawrence & Wishart

Singer, M. (1961), 'A survey of culture and personality theory and research', pp. 9–92 in B. Kaplan (ed.)., *Studying Personality Cross-Culturally*, New York: Harper & Row

Skolnik, A., and Skolnik, J. H. (1974), *Intimacy, Family and Society*, Boston: Little Brown

Slater, P. (1974), 'Parental role differentiation', in R. Coser (ed.), *The Family: Its Structure and Functions*, New York: St Martin's Press

Smelser, N. J. (1959), *Social Change in the Industrial Revolution*, London: Routledge & Kegan Paul

Smelser, N. J. (1963), 'Mechanisms of change and adjustment to change', in B. Hoselitz and W. E. Moore (eds), *Industrialisation and Society*, Unesco–Mouton

Smith, A. (1973), *The Concept of Social Change*, London: Routledge & Kegan Paul

Smith, M. G. (1966), 'Pre-industrial stratification systems', in N. Smelser and S. Lipset (eds), *Social Structure and Mobility in Economic Development*, London: Routledge & Kegan Paul

Smith, P. K. (1974), 'Ethological methods', in B. Foss (ed.), *New Perspectives on Child Development*, Harmondsworth: Penguin

Sorokin, P. A., and Zimmerman, C. C. (1929), *Principles of Rural–Urban Sociology*, New York: Hinny Holt

Spencer, H. (1971), *Structure, Function and Evolution*, readings, edited with an introduction by S. Andreski, London: Nelson

Spergel, I. (1964), *Racketville, Slumtown, Haulburg – an Exploratory Study of Delinquent Subcultures*, Chicago: University of Chicago Press

Spiro, M. E. (1979), *Gender and Culture – Kibbutz Women Revisited*, New York: Schoken

Srinavas, M. (1962), *Caste in Modern India*, New York: Asia Publishing House

Stacey, M. (1969), 'The myth of community studies', *British Journal of Sociology*, vol. 20, no. 2, pp. 34–147

Stammler, O. (1971) (ed.), *Max Weber and Sociology Today*, Oxford: Basil Blackwell

Stanmer, W. (1975), 'Reflections on Durkheim and aborigine religion', in W. Pickering (ed.), *Durkheim on Religion*, London: Routledge & Kegan Paul

Stein, M. (1964), *The Eclipse of Community*, New York: Harper & Row

Steward, J. (1955), *Theory of Culture Change*, Urbana: University of Illinois Press

Stinchcombe, A. (1968), *Constructing Social Theories*, New York: Harcourt Brace & World

Stone, G. P., and Farberman, H. A. (1970), 'On the edge of *rapprochement*: was Durkheim moving towards the perspective of symbolic interaction?', pp. 100–12 in G. P. Stone and H. A. Faberman (eds), *Social Psychology through Symbolic Interaction*, Waltham: Ginn–Blandsell

Stone, M. (1981), *The Education of the Black Child in Britain – the Myth of Multiracial Education*, London: Fontana

Strouse, J. (1974) (ed.), *Women and Analysis*, New York: Dell

Sulloway, J. (1981), *Freud – Biologist of the Mind*, London: Fontana

Sussman, M. B. (1965), 'Relations of adult children with their parents', in E. Shanas and G. Streib (eds), *Social Structure and the Family*, Englewood Cliffs, NJ: Prentice–Hall

Sutherland, E. H. (1961), *White Collar Crime* (1949), New York: Dryden

Sutherland, E. H., and Cressey, D. (1966), *Principles of Criminology*, 7th edn, Philadelphia: J. P. Lippincott

Swanson, G. (1960), *The Birth of the Gods – the origins of primitive belief*, Michigan: University of Michigan Press

Sweezy, P. (1956), *The Theory of Capitalist Development*, New York: Monthly Review Press

Swift, D. (1972), 'What is the environment?', in K. Richardson and D. Speirs (eds), *Race, Culture and Intelligence*, Harmondsworth: Penguin

Talmon, Y. (1972), *Family and Community in the Kibbutz*, Cambridge, Mass.: Harvard University Press

Talmon, Y. (1977), Review of Tiger and Shepher (1976), *Journal of Marriage and The Family*, vol. 39, no. 2, pp. 626–8

Taylor, I. Walton, P., and Young, J. (1973), *The New Criminology*, London: Routledge & Kegan Paul

Taylor, J. (1979), *From Modernization to Modes of Production*, London: Macmillan

Taylor, L. (1972), 'The significance and interpretation of replies to motivational questions: the case of the sex offender', *Sociology*, vol. 6, no. 1, pp. 23–40

Therborn, G. (1978), *What Does a Ruling Class Do When It Rules?* London: New Left Books

Thompson, E. P. (1963), *The Making of the English Working Class*, London: Gollancz

Thompson, E. P. (1965), 'The peculiarities of the English', *Socialist Register*, pp. 311–62

Thompson, E. P. (1967), 'Time, work-discipline and industrial capitalism', *Past and Present*, no. 38, pp. 56–97

Thompson, E. P. (1978), *The Poverty of Theory*, London: Merlin

Tiger, L., and Fox, R. (1974), *The Imperial Animal*, London: Paladin

Tiger, L., and Shepher, J. (1976), *Women in the Kibbutz*, New York: Harcourt Brace & World

Titmuss, R. (1962), *Income Distribution and Social Welfare*, London: Allen & Unwin

Tizard, B., Cooperman, O., Joseph, A., and Tizard, J. (1972), 'Environmental effects on language development', *Child Development*, vol. 43, no. 2, June

Tönnies, F. (1957), *Community and Society*, New York: Harper & Row

Touraine, A. (1974), The Post-Industrial Society, London: Wildwood House

Touraine, A., Durand, C., Pecant, D., and Willener, A. (1965), *Workers' Attitudes to Technical Change*, Paris: OECD

Townsend, P. (1979), *Poverty in the United Kingdom*, Harmondsworth: Penguin

Trotsky, L. (1934), *History of the Russian Revolution*, London: Gollancz

Trotsky, L. (1937), *The Revolution Betrayed*, London: Faber & Faber

Turner, C. (1970), 'Conjugal roles and social networks – a re-examination of an hypothesis' (1967), in C. Harris (ed.), *Readings on Kinship in Urban Society*, Oxford: Pergamon Press

Turner, R. (1974), *Ethnomethodology*, Harmondsworth: Penguin

Vajda, M. (1981), *The State and Socialism – Political Essays*, London: Alison & Busby

Veblen, T. (1939), *Imperial Germany and the Industrial Revolution* (1915), New York: The Viking Press

Veblen, T. (1970), *The Theory of the Leisure Class* (1899), London: Unwin Books

Vernon, P. (1955), *The Assessment of Children*, University of London Institute of Education, Studies in Education no. 7, pp. 189–215, London: Evan

Vernon, P. (1969), *Intelligence and Cultural Environment*, London: Methuen

Vernon, P. (1979), *Intelligence: Heredity and Environment*, San Francisco: University of California Press

Vidich, A. J., and Bensman, J. (1958), *Small Town in Mass Society*, Princeton: Princeton University Press

Vogel, E. F., and Bell., N. W. (1968), 'The emotionally disturbed child as the family scapegoat', in N. Bell and E. Vogel (eds), *A Modern Introduction to the Family*, New York: Free Press

Wallerstein, I. (1974), *The Modern World System*, New York: Academic Press

Wallerstein, I. (1980), *The Modern World System II*, New York: Academic Press

Warner, W. L., and Low, J. O. (1957), *The Social System of a Modern Factory*, Yale University Press

Warren, R. (1963), *The Community in America*, Chicago: Rand McNally

Washburn, S. L. (1980), 'Human and animal behaviour', in A Montague (ed.), *Sociobiology Re-examined*, Oxford: Oxford University Press

Weber, M. (1930), *The Protestant Ethic and the Spirit of Capitalism*, London: Unwin University Books

Weber, M. (1947), *The Theory of Social and Economic Organisation*, trans. A. M. Henderson and T. Parsons, Glencoe, Illinois: Free Press

Weber, M. (1948), *From Max Weber: Essays in Sociology*, edited with an introduction by H. H. Gerth and C. W. Mills, New York: Oxford University Press, 1946: London: Routledge & Kegan Paul, 1948

Weber, M. (1949), *The Methodology of the Social Sciences*, trans. E. Shils and A. M. Henderson, Glencoe, Illinois: Free Press

Weber, M. (1961), *General Economic History*, New York: Collier Books

Weber, M. (1968), *Economy and Society – an Outline of Interpretative sociology*, trans. G. Roth and G. Wittich, New York: Bedminster Press

Weber, M. (1978), Anti-Critical Last Word on *The Spirit of Capitalism*, *American Journal of Sociology*, vol. 83, no. 5, pp. 1105–11

Weinberg, I. (1969), 'The problem of convergence – a critical look at the state of a theory', *Comparative Studies in Society and History*, vol. 11, pp. 1–15

Wesolowski, W. (1969), 'The notions of strata and class in socialist society', in A. Betteille (ed.), *Social Inequality*, Harmondsworth: Penguin

West, J. (1982) (ed.), *Work, Women and the Labour Market*, London: Routledge & Kegan Paul

Westergaard, J. (1970), 'The rediscovery of the cash nexus', *Socialist Register*, pp. 111–38

Westergaard, J., and Resler, H. (1975), *Class in a Capitalist Society*, London: Heinemann

White, L. A. (1959), *The Evolution of Culture*, New York: McGraw–Hill

Whyte, W. H. (1957), *The Organisation Man*, Harmondsworth: Penguin

Williams, R. (1960), *Culture and Society, 1780–1850*, Harmondsworth: Penguin

Williams, R. (1961), *Culture and Society*, Harmondsworth: Penguin

Williams, R. (1973a), *The Country and the City*, London: Chatto & Windus

Williams, R. (1973b), 'Base and superstructure', *New Left Review*, no. 82

Williams, W. M. (1963), *A West Country Village*, London: Routledge & Kegan Paul

Willie, C. V. (1976), *A New Look at Black Families*, New York: General Hall

Willis, P. (1978), *Learning to Labour*, Farnborough: Saxon House

Willman, P. (1982), *Fairness, Collective Bargaining and Income Policy*, Oxford: Oxford University Press

Willmott, P., and Young, M. (1960), *Family and Class in a London Suburb*, London: Routledge & Kegan Paul

Wilson, E. O. (1976), *Sociobiology – the New Synthesis*, Cambridge, Mass.: Harvard University Press

Wilson, E. O. (1978), *On Human, Nature*, Cambridge, Mass.: Harvard University Press

Winkler, J. (1976), 'Corporatism', *European Journal of Sociology*, vol. 17, no. 1

Wirth, L. (1938), 'Urbanism as a way of life', *American Journal of Sociology*, vol. 44, no. 1, pp. 1–24

Wolf, E. (1969), *Peasant Wars in the Twentieth Century*, New York: Harper & Row

Wolpe, H. (1970), 'Some problems concerning revolutionary consciousness', *Socialist Register*, pp. 251–80

Wood, S. (1982) (ed.), *The Degradation of Work*, London: Hutchinson

Woodward, J. (1965), *Industrial Organisation – Theory and Practice*, Oxford: Oxford University Press

Wootton, B. (1955), *The Social Foundation of Wages Policy*, London: Allen & Unwin

Worsley, P. (1956), 'Emile Durkheim's theory of knowledge', *Sociological Review*, vol. 1, no. 4

Wright, E. O. (1976), 'Class boundaries in advanced capitalist societies', *New Left Review*, no. 93

Wright, E. O. (1978), *Class, Crises and the State*, London: New Left Books

Wrong, D. (1967), 'The oversocialised conception of man in modern sociology', in H. J. Demerath and R. Peterson (eds), *System Change and Conflict*, New York: Free Press/ Macmillan

Yanowitch, M. (1977), *Social and Economic Inequality in the Soviet Union*, London: Martin Robertson

Young, J. (1971), *The Drug Takers – the Social Meaning of Drug Use*, London: MacGibbon & Kee

Young, J. (1974), 'New directions in sub-cultural theory', in J. Rex (ed.), *Approaches to Sociology*, London: Routledge & Kegan Paul

Young, M., and Willmott, P. (1957), *Family and Kinship in East London*, London: Routledge & Kegan Paul

Young, M., and Willmott, P. (1973), *The Symmetrical Family*, London: Routledge & Kegan Paul

Zaslavsky, V. (1979), 'The regime and the working class in the USSR', *Telos*, no. 42, Winter

Zeitlin, I. (1971), *Ideology and Social Theory*, Glencoe, Illinois: Free Press

Zeitlin, M. (1974), 'Corporate ownership and control – the large corporation and the capitalist class', *American Journal of Sociology*, vol. 79, no. 5

Zukin, S. (1978), 'The problem of social class under socialism', *Theory and Society*, pp. 403–11

Zweig, F. (1961), *The Worker in an Affluent Society*, London: Allen & Unwin

Index